THE BRITISH TELEVISION PILOT EPISODES RESEARCH GUIDE 1936 - 2015

EDITED BY

CHRISTOPHER PERRY

SIMON COWARD AND RICHARD DOWN

Kaleidoscope Television Archives

ISBN 978-1-900203-62-3

The British Television Pilot Episodes Research Guide 1936-2015

Edited by Christopher Perry with Simon Coward and Richard Down

Copyright © 2015 Kaleidoscope Television Archives Ltd

Original Kaleidoscope logo design by Clayton Hickman

Guide section generated by the Kaleldoscope Database, designed by Simon Coward

Kaleidoscope Television Archives Ltd
42 Victoriana Way
Handsworth Wood
B20 2SZ
United Kingdom

GUIDE FORMAT

The layout of the listings may seem a little daunting at first, but trying to pack this much information into a book does necessitate some compromises over instant readability. Much of this information will only to apply to a handful of entries, such as Comedy Playhouse where the entry contains numerous episodes. Where a single pilot only is show, the listing will be more straightforward.

At most, each listing is split into up to four levels of information, though nearly all use three or fewer. The first of these levels reflects the information that relates to the programme as a whole. Now this "programme" might be a one-off special, a single six-part series, or a long-running programme with several hundred editions. Details which remain constant throughout the whole of the programme's run will be listed here. In most cases this means that the companies which commissioned and made the programme will be listed here, as would any writer, director or producer who fulfilled that role throughout. The duration, in minutes, will be generally found here too, as will the name of the company whose broadcast dates are used in the episode section. Here's a fictitious sample entry:

PACK MY BOX WITH FIVE DOZEN LIQUOR JUGS

Produced by BBC Birmingham for BBC1. Transmission details are for BBC1. Duration: 50 minutes.

Main regular credit(s): Music by Carry Goffin; executive producer Gerald Roy.
Main regular cast: Carlton Simon (Quiz-Master); Jesamine Taylor (Hostess).

Where a programme is split into more than one series, the next entry will be for the first series. This may be no more than a simple entry saying just "SERIES 1", but it can contain the same types of information as found at programme level. For example:

SERIES 1
Main regular credit(s): Produced by Di Vengram.

In this case, no single producer worked throughout the various series of **Pack My Box with Five Dozen Liquor Jugs** but Di Vengram fulfilled this role on the first series, so she gets credited here. Someone else will no doubt be credited for the second and third series. We'll come back to the third level in a moment, but in most cases, the next set of entries will be the episodes. Here's another fictional sample:

	Production No	VT Number	Holding / Source Format
##.##.#### **[untransmitted pilot]**	K22/456	T1029	R1N|n / 40

Programme associate Hedley McIlroy; directed by T. S. Wilson.
Gerry Knox, Frank Allaway.

23.12.1968 **[second pilot]**
Carlton Simon quizzes a group of celebrities in the special festive edition.
Programme associate Walter Hobday; directed by T. S. Wilson.
Winnie Wise, Stephen Harland, Audrey Godwin, Old Bill White*.

	Production No	VT Number	Holding / Source Format
—.—.—— **[third pilot]**	K22/459	T1033	R1 / 40

Alternative transmissions: BBC 2: 30.12.1968
Programme associate Hedley McIlroy; directed by Brian Hobday.
Fred Dunn, Doreen Rogers.

Each entry has a similar pattern. It starts with a transmission date and is followed by the episode title. Where a programme doesn't use episode titles, there will sometimes be a short description in its place and these will always be put in "speech marks" like this. Where the information is available, a production number and/or video tape recording number will be included. Finally, we list the current archive holding status of the episode and the original transmission format where we know it. See the end of the book for a list of archive and transmission format codes and other formatting symbols.

Lastly, the credits and cast for the particular episode are shown, excluding any regulars who have already been listed at programme or series level. Where a performer appears in multiple episodes in a particular named role, that role will be noted, otherwise just the name of the performer is listed. Sometimes, for quite long-running series, only those performers appearing most frequently will have their role recorded. If a performer appears in almost every episode of a long running series, he or she will sometimes be credited at programme level as though in every episode and the episodes they did not appear in will carry a note "So-and-so did not appear in this edition". Lastly, you may see some cast or credit information highlighted with an asterisk as in Old Bill White's credit in the second edition listed above. This shows that the apperance in question was uncredited and, while we believe the information to be correct, in many cases this is based upon unpublished information and so may not be separately verifiable.

Each section may be complemented by a synopsis which, if present, will appear towards the top of the section and/or some brief (or in some cases, not so brief) notes, which follow the entry.

A list of the codes used in the Holding / Source Format column may be found at the end of the book.

OTHER CONVENTIONS USED

All dates are shown in standard UK format: day, then month, then year – e.g. 7th June 2005 is shown as 07.06.05 or 07.06.2005.

Where a transmission date is shown as —.—.—— then no transmission has been found for the particular standard channel or BBC region whose dates form the main listing for the programme. There are, however, alternative transmission details, for another channel or region – and these will be shown below.

Where a transmission date is shown as ##.##.#### then in most cases, the programme in question was either not made or was made but is known to have never been transmitted. In a few cases, the programme may have been shown but we will have been unable to trace a tx date. Usually, where this is unclear, an explanatory note will accompany the entry.

Sometimes while reading this Guide, under the actual entry for a series or play you might find an unusual note:

07/05/62 - PANORAMA (LCA6861D) - front: great big chunk of end of "This Is Your Life: Ellaline Terris"; 'UK' logo with announcement 'This is BBC Television' (as above). End: 'Circle' logo, no narration; in-vision announcer, start of verbal trail for play in the series "Suspense" after the news - recording speeds up; obscured bit of News presented by Michael Aspel, snatch of sound at start.

This footnote refers to a piece of continuity film held by the BBC archives on R1, R3 or D3 (for later post-1969 sequences.) It was standard practice in the earlier days of television for telerecordings to start early before the actual intended programme started, or finish late to ensure the whole show was kept. Many of these examples of trailers, BBC globes and in-vision announcers that survive, are kept on the starts or ends of programmes shown live.

To read the extract above: 07/05/62 - PANORAMA (LCA6861D) The date is the date that the trailer/continuity was recorded, the title in capital letters is the live show on the film reel and the number in brackets is the BBC accession number to find the sequence. What follows is then a shot by shot description of the actual footage. Most of these continuity trails are not formally catalogued on the BBC's system, and are included in this guide to help researchers examining programmes that suffered timeslot changes or other unforseen circumstances not reflected in the Radio Times. It also shows that many clips exist from shows officially catalogued as wiped, which may help future broadcasters looking for the early work of Michael Caine or the first ever title sequence to Top of The Pops (which only survives in this format).

Entries marked with an asterisk in the "See Also" lists appear in *Kaleidoscope*'s other guides but are not contained in this volume.

10 THINGS YOU DON'T KNOW ABOUT YOUR MUM

A Twenty Twenty Television production for BBC 3. Untransmitted.

	Holding / Source
##.##.#### [untransmitted pilot]	HD/DB /

THE 11 O'CLOCK SHOW

Alternative/Working Title(s): THE NEWS ALTERNATIVE

A Talkback production for Channel 4. Transmission details are for Channel 4. Duration: 25 minutes.

SERIES 1

	Holding / Source
##.##.#### [untransmitted pilot]	DB / DBS

13B ADAM AND EVE MEWS

A Four Winds Films production for a variety of companies (see details below). Untransmitted. Duration: 25 minutes.

Written by Paul Davis; produced and directed by Paul Davis.

Natasha Pyne, Carol Cleveland, Myles Reitherman.

	Holding / Source
##.##.#### [untransmitted pilot]	J /

According to The Stage and Television Today in August 1970, a pilot was made and Four Winds received finance [we are unsure from whom] to make nine more episodes. We don't know whether any or all of these additional episodes were made.

15 STOREYS HIGH

A BBC production for BBC 3. Transmission details are for BBC 3. Duration: 28 minutes.

Main regular cast: Sean Lock (Vince), Benedict Wong (Errol).

	Holding / Source
##.##.#### Dead Swan [untransmitted pilot]	DB /

2

A Granada production. Transmission details are for the Granada region. Duration: 24 minutes.

Written by Chris Middleton and Jonathan Kydd; script editor Paul Spencer; theme music by John Hegley and Nigel Piper; designed by Taff Batley; executive producer David Liddiment; production manager Pete Roos; produced by Mark Robson; directed by Richard Signy.

Doon Mackichan (Sarah), Rob Sprackling (Stephen), Steve Coogan (Andrew / Waiter), Paul B. Davies (Damian / Postman), Nick Hancock (Hugo / Teddy's Voice), Jonathan Kydd (Raoul), Phil Nice (Mr Green / Compere), Jo Unwin (Fiona).

	Production No	Holding / Source
07.09.1990	P1563	DB / 1"

THE 21ST CENTURY SHOW

A BBC production. Untransmitted. Duration: 21 minutes.

Written by Graeme Garden and Bill Oddie; costume Rupert Jarvis; make-up Pauline Cox; music by Dave MacRae; designed by John Stout; produced and directed by Jim Franklin.

Graeme Garden (Narrator), Ann Hamilton, Henry McGee, Andrew Ray, Judy Loe, Judith Alderson, Stuart Fell, The Santus Brothers, James Muir, Leigh Marsh and her Dogs, Dora the Elephant, Jan Murzynowski, Malcolm Franklin.

	Production No	Holding / Source
##.##.#### [1979 pilot]	LLCA711A/71	DB-D3 / 2"

Originally scheduled for 12.04.1979.

There are two versions/edits of the show - the 72 and 73 edits, both were made in 1979.

2DTV

A 2D Productions production for ITV 1. made in association with Channel Television. Transmission details are for the Central region. Duration: 25 minutes.

Main regular credit(s): Produced by Giles Pilbrow; directed by Tim Searle.

Main regular cast: Jon Culshaw, Dave Lamb, Jan Ravens.

	Holding / Source
27.03.2001	DB / DBSW

With Alistair McGowan.

Satirical animation show.

3 2 1

A Yorkshire Television production. Transmission details are for the ATV/Central region. Duration: 50 minutes.

Main regular credit(s): Theme music by Johnny Pearson.

Main regular performer(s): Ted Rogers (Host).

	VT Number	Holding / Source
##.##.#### [untransmitted pilot]	Y/1737/0001	J / 2"

Recorded in August 1977.

THE 3RD XI

An Avalon Television production for BBC 3. Transmission details are for BBC 3. Duration: 28 minutes.

Written by Marek Larwood, Katherine Parkinson, Laura Solon and Ben Willbond; script supervisor Diane Taylor; assistant director Julie Sykes; art director Neil Barnes; designed by James Dillon; production associate Alison Carpenter; executive producers Richard Allen-Turner, Sally Debonnaire and Jon Thoday; production manager Chris Iliffe; produced by Sioned Wiliam; directed by Lissa Evans and Paul King.

Marek Larwood, Katherine Parkinson, Laura Solon, Ben Willbond, James Rawlings, Rufus Jones, Paul Robinson.

	Holding / Source
##.##.#### **[untransmitted pilot]**	DB /

Recorded in 2007.

See also: LAURA, BEN AND HIM

6 DATES WITH BARKER

An LWT production. Transmission details are for the ATV midlands region. Duration: 25 minutes.

Produced by Humphrey Barclay; directed by Maurice Murphy.

Ronnie Barker (Various Roles).

	Production No	Holding / Source
15.01.1971 **1899 A.D.: The Phantom Raspberry Blower Of Old London Town**	9L/00594	D2 / 2"

Written by Spike Milligan; designed by David Catley.

With Ronnie Barker (Inspector Alexander / Disraeli / Home Secretary), Alan Curtis (The Phantom), Larry Noble (Sergeant Bowles), John Sharp (Butler), David Jason (Raspberry Sounds Throughout), Christine Ozanne (Duchess), Moira Foot (Maureen Body), John Lawrence, Pat Gorman, Astley Harvey, Tony Joyce.

This play was later adapted into a serial for The Two Ronnies.

See also: HARK AT BARKER* / THE TWO RONNIES

THE $64,000 QUESTION

A Central production. made in association with Talbot TV Ltd. Transmission details are for the Central region.

Main regular credit(s):   Created by Cinecor Associates; music by Ed Welch; produced by Peter Harris.

Main regular performer(s): Bob Monkhouse (Presenter).

	VT Number	Holding / Source
##.##.#### **[untransmitted pilot]**	4754/89	DV / 1"

Duration: 41 minutes.

Directed by Peter Harris.

Recorded 16.11.89.

There are no end credits, just music.

'68 STYLE

An ABC production. Untransmitted.

Talent show pilot for younger stars.

Written by George Evans, Denis Goodwin and Derek Collyer; dances staged by Lionel Blair; choreography by Lionel Blair; produced and directed by Pat Johns.

Johnny Hackett, Chris Langford, Dilys Watling, Bob Sharples and his Orchestra.

	Holding / Source
##.##.#### **[untransmitted pilot]**	J / 40

Recorded at Teddington on 17.03.1968.

THE ABBEY

A Baby Cow Productions production for ITV 1. Transmission details are for the Central region. Duration: 25 minutes.

Set in a low-rent alternative to the Priory run by a recovering rock chick. The characters — a bulimic model who eats tissues, a sexaddicted OAP and a DJ who snorts the gas from a squirty cream can.

Written by Morwenna Banks; executive producer Henry Normal; produced by Alison MacPhail; directed by Jonny Campbell.

Morwenna Banks (Marianne Hope), Omid Djalili (Tony), Russell Brand (Terry), Reece Shearsmith (Doctor Darren), Miranda Hart (Helen), Liz Smith (Elsie), Tamsin Egerton (Tiffany), Marti Pellow (Eddie Coogan), Rasmus Hardiker (Dean).

	Holding / Source
14.02.2007	DB / DBSWF

ITV commissioned a full series of The Abbey for broadcast on ITV2 in 2008. Filming was due to begin in January 2008, but the series was later cancelled

ABOVE THEIR STATION

A Granada production for BBC 3. Transmission details are for BBC 3. Duration: 30 minutes.

Written by Rhys Thomas; script supervisor Suzanne Baron; director of photography John Simmons; art director Jo Sutherland; designed by Neil Griffiths, Sam Harley and James Dillon; production executive Grace Boylan; executive producers Simon Lupton and Saurabh Kakkar; production manager Jo Alloway; produced by Jon Rolph; directed by Tony Dow.

Luke Gell (Len), Ashley Madekwe (Kelly), Rhys Thomas (Perry), Sonny Rooney (Danny), Andy Linden (Dino), Andrew Brooke (Police Constable Preston), Dudley Sutton (Chester Thompson), Denis Lawson (Keith Boone), Ruth Connell (Olga), Tony Way (Techno Benson), Simon Day (Doctor Barry Clack).

	Holding / Source
22.02.2010	HD/DB / HDC

ABRACADABRA

An Associated-Rediffusion production. Transmission details are for the ATV midlands region. Duration: 25 minutes.

A word game.

Main regular credit(s):   Devised by Roy Ward Baker.

SERIES 1

Main regular credit(s):   Directed by Tig Roe.

Main regular performer(s): With Roy Ward Dickson (Host), Shirley Dickson.

	VT Number	Holding / Source
##.##.#### [dummy run]	W1197/218	J / 40

Recorded 25.01.1961.

See also: ABRACADABRA!*

ABRACADIGANCE

A John Kaye Cooper Productions production for LWT. Transmission details are for the London Weekend Television region.

Main regular credit(s):   Produced and directed by John Kaye Cooper.

Main regular performer(s): Richard Digance.

	Holding / Source
27.08.1988	D2 / 1"

Duration: 40 minutes.

Written by Richard Digance; programme associates Robin Sieger and Colman Hutchinson; theme music by Alan Parker; designed by Quentin Chases.

With Mr Pip's Marching Up and Down Band, Vilma Hollingbery.

ABSOLUTELY

An Absolutely production for Channel 4. Transmission details are for Channel 4. Duration varies - see below for details.

Main regular credit(s):   Written by Pete Baikie, Morwenna Banks, Jack Docherty, Moray Hunter, Gordon Kennedy and John Sparkes.

Main regular cast: Pete Baikie, Morwenna Banks, Jack Docherty, Moray Hunter, Gordon Kennedy, John Sparkes.

	Holding / Source
##.##.#### [untransmitted pilot]	DB / 1"

See also: MR DON AND MR GEORGE*

AC/DC - THE CURRENT SCENE

An LWT production. Untransmitted. Duration: 40 minutes.

A pop music programme with performers and dancers in studio.

Choreography by Jackie Dalton; designed by Bryce Walmsley; produced and directed by David Bell.

Jimmy Helms, Kiki Dee, The Majestics, Doris Troy, Tony Cole, Peter London, Doreen & Irene Chanter [as Irene & Doreen Chanter], Pull & Thrust, Uppers & Downers.

	VT Number	Holding / Source
##.##.#### [untransmitted pilot]	9L/09296	DB / 2"

Recorded 09.10.1973.

ACCORDING TO DAISY

A HTV Wales production. Untransmitted. Duration: 25 minutes.

This was a pilot episode written for Su Pollard. Her character was a journalist who needed help to keep her unruly kids out of trouble. Advertising for a Home Help, along came strict George Pym. Although recorded, transmission was held back until a full season was commissioned. Unfortunately Su Pollard was tied up with other projects until late 1989, by which time Jackson had fallen ill. Although Jeremy Brett was considered to replace Gordon, the project was shelved.

Gordon Jackson (George Pym), Su Pollard.

	Holding / Source
##.##.#### **[untransmitted pilot]**	J / 1"

Tape currently missing from shelf.

ACE HIGH

A BBC production. Untransmitted.

	VT Number	Holding / Source
##.##.#### **[untransmitted pilot]**	16/P/10941	J /

Recorded 11th February 1961.

ACES HIGH

A Tyne Tees Television production. made in association with Celador International. Untransmitted. Duration: 25 minutes.

A card game show.

Research Trevor Hearing; executive producer Heather Ging; produced by Christine Williams; directed by James Whiteley.

David Rogers (Host).

	Holding / Source
##.##.#### **[untransmitted pilot]**	J / 1"

Recorded November 1984.

ACES HIGH

Commissioned by ITC. Not made.

Executive producer Robert S. Baker.

	Holding / Source
##.##.####	NR /

Mentioned in Television Today on 02.11.1967 as being one of two series to go into production, the other being Department S.

ACTS OF PASSION

Produced for Channel 4 by a variety of companies (see details below). Transmission details are for Channel 4. Duration: 25 minutes.

	Holding / Source
31.08.1999 **Heterosexuality**	DB / C1S

A Vicarious Productions production.

Written by Rikki Beadle-Blair; script associate Carolyn Young; script supervisor Emma Thomas; music by Mark Hawkes and Rikki Beadle-Blair; designed by Katrina Lindsay; executive producer Roger Brown; produced by Carol Harding; directed by Rikki Beadle-Blair.

With Noel Clarke (Kwame), Rikki Beadle-Blair (Max), Karl Collins (Jordan), Paul Keating (Dean), Rebecca Varney (Asha), Frances Lima (Gerri), Arin Alldridge (Daniel), Carleen Beadle (Cindy), Dee Dee Samuels (Doris), Michael Dotchin (Robin), Davey Fairbanks (Bambi), Lisa Harmer (Peggy), Gavin Delaney (Pablo), David Squire (Asha's Dad), Helen Sheals (Hilly).

See: METROSEXUALITY.

AD LIB

A Yorkshire Television production. Transmission details are for the ATV midlands region. Duration: 25 minutes.

Main regular cast: Duncan Goodhew (Presenter), Tilly Vosburgh (Presenter).

SERIES 1

Main regular credit(s): Designed by Robert Scott; executive producer Joy Whitby; produced by Peter Murphy; directed by Alister Hallum.

Main regular cast: With Ian Bartholomew, Oona Kirsch, Liz Lewis, Craig Lynn, Beverley Martin, David Nunn, Nick Rowan.

		VT Number	Holding / Source
30.03.1981	**[pilot 1]**	C300	1" / 2"
06.04.1981	**[pilot 2]**	C301	1" / 2"
13.04.1981	**[pilot 3]**	C302	1" / 2"

ADAM ADAMANT

A BBC production for BBC 1. Transmission details are for BBC 1. Duration: 50 minutes.

Gerald Harper (Adam Adamant), Ann Holloway (Georgina Jones), Peter Ducrow (The Face), Veronica Strong, Vernon Joyner, Norman Mitchell, Grenville Steel, Norman Claridge, Michael Latimer, Ian Kingsley, Mary Hignett, Eric McCaine.

	Holding / Source
##.##.#### **Adam Adamant Lives**	J / 40

Written by Donald Cotton; based on material by Richard Harris; story editor Ken Levison; directed by William Slater.

With Gordon Gardner, Frank Tregear, Carol Passmore, Kenneth Benda, Gordon Faith, Nicholas Brett.

See also: ADAM ADAMANT LIVES!* / MAGNUS HAWKE / TOM DEVISES

ADAM SMITH

Alternative/Working Title(s): ADAM SMITH D.D.

A Granada production. Transmission details are for the ATV midlands region. Duration: 25 minutes.

The life of a Church of Scotland minister.

Main regular cast: Andrew Keir (Adam Smith).

	Holding / Source
##.##.#### [untransmitted pilot]	J / 2"

The story was set in the present day and centred around a 47-year-old minister, who is a widower, and his family.

Written by George Byatt; executive producer June Howson.

Made in partnership with STV in June 1971.

	Holding / Source
##.##.#### [second untransmitted pilot]	J / 2"

Written by George Byatt.

Made in partnership with STV in June 1971.

ADMIN

A Channel X production for BBC Manchester. Transmission details are for BBC 3. Duration: 30 minutes.

Comedy pilot set in a solicitors' office. Young Darrel is keen to impress the boss.

Created by David Isaac; written by David Isaac; script supervisor Jane Houston; theme music by Little Man Tate; designed by Gavin Lewis; production executive Claire Asbury; executive producers Jon Mountague and Alan Marke; produced by Matt Tiller; directed by Michael Buffong.

Neil Fitzmaurice (Mike), Peter Slater (Mr Jordan), Chris Hannon (Darrel), Christian Foster (Kenny), Abdullah Afzal (Asif), Rachel Rae (Shelley), Jessica Hall (Tania), Sian Reeves (Gloria), Kulvinder Ghir (Mohammed), Samira Chahhary (Receptionist), Chereen Buckley (Lee Ann), Jarrod Cooke (Danny), Mohammed Rafique (Mr Ahmed).

	Holding / Source
12.05.2008	DB / DBSWF

THE ADS SHOW

A Kaleidoscope Television production for Big Centre TV. Transmission details are for Big Centre TV.

Main regular credit(s):   Introduced by Tim Disney; written by Simon Coward; theme music by Barry Gray; edited by Simon Coward; titles by Dave Jeffery; executive producer Chris Perry; directed by Simon Coward.

	Production No	Holding / Source
##.##.#### [untransmitted pilot]	ADS00A	MXF / MXF

Duration: 24 minutes.

Much of the material in the pilot was re-used in programme 1. Tim Disney did not introduce this edition, and the opening and closing title sequences were little more than place-holders.

THE ADVENTURE GAME

A BBC production for BBC Children's Department. Transmission details are for BBC 2.

SERIES 1

Transmission details are for BBC 1.

	Holding / Source
##.##.#### [untransmitted 1980 pilot]	2"|n / 2"

ADVENTURE WEEKLY

A BBC production for BBC 1. Transmission details are for BBC 1.

Main regular credit(s):   Produced by John McRae.

Main regular cast: Brent Oldfield (Peter Perkins), Ian Ellis (Tubby Taylor), Frank Barry (Swot English), Bartlett Mullins (Mr Filling), Michael Wisher (Police Constable Cullis).

A BBC production.

	Holding / Source
##.##.#### Into Print [untransmitted pilot]	R1 /

Duration: 28 minutes.

Written by Shaun Sutton; script editor Kenneth Poolman [credited as Ken Poolman]; directed by Barry Letts.

With John Gugolka (Andy Rogers), Robert Dean (Mr Perkins), Frederick Danner, Bill Lyons, Chubby Oates, Arthur Hewlett, Harry Littlewood, Joseph Greig.

THE ADVENTURES OF ALI BABA

A The Danzigers production. Untransmitted. Duration: 25 minutes.

Produced by The Danzigers.

Daniel Massey (Ali Baba).

This programme was mentioned, along with The Cheaters and Richard The Lionheart as being a forthcoming Danzigers' production in The Stage (28.01.1960). Quite probably, it was never made.

ADVENTURES OF AN ELEPHANT BOY

A K and H Films Productions Ltd production. Untransmitted. Duration: 25 minutes.

Main regular credit(s):   Written by Kenneth Hume; produced and directed by Kenneth Hume.

Main regular cast: David Wyman.

		Holding / Source
##.##.#### **[first pilot]**		J / B3
##.##.#### **[second pilot]**		J / B3
##.##.#### **[third pilot]**		J / B3

Made in Ceylon, the finance came from John Kennedy, the agent of Tommy Steele and Kenneth Hume. In March 1959, ATV and NBC were interested. Hume had written 26 scripts. It likely failed to attract interest because ABC made 'The Adventures of a Jungle Boy' at the same time!

THE ADVENTURES OF DANIEL

A BBC Scotland production for BBC 3. Transmission details are for BBC 3. Duration: 30 minutes.

Comedy.

Written by Stewart Williams and Tim Allsop; additional material by Daniel Sloss; executive producer Jemma Rodgers; directed by Ben Gosling Fuller.

Daniel Sloss (Daniel), Jenny Hulse (Emma), Jordan McCurrach (Matt), Kevin Guthrie (James), Laura Aikman (Suzie), Finlay Johnston (Daniel's brother), Bailey Edmondson (Daniel's brother), Jonathan Slinger (Mr Wallace), Imogen Stubbs (Mrs Wallace), Susan Vidler (Daniel's mum), Ed Byrne (Xantar), Robert McDevitt (Warrior).

	Holding / Source
23.08.2010	HD/DB / HD/DB

THE ADVENTURES OF MR. HERO!

A TV Cartoons Ltd production. Untransmitted. Duration: 7 minutes.

Story by Roberta Leigh; lyrics by Roberta Leigh; music by Roberta Leigh; designed by Harry Hess; produced by Roberta Leigh; directed by Harry Hess.

	Holding / Source
##.##.#### **[untransmitted pilot]**	DB / C1

Animated cartoon.

AFFAIRS OF THE HEART

A Granada production. Transmission details are for the Central region.

A heart-attack victim finds life difficult once he becomes well again.

Main regular credit(s):   Written by Paul Daneman; produced by Brian Armstrong.

Main regular cast: Derek Fowlds (Peter Bonamy), Sarah Badel (Jane Bonamy).

Credits: Directed by Richard Cornwell.

	Production No	Holding / Source
23.08.1983	P1171/8801	1" / 1"

Duration: 23 minutes.

Directed by Richard Cornwell.

With Elizabeth Anson, Frances Bennett, Eamon Boland, Alan Hulse, John Barrard, Larry Martyn, Alison Lloyd, Rosalie Williams, Ann Aris.

AFTER ALL THAT THIS

A Granada production. Transmission details are for the Granada region. Duration: 14 minutes.

Main regular credit(s):   Produced by Nick Turnbull; directed by Peter Walker.

Main regular performer(s): Nick Turnbull (Presenter).

	Production No	Holding / Source
##.##.#### **[untransmitted pilot]**	P998/8801	DB / 2"

AFTER HENRY

Produced for Thames Television by a variety of companies (see details below). Transmission details are for the Central region. Duration: 25 minutes.

Main regular credit(s):   Written by Simon Brett.

Main regular cast: Prunella Scales (Sarah France), Joan Sanderson (Eleanor Prescott), Janine Wood (Clare France), Jonathan Newth (Russell Bryant).

SERIES 1

A Thames Television production.

Main regular credit(s):   Theme music by George Gershwin and Ray Cook; produced and directed by Peter Frazer-Jones.

	VT Number	Holding / Source
11.01.1988 **Phonecalls**	38734	1" / 1"

Designed by Philip Blowers.

With Robert Austin.

The DVD release featured a different title sequence and musical arrangement which suggests that it was a pilot version that Kaleidoscope believes was identical to the transmitted episode, except for its titles. Upon viewing the transmitted episode two it bears no episode title and the set is a totally different design, so this bears out the view that the pilot was re-titled and transmitted as episode two in the series.

See also: AFTER HENRY (RADIO)*

AGATHA CHRISTIE'S THE SECRET ADVERSARY

An LWT production. Transmission details are for the Central region. Duration: 115 minutes.

Adapted by Pat Sandys; based on a book by Agatha Christie; music by Joseph Horovitz; edited by Ray Helm; director of photography Mike Humphries; assistant director John Quilty; designed by Bryan Bagge; associate producer Ron Fry; production manager Peter McKay; produced by Jack Williams; directed by Tony Wharmby.

Francesca Annis (Tuppence Cowley), James Warwick (Tommy Beresford), Gavan O'Herlihy (Julius P. Hersheimmer), Alec McCowen (Sir James Peel Edgerton), Honor Blackman (Rita Vandemeyer), Peter Barkworth (Mr Carter), Toria Fuller (Annette / Jane Finn), John Fraser (Kramenin), George Baker (Whittington), Donald Houston (Boris), Joseph Brady (Doctor Hall), Wolf Kahler (The German), Reece Dinsdale (Albert), Peter Lovstrom (Henry), Matthew Scurfield (Conrad), Holly Watson (Child on Beach), Phyllida Hewat (Woman in tea shop), James Walker (First clerk), Mike Elles (Second clerk), Gabrielle Blunt (Annie), Norman Hartley (Florist), Roger Ostime (Ritz receptionist), Nicholas Geake (Watson), Simon Watkins (Man at Astley Priors), Steve Fletcher (Messenger boy).

	VT Number	Holding / Source
09.10.1983	10240	DB / C1

See also: AGATHA CHRISTIE'S "PARTNERS IN CRIME"

THE AL LOGAN SHOW

An Ulster Television production. Not made.

Music series with showband singer Al Logan.

Al Logan.

This was planned as a spin-off from Hullo There, UTV's most popular music series. Al Logan was its most popular guest artist and, hoping to exploit his popularity, UTV offered him two pilots in 1968. These were never produced due to internal politics involving the abrupt departure of Geoffrey Gilbert, UTV's programme controller.

AL READ

A BBC production. Untransmitted. Duration: 30 minutes.

Al Read.

	VT Number	Holding / Source
##.##.#### [untransmitted pilot]	VTC/6HP/53464	J / 2"

Recorded 21st August 1969.

ALEXANDER ARMSTRONG'S BIG ASK

Alternative/Working Title(s): WHAT DO YOU KNOW?

A Black Dog Television production for Dave. made in association with So Television. Transmission details are for Dave. Duration: 25 minutes.

Written by Dan Gaster, Will Ing and Paul Powell.

Alexander Armstrong (Host), Dave Lamb, Katy Brand, Griff Rhys Jones, Robert Webb.

	Holding / Source
30.05.2011	HD/DB / HD/DB

ALISTAIR MCGOWAN'S BIG IMPRESSION

A Vera production for BBC 1. Transmission details are for BBC 1. Usual duration: 30 minutes.

Main regular cast: Alistair McGowan (Various roles).

	Holding / Source
02.09.1999	DB / DBSW

Produced by Charlie Hanson; directed by Gareth Carrivick.

With Julian Dutton, Alan Francis, Ronni Ancona.

See also: ALISTAIR MCGOWAN'S BIG JUBILEE* / ALISTAIR MCGOWAN'S BIG WORLD CUP*

ALL NIGHT LONG

A BBC production for BBC 1. Transmission details are for BBC 1. Duration: 30 minutes.

Main regular credit(s):   Written by Dick Fiddy and Mark Wallington; associate producer Justin Sbresni; produced and directed by Harold Snoad.

Main regular cast: Keith Barron (Bill Chivers).

	Holding / Source
##.##.#### In The Dark [untransmitted pilot]	DB / D3S

ALL YOU NEED IS EARS

A Whitement production for Channel 4. Transmission details are for Channel 4. Duration: 25 minutes.

Written by George Martin; produced by Aubrey Singer and Tom Gutteridge.

	Holding / Source
##.##.#### [untransmitted pilot]	J / 1"

ALL YOURS

An LWT production. Untransmitted. Duration: 25 minutes.

Written by Jan Etherington and Gavin Petrie; designed by John Anderson; executive producer Lisa Clark; produced and directed by Lissa Evans.

Lynda Bellingham (Gemma), Brian Protheroe (Dan), Simon Greenall (Francis), Emma Kennedy (Paulette), Tabitha Wady (Sophie), Kevin Bishop (Liam), Charlie Eva (Simon the Grandchild), Peter Greenhough (Clinic Patient), Pam Buckley (Clinic Patient).

	VT Number	Holding / Source
##.##.#### [untransmitted pilot]	9L/94668	DB / DBSW

'ALLO 'ALLO!

A BBC production for BBC 1. Transmission details are for BBC 1. Duration varies - see below for details.

Main regular credit(s):   Created by Jeremy Lloyd and David Croft; theme music by David Croft and Roy Moore.

Main regular cast: Gorden Kaye (René Artois), Carmen Silvera (Edith Melba Artois), Vicki Michelle (Yvette Carte-Blanche), Kirsten Cooke (Michelle Dubois), Richard Marner (Herr Colonel Kurt Von Strohm), Guy Siner (Lieutenant Hubert Gruber), Kim Hartman (Helga Geerhart).

	Holding / Source
30.12.1982	DB-D3 / 2"

Duration: 35 minutes.

Rene, a cafe proprietor in occupied France, suddenly finds himself the centre of the organisation devoted to helping escaping RAF officers to get back to England.

Written by Jeremy Lloyd and David Croft; designed by Shelagh Lawson; production manager Susan Belbin; produced and directed by David Croft.

With Francesca Gonshaw (Maria), Richard Gibson (Herr Otto Flick), Jack Haig (Monsieur Roger Leclerc), Sam Kelly (Captain Hans Geering), Rose Hill (Fanny, the Mother), John D. Collins (Flying Officer Fairfax), Nicholas Frankau (Flying Officer Carstairs), Richard Cottan (Claud).

See also: REX MILLIGAN* / STARS REUNITED*

ALPINE PILOT

A Caesar Film Productions production. made in association with Atlantic Films. Untransmitted.

	Holding / Source
##.##.####	J /

Written by Frank Driscoll.

According to Television Today [18.01.1962] shooting was to begin in March for a pilot film for what was hoped to be a series of 26 x 25-minute episodes.

ALRIGHT NOW!

A Tyne Tees Television production. Transmission details are for the Tyne Tees region. Duration varies - see below for details.

Main regular credit(s):   Designed by Tim Trout; executive producer Andrea Wonfor; produced by Malcolm Gerrie; directed by Gavin Taylor.

SERIES 1

Main regular performer(s): With Den Hegarty (Host).

	Holding / Source
##.##.#### [untransmitted pilot]	DBSEQ / 2"

Duration: 52 minutes.
With The Showbiz Kids, The Steve Gibbons Band, David Sandison, Young Bucks.
Recorded 17.01.1979

THE AMBASSADOR'S DAUGHTER

An Unknown production for ITC. Not made.

Written by Seeman & Rose.

The Stage reported on 17.03.1960 of an ITC pilot for a series "based on the colourful Sharman Douglass".

AN EVENING AT THE CANDLELIGHT

A BBC production. Untransmitted.

	VT Number	Holding / Source
##.##.#### Scarborough Night Club [untransmitted pilot]	35/P/T/8955	J / R3

Recorded 17th August 1960.

AND NOW THE GOOD NEWS

A BBC Manchester production for BBC 2. Transmission details are for BBC 2. Duration: 25 minutes.

Main regular credit(s):   Written by Richard Stilgoe; produced by Ken Stephinson; directed by Tom Gutteridge.

Main regular performer(s): Richard Stilgoe (Host).

	Holding / Source
##.##.#### [untransmitted pilot]	DB-D3 / 2"

With Richard Stilgoe.
Pilot.

ANGLIAN LIVES

A Talkback production for BBC 2. Transmission details are for BBC 2. Duration: 29 minutes.

Written by Peter Baynham, Steve Coogan and Armando Iannucci; art director Simon Rogers; designed by Dennis De Groot; production team Penny Anderson, Suzanne Baron, Sarah Daman, Cathy McLoughlin and Holly Sait; associate producer Peter Baynham; production executives Sally Debonnaire and Jenny Hay; executive producer Peter Fincham; production manager Jo Hunter; produced and directed by Adam Tandy.

Steve Coogan (Alan Partridge), Peter Baynham (Ray Woollard), Amelia Bullmore, Simon Greenall, Melanie Hudson.

	Holding / Source
24.03.2003	DB / DBSW

ANIMAL CRACKERS

An LWT production. Untransmitted. Duration: 30 minutes.

Main regular performer(s): Bob Carolgees (Host).

	Production No	VT Number	Holding / Source
##.##.#### [first pilot]	91782	9C/91782	1" / 1"

With Nerys Hughes, Matthew Kelly.

		VT Number	Holding / Source
##.##.#### [second pilot]		9C/20699	DB / 1"

With Michaela Strachan, Mick Brown.

This edition is retained as a studio recording which includes a couple of instances where the programme has to stop while technicians repair parts of the set.

ANIMAL GAME

A BBC production. Transmission details are for BBC.

	VT Number	Holding / Source
20.11.1973	VTC/6HP/85042	J / 2"

Recorded 11.09.1973.

ANIMAL, VEGETABLE AND MINERAL

A BBC production. Transmission details are for BBC 1.

	VT Number	Holding / Source
##.##.#### [untransmitted pilot]	– VTC/6HP/65476	J / 2"

Recorded 23rd March 1971.

Surviving material only.

THE ANN LOVINGTON DREAM SHOW

Alternative/Working Title(s): THE ANN LOVINGTON HOUR

A Thames Television production. Untransmitted. Duration: 50 minutes.

Written by Howard Schuman; produced by Andrew Brown.

Julie Covington (Ann Lovington).

	VT Number	Holding / Source
##.##.####	124369	J / 2"

This was intended as Schuman'Brown/Covington's next project after ROCK FOLLIES OF 77. It isn't clear whether material was recorded for this programme but none survives now. Given the legal fracas over the casting and origination of ROCK FOLLIES and the fact that one of those involved was Annabel Leventon, picking such a similar-sounding name for the lead character in their next show seems careless at best. What were they thinking of?

ANNA LEE

A Carnival Films production for LWT. made in association with Chestermead Ltd. Transmission details are for the Central region. Duration: 100 minutes.

Main regular credit(s): Based on books by Liza Cody; executive producers Sarah Wilson and Nick Elliott.

Main regular cast: Imogen Stubbs (Anna Lee), Brian Glover (Selwyn Price).

Credits: Music by Richard Hartley; designed by Mike Oxley; executive producer Nick Elliott; produced by Sue Birtwistle.

Cast: With Michael Bryant (Commander Brierly), Ken Stott (Bernie Schiller), David Harewood (Stevie Johnson), Barbara Leigh-Hunt (Beryl Doyle).

	VT Number	Holding / Source
10.01.1993 **Headcase**	12205	D2 / V1S

Ex-policewoman Anna Lee joins the Brierly Detective Agency as a private investigator, and her first assignment appears to be a straightforward missing person's case until one man disappears and another turns up dead.

Dramatised by Andrew Davies; developed by Chestermead Ltd; directed by Colin Bucksey.

With Alan Howard, Kate Beckinsale, Shirley Anne Field, Richard Dempsey, Clive Merrison, Paul Guilfoyle, Roger Lloyd Pack, Eoin McCarthy, Robin Soans, Paul Kember, Nicholas Hewetson, Tim Wylton, Anthony May, Linda Hartley, Doreen Andrew, Gillian Raine, Edward Jewesbury, Julia St. John, Jack Ellis, Wendy Allnutt, Jan Chappell, Alfred Le Prevost, Reuben Le Prevost, Judith Coke, Albert Moses, Jason Sulhey, Jonathan Magnanti.

ANONYMOUS

A Tiger Aspect production for ITV 1. Transmission details are for the Central region.

Written by Adrian Lynch, Darren Smith and David Reilly; executive producers Deborah Sargeant and Clive Tulloh; produced by Richard Cook and Matt Smith; directed by Gary Brooks and Chris Faith.

Stephen Mulhern (Presenter), Matt Dawson, Jennie McAlpine, Louis Walsh, Richard Arnold, Austin Healey, Michelle Keegan, Shayne Ward.

	Holding / Source
18.07.2009	HD/DB /

ANT AND DEC'S SATURDAY NIGHT TAKEAWAY

A Granada/ITV Productions production for ITV 1. Transmission details are for the Central region. Duration varies - see below for details.

Main regular credit(s):   Theme music by Will Slater and Rumble Music; executive producers Anthony McPartlin and Declan Donnelly.

Main regular performer(s): Anthony McPartlin (Himself), Declan Donnelly (Himself).

SERIES 3

A Granada production.

Main regular credit(s):   Produced by James Sunderland; directed by Chris Power.

Main regular performer(s): With Marc Silk (Voice Over), James Pallister (Little Ant), Dylan McKenna Redshaw (Little Dec).

	VT Number	Holding / Source
##.##.#### **Ant And Dec 6 Puppet [untransmitted pilot]**	9L/51081	DB / DBSW

Untransmitted pilot to test a new strand of the show.

ANYTHING GOES

A BBC Manchester production for BBC. Untransmitted.

	Holding / Source
##.##.#### **[untransmitted pilot]**	J / 1"

APE

A Green inc production for E4. Transmission details are for E4. Duration: 25 minutes.

Written by Liam Hourican, David Crann, George Kane and Keith Martin; music by Conner Dougan; designed by Laura Ng; executive producers Stephen Stewart and Chris Jones; produced by Keith Martin; directed by George Kane.

Liam Hourican, Diarmuid Corr, Jim Roche, Olga Wehrly.

	Holding / Source
31.07.2008	DB / DBSWF

APPOINTMENT WITH FEAR

A Troublefree production for TVS. Transmission details are for the Central region. Duration: 25 minutes.

Written by Ian Stuart Black; script executive Corinne Cartier; music by Nigel Hess; associate producer Lars Macfarlane; produced by Graham Benson; directed by Herbert Wise.

Lisa Orgolini (Sonia Stafford), Jeremy Northam (Gerald Stafford), Matyelok Gibbs (Mrs Gilbert), Mary Wimbush (Mrs Stafford).

	VT Number	Holding / Source
04.04.1992 **House Of Glass**	22693	B / C1

Ghostly thriller set in a country house. Sonia arrives at her new husband's family seat to find his ancestors still in evidence.

ARCADIA

A Talkback Thames production for BBC. Untransmitted. Duration: 28 minutes.

Written by Jim Poyser and Paul Viragh.

Fritz Bragpuss, Georgine Anderson, Jamie Kenna, Martha Howe-Douglas, Matt Green, Nick Mohammed, Paul Viragh, Thomas Nelstrop, Adrian Phillips, Andy Taylor, Charlie Covell, Chloe Bale.

	VT Number	Holding / Source
##.##.#### **[untransmitted pilot]**	366900	DB / DBSW

Recorded 2008.

No on-screen end credits.

THE ARMANDO IANNUCCI SHOWS

A Talkback production for Channel 4. Transmission details are for Channel 4. Duration: 24 minutes.

Main regular credit(s):   Written by Armando Iannucci, Kevin Cecil and Andy Riley; director of photography John Rosenberg; production executive Joanna Beresford; executive producer Peter Fincham; production manager Jo Kay.

Main regular cast: Armando Iannucci (Presenter).

	Holding / Source
##.##.#### **[untransmitted pilot]**	DB / DBSW

Produced by Alison MacPhail.

Recorded 11.06.1999.

ARMCHAIR CINEMA

A Euston Films production for Thames Television. Transmission details are for the ATV midlands region. Duration varies - see below for details.

Executive producers Lloyd Shirley and George Taylor.

	Production No	Holding / Source
04.06.1974 **Regan**	60081	DB / C1

Alt.Title(s): *The Outcast*

Duration: 90 minutes.

Jack Regan is a good copper. But his tough, intuitive style has gone out of fashion at Scotland Yard. When a policeman is mysteriously murdered, Regan breaks all the rules to track down the killer. He finds, however, that there are men in the Flying Squad prepared to break him ...

Written by Ian Kennedy Martin; associate producer Mary Morgan; produced by Ted Childs; directed by Tom Clegg.

With John Thaw (Detective Inspector Jack Regan), Dennis Waterman (Detective Sergeant George Carter), Lee Montague (Arthur Dale), Garfield Morgan (Detective Chief Inspector Frank Haskins), David Daker (Tusser), Janet Key (Kate), Maureen Lipman (Annie), Morris Perry (Detective Superintendent Maynon), Stephen Yardley (Detective Inspector Laker), Barry Jackson (Morton), Miquel Brown (Miriam), Peter Blythe (Peter), Carl Rigg (Detective Sergeant Kent), Michael da Costa (South), Ronald Pember (Landlord), Jonathan Elsom (Interviewer), Betty Woolfe (Mrs Berry), Seymour Matthews (Doctor), Don Henderson (Strip-Club Heavy), Nancy Gabrielle (Johno's Wife), Del Baker (Detective Sergeant Cowley).

See also: THE SWEENEY*

THE ARMCHAIR DETECTIVE

A Central production. Transmission details are for the Central region. Duration: 30 minutes.

Audience participation whodunnit mystery drama, in the style of Agatha Christie.

Created by Diane Campbell; executive producer Tony Wolfe; produced by Diane Campbell; directed by David Dunn.

Matthew Kelly (Presenter), Max Wall, Jean Alexander, Richard Gibson, Ken Morley, Caroline Munro.

	Production No	Holding / Source
05.01.1990	4451	1" / 1"

Recorded May 1989.

ARMCHAIR THEATRE

An ABC/Thames production. Transmission details are for Various ITV Companies. Usual duration: 50 minutes.

SERIES 2

An ABC production. Transmission details are for the ABC midlands region. Duration: 50 minutes.

SUMMER ARMCHAIR THEATRE

Duration: 50 minutes.

Main regular credit(s):   Produced by Harry Alan Towers.

	Holding / Source
16.08.1959 **You'll Never See Me Again**	B3 / B3

Alternative transmissions: ABC: 16.08.1959.

Jim, an American architect living in England, is suspected of murdering his missing wife, but saves himself by an architectural hunch.

Written by Cornell Woolrich; adapted by Joel Murcott; produced by Harry Alan Towers; directed by Ted Post.

With Ben Gazzara (Jim Mason), Leo Genn (Inspector Stillman), Brenda de Banzie (Mrs Alden), James Hayes (Joe Alden), Derek Aylward (Bob Roberts), Jacqueline Ellis (Myra), Ivor Salter (Sergeant Mitchell), Betty McDowall (Anne Roberts).

Pilot for a series called Crime Club. Production began on 29th June 1959. A further script for a planned episode two was ready.

30.08.1959 **Invitation To Murder**	B3|n / B3

Alternative transmissions: ABC: 30.08.1959.

An eccentric millionaire writes a new will, leaving small amounts each week for life to five people, with the bulk of the estate to the last survivor. Very soon, the struggle to survive becomes a murder race.

Written by Joel Murcott; produced by Harry Alan Towers; directed by Robert Lynn.

With Robert Beatty (Michael Steel), Ernest Thesiger (Andrade), Lisa Daniely (Joan), Douglas Wilmer (Inspector Marquand), Catherine Feller (Leona), John Howlett (Sergeant Colbert), Bud Knapp (Boland), Denis Shaw (Karim), Guy Kingsley Poynter (Curtis), Keith Pyott (Doctor), Tony Thawnton (Waiter), Olga Dickie (Nurse Slagg).

Pilot for planned series that never happened. Television Today suggests this may have started life as The Saint, but Towers could not secure the rights to the name.

06.09.1959 **Young David**	J / B3

Alternative transmissions: ABC: 06.09.1959.

The early life of David Copperfield dramatised from Charles Dickens' famous novel.

Introduced by Fredric March; written by Charles Dickens; production supervised by Frank Sherwin Green; produced by Harry Alan Towers; directed by Robert Lynn.

With Robert Morley (Mr Micawber), Alan Wheatley (Mr Murdstone), Patricia Jessel (Miss Murdstone), Martin Stephens (David), Irene Handl (Mrs Micawber), Barbara Ogilvie (Peggotty), Ann Gudrun [as Anne Gudrun] (Mrs Copperfield), Fred Kitchen (Mr Quinion), Peter Bull (Mr Creakle), Marjorie Fleeson (Mrs Creakle), Michael Scoble (Mealy), Keith Smith (Captain Hopkins), Robert Raglan (First Creditor), Frank Pemberton (Second Creditor).

The TV Times notes that this "acts as a preview of the ABC series TALES FROM DICKENS, which is to be shown in the New Year."

SERIES 4

An ABC production. Transmission details are for the ABC midlands region.

Main regular credit(s):   Produced by Sydney Newman.

Holding / Source

24.06.1962 **Dumb Martian**   J|c / 40

Alternative transmissions: ABC: 24.06.1962.

Duncan Weaver, a space pilot, has reached 35, the age limit for flying. Duncan has consistently gambled away his pay So he accepts a job on a space station. The prospect of two years alone on the almost airless "pebble," less than 40 miles across, seems interminable.

Even a microfilmed library and a huge collection of taped music would not compensate for only one ship a month calling to re-fuel.

So to offset the loneliness, and to help with the chores, Duncan buys Lellie, a Martian girl. At first the "Mart's" lisping speech seems cute to Duncan. But as the novelty wears thin Duncan's boorishness emerges.

To him Marts are little better than dumb animals. He pushes Lellie around, treating her as a fool. A rare visitor is Dr. Alan Whint, a geologist. Whint is the opposite of Duncan. He's a thinking man and he doesn't underrate the
Marts. Lellie, naturally, becomes the sparking point of conflict between the two men. It is Lellie, too, who produces some surprises.

Based on a story by John Wyndham; designed by James Goddard; directed by Charles Jarrott.

With William Lucas (Duncan Weaver), Ray Barrett (Alan Whint), Hilda Schroder (Lellie), Garfield Morgan (Reception Clerk), Charles Morgan (Chief), Michael Bird (Harry), Mike Pratt (Mac), Morris Perry (Alastair), Raymond Adamson (Withers).

See also: OUT OF THIS WORLD.

SERIES 9

An ABC production. Transmission details are for the ABC midlands region. Duration: 50 minutes.

Main regular credit(s):   Produced by Leonard White.

Holding / Source

04.02.1967 **A Magnum For Schneider**   1"-R1|n / 40

Callan is a killer—but a reluctant one, prematurely retired at the age of 35 to become a clerk, because of a tendency to question orders and to show clemency to the targets assigned him. At the start of A Magnum for Schneider, Callan is offered his old job back — provided he kills Rudolph Schneider, a bluff German working in London.

Written by James Mitchell; story editor Terence Feely; designed by David Marshall; directed by Bill Bain.

With Edward Woodward (David Callan), Russell Hunter (Lonely), Ronald Radd (Colonel Hunter), Peter Bowles (Toby Meres), Joseph Furst (Rudolph Schneider), Ivor Dean (Waterman), Martin Wyldeck (Detective Inspector Pollock), John Scarborough (Detective Sergeant Jones), Helen Ford (Miss Brewis), Francesca Tu (Jenny), Judy Champ (Secretary).

See also: CALLAN.

18.02.1967 **Never Mind The Quality, Feel The Width**   J / 40

The play tells of a quarrel between Irish trouser maker Kelly and Jewish jacket maker Morris Cohen (John Bluthal). After winning an order for a suit from a betting shop proprietor (Dudley Foster). Kelly seeks a partnership with Cohen for whom he has worked for 15 years. But Cohen refuses. Even the priest and the rabbi. consorting over glasses of kosher rum, cannot reconcile them.

Written by Vince Powell and Harry Driver; story editor Terence Feely; designed by Stan Woodward; directed by Patrick Dromgoole.

With Frank Finlay (Patrick Kelly), John Bluthal (Emmanuel Cohen), Dudley Foster (George Gladwin), Venetia Maxwell (Rita), Charles Lamb (Wally), Michael McKevitt (Clerk), Christopher Benjamin (Rabbi Levy), Denis Carey (Father Ryan).

This became a successful ABC/Thames sitcom.

Billed as the second half of the 11th season.

See also: AFTER THE FUNERAL (RADIO)* / CALLAN* / CRIME CLUB / HOT SUMMER NIGHT (RADIO)* / LENA, OH MY LENA (RADIO)*

ARMCHAIR THRILLER

Produced for Thames/Southern by a variety of companies (see details below). Transmission details are for the ATV midlands region. Usual duration: 25 minutes.

Main regular credit(s):   Devised by Andrew Brown; theme music by Andy Mackay.

SERIES 1

A Thames Television production.

Quiet As A Nun

A nun dies of starvation in a convent tower. Jemima Shore is asked to investigate...

Main regular credit(s):   Adapted by Julia Jones; based on a book by Antonia Fraser; script executive Joan Rodker; story editor Robert Banks Stewart; music by
                                             Roger Webb; designed by Bill Palmer; produced by Jacqueline Davis; directed by Moira Armstrong.

Main regular cast: With Maria Aitken (Jemima Shore), Renée Asherson (Mother Ancilla), Doran Godwin (Sister Lucy).

	VT Number	Holding / Source
11.04.1978 **The Tower**	17745	D3 / 2"

With Brenda Bruce (Sister Elizabeth), James Laurenson (Alexander Skarbek), Margaret D'Arcy (Sister Clare), Linda Slater (Dodo), Sarah Webb (Margaret), Patsy Kensit (Tessa), Catrina Hylton (Mandy), David Burke, Michèle Winstanley, Kate Binchy, Mary Healey, James Appleby.

13.04.1978 **The Chapel**	17746	D3 / 2"

With Susan Engel (Sister Agnes), James Laurenson (Alexander Skarbek), Sylvia Coleridge (Sister Boniface), Margaret D'Arcy (Sister Clare), Linda Slater (Dodo), Sarah Webb (Margaret), Michèle Winstanley (Blanche), David Burke, Kate Binchy, Mary Healey.

18.04.1978 **The Black Nun**	17747	D3 / 2"

With Brenda Bruce (Sister Elizabeth), Sylvia Coleridge (Sister Boniface), Margaret D'Arcy (Sister Clare), Linda Slater (Dodo), Sarah Webb (Margaret), Michèle Winstanley (Blanche), Patsy Kensit (Tessa), Catrina Hylton (Mandy), Ronald Mayer.

| 20.04.1978 | **Witness And Wills** | | 17748 | D3 / 2" |

With Brenda Bruce (Sister Elizabeth), Susan Engel (Sister Agnes), Sylvia Coleridge (Sister Boniface), Margaret D'Arcy (Sister Clare), Linda Slater (Dodo), Sarah Webb (Margaret), Michèle Winstanley (Blanche), Patsy Kensit (Tessa), Catrina Hylton (Mandy), David Burke, Mary Healey, Elvi Hale, John Bryans, Helen Brindle.

| 25.04.1978 | **Powers Of Darkness** | | 17749 | D3 / 2" |

With Susan Engel (Sister Agnes), Sylvia Coleridge (Sister Boniface), Patsy Kensit (Tessa), Catrina Hylton (Mandy), Elvi Hale, John Bryans.

| 27.04.1978 | **Death And Decisions** | | 17750 | D3 / 2" |

With Brenda Bruce (Sister Elizabeth), Susan Engel (Sister Agnes), James Laurenson (Alexander Skarbek), Sylvia Coleridge (Sister Boniface), Margaret D'Arcy (Sister Clare), Linda Slater (Dodo), Sarah Webb (Margaret), Michèle Winstanley (Blanche), Patsy Kensit (Tessa), Catrina Hylton (Mandy)

The adventures of Jemima Shore proved so popular, that Thames went on to make Jemima Shore Investigates.

See also: THE CHELSEA MURDERS* / JEMIMA SHORE INVESTIGATES*

ARRIVEDERCI RHONDDA

A BBC Wales production for BBC 1 Wales. Transmission details are for BBC 1 Wales. Duration. 30 minutes.

Written by Robin Edwards and Johnny Tudor; produced by Robin Edwards; directed by Huw Thomas.

Windsor Davies (Archie McCarthy), Ruth Madoc (Kinkie Katinka), Johnny Tudor (Tony Bellini), Siôn Probert (Tyrone Powell), Patricia Kane (Maria Bellini), Melanie Walters (Sian Madog).

	Holding / Source
26.02.1995	DB / D3S

ART ... ADRIFT

A BBC Birmingham production for BBC. Never intended for transmission. Duration: 30 minutes.

Written by Peter Terson; script editor Tara Prem; music by Sidney Sager [credited as Sidney Sagar]; designed by Michael Edwards; produced by David Rose; directed by Eric Davidson.

Brian Glover (Art), Anne Raitt (Meg), Christopher Martin (Neville), Tony Caunter (Mason), Merelina Kendall (Lecturer), Roger Milner (Official), Terence Woodfield (Official).

	Production No	VT Number	Holding / Source
##.##.#### [untransmitted pilot]	01743/1750	VTC/6HT/89864/BM	DB / 2"

Recorded 1974.

See: PLAY FOR TODAY - The Fishing Party / Shakespeare Or Bust.

ART ATTACK

Produced for ITV by a variety of companies (see details below). Transmission details are for the Central region. Duration: 25 minutes.

Main regular cast: Neil Buchanan (Presenter).

SERIES 1

A TVS production.

	Holding / Source
##.##.#### [untransmitted pilot]	1" / 1"

Recorded 17.03.89.

ARTHUR AND PHIL GO OFF...

A Vulgar Productions production for Channel 4. Transmission details are for Channel 4. Duration varies - see below for details.

Main regular credit(s): Written by Phil Nice and Arthur Smith [jointly credited as Fiasco Job Job]; produced by Sue Hayes.

Main regular cast: Arthur Smith, Phil Nice.

	Holding / Source
16.12.1985 **To Boulogne**	1" / 1"

Duration: 40 minutes.

Directed by Geoff Wonfor.

With Jan Rhodes, Maxine Ostwold, Babs Sutton, Adam Wide.

ASK ODDIE

A HTV production. Transmission details are for the Central region.

Main regular cast: Bill Oddie (Presenter).

SERIES 1

Main regular credit(s): Produced by Peter Curtis; directed by Ken Price.

	Holding / Source
##.##.#### [untransmitted pilot]	1" / 1"

Duration: 20 minutes.

AT HOME WITH LARRY GRAYSON

An LWT production. Transmission details are for the Central region. Duration: 25 minutes.

Executive producer Barry Cox; produced by Paddy Haycocks; directed by Daniel Wiles and Peter Swain.

Larry Grayson (Host), Janet Street-Porter, Noele Gordon, John Hanson, Arthur Marshall.

	Holding / Source
26.08.1983	D2 / 1"

Originally made for Channel 4.

ATLETICO PARTICK

A BBC Scotland production for BBC 1. Transmission details are for BBC 1. Duration: 30 minutes.

Main regular credit(s):   Written by Ian Pattison; produced and directed by Colin Gilbert.

Main regular cast: Gordon Kennedy (Jack Roan).

Holding / Source

28.08.1995   DB-D3 / D3S

Things are looking gloomy for Atletico Partick AFC. The attendance on and off the pitch is atrocious and the team may soon disband. Only one manager can hope to recapture the glory days for Scotland's least successful Sunday
league side - and that's Jinky Baird.

With Clive Russell (Jinky Baird), Terry Neason (Minnie Baird), Aline Mowat (Karen Roan), Jonathan Watson (Budd), Tom McGovern (Ally), Steven McNicoll (Lachie), Gavin Mitchell (McStick), Iain McColl (Pettigrew), Gary Grochla (Barrhead Winger), Gordon Cameron (Social Worker), Iain Stuart Robertson (Marital Therapist), Libby McArthur (Trish), Johnny Irving (News Vendor), Stacey McKinnon (Girl With Dog), Douglas Paul (Ref).

AU PAIRS

An April Television Production production for Au Pair Holdings Ltd. Untransmitted. Duration: 24 minutes.

Created by Mike Prince; titles by Graham Holloway; developed by Jane Rossington; produced by Mike Prince.

Jane Rossington (Jennifer Jones).

Holding / Source

##.##.####   **Sylvie From Brittany**   B /

Written by Harriet Mills; songs by Ashley Hamilton-Jones; music by Dave Lowe and Julian Ronnie; directed by Graham Holloway.

With Maggie Moon, Anne Caris, Muge Milli, Ashley Hamilton-Jones, Andrew Westfield, Rebekah Savage, Tim Vincent, Sarah Reeves, Leti Oyam Buru, Dale Grimston, Julian Ronnie, Philip Sydney, Natalie Forbes, Lola De La Aguilera Patino, Andrea Bartenschlager, Catherine Brevin, Laura Fracasso, Candice Gair, Tina Garcia, Kerry Matthews, Eva Pecci-Fernandez, Susanen Pecci-Fernandez, Aurore Petin, Belen Rodriguez-Villar, Severine Roux, Lizzi Sanchez, Didem Serbetciougl, Maribel Torres.

1992 untx pilot

THE AUCTION GAME

An LWT production. Untransmitted. Duration: 23 minutes.

	Production No	Holding / Source
##.##.#### [untransmitted pilot]	9L/00025	J /

Made in 1968.

AUNTIE'S BLOOMERS

A BBC production for BBC 1. Transmission details are for BBC 1. Duration varies - see below for details.

Holding / Source

29.12.1991   DB / 1"S
A Celador production.
Produced by Paul Smith; directed by Patricia Mordecai.
With Terry Wogan (Host).

BADGER'S SET

A Yorkshire Television production. Transmission details are for the ATV midlands region. Duration: 50 minutes.

Written by Barry Took; music directed by Ken Jones; designed by Colin Pigott; produced by Paddy Russell.

Julian Orchard (Eric Badger / Doctor Badger), Gwen Taylor (Leila), Diane Mercer (Natasha Karavanovna), Beryl Cooke (Mrs Badger), Maggie Flint (Mrs Robash), Barry Halliday (Lee Kwan), Gwyn Gray (Trubshawe).

	Holding / Source
23.09.1974	1" / 2"

BALLAD OF JOHNNY VANGUARD

A TVS production. Untransmitted. Duration: 25 minutes.

Written by Dick Fiddy and Mark Wallington; produced by Humphrey Barclay.

Jeffrey Holland (Johnny Vanguard), John Bird (Agent), Lesley Joseph (Secretary), Nicky Croydon (Traffic Warden), Diane Bull (Fan), Pamela Cundell (Johnny's Mother), Fine Time Fontayne (Record Shop Owner), Peter Capaldi (Punk Rocker).

	Holding / Source
##.##.#### [untransmitted pilot]	1" / 1"

BARELY LEGAL

A the Comedy Unit production for BBC 3. Transmission details are for BBC 3. Duration: 30 minutes.

Written by Dave Baird, Tony Carter, Daniel Coombes, Joe da Costa, Iain Davidson, Chuck Gee, Chris Grudy, Alistair Griggs, Ginger Kidd, Andrew Mettam, Dominique Moore, Tim Telling, David Weir and Huw Williams; theme music by Action Group; designed by Laura Donnelly; production executive Susan Haynes; executive producers Rab Christie and Jon Rolph; produced by Gavin Smith; directed by William Andrew [credited as William Andrews].

Ellie Bird, Joe da Costa, David Hayler, Sophie McCabe, Dominique Moore, Ekow Quartey, Michael Kelly.

	Holding / Source
26.05.2008	DB / DBSWF

THE BARKING PARROT SHOW

A BBC Bristol production. Untransmitted.

Mark Curry (Host), Shyama Perera (Host), Jake Thackray.

	Holding / Source
##.##.#### [untransmitted pilot]	1" / 1"

BARNET

A BBC production for BBC 2. Transmission details are for BBC 2. Duration: 30 minutes.

Maurice, who was once employed by Ponsonby's Hairdressing in London's West End, has been left with a set of values that have no place in the tatty East End establishment he now runs. The carping remarks of his disillusioned wife. Phoebe, her shady relatives and Petal, her daughter by a previous marriage, all serve to make his life pretty unbearable. Will going unisex really help matters?

Written by Doris Richards and Allen Sadler; lighting by Peter Smee; sound Len Shorey; designed by Tony Snoaden; produced by Harold Snoad; directed by Mandie Fletcher.

Donald Churchill (Maurice Barnet), Patrick Cargill (Clive Parmeter), Toni Palmer (Phoebe), Andrew Paul (Cliff), Sarah Webb (Petal), Brian Peck (Alf), Tony Calvert (Skinhead), Ian Halcrow (Skinhead).

	Holding / Source
03.04.1985	DB / 1"

BARNEY IS MY DARLING

A BBC production for BBC 1. Transmission details are for BBC 1. Duration: 30 minutes.

Main regular credit(s):   Written by Marty Feldman and Barry Took; music by Max Harris; designed by Peter Seddon; produced and directed by James Gilbert.

Main regular cast: Irene Handl (Ramona Pank), Bill Fraser (Barney Pank).

	Holding / Source
17.12.1965 **Home Is The Sailor**	J /

With Angela Crow, George Tovey, Margaret Flint, Peter Cleall.

BARRYMORE

An LWT production. Transmission details are for the Central region. Duration varies - see below for details.

Main regular performer(s): Michael Barrymore (Host).

	Production No	Holding / Source
##.##.#### [untransmitted pilot]	92388	D2 / 1"

Duration: 52 minutes.

Written by Geoff Atkinson, Simon Ball, Richard Herring, Stewart Lee and Andy Walker; research Carolynne Chandler, Peter Gwyn and Rhona Howat; designed by Margaret Howat; associate producer Chris O'Dell; executive producer John Kaye Cooper; production manager Barry Read; produced and directed by Ian Hamilton; location sequences directed by Chris Fox.

With Don Hunt and his Orchestra.

Recorded 29.06.91

BARTHOLOMEW BINKS

A Kingston Films production for a variety of companies (see details below). Untransmitted. Duration: 25 minutes.

Comedy about a naive policeman.

Produced by Robert Kingston; directed by Gordon Shadrack.

Stephen Lewis (Bartholomew Binks), Fiona Curzon, George Moon, Tom Collister, David Boliver, Sally Douglas, Alan Granville.

	Holding / Source
##.##.#### **[untransmitted pilot]**	J /

According to the Stage and Television Today [03.09.1970] a pilot was made for this series.

BASH

A BBC production for BBC 3. Transmission details are for BBC 3. Duration: 30 minutes.

A woman organises a Halloween party to impress her boss but her plans come to naught as the evening descends into chaos.

Written by Robin French and Kieron Quirke; script supervisor Victoria Peacock; production executive Sarah Hitchcock; executive producers Micheal Jacob and Paul Schlesinger; produced by Adam Bromley; directed by Dominic Brigstocke.

Susan Earl (Stacey), Ben Willbond (Henry), Andrew Garfield (Dylan), Leo Bill (Boghead), Kevin R. McNally (Mr West), Daisy Haggard (Ness), Rasmus Hardiker (Neil), Rez Kempton (Conor), Andrea Green (Sarah), Naomi Bentley (Rachel).

	Holding / Source
05.02.2007	DB / DBSWF

BATTLE OF THE FANTASY BANDS

A BBC production for BBC 1. Transmission details are for BBC 1.

Terry Wogan (Host), Ulrika Jonsson (Host).

	Holding / Source
19.01.2001	DB / DBSW

BBC NEW TALENT WEEK

A BBC production for BBC 3. Transmission details are for BBC 3. Duration: 30 minutes.

	Holding / Source
21.03.2005 **I'm With Stupid**	DB / DBSWF

A BBC Manchester production.

Written by Daniel Peak; from an idea by Peter Keeley; script supervisor Sian Prosser; production executive Claire Asbury; executive producer Kenton Allen; produced by Jon Mountague; directed by Dominic Brigstocke.

With Paul Henshall (Paul), Mark Benton (Sheldon), Steve Edge (Sergeant Swithenbank), Ruth Jones (Jean), Alan Martin (Graham), Kevin Davies (Syd), Olivia Jardith (Old Lady), Seymour Mace (Homeless Man), Dennis Conlon (Shopkeeper), Michael Hugo (Police Constable Darren Rodgers).

22.03.2005 **10:96**	DB / DBSWF

A BBC Manchester production.

Two policemen who spend a claustrophobic evening in their patrol car under the call sign 10:96. Sergeant Barnes has high blood pressure and low self esteem but means well, while PC Sands is Anglo-Indian and soon becomes the victim of his boss's comical attempts to be politically correct.

Written by Tony Burgess; produced by Kenton Allen; directed by Noreen Kershaw.

With Neil Fitzmaurice (Sergeant Gary Barnes), Chris Bisson (Constable David Sands), Kaleem Janjua, Fiona Clarke, Tony Nyland, Miriam Ali, Mo Manir, Mushi Noor, Ben Thomson, Tony Skipp.

23.03.2005 **Marigold**	DB / DBSWF

Written by Robin Taylor; script supervisors Victoria Peacock and Teresa Powick; script editor Brian Dooley; music by Lorraine Bowen; production executive Sarah Hitchcock; executive producers Sophie Clarke-Jervoise and Micheal Jacob; produced by Eirwen Davies; directed by Martin Dennis.

With Selina Griffiths (Marigold), Angus Deayton (Kenneth), Augustus Prew (Jack), Amy Yamazaki (Charlotte), William Thomas (Milkman), Liam Noble (Dave), Antony Worrall Thompson (Himself), Sarah Whittuck (Passer By), Helen Modern (Record Shop Assistant), Bella Hewitt (Young Marigold).

Pilot episodes for possible series.

See also: I'M WITH STUPID

BE MORE ETHNIC

A BBC production for BBC 3. Transmission details are for BBC 3. Duration: 30 minutes.

Fitting in isn't easy in the world of Sol De Silva - his best mate thinks he's great, his new flatmate thinks he's psychotic, and his dad thinks he's a doctor.

Christopher Simpson, Keith Duffy, Laura Donnelly.

	Holding / Source
18.03.2007	DB / DBSW

BEADLE'S HOT SHOTS

An LWT production. Transmission details are for the Central region.

Main regular cast: Jeremy Beadle (Presenter).

	Holding / Source
##.##.#### **[untransmitted pilot]**	DV /

BEADLE'S PEOPLE

A Tintagel production for Beadle Productions. Untransmitted. Duration: 22 minutes.

Jeremy Beadle (Presenter).

	Holding / Source
##.##.#### [untransmitted pilot 1998]	DV /

Recorded 30.06.1998 at Molinare.

BEASTS

An ATV production. Transmission details are for the HTV West region. Duration: 50 minutes.

Written by Nigel Kneale; produced by Nicholas Palmer.

	Production No	VT Number	Holding / Source
##.##.#### During Barty's Party [untransmitted pilot]	1755	1755/75	

Designed by Anthony Waller; directed by Don Taylor.

Recorded 05.09.1975.

BEAT YOUR NEIGHBOUR

A BBC production. Untransmitted.

	VT Number	Holding / Source
##.##.#### [untransmitted pilot]	16/A/19261	J /

Recorded 1963.

BEATS PER MINUTE

A Music Box production for Granada. Transmission details are for the Granada region. Duration: 25 minutes.

SERIES 1

	Production No	Holding / Source
12.12.1992 [first pilot]	1/8240/0001	DB / D3
19.12.1992 [second pilot]	1/8240/0002	DB / D3

BEFORE THEY WERE FAMOUS

A BBC Light Entertainment production for BBC 1. Transmission details are for BBC 1. Duration varies - see below for details.

Clips of famous people in early roles.

	Holding / Source
31.03.1997	DB-D3 / D3S

Duration: 40 minutes.

Produced by Caroline Wright; directed by Stuart McDonald.

With Angus Deayton (Presenter).

BEING HUMAN

A Touchpaper Television production for BBC Wales. Transmission details are for BBC 3. Duration: 60 minutes.

Main regular credit(s):	Created by Toby Whithouse.
Main regular cast:	Russell Tovey (George).

	Holding / Source
18.02.2008	DB / DBSWF

Pilot about the friendship between three unusual flatmates. Mitchell and George are a vampire and a werewolf, while their agoraphobic pal Annie also harbours a macabre secret.

Written by Toby Whithouse; script supervisor Vicki Howe; music by Sam Watts; designed by Andrew Purcell; production executive Helen Municchi; executive producer Rob Pursey; produced by Matthew Bouch; directed by Declan O'Dwyer.

With Guy Flanagan (Mitchell), Andrea Riseborough (Annie), Claire Foy (Julia), Adrian Lester (Herrick), Dominique McElligott (Lauren), Dylan Brown (Seth), Saikat Ahamed (Mortuary Attendant), Charmaine Hibberd (Neeru), Zara Ramm (Cathy), Huw Davies (Rory), Will Irvine (Peter), Nathalie Armin (Eleanor).

See also: BECOMING HUMAN*

BELMINSTER BREW

A Central production. Untransmitted.

Created by John Hawkesworth and Jeremy Burnham; developed by John Hawkesworth.

	Holding / Source
##.##.#### [untransmitted pilot]	J / 1"

BERNIE CLIFTON ON STAGE

An ATV production. Transmission details are for the ATV midlands region. Duration: 25 minutes.

Written by David Renwick, Andrew Marshall and Max Sherrington; designed by Mike Perry; produced and directed by Royston Mayoh.

Bernie Clifton (Host), Superhoof, Rusty Goffe, Carol Asti, Denny Piercey, Michael Clifton, Geoff Thacker, Dickie Davies, Aiden J. Harvey.

	Holding / Source
06.07.1980	DB / 2"

BEWITCHED

A BBC production. Untransmitted. Duration: 30 minutes.

2008 remake of the classic American sitcom.

Sheridan Smith (Samantha), Tom Price (Darrin), Frances de la Tour (Endora).

	Holding / Source
##.## #### [untransmitted pilot]	HD/DB / HD/DB

BIG BREAK - A CELEBRITY CHRISTMAS SPECIAL

A BBC production for BBC 1. Transmission details are for BBC 1. Usual duration: 30 minutes.

Main regular performer(s): Jim Davidson (Presenter), John Virgo (Referee).

	Holding / Source
##.##.#### [untransmitted pilot]	DB / 1"

With Mike Reid (Presenter).

THE BIG MATCH

A Granada production for Granada Media Group. Untransmitted. Duration: 50 minutes.

A studio-based dating show in which 100 guys compete in a series of light-hearted compatibility games in order to win a date with one dream girl. Everyone arrives with their bags packed because at the end of the show, the lucky last man standing and the girl depart immediately for a fantasy vacation.

Executive producers Dwight Smith and Michael Agbabian; produced by Mark Johnson.

Cat Deeley (Presenter).

	Production No	Holding / Source
##.##.#### [untransmitted pilot]	P6845/1	DB / DBSW

Made for Granada USA (Los Angeles).

BIG NIGHT IN

A BBC production for BBC 2. Transmission details are for BBC 2. Duration: 30 minutes.

Executive producer Sue Davidson; produced by Duncan Gray.

The Knowles Family (Presenters).

	Holding / Source
10.11.1995	DB / D3S

BIG TRAIN

A Talkback production for BBC 2. Transmission details are for BBC 2. Duration: 29 minutes.

Main regular credit(s): Director of photography John Rosenberg; production designer Dennis De Groot; executive producers Peter Fincham and Geoffrey Perkins; production manager Jo Hunter.

	Holding / Source
##.##.#### [untransmitted pilot]	J / DBS

Written by Graham Linehan and Arthur Mathews; produced by Caroline Leddy; directed by Christopher Morris.

BILLY DAINTY, ESQ.

A Thames Television production. Transmission details are for the ATV midlands region.

Main regular credit(s): Produced and directed by Dennis Kirkland.

Main regular performer(s): Billy Dainty.

	Holding / Source
17.09.1975	J / 2"

Duration: 50 minutes.

Over 38 years ago, Billy Dainty started rolling 'em in the aisles. Now this veteran comedian, singer, sketch-man and dancer has his own variety show on television.

Written by Vince Powell and Brian Cooke; designed by Patrick Downing.

With Michael Robbins, Victor Spinetti, Sheila White, Kate Williams, Keith Fordyce, Janet Webb, The Lionel Blair Dancers, The Mike Sammes Singers.

THE BILLY WEST SHOW

A Granada production. Untransmitted.

Designed by Colin Pocock; directed by John Birt.

Tim Davies, Richard Harbord, Paul McDowell, Mick Sadler, Hilary Pritchard.

	Production No	Holding / Source
##.##.#### [untransmitted pilot]	P659/DR	J / 2"

Recorded 22nd May 1970.

BIRD'S-EYE VIEW

A BBC production for BBC 2. Transmission details are for BBC 2. Duration: 50 minutes.

Main regular credit(s): Series editor Edward Mirzoeff.

	Holding / Source
24.12.1967 **Birds-Eye View Of Great Britain**	C1 / C1

A BIT OF AN ADVENTURE

A Yorkshire Television production. Transmission details are for the ATV midlands region. Duration: 55 minutes.

Mable Maple, wife of writer Gordon, is used to creative problems and the people concerned. But in this play, even she draws the line at Jean Paul, a French film director with a limitless capacity for destroying everything and everyone in sight.

Over smoked salmon and white wine, Mable and Jean Paul do battle, with Gordon the unwilling buffer.

Written by Charles Wood; designed by Alan Pickford; executive producer Peter Willes; directed by Marc Miller.

George Cole (Gordon Maple), Gwen Watford (Mabel Maple), Pierre Vaneck (Jean Paul), Fanny Rowe (Gordon's Mother), Raymond Francis (Gordon's Father), Kim McDonald (Catherine Maple), Merlin Ward (Nigel Maple).

	VT Number	Holding / Source
21.07.1974	Y/0155/0001	B / 2"

See also: DON'T FORGET TO WRITE!"

THE BIZZ

A Thames Television production. Transmission details are for the Central region. Duration: 25 minutes.

Main regular credit(s):   Produced by Kate Marlow; directed by Graeme Matthews.

Main regular performer(s): Lisa Maxwell (Presenter), Kelly Temple (Presenter).

	VT Number	Holding / Source
##.##.#### Untransmitted pilot	34374	1" / 1"

With Arcadia, Billboard, Duran Duran, The Housemartins, Jelly's, Katrina, Paul King, Freddie Mercury, Billy Ocean, Swimwear, Video Cafe.

BLACKPOOL NIGHT OUT

An ABC production. Transmission details are for the ABC midlands region. Duration: 52 minutes.

	Holding / Source
##.##.#### [untransmitted pilot]	J / 40

From the ABC Theatre, Blackpool

THE BLACKPOOL SHOW

An ABC Manchester production for ABC. Transmission details are for the ABC midlands region. Duration: 52 minutes.

	VT Number	Holding / Source
##.##.#### [untransmitted pilot]	VTR/5789	J / 40

With Tony Hancock (Compere), Keith Harris, Gordon and Bunny Jay, Toni Eden, Al Saxon.

RX: 12/06/1966.

From the ABC Theatre, Blackpool.

BLANKETY BLANK

A BBC production for BBC 1. made in association with Mark Goodson / Talbot TV Ltd. Transmission details are for BBC 1. Duration varies - see below for details.

Main regular credit(s):   Theme music by Ronnie Hazlehurst.

Main regular performer(s): With Terry Wogan (Host).

	Holding / Source
##.##.#### [first untransmitted pilot]	DB-D3 / 2"
##.##.#### [second Untransmitted pilot]	DB-D3 / 2"

BLIND DATE

An LWT production. Transmission details are for the Central region.

Cilla Black made this series her own! Love matches or not!

Duncan Norvelle (Presenter).

	Holding / Source
##.##.#### [untransmitted pilot]	J / 1"

BLISS

An Abbey Films production for Carlton UK. Transmission details are for the Central region. Usual duration: 75 minutes.

Main regular credit(s):   Devised by Michael Stewart; produced by Jacky Stoller.

Main regular cast: Simon Shepherd (Doctor Sam Bliss), Siân Webber (Doctor Melanie Kilpatrick), Sarah Smart (Zoe Bliss), Zoe Hart (Louise Bliss).

	Production No	Holding / Source
11.10.1995	CAR/00432/0001	D2 / V1S

"We are at the stage where we can write our own biological destinies. But do we understand the moral implications? At root, to whom does life belong?" This is the question at the ethical heart of this thriller about murder, the quest for eternal youth and the scientific mind. Dr Sam Bliss, a Cambridge medical researcher who gets drawn into the mystery surrounding the deaths of two young women. It transpires that these women were descendents of a community which, by some genetic mutation, lived to more than 150 years. And they both died by being bled to death. Is someone trying to harvest the longevity gene carried in their blood and can Bliss and his assistant Dr Melanie Kilpatrick track down the killer before he gets to his third victim?

Written by Michael Stewart; script supervisor Sue Clegg; music by Daemion Barry; associate producer Dominic Fulford; directed by Marc Evans.

With Jonathan Hyde, Reece Dinsdale, Eva Marie Bryer, Jennifer Hilary, Deborah Norton, Robert Morgan, John Normington, Peter Penry Jones, Doyne Byrd, Chris Larkin, Wendy Nottingham, Stanley Townsend, Neville Phillips, Philip Fowke, Michael Stewart, Jackie Murray, Samantha Cones, Susannah Wise, Selma Alispahic.

BLISTERS

A BBC production. Untransmitted. Duration: 30 minutes.

Patsy Kensit, William Gaunt.

	Production No	Holding / Source
##.##.#### [untransmitted pilot]	LLCE328L/72	DB / 1"

No end credits.

BLOCKBUSTERS

A Central production. Transmission details are for the Central region. Duration: 25 minutes.

	Production No	VT Number	Holding / Source
##.##.#### [untransmitted pilot]	9245/81	14196x6	J / 2"

Recorded 17.12.1981.

BLUNDER

A Channel X production for Channel 4. Transmission details are for Channel 4. Duration: 25 minutes.

Main regular credit(s):   Written by Nina Conti, Simon Farnaby, Tom Meeten, David Mitchell, Rhys Thomas and Tony Way; additional material by Steve Burge and Glynne Wiley; script supervisor Katie Harlow; script editor Charlie Higson; theme music by Matt Berry; music by Trellis and Steve Burge; director of photography Andy Hollis; titles by Mr and Mrs Wheatley; art directors Phil Barber and Doug Slocombe; designed by Greg Shaw; series producers Alan Marke and Jim Reid; line producer Rebecca Ferrand; directed by Richard Valentine; additional direction by Joe Cornish.

Main regular cast: Tony Way, Nina Conti, Simon Farnaby, Tom Meeten, David Mitchell, Rhys Thomas.

	Holding / Source
##.##.#### [untransmitted pilot]	DB / DBSW

All of David Mitchell's appearances derive from the untransmitted pilot.

BOB AND MARGARET

A Snowden Fine Animation production for Channel 4. made in association with Global / National Film Board of Canada / Nelvana. Transmission details are for Channel 4.

Main regular credit(s):   Created by Alison Snowden and David Fine; written by Alison Snowden and David Fine; executive producers Michael Hirsh, Patrick Loubert and Clive Smith; produced by Alison Snowden and David Fine; directed by Alison Snowden, David Fine and Jamie Whitney.

Main regular cast: Andy Hamilton (Bob), Alison Snowden (Margaret).

	Holding / Source
26.03.1995 **Bob's Birthday**	C1 / C1S

Duration: 15 minutes.

Animated series.

BOBBY DAVRO ON THE BOX

A TVS production. Transmission details are for the Central region.

Main regular credit(s):   Music by Andy Street; designed by Greg Lawson; associate producer Alan Nixon; produced by John Kaye Cooper.

Main regular cast: Bobby Davro, Jessica Martin, Alyn Ainsworth and his Orchestra.

	Holding / Source
19.05.1985	1" / 1"

Duration: 40 minutes.

Written by Geoff Atkinson, Paul Minett and Brian Leveson; choreography by Chris Power; directed by John Kaye Cooper.

With Jim Sweeney, The Chris Power Dancers.

BOBBY DAVRO'S TV WEEKLY

A TVS production. Transmission details are for the Central region. Duration varies - see below for details.

Main regular cast: Bobby Davro, Jessica Martin, Alyn Ainsworth and his Orchestra.

	Holding / Source
27.12.1986 **Bobby Davro's TV Annual**	1" / 1"

Duration: 40 minutes.

Written by Geoff Atkinson, Charlie Adams, Eric Davidson, Russel Lane, Paul Minett and Brian Leveson; designed by Quentin Chases; associate producer Alan Nixon; produced by John Kaye Cooper; directed by Nigel Lythgoe.

With No guest cast.

BOBBY'S YOUR UNCLE

A BBC production for BBC Radio 4. Not made. Duration: 30 minutes.

Written by Bob Monkhouse.

Bob Monkhouse ('Uncle' Bobby Mason).

	Holding / Source
##.##.#### **The Return Of Francis X. Bushman**	NR /

Sitcom about a DJ called 'Uncle' Bobby Mason pitched but never made.

BOB'S FULL HOUSE

A BBC production for BBC 1. Transmission details are for BBC 1. Usual duration: 35 minutes.

Main regular credit(s):   Devised by Terry Mardell and David Moore; theme music by John Mealing.

Main regular performer(s): Bob Monkhouse (Host).

	Holding / Source
##.##.#### **Top Of The Shop [first pilot]**	DB|a / 1"
Duration: 31 minutes.	
## ## #### **Top Of The Shop [second pilot]**	DB|a / 1"
Duration: 39 minutes.	
##.##.#### **[untransmitted pilot]**	DB / 1"
Recorded 11.06.84.	

The on-screen title omits the apostrophe in the opening credits but often includes it during the end titles.

BOB'S YOUR UNCLE

A Central production. Transmission details are for the Central region.

Main regular performer(s): Bob Monkhouse (Host).

Duration: 50 minutes.

	VT Number	Holding / Source
##.##.#### **[first pilot]**	5572/90	DV / 1"
Recorded 09.10.90.		
##.##.#### **[second pilot]**	5573/90	DV / 1"
Recorded 09.10.1990.		

BODYGUARDS

A Zenith Films production for Carlton. Transmission details are for the Central region. Duration: 50 minutes.

Main regular credit(s):   Created by Jeffrey Caine; produced by Nigel Stafford-Clark.

Main regular cast: Louise Lombard (Liz Shaw), Sean Pertwee (Ian Worrell), John Shrapnel (Alan MacIntyre).

	Holding / Source
10.04.1996	D2 / V1S

The premise of the series (about the work of the Close Protection Group, a handpicked team dedicated to protecting politicians, celebrities and royalty) also gives the stars Louise Lombard, Sean Pertwee and John Shrapnel plenty of opportunity to stride about looking in turns tense, cool, alert and efficient. In this pilot for a possible series, Josette Simon and George Harris play rival candidates for the presidency of an African country in need of protection while attending a high-level governmental conference.

Written by Jeffrey Caine; associate producer Dominic Fulford; directed by Robert Bierman.

With Josette Simon, Stefan Kalipha, George Harris, Jeffry Wickham, Terence Harvey, Jonathan Coy, Geoffrey Beevers, Matt Bardock, Peter McNamara, Giorgio Serafini, Sam Lathem, Trevor Cooper, Mark Womack, Robert Horwell, Ged Simmons, Raymond Johnson, Matthew Brenher, Andreas Petrides, Colin Mace, Frank Jarvis, Freddie Stuart, Michael Bell.

BONKERS!

An ATV production. Transmission details are for the ATV midlands region. Duration: 25 minutes.

Main regular credit(s):   Written by Jack Burns, David Pollock and Elias Davis; additional material by Bob Monkhouse; music by Jack Parnell and his Orchestra; choreography by Norman Maen; executive producer Thomas M. Battista; production manager Harry Bell; produced by Jack Burns; directed by Peter Harris.

Main regular cast: Bob Monkhouse (Host), The Hudson Brothers, The Bonkettes, Jack Parnell and his Orchestra.

	VT Number	Holding / Source
14.07.1979 **[second pilot]**	2420/78	DB / 2"
Designed by Ken Wheatley.		
With Rita Moreno.		
28.07.1979 **[first pilot]**	2419/78	DB / 2"
Designed by David Chandler.		
With Sandy Duncan.		

Each VTR number was given a /PAL and /NTSC suffix. There appear to be different designers for each country.

Shaun O'Riordan at a later date re-recorded many Bob Monkhouse links on the /PAL VTR number to make the show's more English.

BOOK 'EM AN' RISK IT

A Bright Thoughts Company production for Channel 4. Transmission details are for Channel 4. Duration: 50 minutes.

Written by The Cast; music directed by Kenny Clayton; produced by Neil Anthony and Bryan Izzard; directed by Bryan Izzard.

Jim Barclay, Arnold Brown, Jock McLog and McNikki, The Oblivion Boys, Adrian Hedley, Trimmer and Jenkins, The Chip Shop Show, The Joeys, Steve Dixon.

	Holding / Source
11.08.1983	1"|n / 1"

BOOK OF LISTS

An LWT production. Never intended for transmission.Duration: 45 minutes.

Jeremy Beadle (Presenter), Bill Oddie, Bernard Manning, Suzi Quatro, Nigel Dempster.

	Holding / Source
##.##.#### [untransmitted pilot]	DV / 2"

Recorded 20th December 1983

THE BOOK PROGRAMME

A BBC production. Untransmitted.

	VT Number	Holding / Source
##.##.#### [untransmitted pilot]	16/P/7905	J /

Recorded 01.03.1960.

	VT Number	Holding / Source
##.##.#### [untransmitted pilot film insert]	35/P/T/8264	J /

Recorded 29.03.1960.

BOOKIE

A Scottish Television production. Transmission details are for the Central region. Duration: 50 minutes.

Transmission details are for the Scottish Television region. Duration: 54 minutes.

Credits: Written by Allan Prior; executive producer Robert Love; produced and directed by Leonard White.

Cast: With Robert Urquhart (Sam), Jeananne Crowley (Jill), Elizabeth Millbank (Sarah), Michael Mackenzie (Tom), Phil McCall (Alec), John Murtagh (Tony), Betty Gillin (Annie), Patrick Lewsley (Pat).

	VT Number	Holding / Source
06.12.1983	7232	1" / 2"

The pilot was only shown in the Scottish region.

BOTH ENDS MEET

An ATV production. Untransmitted. Duration: 25 minutes.

A bicycle shop owner resists selling her shop when the neighbourhood becomes more fashionable.

Written by Jan Butlin; produced and directed by Bob Spiers.

Barbara Windsor (Doris White), John Blundell (Chalky White), Pauline Quirke (Cissy White), Sue Holderness (Prue Saunders), Jeremy Sinden (Timothy Saunders), Ronald Leigh-Hunt (Sir Roland McFarn), Richard Clifford (Toby), Reginald Marsh (Sir Henry Blair), Gorden Kaye (Mr Wright), Hugh Quarshie (Malcolm St. John Peterson), Joan Benham (Nora Pritchard), Pat Keen (Monica Blythe).

	Production No	VT Number	Holding / Source
##.##.#### [untransmitted pilot]	5872	5872/80	DB / 2"

Location filming 23.09.1980; studio recording 30.09.1980.

BOTTLE BOYS

An LWT production. Transmission details are for the Central region. Duration: 25 minutes.

Main regular credit(s):   Created by Vince Powell; produced and directed by Stuart Allen.

Main regular cast: Robin Askwith (Dave Deacon), Oscar James (Joe Phillips).

	Holding / Source
##.##.#### Lotta Bottle [untransmitted pilot]	2"|n / 2"

BOWLING GREEN

An Associated-Rediffusion production. Untransmitted. Duration: 25 minutes.

	VT Number	Holding / Source
##.##.#### [first pilot]	W1801/137	J / 40

Written by Alun Falconer; directed by Joan Kemp-Welch.

With Dorothy Bromley (Jennifer), Naomi Chance (Helen), Ivor Danvers (Hugh), Alexander Davion (Ray), Brian McDermott (John), Frederick Peisley (Frank), Wensley Pithey (Jacob), Elsie Wagstaff (Aunt Beatrice), Dermot Walsh (David).

		Holding / Source
##.##.#### Episode One [second pilot attempt]		J / 40

Directed by Ian Fordyce.

With Richard Caldicot (Jacob Cresswell), Naomi Chance (Helen Cresswell), Dorothy Bromiley (Jennifer Cresswell), Robin Culver (John Cresswell), Daphne Riggs (beatrice Cresswell), John Lee (David Masters), Noëlle Middleton (Moyra Middleton), Natasha Pyne (Meg Masters), James Donnelly (Ray Hudson), Noel Coleman (Richard Black), Frederick Peisley (Frank Hudson), Wendy McClure (Joan Strange), Stephen Hancock (Hugh Williams).

Recorded 20.06.63.

		Holding / Source
##.##.#### Episode Two [second pilot attempt]		J / 40

Directed by Ian Fordyce.

With Richard Caldicot (Jacob Cresswell), Naomi Chance (Helen Cresswell), Dorothy Bromily (Jennifer Cresswell), Robin Culver (John Cresswell), Daphne Riggs (Beatrice Cresswell), John Lee (David Masters), Noëlle Middleton (Moyra Masters), Natasha Pyne (Meg Masters), James Donnelly (Ray Hudson), Noel Coleman (Richard Black), Frederick Peisley (Frank Hudson), Wendy McClure (Joan Strange), Stephen Hancock (Hugh Williams), Edward Jewesbury (Doctor), Vernon Morris (Peter).

Recorded 21.06.63.

Pilots for a proposed series which was never made.

THE BOYS FROM IPANEMA

An ATV production. Untransmitted. Duration: 25 minutes.

Written by Andrew Nickolds and Stan Hey; theme music by Christopher Neil; produced and directed by Bob Spiers.

Paul Nicholas (Ronald/Paul Pope), Tony Melody (Mr Wilkinson), Christopher Neil (Chris Wilkinson).

	Production No	VT Number	Holding / Source
##.##.#### **With A Song In My Love-Heart**	5744	5744/80	2" / 2"

Filming 19.05.1980; studio recording 03.06.1980.

BOYS FROM THE BLACKSTUFF

A BBC production for BBC 2. Transmission details are for BBC 2. Duration varies - see below for details.

Main regular credit(s): Written by Alan Bleasdale.

Main regular cast: Michael Angelis (Chrissy/Chrissie Todd), Tom Georgeson (Dixie Dean), Alan Igbon (Loggo Logmond), Gary Bleasdale (Kevin Dean), Peter Kerrigan (George Malone), Bernard Hill (Yosser Hughes).

	Holding / Source
02.01.1980 **The Black Stuff**	DB-D3 / C1

A BBC Manchester production. Duration: 110 minutes.

A Merseyside tarmac gang at work on Teeside.

Script editor Michael Wearing; designed by Chris Edwards; produced by David Rose; directed by Jim Goddard.

With Jean Warren (Maureen), Janine Duvitski (Student), Edward Peel (Clerk of Works), David Calder (McKenna), Valerie Lilley (Doris), Sean Lynch (Brendan), Alan Lake (Dominic), Lois Baxter (Masseuse), Michael Wardle (Lorry Driver), David Theakston (Bank Manager), Derry Jordan (Bank Clerk), Juliet Cooke (Hotel Manageress), Neville Wright (Businessman), Adrian Nolan (First Irishman), Brendan McIlduff (Second Irishman), Kathryn Apanowicz (Girl in House), Georgina Smith (Service Station Lady), Alison Ambler (Shop Assistant), Ralph Hawkes (Farmer).

David Attwood was the Production Assistant.

THE BRADLEY WALSH SHOW

An ITV Productions production for ITV 1. Untransmitted.

	Holding / Source
##.##.#### **[untransmitted pilot]**	DB / DBSW

BRAINWAVES

A Roxy Films production. Untransmitted. Duration: 25 minutes.

The series was to be based on Sykes' reactions to the peculiar, crazy, or bizarre inventions of the last century. Real working models of these contraptions would be made—and Sykes let loose among them.

Produced and directed by B. Charles-Dean.

Eric Sykes.

	Holding / Source
##.##.#### **[untransmitted pilot]**	J / B3

Made in August 1960. 26 x 25mins were planned.

BRASS

A Granada production. Transmission details are for the Central region. Duration: 25 minutes.

Main regular credit(s): Written by John Stevenson and Julian Roach; theme music by Kenyon Emrys-Roberts.

Main regular cast: Timothy West (Bradley Hardacre), Caroline Blakiston (Lady Patience), Barbara Ewing (Agnes Fairchild), David Ashton (Doctor Macduff), James Saxon (Morris Hardacre), Gail Harrison (Isobel Hardacre), Emily Morgan (Charlotte Hardacre), Shaun Scott (Jack Fairchild), Gary Cady (Matthew Fairchild).

SERIES 1

Transmission details are for the Central region.

Main regular credit(s): Produced by Bill Podmore; directed by Gareth Jones.

Main regular cast: With Geoffrey Hinsliff (George Fairchild), Robert Reynolds (Austin Hardacre).

	Production No	Holding / Source
21.02.1983 **Episode 1**	P1034/1	1" / 2"

Designed by Chris Wilkinson.

With Bill Monks (Job Lott).

BRAVE YOUNG MEN

A Baby Cow Productions production for BBC 3. Transmission details are for BBC 3. Duration: 30 minutes.

Two friends must combat global disasters.

Written by Sam Leifer and Tom Basden; music by Kevin Sargent; designed by Paul Cripps; executive producers Henry Normal, Alison MacPhail and Simon Lupton; produced by Teddy Leifer; directed by Sam Leifer.

Marc Wootton (Owen Malloy), Tom Basden (Jamie Husband), Patrick Barlow (?), Dominic Coleman (Iain Beasley), Joanna Neary (Miss Violet), Jonny Sweet (Mr Knowles), Daniel Lawrence Taylor (Eric), Ruth Sheen (Stephanie Molloy), Chloe Palmer (Jasmine Malloy), Mathew Baynton (Dylan), Tom Joseph (Wiseman).

	Holding / Source
22.03.2009	HD/DB / HD/DB

BRIDGE

A BBC production. Untransmitted.

	VT Number	Holding / Source
##.##.#### [untransmitted 1976 pilot]	VTC/6HP/B	DB / 2"

BRITAIN IN BRIEF

An Ulster Television production. Untransmitted.

Round-up of off-beat stories filmed by ITV's regional companies.

Brian Connell (Host).

	Holding / Source
##.##.####	J /

The pilot was shown on closed circuit television to help journalists understand the format. Four episodes were planned to be made.

THE BRITISH SITUATION

A Thames Television production. Untransmitted. Duration: 25 minutes.

Written by Howard Schuman; produced by Andrew Brown; directed by Marilyn Gaunt.

Denis Lawson, Ian McDiarmid, Eleanor Bron, Richard Beckinsale.

	Holding / Source
##.##.####	DB|n / 2"

Sitcom written to show at the 1978 Edinburgh Television Festival.

BROTHERLY LOVE

A Yorkshire Television production. Transmission details are for the ATV midlands region. Duration: 25 minutes.

It is possible, says Mike Hanson, to get on in this world - but heaven help you if you've a family who won't let you, especially if that family comes in the shape of a less than helpful brother.

Written by Roy Bottomley and Tom Brennand; designed by Gordon Livesey; produced and directed by Derrick Goodwin.

Keith Barron (Mike Hanson), David Swift (Eddie Hanson), Bridget Armstrong (Sarah), Jay Neill (Waiter).

	Holding / Source
16.09.1974	DB / 2"

BROTHERLY LOVE

A BBC Scotland production for BBC 1. Transmission details are for BBC 1. Duration: 30 minutes.

Main regular credit(s):   Written by Bernard McKenna; executive producer Mike Bolland; produced by Ian Burgoyne; directed by Ron Bain.

Main regular cast: Gregor Fisher (Hector Robertson), James Fleet (Frank Robertson).

	Holding / Source
08.10.1999	DB / DBSW

THE BROWN MAN

A BBC Scotland production for BBC 2. Transmission details are for BBC 2. Duration: 30 minutes.

Written by Jonathan Bernstein; music by David McNiven; produced by Colin Gilbert; directed by David Blair.

Arnold Brown (The Brown Man), Gemma Craven (Angel Bailey), Lou Hirsch (Marty Hyphen), Katy Murphy (Hilary Preminger), James Ryland (Lance Bowley), Andy Gray (Ne'Ville), Celia Imrie (Anne Ratner), Forbes Masson (Floyd The Fan), David Tennant (Billy The Boyd), Lindy Whiteford (Lydia), Maria Miller (Mimsy), George Drennan (Jim), Lisa Wiggins (Dinky-Sue), David McNiven (Club Band), Jim Condie (Club Band), Nick Jones (Club Band), Aileen Wilkie (Fire Eater).

	Holding / Source
07.09.1993	DB-D3 / V1S

THE BUBBLE

A Hat Trick production for BBC 2. Transmission details are for BBC 2. Duration: 30 minutes.

Main regular credit(s):   Created by Pic and Roll; format by Avri Gilad and Armoza Formats; programme associate Colin Swash; script supervisor Jo Newey; music by Karl Sadler; titles by Component Graphics and Chris Scott; art director Shaun Burley; designed by Dennis De Groot; assistant producers Jimmy Baker, Rebecca Fleckney, Sophie Waldron and Ruth Wilson; executive producers Richard Wilson and Katie Taylor; head of production Laura Djanogly; production manager Julie Rose; series producer Nick Martin; produced by Paul McGettigan and Ben Wicks; directed by Lissa Evans.

Main regular cast: David Mitchell (Presenter).

	Holding / Source
##.##.#### [untransmitted pilot]	HD/DB / HDC

THE BUCCANEERS

A Weinstein production for Sapphire Films. made in association with ITP. Transmission details are for the ATV midlands region. Duration: 25 minutes.

Main regular credit(s):   Executive producer Hannah Weinstein.

Main regular cast: Robert Shaw (Dan Tempest), Peter Hammond (Lieutenant Beamish (until 20.03.57)), Edwin Richfield (Armando).

	Holding / Source
##.##.#### [five untransmitted pilots]	J / B3

Television Today in February 1957 reported that Robert Shaw was one of five actors chosen to play Dan Tempest originally. Five pilots were filmed and Shaw was chosen.

The majority of the information detailing the real writers behind the on-screen pseudonyms was collated by Steve Neale and has previously been published in "Pseudonyms, Sapphire and Salt" (Historical Journal of Film, Radio and Television, Vol. 23, No. 3, 2003), "Swashbucklers and Sitcoms, Cowboys and Crime, Nurses, Just Men and Defenders: Blacklisted Writers and TV in the 1950s and 1960s" (Film Studies, Issue 7, Winter 2005) and "Un-American Hollywood: Politics and Film in the Blacklist Era" (Rutgers University Press, 2008).

THE BUDS OF NOVEMBER

Alternative/Working Title(s): BUDS IN NOVEMBER

A Regent Productions production for TVS. Untransmitted. Duration: 25 minutes.

Two brothers have a reunion after many years apart. One is the black sheep, the other is a living bore. Both disapprove of the other's lifestyle. They are forced to live with their spinster sister.

Written by Barry Pilton; produced and directed by William G. Stewart.

Timothy West, Donald Churchill.

	VT Number	Holding / Source
##.##.#### [untransmitted pilot]	5299	1" / 1"

TVS VTR 5299 R/T 13:51/12:27 .

Recorded February 1985.

BULLSEYE

An ATV/Central production. made in association with Chatsworth Television. Transmission details are for the ATV/Central region. Usual duration: 35 minutes.

Main regular credit(s):   Devised by Andrew Wood and Norman Vaughan; theme music by Johnny Patrick [credited as John Patrick].

Main regular performer(s): Jim Bowen (Presenter).

	Holding / Source
##.##.#### [first pilot]	J / 2"
Directed by Peter Harris.	
##.##.#### [second pilot]	J / 2"
Directed by Peter Harris.	

Surviving production paperwork refers to the first broadcast series as programmes 3 to 15, leading to the obvious conclusion that there were two unbroadcast pilots. Whether they were actually recorded and then junked or never recorded, we don't know. Peter Harris claims Jim Bowen was so bad they had to junked, literally burned!

SERIES 3

Transmission details are for the Central region.

Main regular credit(s):   Script associate Howard Imber; produced by Peter Holmans; directed by Bob Cousins.

Main regular performer(s): With Tony Green (Scorer), Tony Green (Out Of Vision Scorer).

	Holding / Source
25.12.1983 **Christmas Special**	J / 1"

With Anne Aston (Hostess), Eric Bristow, Keith Deller, Maureen Flowers, Kenneth Kendall, Anne Diamond, Judith Hann.

THE BULLSHITTERS

A Michael White/Dinky Doo production for Channel 4. Transmission details are for Channel 4. Duration: 41 minutes.

Spoof version of The Professionals.

Written by Keith Allen and Peter Richardson; music by King Cobra; film editor Geoff Hogg; assistant director Simon Hinkly; art director Celia Barnett; executive producer Michael White; produced by Elaine Taylor, Keith Allen and Peter Richardson; directed by Stephen Frears.

Keith Allen (Bonehead), Peter Richardson (Martin Foyle), Robbie Coltrane (Commander Jackson), Alan Pillay [as Alana Pellay] (Herself), Jimmy Fagg (Himself), Fiona Hendley (Janie), Al Matthews (Admiral), George Khan (Thompson), Kevin Allen (Chuck), Gary Martin (Stig), John Sarbutt (Dean), David Farringdon (Troy), Anthony Sharp [as Anthony Sharpe] (Father), Patience Tomlinson (Daughter), Esther Freud (Girl Backstage), Michael White (Himself), Julian Firth (R.A.D.A. Student), Malcolm Hardee (Builder), Suzanne Jerome (Knobs Receptionist), Elvis Costello (Stone Deaf A & R Man), Suzy Serome, Malcolm Hardy.

	Holding / Source
03.11.1984 **Roll Out The Gunbarrel**	1" / C1

See also: THE PROFESSIONALS*

BUNCH OF FIVE

Produced for Channel 4 by a variety of companies (see details below). Transmission details are for Channel 4. Duration: 25 minutes.

Comedy pilots.

	Holding / Source
03.06.1992 **Dead At Thirty**	1" / 1"S

A Tiger Television production.

Four flat-sharers' weekend plans are destroyed by a computer game and a plumber.

Written by Charlie Higson and Paul Whitehouse; produced by David Tyler; directed by John Stroud.

With Paterson Joseph, Jesse Birdsall, Lou Curran, Mark Williams.

10.06.1992 **Blue Heaven**	1" / 1"S

A John Blair Films production.

Frank wants to leave home, be famous and, of course, get the girl. But things don't go according to plan.

Written by Frank Skinner; produced by Jo Sargent; directed by Tony Dow.

With Frank Skinner (Frank), Conleth Hill (Roache).

SEE: Blue Heaven.

17.06.1992 The Weekenders – The Meat Festival   1" / C1

A Granada production.

Two chums in search of a quality sausage. Their journey takes them to an open-air fete where they find the ideal length of meat. The only snag is that invading aliens need the sausage.

Written by Jim Moir and Bob Mortimer; music by The Human League; executive producer David Liddiment; produced by Mark Robson; directed by Sandy Johnson.

With Vic Reeves (Jim), Bob Mortimer (Bob), Paul Whitehouse (Spencer Pendel), Tommy Cockles (Slow Police Constable), Brendan O'Sullivan (Slow Burglar), Wilfred Harrison (Father), Russell Dennett (Electric Russell), Philip Oakey (Speciality Meat Seller), David Boyce (Alien Leader), Richard Ashton (Tall Alien), Colin Burgess (Short Alien), Ina Clough (Seepage Seller), Harry Beety (Boiled Onion Seller), Louise Yates (Receptionist), John Patrick-Thomson (Policeman), Mike Wattam (Policeman 2), Kate Layden (Queen Alien).

24.06.1992 Shall We Gather At The River?   1" / 1"S

An etc productions production.

Young Herbert wants to know what his grandfather had to do with a woman who he is about to be buried by.

Written by Timothy Keen; produced by Esta Charkham; directed by John Henderson.

With Beryl Reid (Gran), Gwilym Cox (Herbert Alcock), Rosemary Leach (Mrs Alcock), Francis Matthews (Mr Strathclyde), Michael Troughton (Hedley).

01.07.1992 Miles Better   1" / 1"S

A Childsplay production.

Set in Glasgow, Andy Gray and Ann Scott-Jones star as thirtysomething Miles and his Stalinist granny.

Written by Peter Arnott and Peter Mullan; executive producer Esta Charkham; produced by Peter Tabern; directed by David G. Hillier.

With Andy Gray (Michael Miles), Ann Scott-Jones (Gran), Jenny McCrindle (Nita), Alison Peebles (Linda).

BUNCLARKE

A BBC production. Untransmitted. Duration: 30 minutes.

Pilot using a Tony Hancock script. Sid was Tony's brother-in-law in this planned new series.

Written by Ray Galton and Alan Simpson.

Arthur Lowe (Tony), James Beck (Sid).

	Holding / Source
##.##.#### The Economy Drive [untransmitted pilot]	J / 2"

BUNK BED BOYS

A BBC production for BBC 3. Transmission details are for BBC 3. Duration: 30 minutes.

A comedy about two 20-something brothers still living with their mother and sharing a bedroom.

Written by Daniel Peak; executive producers Myfanwy Moore and Graham Smith; produced by Simon Lupton; directed by Gareth Carrivick.

Bryan Dick (Phil), Rob Rouse (Jim), Geraldine McNulty (Mum), Sally Hawkins (Helen), David Cann (Zookepper).

	Holding / Source
22.03.2004	DB / DBSWF

This play won BBC Talent's New Sitcom Writers' Award.

BURNISTOUN

A the Comedy Unit production for BBC 2 Scotland. Transmission details are for BBC 2 Scotland. Duration: 30 minutes.

Main regular credit(s):   Theme music by John Mark Williams.

	Holding / Source
25.02.2009	HD/DB /

Written by Robert Florence and Iain Connell; designed by David Jennings; executive producers Colin Gilbert and Ewan Angus; produced by Rab Christie; directed by Iain Davidson.

With Robert Florence, Iain Connell, Leah Macrae, Allan Miller, Richard Rankine.

THE CABBAGE PATCH

A Central production. Transmission details are for the Central region. Duration: 25 minutes.

A view of family life from one key perspective - the mother's/wife's - The Cabbage Patch focused on Janet, a suburban housewife who, at the age of 36, has allowed herself to go to seed and is maniacal in the easily distracted, bad-tempered way that she deals with her domestic strife. Young daughters Kate and Elizabeth, while not uniquely problematic, cause her plenty of turmoil, and husband Tony's work in computers affords him the right, he thinks, to loll about at the house in a 'notice-me!' kind of way. Janet also has to endure her friends Ruth and Susie, who consider themselves superior, and her meddlesome mother, Lillian, whose idea of encouragement is to suggest that her daughter quit the scene and marry somebody else.

Main regular credit(s): Written by Joan Greening; music by Robert Farnon; designed by David Chandler; produced by Shaun O'Riordan.

Main regular cast: Julia Foster (Janet), Betty Marsden (Lillian), Emlyn Price (Tony), Natasha Byrne (Kate), Amelia Lowdell (Elizabeth), Jill Benedict (Ruth), Jeni Barnett (Amanda), Belinda Lang (Susie).

	Production No	Holding / Source
##.##.#### [untransmitted pilot]	9389	J / 2"

Produced and directed by Shaun O'Riordan.

With Nerys Hughes, Jack Galloway, Elspeth March, Jeni Barnett, Janette Legge, Jill Benedict.

Listed to be recorded for 29/07/82 but subsequently postponed to following week.

CABBAGES AND KINGS

A BBC Children's Department production for BBC 1. Transmission details are for BBC 1.

	Holding / Source
##.##.#### [untransmitted pilot]	DB-D3 / 2"

THE CAFE

A BBC Wales production. Transmission details are for BBC Wales. Duration: 30 minutes.

Written by David Powell; produced and directed by Jack Williams.

	Holding / Source
##.##.#### [untransmitted pilot]	NR / 2"

Comedy pilot being cast according to The Stage, 22.03.1973.

CALENDAR COUNTDOWN

A Yorkshire Television production. Transmission details are for the Yorkshire Television region. Duration: 27 minutes.

Main regular performer(s): Richard Whiteley (Presenter).

	Holding / Source
##.##.#### [untransmitted pilot]	B / 1"

See also: COUNTDOWN* / COUNTDOWN CHRISTMAS SPECIAL*

CALL EARNSHAW

Alternative/Working Title(s): THE GLASS EYE

A Yorkshire Television production for Channel 4. Transmission details are for Channel 4. Duration: 25 minutes.

Main regular credit(s): Written by Graham White; designed by Allan Anson; produced and directed by Alan Tarrant.

Main regular cast: Trevor Bannister (Earnshaw), Derek Royle (Higgins), Pearl Hackney (Ethel), Peter Spraggon (Chopper Stevens), Keith Marsh (Sergeant Feather), Diana Rayworth (Mavis), Sandra Gough (Rose).

	Holding / Source
17.12.1984 **Forget It**	1"|n / 1"
##.##.#### **Forget It** [dress run]	1" / 1"

Reported in The Stage 08.12.83 - The Glass Eye was to be part of a series of either four or five comedy pilots - along with LANGLEY BOTTOM, WE'RE GOING TO BE ALRIGHT (later IT'S GOING TO BE ALRIGHT) and one or two still to be decided.

The tape box for the one-inch edited master contained a different tape altogether, and ITV cannot track back to find the tape that should be in there, so it's classified as missing. Fortunately, the NFA have kept it.

There is an unedited master of the Dress Run. It has front titles, but no end credits, and scenes stop and start again.

CALL ME MISTER

A BBC production for BBC 1. made in association with Australian Broadcasting Corporation. Transmission details are for BBC 1.

Main regular credit(s): Created by Robert Banks Stewart; script editor Bob Baker; produced by Robert Banks Stewart.

Main regular cast: Steve Bisley (Jack Bartholomew), Dulice Liecier (Julie Columbus), David Bamber (Fred Hurley), Dermot Crowley (Detective Sergeant McBride).

	Holding / Source
05.09.1986 **Long Shot**	DB / C1

Duration: 80 minutes.

Written by Robert Banks Stewart; directed by Colin Bucksey.

With Haydn Gwynne (Bridget Bartholomew), Rupert Frazer (Philip Bartholomew), Norman Kaye, Hugh Fraser, Clive Merrison, Tara Shaw, Steven Grives, Brian McDermott, Kate Fitzpatrick, Tom Oliver, Julia McCarthy, Ben Aris, Kathy Burke, Trader Faulkner, Roger Leach, Arky Michael, Kevin Stoney, Tattiana Colombo, Stephanie Kapsza, Simon Watkins, Richard Bonehill, Julian Littman, Adam Ross, Chris Bradshaw, Nigel Mogg, Steve Brown, Graeme Lyndon, Ronald Meelee, Christine James.

The Creative Accountant and Running Time have never been repeated on terrestial television.

CANNON AND BALL

An LWT production. Transmission details are for the ATV/Central region. Duration varies - see below for details.

Main regular cast: Cannon and Ball (Hosts).

	Holding / Source
##.##.#### **[proper series - untransmitted pilot]**	J / 2"

See also: BRUCE FORSYTH'S BIG NIGHT*

CANNON AND BALL'S CASINO

A Yorkshire Television production. Transmission details are for the Central region.

Main regular credit(s):   Written by Robert Lewis, Louis Robinson and Bryan Blackburn; produced and directed by Graham Wetherell.

Main regular cast: Cannon and Ball (Hosts).

	Holding / Source
##.##.#### **[untransmitted pilot]**	1" / 1"

Duration: 50 minutes.

With Tricia Dusky, George Marshall.

CANTOR'S CRACKERS

A Yorkshire Television production. Untransmitted.

Written by Kenny Cantor and Terry Cantor; produced by John Duncan; directed by David Mallet.

Kenny Cantor, Jimmy Patton, Brian Patton, Jane Terry.

	Holding / Source
##.##.#### **[untransmitted pilot]**	J / 2"

This production was reported in The Stage 02.04.1970.

CAPTAIN SCARLET AND THE MYSTERONS

A Century 21 production for ITC. made in association with ATV. Transmission details are for the ATV midlands region.

Main regular credit(s):   Format by Gerry Anderson and Sylvia Anderson; characters created by Sylvia Anderson; script editor Tony Barwick; music by Barry Gray; associate producer John Read; executive producer Gerry Anderson; produced by Reg Hill; director supervising series Desmond Saunders [credited as Des Saunders].

Main regular cast: Francis Matthews (Voice of Captain Scarlet), Sylvia Anderson (Voices), Edward Bishop (Voices), Cy Grant (Voices), Donald Gray (Voices), Janna Hill (Voices), Paul Maxwell (Voices), Liz Morgan (Voices), Charles Tingwell (Voices), Jeremy Wilkin (Voices).

	Holding / Source
29.09.1967 **The Mysterons**	DB / C3

Duration: 27 minutes.

Written by Gerry Anderson and Sylvia Anderson; directed by Desmond Saunders.

This episode title does not appear on screen.

See also: CAPTAIN SCARLET*

CAPTAIN SCARLET AND THE RETURN OF THE MYSTERONS

Alternative/Working Title(s): CAPTAIN SCARLET - THE NEW MILLENNIUM

An Anderson Entertainment production for Carlton. Transmission details are for the Central region. Duration: 4 minutes.

Written by Gerry Anderson and John Needham; designed by Mark Harris; executive producers Gerry Anderson and John Needham; directed by Gerry Anderson and John Needham.

Francis Matthews (Voice of Captain Scarlet), Ed Bishop (Voice of Captain Blue), Gary Martin (Voice of Captain Black and the Mysterons), Leone Connery (Voice of Destiny Angel).

	Holding / Source
##.##.#### **[untransmitted pilot]**	DB / DBSW

Made in 2000.

CARTOON ALPHABET

A Yorkshire Television production. Transmission details are for the Central region. Duration: 25 minutes.

Main regular credit(s):   Written by Richard O'Keeffe; produced by Richard Evans; directed by Don Clayton.

Main regular cast: Tim Brooke-Taylor (Presenter), George Melly (Singer).

	Holding / Source
##.##.#### **[untransmitted pilot]**	1" / 1"

CASA MIA

A BBC North production. Untransmitted. Duration: 30 minutes.

Written by Geoff Atkinson; produced by Alan Nixon; directed by Nic Phillips.

Kate Lock, Peter Hugo Daly.

	Holding / Source
##.##.#### **Friends And Neighbours [untransmitted pilot]**	J / 1"

BBC say: "all the 1" recordings were junked. There was no actual tx tape made, just one logged as 'part edit'. Someone made a VHS of that in 1990 which later went missing, anyone's guess what happened to it."

Cancelled after a scene-shifters' strike. Made circa late 1980s.

THE CASE OF THE MUKKINESE BATTLEHORN

The companies who commissioned and produced this production are not known. Transmission details are for the TWW (General) region. Duration: 25 minutes.

Peter Sellers, Spike Milligan, Dick Emery, Pamela Thomas.

	Holding / Source
	B3 / B3

26.07.1962

Alternative transmissions: Anglia: 18.04.1962; Associated-Rediffusion: 10.04.1962; Scottish Television: 10.04.1962; Southern Television: 10.04.1962; Westward Television: 10.04.1962.

According to Television Today this was a TV pilot film, picked up for cinematic distribution. It was certified for cinema release less than a month after that piece appeared in the paper which didn't suggest they were that serious about it being for TV.

CASTING COUCH

A Granada production. Transmission details are for the Central region. Duration: 25 minutes.

A satirical celebrity-based panel game.

Main regular credit(s):   Executive producers Andy Harries and Justin Judd; produced by Robert Popper.

Main regular performer(s): Mel Giedroyc (Host), Sue Perkins (Host).

	VT Number	Holding / Source
##.##.#### **[untransmitted pilot]**	1/3047/0001	DB / DBSW

Directed by Ian Latimer.

With John Moloney, John Thomson, Craig Kelly, Ed Byrne, Maria McErlane, Saeed Jaffrey.

Recorded 1999.

THE CASTLE GAME

A Chatsworth Television production for Channel 4. Untransmitted. Duration: 50 minutes.

Produced and directed by Paul Stewart Laing.

Peter Purves (Presenter).

	Holding / Source
##.##.#### **Untransmitted pilot**	DV / 1"

No proper credits, just an assembly run-through.

CBS SUMMER PLAYHOUSE: OUTPOST

A Linnea Productions production for HTV. made in association with Columbia Pictures Television. Untransmitted. Duration: 47 minutes.

Written by Jeff Melvoin; based on a story by Jeff Melvoin and Michael Bryant; executive producers Patrick Dromgoole and Johnny Goodman; produced by Jeff Melvoin; directed by Tommy Lee Wallace.

Joanna Goring (Marshal Rachel Morgan), Ben Marley (Drew), Jeremy Flynn (Cray), David Robb (Jason Stockwell), Neil Dickson (Cooper), Marissa Dunlop (Kelly), Joseph Marcell, Badi Uzzaman, Major Wiley, Christopher Rozycki, Eiji Kusuhara, Niall Padden, Terry Kingly.

	Holding / Source
##.##.#### **[untransmitted pilot]**	1" / V1S

CELEBRITY SQUARES

A So Television production for Channel 5. Transmission details are for Channel 5.

	Holding / Source
##.##.#### **[untransmitted pilot]**	DB / DBSW

With Tom Binns (Presenter), Ed Byrne, Brigitte Nielsen, Coolio, Anneka Rice, Mel Giedroyc, Sue Perkins, Phil Tufnell, Tess Daly, Richard Blackwood, Joan Rivers.

c. 2003.

CELEBRITY SQUARES

Alternative/Working Title(s): BOB AND THE BIG BOX GAME! / BOB'S GALAXY GAME / BOB'S SUPERSQUARES / THE ATV SUNDAY QUIZ / THE BIG NAME GAME!

An ATV production. Transmission details are for the ATV midlands region. Duration: 39 minutes.

Main regular credit(s):   Devised by Merrill Heatter and Bob Quigley; music by Jack Parnell.

Main regular performer(s): Bob Monkhouse (Presenter).

Main regular credit(s):   Written by Dennis Berson; produced and directed by Paul Stewart Laing.

Main regular performer(s): With Kenny Everett (Voice Only).

	Holding / Source
##.##.#### **[first pilot]**	DV / 2"
With Showaddywaddy.	
##.##.#### **[second pilot]**	DV / 2"
With Sweet Sensation.	

Bob himself named this quiz show which was based on the U.S. show Hollywood Squares.

Have you ever seen Bob's Supersquares, The ATV Sunday Quiz or Bob and the Big Box Game? No, because they were all Bob's own titles for a gameshow that began life in the USA as Hollywood Squares.

Devised by Merrill Heatter and Bob Quigley, Lew Grade acquired the rights to Hollywood Squares. The concept involving celebrities sitting in noughts or crosses boxes. Contestants would be asked a question, hear a plausible answer from the star and decide if their answer was true or false. A correct guess and you could try to form three noughts or crosses in a row and win the game.

CELEBRITY SQUARES

ATV keen to keep Bob Monkhouse after his work on The Golden Shot gave the task of creating the new show to Francis Essex and Paul Stewart Laing. Essex wanted a wide variety format with musical acts so two pilots were made with musical contributions from Showaddywaddy and Sweet Sensation. Both acts had become famous on New Faces, directed by Paul Stewart Laing. Laing thought the music acts were poor, Essex agreed and they were dropped in favour of a charity quiz game called Bob's Full House.

From the outset ratings were high with many critics praising the witty quips from the guest stars, who included Willy Rushton, Diana Dors, Harry H. Corbett and Alfred Marks. Choosing a voice over artist was tricky, Laing insisted they use an ex-Radio 1 DJ who had fallen out with the BBC and was now unemployable. At the readthrough for Francis Essex the DJ was very straight-laced, but once he got the part, the real madcap Kenny Everett came to the fore, and his career was relaunched.

The witty jokes from the guest stars were not actually ab-libs, they were carefully scripted by Dennis Berson who wrote the jokes uncredited. Laing would brief contestants and never give them the answers. Only once did Diana Dors ask for an answer and she told the audience, much to Laing's anger. Anthea Redfern also insisted on the correct answers, but Laing told her the wrong answers, much to the amusement of her husband Bruce Forsyth who was watching the show.

Many of the answers were based on unusual trivia facts compiled by Jeremy Beadle. When the first series began to be transmitted, letters began to arrive complaining that the answers were factually wrong. Laing summoned Jeremy Beadle to his office and asked, "How do you get your answers?" Beadle replied he often made up the answers if they sounded "close enough"! After that, the answers had to be checked by an outside body.

Hollywood Squares finished with the winner being given the keys to a car. The IBA, the regulatory body that ran ITV, objected and said winners must earn their prize so Laing and Berson devised an endgame involving the winner answering nine questions on a theme to win the prize. The question one week was "Name nine types of bread?" One of the answers was bread rolls. ATV received complaints that bread rolls were not a type of bread. Laing replied by asking the irate complainers if they had the courage to contact the winner and ask for the prize back.

Eventually Laing left to become a freelance director working on This Is Your Life and London Night Out. Bob left to become the host of Family Fortunes. He returned in 1993 to remake the show for Central Television in association with Grundy Television. The concept remained similar, but the charity round was dropped. Guest start included John Inman, Wendy Richard, the Chippendales and new comedians such as Shane Richie and Joe Pasquale. The gags this time were created by Bob and Colin Edmonds, again uncredited. Bob Monkhouse died in 2003 and did not take part in a third remake from So! Television who made a pilot for Channel 5.

CELEBRITY SQUARES

A Reg Grundy Productions production for Central. Transmission details are for the Central region.

Main regular performer(s): Bob Monkhouse (Presenter).

	Production No	Holding / Source
##.##.#### **Dummy Run**		DV / 1"
Recorded 03.12.92.		
##.##.#### **Rehearsal Show**		DV / 1"
Recorded 10.11.93.		
##.##.#### **Dry Run**	011127	DV / 1"

CHAIN LETTERS

A Tyne Tees Television production. made in association with Action Time / Barry & Enright Productions. Transmission details are for the Central region. Duration: 25 minutes.

Main regular credit(s):   Produced by Christine Williams.

Main regular performer(s): Jeremy Beadle (Presenter).

Main regular credit(s):   Directed by Jim Brown.

	Holding / Source
	1" / 1"
##.##.#### **[pilots x 2]**	

CHALK AND CHEESE

A Thames Television production. Transmission details are for the ATV midlands region. Duration: 25 minutes.

Main regular credit(s):   Written by Alex Shearer; designed by Colin Andrews; produced and directed by Michael Mills.

Main regular cast: Robin Hawdon (Scott).

Transmission details are for the Thames Television region.

	Holding / Source
	DB|n / 2"
09.11.1977 **Spasms**	

With Jonathan Pryce (Finn), Miriam Margolyes (Rose Finn), Jenny Cox (Amanda Scott).

See also: SPASMS*

THE CHAMBER

A BBC production for BBC 1. Transmission details are for BBC 1. Duration: 30 minutes.

There are local government machinations in the mythical
Metropolitan Borough of Dunsall. When the leader of the Conservative-run council dies. a battle ensues to find his successor, resulting in much in-fighting and backstabbing.

Written by John Bird; produced and directed by Richard Boden.

John Bird (Councillor Percy Lygoe), John Wells (Councillor Graham Tombs), Diane Fletcher (Evelyn Tombs), Lesley Vickerage (Beebie Singleton), Geoffrey McGivern (Fletcher Mills), Karen Salt (Melanie Singleton), John Barron (Neville Transon), Owen Brenman (Eric Bradley), Tara Ward (Margot Prean), Milton Johns (Les Driffield), Michael Bertenshaw (Noel Washburn), Phil Nice (Slaney), Andrew Nyman (The Priest).

	Holding / Source
	DB-D3 / D3S
11.09.1995	

CHANCE IN A MILLION

A Thames Television production for Channel 4. Transmission details are for Channel 4. Duration: 25 minutes.

Main regular credit(s):   Written by Andrew Norriss and Richard Fegen; theme music by Ronnie Aldrich; produced and directed by Michael Mills.

Main regular cast: Simon Callow (Tom Chance), Brenda Blethyn (Alison Little).

	VT Number	Holding / Source
##.##.#### [untransmitted pilot]	27882	D3 / 2"

Designed by Alison Waugh.

With Ralph Nossek, Brian Croucher, Debbi Blythe, Bill Pertwee, Joe Dunlop, Simon Sutton, Richard McNeff, John Golightly.

THE CHANGE

A BBC production. Untransmitted.

	Holding / Source
##.##.#### [untransmitted pilot]	DB /

THE CHARLESTON YEARS

A Granada production. Not made. Duration: 25 minutes.

Written by Sid Colin.

A planned twenty-six episode, half-hour comedy series with Sid Colin as the lead writer. Set in London in the late 1920s / early 1930s. Mentioned in The Stage in August 1961 and presumably a victim of the six month Equity strike which started a couple of months.

CHARLOTTE MOVES... AND TAMBOURINES PLAY

An ABC production. Transmission details are for the ABC midlands region. Duration: 50 minutes.

Charlotte from the university — and Frankie from nowhere! What can they have to say to each other, and what will their friends think?

Narrated by Roger McGough; written by Roy Bottomley and Tom Brennand; story editor John Kershaw; designed by Mike Hall; produced by Reginald Collin; directed by James Goddard.

Gabrielle Drake (Charlotte), Richard O'Callaghan (Frankie), Christian Roberts (Peter), John Wreford (Paddy), Sandra Bryant (Rita), Gordon Reid (Mike), William Victor (Norman), George Betton (Frankie's Father), Ann Holloway (Brenda), Doel Luscombe (Barman), Bill Lyons (Judder), Mike Lucas (Johnny), Tom Wallwork (Boy), Glen Stowther (Boy).

	Holding / Source
02.07.1967	J / 40

See also: SAT'DAY WHILE SUNDAY*

CHAS & DAVE'S KNEES-UP

An LWT production. Transmission details are for the Central region.

Main regular performer(s): Chas & Dave (Hosts).

	Holding / Source
25.12.1982 **Chas & Dave's Christmas Knees-Up**	D2 / 1"

Duration: 50 minutes.

Designed by Michael Minas; produced by David Bell; directed by Alasdair MacMillan.

With Jim Davidson, Eric Clapton, Lenny Peters, Jimmy Cricket, Albert Lee, Cosmotheka, Alyn Ainsworth and his Orchestra.

CHEAP AT HALF THE PRICE

A Thames Television production. Transmission details are for the ATV midlands region. Duration: 25 minutes.

Jimmy Wilcox, proprietor of the "Treasure House," an antique shop in Chelsea, is a raconteur, philosopher - and dutiful husband. He sees himself as a future antique expert. But this ambition is constantly thwarted - by his dim-witted assistant, by his long-suffering wife, and by his own magnificent incompetence.

Written by Vince Powell and Harry Driver; research Martin Weitz; designed by Graham Guest; produced and directed by Les Chatfield.

Roy Kinnear (Jimmy Wilcox), Doug Fisher (Charlie), Joan Peart (Lady Customer), Paul Haley (Detective), Marjie Lawrence (Madge), Raymond Mason (Mr Martin).

	VT Number	Holding / Source
22.05.1972	5852	J / 2"

THE CHEAPEST SHOW ON THE TELLY

A BBC Birmingham production for BBC 1 Midlands. Transmission details are for BBC 1 Midlands. Duration: 30 minutes.

Main regular credit(s):   Devised by Don Maclean.

Main regular cast: Don Maclean, Lenny Henry.

	Holding / Source
##.##.#### [untransmitted pilot]	DB-DV / 2"

Written by Howard Imber and Don Maclean; music by Colin Thomas, Aiden Ford and Mike Hadley; designed by Mary Spencer; produced by John Clarke.

With Jane Galloway, Alan Devereaux (Golden Voice).

Recorded 23.04.1978. Ex-1500 cassette owned by Kaleidoscope.

Shown as part of the CONTACT strand.

CHEGGERS PLAYS POP

A BBC Manchester production for BBC 1. Transmission details are for BBC 1.

Main regular performer(s): Keith Chegwin (Presenter).

SERIES 1

	Holding / Source
##.##.#### **[untransmitted pilot]**	DB-D3 / 2"
Recorded April 1978	

CHILLER

A Yorkshire Television production. Transmission details are for the Central region.

Theme music by Colin Towns; executive producer David Reynolds; produced by Lawrence Gordon Clark and Peter Lover.

Transmission details are for Channel 4.

	Holding / Source
30.12.1991 **Gray Clay Dolls**	1" / 1"

Duration: 25 minutes.

With Ronald Pickup (Leonard Gray), Robert Hines (Elton).

THE CHIP SHOW

Alternative/Working Title(s): RISTORANTE LA BAXA

A BBC production. Untransmitted. Duration: 30 minutes.

Jim Broadbent*, Tim McInnerny*, Tony Robinson*.

	Holding / Source
##.##.#### **[untransmitted November 1984 pilot]**	DB-D3 / 2"

There are no end credits. A role of 'Mama' is played by an unknown actress.

CHOPRATOWN

A Hat Trick production for BBC 1. Transmission details are for BBC 1. Duration: 60 minutes.

Created by Anil Gupta, Richard Pinto and Sharat Sardana; written by Richard Pinto; script supervisor Po San Wong; music by Andy Britton and David Goldsmith; production executives Sacha Whitmarsh and Jessica Sharkey; executive producers Anne Mensah, Sally Woodward Gentle [credited as Sally Woodward] and Mark Redhead; produced by Anil Gupta; directed by Sean Grundy.

Sanjeev Bhaskar (Vik Chopra), Natalie Casey (Annie Deever), Neil Stuke (Detective Inspector Nigel Caro), Omid Djalili (Ali Ergun), Basienka Blake (Yasemine Ergun), Morwenna Banks (Victoria), Sam Dastor (Subhash Chopra), Lalita Ahmed (Swaren Chopra), Jimmy Roussounis (Mehmet), Paul Bazely (Doctor Mamoulian), Philip Arditti (Ozdemir Ergun), Daisy Dunlop (Maeve), Adjoa Andoh (Abebe), Manish Patel (Ash Desai), Madhav Sharma (Mr Das), Andy McEwan (Brian), Jess Dickens (Olivia), Neil McDermott (Henry).

	Holding / Source
19.12.2005	DB / V1SW

CIRCLES OF DECEIT

A Yorkshire Television production. Transmission details are for the Central region. Duration varies - see below for details.

Main regular credit(s):	Based on novels by Jill Arbon.
Main regular cast:	Dennis Waterman (John Neil).

	Production No	VT Number	Holding / Source
16.10.1993 **Circle Of Deceit: The Wolves Are Howling**	Y/0360/0001	L617	DB / V1S

Duration: 99 minutes.

John Neil, still haunted by his tragic past, is ordered back into action by his superiors. His mission is to infiltrate the IRA In Belfast, posing as Jackie O'Connell - an Irishman who has recently been killed in a car crash, having lived in London since boyhood.

Adapted by Wesley Burrowes; music by Tim Souster; associate producer Peter Richardson; executive producer David Reynolds; produced by Andrew Benson; directed by Geoffrey Sax.

With Peter Vaughan, Clare Higgins, Ian McElhinney, Tony Doyle, Derek Jacobi, Robert Swann, Sean O'Neill, Cindy O'Callaghan, Barnaby Meredith, Gerard Crossan, Andrew Connolly, Hellena Schmied, Carmel McSharry, Colum Convey, Colum Callivan, John O'Toole, Nicky Evans, Patrick Connolly, Stuart Fox, Martin Pearson, Graham Wicinskj, John Laing, Melee Hutton, Elizabeth Rees-Morgan, Ian Scott Owen, Martin Folity, Fizzie Lizzie, Rhubarb, Albert the Idiot.

CITY LIGHTS

A BBC Scotland production for BBC 1 Scotland. Transmission details are for BBC 1 Scotland. Duration: 30 minutes.

Main regular credit(s):	Written by Bob Black.
Main regular cast:	Gerard Kelly (Willie Melvin).

	Holding / Source
21.12.1984	DB / 1"

Produced by Colin Gilbert.

With Billy Greenless (Chancer), Gwyneth Guthrie (Mum), Kirsty Miller (Janice McLachlan).

CLARE IN THE COMMUNITY (RADIO)

Produced for BBC Radio 4 by a variety of companies (see details below). Transmission details are for BBC Radio 4.

Main regular credit(s): Written by Harry Venning and David Ramsden; based on material by Harry Venning.

Main regular cast: Sally Phillips (Clare), Nina Conti (Megan), Gemma Craven (Helen), Alex Lowe (Brian), Richard Lumsden (Ray), Ellen Thomas (Irene), Andrew Wincott (Simon).

	Holding / Source
##.##.#### [untransmitted pilot]	DB / DBSW

A Tiger Aspect production for ITV.

With Julia Sawalha (Clare).

In 2002 ITV commissioned a sitcom based on Harry Venning's comic strip. Two episodes were commissioned and a pilot episode. The pilot wasn't picked up for a full series and has never been broadcast.

Clare in the Community is a British comic strip in The Guardian newspaper, written by Harry Venning. The title is a pun on care in the community.

Clare is a social worker who likes to sort out other people's problems while ignoring her own. She is white, middle class and heterosexual - but doesn't like to be reminded of it. She is a control freak but both her personal and professional lives are out of control.

CLARK AND MURRAY SHOW

A Scottish Television production. Untransmitted. Duration: 25 minutes.

Written by Stan Mars; produced and directed by James Sutherland.

Gracie Clark, Colin Murray.

	Holding / Source
##.##.#### [untransmitted pilot]	J /

Recorded 3rd July 1969.

A CLASS BY HIMSELF

A HTV production. Transmission details are for the ATV midlands region. Duration: 25 minutes.

Main regular credit(s): Written by Richard Stilgoe; designed by Doug James; executive producer Patrick Dromgoole; produced and directed by David Boisseau.

Transmission details are for the HTV region.

	Holding / Source
14.01.1971 **The Thumb Of Barnaby Locke**	J / 2"

With John Le Mesurier (Lord Shepton), Peter Madden (Clutton), Richard Stilgoe (Hitch-Hiker).

CLIPJOINT

A Mike Mansfield Television production for Carlton UK. Untransmitted.

Executive producer Richard Holloway; produced and directed by Mike Mansfield.

Jonathan Coleman (Host), Tony Slattery (Team Captain), Noddy Holder (Team Captain), Wendy Lloyd, Davina McCall, Kriss Akabusi, Tony Hadley.

	Holding / Source
##.##.#### [untransmitted pilot]	DB / DBS

CLIPJOINT

An LWT production. Untransmitted. Duration: 28 minutes.

Written by Bob Monkhouse; designed by Rodney Cammish; production manager Brian Penny; produced and directed by Bryan Izzard.

Windsor Davies (Llewellyn Evan), Jack Douglas (Alfred), Andrew Sachs (Francis St John Allison), Colin Jeavons (Councillor Honk).

	VT Number	Holding / Source
##.##.#### **The Razor's Edge [untransmitted pilot]**	99043	DB / 2"

Recorded 13.04.77.

CLOSE TO HOME

An LWT production. Transmission details are for the Central region. Duration: 25 minutes.

Main regular credit(s): Created by Brian Cooke.

Main regular cast: Paul Nicholas (James Shepherd), Angharad Rees (Helen DeAngelo), Jane Briers (Rose).

	Production No	Holding / Source
##.##.#### **Starting From Scratch [untransmitted pilot]**	92015	1" / 1"

Written by Brian Cooke.

With Paul Nicholas, Diana Weston, Lucy Benjamin, Stephen Frost.

CODENAME

A BBC production for BBC 2. Transmission details are for BBC 2. Duration: 50 minutes.

Main regular credit(s):   Devised by David Proudfoot and Bill Hays.

	Holding / Source
07.08.1969 **Codename: Portcullis**	C1 / C1

A BBC 1 production.

Martyrs' Hall is a distinguished Cambridge college. The Master, Sir Iain Carfax, has recently left the Cabinet and now enjoys life at his old college with his daughter Diana. The dignified serenity is, however , a cover for the United Kingdom's most important spy cell, 'Codename: Portcullis.'

This play concerns the enlistment of a new co-spy and the provention of a dangerous formula in the germ-warfare arsenal from leaving the country.

Written by Bill Hays; costume Ursula Reid; make-up Heather Stewart; music by John Baker; designed by Peter Brachacki; produced by David Proudfoot; directed by Bill Hays.

With Clifford Evans (Sir Iain Carfax), Jennifer Daniel (Diana Carfax), Peter Jeffrey (Philip Skelton), John Turner (Roger Cooper), James Grout (Doctor Maurice Owen), John White (Dick Culliford), Michael Moyer (Doctor Carel Kapec), Hazel Bainbridge (Housekeeper), James Garbutt (The Dean), Keith Smith (Chief Inspector Sheard), Marguerite Young (Woman On Beach).

COLD BLOOD

A Granada production for ITV 1. Transmission details are for the Central region. Duration: 75 minutes.

Written by Tom Needham; music by Colin Towns; director of photography Tony Coldwell; art director Emma Dibb; production executive David Noble; produced by Ian White.

Jemma Redgrave (Detective Sergeant Eve Granger), John Hannah (Jake Osbourne), Ace Bhatti (Detective Constable Ajay Roychowdury).

A Granada production.

	Holding / Source
19.10.2005	DB / V1SW

Script supervisor Angie Pontefract; script editor Harry Oulton; designed by Margaret Coombes; associate producer Howard Ella; executive producer Carolyn Reynolds; directed by Stuart Orme.

With Matthew Kelly (Brian Wicklow), Patrick Drury (Tom Welburn), David Calder (Professor Kerr), Kerry Fox (Jan), Elizabeth Bennett (Annie Granger), Jane Lowe (Mary Osbourne), Jack Brady (Ray Jackman), Paul Oldham (Kevin Honeycutt), Ann Beach (Lynn), Loreto Murray (Doctor), Andrew Mchugh (Journalist), Paul Gabriel (Police Constable Neal Doyle).

See also: COLD BLOOD II*

COLD FEET

A Granada production. Transmission details are for the Central region. Duration varies - see below for details.

Main regular cast: James Nesbitt (Adam Williams), Helen Baxendale (Rachel Bradley), John Thomson (Pete Gifford), Fay Ripley (Jenny Gifford), Robert Bathurst (David Marsden), Hermione Norris (Karen Marsden), Jacey Salles (Ramona Ramirez).

	Holding / Source
30.03.1997	DB / V1SS

Duration: 51 minutes.

A group of thirtysomethings struggle with commitment, romance, fertility charts and babies in a tale of love, mating and supermarket dating. Shot in and around Manchester, this comic romp deals with some of the love dilemmas facing nineties man and woman.

Written by Mike Bullen; executive producer Andy Harries; produced by Christine Langan; directed by Declan Lowney.

With Stephen Mapes (Simon Atkinson), Kathryn Hunt, John Griffen, Mark Andrews, Mark Crowshaw, Mike Bullen, Lewis Hancock, Pauline Jefferson, Jeremy Turner-Welch, David Harewood.

This episode featured some scenes on videotape.

COLIN'S SANDWICH

A BBC production for BBC 2. Transmission details are for BBC 2.

Main regular credit(s):   Written by Paul Smith and Terry Kyan.

Main regular cast: Mel Smith (Colin Watkins).

	Production No	Holding / Source
##.##.#### **[untransmitted 1987 pilot]**	LLCJ300L/71	DB / 1"

Duration: 32 minutes.

Costume Judy Pepperdine; make-up Lisa Pickering; designed by Jo Day; production manager Andy Smith; produced and directed by John Kilby.

With Frances Tomelty (Jenny), Jane Booker (Sarah), Nicholas Pritchard, Simon Shepherd (Richard), Andrew Robertson (Travers), Kim Clifford (Mandy), Tony Haase, Richard Wycomb (Trevor), Ken Campbell (Ted), Michael Medwin, David Lyon (John Langley), Mike Grady (Des).

A discontinuous studio recording running approx 88 minutes also survives.

COMBAT KARATE

A Limehouse production for Channel 4. made in association with Fugitive TV. Untransmitted.

Pilot about full contact karate.

Executive producer Terence Pritchard; produced by Dominic Anciano and Ray Burdis; directed by David MacMahon.

	Holding / Source
##.##.#### **[untransmitted pilot]**	J / 1"

COMBAT SHEEP

A Baby Cow Productions production for BBC 1. made in association with Childrens Company. Transmission details are for BBC 1. Duration: 30 minutes.

Written by Tim Firth; additional material by Peter Baynham and Graham Duff; executive producers Steve Coogan and Henry Normal; produced by Robert Howes; directed by Dominic Brigstocke.

Steve Coogan (Harris), Ronni Ancona (Peaches), Mark Williams (Moose), Kevin Eldon (Cooper), Chris Ellison (Detective Inspector Hindle).

	Holding / Source
30.12.2001	DB /

Animated comedy.

COME BACK MRS. NOAH

A DDC production for BBC 1. Transmission details are for BBC 1. Duration: 30 minutes.

Main regular credit(s): Written by Jeremy Lloyd and David Croft; produced by David Croft.

Main regular cast: Mollie Sugden (Mrs Gertrude Noah), Ian Lavender (Clive Cunliffe), Donald Hewlett (Carstairs), Michael Knowles (Fanshaw).

	Holding / Source
13.12.1977	DB-D3 / 2"

The year is 2050. Mrs Noah - prize-winning housewife - is being shown round Great Britain's new Space Exploration Vehicle.

Lighting by Howard King; sound Laurie Taylor; designed by Don Giles; directed by David Croft.

With Gorden Kaye (Nicky Manson), Joe Black (Mr Garstang), Robert Gillespie (Mission Controller), Ann Michelle (Assistant Controller), Jennifer Lonsdale (Technician).

THE COMEDIANS

A Granada production. Transmission details are for the ATV midlands region. Usual duration: 25 minutes.

SERIES 1

Main regular credit(s): Designed by Colin Rees; produced by John Hamp; directed by Walter Butler.

	Production No	Holding / Source
12.06.1971	P712/1	D2 / 2"

Produced by John Hamp; directed by Walter Butler.

With Frank Carson, Bernard Manning, George Roper, Charlie Williams, Ken Goodwin, Duggie Brown, Mike Coyne, Paul Melba, Shep's Banjo Boys.

THE COMEDY CROWD

A Thames Television production. Transmission details are for the Central region. Duration: 25 minutes.

Written by Bryan Blackburn, Peter Corey, Richard Eadie, Phil Haynes, Russel Lane, Gerald Mahlowe, Trevor McCallum, Paul Minett, Brian Leveson and Peter Vincent; script editor Bryan Blackburn; script consultant Ian Davidson; music by Ray Monk; designed by Jane Moorfoot; produced and directed by David Bell.

Allan Stewart, Aiden J. Harvey, Tony Slattery, Martin Connor, Sherrie Hewson.

	Holding / Source
05.04.1988	1" / 1"

COMEDY EXCHANGE

A Tiger Aspect production for Dave. Transmission details are for Dave. Duration: 48 minutes.

Created by Bart Coleman and Olivia Wingate; executive producers Lisa Perrin and Gary Chippington; produced by Shannon Vandermark.

	Holding / Source
19.03.2010	DB / DBSW

Production executive Caroline Bourne; executive producers Bart Coleman, Olivia Wingate, Lisa Perrin and Gary Chippington; head of production Rebecca Mulraine; production manager Claire Askew; produced and directed by Shannon Delwiche.

With Isy Suttie (Narrator), Phill Jupitus, Eugene Mirman.

COMEDY FIRST

Produced for ITV by a variety of companies (see details below). Transmission details are for the Central region. Duration: 25 minutes.

Comedy pilots.

	Production No	Holding / Source
10.07.1995 **Barbara - Rivals**		D3 / D3S

A Central production for Carlton.

A plain-speaking Yorkshire woman who can't stop meddling in her family's business.

Written by Mark Bussell, Rob Clark, Ramsay Gilderdale and Graham Mark Walker; executive producer Paul Spencer; produced by Mark Bussell; directed by Les Chatfield.

With Gwen Taylor (Barbara Liversidge), Sam Kelly (Ted Liversidge), Shirley Anne Field (Jean), Caroline Milmoe (Linda), Glen Davies (Martin), Madge Hindle (Doreen), Dee Orr (Mrs Evans), Bill Gavin (Mr Meeks).

SEE: Barbara.

17.07.1995 **Sometime Never**		DB / D3S

A Witzend production for Meridian.

Today is drama teacher Max Bailey's 31st birthday. Reflecting on her lot in life, she wonders what happened to the sophisticated, stylish woman she had imagined she would grow up to be. She turns to best friend Bernice for comfort, but she has opened the cooking sherry.

Written by Jenny Lecoat; associate producer Julian Meers; executive producer Allan McKeown; produced by Tony Charles; directed by Baz Taylor.

With Sara Crowe (Maxine Bailey), Ann Bryson (Bernice), Saeed Jaffrey (Harry), Lucinda Fisher (Miss Louise Kilgariff), Sean Carnegie (Jason Williams), Harry Burton (Ian).

24.07.1995 **Sardines - Officer's Watch**   D3S / D2S

A Talkback production for Carlton.

Petty Officer Davy Kotowski wheels and deals his way round a naval submarine and rarely gets caught. This episode finds him in trouble for running a gambling ring and plotting his revenge by "unleashing the monster that lies at the murky bottom" of his dim sidekick's mind. Alternatively, he could just set up a double-cross that will raise the hairs on the neck of his bewigged rival.

Written by Gareth Edwards, Chris Langham and Ben Miller; executive producer Peter Fincham; produced and directed by Charlie Hanson.

With Griff Rhys Jones (Davy Kotowski), Anthony Smee (Mr Tench), Ian Bartholomew (Lionel Pinner), William Ivory (Chris), John Docherty (Captain), Paul Shearer (Proudlove), Peter Hugo Daly (Galloway), Perry Benson (Coxswain), Ben Miller (Simon), Alexander Armstrong (Alistair), Jake Abraham (Mlckey).

31.07.1995 **Waiting - Unnatural Selection**   DB / D3S

A Mentorn Films production for Scottish Television.

Comedy pilot about the staff of a medical centre.

Written by Jim Hitchmough; executive producer Tom Gutteridge; produced and directed by Charlie Hanson.

With Patrick Barlow (Mr Horation Reginald Therapy / Maurice Ribley), Peter Jones (Doctor Roger Captsick), Sarah Lam (Doctor Anna Chen), Simon Slater (Doctor Duncan Pettifer), Brigit Forsyth (Beryl Oldham), Ashley Jensen (Amanda Cookson), Derek Hutchinson (Mr MacIntyre), Fraser Downie (Mr Kellgreen), Terence Maynard (Colin), David Carey (Tommy).

07.08.1995 **The Smiths - Swapping Cogs**   1/1942/0001   D2 / D2S

A Granada production.

These Smiths are a downbeat family dogged by misfortune whose idea of a good time is a romp in the back of an old Cortina. When it comes to a monopoly on domestic misery, Clive and Carol Smith and their teenage off-spring Wayne and Debbie are a family for whom the glass of life is defintely half-empty. With the walls of their terraced house paper thin, there's only one place for mum and dad to escape and re-light the fire of their passionate youth - in the car.

Written by Julian Roach; executive producer Andy Harries; produced by Anthony Wood; directed by Tim Poole.

With Kevin McNally (Clive), Rebecca Lacey (Carol), Scott Neal (Wayne), Heather Jones (Debbie), Rowland Rivron (Geoff), Geoffrey Hughes (Dooley), Jackie Downey (Carol's Best Friend), Sonia Evans (Donna).

14.08.1995 **Now What**   D3 / D3S

A Crucial Films production for Carlton.

Comedian Lenny Henry helped produce this final programme in the series, which takes a different form from previous Comedy First offerings. A compilation of sketches.

Written by Andrew Barclay, Will Buckley, Jane Bussman, David Coe, Geoff Deane, Carlton Dixon, Sharon Foster, Jeremy Front, Tony Gardner, Paul Henry, Paul Johnson, Jo Martin and David Quantick; script editor Jim Pullin; executive producers Lenny Henry and Polly McDonald; produced by Lenny Barker; directed by Chris Bould.

With Curtis Walker, Don Gilet, Fiona Allen, Angela Wynter, Alan Marriott.

See also: BARBARA* / SOMETIME, NEVER*

COMEDY FOUR

A Granada production. Transmission details are for the ATV midlands region. Duration: 25 minutes.

Comedy pilots.

	Production No	Holding / Source
06.06.1963 **Tea At The Ritz**	P395/1	J /

Written by James Kelly and Peter Miller; script editor Barry Took; designed by Darrell Lass; produced by Peter Eton; directed by Graeme McDonald.

With Norman Rossington (George Podmore), Ronnie Stevens (Arnold Barnes), Ann Lancaster (Rene Barnes), Rita Webb (Mrs Gutter), Jack Bligh, David Gregory, Sonya Petrie, Howard Knight, Alfred Maron, Varley Thomas.

13.06.1963 **Fit For Heroes**   P395/3   DB / 40

Written by James Kelly and Peter Miller; script editor Barry Took; designed by Darrell Lass; produced by Peter Eton; directed by Graeme McDonald.

With Kenneth Connor (Corporal Bill Rust), Deryck Guyler (Major Rodney Heppelwaite), Donald Morley, Bartlett Mullins, Fred McNaughton, Philip Stone, Graham Crowden, Michael Earl, Ryan Jelff, Gordon Lang, Ernest McKennan [as Ernest McKinnon], Terry Brooks, Peter Ross, Peter Evans.

Recorded 11.06.63.

Five more scripts were written - The Reunion, Not Wanted On Voyage, The Rivals, The Lollipop Men and The Suit (6th in the series).

20.06.1963 **Scoop**   P395/4   DB / 40

Written by James Kelly and Peter Miller; script editor Barry Took; designed by Stanley Mills; produced by Peter Eton; directed by Graeme McDonald.

With Miriam Karlin (Maria), Warren Mitchell (Albert Tavistock), Lloyd Lamble (The Editor), Nora Gordon (Betty), Arnold Diamond (The Hotel Manager), Michael Oxley (The Hotel Manager's Assistant), Joyce Marlow, Fredric Abbott.

Recorded 18.03.1963

27.06.1963 **Home From Home**   P395/5   DB|c / 40

Written by James Kelly and Peter Miller; script editor Barry Took; designed by Darrell Lass; produced by Peter Eton; directed by Graeme McDonald.

With Eddie Byrne (Paddy), Harry Fowler (Max), Neil McCarthy (Nigel), Richard Caldicot (The Governor), Tenniel Evans (The Vicar), Sydney Arnold (Ronald), Keith Pyott (Mr Rawson), John Kidd (Woodthorpe), Ann Way (Miss Hope Evans), Diane Appleby (Deirdre), Fred McNaughton (Milton).

Recorded 25.06.63

##.##.#### **Home From Home**   NR|c / NM

Alt.Title(s): *Be It Ever So Humble*

Written by Dennis Spooner and Richard Harris; script editor Barry Took.

Two further productions were made under this banner title but were never billed as part of this series. In fact the umbrella title never appears on screen at all, other than on the VT clock and there, quite possibly because of space considerations, it's always written as COMEDY 4. A source of confusion over the years has been the play "Home From Home" which various sources (including extant ITV documentation passed to ITN) attribute to Dennis Spooner and Richard Harris while the TV Times and the programme's own end credits list James Kelly and Peter Miller. In fact there were two plays of this title written for the series, having enough similarity within their general premise to suggest that perhaps the same idea was suggested to both writing teams by Barry Took, but - broadly - with different plots and characters in each case. While we have found no evidence to suggest that it was made, the Spooner/Harris script survives: it includes an alternative title ("Be It Ever So Humble") and refers to the series as a whole as COMEDY SEVEN. Finally, the TV Times regularly credited Barry Took as co-writer rather than Script Editor but nothing in the surviving script or video material supports the idea that Took was a co-writer on any of them.

See also: A LITTLE BIG BUSINESS / TIN PAN ALICE

COMEDY LAB

Produced for Channel 4 by a variety of companies (see details below). Transmission details are for Channel 4. Usual duration: 25 minutes.

SERIES 1

		Holding / Source
25.11.1998 **Trigger Happy TV**		DB / DBSW

An Absolutely production.

With Dom Joly.

SERIES 2

		Holding / Source
16.09.1999 **Roy Dance Is Dead**		DB /

An Angel Eye Media production.

Written by Cliff Kelly, Adam G. Goodwin and Dan Clark; executive producer James Harding; produced and directed by Richard Osborne.

With Barry J Gordon (Roy Dance), Cliff Kelly (Mark), Adam G. Goodwin (Mark), Dan Clark (Jerry).

SERIES 8

		Holding / Source
10.05.2006 **FM**		DB / DBSWF

A Room 5 Productions production.

Written by Oliver Lansley and Ian Curtis; script supervisor Laure Brégevin; costume Chloe Croft; make-up Amie Morris; music by Tomas Gisby and Neil Townsend; edited by Mark Williams; director of photography Johnny Morrison; art director Matthew Dutton; production designer Mari Luccacini; production manager Tim Riddington; produced by Johnny Morrison; directed by Ian Curtis.

With Oliver Lansley (Neil), Warwick Davis (Dom), Dean Lennox Kelly (Lindsay), Raquel Cassidy (Jane), Robin Weaver (Kate), Phil Nichol (Keith), Daisy Haggard (Sarah), Matt King (Seb), Tony Blackburn (Himself), Steve Jones (Himself), Brakes (Themselves).

See also: FM* / FONEJACKER*

COMEDY MADHOUSE

An LWT production. Untransmitted. Duration: 25 minutes.

	Holding / Source
##.##.####	J / 2"

COMEDY PLAYHOUSE

A BBC production. Transmission details are for BBC. Usual duration: 30 minutes.

In recent years modern viewers may have enjoyed Comedy Showcase on Channel 4. A chance to try out a selection of comedy one-offs that may become a series. Nowadays the comedy pilot or single play is a rare beast, hunted to near extinction by TV executives who find them costly to make and impossible to sell abroad, thereby limiting their financial efficiency. But forty years ago the single play – comedy or drama – was at the height of its power.

In 1961 Ray Galton and Alan Simpson had finished working with Tony Hancock, and wanted to find a new successful sitcom to keep them in work. They pitched a number of ideas to the BBC who were unsure which ones were the frontrunners. Instead they were commissioned to write a whole series of comedy plays, each 30 minutes duration. Ray recalls that each edition took them a week to write, and the ideas flowed freely, until the second series when they found themselves lost for words in March 1963. One of their greatest works, 'Impasse', about two drivers who block a country lane, was written in one day as a last resort.

The original two seasons of Comedy Playhouse spawned only one series – a piece called Steptoe and Son that has passed into TV legend. Having found their next sitcom, Galton and Simpson were then replaced by a plethora of great comedic writers – Jack Rosenthal, Johnny Speight, John Chapman, Richard Harris, Dennis Spooner, Marty Feldman and Roy Clarke to name but a few.

This short column cannot fully explore the sheer amount of plays produced, so consider this part one of a tale that will be told more fully in 2010. The series can be broadly split into two bodies of work: the one-offs and the pilots that became successful series.

Firstly, perhaps you remember some of those one-offs plays? Paul Merton remade many of them in the 1990s. Marty Feldman and Barry Took's 'Barnaby Spoot And The Exploding Whoopee Cushion' gave John Bird and John Le Mesurier the spotlight in May 1965. Hugh Lloyd tried to go solo in 'Hughie' in May 1967. Barbara Windsor and Pat Coombs were 'Meter Maids' in August 1970 and Asian actors took centre stage in April 1971 for a rare comedic outing that did not use race as a source of comedy. Renu Setna portraying the gentle but funny 'Uncle Tulip' very well. Sadly, many of these plays are now destroyed, and exist only as fond memories.

The pilots for successful spin-off series exist in more abundance, as do the series themselves. Some series were shortlived. Do you remember Bill Fraser as the undertaker Basil Bulstode in 'That's Your Funeral', or smooth operator Terry Thomas as 'The Old Campaigner' James 'F.J.' Franklin-Jones? Some series ran for more than one series – 'Are You Being Served', 'Till Death Us Do Part', 'Up Pompeii' and 'It Ain't Half Hot Mum' are good examples. 'Are You Being Served' was considered to be awful when viewed by TV executives who shelved all plans to show it, but when members of the Israeli Olympic team were taken hostage and eventually killed at the 1972 Summer Olympics in Munich, Germany, TV executives needed a quick programme filler and Grace Brothers opened its doors for the first time. Another unsuccessful play that was initially pulled was Talbot Rothwell's 'Up Pompeii' about a Roman slave called Lurcio. The up-down career of Frankie Howerd had been sliding again until his work for the Carry On films gave him fresh appeal. His valiant attempts to finish the Prologue and rewrite the rude endings of the poems written by his master's son, Nausius, entertained Britain for two seasons, two specials and made the theatrical technique of the 'aside' (when the actor speaks to the audience) a popular form of comedy acting still copied now by artistes such as Frank Skinner and Miranda Hart.

Main regular credit(s):   Theme music by Ron Grainer.

SERIES 1

Transmission details are for BBC.

Main regular credit(s):   Written by Ray Galton and Alan Simpson; music by Ron Grainer.

	Holding / Source
15.12.1961 **Clicquot Et Fils**	J /

Produced and directed by Duncan Wood.

With Eric Sykes, Warren Mitchell, Henry Oscar, Joan Hickson, Terence Knapp, Charles Lloyd Pack, Michael Logan, Frank Thornton, Barbara Hicks.

22.12.1961 **Lunch In The Park**	J /

Produced and directed by James Gilbert.

With Stanley Baxter, Daphne Anderson, Bernard Hunter, Roger Avon.

29.12.1961 **The Private Lives Of Edward Whiteley**	J /

Produced and directed by Duncan Wood.

With Tony Britton, Raymond Huntley, Terence Alexander, Priscilla Morgan, Annabelle Lee, Gwenda Ewen, Dorothy Gordon, Bruno Barnabe.

05.01.1962 **The Offer**	DB-D3-R1 /

Conducting a rag-and-bone business means two things-collecting the stuff and Bogging it. The old-established firm of Steptoe and Son are doing quite well on the first count, but on the second.....

Designed by Malcolm Goulding; produced and directed by Duncan Wood.

With Harry H. Corbett (Harold), Wilfrid Brambell (Dad).

12.01.1962 **The Reunion**	J /

Produced and directed by Duncan Wood.

With Lee Montague, J. G. Devlin, Dick Emery, Patrick Cargill, Jerold Wells, Bernard Goldman, David Gregory, Cameron Hall.

19.01.1962 **The Telephone Call**	J /

Produced and directed by James Gilbert.

With Peter Jones, June Whitfield, Richard Caldicot, Derek Bond, Harold Lang, John Grieve, Alister Smart, Roger Avon.

26.01.1962 **The Status Symbol**	J /

Produced and directed by Graeme Muir.

With Alfred Marks, Graham Stark.

02.02.1962 **Visiting Day**	J /

Produced and directed by G. B. Lupino.

With Bernard Cribbins, Betty Marsden, Wilfrid Brambell, Hugh Lloyd, Priscilla Morgan, Molly Weir, Harold Goodwin.

24.09.62 - BRITAIN ON THE BRINK (LCA5122S) – front: glimpse (reasonably long, c. 10 seconds, showing Sheila Hancock as a 'pirate', Peter Jones and unidentified other actor) and end caption 'Produced by Dennis Main Wilson' of "The Rag Trade"); caption 'On BBC tv Tomorrow'; trailer for "Comedy Playhouse: Visiting Day" (does not exist, though this looked specially shot – inc footage of Bernard Cribbins) at 7.55pm; 'UK' logo with announcement 'This is BBC Television'. End: 'Circle' logo briefly; in-vision female announcer, plug for return of "Panorama" next Monday at 8.30 after summer break, details of rest of evening's programmes – after the News, at 9.25, Inspector Maigret returns in the first of a new series, then at 10.15, "Come Dancing" (sound cuts, picture continues for a short while).

09.02.1962   **Sealed With A Loving Kiss**   J /

Produced and directed by James Gilbert.

With Ronald Fraser, Avril Elgar, Gladys Henson, Vic Wise, Rita Webb.

16.02.1962   **The Channel Swimmer**   J /

Produced and directed by G. B. Lupino.

With Sydney Tafler, Warren Mitchell, Michael Brennan, Frank Thornton, Bob Todd, Joe Gibbons.

SERIES 2

Transmission details are for BBC. Duration: 25 minutes.

Main regular credit(s):   Written by Ray Galton and Alan Simpson; music by Ron Grainer.

                                                         Holding / Source

01.03.1963   **Our Man In Moscow**   R1 /

Produced and directed by Duncan Wood.

With Robert Morley, Patrick Wymark, Frank Thornton, Anthony Newlands, Michael Earl, Frank Littlewood, Leon Thau, Peter Thompson.

08.03.1963   **And Here, All The Way From...**   R1 /

Produced and directed by Duncan Wood.

With Eric Barker, Terence Alexander, Harry Locke, Richard Waring, Erica Rogers, Bernard Goldman, Roger Delgado, David Lander, Roger Avon, Margaret Wedlake, Michael Stainton, Peggy Ann Clifford, Herbie Nelson.

15.03.1963   **Impasse**   R1 /

Produced and directed by Duncan Wood.

With Leslie Phillips, Bernard Cribbins, Harry Locke, Duncan Macrae, Georgina Cookson, Yootha Joyce, Campbell Singer.

The premise - of two car drivers meeting on a narrow country lane and neither being prepared to back-up to allow the other through - was re-used by Galton and Simpson for the 'Pride' segment of the 1971 portmanteau film "The Magnificent Seven Deadly Sins".

29.03.1963   **Have You Read This Notice?**   J /

Produced and directed by Graeme Muir.

With Frankie Howerd (Norman Fox), Bill Kerr (Customs Officer), Edwin Apps (Passenger), Derek Prentice, Graham Ashley, Claire Collins, François Landry, David Gregory, Valerie Stanton.

05.04.1963   **A Clerical Error**   R1 /

Produced and directed by Graeme Muir.

With John Le Mesurier, Russell Napier, Yootha Joyce, Blake Butler, Harry Landis, Amy Dalby, Rosemary Davis, Barry Johns, Raymond Hodge, David Gregory, Andy Devine, Jeanne Davis, George Betton, Ken Roberts, John Caesar.

12.04.1963   **The Handyman**   R1 /

Produced and directed by Duncan Wood.

With Alfred Marks, Anthony Sharp, Damaris Hayman, Anthony Sagar, Frank Williams, John Harvey, Edwin Apps, Julian Orchard, Cameron Hall, Joan Ingram, Robert Raglan, Barney Gilbraith, Reg Thompson, William Raynor.

SERIES 3

Transmission details are for BBC.

                                                         Holding / Source

28.09.1963   **On The Knocker**   J /

Written by Harry Driver and Jack Rosenthal; music by Ron Grainer; designed by Barry Newbery; produced and directed by Douglas Moodie.

With Ronald Fraser (Ronnie Fender), Alfred Burke (Frank), Diana Hope (Carole Lewisham), Noel Johnson (Arthur Lewisham), Betty England (Mrs Soames), Beatrix Thompson (Mrs Marsden), Ruth Lodge (Mrs Hughes), Richard Coleman (Charles Pratt).

05.10.1963   **Underworld Knights**   J /

Written by Trevor Peacock; based on a story by A. J. Bacon; music by Ron Grainer; designed by Stanley Dorfman; produced and directed by Philip Barker.

With Ron Moody (Vogler), Bryan Pringle (Froggy), Frank Sieman (Sailor), Robert Raglan (Publisher), George Roderick (Boopy), Blake Butler (Crook 1), Trevor Peacock (Crook 2), Pat Coombs (Café Server), Fred McNaughton (Guard), Frank Littlewood (First Man In Café), Anthony Sagar (First Policeman), Henry McGee (Second Man In Café), Patrick Kavanagh (Second Policeman).

12.10.1963   **Fools Rush In**   HD-R1 /

Written by Vince Powell and Frank Roscoe; music by Ron Grainer; designed by Tim Harvey; produced and directed by John Ammonds.

With Deryck Guyler (The Major), Patrick Newell (Barney), Gordon Rollings (Wilfred).

12.10.63 - GALLERY: CONSERVATIVE PARTY CONFERENCE: HIGHLIGHTS (LCA5069P) – front: end titles of "Comedy Playhouse: Fools Rush In"; caption 'BBC tv'; in-vision announcer (Meryl O'Keefe?) announces "Gallery"; globe with announcement 'This is BBC Television' (by male announcer!)

19.10.1963   **Shamrot**   J /

Written by Johnny Speight; music by Ron Grainer; designed by Jane Martin; produced and directed by Philip Barker.

With Dermot Kelly (Dermot), Kathleen Harrison (Woman), Thomas Baptiste (Coloured Boy), Arthur Mullard (Man In Labour Exchange), Alan Simpson (First Irishman), Tony Doyle (Second Irishman).

26.10.1963   **The Bachelor Girls**   J /

Written by John Chapman; music by Ron Grainer; designed by Roy Oxley; produced and directed by Douglas Moodie.

With Tracy Reed (Sally Trent), Anna Palk (Joan Hunter), André Maranne (Artist), Terence de Marney (Meter Man), Edward Fox (Peter), Dennis Ramsden (Vicar), Jill Hyem (Girl-Friend).

02.11.1963   **The Plan**   J /

Written by Richard Harris and Dennis Spooner; music by Ron Grainer; designed by Fanny Taylor; produced and directed by Sydney Lotterby.

With Peter Cushing (Albert Fawkes), P. G. Stephens (Seamus McMichael), Alan Kemp (First Boy), Vincent Everett (Second Boy), Leslie Hart (Third Boy), Michael Segal (Shopkeeper), Philip Howard (First City Gent), Ray Browne (Second City Gent), James McManus (Left Luggage Attendant), John Snagge (Newsreader), David Coote (Police Constable), David Davies (Police Superintendent), Stuart Saunders (Police Sergeant), Graham Stark (Lieutenant Mills), Francis Matthews (Captain Hawkins).

09.11.1963 **A Picture Of Innocence**   J /

Written by Jack Rosenthal and Harry Driver; music by Ron Grainer; designed by Lionel Radford; produced by Douglas Moodie; directed by Douglas Argent.

With Patricia Burke (Bette Berry), Frederick Peisley (Arthur Berry), Marian Spencer (Ada), Charles Lloyd Pack (Arnold Slater), Dorothy Bart (Sylvia), David Selwyn (Jimmy), Frank Pettitt (Alf Stringer), Harry Littlewood (Harry Glass), Harry Shacklock (Fred), Bernard Hopkins (Geoffrey), Stephen Hancock (Scout Master).

16.11.1963 **Nicked At The Bottle**   J /

Written by Marty Feldman; music by Ron Grainer; designed by Raymond Simm; produced and directed by Michael Mills.

With George Cole (Mossy), Margaretta Scott (Mrs Emily Trout), Doris Hare (Mrs Martin), James Villiers (Jeremy Trout), Charles Heslop (Mr McMurtrie), Gabriella Licudi (Samantha Trout), Joan Ingram (Lady In The Tube), Anthony Mayne (Man In The Tube), Tim Buckland (Magistrate), Peter Stephens (Nosher Fawkes), Richard McNeff (Policeman), Dennis Ramsden (Judge).

23.11.1963 **The Chars**   J|a /

Written by Harry Driver and Jack Rosenthal; music by Ron Grainer; designed by John Cooper; produced and directed by Douglas Moodie.

With Elsie Waters (Flo), Doris Waters (Cissy), Ann Lancaster (Amanda), Michael Balfour (Cyril, Bus Driver), James Beck (Sydney, Conductor), Arthur Lovegrove (Frank, Commissionaire), Betty Aubrey (Char), Grace Newcombe (Char), Betty Cardno (Char), Derek Nimmo (Mr Thornton).

30.11.1963 **Comrades In Arms**   J /

Written by Donald Churchill; music by Ron Grainer; designed by Ridley Scott; produced and directed by Graeme Muir.

With Graham Stark (Ted), Fenella Fielding (Julie), Ian Bannen (Bernard), Elvi Hale (Bernard's Wife), Virginia Hewett, Sydney Dobson.

14.12.1963 **The Walrus And The Carpenter**   J /

Written by Marty Feldman and Barry Took; music by Ron Grainer; designed by Sheila Toye; produced and directed by Michael Mills.

With Felix Aylmer (Gascoigne Quilt), Hugh Griffith (Luther Flannery), Doris Hare, Harry Pringle, Richard Klee.

28.12.1963 **The Bed**   R3 /

Written by Ronald Wolfe and Ronald Chesney; music by Don Banks; designed by Charles Carroll; associate producer Philip Barker; produced and directed by John Paddy Carstairs.

With Thora Hird (Thora), Freddie Frinton (Freddie), Brian Oulton (Salesman), Lesley Allen (Young Newly-Wed), Patrick Scanlan (Young Newly-Wed).

03.01.1964 **The Mate Market**   R1 /

Written by Gerry Jones; music by Ron Grainer; designed by John Cooper; produced and directed by Dennis Main Wilson.

With Jeremy Young (Alan), Lance Percival (John Cook), Francesca Annis (Ann), Jean Conroy (Jill), Dilys Laye (Jean), Richard Caldicot (Mr Steel), Cal McCord (Waiter), Hazel Coppen (Lady), Betty Huntley-Wright (Mrs Steel).

10.01.1964 **The Hen House**   J /

Written by George Evans and Derek Collyer; music by Don Banks; designed by Charles Carroll; produced and directed by Michael Mills.

With Beryl Reid (Mrs Teresa Fanwyn), Barbara Windsor (Cynthia Spooner), Dermot Kelly (Edwin Russell), Anthony Wager (Fred), Carol Austin (Diane Brewer), Sasha Waddell (Pat Henderson), Madeleine Mills (Josie Evans), Paddy Glynn (Ronnie Blake), Margaret Read, Lesley Hill, Roger Darrack, Rod Ford, Terry Long, Graham Weston, Philip Bunn.

17.01.1964 **The Siege Of Sydney's Street**   DB-R1 /

Written by Richard Harris and Dennis Spooner; music by Don Banks; designed by Malcolm Goulding; produced and directed by Dennis Main Wilson.

With Roy Kinnear (Sydney Lord), Gordon Rollings (Roger Matthews), Eleanor Darling (Elderly Lady), Eric Dodson (Police Constable), Sheila Bonargee (Indian Girl), Barbara Keogh (Elsie), Arthur Barrett (Arthur), Bill Cartwright (Quiz-Master), David Gregory (Contestant), George Benson (Mr Wilkes), Laura Thurlow (Laura), Gerry Jones (Reporter), Alan Kemp (Small Boy), Arthur Mullard (First Bailiff), Peter Thomas (Second Bailiff).

24.01.1964 **The Mascot**   J /

A BBC North production.

Written by Vince Powell and Frank Roscoe; designed by Kenneth Lawson; produced and directed by John Ammonds.

With Dudley Foster (Mr Gibson), Robert Dorning (Billy Carter), Joe Gladwin (Arnold Birtwistle), Clare Kelly (Doris Birtwistle), Jimmy Gay (Jimmy Martin), Ken Parry (Neville Turner), Frederick Farley (Mr Braithwaite), Meg Johnson (Office Girl), Tony Melody (Referee), Orrena Elder (Miss Morgan), The Larry Gordon Dancers (Majorettes).

31.01.1964 **Good Luck Sir, You Got A Lucky Face**   J /

Written by Marty Feldman; music by Don Banks; designed by Eva Swiderska; produced and directed by Dennis Main Wilson.

With Graham Stark (Gomorrah Weevil), Derek Francis (Mr Harbinger), Frank Thornton (Jessop), Thelma Ruby (Mrs Harbinger), Geoffrey Dunn (Lord Fenwick), Bernard Egan (Taxi Driver).

SERIES 4

Transmission details are for BBC 1. Duration: 25 minutes.

Holding / Source

28.05.1965 **Barnaby Spoot And The Exploding Whoopee Cushion**   J /

Written by Marty Feldman and Barry Took; music by Dennis Wilson; designed by Roger Andrews; executive producer Graeme Muir; produced and directed by Dick Clement.

With John Bird, John Le Mesurier, Ronald Lacey, Sheila Steafel, Alister Williamson, Jane Thorne, Bart Allison, Bill Burridge, Harry Hutchinson, Sidney Johnson, Toby Lenon, Donald McCollum, Bert Simms, James Ure.

04.06.1965 **Mother Came Too**   J /

Written by John Waterhouse; music by Dennis Wilson; designed by Paul Allen; executive producer Graeme Muir; produced and directed by Philip Barker.

With Peggy Mount, Graham Stark, Robert Webber, Sally Anne Shaw, Tom Gill, Tony Hilton, Maitland Moss, Totti Truman Taylor, Amy Dalby.

11.06.1965 **Here I Come Whoever I Am**   J /

Written by Marty Feldman; music by Dennis Wilson; executive producer Graeme Muir; produced and directed by Dennis Main Wilson.

With Bernard Cribbins, Helen Fraser, Caron Gardner, Mike Pratt, Edward Evans, Annie Leake, Johnny Clayton, George Day, Kathy Fitzgibbon, Fiona Frazer, Maureen Lane, Pam Oswald, Valerie Stanton.

11.06.65 - INTERNATIONAL SWIMMING (LOS5728Y) – front: end credits of "Comedy Playhouse: Here I Come Whoever I Am"; trailer for "Stage Coach"; globe with announcement.

18.06.1965 Happy Family   J /
Written by Dick Hills and Sid Green; music by Dennis Wilson; executive producer Graeme Muir; produced and directed by Bryan Sears.
With Ted Ray, Daphne Anderson, Patrick Westwood, Robert Raglan, Lyn Pinkney, Mary Maude, Judith Geeson, Carla Challoner, Janet Hannington.

02.07.1965 Memoirs Of A Chaise Longue   J /
Written by Marty Feldman and Barry Took; music by Dennis Wilson; produced and directed by Graeme Muir.
With Alan Melville (The Chaise Longue), Fenella Fielding, Terence Morgan, Jack Watling, Sally Bazely, Jean Rogers, Betty Marsden, John Le Mesurier, J. G. Devlin, Shay Gorman, Patrick Durkin, Gerald McAllister, Mary Jordan.

08.07.1965 Murray And Me   J /
Written by John Law; music by Dennis Wilson; designed by Roger Andrews; executive producer Graeme Muir; produced and directed by Philip Barker.
With Chic Murray (Himself), Alan Baulch (Tommy), Harry Locke, Diana Hope, Ann Lancaster, Betty Romaine, Mary Jordan, Bill Treacher, Michael Newport.

15.07.1965 Hudd   J /
Written by George Evans and Derek Collyer; music by Dennis Wilson; designed by Roger Cheveley; executive producer Graeme Muir; produced and directed by John Paddy Carstairs.
With Noël Dyson, Tony Hilton, Maureen Crombie.

22.07.1965 Till Death Us Do Part   JSEQ /
Alf Garnett is an ardent West Ham supporter. But a racist? He thinks not.
Written by Johnny Speight; music by Dennis Wilson; designed by Ken Jones; executive producer Graeme Muir; produced and directed by Dennis Main Wilson.
With Warren Mitchell (Alf Ramsey), Anthony Booth (Mike), Una Stubbs (Rita), Gretchen Franklin (Else Ramsey), Robert Dorning, Derek Nimmo, Eric Dodson, Colin Welland.

29.07.1965 The Time And Motion Man   J /
Postponed from 25.06.1965.
Written by Dick Clement and Ian La Frenais; music by Dennis Wilson; designed by Michael Young; produced and directed by Graeme Muir.
With Leslie Phillips, Pauline Delany, Richard Moore, Billy Milton.

05.08.1965 Sam The Samaritan   J /
Adapted by David Climie; based on a story by W. W. Jacobs; designed by Darrol Blake; executive producer Graeme Muir; produced and directed by Michael Mills.
With Wilfrid Brambell (Sam Small), Roy Kinnear (Ginger Dick), John Junkin (Peter Russet), Edwin Brown (Landlord), Miriam Raymond (Barmaid), Alexandra Dane (Barmaid), Harold Goodwin (Widden), Joseph Sealy (Worple), Helen Forde, Paddy Glynn, Ruth Harrison, Kathleen Saintsbury, John Scott Martin.

12.08.1965 The Vital Spark   J /
Alt.Title(s): *Para Handy*
A BBC Scotland production.
Written by Bill Craig; based on characters created by Neil Munro; theme music by Ian Gourlay; designed by Guthrie Hutton; executive producer Graeme Muir; produced and directed by Pharic Maclaren.
With Roddy McMillan (Para Handy), Robert Urquhart (Dougie), John Grieve (Dan Macphail), Alex McAvoy (Sunny Jim), James Gibson, Phil McCall, Roy Hanlon, Wallace Campbell.

19.08.1965 Betsy Mae   J /
Written by Ken Hoare and Mike Sharland; music by Bill McGuffie; designed by Jeremy Davies; executive producer Graeme Muir; produced and directed by Douglas Moodie.
With Hermione Gingold (Betsy Mae Meadows), Nicholas Phipps (Roger Kaye), Michael Newport (John Plowman), Peter Elliott (Cyrus), Gina Bon (Irma), Frank Cowley (Station Porter), Michael Gover (Chauffeur), Zena Skinner (Herself).

SERIES 5
Transmission details are for BBC 1.

                                                                                   Holding / Source

17.05.1966 The Bishop Rides Again   DB-R1 /
Written by Pauline Devaney and Edwin Apps [jointly credited as John Wraith]; theme music by Ron Grainer; music by Dennis Wilson; designed by Peter Kindred; produced and directed by Stuart Allen.
With Robertson Hare (The Archdeacon), William Mervyn (The Bishop), Derek Nimmo (The Reverend Mervyn Noote), John Barron (The Dean), James Beck (Policeman), Ruth Kettlewell (Mrs Beems), Christina Couldrey (Norma), Cheryl Molineaux (Young Girl), Robert Anthony (Young Man), Gaynor Jones (Child).

24.05.1966 Beggar My Neighbour   J /
Written by Ken Hoare and Mike Sharland; music by Bryan Daly; designed by Michael Young; produced and directed by David Croft.
With Peter Jones, June Whitfield, Reg Varney, Pat Coombs, John Junkin.

31.05.1966 A Little Learning   J /
Written by Christopher Bond; music by Bill McGuffie; designed by Gordon Toms; produced and directed by Eric Fawcett.
With Jack Hulbert, Cicely Courtneidge, Clive Morton, Ronald Adam, James Chase, Pamela Conway, Mirabelle Thomas, Ray Emmins.

07.06.1966 Judgment Day For Elijah Jones   J /
Written by Marty Feldman; music by Dennis Wilson; designed by Austen Spriggs; produced by Dennis Main Wilson; directed by John Street.
With Clive Dunn (Elijah Jones), Bernard Cribbins (Brother Arnold), Priscilla Morgan (Mrs Jones), Tony Melody, Peter Diamond, Derek Martin, John Mulgrew.
Filmed partially at Chessington Zoo. In real life Priscilla Morgan was Clive Dunn's wife.

14.06.1966 Room At The Bottom   J /
Written by John Esmonde and Bob Larbey; designed by Donald Homfray; produced and directed by David Askey.
With Kenneth Connor (Gus Fogg), Deryck Guyler (Mr Powell), Francis Matthews (Mr Dillington), Richard Pearson (Happy Brazier), Brian Wilde (Mr Salisbury), Barry Halliday (Dennis Timms), Erik Chitty (Uncle Wilf), Godfrey James (Monty).

21.06.1966 The End Of The Tunnel   J /
Written by Richard Waring; music by Dennis Wilson; designed by John Hurst; produced and directed by Graeme Muir.
With George Cole (Charles), Lynn Redgrave (Sheila), Henry McGee (Harry), Tenniel Evans (Bernard), Anne Jameson (Mary), Michael Anthony (Freddie), Peter Hughes (Porter), Michael Spice (Ted).

28.06.1966 **Seven Year Hitch**   J /

Written by Fred Robinson; designed by Austin Ruddy; produced and directed by Vere Lorrimer.

With Harry H. Corbett (Ern), Joan Sims (Is), Derek Royle (Mr Swann), Dawn Beret (Deirdre), Kenneth Nash (Kevin), Hazel Coppen (Daisy), John Baskcomb (Bert), Bert Simms (Grandpa), Ross Parker (Uncle George), Joyce Hemson (Aunt Glad).

05.07.1966 **The Mallard Imaginaire**   J /

Written by Alan Melville; music by Dennis Wilson; designed by Peter Brachacki; produced and directed by Graeme Muir.

With Robert Coote (Right Honourable Mervyn Pugh), Moira Lister (Janet Pugh), Jonathan Cecil (Roger), Nan Munro (Miss Dempster), Arthur Howard (Mr Harrison), Daphne Anderson (Mrs Nicholson), Michael Wennick (David), Valetta Johnson (Esmeralda), Tom Gill (Interviewer).

02.08.1966 **The Reluctant Romeo**   J /

Written by George Evans and Derek Collyer; music by Bill McGuffie; designed by Luciana Arrighi; produced and directed by Eric Fawcett.

With Leslie Crowther (Thomas Jones), Amanda Barrie (Geraldine), Margo Jenkins (Sally), Dorothy Frere, John Gabriel, Cicely Paget-Bowman, Keith Pyott, Sheila Steafel, Geoffrey Sumner.

SERIES 6

Transmission details are for BBC 1.

	Production No	Holding / Source

19.05.1967 **Hughie**   J /

Written by Johnnie Mortimer and Brian Cooke; based on an idea by Alexander Doré; music by Dennis Wilson; designed by Oliver Bayldon; produced and directed by Robin Nash.

With Hugh Lloyd (Hughie), Patrick Cargill (Mr Gates), Ann Lancaster (Mrs Green), Robert Gillespie (Padre), Geoffrey Lumsden (Prison Governor), Patricia Clapton (Mandy), Stuart Sherwin (Postman), Penny Morrell (Girl In Car), Robert Arnold (Policeman), Michael Sheard (Magistrate's Clerk), Anthony Sharp (Magistrate).

26.05.1967 **House In A Tree**   J|a /

Written by Richard Waring; music by Dennis Wilson; designed by Gordon Toms; produced and directed by Graeme Muir.

With Wendy Craig (Jennifer), Paul Daneman (Henry), Fanny Rowe (Mother), Rosalind Knight (Biddy), Roberta Tovey (Trudi), John Moulder-Brown (Robin), Jill Riddick (Amanda), Keneth Thornett (Police Sergeant), George Day (Prison Officer), Sydney Dobson (Tipstaff).

02.06.1967 **Spanner In The Works**   J|a /

Written by Vince Powell and Harry Driver; music by Bill McGuffie; designed by Stephan Paczai; produced and directed by Stuart Allen.

With Jimmy Jewel (Jimmy), Norman Rossington (Norman), Fyfe Robertson, Cliff Michelmore, Julian Holloway, Colin Douglas, Blake Butler, Peter Bathurst, Eric Dodson, Arnold Peters, Jon Rollason, Jill Allen, Michael Slater.

09.06.1967 **Heirs On A Shoestring**   J|a /

Written by Dave Freeman; music by Dennis Wilson; designed by Gillian Howard; produced and directed by John Street.

With Jimmy Edwards (James), Clive Dunn (Uncle Charles), Sam Kydd (Alfred), Frances Bennett (Winifred), Eileen Way (Mrs Jibbet), Hugo Burns (Father Melody).

16.06.1967 **Uncle Fred Flits By**   J /

Adapted by Michael Mills; based on a book by P. G. Wodehouse; designed by Peter Julien; produced and directed by Michael Mills.

With Wilfrid Hyde-White (Uncle Fred), Avis Bunnage (Connie Parker), Jonathan Cecil (Pongo Twistleton), Richard McNeff (Commissionaire), Gerald Case (Link Man), Michael Trubshawe (Old Bean), Raymond Clarke (Old Crumpet), Kate Brown (Maid), George Pensotti (Wilberforce Robinson), Gordon Rollings (Claude Parker), Janina Faye (Julia Parker), Ballard Berkeley (Mr Roddie).

23.06.1967 **Loitering With Intent**   11/1/7/0561   J / Live

Written by Myles Rudge; music by Bill McGuffie; designed by Dennis Gordon-Orr; produced and directed by Stuart Allen.

With David Tomlinson (Charles Pinfold), Daphne Anderson (Louise Pinfold), John Nettleton, Barry Fantoni, Madeline Mills, Rudolph Walker.

29.06.1967 **To Lucifer - A Son**   J|a /

Written by Johnny Speight; music by Dennis Wilson; designed by Daphne Shortman; produced and directed by Dennis Main Wilson.

With Jimmy Tarbuck, John Le Mesurier, Dermot Kelly, Pat Coombs, Rita Webb, Eddie Malin, Tommy Godfrey, Gladys Dawson, Arthur English, Gabor Baraker.

30.06.1967 **The Old Campaigner**   DB-D3-R1 /

Written by Michael Pertwee; music by Jack Emblow; designed by Bob Macgowan; produced and directed by Robin Nash.

With Terry-Thomas (James 'F.J.' Franklin-Jones), Susan Jameson (Picture of Isobel), Beatrix Mackey (Louise Tchernik), Helena McCarthy (Karina Tabor), Derek Fowlds (Peter Clancy), Lois Penson (Miss Pinto), Norman Claridge (L.B.), Brian Cullingford (Porter), Erika Raffael (Yvette), Nadja Regin (Frederique Duval), Andrew Andreas (Walter), Julie Martin (Frances Renaud), André Maranne (Businessman), John Serret (Doctor).

SERIES 7

Transmission details are for BBC 1.

	Holding / Source

26.04.1968 **State Of The Union**   J /

Written by Ronnie Taylor; music by Ronnie Hazlehurst; designed by Gwen Evans; produced and directed by John Ammonds.

With Les Dawson (Les, Union Sec., N.U.W.), Patsy Rowlands (Gladys, His Wife), Michael Robbins (Ernie, Shop Steward), Melvyn Hayes (Russell), Edward Evans (Mr Lockerby, Works Manager), Roma Tomelty (Canteen Girl).

03.05.1968 **View By Appointment**   J /

Written by Jennifer Phillips; music by Max Harris; designed by Richard Hunt; produced and directed by Robin Nash.

With Beryl Reid (Irene Jelliot), Hugh Paddick (Sydney Jelliot), Derek Fowlds (Jimmy), Pauline Collins (Marjorie), Diana King (Mrs Quincy-Smith), John Harvey (Mr Quincy-Smith), Anthony Sharp (Mr Bumbry).

10.05.1968 **The Family Of Fred**   J /

Written by Peter Robinson; music by Judd Proctor; designed by Evan Hercules; produced and directed by Douglas Argent.

With Freddie Frinton (Fred Holmes), Mike Lucas (Albert Pike), Pamela Pitchford (Mrs Lester), Judi Bloom (Carol Holmes), Carolyn Moody (Janet Holmes), Roberta Rex (Vicki Holmes), Jean Kent (Aggie Plunkett), Gerald Moon (Robert Bean).

17.05.1968 Stiff Upper Lip   J /

Adapted by Barry Took; based on a story by Lawrence Durrell; music by Ronnie Hazlehurst and Handel; designed by Colin Shaw; produced and directed by Michael Mills.

With Richard Vernon (Sir Reginald Polk-Mowbray), Michael Bates (Antrobus), George Baker (Commander Benbow), Derek Aylward (Captain Gore-Strangely), John Glyn Jones (Drage), Bernard Bresslaw (Percy), Nadja Regin (Smyrna), Vivien Hellbron (Secretary To Antrobus), Artro Morris (Comrade Bobok), Denis Bernard (Comrade Kockchick), Robert Lee (Comrade Ping Ho), Corbet Woodall (Newsreader), Rodney Lovick (Sir Lumsden Rees-Mountauk).

24.05.1968 Wild, Wild Women!   J /

Written by Ronald Chesney and Ronald Wolfe; music by Dennis Wilson; designed by Jeremy Davies; produced and directed by Philip Dale.

With Barbara Windsor (Millie), Derek Francis (Mr Harcourt), Ronnie Stevens (Clarence), Jennie Paul (Blossom), Penelope Keith (Daisy), Sonia Fox (Ruby), Paul Gillard (Waiter), David Stoll (Lord Hurlingham), Zena Howard (Lady Hurlingham), Jacquie-Ann Carr (Milliner), Colette Gleeson (Milliner), Janice Gordon (Milliner), Virginia McCarthy (Milliner), Frances Nicholson (Milliner), Jeannette Wild (Milliner).

24.05.68 - WORLD CHAMPIONS ON ICE (LOS8453K) - front end titles of "Going for a Gong", trailer for "Comedy Playhouse. Wild, Wild Women" (inc. clips - Barbara Windsor, Derek Francis, Ronnie Stevens, Penelope Keith etc); globe with announcement inc. plug for "The Newcomers". End: start of trail for BBC2 Sammy Davies Jnr programme...

31.05.1968 Thank You Sir, Thank You Madam   J /

Written by George Evans and Derek Collyer; produced and directed by James Gilbert.

With David Lodge (Wally), Peter Glaze (Ralph), Gordon Rollings (Flipper), John Grieve (Alec), Veronica Clifford (Barmaid).

##.##.#### Current Affairs   J /

Originally scheduled for 31.05.1968.

Written by George Wadmore and Pat Dunlop; music by Dennis Wilson; designed by Bernard Lloyd-Jones; produced and directed by Philip Barker.

With Harold Goodwin, Arthur White, Kenneth Fortescue, Ken Parry, Robert Dorning, Damaris Hayman, Bruce Wightman, Ernest Arnley, Frank Sieman, Tom Macaulay, Roger Avon, Donna Reading, Eric Francis, John Newbury.

07.06.1968 B-And-B   R1 /

Written by Michael Pertwee; music by John Dankworth; designed by Peter Kindred; produced and directed by Michael Mills.

With Bernard Braden (Bernie), Barbara Kelly (Barbara), Kim Braden (Sally), Mark Griffith (Johnny), Pauline Collins (Chantal), Tom Macaulay (Al Thompson).

14.06.1968 Me Mammy   J /

Written by Hugh Leonard; music by Max Harris; designed by Roger Ford; produced and directed by James Gilbert.

With Milo O'Shea (Bunjy), Anna Manahan (Mrs Kennefick), Yootha Joyce (Miss Argyll), Neil Hallett (Mr Graham), Diana Coupland (Mrs Cattermole), John Welsh (Father John).

28.06.1968 The Gold Watch Club   J /

Written by Richard Waring; based on an idea by Max Kester; music by Dennis Wilson; designed by Alan Hunter-Craig; produced and directed by Graeme Muir.

With Dennis Price (Edward Wilkins), Avice Landon (Sarah Wilkins), Peter Bayliss (Brown), Derek Waring (Poulson), Bob Todd (Cartwright), Barbara Clift (Rosie), Barbara Leake (Mrs Hanley), Roger Avon (Newsagent), Norman Mitchell (Victor), Amy Dalby (Old Lady), Sonia Graham (Barmaid), Jack Allen (Manders).

SERIES 8

Transmission details are for BBC 1.

                                                                                                            Holding / Source

14.04.1969 The Liver Birds   J / 2"

Dawn and Beryl are two Liverpudlian girls. 'The Liver Birds' share a flat in Liverpool. In fact they share everything-clothes, food, drink, coathangers. They're great friends. Except when it comes to sharing boyfriends ...

Written by Carla Lane, Myra Taylor and Lew Schwarz; theme music by The Scaffold; music by Ronnie Hazlehurst; designed by Gillian Howard; produced and directed by Sydney Lotterby.

With Pauline Collins (Dawn), Polly James (Beryl), Roy Marsden (Nigel), Hugh Walters (Terence).

21.04.1969 The Valley Express   J / 2"

Written by John Lloyd; music by Max Harris; designed by Valerie Warrender; produced and directed by James Gilbert.

With David Baxter (Stan), Richard Davies (Reg), Nerys Hughes (Jenny), Jessie Evans (Pet-Shop Owner), Graeme Garden (TV Director), Harry Walker (Cameraman), James Appleby (Sound Man).

28.04.1969 Tooth And Claw   J|a / 2"

Written by Marty Feldman and Barry Took; music by Ken Jones; designed by Raymond London; produced by G. B. Lupino; directed by Roger Race.

With Warren Mitchell (Reuben Tooth), Marty Feldman (Sydney Claw), Ronald Fletcher (Narrator), Richard Caldicot, Anthony Dawes, Arnold Diamond, Norman Chappell, David Rowlands, Harry Brooks Jr, Gordon Craig.

05.05.1969 As Good Cooks Go   J / 2"

Good cooks often have their trials and tribulations and some of them have to deal with more than just kitchen problems.

Written by John Warren and John Singer; music by Dennis Wilson; designed by Barry Newbery; produced and directed by John Howard Davies.

With Tessie O'Shea (Blodwen O'Reilly), Robert Dorning (Mr Bullock), Georgina Patterson (Receptionist), Barry Keegan (Mick), Nosher Powell (Wally), Tommy Godfrey (Charlie), Norman Chappell (Sid), Alex McAvoy (Jock), Brian Grellis (Harry), Raymond Boyd (Willie), Bruno Barnabe (Columnist), James Appleby (Joe), Hilary Pritchard (Susan), Bobby Campbell (Violinist), John Lawrence (Vicar), David Brook (Executive).

12.05.1969 The Loves Of Larch Hill   J|a / 2"

Written by Anne Burnaby; music by Dennis Wilson; designed by James Bould; produced and directed by Eric Fawcett.

With Robert Dorning (Robert Love), Jan Holden (Liz Love), David Munro (Keith Love), Gillian Blake (Alison 'Smudge' Love), Marigold Russell (Rosemary Love), Nan Braunton (Mrs Love Sr), Denis Cleary (Taxi Driver), Hazel Hughes (Mrs Basiljet), Lois Penson (Matron), Joyce Hemson (Mrs Basiljet's Daughter), Jack Allen (Henry Maddox), Suzanna Pinney (Barmaid).

19.05.1969 The Making Of Peregrine   J|a / 2"

Written by Marty Feldman and Barry Took; music by Ken Jones; designed by David Spode; produced and directed by G. B. Lupino.

With Dick Emery (Stanley Mold), Pat Coombs (Minerva Mold), Andrew Ray (Peregrine Mold), Sam Kydd (Rory), Sean Gerrard (Kevin), John Blyth (Cyril Cudlipp), Julia Goodman (Girl At The Bar), Diana Crawford (Miss Erotica).

17.09.1969 **Up Pompeii!**   DB-D3 / 2"

Duration: 35 minutes.

The adventures of Lurcio the slave.

Written by Talbot Rothwell; music by Alan Braden; designed by Sally Hulke; produced and directed by Michael Mills.

With Frankie Howerd (Lurcio), Max Adrian (Ludicrus), Ruth Harrison (Cassandra), Georgina Moon (Erotica), Elizabeth Larner (Ammonia), Kerry Gardner (Nausius), Walter Horsbrugh (Plautus), Aubrey Woods (Bilius), Julia Goodman (Cilla), John Junkin (Odius), Richard McNeff (Senator).

SERIES 9

Transmission details are for BBC 1.

Holding / Source

18.12.1969 **Joint Account**   J|a / 2"

Written by Mike Seddon; designed by Pamela Lambooy; produced and directed by Michael Mills.

With Keith Barron (rodney), Sarah Atkinson (Celia), Geoffrey Whitehead (George), Bossie The Dog (Jaguar), Barbara Lindley (New Arrival).

01.01.1970 **The Jugg Brothers**   J / 2"

Written by Bob Grant and Stephen Lewis; designed by Philip Lindley; produced and directed by Dennis Main Wilson.

With Stephen Lewis (Stephen Jugg), Bob Grant (Robert Jugg), Fanny Carby (Lilly Dolly), Queenie Watts (Annie Bundle), Nancy Nevinson (Meg), Winifred Sabine (Kate), Edward Caddick (George Fryer), Ian Ramsey (Boy), Gerald Rowland (Boy).

08.01.1970 **An Officer And A Gentleman**   J / 2"

Written by Myles Rudge; music by Dennis Wilson; designed by James Bould; produced and directed by Robin Nash.

With James Grout (Major Gissing), Ken Wynne (Sid Coil), Patricia Hayes (Mrs Telfer), Diana King (Miss Jellicoe), Raymond Westwell (Dimitri Yevgenyvitch).

15.01.1970 **Who's Your Friend?**   J / 2"

Written by Terence Edmond; music by Dennis Wilson; designed by Stuart Walker; produced and directed by Graeme Muir.

With Bernard Cribbins (Jimmy Sampson), Maggie Fitzgibbon (Laura Marshall), Frank Thornton (Mr Walters), Jane Muir (Secretary), Alan Tilvern (Manny Wolfe), Frank Williams (Warrender), Donal McCann (Doyle), John Mulgrew (Sydney Pratt), John F. Landry (Reporter).

SERIES 10

Transmission details are for BBC 1.

Holding / Source

11.03.1970 **Keep 'Em Rolling**   J|a / 2"

Written by David Climie and John Law; music by Arthur Dulay; designed by Austin Ruddy; produced by Michael Mills; studio sequences directed by Michael Mills; film sequences directed by Jim Franklin.

With Derek Nimmo (Reggie Turpin), Peter Bayliss (C. D. Birtwistle), Sheila White (Gladys Smith), Timothy Bateson (Brownie Brown), Fabia Drake (Duchess of Haverstock), Jonathan Cecil (Major Fitzwarren), Walter Horsbrugh (Duke of Haverstock), Roland Macleod (Mr Murchison), Anthony Dawes (The Vicar), Gordon Rollings (The Drunk), Michael Collins (Signpainter), Valerie Stanton (The Bride), Peter Diamond (The Sergeant).

18.03.1970 **Better Than A Man**   J|a / 2"

Written by Kenneth Eastaugh; music by Ronnie Hazlehurst; designed by Austin Ruddy; produced and directed by Sydney Lotterby.

With Sheila Hancock (Wendy), Leslie Sands (George Hillbright), Allan Cuthbertson (Llewellyn Chadwick), Willoughby Goddard (Sir Michael Binns), John Warner (Arnold Pollock), Bartlett Mullins, John Rae, John Cazabon, Helen Cotterill, Frank Abbott, Richard Young, Samantha Birch.

25.03.1970 **Last Tribute**   R1 / 2"

Written by Peter Lewis; music by Ronnie Hazlehurst; designed by John Burrowes; produced and directed by Michael Mills.

With Bill Fraser (Basil Bulstrode), Raymond Huntley (Emanuel Holroyd), David Battley (Percy), David King (Charlie), Tony Melody (Policeman), Jack Arrow (Police Sergeant).

01.04.1970 **Haven Of Rest**   J / 2"

Written by Alan Melville; music by Dennis Wilson; designed by Valerie Warrender; produced and directed by Robin Nash.

With Julian Orchard (Rupert Haliburton), Vivienne Bennett (Miss Barnett), Ballard Berkeley (Colonel Satchwell-Simpson), Janie Booth (Bessie), Lally Bowers (Daphne Delaney), Joyce Carey (Lady Henderson), Judith Furse (Muriel Crump), Colin Gordon (Arthur Plenderleith), Deryck Guyler (Mr Benson), Patricia Hayes (Miss Batchelor), John Le Mesurier (Mr Prentice), Tony Sympson (Thatcher).

SERIES 11

Transmission details are for BBC 1.

Holding / Source

08.07.1970 **Mind Your Own Business**   J|a / 2"

Written by Tony Bilbow and Mike Fentiman; designed by Graham Oakley; produced and directed by Dennis Main Wilson.

With Tony Selby (Bill), Derek Griffiths (Ernie), Norman Bird (Dad), Hilda Fenemore (Mum), Cheryl Hall (Audrey), Adrienne Posta (Muriel), Eugenie Cavanagh, Ian Ramsey, Michael Reynell.

15.07.1970 **The Old Contemptible**   J / 2"

Written by John Waterhouse; designed by Oliver Bayldon; produced by Dennis Main Wilson; directed by Vere Lorrimer.

With Billy Russell (Sam Oakley), Arthur English (Arthur Oakley), Gretchen Franklin (Lily Oakley), Tamara Ustinov (Josie Oakley), John Sharp (Mr Ludlow), Joyce Carpenter (Mrs Ludlow), Michael Osborne (Simon), Derrick Gilbert (Protester), Keneth Thornett (Landlord), Laurence Archer (Old Contemptible), Walter Swash (Old Contemptible).

29.07.1970 **Don't Ring Us... We'll Ring You**   J / 2"

Written by Mike Craig and Lawrie Kinsley; lyrics by John Junkin; music by Denis King; designed by Valerie Warrender; produced and directed by Dennis Main Wilson.

With John Junkin (Ernie Babcock), Norman Rossington (Jimmy Duffy), Colin Welland (Dave Sullivan), Barbara Mullaney (Ethel), Joe Gladwin (Reg Aveyard), Tony Melody (Gas Man), Gael West (Pat Morgan), Pamela Manson (Gloria), Sandy Powell (Joe Ridsdale).

05.08.1970   **Meter Maids**   J / 2"

Written by Louis Quinn and Robin Hawdon; music by Alan Braden; designed by Oliver Bayldon; produced and directed by Douglas Argent.

With Barbara Windsor (Polly), Joan Sanderson (Smythe), Pat Coombs (Crocker), Martin Wyldeck (Superintendent Craddock), Bob Todd (Sergeant McKenzie).

SERIES 12

Transmission details are for BBC 1.

Holding / Source

01.04.1971   **Just Harry And Me**   J / 2"

Written by Charles Laurence; designed by Christine Ruscoe; produced and directed by Duncan Wood.

With Sheila Hancock (Claire), Donald Houston (Harry), Lynne Frederick (Jenny), Tony Melody, Joan Ingram, Harry Burgess Wall, Nigel Bradshaw.

08.04.1971   **Uncle Tulip**   J / 2"

Written by Rene Basilico; music by Max Harris; designed by Christine Ruscoe; produced and directed by Douglas Argent.

With Renu Setna (Uncle Tulip), Frank Olegario (Uncle Ranjit), Geoffrey Lumsden (Doctor Johnson), Yasmin (Anna), Madhav Sharma (Charlie), Mary Hignett (Mrs McMichael), Vivienne Stephens (Servant Girl), Mohan Singh (Gulam), Sahab Qizilbash (Sandri).

15.04.1971   **It's Awfully Bad For Your Eyes, Darling...**   J / 2"

When mother arrives at Samantha's flat, it takes a lot of imagination to disguise Sam's boy-friend among her more feminine flat-mates.

Written by Jilly Cooper and Christopher Bond; music by Don Rendell and Ian Carr; designed by Michael Young; produced and directed by John Howard Davies.

With Jane Carr (Gillian Page-Wood), Anna Palk (Virginia Walker), Joanna Lumley (Samantha Ryder-Ross), Jeremy Lloyd (Bobby Dutton), Timothy Carlton (Jeremy Bathurst), Jim Collier (Unidentified Drunk), Marion Mathie (Mrs Ryder-Ross).

22.04.1971   **The Rough With The Smooth**   DB / 2"

See how the Fates their gifts allot For A is happy - B is not. Yet B is worthy, I daresay Of more prosperity than A!

If I were Fortune- which I am not B should enjoy A's happy lot And A should die in misery. That is, assuming I am B.

Written by John Junkin and Tim Brooke-Taylor; theme music by Denis King; music by Dennis Wilson; designed by Peter Blacker; produced and directed by Leon Thau.

With Tim Brooke-Taylor (Richard Woodville), John Junkin (Harold King), Eleanor Smale, Jenny Till, Richard McNeff, Timothy Carlton, Graham Tonbridge, Clovissa Newcombe, Terence Brook.

29.04.1971   **Equal Partners**   J / 2"

Written by John Lloyd and Graeme Garden; music by Dennis Wilson; designed by Valerie Warrender; produced and directed by Graeme Muir.

With Nicky Henson (Nicky), Angela Scoular (Pauline), Jessie Evans (Mrs Jones), Hilary Pritchard (Mary).

06.05.1971   **The Importance Of Being Hairy**   J / 2"

Written by Kingsley Amis; music by Dennis Wilson; designed by Richard McManan-Smith; produced and directed by Graeme Muir.

With Gerald Flood (Peter Hastings), George Howe (Professor Shillito), John Cater (Doctor Chatterjee), Betty Goulding (Sally Train), Louie Ramsay (Jill Hastings), Victor Platt (Fortnum), Doug Fisher (Tom Potts), Pearl Hackney (Dora Leach), Paul Thompson (Snibb), George Janson (Lawson Jones), Sally Avery (Girl Candidate), Richard Penny (Boy Friend), Gilly Flower (Miss Travers), David Simeon (Watchdog), James Copeland (Professor Macdonald).

SERIES 13

Transmission details are for BBC 1.

	Production No	VT Number	Holding / Source

14.01.1972   **Idle At Work**   J / 2"

Written by Graham Chapman and Bernard McKenna; music by Max Harris; designed by David Chandler; produced by James Gilbert; directed by Harold Snoad.

With Ronnie Barker (George Idle), Graham Crowden (Mr Chesterton), Derek Francis (Restaurant Manager), Mary Merrall (Auntie), William Kendall (The 'General'), Roland Macleod (The 'Bishop'), Annabel Leventon (Saunders), Timothy Carlton (Naismith), Janet Mahoney (Miss Pettifer), Anne De Vigier (Wendy), Alec Bregonzi (Ken), Michael Stainton, Ian Gray, John Owens, Robert Yetz, Desmond Cullum-Jones.

21.01.1972   **And Whose Side Are You On?**   J / 2"

Written by David Hardie, Di Hardie and Terence Edmond; music by Burt Rhodes; designed by Pamela Lambooy; produced and directed by Leon Thau.

With Patrick Newell (Major Sperling), Tim Barrett (Pomfret), Freddie Earlle (Gaston), Terence Edmond (Lieutenant Dunkel), John Hollis (Muller), Olivia Breeze (Waitress), Laurie Webb (Postman), Roy Evans (Maurice), Derek Chafer (Aide).

28.01.1972   **Born Every Minute**   DB-D3 / 2"

Written by Jack Popplewell; designed by Roger Lowe; produced and directed by David Croft.

With Juliet Harmer (Girl), Campbell Singer (Sir Rufus), Mollie Sugden (Lady Wright), Harry Landis (Joe), Gordon Peters (Ticket Collector), Edward Sinclair (Head Waiter), Michael Stainton (Chauffeur), Balfour Sharp (Page-Boy), Ronald Fraser, James Beck.

27.03.1972   **The Dirtiest Soldier In The World**   DB-D3 / 2"

Alt.Title(s):   *The General Danced At Dawn*

Adapted by David Climie; based on a book by George Macdonald Fraser; music by George Alexander; designed by Paul Joel; produced and directed by Michael Mills.

With John Standing (Lieutenant Macneill), Freddie Earlle (Private McAuslan), Jack Watson (RSM), Moray Watson (CSM), Allan Cuthbertson (Colonel Gordon), Ben Aris (The Adjutant), Andrew Downie (Major Chisholm), Jay Neill (Sergeant of The Guard), Stephen Temperley (Corporal of The Guard), Kevin Moran (Private MacFarlane), Christopher Holmes (Private MacDonald), Clive Woodward (Private Hobbs), Ricky Newby (Private Fraser), Ben Gaule (Private Grant), Pauline Crow (The Duchess), George C. Robb (The Duke).

07.09.1972   **Weren't You Marcia Honeywell?**   11/4/2/3137   VTC/6HT/79784/ED   J / 2"

Written by Ken Hoare; music by Max Harris; produced and directed by Douglas Argent.

With Betty Marsden (Betty Marsden), Hugh Paddick (Hugh Paddick), Jo Garrity (Pearl, Young Girl), Hilda Fenemore (Mrs Tucker, Housekeeper), Royce Mills (Graeme Thoms, TV Producer), John Brand (Voiceover).

08.09.1972 **Are You Being Served?**   DB-D3-R1 / 2"

A new comedy that takes a close look at the small world of a department store

Written by Jeremy Lloyd and David Croft; theme music by Ronnie Hazlehurst; designed by James Bould; produced and directed by David Croft.

With Trevor Bannister (Mr Lucas), Mollie Sugden (Mrs Betty Slocombe), Frank Thornton (Captain Stephen Peacock), Arthur Brough (Mr Ernest Grainger), John Inman (Mr Wilberforce Humphries), Wendy Richard (Miss Shirley Brahms), Nicholas Smith (Mr Cuthbert Rumbold), Larry Martyn (Mr Mash), Michael Knowles (The Customer), Harold Bennett (Young Mr Grace), Stephanie Gathercole (The Secretary).

SERIES 14

Transmission details are for BBC 1.

Holding / Source

04.01.1973 **Last Of The Summer Wine - Of Funerals And Fish**   DB-D3 / 2"

Blamire, Compo and Clegg are three opposites with one thing in common - determination to make each day as full as possible.

Written by Roy Clarke; music by Ronnie Hazlehurst; designed by Andrew Dimond; produced and directed by James Gilbert.

With Michael Bates (Cyril Blamire), Bill Owen (Compo), Peter Sallis (Clegg), Blake Butler (Mr Wainwright), Rosemary Martin (Mrs Partridge), Michael Stainton (Vicar), John Comer (Sid), Jane Freeman (Ivy), Kathy Staff (Mrs Nora Batty), Derek Etchells (Van Driver), Pat Bonna (First Woman), Jean McLaren (Second Woman), John Barratt.

June Howson, the director, recalls: "I originally commissioned Roy Clarke to write a pilot for Adam Smith which was never made. It was basically about three old men who went fishing together - one of whom was the Minister. It was gentle and charming and I loved it although it wasn't quite what Denis Forman at Granada had in mind so sadly, on my part, it was rejected. He took it to the BBC and a revamped version became Last of The Summer Wine."

11.01.1973 **The Rescue**   R1 / 2"

Written by Peter Jones; music by Dennis Wilson; produced and directed by John Howard Davies.

With Peter Jones (Clive), Nicholas Parsons (Guy Shelmerdine), Moyra Fraser (Connie Shelmerdine), Lucita Lijertwood (Mrs Harris).

18.01.1973 **Elementary, My Dear Watson**   DB-D3 / 2"

Alt.Title(s): *The Strange Case of the Dead Solicitors*

Duration: 31 minutes.

What is the tenuous thread that links five dead solicitors with Fu Manchu and the panel of Call My Bluff?

What is the curse of the Belling-ham-Datchetts?
Is Dr Watson becoming too surreal for his own good?

Sherlock Holmes finds Edwardian solutions to these problems of 1973.

Written by N. F. Simpson; music by Burt Rhodes; designed by Raymond Cusick; produced by Barry Took; directed by Harold Snoad.

With John Cleese (Sherlock Holmes), William Rushton (Doctor Watson), Josephine Tewson (Lady Cynthia), Norman Bird (Inspector Street), Chic Murray (Constable), Bill Maynard (Frank Potter), Larry Martyn (Fu Manchu), Michael Gover (Superintendent Truscott), Michael Knowles (Rupert), Helen Lambert (Secretary), Rosemary Lord (Mabel), Ivor Salter (Airport Loader), Gordon Faith (Security Man), Colin Bean (Newsboy), Rose Hill (The Lady), John Wells (Prime Minister), Frank Muir, Dawn Addams, Alan Coren, Patrick Campbell, Morag Hood, John Carson, Robert Robinson.

25.01.1973 **The Birthday**   DB-D3 / 2"

The party - Sodom and Gomorrah with sandwiches. But nobody comes. The solution? Rentabird.

Written by Eric Davidson; drawings by Franklin; music by Ken Jones; designed by Peter Brachacki; produced and directed by Dennis Main Wilson.

With Gordon Peters, Mary Millar, Gary Raymond, Frank Thornton, Bill Pertwee, Pamela Cundell, Ritchie Stewart, Edward Evans.

01.02.1973 **Marry The Girls**   J / 2"

Written by Godfrey Harrison; music by Dennis Wilson; designed by Michael Young; produced and directed by Graeme Muir.

With John Le Mesurier (Luke Elms), Barbara Murray (Lottie Elms), Sally Stephens (Sarah Elms), Sally Thomsett (Miranda Elms), Briony McRoberts (Julie Elms), John Leeson (Hippy), Yvette Vanson (Emma Elms), Heather Bell (Kate Elms), David Simeon (Ian Hollis), Maggie Hanley (Celia Harvey).

08.02.1973 **Home From Home**   R1 / 2"

Written by Eric Davidson; music by Alan Braden; designed by John Burrowes; produced and directed by Harold Snoad.

With Michael Robbins (Bill Collins), Yootha Joyce (Lil Wilson), Carmel McSharry (Pam Collins), Tony Selby (Ron Bates), Olive Mercer (The Neighbour).

03.01.1974 **It Ain't Half Hot Mum**   DB-D3 / 2"

1945 - The 'quit India' movement is gaining momentum and the sun would appear to be setting on this corner of the British Empire.

Written by Jimmy Perry and David Croft; theme music by Jimmy Perry and Derek Taverner; designed by Paul Joel; produced and directed by David Croft.

With Michael Bates (Rangi Ram), George Layton (Bombadier Solomons), Windsor Davies (BSM Williams), Melvyn Hayes (Gunner Beaumont), Christopher Mitchell (Gunner Parkins), John Clegg (Gunner Graham), Donald Hewlett (Colonel Reynolds), Michael Knowles (Captain Ashwood), Stuart McGugan (Gunner Mackintosh), Don Estelle (Gunner Sugden), Mike Kinsey (Gunner Evans), Kenneth MacDonald (Gunner Clark), Nik Zaran (Inspector Singh), Dino Shafeek (Char Wallah Muhammed), Babar Bhatti (Punka Wallah Rumzan), Ashwin Patel.

"In Vision", BBC2, tx: 28.5.1974, looked at Comedy Playhouse and in particular Steptoe and Son and Till Death Us Do Part. Produced and directed by Peter Foges. 45 mins.

SERIES 15

Transmission details are for BBC 1.

Production No   Holding / Source

##.##.#### **Bird Alone**   J / 2"

With Liz Smith, Yootha Joyce.

Recorded 02.04.1974. The 2" of this pilot existed until 1989 but seems to have gone missing during the transfer to D3 project. It's spool number was 42452, programme ID 01144/315901.

16.04.1974 **No Strings: Friend Or Woman**   DB-D3 / 2"

Derek advertises for a flatmate. When Leonora arrives his tidy bachelor domain is soon disrupted by a feminine touch.

Written by Carla Lane; music by Ken Jones; designed by Don Giles; produced and directed by Roger Race.

With Rita Tushingham (Leonora), Keith Barron (Derek), Lindsay Ingram (Iris), Eric French (Man In Street), Jennifer Guy (First Girl In Flat), Valerie Braithwaite (Annabel), Cunitia Knight (Clare), April Walker (Angela).

23.04.1974 **Franklyn And Johnnie**   J / 2"

Written by Richard Waring; music by Dennis Wilson; designed by Christine Ruscoe; produced and directed by Graeme Muir.

With Ronnie Barker (Johnnie Wetherby), Geoffrey Bayldon (Franklyn Sims), Richard Hurndall (Mr Mawson), Joyce Heron (Dora Phillips), Sydney Bromley (Bernard Watson), Hugh Morton (Vicar), Ian Price (James Kilpatrick), Peter Hughes (Factory Foreman), Raymond Bowers (Anderson), Anthony Brothers (Estate Agent).

30.04.1974 **Howerd's History Of England**   J|a / 2"

Written by Barry Took and Michael Mills; designed by Paul Allen; produced and directed by Michael Mills.

With Frankie Howerd (Host), Patrick Newell, Patrick Holt, Brian Oulton, Taiwo Ajai, John Cazabon, Maggy Maxwell, Frances Lee, Linda Cunningham, Barbara Lindley, Gail Playfair, Cyril Appleton, Tony Sympson, Leon Greene.

07.05.1974 **Happy Ever After**   DB-D3 / 2"

The Fletchers' family have grown up and flown. For the first time in 23 years there'll be no children around the house but the unaccustomed freedom brings its problems.

Written by John Chapman and Eric Merriman; designed by Ray London; produced and directed by Peter Whitmore.

With Terry Scott (Terry Fletcher), June Whitfield (June Fletcher), Roger Davis (Gordon), Lena Clemo (Susan Fletcher), Caroline Whitaker (Debbie Fletcher), Paul Greenwood (David Turner), Beryl Cooke (Aunt Lucy), David Carter (Driver), Philip Ryan (Driver).

14.05.1974 **The Dobson Doughnut**   J / 2"

Written by Raymond Allen; music by Alan Roper; designed by Paul Allen; produced and directed by Michael Mills.

With Milo O'Shea (Henry Medway), Bernard Spear (Dobson), Jo Kendall (Alison), Brian Miller (Ken), Robert Prince (Newspaper Reporter), John Ringham (Bates), Geoffrey Whitehead (Thomas), Jim Smilie (TV Announcer), Harry Locke (Shaw), Ken Haward (Police Sergeant), The Portsmouth Youth Band.

21.05.1974 **The Big Job**   DB-D3 / 2"

'Half a million in used notes' - Eddie's perennial dream. But when he tries his hand at kidnapping, the results are disastrous.

Written by Peter Jones; music by Ken Jones; designed by Paul Munting; produced by Dennis Main Wilson; directed by Gareth Gwenlan.

With Peter Jones (Eddie), Prunella Scales (Dolly), Andonia Katsaros (Norma), Nick Brimble (Ginger), Alfred Marks (Mr Oldenshaw), Aubrey Woods (Grimes).

28.05.1974 **It's Only Me - Whoever I Am**   1143/3179   J / 2"

Written by Roy Clarke; music by Max Harris; designed by Raymond Cusick; produced and directed by Sydney Lotterby.

With David Jason (Quentin), Patricia Hayes (Blanche), Christine Ozanne (Brenda), Daphne Heard (Aunty Vee), Olive Mercer (Housekeeper), Edward Burnham (Father Keane), Paul Greenwood (Maurice), Adrienne Burgess (Janet), David Rhys Anderson (Actor), Bernard Spear (Producer), Elaine Baillie (Maggie).

04.06.1974 **The Last Man On Earth**   1164/3160   DB-D3 / 2"

Written by Ray Galton and Alan Simpson; music by Dennis Wilson; designed by Valerie Warrender; produced and directed by Graeme Muir.

With Dandy Nichols (Mother), Ronald Fraser (Henry).

The surviving recording is the complete studio recording, circa 51 minutes.

11.06.1974 **Sitting Pretty**   J / 2"

Written by Pauline Devaney and Edwin Apps; music by Dennis Wilson; designed by Robin Tarsnane; produced and directed by Graeme Muir.

With Nicky Henson, Una Stubbs, James Cossins, Anne Jameson, Benny Lee.

25.06.1974 **Pygmalion Smith**   DB-D3 / 2"

Written by Roy Clarke; designed by Barrie Dobbins; produced and directed by Roger Race.

With Leonard Rossiter (Smithy), T. P. McKenna (Brewster), Barbara Courtney (Auriol Pratt), Margaret Burton (Mrs Kintoul).

03.07.1974 **A Girl's Best Friend**   J / 2"

Written by Donald Churchill; music by Ken Jones; designed by Cynthia Kljuco; produced and directed by John Howard Davies.

With Zena Walker (Audrey Dalton), Carolyn Courage (Lynn Dalton), Reginald Marsh (Arnold), David Knight (Jack Shepherd).

09.07.1974 **The Reverent Wooing Of Archibald**   J / 2"

What has a pin-headed young man like Archie Mulliner to offer a bally goddess like Aurelia Cammerleigh ?

Adapted by David Climie; based on a book by P. G. Wodehouse; music by Dennis Wilson; designed by Jeremy Bear; produced by Graeme Muir; directed by Jeremy Bear and Graeme Muir.

With William Mervyn (Mr Mulliner), Betty Romaine (Miss Postlethwaite), June Conniff (Flapper), Billy Milton (Draught Stout), Harry Goodier (Tankard), John Dunbar (Bass), Julian Holloway (Archibald Mulliner), John Leeson (Tuppy Glossop), Madeline Smith (Aurelia Cammerleigh), Joan Benham (Aunt Cora), Julian Fox (Algy Wymondham-Wymondham), Jenny Cox (Doris), Philip Howard (Simmons), Jennifer Croxton (Muriel).

##.##.#### **French Relish**   J / 2"

Originally scheduled for 16.07.1974.

Written by Pauline Devaney and Edwin Apps; designed by Peter Kindred; produced and directed by Harold Snoad.

With Derek Nimmo (Simon Pollock).

On this date, the usual Comedy Playhouse slot had a repeat of Seven Of One: Open All Hours.

12.12.1974 **Too Much Monkey Business**   J / 2"

Written by Roy Kendall; music by Denis King; designed by Cynthia Kljuco; produced and directed by Douglas Argent.

With Norman Rossington (Jim), Pat Heywood (Laura), George Innes (Andy), John Ringham (Mr Barnes), Harold Goodwin (Barry), Michael O'Hagan (Brian).

11.06.1975 **The Melting Pot**   UM / 2"

Written by Spike Milligan and Neil Shand; music by Iain Sutherland and John Mayer; designed by Paul Allen; produced and directed by Roger Race.

With Spike Milligan (?), John Bird (?), Peter Jones (?), Harry Fowler (?), Frank Carson (Irish Landlord), Alexandra Dane (South African Landlady), Alister Williamson (Australian Bookie), Anthony Brothers (Scottish Arab), Wayne Browne (Coloured North Countryman), Freddie Earlle (Orthodox Jew), Robert Dorning (Colonel), Rita Webb (Daily Help).

18.06.1975 **Only On Sunday**   J / 2"

Written by Dick Clement and Ian La Frenais; music by Ken Jones; designed by Cynthia Kljuco; produced and directed by Gareth Gwenlan.

With Trevor Bannister (Geoffrey), Peter Bowles (Patrick), Jacqueline Clarke (Linda), Caroline Dowdeswell (Lisa), Gaynor Stuart (Beth), Linda Cunningham (Alison), Evan Ross (Vicar).

25.06.1975 For Richer... For Poorer   J / 2"

Written by Johnny Speight; designed by Valerie Warrender; produced and directed by Dennis Main Wilson.

With Harry H. Corbett (Working-Class Hero), Eric Pohlmann (Ugly Face of Capitalism), David Battley (Nigel The Idle), Don Henderson (Mediator).

02.07.1975 Captive Audience   J|a / 2"

Written by Dick Clement and Ian La Frenais; designed by Ken Ledsham; produced and directed by Roger Race.

With Derek Fowlds (Leonard), Daphne Heard (Mum), Leslie Dwyer (Uncle Jeffrey), Cheryl Hall (Avril), Léon Vitali (Eric).

09.07.1975 Going, Going, Gone...Free?   DB-D3 / 2"

Written by Carla Lane; designed by Cynthia Kljuco; produced and directed by Gareth Gwenlan.

With Pauline Yates (Jen), Beryl Cooke (Molly), Peter Duncan (Mark), Madge Ryan (Mrs Dean), Gillian McCutcheon (Brenda), John Clegg (Gerald), Geoffrey Palmer (Ralph), Brian Hayes (Policeman).

See also: IT AIN'T HALF HOT MUM* / LAST OF THE SUMMER WINE* / THE LIVER BIRDS* / ME MAMMY* / MR BIG* / NO STRINGS* / THE OLD CAMPAIGNER* / STEPTOE AND SON* / UP POMPEII!* / WODEHOUSE PLAYHOUSE*

COMEDY PLAYHOUSE

Produced for Carlton by a variety of companies (see details below). Transmission details are for the Central region. Duration: 25 minutes.

Holding / Source

23.02.1993 The 10%ers   D2 / D2S

A Grant/Naylor production.

Exploits of a talent agency in London's West End.

Written by Rob Grant and Doug Naylor; script supervisor Judy Packman; music by David Mindel; produced by Rob Grant and Doug Naylor; directed by Doug Naylor and Rob Grant.

With Clive Francis (Dominic), Benedict Taylor (Atin), Gabrielle Cowburn (Helen), Colin Stinton (Tony), Elizabeth Bennett (Joan), Denis Lill (Murray), Beatie Edney (Monica), Madge Ryan (Gloria), Clive Panto (Ernie), Julie Peasgood (Trudy), Gordon Langford-Rowe (Eamon), Elizabeth Hickling (Natalie), Tom Petheram (Priest), Simon Oates (Roddy Preston), Walter Plinge (Security Guard).

02.03.1993 Wild Oats   D2 / D2S

A Celador production.

Roland is getting along fine as a carefree bachelor, until the day his son arrives in London from the north seeking his fortune.

Written by Steve Knight and Mike Whitehill; produced and directed by Nic Phillips.

With Leslie Grantham (Roland Jackson), Jonathon Morris (David Jackson), Julie Bramall (Jennifer), Eve Ferret (Deirdre), Fraser James (Paul), Max Cane (Photographer), Edward Clayton (Mr Stubbs).

09.03.1993 Brighton Belles   D2 / D2S

A Humphrey Barclay Productions production.

From the popular American comedy series The Golden Girls. Frances, Annie and Bridget are three frank and funny friends who share a beautiful house and a life of harmony, until Frances's 80-year-old mother turns up, homeless.

Adapted by Christopher Skala; based on material by Susan Harris; executive producer Al Mitchell; produced by Humphrey Barclay and Christopher Skala; directed by James Cellan Jones.

With Sheila Hancock (Frances), Wendy Craig (Annie), Sheila Gish (Bridget), Jean Boht (Josephine).

16.03.1993 Stuck On You   D2 / D2S

A Central production.

Danny and Beth were once in love but are now at each other's throats. The problem is, they can't sell their dingy London flat, so they agree to live together but under new rules.

Written by Mark Bussell and Justin Sbresni; produced by Paula Burdon; directed by Nick Hurran.

With Neil Morrissey (Danny), Amelia Bullmore (Beth), Tom Watt (Gordon), Caroline Milmoe (Hazel), Jeremy Gittins (Mike), Anthony Dunn (Cliff), Roger Frost (Policeman), Steven Brough (Neighbour), William Lawrance (Richard).

23.03.1993 Once In A Lifetime   D2 / D2S

A Noel Gay Television production.

When Helen meets Mojo on the television game show Once in a Lifetime, both of their lives are changed forever.

Written by Nick Symons, Sandi Toksvig and Joolz; script editor Nick Revell; executive producer Charles Armitage; produced by Nick Symons; directed by Sylvie Boden.

With Pam Ferris (Roger), Lisa Maxwell (Mojo), Maria McErlane (Helen Steel), Kate Robbins (Bella White), Ramsay Gilderdale (Roger).

30.03.1993 Cut And Run - The Badger Watch   D2 / D2S

A Zenith North production.

As part of a campaign to stop a golf course being built on open countryside, an independent video company is asked to film the badgers that live there. It all sounds simple enough.

Written by Tim Firth; script editor Paul Mayhew-Archer; executive producer Ian Squires; produced and directed by Alan J. W. Bell.

With Tim Healy (Stan), Wayne Foskett (Jerry), Christopher Lang (Peter Bennett), Carla Mendonca (Imo), Gary Waldhorn (Mr Hogson), Steph Bramwell (Mrs Genevieve Hogson), Paul Kynman (Steve), David Miller (Chippy), Marcello Magni (Luigi).

13.04.1993 The Complete Guide To Relationships   D2 / D2S

A Kudos Productions production.

Mike and Julia have split up for the sixth time. Sarah is wondering how to chuck Tony. Val has been dumped by The Jerk. When Sarah meets Mike and there is an instant attraction, things become even more complicated.

Written by Kim Fuller; executive producer Stephen Garrett; produced by Kim Fuller; directed by Juliet May.

With Michael Maloney (Mike), Anna Chancellor (Julia), Michael Simkins (Tony), Maria Friedman (Sarah), Sophie Thompson (Val), David Bamber (Chris), Diane Parish (Donna), Tony Whithouse (Gary), Enn Reitel (Narrator).

20.04.1993 Sailortown - Where There's A Will   D2 / D2S

An Ulster Television production for Central.

The owner of a bar in Belfast's dockside area has died, and in the absence of a will, his son-in-law and grandson compete to take control.

Written by Mark Bussell and Martin Lynch; music by The Pogues; executive producer Paul Spencer; produced by Trevor McCallum; directed by Nick Hurran.

With James Nesbitt (Skeebal), Pat Laffan (Danny), Mark Mulholland (Tamala), Brendan Conroy (Billy), Simon Magill (Brad), John Rogan (Father Francis), Olivia Nash (Mrs Mac), Joe McPartland (Gerry).

See also: BRIGHTON BELLES*

COMEDY PREMIERE

An ATV production. Transmission details are for the ATV midlands region. Duration: 25 minutes.

	Production No	VT Number	Holding / Source
07.08.1975 What A Turn Up	9910	9910/75	J / 2"

Grandad's unexpected arrival on the day of his grand-daughter's wedding causes great upheaval in the Warner household— to say nothing of speculation as to whether or not he made a fortune in Australia ...

Written by Brian Clemens and Dennis Spooner; theme music by John Montgomery; designed by Gerry Roberts; produced and directed by John Scholz-Conway.

With Bernard Lee (Wally Warner), Vivian Pickles (Margaret Warner), Anton Rodgers (George Warner), Diana King (Mrs Fennell), Ronald Leigh-Hunt (Mr Fennell), Nina Thomas (Lesley Warner), David Neville (Simon Fennell), Martin Neil (Justin Warner).

14.08.1975 For Richer For Poorer	9911	9911/75	J / 2"

Being short of a pound or two is everyone's lot nowadays, but Richard and Fiona Bunting have their own way of solving the money shortage...

Written by Jon Watkins; designed by Gerry Roberts; produced and directed by John Scholz-Conway.

With George Layton (Richard Bunting), Ian Ogilvy (Nigel Benson), Susan Dury (Fiona Bunting), Jane How (Penelope Benson), Peter Hill (Man From Finance Company).

21.08.1975 Honey	9909	9909/75	J / 2"

"Come and stay with us when you're round our way", is a common enough expression. Most people don't expect to be taken at their word but Honey Jones did...

Written by Mike Craig, Lawrie Kinsley and Ron McDonnell; designed by Gerry Roberts; produced and directed by John Scholz-Conway.

With Michael Bates (Reg Forrester), Kathleen Byron (Vera Forrester), Sandra Dickinson (Honey Jones), Bernard Holley (Peter Forrester), Barbara Kellerman (Susan), Ronnie Brody (Wine Waiter), Frank Coda (Head Waiter).

28.08.1975 The Truth About Verity	9912	9912/75	J / 2"

The old adage says: "People in glass houses shouldn't throw stones." It's perhaps better not to throw advice, either — especially if you're a female "Jeckyll and Hyde." But what really is the truth about Verity Martin?

Written by Jon Watkins [credited as John Watkins]; designed by Gerry Roberts; produced and directed by John Scholz-Conway.

With Sylvia Syms (Verity Martin), John Savident (Mr Frisby), Jenny Hanley (Alison Bentley), John Carlin (Hugh), Ed Devereaux (Roger), Jo Anderson (Miss Tudor), Frank Coda (Mr Mendoza).

31.08.1975 Home Sweet Home	9914	9914/75	J / 2"

How does one get rid of an unwanted house guest, especially if it's a relative? Little George has a number of ideas of his own-which have quite an effect on the entire household...

Written by John Kane; theme music by John Montague and John Montgomery; designed by Gerry Roberts; produced and directed by John Scholz-Conway.

With Russell Lewis (George), Rosamond Burne (Auntie Agnes), Christine McKenna (Jess), Nigel Greaves (Willy), Gaynor Hodgson (Binny), Derek Deadman (Taxi Driver), Susan Brown (Miss Hayes).

Billed as Children's Comedy Premiere. Specially-written for the cast of 'The Kids from 47A'.

26.11.1975 Milk-O	9913	9913/75	J / 2"

Milkman Jim oversleeps, and with a £10 prize for the winner of the Empty Milk Bottle Competition at stake . .

Written by Anthony Marriott and Bob Grant; theme music by John Montgomery; designed by Gerry Roberts; produced and directed by John Scholz-Conway.

With Bob Grant (Jim Wilkins), Anna Karen (Rita Wilkins), Leslie Dwyer (Dad), Alan Curtis (Norman Fish), Peter Greene (Charlie Morris), Paul Moriarty (Dennis Green), Helen Keating (Housewife), Mike Savage (Frank Richards).

This run was originally intended to begin on 09.06.75 but was moved to allow a repeat run of MAN ABOUT THE HOUSE to be scheduled further away from a new run of the same series in the Autumn.

COMEDY SHOWCASE

Produced for Channel 4 by a variety of companies (see details below). Transmission details are for Channel 4. Duration: 25 minutes.

SERIES 1

	Holding / Source
05.10.2007 Other People	DB / DBSWF

A Company Pictures production.

Written by Toby Whithouse; executive producers George Faber, Charles Pattinson and Tom Grieves; produced by Emma Burge; directed by William Sinclair.

With Martin Freeman (Greg Wilson), Nicholas Burns (Rick Parish), Emma Kennedy (Sally), Siobhan Finneran (Shirley), Matt Green (Mr Kane), Phil Davis (Police Sergeant), James Rochfort (Prosecutor), John Fortune (Magistrate).

12.10.2007 Ladies And Gentlemen	DB / DBSWF

A Talkback Thames production.

Created by James Bobin, Jesse Armstrong and Sam Bain; written by Sam Bain and Jesse Armstrong; script editor Arthur Mathews; music by Ben Bartlett; designed by Dennis De Groot; executive producers Phil Bowker, Jesse Armstrong and Sam Bain; head of production Beatrice Gay; produced by Derrin Schlesinger; directed by Becky Martin.

With Reece Shearsmith (Freddy), Darren Boyd (Horatio), Adam Buxton (Jack), Lucy Punch (Alice), Rosie Cavaliero (Louisa), Cara Horgan (Emily), Christina Cole (Elizabeth), Dominic Coleman (Police Constable Jackson), Neil Edmond (Servant), Karl Johnson (Uncle Philip), Jessica Regan (Susanna), Jonathan Slinger (Mr Lupton), Geoffrey Whitehead (Lawyer).

COMEDY SHOWCASE

19.10.2007 **Plus One**   DB / DBSWF

A Kudos Film & Television production.

Written by Tim Allsop and Stewart Williams; script supervisor Chrissie Bibby; designed by Greg Shaw; associate producers Tim Allsop and Stewart Williams; executive producer Derek Wax; head of production Alison Barnett [credited as Alison Barnet]; produced by Kate Crowe; directed by Simon Delaney.

With Rory Kinnear (Rob Black), Duncan James (Duncan from Blue), Miranda Raison (Linsey), Nigel Harman (Rich), Steve John Shepherd (Paul), Ingrid Oliver (Rebecca), Ruth Bradley (Laura), Gemma Atkinson (Herself), Manjinder Virk (News Reporter), Eric Carte (Uncle Phil), Jan Goodman (Barbara), Sapphire Elia (Kerry), Laura Haddock (Nicky).

26.10.2007 **The Eejits**   DB / DBSWF

An Objective Productions production.

Written by Arthur Mathews and Paul Woodfull; script supervisor Pam Wylde; music by Paul Woodfull; designed by Dick Lunn; executive producers Phil Clarke and Andrew O'Connor; head of production Debi Roach; produced by Saskia Schuster; directed by Steve Connelly.

With Dessie Gallagher (Maurice), Patrick McDonnell (Gerard), Paul McGlinchey (Tom Grace), Mark Huberman (Rory McWilliams), Ned Dennehy (Bob Salmon), Debbie Chazen (Garvey), Eamon Geoghegan (Balaclava Man), Finbar Lynch (Concrete O'Hara), Kathy Burke (Virgin Mary), Arthur Mathews, Edward McLiam, Paul Woodfull.

09.11.2007 **Free Agents**   DB / DBSWF

A Big Talk Productions production.

Written by Chris Niel; script supervisor Angelica Pressello; music by David Arnold; designed by Dick Lunn; executive producers Iain Morris and Damon Beesley; head of production Karen Beever; produced by Nira Park; directed by Richard Laxton.

With Stephen Mangan (Alex), Sharon Horgan (Helen), Anthony Head (Stephen), Nick Barber (Tod), Frances Tomelty (Sylvia), Richard Dillane (Theatre Actor).

In association with Bwark Productions.

23.11.2007 **Kevin Bishop**   DB / DBSWF

An Objective Productions production.

Written by Kevin Bishop, Lee Hupfield, Tim Allsop, Stewart Williams, The Dawson Brothers, Ed Hall, Samantha Martin, Gary Monaghan, Nico Tatarowicz and David Cadji-Newby; script supervisor Anne Patterson; music by Mark Thomas; designed by Jonathan Paul Green; assistant producer Samantha Martin; associate producer Kevin Bishop; production executive Jenny Hay; executive producers Phil Clarke and Andrew O'Connor; head of production Debi Roach; produced by Lee Hupfield; directed by Elliot Hegarty.

With Kevin Bishop (Host), Jim Howick, Katie Males, Oliver Maltman, Vanessa Feltz.

SERIES 2

                                                                                                                       Holding / Source
12.11.2009 **Campus**   HD/DB / HD/DB

A Monicker Pictures production.

Written by Robert Harley, James Henry, Oriane Messina, Gary Parker, Victoria Pile, Richard Preddy, Fay Rusling and Christian Sandino-Taylor; script supervisor Angelica Pressello; music by Trellis; director of photography Danny Cohen; art director Lucy Spink; designed by Dick Lunn; associate producer Robert Harley; executive producer Caroline Leddy; line producer Rachel Salter; produced and directed by Victoria Pile.

With Will Adamsdale (Jason Armitage), Lisa Jackson (Imogen Moffat), Joseph Millson (Matt Bear), Andy Nyman (Jonty De Wolfe), Sara Pascoe (Nicole Huggins), Dolly Wells (Lydia Tennant), Alison Lintott (Grace), Ahir Shar (Student), Will Abbott (Student), Daniel Castella (Student).

13.11.2009 **PhoneShop: New Man**   HD/DB / HD/DB

A Talkback Thames production.

Written by Phil Bowker; additional material by The Cast and Jon MacQueen; script supervisor Penelope Chong; script editor Ricky Gervais; director of photography Martin Hawkins; art director Holly Berk; designed by Simon Rogers; head of production Beatrice Gay; line producer Caroline Wyard; produced and directed by Phil Bowker.

With Andrew Brooke (Ashley), Javone Prince (Jerwayne), Tom Bennett (Christopher), Emma Fryer (Janine), Martin Trenaman (Lance), Ellena Stacey, Paul Pariser, Claire Vousden, Kobna Holdbrook-Smith.

27.11.2009 **The Increasingly Poor Decisions Of Todd Margaret**   HD/DB / HD/DB

A RDF Television production.

Written by Shaun Pye and David Cross; script supervisor Suzanne Baron; director of photography James Hawkinson; art director Jane Shepherd; designed by Dennis De Groot; associate producer David Cross; production executive Helen Municchi; executive producer Clelia Mountford; production manager Kezia Walker; line producer Caroline Wyard; produced by Michael Livingstone; directed by Anthony Russo and Joe Russo.

With David Cross (Todd Margaret), John Fortune (Magistrate), Will Arnett (Brent Wilts), Amber Tamblyn (Girl), Matt King (Taxi Driver), Sharon Horgan (Alice), Kayvan Novak (Bomb Disposal Officer), Russell Tovey (Dave), John Bishop (Man At Trivia Machine), Sara Pascoe (Woman At Trivia Machine).

04.12.2009 **The Amazing Dermot**   HD/DB / HD/DB

A Roughcut production.

Written by Harry Williams and Jack Williams; script supervisor Sue Davies; music by Phase Music; director of photography Andy Hollis; titles by Sprout; art director Emma Lovell; designed by Julie Harris; executive producer Ash Atalla; line producer Tim Sealey; directed by Martin Dennis.

With Rhys Darby (Dermot / Lesley), Darren Boyd (Mickey), Alex Macqueen (Neil), Sinéad Keenan (Wendy), Thaila Zucchi (Lucille), Genevieve Barr (Jessica), John Biddle (Journalist), Richard Dixon (Auctioneer), Travis Oliver (Frank).

11.12.2009 **Guantanamo Phil**   HD/DB / HD/DB

A Hat Trick production.

Written by Mark Bussell and Justin Sbresni; script supervisor Jane Berry; director of photography Len Gowing; designed by Gavin Lewis; executive producer Jimmy Mulville; head of production Jessica Sharkey; line producer Donna Molloy; produced by Mark Bussell and Justin Sbresni; directed by Mark Bussell and Justin Sbresni.

With Steve Edge (Phil), Rebekah Staton (Carly), Martin Savage (Brendon), Beverley Rudd (Katie), Sally Bankes (Jance), Justin Edwards (Simpson-Jones), Ted Robbins (Lee Parsons), Tony Mooney (Dale), Conor Alexander (Abou Issa), Nayif Rashed (Abou Iss's Dad), Richard Standing (Martin Qual), Catherine Tyldesley (Louise), Anthony Gibbons (Securitiy Guard).

In association with Busby Productions.

18.12.2009 **Girl Friday**   HD/DB / HD/DB

An Objective Productions production.

Written by Lu Corfield, Kathryn Drysdale, Kerry Howard, Josie Long, Nat Luurtsema and Sara Pascoe; additional material by Lee Hupfield and Samantha Martin; script supervisor Anne Patterson; director of photography Pete Rowe; art director Louisa Morris; designed by Jonathan Paul Green; production executive Jenny Hay; executive producers Lee Hupfield and Andrew O'Connor; head of production Debi Roach; production manager Charlotte Cinalli; produced by Samantha Martin; directed by Ben Palmer.

With Lu Corfield, Kathryn Drysdale, Kerry Howard, Josie Long, Nat Luurtsema, Sara Pascoe, Matthew Crosby, Tom Parry.

SERIES 3

Holding / Source

02.09.2011 **Chickens**   HD/DB / HD/DB

A Big Talk Productions production.

Written by Simon Bird, Jonny Sweet and Joe Thomas; script supervisor Chrissie Bibby; director of photography Erik Wilson; art director Julian Weaver; designed by Jeff Sherriff; production executive Lyndsay Robinson; executive producer Kenton Allen; line producer Martin Coates; produced by John Rushton; directed by Steve Bendelack.

With Simon Bird (Cecil), Jonny Sweet (Bert), Joe Thomas (George), Jessica Barden (Barmaid), Thomas Benn-Wooley (Archie), Sarah Daykin (Winky), Emerald Fennell (Agnes), Olivia Hallinan (Gwyneth), Felicity Montagu (Merel), Alfie Nash (Mrs Honeywell's Son), Joanna Scanlan (Mrs Snedden), Flora Spencer-Longhurst (Gracie), Catherine Tydesley (Mrs Honeywell), Rupert Vansittart (Headmaster).

See also: CAMPUS* / FREE AGENTS* / THE KEVIN BISHOP SHOW* / PLUS ONE*

COMEDY SPECIAL

A BBC production for BBC 1. Transmission details are for BBC 1. Duration: 30 minutes.

Holding / Source

30.08.1972 **No Peace On The Western Front**   DB-D3 / 2"

A Prussian private and a Glaswegian Seaforth Highlander meet on the Somme in 1916.

Written by Dennis Pitts; designed by Tony Snoaden; produced and directed by Dennis Main Wilson.

With Ronald Fraser (Private Magnus 'Jock' MacMillan), Warren Mitchell (Fritz Von Scharngnan Clausewitz).

05.04.1977 **A Roof Over My Head**   DB-D3 / 2"

Have you ever tried to buy a house? This is a story of a man who did and the disasters that befell him.

Adapted by Barry Took; based on a book by Michael Green; music by Denis King; designed by Barrie Dobbins; produced and directed by Douglas Argent.

With Brian Rix (James), Lynda Baron (Sheila), Peter Bowles (Jack Askew), Richard Hurndall (Sir Phillip), Gail Harrison (Gaye), Deborah Watling (Maureen), Sheila Keith (Mrs Bagworth), Donald Gee (House Agent), Michael Stainton (Barman), Terence Conoley (Houseowner), Andy Ho (Houseowner).

12.04.1977 **Citizen Smith**   DB-D3 / 2"

A young Londoner sees himself as the Che Guevara of Tooting.

Written by John Sullivan; costume Robin Stubbs; make-up Kim Burns; designed by Gloria Clayton; produced and directed by Peter Whitmore.

With Robert Lindsay (Wolfie Smith), Cheryl Hall (Shirley), Mike Grady (Ken), Anthony Millan (Tucker), Artro Morris (Dad), Hilda Braid (Mum).

19.04.1977 **Michael Bentine's Square World**   DB-D3 / 2"

More than a decade ago, It's a Square World was a comedy innovation. Tonight, for this one programme, the ingenious Michael Bentine is back with a world squarer than ever!

Written by Michael Bentine and John Ennis; designed by Paul Joel; produced and directed by Jim Franklin.

With Michael Bentine, Jack Haig, Stuart Fell, Jan Hunt, Barrie Manning, Fiona MacNaughton, Pamela Manson, Bill Maxam, RAF Gymnastic Team.

26.04.1977 **The Boys And Mrs B**   DB-D3 / 2"

Written by Ronald Wolfe and Ronald Chesney; music by Ronnie Hazlehurst; lighting by Peter Smee; sound Hugh Barker; designed by Marjorie Pratt; produced and directed by Dennis Main Wilson.

With Michael Deeks (Dodger), Sean Clarke (Pete), Simon Henderson (Billy), Herbert Norville (Nick), Tony Robinson (Mark), Jeff Stevenson (Tiny), Lynette McMorrough (Hilda), Sue Upton (Jackie), Richard Caldicot (Councillor Cooper), John Tordoff (Joe Bates), Gorden Kaye (Mr Hobkirk), Luan Peters (The Stripper), Peter Cleall (Lenny).

03.05.1977 **Maggie - It's Me!**   DB-D3 / 2"

When Allie leaves her boyfriend - just to teach him a lesson - where else shall she go but to Maggie?

Written by Bernard Taylor; music by Dennis Wilson; designed by Roger Murray Leach; produced and directed by Graeme Muir.

With Frances de la Tour (Maggie), Rosemary Martin (Allie).

See also: CITIZEN SMITH* / A ROOF OVER MY HEAD*

COMEDY TONIGHT

Produced for ITV by a variety of companies (see details below). Duration: 25 minutes.

An ABC production. Transmission details are for the ABC midlands region.

Holding / Source

25.11.1967 **Just Good Friends**   J / 40

Derek Nimmo plays a boy who is saving up to get married to his girlfriend, and who takes a night job at what he tells her is a garage, to earn more money.

Written by John Esmonde and Bob Larbey; produced and directed by John Paddy Carstairs.

With Derek Nimmo, Amanda Barrie.

02.12.1967 **Daft As A Brush**   HF / 40

Written by Alec Travis; designed by Michael Perry; produced and directed by Pat Johns.

With Ken Platt (Ken), Betty Driver, Sheila Bernette, Michael Cadman, Geoffrey Reed, Aimi MacDonald.

09.12.1967 **Thicker Than Water**   J / 40

Written by Derek Collyer and George Evans; designed by Michael Perry; produced and directed by Pat Johns.

With Beryl Reid (Rose), Sheila Hancock (Charlotte), Martin Wyldeck, Lola Morrice.

An LWT production. Transmission details are for the ATV midlands region.

	Production No	Holding / Source
23.03.1980 **Tell It To The Judge**		DB|n / 2"

Written by Sid Green; designed by David Catley; produced and directed by Derrick Goodwin.

With Dave King (Detective Inspector Vic Saggers), Linal Haft (Detective Constable Ossie Sullivan), Nell Curran (Woman Detective Sergeant Kathleen Mulligan), Steven Pacey (Detective Constable Roger Wilson), John Grieve (Detective Sergeant Jock Stuart), Michael Cronin (Detective Constable Dai Thomas), Jay Neill (First Police Constable), Robin Parkinson (Mr Jackson), Betty Alberge (Elsie Brownley), Frank Lee (Monty Bergman), Karl Howman (Detective Constable Martin Walters), Paul Barber (Detective Constable Dennis Baxter), Kenneth Waller (Desmond Carter), David Purcell (Second Police Constable), Ben Ellison (Franklyn Butey), Michael Shilling (Third Police Constable), Jessica Turner (Jennifer Wilson), Lionel Ngakane (Lord Butey).

01.06.1980 **Him & His Magic**   99551   DB / 2"

Written by Geoff Rowley; theme music by Pilot; designed by Diana Bates; production manager Mike Hack; produced by Humphrey Barclay; directed by Geoffrey Sax.

With Philip Martin Brown (Stanley), Paul Luty (Uncle Ernie), Joan Scott (Mum [Voice]), Pravin Chouhan (Nijaz), Saad Ghazi (Hamid), Pamela Cundell (Woman in Shop), Renu Setna (Uncle Zabat), Betty Hardy (Gran [Voice]), Linda Lou Allen (Darlene), Babu Rao (Baba).

COMEDY WAVELENGTH

A Chapter One production for Channel 4. Transmission details are for Channel 4. Duration: 25 minutes.

Main regular credit(s):   Produced by Bob Clarke and David MacMahon.

Main regular cast: Paul Merton (Host).

	Holding / Source
17.02.1987 **[pilot 1]**	1" / 1"

Directed by David MacMahon.

With Terry Morrison, The Bouncing Czechs, Jonathan Kydd.

24.02.1987 **[pilot 2]**   1" / 1"

Directed by David MacMahon.

COMEDY WORKSHOP

A Granada production. Untransmitted. Duration: 25 minutes.

Written by Ian Davidson and The Cast; designed by Michael Grimes; produced by Barry Took; directed by Mike Newell.

Norman Chappell (Shoe Salesman), Joyce Grant (Madame Zora), Brian Murphy (Guardsman / Tramp), Julian Orchard (His Lordship / Guards Officer), Anton Rodgers (P.R.O. / Window Dresser), Patsy Rowlands (Maud Carver).

	Production No	Holding / Source
##.##.#### **Love And Maud Carver**	P447	DB-4W / 40

Recorded 05.06.1964.

COMIC ASIDES

A BBC production for BBC 2. Transmission details are for BBC 2. Duration: 30 minutes.

SERIES 1

	Holding / Source
12.05.1989 **KYTV - Siege Side Special**	DB / 1"

Britain's newest and most prestigious satellite broadcasting network, KYTV, links up with BBC2 for half-an-hour of quality programming.

Written by Angus Deayton and Geoffrey Perkins; designed by John Asbridge; produced by Jamie Rix and John Kilby; directed by Jamie Rix and John Kilby.

With Helen Atkinson Wood, Angus Deayton, Geoffrey Perkins, Philip Pope, Michael Fenton Stevens, Peter Cellier, Caroline Leddy, Steve Nallon.

19.05.1989 **Tygo Road**   DB / 1"

A Pola Jones Film production.

Rising proudly above the decay of the inner-city and dominating the desolate landscape between the Town Hall and Wat Tyler Infants stands the last bridgehead against the remorseless march of Thatcherism - Tygo Road Community Centre.

Written by Richard Cottan and Christopher Douglas; designed by Jo Day; executive producers John Kilby and Jamie Rix; produced by André Ptaszynski; directed by Bob Spiers.

With Kevin McNally (Adam), Deborah Norton (Clare), Steven O'Donnell (Leo), Vas Blackwood (Gary), Bill Bailey (Spinnij), Leila Bertrand (Val), Alisa Bosschaert (Selina), Ben Thomas (Gandalf), Arthur Cox (Agoraphobic), Bernard Strother (Unassertive), Sophie Thompson (Sophie's Voice), Gordon Gostelow (Lionel).

26.05.1989 **Dowie**   DB / 1"

Dust to dust, ashes to ashes, fun to funky, praise the Lord, Dowie's dead.

Written by John Dowie; music by Tony De Meur and James Compton; designed by Jo Day; produced by Jamie Rix and John Kilby; directed by John Kilby.

With John Dowie, Cathryn Harrison, Steve Steen, Jim Sweeney, Hepburn Graham, Ronnie Golden Band, Max Wall, Anna Wing.

02.06.1989 **The Stone Age**   DB / 1"

A Jon Blair Film Company production.

Dave Stone is a rock legend. He is super rich. super successful and super bored.

Written by Ian Hislop and Nick Newman; designed by John Asbridge; executive producers John Kilby and Jamie Rix; produced by Jon Blair; directed by Mandie Fletcher.

With Trevor Eve (Dave Stone), David Barrass (Mike), William Vanderpuye (PR Man), Paul Mark Elliott (Harvey), Rupert Holliday Evans (Justin Snell), Shelley Pielou (Waitress), Christina Shepherd (Sandra), Carmen Du Sautoy, Jonathan Coy, Roger Lloyd Pack, Bob Goody, Clive Anderson.

09.06.1989 **I, Lovett**   DB / 1"

A BBC Scotland production.

I, Lovett, am an inventor. I, Lovett, invent some quite interesting inventions. Well, I, Lovett, find them interesting. I, Lovett, live with my dog Dirk. He's a bit of a lad. My next-door neighbour, he's another bit of a lad. We're all hopeful about my latest invention. It could make me a millionaire. Only time will tell. Watch this space is the advice from I, Lovett.
Yours sincerely, Norman.

Written by Norman Lovett; music by David McNiven; designed by Dugald Findlay; produced and directed by Colin Gilbert.

With Norman Lovett (Norman), Geoffrey Hughes (Voice of Dirk), Dicken Ashworth (Darren), Russell Hunter (Chin Gutter), Nick Revell (Policeman), Iain Sexon (Voice of Godfly), Arnold Brown (Archie McKenzie), Simon Donald (Desmond Flounder), Eric Cullen (Man With House), Mary Riggans (Voice of Spider), Leon Sinden (Voice of Horse), Magnus Magnusson (Himself).

16.06.1989 **Mornin' Sarge - The New Constable**   DB / 1"

It's not all masonic lodges, call girls and international cocaine smuggling ... some police work is pretty boring too.

Written by Tony Haase, Pete McCarthy and Rebecca Stevens; designed by Richard McManan-Smith; produced by Jamie Rix and John Kilby; directed by John Kilby.

With Robin Driscoll (Ted), Tony Haase (Ben), Pete McCarthy (Kevin), Rebecca Stevens (Wendy), Paul Brooke (Sarge), Anna Manahan (Old Lady), Gerald Flood (Journalist), Chubby Oates (Bobby), Suzette Llewellyn (Mother), Curt Clement-Fletcher (Boy).

SERIES 2

Untransmitted.

	Production No	Holding / Source

##.##.#### **Us Girls**   1/LLC/C522R/71   DB / 1"

Written by Lisselle Kayla; script editors Heather Peace and Justin Sbresni; costume Paula Bruce; make-up Yvonne Brockbank; designed by Rob Hinds; production manager Johanna Kennedy; produced and directed by David Askey.

With Joanne Campbell (Bev), Carmen Knight (Selina), Nick Pickard (Sean), Marlaine Gordon (Aisha), Kerry Potter (Catherine), Mona Hammond (Grandma), Allister Bain (Grandad), Nirjay Mahindru (Vijay).

Recorded 16/10/1991.

##.##.#### **Flick**   LLCB841E/72   DB-D3 / D3S

Written by Ann Caulfield, Leo Chester, Paul Henry, Carol Williams, Llewella Gideon, Laurence Gouldbourne, Collette Johnson, Paul McKenzie, Ishmael Thomas and Curtis Walker; script consultants Kim Fuller, Lenny Henry and Trix Worrell; costume Ann Doling; make-up Tracy Drury; music by John Collins; designed by Nigel Jones; production manager Babara Jones; produced by Charlie Hanson; directed by John Kilby.

With Curtis Walker, Leo Chester, Perry Benson, Kathy Burke, Llewella Gideon, Collette Johnson, Ishmael Thomas.

Sketch show dominated by gags and performances by black actors. Very funny.

##.##.#### **Jerry Sadowitz**   LLCB842Y/71   DB-D3 / D3S

Alt.Title(s): *The Pall Bearer's Review*

Written by Jerry Sadowitz; costume Gini Hardy; make-up Christine Vidler; music by Steve Brown; designed by Sally Engelbach; production manager John Spencer; produced by Jamie Rix; directed by Tony Newman.

With Gilly Flower, Jerry Sadowitz, Dreenagh Darrell, Johnny Immaterial, Los Propotos, Daniel Strauss.

Recorded in 1990.

##.##.#### **Small World: The Island Of Pentness**   LLCB844L/71   DB-D3 / D3S

Duration: 35 minutes.

Written by John Sullivan; costume Jeremy Turner; make-up Christine Vidler; music by Kenny Craddock and Colin Gibson; designed by Andrew N. Gagg; production manager John L. Spencer; produced and directed by Bob Spiers.

With Alexei Sayle (Sir Roland Crust / Winston), John Fortune (Major Piles), Lee Montague (Sergeant Spinks), Phil Nice (Lawrence), Eddy Seager (Monty), Mark Tandy (Gerry), Ron Tarr (The Heap), Lusan Wong (Leading Seaman), Patrick Lunt (News Commentator).

Sitcom set on an atomic affected island.

	Holding / Source

12.07.1991 **Joking Apart**   DB / 1"

A black comedy about a scriptwriter whose work takes over his life. Mark Taylor 's wife finally leaves him, after an eventful marriage which begins at a funeral and finishes at a surprise party.

Written by Steven Moffat; produced by André Ptaszynski; directed by John Kilby.

With Robert Bathurst (Mark Taylor), Fiona Gillies (Becky Johnson Taylor), Tracie Bennett (Tracy Glazebrook), Paul Raffield (Robert Glazebrook), James Greene, Paul Rainbow, Rhoda Lewis, Frank Lee.

For full details see the series listing.

25.05.1993 **It's A Mad World, World, World, World**   DB-D3 / D3S

A Pozzitive production.

Witness the weirdest snooker match ever played and discover how earthquakes were invented in this comedy sketch show. Adapted from Radio 4's award-winning And Now in
Colour series.

Written by The Cast; produced by David Tyler; directed by Geoff Posner.

With Caroline Aherne, Tim De Jongh, Alistair McGowan, William Van Dyck, Flip Webster.

SERIES 3

	Holding / Source

09.01.1994 **The High Life**   DB-D3 / D3

Two air stewards have become frustrated by their daily grind. Sebastian longs for glamour.
Steve just wants a girlfriend

Written by Alan Cumming and Forbes Masson; produced and directed by Tony Dow.

With Alan Cumming (Sebastian Flight), Forbes Masson (Steve McCracken), Siobhan Redmond (Shona Spurtle), Patrick Ryecart, Gerda Stevenson, Alex Norton, Geoffrey Toone, Hilary Lyon, Stuart Quarrie.

COMIC ASIDES

16.01.1994 **Woodcock**   DB-D3 / D3

A young cabin boy is pressganged on to a clapped-out old tug in 1793. He looks forward to the voyage of his dreams, until he meets the crazy crew.

Written by Ian McPherson; produced and directed by Michael Leggo.

With Prunella Scales (Captain), Frank Skinner (Jasper, Ship's Parrot), Jonathan Hyde (Slyme, Evil First Mate), Michael Angelis (Cyril), Phelim McDermott (Woodcock), Imelda Staunton (Edna), John Bett (Doctor McGregor), John Rogan (Father), Andy Hockley (Dai), James Warrior (Gareth).

23.01.1994 **The Last Word**   DB-D3 / D3

Alt.Title(s): *Obit*

Everyone hates journalist Michael Dimmock. He's vicious, arrogant, rude and boorish. And successful. Or he was....

Written by Tony Bagley; produced by Justin Sbresni; directed by Roy Gould.

With Mark McGann (Michale Dimmock), Michael N. Harbour (Andy), Paul Shelley (Donald), Hazel Ellerby (Gill), Philip Fox (Paul).

30.01.1994 **The Honeymoon's Over**   DB-D3 / D3

The fun's over and Phil and Helen return to their tiny flat, their dead-end jobs and the cat.

Written by Paul Whitehouse and Charlie Higson; script editor Sean Hardie; produced by Charlie Higson and Paul Whitehouse; directed by John Birkin.

With Alex Lowe (Phil), Angela Clarke (Helen), Georgina Hale (Norma), Paul Whitehouse (Billy), Des McAleer (Skippy), Mark Williams (Martin), Jim Moir (Ginger).

SERIES 4

Holding / Source

18.08.1995 **Pulp Video**   DB-D3 / D3S

A BBC Scotland production.

A comic look at issues of the day.

Executive producer Colin Gilbert; produced by Philip Differ and Dave Behrens; directed by Philip Differ and Dave Behrens.

With Ford Kiernan, Andrew Fairlie, Greg Hemphill, Jane McCarry, Gavin Mitchell, Fred Macaulay, Parrot, Marc Riley, David McGowan, Veronica Leer, Mark Radcliffe, Nicola Park.

25.08.1995 **N7**   DB-D3 / D3S

Nick Revell 's tale follows a "creative and depressed" writer whose difficult domestic situation leads him to seek solace among his talking geraniums.

Written by Nick Revell; executive producer Susan Belbin; directed by Angela De Chastelai Smith.

With James Larkin (Nick), John Stratton (Craig), Louise Beattie (Shonagh), David Westhead (James), Cliff Parisi (Alvin), Phil Daniels (Vince), Andrew Lincoln (Andy), Simon Clayton (Brian), Charles McKeown (Denis).

01.09.1995 **Mac**   DB-D3 / D3S

A BBC Scotland production.

Mac. A rabid nationalist and self-appointed saviour of Scotland, Mac is driven to despair when his brother Findlay seems set to hire an Englishman to run the family business.

Written by Jack Docherty; executive producer Colin Gilbert; produced by Caroline Roberts and Jack Docherty; directed by Caroline Roberts.

With Jack Docherty (Mac), Gordon Kennedy (Findlay), Nick Hancock (Van Webster), Elaine Collins (Aileen), Primrose Milligan (Mrs Hunter).

08.09.1995 **Felix Dexter On TV**   DB-D3 / D3S

Felix Dexter on TV. Stand-up comedian Felix Dexter , from The Real McCoy, introduces a range of oddball characters.

Written by Felix Dexter; script editors Paul Whitehouse and Charlie Higson; executive producer Bill Wilson; produced by Janice Thomas; directed by Chris Bould.

With Felix Dexter (Host), Adrian Lester, Phil Cornwell, Pip Torrens, Brian Bovell, Wilbert Johnson, Eileen Dunwoodie.

See also: THE HIGH LIFE* / KYTV* / US GIRLS

THE COMIC SIDE OF 7 DAYS

A BBC production for BBC 3. made in association with Pozzitive Television. Transmission details are for BBC 3. Duration: 30 minutes.

Main regular credit(s):   Created by Andy Marlatt and Tony Roche.

Holding / Source

##.##.#### **[untransmitted pilot]**   DB /

Written by Andy Marlatt and Tony Roche; research Nerys Evans; make-up Ally Williams; sound Glenn Calder; production executive Jez Nightingale; executive producer Jon Plowman; production manager Jill Hallowell; produced and directed by David Tyler.

With Ewan Bailey (Voices), Tony Gardner (Voices), Emma Kennedy (Voices), Rowland Rivron, Armando Iannucci, Inder Manocha, Julia Morris, Rob Rouse, Mark Steel, Andy Marlatt, John Oliver.

Recorded 16/06/2004.

THE COMIC STRIP PRESENTS

Produced for Channel 4 by a variety of companies (see details below). Transmission details are for Channel 4. Duration varies - see below for details.

A Filmworks/Comic Strip production. made in association with Filmworks. Duration: 30 minutes.

Holding / Source

02.11.1982 **Five Go Mad In Dorset**   C1 / C1

Written by Peter Richardson and Peter Richens; assistant director James Corbett; art director Adrian Smith; production manager Elaine Taylor; produced by Peter Richardson, Michael White, Victoria Poushkine-Relf and Michael Hall; directed by Bob Spiers.

With Adrian Edmondson (Dick), Dawn French (George), Peter Richardson (Julian), Jennifer Saunders (Anne), Daniel Peacock (Toby Thurlow), Robbie Coltrane (Gipsy/Shopkeeper), Ronald Allen (Uncle Quentin), Raymond Francis (Police Inspector), Sandra Dorne (Aunt Fanny), Nosher Powell (Fingers), Ron Tarr (Dirty Dick), Barney Sharpe (Policeman), Bimbo (Timmy).

Later credited to Michael Pidcock and Partners.

See also: THE COMIC STRIP*

COMIC TIMING

A Granada production. Transmission details are for the Granada region. Duration: 25 minutes.

Executive producer Andy Harries.

	Production No	Holding / Source
01.11.1993 **No Worries**	P1933	DV / D3S

Duration: 26 minutes.

Mark Little and Les Hill star in a tale of a young Australian lawyer who comes to work in Britain.

Written by Stephen Ward; designed by Paul Rowan; executive producer Andy Harries; produced and directed by Spencer Campbell.

With Mark Little (Warren Brown), Les Hill (Wayne Gibson), Victoria Wicks (Sarah St. John Walderbury), Frederick Treves (Charles St. John Walderbury), Richard Lintern (Peter Howard), Ravin Ganatra (Customs Officer), Andrew Peisley (Deano), Rod Arthur (Immigration Officer), Helen Atkinson Wood (Customs Lady), Michael Buffong (Cabby), Fine Time Fontayne (Mr Featherstonehaugh), Rosalie Williams (Eleanor St. John Walderbury).

	Production No	Holding / Source
08.11.1993 **Arthur Smith Sings Andy Williams**	P2043	D3 / D3S

With Arthur Smith (Arthur Craven), Tony Hawks (Piano Player).

	Production No	Holding / Source
16.11.1992 **Pure Raunch**	P1975	B / D3S

Produced by James Maw; directed by Nick Peake.

With Jeff Green (Host), Jo Brand, Doug Anthony All-Stars.

	Production No	Holding / Source
22.11.1993 **A Load Of Old Bob**	P2044	D3 / D3S
09.11.1992 **The Dead Good Show**	P1935	D3 / D3S

Alt.Title(s): *Local Comedy*

Written by Caroline Aherne, Steve Coogan and John Thomson; script editor Kim Fuller; designed by Paul Rowan; production manager Paul Wroblewski; produced by James Maw; directed by Andrew Humphries and David MacMahon.

With Caroline Aherne, Steve Coogan, John Thomson.

Recorded 19th-20th May 1992.

	Production No	Holding / Source
06.12.1993 **That Nice Mrs Merton**	P2092	D3 / D3S

A Granada In The North West production.

Written by Caroline Aherne, Craig Cash and Henry Normal; designed by Christopher Wilkinson; produced by Peter Kessler; directed by Richard Signy.

With Caroline Aherne (Mrs Merton), Carol Thatcher, Doctor Mark Porter, Terry Christian, Steve Halliwell, CNN.

	Holding / Source
13.12.1993 **Shuttleworth Showtime**	D3 / D3S

Comedy pilots.

See also: THE MRS MERTON SHOW

COMING HOME

A BBC production for BBC 1. Transmission details are for BBC 1. Duration: 30 minutes.

Main regular credit(s):   Written by David Fitzsimmons; music by Ronnie Hazlehurst.

	Production No	Holding / Source
##.##.#### **[untransmitted 1980 pilot]**	LLCB691H/71	DB-D3 / 2"

Costume Laura Ergis; make-up Jean Steward; designed by Ken Ledsham; produced and directed by Martin Shardlow.

With Paul Copley (Donald), Sharon Duce (Sheila), Lynda Marchal (Muriel), Roger Sloman (Ben), Eva Griffith (Ruth), David Thackwray (Joey), Peter Schofield (Ernest), Janet Davies (Lucy), Rose Power (Aunt Eunice), John Blain (Uncle Reg), Linda Polan (Miss Rothwell), Tilly Vosburgh, Joanne Whalley, Jane Croft.

The BBC have this listed as an untransmitted episode, but it's actually an untransmitted pilot.

COMING OF AGE

A BBC production for BBC 3. Transmission details are for BBC 3. Duration: 30 minutes.

Main regular credit(s):   Created by Tim Dawson.

Main regular cast: Tony Bignell, Dani Harmer.

	Holding / Source
	DB / DBSWF
21.05.2007	

Comedy pilot following the exploits of a group of teenage friends.

Written by Tim Dawson; executive producer Micheal Jacob; produced by Stephen McCrum.

With Dani Harmer (Chloe), Tony Bignell (Matt).

See also: TWO PINTS OF LAGER AND A PACKET OF CRISPS*

THE COMMUNICATORS

A BBC production. Untransmitted.

	VT Number	Holding / Source
##.##.#### **[untransmitted pilot]**	VT/P/16892	J / 40

Recorded 9th December 1962.

COMPANY OF EIGHT

A BBC production. Untransmitted.

	VT Number	Holding / Source
##.##.#### **[untransmitted pilot]**	16/P/19268	J /
##.##.#### **[untransmitted pilot]**	16/P/19303	J /

Recorded 28.07.1963.

THE COMPLETE DRAMATIC WORKS OF WILLIAM SHAKESPEARE

Alternative/Working Title(s): THE SHAKESPEARE PLAYS

A BBC production for BBC 2. made in association with Time-Life Television. Transmission details are for BBC 2. Duration varies - see below for details.

Written by William Shakespeare.

Holding / Source

##.##.####   Much Ado About Nothing [untransmitted pilot]   DB-D3 / 2"

Duration: 145 minutes.

Script editor Alan Shallcross; theme music by Sir William Walton; music by Philip Pickett and The New London Consort; produced by Cedric Messina; directed by Donald McWhinnie.

With Michael York (Benedick), Penelope Keith (Beatrice), Nigel Davenport (Don Pedro), Ian Richardson (Don John), Anthony Andrews (Claudio), Ciaran Madden (Hero), Bruce Purchase (Leonato), Arthur Lowe (Dogberry), Nina Thomas (Ursula), Leon Sinden (Antonio), David Battley (Verges), Rayner Bourton (Borachio), Christopher Reich (Conrade), Jenny Twigge (Margaret), David Hillman (Balthazar), Gerald James (Friar Francis), Ashley Knight (Messenger), Leslie Sarony (First Watch), Jimmy Gardner (Second Watch), Harold Reese (Sexton).

Made in 1978 but not transmitted.

COMRADE DAD

A BBC production for BBC 2. Transmission details are for BBC 2. Duration: 30 minutes.

Londongrad, 1999.

Main regular credit(s):   Written by Peter Vincent and Ian Davidson; produced and directed by John Kilby.

Main regular cast: George Cole (Reg Dudgeon / Dad).

Holding / Source

17.12.1984   "The Rabbit"   DB / 1"

Alternative transmissions: ABC: .

Designed by Chris Hull.

With Lee Whitlock (Bob), Claire Toeman (Zoe), Colette O'Neil (Katrina / Mum), Anna Wing (Gran), Damien Nash (Scath), George Innes (Blackmarketeer), Lisa Anselmi, David Hatton, Paul McDowell, David McKail, Kathleen St. John, Stella Tanner.

CORONATION STREET

Alternative/Working Title(s): FLORIZEL STREET

A Granada/Granada Manchester Television production for Granada. Duration varies - see below for details.

Main regular credit(s):   Created by Tony Warren; theme music by Eric Spear.

Holding / Source

##.##.####   [episode 1 dry-run]   J / 40

With Doris Hare.

##.##.####   [episode 3 dry-run]   J / 40

With Doris Hare.

See also: AN AUDIENCE WITH CORONATION STREET* / THE BETTY DRIVER STORY* / THE BROTHERS McGREGOR* / CORONATION STREET SPECIAL* / CORONATION STREET: 50 YEARS, 50 MOMENTS* / CORONATION STREET: THE BIG 50* / CORRIE EXTRA: GARY'S ARMY DIARIES* / PARDON THE EXPRESSION / REST ASSURED / THE ROAD TO CORONATION STREET* / A ROYAL GALA* / STARS ON THE STREET* / TURN OUT THE LIGHTS*

COSMO AND THINGY

An LWT production. Transmission details are for the London Weekend Television region. Duration: 28 minutes.

Written by John Esmonde and Bob Larbey.

Graham Stark (Cosmo), Ronnie Brody (Thingy).

Holding / Source

29.10.1972   DB / 2"

COUNTDOWN

A Southern Television production. Transmission details are for the Southern Television region. Duration: 25 minutes.

Main regular credit(s):   Designed by Gregory Lawson; produced and directed by Mike Mansfield.

Main regular performer(s):   Muriel Young (Host), Don Wardell, The Johnny Pearson Orchestra.

Holding / Source

02.04.1966   J / Live

Quiz show.

COUNTERSTRIKE

A BBC production for BBC 1. Transmission details are for BBC 1. Usual duration: 50 minutes.

Main regular credit(s):   Narrated by Dick Graham; created by Tony Williamson.

Holding / Source

##.##.####   Mark Of Cain [untransmitted pilot]   J / 40

Alt.Title(s):   *The Wheel*

Adapted by Patrick Alexander; based on a story by Tony Williamson; produced by Anthony Kearney; directed by Geoffrey Nethercott.

With Barrie Ingham (Martin Cain), Jennifer Daniel (Doctor Mantha Scott), John Paul, Stephen Whittaker, Peter Vaughan, Julian Holloway, June Watts, Billy Milton, Patrick Godfrey, Phillip Ross, Judy Ferguson, David Morrell, Geoffrey Lumsden.

Recorded in 1966.

1967 season commissioned but scrapped.

Unused storylines include - commissioned in 1966 unless stated: 'The Final Harvest' by Malcolm Hulke; 'Virus Story' by Dick Sharples; 'Infiltrator by Richard Harris; 'The Four Letter Word' by Anthony Skene - slot becomes 'Nocturne' but it is a different script; 'A Sound Like Thunder' by Tony Willamson; 'Still Life' aka 'The Sleepers' and '1066 or 7' by George F. Kerr; 6 further, untitled scripts by Tony Williamson; 'Blackout; by John Lucarotti; 'The Lonely People' by Anthony Skene; 'Equation To Kill' aka 'The Genius Factor' by Jack Gerson - script; 'The Colony' by Michael Winder - script; an untitled idea by James Mitchell and 'New Morning Glory by George Kerr.
Commissioned in 1968: 'The Pill' by Ray Bowers; 'Whispers Who Dares' by Gerald Wilson; and untitled script by David Lingstone; an untitled script by Keith London; 'Backlash' aka 'Onward Christian Soldiers' or 'The General Is Right' or 'God For Harry, England And St George!' and 'Alive And Kicking by George Kerr.

COUNTRY BOY

A Southern Television production. Transmission details are for the ATV midlands region. Duration: 25 minutes.

Main regular credit(s):   Presented by Jack Hargreaves; directed by George Egan.

	Holding / Source
	J /

##.##.#### [untransmitted pilot]

Introducing a city child to the wonders of the countryside.

With Oliver Kite.

COURIER

A Tyburn Productions production. Not made.

Created by Edward Abraham and Valerie Abraham; script supervisor Dennis Spooner; story editor Gillian Garrow; executive producer Kevin Francis.

	Holding / Source
	NR|c / NM

##.##.#### **Now You See Him [unmade pilot]**

Written by Philip Broadley.

Planned filmed series that never got made.

COVINGTON CROSS

A Gil Grant Productions production for Thames TV International. made in association with Reeves Entertainment. Transmission details are for the Central region.

Main regular credit(s):   Executive producer Gil Grant; produced by Aida Young.

Main regular cast: Nigel Terry (Sir Thomas Grey), Cherie Lunghi (Lady Elizabeth), James Faulkner (John Mullens), Jonathan Firth (Richard), Ben Porter (William Grey), Glenn Quinn (Cedric), Ione Skye (Eleanor).

	Holding / Source
31.08.1992	D3 / C1

Duration: 75 minutes.

Written by Gil Grant; directed by William Dear.

With Jad Mager, Paul Brooke, Rosalind Bennett, Greg Wise, Miles Anderson, Richard Cordery, Terence Beesley, Oliver Haden, Daniel Craig, Shay Gorman, Devon Dear.

Series was not transmitted in this country.

COWS

A Pozzitive / Ella Communications production for Channel 4. Transmission details are for Channel 4. Duration: 50 minutes.

Created by Eddie Izzard; written by Eddie Izzard and Nick Whitby; script supervisor Anna Staniland; graphics by Andy Carroll; costume Anna Stubley; make-up Lisa Cavalli-Green; music by Simon Pilton and Sarah Townsend; choreography by Sue Lefton; lighting by Rob Kitzmann; sound Keith Nixon; camera supervisor Peter Edwards; designed by Les Stephenson; associate producer Nick Whitby; production manager Lesley Davies; co-produced by Eddie Izzard; produced by David Tyler and Geoff Posner; directed by Geoff Posner.

Pam Ferris (Boo Johnson), James Fleet (Thor Johnson), Patrick Barlow (Great-Aunt Grace), Jonathan Cake (Rex Johnson), Kevin Eldon (Toby Johnson), Nicola Walker (Shirley Johnson), Sally Phillips (Pinky), Iain Mitchell (Fetch), Geoffrey Leesley (Mr Pinky), Caroline Holdaway (Mrs Pinky), Adrian Scarborough (Vicar), Deddie Davies (Cook), Gregor Truter (Young Politician), Bernard Gallagher (Party Chairman), Richard Turner (Gardener), Neil McCaul (Theatre Director), Phil Nice (Theatre Manager), Eddie Izzard (The Pantomime Cow).

	Holding / Source
01.01.1997	D3 / D3S

CRAWFORD PARK

A Pozzitive Productions production. Untransmitted.

Written by Shaun Pye and Alan Connor.

Celia Imrie (Doctor Fleishmann), Marcus Brigstocke (Alan), Victoria Hamilton.

	Holding / Source
	J /

##.##.#### [untransmitted pilot]

Recorded in 2006. Additional details purloined from www.comedy.co.uk.

CRIBB

Alternative/Working Title(s): SERGEANT CRIBB

A Granada production. Transmission details are for the ATV midlands region. Duration: 50 minutes.

Main regular credit(s):   Based on novels by Peter Lovesey; theme music by Derek Hilton; produced by June Wyndham-Davies.

Main regular cast: Alan Dobie (Detective Sergeant Cribb), William Simons (Detective Constable Thackeray).

	Production No	Holding / Source
23.12.1979 **Waxwork [screenplay]**	P790/19	D3 / 2"

See also: SCREENPLAY / SWING, SWING TOGETHER (RADIO)*

CRIME CLUB

A Towers of London Productions production for ABC. Transmission details are for the ABC midlands region. Duration: 50 minutes.

Produced by Harry Alan Towers.

	Holding / Source
22.12.1963 **You'll Never See Me Again**	B3 / B3

This is a repeat tx date of the Summer Armchair Theatre.

Planned series that never went further than a pilot shown in Summer Armchair Theatre, August 1959.

See also: ARMCHAIR THEATRE

CRISS CROSS QUIZ

A Granada production. Untransmitted. Duration: 25 minutes.

Produced by John Huntley; directed by Ric Mellis.

	Holding / Source
##.##.#### **[untransmitted pilot]**	J / 1"

Recorded Winter 1984.

"CROSSWORD" PILOT

A BBC production. Untransmitted. Duration: 30 minutes.

Celebrities compete to complete a crossword puzzle.

Produced by Brian Patterson.

Jill Townsend, Chris Serle, Irene Thomas, David Hunt.

	Holding / Source
##.##.#### **[untransmitted pilot]**	J / 2"

Recorded 1980.

CRUNCH

A BBC Birmingham production for BBC. Untransmitted. Duration: 30 minutes.

Another variation on the 'Gong Show' idea, only in this instance the contestants were pushed, dropped or knocked into large containers of water once 50% of the audience had got fed up with them.

Music by Harold Rich; lighting by Bob Gell; sound Davie Hughes; designed by Charles Carroll; produced by John Smith; directed by Richard Tilling.

Terry Wogan (Host), Ray Barrett (Star Guest), The Suedelles, William Neary, Tony Kent, Tony Vale, Pepper Village, George Webb and Pamela, Don Juan Burns, Barbara Lindsay, Lance Harvey.

	Holding / Source
##.##.#### **[untransmitted 1975 pilot]**	DB / 2"

CRUSH A GRAPE

A Border Television production. Transmission details are for the Central region.

Main regular credit(s):   Designed by Ian Reed; associate producer Tony Nicholson; executive producer Paul Corley; produced and directed by Harry King.

Main regular cast: Stu Francis (Presenter), Charlie Cairoli, Linda Nolan, Nikki Ellen.

	Holding / Source
30.12.1987	1" / 1"

Duration: 30 minutes.

Join Stu for a great Christmas party.

With Keith Harris & Orville, Pepe and Friends.

CRY WOLF

An Alomo production for BBC 1. Transmission details are for BBC 1. Duration: 29 minutes.

Doctor Wolf, noted in her profession, agrees to join a GP's surgery run by Doctor Hook and some very eccentric characters.

Main regular credit(s):   Written by Anne Rabbitt.

	VT Number	Holding / Source
##.##.#### **[untransmitted pilot]**	106590	DB / DBSW

Doctor Wolf leaves hospital practice to join Doctor Hook's GP's surgery.

She finds Bambi, the receptionist, who gives prescriptions, a Health Visitor who eats on duty and Cherry the patient with nothing wrong with her.

Then Doctor Wold reveals she is pregnant, is it Doctor Hook's who she had a one night stand with some months before?

Script supervisor Emma Thomas; costume Caroline Pitcher; make-up Lisa Cavalli-Green; lighting by Keith Reed; sound Richard Bradford; camera supervisor Tony Keene; designed by David Ferris; executive producer Claire Hinson; supervising producers Laurence Marks and Maurice Gran; production manager Sue Landsberger; produced by Micheal Jacob and Julian Meers; directed by Liddy Oldroyd.

With Phyllis Logan (Doctor Wolf), Bill Paterson (Doctor Hook), Sarah Parish (Bambi), Siobhan Hayes (Cherry), Paul Trussell (Jason), Alison Lomas (Julie), Ted Robbins (Man In Restaurant), Angela Sims (Woman In Restaurant), Lizzie Roper (Woman In Restaurant), Rhodri Hugh (Man In Surgery), Raji James (Waiter).

Held by Fremantle Media.

Production material for episodes 1-2 was edited into a single episode 1 for transmission.

THE CRYSTAL CUBE

A BBC production for BBC 2. Transmission details are for BBC 2. Duration: 30 minutes.

Written by Stephen Fry and Hugh Laurie; produced and directed by John Kilby.

Stephen Fry, Hugh Laurie, Emma Thompson, Robbie Coltrane, Arthur Bostrom, Fanny Carby, Roy Heather, John Savident, Paul Shearer.

	Holding / Source
07.07.1983	DB-D3-2" / 2"

CRYSTAL TIPPS AND ALISTAIR

A BBC production for BBC 1. Transmission details are for BBC 1. Duration: 4 minutes.

	Holding / Source
10.06.1971 **Hide And Seek**	DB-D3 / C1

Written by Hilary Hayton and Graham McCallum; produced and directed by Michael Grafton-Robinson.

CUFFY

An Elstree Company production for Central. made in association with Central Independent Television. Transmission details are for the Central region. Duration: 25 minutes.

A sitcom spin-off from the six-part comedy-drama Shillingbury Tales, CUFFY focused on the life of the rag-tag ragamuffin man who lived in discomfort in his tawdry caravan and moped around the village of shillingbury wearing a grubby coat, flat cap and stubble. Underneath it all, though, the tinker had a heart of something approaching gold.

Main regular credit(s):	Written by Francis Essex; based on an idea by Bob Monkhouse; music by Ed Welch; executive producer Greg Smith; produced and directed by Paul Harrison.
Main regular cast:	Bernard Cribbins (Cuffy), Jack Douglas (Jake), Nigel Lambert (Norris), Linda Hayden (Mandy), Diana King (Mrs Simpkins).

	Production No	Holding / Source
10.04.1983 **Cuffy And A Downpour**	9312	1" / 2"

Written by Francis Essex; produced by Greg Smith and Chris Baker; directed by Chris Baker.

With No guest cast.

Diana King is not in this episode.

Essex mentions in the 'Authors Note' which he wrote at the start of his 'Shillingbury Tales' novelisation, published by New English Library, 1981. To quote:

"The series was written during the winter and spring of 1980 during early morning and late night sessions. By June I was two scripts behind schedule and beginning to worry. One Saturday afternoon the front doorbell chimed and my close friend Bob Monkhouse stood there. He gave me, actually gave me, three typewritten pages outlining the basic story of Cuffy the Tinker. "I thought it might come in handy," was all he said. Come in handy.....!"

See also: SHILLINGBURY TALES

CUSTARD PIE PARADE

An LWT production. Untransmitted.

Leslie Crowther.

	Holding / Source
##.##.#### [untransmitted pilot]	DB|n / 2"

A CUT ABOVE

Alternative/Working Title(s): A CUT ABOVE THE REST

An ATV production for Central. made in association with Witzend. Transmission details are for the Central region. Duration: 25 minutes.

A barber's son aspires to own his own shop. 1960s setting.

Written by Andrew Nickolds and Stan Hey; executive producer Allan McKeown; produced by Tony Charles and Bob Spiers; directed by Bob Spiers.

Michael Deeks (Ray Bishop), Mark Kingston (Mr Sargent-Smith), Tracey Ullmann (Samantha), Angela Browne (Mrs Sargent-Smith), Gorden Kaye (Stanley), Janet Davies (Beryl), Lala Lloyd (Mrs Eastman), George Tovey (Mr Eastman), Wayne Watkins (Boy).

	VT Number	Holding / Source
27.08.1982	1449/82	D2 / 2"

THE CUT PRICE COMEDY SHOW

A TSW production for Channel 4. Transmission details are for Channel 4. Duration: 25 minutes.

Main regular credit(s):	Written by Peter Cave, Kevin Goldstein-Jackson and Lenny Windsor; music by David Glasson and Tatty Ollity; designed by David Drewery; executive producer Kevin Goldstein-Jackson; produced and directed by Stephen Wade.
Main regular cast:	Roger Ruskin Spear, Stefanie Marrian, Royce Mills, Caroline Ellis, Lenny Windsor.

	Holding / Source
##.##.#### [untransmitted pilot]	J / 2"

Recorded Summer 1981.

CYDERDELIC

A BBC production for BBC 2. Transmission details are for BBC 2. Duration: 30 minutes.

Having won BBC2's 2000 Greenlight Entertainment Award for new talent. West Country dance collective and political activists Cyderdelic are furnished with the prize of a documentary, following them as they embark on a summer of action.

Written by Ian Pearce, Mark Steel and Jennifer Armitage; executive producer Jon Plowman; produced by Phil Bowker; directed by Becky Martin.

Ian Pearce (Beetle Smith), Mark Steel (Su Long), Jennifer Armitage (Frogger), John Peel (Narrator).

Holding / Source

07.01.2002

DB / DBSW

D.O.A

A Channel K production for BBC 3. Transmission details are for BBC 3. Duration: 28 minutes.

Comedy pilot which follows mismatched paramedic duo Tom and Julie on their first, chaotic night shift together. Tom is a junior doctor, currently suspended pending a malpractice inquiry and working as a paramedic while he fights to clear his name. Julie is an experienced hand, with a dry wit and a sideline in adult sex toys and lingerie, which she sells from the back of the ambulance. Tom is also in danger of losing his snooty fiancee Lucy and has to fend off the advances of a stalker ex-patient.

Written by Roger Beckett and Gary James Martin; script supervisor Rachel Stephenson; music by Philip Zikking; director of photography John Lynch; assistant director Sam Ferguson; art director Kirsty Crumpton; production designer Paul Rowan; production associate Gary Matsell; executive producers Jon Rolph, Alan Marke and Matt Tiller; line producer Rebecca Christensen; produced by Sally Martin; directed by Ben Gregor.

Kris Marshall (Tom Lassiter), Karen Taylor (Julie Wade), Kevin Eldon (Carl), Kerrie Hayes (Sharon Selby), James Quinn (Brian Selby), Greg Wagland (Senior Consultant), Richard Glover (The Rat), Catherine Shepherd (Lucy Harrington), Tom Price (Luke Chambers), Lee Boardman (Terrence Mowbury), Daniel Lawrence Taylor (Bandages), Robert Wilfort (Danny), Simon Greenall (Priest), Finn Atkins (Goth Girl), Cavan Clerkin (Rob Krizzo), John Branwell (Clive), Pauline Daniels (Clive's Wife).

	Holding / Source
24.10.2010	HD/DB / HD/DB

D'ABO

A BBC production. Untransmitted. Duration: 33 minutes.

Designed by Christine Ruscoe; produced and directed by Peter Ridsdale Scott.

Michael D'Abo (Presenter), Derek Griffiths.

	Production No	VT Number	Holding / Source
##.##.#### 30/07/1971 Untransmitted pilot	3341/1327	/6HP/67993	DB / 2"

DAD YOU'RE A SQUARE!

An ATV London production. Untransmitted. Duration: 29 minutes.

Devised by Barry Langford; designed by Bill McPherson; produced and directed by Albert Locke.

Bill Owen (Chairman).

	Production No	VT Number	Holding / Source
##.##.#### [dummy run]	7823	TR3858	B-R1 / 40

Alternative transmissions: Southern Television: .

With Edward Starr (Member of 'Cats' panel), Max Solomons (Member of 'Squares' panel), Roy Solomons (Member of 'Cats' panel), Joe Richman (Member of 'Squares' panel).

Recorded in front of an audience at the Wood Green Empire studio on 08.08.1961. The panellists were made up of three members of the Compayne Gardens Jewish Youth Club and their fathers. On the surviving copy only four of the six panellists are introduced by Bill Owen although there is some damage near the start of the programme so it may be that the full introductions have been lost. At the opening of the programme, Owen states that he had only just arrived at the studio having come straight to Wood Green from where he was working earlier in the evening, so he hadn't yet been introduced to the panellists, something which may have contributed to the chaos. Owen closes the production by saying "see you next week" but this appears to have been ATV's only production under this title.

See also: DAD, YOU'RE A SQUARE

DAD, YOU'RE A SQUARE

A Southern Television production. Transmission details are for the Southern Television region. Duration: 25 minutes.

Main regular credit(s):   Devised by Barry Langford.

	Holding / Source
##.##.#### [dry run, not transmitted]	NR /

Produced and directed by Angus Wright.

With Barry Langford (Chairman).

In the studio some time during the last week of March, but the exact date isn't currently known.

	Holding / Source
##.##.#### [dry run, not transmitted]	NR /

Produced and directed by Angus Wright.

With Barry Langford (Chairman).

In the studio on 09.05.1963.

Sandra Stone was a regular on the programme in its early days, but we do not know for how many editions. Similarly, later on, Doug Bartram was described in Television Today (24.10.1963) as being a "current member of the panel".

Based on information in the press, Southern Television considered this run to consist of three separate production series even though the broadcast run was continuous. It seems likely that the OB editions were considered to be a separate production run to the earlier, studio-based, programmes but whether that is actually the case and where the earlier season break occurred we do not know.

See also: DAD YOU'RE A SQUARE!

DADS

A Humphrey Barclay Productions production for Granada. Untransmitted. Duration: 25 minutes.

The Dad in this comedy is left holding the baby whilst his wife is away for a few days pursuing her career interests. In need of somebody to look after his son Danny during working hours he's made an arrangement with a widowed father he met in the supermarket the day before, but will things go as smoothly as intended?

Written by Mike Stott; designed by Quentin Chases; production executive Tony Humphreys; executive producers David Liddiment and Al Mitchell; produced by Humphrey Barclay; directed by Les Chatfield.

Tom Watt (Colin), Ian Sharrock (Dave), Jackie Downey (Annie), Marie Critchley (Sue-Ann), Ruth Sheen (Nessa), Philip Whitchurch (Mr Fishwick), Judy Holt (Donna).

	Production No	Holding / Source
##.##.#### [untransmitted pilot]	1/8183/0001	DV / 1"

Made in 1991. Only retained on VHS by the archives.

DAPPERS

A Mammoth Screen production for BBC Wales. Transmission details are for BBC 3. Duration: 30 minutes.

Created by Catherine Johnson; written by Catherine Johnson; script supervisor Elaine Matthews; script editor Huw Williams; director of photography Nick Dance; designed by Amelia Shankland; executive producers Michele Buck, Catherine Johnson and Damien Timmer; head of production Jon Williams; production manager Samantha Waite; produced by Jane Harrison; title sequence directed by Ray Leek; directed by Greg Fay.

Chiara Haidapour (Angel), Finn Goggin (Daisy), Ty Glaser (Faye), Lenora Crichlow (Ashley), Ravin J. Ganatra (Shop Keeper), Darren Boyd (Ben), Olivia Poulet (Anna), Jack Ashton (Ryan), Tom Ellis (Marco), Eddie Large (Barney), Hamilton Lee (The Homeless), Juliet Cowan (Jasmine), Gwen Taylor (Wendy).

	Holding / Source
10.06.2010	HD/DB / HDC

THE DAVE CASH RADIO PROGRAM

A HTV production. Transmission details are for the ATV midlands region. Duration: 25 minutes.

Main regular credit(s):   Created by Dave Cash and Richard W. Jackman; written by Richard Kenning and K. C. Hayward; associate producers Leon Auerbach and Derek Clark; executive producer Patrick Dromgoole; produced by Richard W. Jackman; directed by Tom Clegg and Richard W. Jackman.

Main regular performer(s): Dave Cash (DJ).

	Holding / Source
##.##.#### **[untransmitted pilot]**	C3SEQ|n / C3

Production material only.

THE DAY AFTER TOMORROW

A Gerry Anderson production for BBC 1. Transmission details are for BBC 1.

	Holding / Source
11.12.1976	DB / C1

See also: INTO INFINITY

THE DAY TODAY

A Talkback production for BBC 2. Transmission details are for BBC 2. Duration varies - see below for details.

Main regular credit(s):   Devised by Christopher Morris and Armando Iannucci; written by Christopher Morris, Armando Iannucci, Peter Baynham and The Cast; programme associates Nick Ganner and Susie Gautier-Smith; music by Jonathan Whitehead and Christopher Morris; designed by Dennis De Groot; executive producer Peter Fincham; production manager Alison MacPhail; co-produced by Christopher Morris; produced by Armando Iannucci; directed by Andrew Gillman.

Main regular cast: Christopher Morris, Steve Coogan, Doon Mackichan, Patrick Marber, Rebecca Front, David Schneider, Michael Alexander St. John.

	Holding / Source
##.##.#### **[untransmitted pilot]**	D3 / D3S

Duration: 35 minutes.

Additional material by Peter Baynham, Andrew Glover, David Quantick and Steven Wells; script associate Peter Baynham.

With John Thomson, Andrew Birt, Andy Linden, Minnie Driver.

Baynham's credit is misspelt "Associate". Christopher Morris is credited as 'Chris Morris' on this programme which also doesn't carry the 'Devised by' or 'Co-Producer' credits. Because the pilot used a different, and presumably cheaper, news-studio set, where ideas from the pilot were used in the series, the "studio" material was re-recorded. In contast, where appropriate, most of the pilot's location footage was re-used.

	Holding / Source
##.##.#### "Post-Programme Update" [untransmitted pilot]	D3 / D3S

Duration: 5 minutes.

The short editions carried no credits and, apart from a pilot entry, acted as a promo for the following day's full-length programme – the descriptions for the longer programmes come from these promos. Each of the longer programmes carried at least one bizarre fictional credit - see individual entries.

DAYBREAK

An ATV production. Untransmitted.

Breakfast show pilot.

	Holding / Source
##.##.####	UM / 2"

Recorded 22.9.1980.

DAYTIME DRAMA: THE GP'S

Alternative/Working Title(s): DAYTIME DRAMA

A Thames Television production. Transmission details are for the Central region. Duration: 25 minutes.

Main regular credit(s):   Written by Tom Brennand and Roy Bottomley.

Main regular cast: Robert Swales, Arthur Kelly, Jan Harvey, Jonathan Newth.

	VT Number	Holding / Source
18.07.1983 **[pilot 1]**	29043	1" / 1"
19.07.1983 **[pilot 2]**	29044	1" / 1"

DEAD ERNEST

A Witzend production for ATV. Untransmitted. Duration: 25 minutes.

Written by John Stevenson and Julian Roach; executive producer Allan McKeown; produced by Tony Charles; directed by John Kaye Cooper.

	Holding / Source
##.##.#### [untransmitted pilot]	J / 2"

Recorded 8th May 1981.

See also: DEAD ERNEST*

DEAD RINGERS

A BBC production for BBC 2. Transmission details are for BBC 2.

Main regular credit(s):   Music by John Whitehall.

	Holding / Source
15.03.2002	DB / DBSW

Duration: 29 minutes.

Written by Tom Jamieson, Nev Fountain, Jon Holmes, Lawrence Howarth and Jon Culshaw; additional material by Jan Ravens and Mark Perry; music by John Whitehall; director of photography Martin Hawkins; art director Liz Lander; designed by Graeme Story; production executive Claire Bridgland; executive producer Jon Plowman; line producer Julia Weedon; produced by Bill Dare; directed by John Birkin.

With Phil Cornwell, Jon Culshaw, Jan Ravens, Kevin Connelly, Mark Perry, Just Us.

DEAR LADIES

A BBC Manchester production for BBC 2. Transmission details are for BBC 2. Duration: 30 minutes.

Main regular credit(s):   Created by Patrick Fyffe and George Logan.

Main regular cast: George Logan (Doctor Evadne Hinge), Patrick Fyffe (Dame Hilda Bracket).

SERIES 1

Main regular credit(s):   Written by Gyles Brandreth; theme music by Patrick Fyffe and George Logan; music by John Golland; designed by Dugald Findlay; produced by Peter Ridsdale Scott; directed by Mike Stephens.

	Holding / Source
15.03.1983 **Look After The Pennies**	DB-D3 / 2"

Script associate Gyles Brandreth; production team Gus Maclean and Anne Comer; assistant producer Martin Hughes.

With Frances Cox, Alick Hayes.

Recorded August 1981.

See also: HINGE AND BRACKET'S NEW YEAR'S EVE PARTY* / A PRIZE PERFORMANCE*

DEAR ME

Alternative/Working Title(s): DAME HETTIE WILTSHIRE MOFFAT REMEMBERS

An LWT production. Untransmitted. Duration: 25 minutes.

A sitcom in which Irene Handl plays Dame Hettie (a sort of Hyacinth Bouquet figure) recalling her colourful life.

Written by N. F. Simpson; produced by Humphrey Barclay; directed by Philip Casson.

Irene Handl (Dame Hettie Wiltshire Moffat), Richard Vernon (Willie), Nigel Pegram (Colin), Noel Howlett (Reverend Craven), Zulema Dene (Mrs Laycock), Elissa Derwent (Hermione).

	Production No	VT Number	Holding / Source
##.##.#### **Life Must Go On**	9281	4494	DB / 2"

Recorded 18.12.73.

DEE TIME

A BBC production for BBC 1. Transmission details are for BBC 1. Usual duration: 45 minutes.

Main regular performer(s): Simon Dee (Host), Alyn Ainsworth and his Orchestra [as The Alyn Ainsworth Orchestra].

	Holding / Source
##.##.#### [untransmitted pilot]	J /

With Joan Turner.

All R1SQ contain artists listed against the programme. The R1 for the edition t/x'd 03.05.69 is missing the opening titles.

DELTA FOREVER

Alternative/Working Title(s): NANCY AND THE PUNKS / ONLINERS

An Angel Eye Media production for BBC 3. Transmission details are for BBC 3. Duration: 30 minutes.

Comedy pilot about the obsessive online fans of a series of novels about teen-hero Delta, whose lives revolve around an unofficial fan-site on which they meet and greet, rubbish their rivals and generally show off. The film studio holds a secret preview screening in London of the first movie adaptation of the beloved Delta series.

Written by Jon Hunter, Misha Manson-Smith, Holly Walsh, Greg McHugh and Ben Bond; designed by Nathan Parker; executive producers Alan Tyler, Cheryl Taylor and Richard Osborne; produced by John O'Callaghan and Kelly McGolpin; directed by Misha Manson-Smith.

Antonia Campbell Hughes (Miranda), Ophelia Lovibond (Roxy), Samantha Blakey (Mags), Greg McHugh (Guantanamo Ray), Alex Macqueen (Alex), Jonny Sweet (Johnny), Daniel Kaluuya (Roger), Holly Walsh (Delta Fan), Joshua Topp (Tramp), Misha Mason-Smith (TV Reporter 1 Out of Vision), Kelly McGolpin (TV Reporter 2 Out of Vision).

	Holding / Source
19.05.2008	DB / DBSWF

There was no cast credited on-screen.

DEMPSEY AND MAKEPEACE

An LWT production. made in association with Golden Eagle Films. Transmission details are for the Central region. Duration varies - see below for details.

James Dempsey, a New York cop, is teamed up with posh totty cop Harriet Makepeace.

Main regular credit(s):   Theme music by Alan Parker; music by Alan Parker; executive producer Nick Elliott.

Main regular cast: Michael Brandon (Lieutenant James Dempsey), Glynis Barber (Detective Sergeant Harriet Makepeace), Ray Smith (Detective Superintendent Gordon Spikings), Tony Osoba (Detective Sergeant Chas Jarvis).

SERIES 1

Main regular credit(s):   Produced by Tony Wharmby.

	VT Number	Holding / Source
11.01.1985 **Armed And Extremely Dangerous**	10429	D2 / C1

Duration: 75 minutes.

Written by Ranald Graham; directed by Tony Wharmby.

With Mark Wing-Davey, William Kearns, Douglas Milvain, David Baxt, Ross Murray, Desmond Cullum-Jones, Norman Chancer, John Barcroft, Cheryl Prime, Ray Jewers, Victor Baring, Eric Kent, Tony Jay, Margot van der Burgh, Peter Brace, Paul Bacon, Andrew Jolly, Knight Mantell, Ralph Michael, Terence Alexander, Laurin Kaski.

Some of the D2 versions appear to have been mastered by Granada International for overseas sale and are slightly trimmed. This list of cuts is compiled from looking at the Portugese and British Network DVD releases:
1. ARMED AND EXTREMELY DANGEROUS
Portuguese version: Unedited. Slightly superior video quality, and noticeably clearer audio.

UK version: Edited - The scene where Dempsey shoots his partner Joey is cut, removing his second shot, and his shot at the fleeing Coltrane.

2. THE SQUEEZE
Both versions almost identical, unedited.

3. LUCKY STREAK
Both versions almost identical, unedited.

4. GIVEN TO ACTS OF VIOLENCE
Portuguese version: Unedited.

UK version: Edited - The scene where Egan kills Ferguson outside the pub is trimmed to remove his 'killing' shot. Also a whole 2 minute scene where Egan and gang take over the railway 'stop' has been removed. Slightly superior video quality (slightly less noise, and much better colours) and noticeably clearer audio.

5. HORS DE COMBAT
Portuguese version: Unedited.

UK version: Edited - The scene where Tommy kills the man at the dog track is cut down to remove the shot of the man slumping over showing the screwdriver in his back. Slightly superior video quality (superior colour) and slightly clearer audio.

6. NOWHERE TO RUN
Portuguese version: Unedited.

UK version: Edited - The shootout at the end of the episode is significantly edited to remove various shots of people being hit/falling, and some of Dempsey's moves and shots. Poor quality edits with noticeable film damage. Slightly superior video quality (superior colour) and slightly clearer audio.

7. MAKE PEACE, NOT WAR
Both versions unedited. UK/Network version has slightly better video and audio quality.

8. BLIND EYE
Both versions unedited. UK/Network version has slightly better video and audio quality.

9. CRY GOD FOR HARRY
Portuguese version: Edited - small clip of dialogue removed.

UK version: Unedited. Slightly superior video & audio quality.

10. JUDGEMENT
Both versions unedited. UK/Network version has slightly better video and audio quality.

DES DAILY

A Talkback Thames production for ITV 1. Untransmitted.

Main regular performer(s): Des O'Connor (Host), David Dickinson, Ricky Tomlinson.

	Holding / Source
##.##.#### **[first pilot]**	DB / DBSW
##.##.#### **[second pilot]**	DB / DBSW

DETECTIVE

A BBC production for BBC 1. Transmission details are for BBC 1. Usual duration: 54 minutes.

Theme music by Ron Grainer.

SERIES 1

Main regular credit(s):   Introduced by Rupert Davies; theme music by John Addison; produced by David Goddard.

Holding / Source

06.04.1964 Cluff : The Drawing   J /

The hero is Detective-Sergeant Caleb Cluff. Embodying the law in the North-country moorland town of Gunnarshaw, he finds violence and passion seething under its dour surface.

Cluff is played by Leslie Sands   Michael Gover plays Harris, a local councillor of Victorian strictness, whose daughter Mona gives Cluff and Inspector Mole (Duel Luscombe) a great deal of trouble.

Written by Gil North; script editors Max Marquis and John Gould; music by Dudley Simpson; designed by Margaret Peacock; directed by Terence Dudley.

With Leslie Sands (Detective Sergeant Cluff), Doel Luscombe (Inspector Mole), Frank Pettitt (Duty Constable), John Rolfe (Constable Barker), Susanna Carroll (Mona Harris), Allan McClelland (Whitaker), Robert Fyffe (Young Clerk), David Kirk (Elderly Clerk), Jeanne Watts (Mrs Cockshott), Margaret Ward (Mrs Whitaker), Polly Murch (Miss Hewson), Michael Gover (Harris), John Kirby (Johnson), Margaret Carlisle (Waitress), Anna Wing (Annie Croft), James McManus (Police Constable), Derek Benfield (Doctor Hamm), Doris Rogers (Cleaner), Mary Fouracres (Nurse).

06.04.64 – PANORAMA (LCA6971W) – front: brief glimpse and end credits of "The Lucy Show"; caption 'BBC Later Tonight'; trailer for "Detective: The Drawing" (pilot for "Cluff" series) (no footage, just graphics); clock (20.25) with announcement 'This is BBC Television, the time now is twenty-five past eight'. End: "Panorama" end credits fade out during first caption – black screen for a second or two, then 'BBC tv' caption, announcement 'This is BBC Television', nothing happens for a few more seconds, then recording stops.

Animals trained by John Holmes.

18.05.1964 Sherlock Holmes : The Speckled Band   R1 / Live

Duration: 50 minutes.

Julia Stoner, step-daughter of the choleric Doctor Grimesby Roylott, has died, apparently of fear, alone in her bedroom. Two years later her sister Helen has a presentiment that she is about to suffer the same fate, and is persuaded to call in Holmes. And so the Master—attended of course by the obtuse Watson—brings his giant mind to bear on a tangle of clues which include strange whistling sounds heard in the night and Julia's dying words about a speckled band.

Adapted by Giles Cooper; based on a story by Sir Arthur Conan Doyle; script editor Max Marquis; designed by Charles Carroll; directed by Robin Midgley.

With Douglas Wilmer (Sherlock Holmes), Nigel Stock (Doctor Watson), Felix Felton (Doctor Grimsby Roylott), Marian Diamond (Julia Stoner), Liane Aukin (Helen Stoner), Nan Marriott Watson (Annie), Mary Holder (Mrs Hudson), Donald Douglas (Percy Armitage).

The R1 for the edition has the title sequence for Sherlock Holmes and the introduction by Rupert Davies is missing.

Animals from Colchester Zoo.

06.07.1964 Doctor Thorndyke : The Case Of Oscar Brodski   R1N / 40

What is the sinister Silas Hickler (George Benson) up to hanging around the railway station? The answer can be found in tonight's story when Dr. Thorndyke investigates the murder of Oscar Brodski.

Adapted by Allan Prior; based on a story by R. Austin Freeman [credited as Austin Freeman]; script editors John Gould and Anthony Read; music by Norman Kay; film camera James Balfour; film editor Ted Hunter; designed by Mary Rea; directed by Richmond Harding.

With Peter Copley (Doctor Thorndyke), Bernard Goldman (Oscar Brodski), George Benson (Silas Hickler), Gerald Sim (Doctor Jervis), Warren Mitchell (Boscovitch), Cameron Hall (Mr Brice), Jack Bligh (Engine Driver), Frank Seton (Fireman), Roy Skelton (Porter), Meadows White (Sergeant Dickens), Wilfred Harrison (Constable).

06.07.64 – PANORAMA (LCA6984T) – front: last caption of "Glynis"; globe, announcement 'This is BBC1'. End: 'BBC1 tv' caption; in-vision announcer, plugs "Detective" after the News (Rupert Davies introduces Austin Freeman's Dr Thorndyke in "The Case of (Oscar Brodski)" (recording cuts during this).

All prints are missing the introduction by Rupert Davies.

See also: CLUFF* / SHERLOCK HOLMES* / THORNDYKE*

DEVENISH

A Granada production. Transmission details are for the ATV midlands region. Duration: 25 minutes.

Main regular credit(s):   Written by Anthony Couch; music by Johnny Pearson; produced by John G. Temple; directed by Brian Mills.

Main regular cast: Dinsdale Landen (Arthur P. Devenish), Terence Alexander (Hugh Fitzjoy), Geoffrey Bayldon (Neville Liversedge), John Kane (Rog Box), Richard Kane (Wilf Braithwaite), Veronica Roberts (Angela Nutall).

SERIES 1

	Production No	Holding / Source
##.##.#### **The Hell Of New Directors [untransmitted pilot]**	P885/1	J / 2"

The original episode was made on 16.01.1977, but was remade on 16.05.1977 before transmission.

THE DEVIL'S HANDS

The companies who commissioned and produced this production are not known. Untransmitted. Duration: 25 minutes.

A suspense thriller.

Holding / Source

##.##.#### **[untransmitted 1961 pilot]**   R3 /

DIAMOND GEEZER

A Granada Yorkshire production for ITV 1. Transmission details are for the Central region.

Main regular credit(s):   Created by Caleb Ranson; written by Caleb Ranson; music by Ray Russell; executive producers David Reynolds and David Jason; produced by David Reynolds.

Main regular cast: David Jason (Des), Stephen Wight (Phil (1st two eps)).

	Holding / Source
20.03.2005	DB / V1SW

Duration: 100 minutes.

David Jason is timid prisoner Des. Des has a stammer and a limp, and is frequently the butt of other prisoners' bullying and brutality. But Des is a man with a secret. He might tour the prison with the tea trolley taking great pains to ensure everyone gets the right strength of their favourite brew, but he has plans—big plans.

Script supervisor Karen Wright; directed by Paul Harrison.

With Paul Bown (Guv'nor), Des McAleer (Martins), Gary Whelan (Benny), Richard Vanstone (Winters), Andrew Grainger (Roberts), Simon Paul Sutton (Denver), Nick Burnell (Callow), Ieuan Rhys (Jenx), Elly Fairman (Gloria), Miranda Pleasence (Miranda), Carli Norris (Betsy), Linda Duffield (Waitress), Reece Andrews (Prison Guard).

DICK TURPIN - HIGHWAYMAN

Produced for ITV by a variety of companies (see details below). Transmission details are for the ATV midlands region. Duration: 25 minutes. Commissioned by ATV.

	Holding / Source
##.##.#### **[untransmitted pilot]**	J /

Originally scheduled for 24.09.1955.

ATV's opening day schedule as released in June 1955 listed this between 1630 and 1700 as "An exciting adventure show filmed in Britain".

	Holding / Source
##.##.#### **[untransmitted pilot]**	J / B3

A Four Seasons production.

Written by Alan Reeve-Jones; story by Jimmy Liggatt; music by Frank Cordell; associate producer Denton De Gray; produced by Bert Page; directed by Max Varnel.

With Alan Browning (Dick Turpin), Jane Hylton (Lady Elizabeth), Michael Balfour (Tom King), Douglas Wilmer, Stratford Johns, Gaynor Jones, Kay Browne, Gerald Case, Robert Dorning, Philip Holles, Christopher Witty, Janina Faye, Peter Diamond, Fred Rawlings.

David Davenport was originally to play Turpin but was injured in an accident on the first day of filming and his role was given to Alan Browning who was originally to play his 'sidekick' Tom King. Six further scripts were ready for production. Production took place in Brighton from 10.08.1959.

Transmission details are for Channel 4.

	Holding / Source
11.11.1990 **[pilot]**	C3 / C3

A Hammer TV production.

Written by Joel Murcott; music by Eric Winstone; produced by Michael Carreras; directed by David Paltenghi.

With Philip Friend (Dick Turpin / 'Mr Palmer'), Diane Hart (Liz), Allan Cuthbertson (Jonathan Redgrove), Hal Osmond (Mac), Raymond Rollett (Hawkins), Norman Mitchell (Rooks), Gabrielle May (Genevieve), John McDonald (Stable Boy), George Mossman (Coachman), Ivor Collin (Ruffian), Barry Du Boulay (Ruffian).

The BFI's database says: An innocent and lively programme filler about the theft of a dowry which Genevieve is bringing her bridegroom, Mr. Jonathan Redgrove. All ends happily. Made circa 1956.

There seem to have been a number of productions either mooted or actually produced under this title. Whether any are related we really don't know.

THE DICKIE HENDERSON SHOW

A Harry Foster TV Productions production for Associated-Rediffusion. Transmission details are for the ATV midlands region. Duration: 25 minutes.

Main regular cast: Dickie Henderson (Dickie).

	Holding / Source
##.##.#### **[untransmitted pilot]**	J / 40

Written by Jimmy Grafton; additional material by Jeremy Lloyd and Alan Fell; produced and directed by Bill Hitchcock.

With June Laverick (June), Richard Wattis (Scoutmaster), Hughie Green (Quizmaster), Jeremy Hawk.

Recorded 29.07.1960. Lionel Murton does not appear in this episode.

	Holding / Source
##.##.#### **[untransmitted pilot]**	J /

Written by Jimmy Grafton and Jeremy Lloyd; produced and directed by Bill Hitchcock.

With Lionel Murton, Peggy Cummins, Eileen Gourlay, Yolande Turner, Davy Kaye, Chic Murray, Peter Graves.

Recorded 15.04.1965. June Laverick does not appear in this episode.

DIDN'T THEY DO WELL

Alternative/Working Title(s): REWIND

A BBC Variety production for BBC 1. Untransmitted. Duration: 30 minutes.

Assistant producers Howard Brenner, Rob Dean and Chris Sussman; production executive Norman Lockhart; executive producer Martin Scott; production manager Andy Bennions; series producer Andy Rowe; directed by Alex Rudzinski.

Bob Monkhouse (Host).

	Production No	Holding / Source
##.##.#### **[untransmitted pilot]**	1/ENTD560A	DB / D3S

DION

A Central production. Untransmitted.

Directed by Frank Hayes.

	Holding / Source
##.##.#### **[untransmitted pilot]**	1" / 1"

Held at MACE.

DIRK GENTLY

An ITV Studios production for BBC Wales. made in association with The Wedded Tandem Picture Company. Transmission details are for BBC 4. Duration: 60 minutes.

	Holding / Source
16.12.2010	HD/DB / HD/DB

Drama featuring writer Douglas Adams's holistic detective Dirk Gently, who operates based on the fundamental interconnectedness of all things. An investigation into a missing cat is inextricably linked to a chance encounter with an old friend, an exploding warehouse, a missing billionaire and a plate of biscuits.

Adapted by Howard Overman; based on a book by Douglas Adams; script supervisor Karen Savage; music by Daniel Pemberton; director of photography Balazs Rolygo; art director Kate Purdy; designed by Dave Arrowsmith; associate producer Howard Overman; production executive Grace Boylan; executive producers Eleanor Moran and Saurabh Kakkar; line producer Kate Dudley; produced by Chris Carey; directed by Damon Thomas.

With Stephen Mangan (Dirk Gently), Helen Baxendale (Susan Harmison), Darren Boyd (Richard Macduff), Doreen Mantle (Ruth Jordan), Jason Watkins (Detective Inspector Gilks), Lisa Jackson (Janice Pearce), Anthony Howell (Gordon Way), Miles Richardson (Doctor Gerstenberger), Billy Boyle (Harry Jordan), Elliot Sutherland (Tom), Gary Pillai (Doctor), Alisha Bailey (Reporter), Joe Hall (Newsagent), Leona Walker (Receptionist), Alex Parry (Barman).

THE DISCRETION OF DOMINICK AYRES

A Southern Television production. Transmission details are for the Southern Television region. Duration: 50 minutes.

Written by David Butler; designed by John Dilly; executive producer Beryl Vertue; produced and directed by David Reid.

Ronald Pickup (Dominick Ayres), Sharon Duce (Mary), Robert Lang (Inspector Waterfield), Hugh Walters (Freddy Challis), Benjamin Whitrow (Lord Kirk), William Humbert (Charles Farmer), Judy Campbell (Lady Shelford), Robert Russell (Crusher King), Joy Shelton (Mrs Majors), Terence Davies (Mick Crawley), John Cording (Sergeant Ramsgard), Katherine Rosenwink (Edyth Ballard), Sheridan Fitzgerald (Emily Lawson), Paul Arlington (Patsy Somers).

	Holding / Source
29.03.1978 **Nightwalker**	DB / 2"

Alternative transmissions: Yorkshire Television: 10.05.1978.

THE DITHERING DETECTIVE

Alternative/Working Title(s): BURGLARY FOR BEGINNERS

A BBC North production. Transmission details are for BBC North. Duration: 25 minutes.

Written by Stan Parkinson; additional material by Ted Taylor; produced and directed by John Ammonds.

Harry Worth (Himself), Paddy Edwards, Campbell Singer, Clive Dunn, William Mervyn.

	Holding / Source
20.03.1959	R3 /

See also: THE TROUBLE WITH HARRY*

DO ME A FAVOUR

A Thames Television production. Transmission details are for the ATV midlands region. Duration: 25 minutes.

Mr. Hadleigh meets Jimmy by chance. But he doesn't know that he is a man who lives on his wits and has an uncomplicated sense of logic that defies argument .. .

Written by Len Walker; designed by Harry Clark; produced and directed by William G. Stewart.

Peter Jones (Jimmy), June Whitfield (Mrs Hadleigh), Terence Alexander (Mr Hadleigh).

	VT Number	Holding / Source
31.03.1971	3722	J / 62

Postponed from 10.02.1971.

DOCTOR WHO

A BBC Drama Serials production for BBC. Transmission details are for BBC 1. Duration varies - see below for details.

Main regular credit(s):　　　Theme music by Ron Grainer.

[original version of first episode]

Transmission details are for BBC 2.

	VT Number	Holding / Source
26.08.1991 **An Unearthly Child**	VT/P/19491	DB-R1 / 40

Alt.Title(s): *100,000 BC*

Duration: 26 minutes.

School teachers Ian Chesterton and Barbara Wright follow mysterious schoolgirl Susan home to a junk yard. They meet her grandfather who seems to have Susan trapped in a police phonebox....

Written by Anthony Coburn; story editor David Whitaker; music by Norman Kay; designed by Barry Newbery; associate producer Mervyn Pinfield; produced by Verity Lambert; directed by Waris Hussein.

With William Hartnell (The Doctor), Carole Ann Ford (Susan Foreman), Jacqueline Hill (Barbara Wright), William Russell (Ian Chesterton), Reg Cranfield, Carole Clarke, Mavis Ranson, Francesca Bertorelli, Heather Lyons, Cedric Schoeman, Richard Wilson, Brinn Thomas.

Recorded 27th September 1963. There is also a 36-minute studio recording on R1, which includes a re-shoot.

The DVD includes three versions including a 2006 re-cut on DB. VidFIREd.

All title sequences except the original exist on film, or VT for the McCoy set.

The test footage for the original title sequence and the 1970 title sequence exist on film.

See also: DOCTOR WHO (RADIO)* / DOCTOR WHO (VIDEO SPIN OFFS)* / DOCTOR WHO CONFIDENTIAL* / DOCTOR WHO: THE ULTIMATE GUIDE* / THE FIVE(ISH) DOCTORS REBOOT* / K.9 AND COMPANY / THE SARAH JANE ADVENTURES / SEARCH OUT SCIENCE: SEARCH OUT SPACE* / TORCHWOOD* / WHATEVER HAPPENED TO SUSAN? (RADIO)*

DOES THE TEAM THINK?

A Thames Television production. Transmission details are for the Central region. Duration: 25 minutes.

Main regular credit(s):　　　Devised by Jimmy Edwards.

Main regular credit(s):　　　Produced and directed by David Clark.

Main regular performer(s):　With Reginald Bosanquet (Chairman), Jimmy Edwards, Tom O'Connor, Roy Hudd, Leslie Crowther, Bernie Winters, David Jason, June Whitfield, Lennie Bennett, Zandra Rhodes.

	Holding / Source
##.##.#### **[untransmitted pilot]**	J / 2"
Recorded October 1980.	
##.##.#### **[second untransmitted pilot]**	J / 2"
Recorded October 1980.	

DOES YOUR MOTHER KNOW YOU'RE WATCHING?

A BBC production. Untransmitted. Duration: 23 minutes.

Designed by Lesley Bremness; produced and directed by Michael Cole.

The Wherehouse, La Mama, London (Presenters).

	VT Number	Holding / Source
##.##.#### **Show 1**	VTC/6HT/58821	DB / 2"
1970s pilot.		

DOGFOOD DAN AND THE CARMATHEN COWBOY

A BBC production for BBC 2. Transmission details are for Central/BBC 2.

Main regular credit(s):　　　Written by David Nobbs.

Transmission details are for the Central region.

	VT Number	Holding / Source
24.07.1982 **[ITV Playhouse]**	D709	DB-1" / 2"

A Yorkshire Television production. Duration: 52 minutes.

Executive producer David Cunliffe; produced and directed by Derek Bennett.

With Gareth Thomas (Aubrey Owen), David Daker (Dan Milton), Janet Allen (Bingo Player), Judi Kent (Club Singer), Helen Cotterill (Myfanwy Owen), David Graham Jones (Compere), Diana Davies (Helen Milton).

DOMINOES

A Central production. made in association with Anthony Gruner / Talbot TV Ltd. Untransmitted. Duration: 25 minutes.

Main regular credit(s):　　　Devised by Ira Skutch and Ernie Frankel; additional material by Garry Chambers; script associate Howard Imber; designed by Giovanni Guarino; produced by Tony Wolfe; directed by Jenny Dodd.

Main regular performer(s):　Lennie Bennett (Host), Michaela Strachan (Domino Damsel).

	Holding / Source
##.##.#### **[first pilot]**	1" / 1"
##.##.#### **[second pilot]**	1" / 1"

DON'T DRINK THE WATER

An LWT production. Transmission details are for the ATV midlands region. Duration: 25 minutes.

Main regular credit(s):　　　Devised by Ronald Wolfe and Ronald Chesney; theme music by Johnny Gregory.

Main regular cast:　　　　　Stephen Lewis (Cyril Blake), Pat Coombs (Dorothy Blake), Derek Griffiths (Carlos).

Credits:　Designed by Andrew Drummond; produced and directed by Bryan Izzard.

	Production No	Holding / Source
##.##.#### **A Place In The Sun [untransmitted pilot]**	9L/09353	2"|n / 2"

With Glynn Edwards, Sandra Dorne, Aubrey Morris, Rita Webb, Nadim Sawalha, Georgio Bosso, Frederick Peisley, Totti Truman Taylor.

Recorded 13.12.73.

See also: ON THE BUSES*

DON'T MOVE NOW

A BBC production. Untransmitted. Duration: 30 minutes.

Written by Raymond Allen; based on an idea by Deborah Morris; costume Mary Woods; make-up Judy Neame; music by Ken Jones; designed by Antony Thorpe; produced and directed by Roger Race.

Dany Clare, Brian Glover, David Kelly, David Battley, Daphne Anderson, Richard Davies, Ann Hamilton, Lennard Pearce, Stan Van.

	Production No	VT Number	Holding / Source
##.##.#### **[untransmitted 1976 pilot]**	1146/3170	VTC/6HT/B10498	DB / 2"

Comedy about Monkton's Removals Firm Ltd.

DON'T SAY A WORD

Alternative/Working Title(s): ACTIONS SPEAK LOUDER / STUMP THE STARS

An Associated-Rediffusion production. Transmission details are for the ATV midlands region. Duration: 25 minutes.

| Main regular credit(s): | Devised by Mike Stokey. |
| Main regular credit(s): | Produced and directed by Robert Fleming. |

	Production No	Holding / Source
##.##.#### **[untransmitted pilot]**	LE/20/17	J /

With Dick Emery, Glen Mason, Libby Morris, Amanda Barrie, Kenneth Connor, Peter Reeves, Joyce Blair, Ray Taylor, Ronan O'Casey.

Recorded 17.05.63.

	Production No	Holding / Source
##.##.#### **[untransmitted pilot]**	LE/20/17	J /

With Ronan O'Casey, Monty Landis, Jill Browne, Una Stubbs, Jimmy Thompson, Harry Fowler, Sheila Matthews, Jackie Lane, Ray Taylor.

Recorded 17.05.63

Although appearing, we are unsure whether Ronan O'Casey hosted either or both of the pilots.

Charades on TV, rather like GIVE US A CLUE.

DON'T SAY GOODBYE, MISS RAGTIME!

A Limehouse production for Channel 4. made in association with Knaves Acre. Transmission details are for Channel 4.

Set in the deep south, 1910, the pilot was recorded at the West India Docks, near Limehouse Studios, on a paddle steamer.

Written by Ian Whitcomb; music directed by Burt Rhodes; choreography by Roger Hannah; programme consultant Dennis Martin; directed by Barney Colehan.

Ian Whitcomb (Presenter), Dawn Hope, Sheila Brand, Scott Sherrin, Keith Nichols, Simon Bowman, Ian Roberts, Richard Drabble, Joanne Campbell, Liz Izen, Nicola Kimber, Pepsi Maycock, Diane Simmons, Kerry Gallagher, Peter Gale.

	Holding / Source
04.01.1985	1" / 1"

DON'T STOP TALKING

An Associated-Rediffusion production. Never intended for transmission.

Anne Cunningham, Peter Reeves, Aubrey Woods, Libby Morris.

	Production No	VT Number	Holding / Source
##.##.#### **[untransmitted pilot]**	LE/10/4	W2140/633	J / 40

Alternative transmissions: Channel 4: .

Recorded 04.03.1964.

DOUBLE FIRST

A BBC production for BBC 1. Transmission details are for BBC 1.

| Main regular credit(s): | Written by John Esmonde and Bob Larbey; produced and directed by Gareth Gwenlan. |
| Main regular cast: | Michael Williams (N. V. Standish), Ann Bell (Mary Webster), Jennifer Hilary (Louise Hobson), Holly Aird (Ellen), Clive Merrison (Derek), Peter Tuddenham (William). |

	Holding / Source
06.09.1988	DB-1" / C1

Duration: 60 minutes.

Designed by Nigel Curzon.

With No guest cast.

DOUBLE TAKE

An LWT production. Untransmitted. Duration: 25 minutes.

	Holding / Source
##.##.#### **[untransmitted pilot]**	2"|n / 2"

rx 19/10/71

THE DOUG ANTHONY ALL-STARS

A Pozzitive Television production for BBC 2. Transmission details are for BBC 2. Duration: 30 minutes.

Produced and directed by Geoff Posner.

The Doug Anthony Allstars, Paul Livingston (Flacco).

	Holding / Source
31.12.1992	DB-D3 / D3S

DOUGLAS FAIRBANKS JR PRESENTS

A Dougfair Corporation production for ITV. Transmission details are for Associated-Rediffusion. Duration: 25 minutes.

Executive producer Douglas Fairbanks Jr.

	Holding / Source
##.##.#### **The Silent Man [untransmitted pilot]**	B3|n / B3

With Tilda Thamar, Robert Ayres.

	Holding / Source
07.03.1958 **Scheherezade**	B1 SO|n / B3

Alternative transmissions: ATV Midlands: 05.09.1956.

Written by Irving Rubine and Selwyn Jepson; produced and directed by Harold Huth.

With Hugh Williams (Shayar), Dermot Walsh (Dubat), Stanley van Beers (Grand Vizier), Maya Koumani (Scheherazade), Elwyn Brook Jones (Yunan), Peter Allenby (Court Official), Lysbeth Rollins (Tse Lao), Harry Baird (Executioner).

Pilot for series that never happened.

03.04.1958 **The Ludlow Affair**	B3 / B3

Alt.Title(s): *Bulldog Drummond and the Ludlow Affair*

Alternative transmissions: ATV Midlands: 23.11.1956.

Adapted by Irving Rubine; based on a story by H. C. (Sapper) McNeile; directed by David McDonald.

With Robert Beatty (Bulldog Drummond), Greta Gynt (Mrs Ludlow), Michael Ripper (Kelly), William Franklyn (Roger Benning), Harry Lane (Kinsella), John Le Mesurier (Inspector Burroughs), Michael Anthony (Doctor Ludlow), Ian Fleming (Churchill).

Some paperwork lists this under the title 'Bulldog Drummond And The Ludlow Affair'. It was made as a pilot for a possible Bulldog Drummond series but when it wasn't picked up it became part of this one.

See also: PLAY GEMS*

DOWN AT THE OLD CLAPHAM GRAND

A Pozzitive Television production for BBC 4. Untransmitted.

Julian Clary (Compere), Milton Jones, Bruce Airhead, Madness, Marcus Brigstocke, Stuart & Barry, Justin Edwards.

	Holding / Source
##.##.#### **[untransmitted 2007 pilot]**	DB /

Held by Pozzitive.

DRAMA PLAYHOUSE

A BBC production for BBC 1. Transmission details are for BBC 1. Usual duration: 50 minutes.

SERIES 1

	Holding / Source
23.11.1970 **The Regiment: The Father Of The Regiment**	R1N / 2"

Duration: 49 minutes.

In June 1895 the Colonel-in-Chief of an Infantry Regiment wrote a letter to The Times daring to criticise the structure of the British Army.

This simple act led to bitter humiliation and social disgrace.

Devised by William Slater; written by Robin Chapman; designed by Barrie Dobbins; produced by Anthony Coburn; directed by William Slater.

With Richard Hurndall (Colonel Freddie Gaunt), Christopher Cazenove (Richard Gaunt), Richard Wordsworth (Lieutenant Colonel Seymour), Wendy Williams (Alice Gaunt), Wendy Allnutt (Charlotte Gaunt), Simon Williams (Eugene), Jeffry Wickham (Captain of Hussars), Lindsay Campbell (Doctor Rumbold), Alister Cameron (Templeton), Earl Green (Carvel), John Dunbar (Editor), Tony Harwood (Captain Grenfell), Art Cross (Mess Sergeant), David Downer (Mess Orderly), Ian Ricketts (Bongo), Peter Davies (Cadet), Robert Fyffe (Reporter), Lauriston Shaw (Jefferson).

30.11.1970 **The Befrienders: Drink A Toast To Dear Old Dad**	J / 2"

The Samaritans will answer any call for help. When there is no one to talk to, nowhere to go, a telephone call can mean the difference between life or death.

Jack has seen the Samaritan poster in the post office. He is alone in London and only 17. Most boys can take their problems to their parents. Unfortunately Jack's parents are his problem.

Written by Harry W. Junkin; designed by Peter Seddon; produced by Anthony Coburn; directed by William Slater.

With Faith Brook (Arabella), Megs Jenkins (Janet), David Griffin (Jack), Basil Hoskins (Philip), Peter Armitage (Chuck), Michael Culver (Jerry), Janet Waldron (Helen), Lucetta Lijertwood (Jamaican Lady), Mary Henry (Mrs Brown), Kenneth Benda (Lawton), Peter Lawrence (Nicholson), Joe Cornelius (Maxwell), John Scholes (Graham), Sharon Campbell (Flightly Girl), Jerry Ram (Indian).

07.12.1970 **The Onedin Line: The Wind Blows Free**	J / 2"

Duration: 51 minutes.

The wind blows free for any man's use. A hundred years ago all a man needed to make a start -and ultimately a fortune-was a ship, the courage to risk his life in her and the cunning to survive in a cut-throat business.

James Onedin found his ship and one other hazard - a woman to match him.

Written by Cyril Abraham; designed by Oliver Bayldon; produced by Anthony Coburn; directed by William Slater.

With Brian Rawlinson (Robert Onedin), Maureen Nelson (Mrs Furlong), Jessica Benton (Elizabeth Onedin), Mary Webster (Sarah Onedin), Peter Gilmore (James Onedin), Edward Chapman (Callon), John Kidd (Agnew), Robert Gillespie (Drummond), Sheila Allen (Anne Webster), James Hayter (Captain Webster), Cyril Shaps (Bragansa), Reg Matthews (Clerk).

SERIES 2

	Holding / Source
23.08.1972 **Sutherland's Law: Man Overboard**	R1N / 2"

The new Fiscal in the town of Glendoran conducts a Fatal Accident Enquiry. But did Ian Campbell fall accidentally or will the Court find a murderer amongst the witnesses?

Written by Anthony Coburn; designed by Robert Berk; produced by Anthony Coburn; directed by David Cunliffe.

With Derek Francis (Mr Sutherland), Gareth Thomas (Alec Duthie), Maev Alexander (Christine), Donald McKillop (Sergeant MacIntyre), Sandra Clark (Janet Campbell), John Mackenzie (Police Constable Merengie), Sheelah Wilcocks (Kate Campbell), Neil Wilson (Archie Campbell), Richard Hampton (Hugh MacPhail), Steve Gardner (Willy Campbell), Roger Hammond (Sheriff), Robert Fyffe (Mr MacPhee), Richard Armour (Mr Robertson), Jill Brooke (Mrs Murray), James Cosmo (Ian Campbell).

30.08.1972 **The Venturers: The Chancer**   HD-R1 / 2"

Bankers put their trust in men. An attractive character and some fast talking can make or lose them a million. How do Prince's assess the worth of Harry Shannon - the carpetbagger?

Written by Donald Bull; designed by Susan Spence; produced by Anthony Coburn; directed by William Slater.

With Douglas Wilmer (Gerald Franklyn), James Kerry (David Aitken), Sebastian Breaks (Tom Prince), Brian Blessed (Harry Shannon), Joy Harrison (Deborah), Kenneth Benda (Grimbold), Mary Hignett (Beryl), Robert Fyffe (Firth), John Saunders (Flood), Geoffrey Toone (Frederick Lessing), John Wilding (Edward), Jacqueline Ellis (Dorothy Aitken), Anne De Vigier (Brenda Shannon), Ray Armstrong (Jason), Czeslaw Grocholski (Stan), John Dunbar (Marshall).

02.10.1972 **The Incredible Robert Baldick: Never Come Night**   DB-D3 / 2"

Alt.Title(s): *The Incredible Dr Baldick*

Postponed from 06.09.1972.

A fear so real, it can kill. A fear so old, it defies reason. A fear which Baldick must overcome - or be smothered by his own terror...

Written by Terry Nation; designed by John Burrowes; produced by Anthony Coburn; directed by Cyril Coke.

With Robert Hardy (Doctor Sir Robert Baldick), Julian Holloway (Thomas Wingham), John Rhys Davies (Caleb Selling), James Cossins (Peter Elmsted), Reginald Marsh (Charles Aldington), Barry Andrews (Seth Marden), Anna Martine (Dead Girl / Boy's Voice).

See also: THE BEFRIENDERS* / THE ONEDIN LINE* / THE REGIMENT* / SUTHERLAND'S LAW* / THE VENTURERS*

DRAMARAMA

Produced for Various ITV Companies by a variety of companies (see details below). Transmission details are for the Central region. Usual duration: 25 minutes.

SERIES 3

Holding / Source

04.06.1984 **Dodger, Bonzo And The Rest**   D3 / 1"

A Thames Television production.

Written by Geoffrey Case; executive producer Pamela Lonsdale; produced by Sheila Kinany; directed by Richard Bramall.

With Lee Ross (Dodger), Sophy McCallum (Bonzo), Lyndon Haynes (Brian), Jenny Jay (Elaine), Joanne Bell (The Rest), Sarah Kerslake (The Rest), David Scaffardi (The Rest), Wayne Watkins (The Rest), Pam Ferris (Dorothy), Mark Fletcher (Ronnie), Cheryl Hall (Mrs Jackson), Liz Gebhardt (Mrs Banks), Ava De Souza (Shop Girl).

SERIES 7

Holding / Source

13.06.1988 **Blackbird Singing In The Dead Of Night**   1" / 1"

A Granada production.

Written by Paul Abbott and Kay Mellor; designed by Christopher George; executive producer David Liddiment; produced by Gareth Morgan; directed by Spencer Campbell.

With Michelle Bernasconi (Kim Taylor), Shula Goldstone (Janie Catlow), Annette Ekblom (Charlotte Morton), Leigh Eaton (James Hanson), Paul Eaton (Dean Hanson), Kate Layden (Mrs Taylor), Scott Fletcher (Danny Phillips), Steve Dixon (Dave Klein), Carl Bewley (Sebastian Crowe), Rosa Roberts (Bella Stevens), Yusuf Sultan (Kahn).

See: CHILDREN'S WARD.

See also: ACE OF WANDS* / DODGER, BONZO AND THE REST* / SHADOWS

DRAW WITH DON

An Ulster Television production. Untransmitted.

Children's series with Irish artist Don Conroy (a local version of Rolf Harris).

Don Conroy (Presenter).

Holding / Source

##.##.#### **[untransmitted 1989 pilot]**   1" / 1"

Note: It's very hard to understand why the pilot was never transmitted. It is well put together and Don had a proven track record in the Republic of Ireland as a children's entertainer/artist. Two versions were made on the same day.

DREAM CASTLE

A Dream Castle Ltd production. Untransmitted.

Bringing to life the dreams of children everywhere.

Music by Barry Gray; executive producer Gerry Brown; produced by George Moreno.

Roy Castle, John McCarthy, Mary McCarthy.

Holding / Source

##.##.#### **[untransmitted pilot]**   J / C1

Recorded January 1973.

THE DRIFTER

A BBC production. Untransmitted.

Ray Barrett.

Holding / Source

##.##.####   J /

Pilot made in 1966.

DROP THE DEAD DONKEY

Alternative/Working Title(s): DEAD BELGIANS DON'T COUNT / DEAD KUWAITIS DON'T COUNT

A Hat Trick production for Channel 4. Transmission details are for Channel 4. Duration: 25 minutes.

Main regular credit(s):	Created by Andy Hamilton and Guy Jenkin; theme music by Matthew Scott.
Main regular cast:	Robert Duncan (Gus Hedges), Neil Pearson (Dave Charnley), Jeff Rawle (George Dent), David Swift (Henry Davenport), Stephen Tompkinson (Damien Day), Victoria Wicks (Sally Smedley).

SERIES 1

Main regular credit(s):	Written by Andy Hamilton and Guy Jenkin; music by Philip Pope; associate producer Guy Jenkin; executive producer Denise O'Donoghue; produced by Andy Hamilton; directed by Liddy Oldroyd.
Main regular cast:	With Haydn Gwynne (Alex Pates).

Holding / Source

##.##.#### "A computer virus begins to reveal secret office files held by Gus..." [untransmitted pilot]   DB / 1"

Theme music by Philip Pope.

DUCK PATROL

An LWT production. Transmission details are for the Central region. Duration: 25 minutes.

'Duck Patrol' follows the fortunes of the Ravensbeck River Police Station and its eight officers who are devoted to maintaining law and order along the banks of the River Thames. Wilson plays Police Constable Rowland Rose, also known as Prof., who likes a quiet life. Nothing makes him happier than a peaceful trip upstream in the police boat with no need to make any entries in the Occurrence Book.

Main regular credit(s):	Created by Jan Etherington and Gavin Petrie; script supervisor Jo Newey; music by Simon Wallace; designed by Harry Banks; associate producers Jan Etherington and Gavin Petrie; executive producer Humphrey Barclay; produced by Jamie Rix; directed by Sylvie Boden.
Main regular cast:	Richard Wilson (Prof), David Tennant (Darwin), Samantha Beckinsale (Marilyn), Trevor Cooper (Ollie), Craig Fairbrass (Hero), Geoffrey Hutchings (Serge), Jason Watkins (Taz), Sue Johnston (Val).

Holding / Source

##.##.#### Of Ducks And Men [untransmitted pilot]   DB / DBS

In the first episode of the series a slow day for the Ravensbeck river police is interrupted when Prof and Darwin encounter a pair of ducks who have mysteriously turned a violent shade of pink. Meanwhile the rest of the staff at the police station are preparing for a wedding.

DUNRULIN'

A Jon Blair Film Company production for BBC 1. Transmission details are for BBC 1. Duration: 30 minutes.

Dulwich: the distant future. Some people never really retire.

	Production No	Holding / Source
##.##.#### [untransmitted 1990 pilot]	LLCB050P	DB / 1"

Written by Alistair Beaton and John Wells; from an idea by Jon Blair; produced by Jon Blair; directed by Richard Boden.

With Angela Thorne (Mrs Thatcher), John Wells (Mr Thatcher), Larry Lamb (Chainsaw Smith), Owen Brenman (Master Thatcher), Hilary Gish (Miss Thatcher), John Cater (Mr Mickey), Jilly Johnson (Mandy), Jestyn Phillips (Registrar), Richenda Carey (1st Nurse), John Dougall [as John Dougal] (Junior Doctor), Janet Palmer (2nd Nurse), Malcolm Rogers (Man In Bed).

23.12.1990 An Active Citizen Is A Healthy Citizen   DB / 1"

Written by Alistair Beaton and John Wells; produced by Jon Blair; directed by Richard Boden.

With Angela Thorne (Mrs Margaret Thatcher), John Wells (Mr Denis Thatcher), Hilary Gish (Ms Carol Thatcher), Owen Brenman (Master Mark Thatcher), Kenneth Cranham (Mr Kneecap Smith), Liz Smith (Mrs Trodd), John Cater (The Vicar), Eiji Kusuhara (Mr Kishimoto), Jilly Johnson (Mandy), Richenda Carey (Sister), Colin Starkey (Senior Doctor), John Dougall (Junior Doctor), Jan Ravens (BBC Announcer).

THE DUSTBINMEN

A Granada production. Transmission details are for the ATV midlands region. Duration varies - see below for details.

Main regular credit(s):	Devised by Jack Rosenthal; music by Derek Hilton.

Holding / Source

30.09.1968 There's A Hole In Your Dustbin Delilah [Playhouse]   B1 / B1

Duration: 75 minutes.

Written by Jack Rosenthal; executive producer H. V. Kershaw; produced by John Finch; directed by Michael Apted.

With Jack MacGowran (Cheese and Egg [C. E. Petty]), Frank Windsor (Bloody Delilah [Mr Sinclair]), Harold Innocent (Heavy Breathing), Graham Haberfield (Winston Platt), Henry Livings (Eric Llewellyn), Marjie Lawrence (Mrs Pride of Jutland), Priscilla Morgan (6 Shakespeare Street), Angela Crow (21 Chaucer Street), John Barrett (Smellie Ibbotson), Pitt Wilkinson (Matthew Pride of Jutland), William Maxwell (Coalman), Maggie Jones (4 Shakespeare Street), Louise Jervis (2 Shakespeare Street), Irlin Hall (19 Chaucer Street), James Beck (Police Sergeant), Peter MacKriel (Milkman), Judy Evans (Helpless Woman), Sheila Irwin (Nurse), Kate Brown (Melanie).

This play was made as part of THE SYSTEM series, but shown in PLAYHOUSE.

The 'devised by' credit only appeared on episodes Jack Rosenthal did not write. The voices - "Ey Mam." "Whaaat?" "The dustbinmen" - at the start of the opening titles might belong to Bernard Padden and Maureen Lipman.

EASY PEASY

A Talkback Thames production for ITV 1. Untransmitted. Duration: 25 minutes.

Written by Paul Smith; script supervisor Emma Thomas; music by Hal Lindes; director of photography Sue Gibson; art director Anna Pearce; designed by Steve Groves; production executive Dean Jones; line producer Kathy Nettleship; produced by Margot Gavan Duffy; directed by Mandie Fletcher.

Peter Davison (George), Amanda Root (Fiona), Josie Lawrence (Phoebe), Jack Connor (Jamie), Shappi Khorsandi (Amira), Hannah Waddingham (Kate Barber).

	Production No	VT Number	Holding / Source
##.##.#### [untransmitted pilot]	PC/6625/04	130257	DB / DBSWF
Recorded 2004.			

EGGHEADS

A BBC production for BBC 2. Transmission details are for BBC 2. Duration: 30 minutes.

	Holding / Source
	Holding / Source
##.##.#### [untransmitted pilot]	DB / DBSW

EGO TRIP

Alternative/Working Title(s): FRANK CARSON'S EGO TRIP

A Granada production. Transmission details are for the Granada region. Duration: 12 minutes.

Irish comic Frank Carson talks about his hilarious life and career. The ebullient Frank talks to Johnnie Hamp, daughter Majella, and journalist Patrick Stoddart about the history of his famous catch phrase - 'It's the way I tell 'em!' - first used in TV in the original series of The Comedians in June, 1971. Flicking back through Frank's early press cuttings, Hamp turns up the headline : 'Death Threats Haunt Frank Carson.' The reason? 'They wanted to shoot me because they said I was degrading the Irish humour, ' says Frank. Frank also demonstrates his famous stage drunk routine which has the audience in stitches and is a particular favourite of his show-biz friend Billy Connolly.

Main regular credit(s):   Produced by John Hamp; directed by David Liddiment.

Main regular cast: Frank Carson, Majella Carson, John Hamp, Patrick Stoddart.

	Production No	Holding / Source
25.03.1983	P1133/1	1" / 1"
25.03.1983	P1133/2	1" / 1"

Shown as a single 25m pilot, made for the Showcase strand. Retained as two smaller versions.

See also: SHOWCASE

THE ELECTRONIC HOOK

Alternative/Working Title(s): THE FAME GAME

A Granada production. Transmission details are for the Granada region. Duration: 40 minutes.

A talent contest where viewers voted for the acts via a talkback system installed in the Granada area by AGB Cable. Singers competed and Gina Johnson won. Comedians also competed. Poor joke-tellers could be cut off early and a graphic of a bomb would appear instead. The bomb would then explode.

Faith Brown (Host), Gina Johnson.

	Holding / Source
01.08.1984	J / 1"

John Hamp says: "This was (I believe) the first time there was interaction between 100 selected viewers and a computer in the studio, which translated their phone signals into a moving graphic on screen, which indicated their reactions to an artist's performance - live. It was the pilot for The Fame Game - the talent show. I had to pilot it to see if my idea to use the new fangled computers would do the job.

The pilot was hosted by Faith Brown, who did a good job, but the Granada programme controller insisted on a male host for The Fame Game!!! Twit!

I don't have a copy of the pilot - shame if its wiped - possibly a bit of TV history!"

The opening titles exist on 16mm film.

ELLINGTON

A Yorkshire Television production. Transmission details are for the Central region.

A hard-headed sports agent who tries to keep his hands clean in a dirty world.

Main regular credit(s):   Created by Don Webb; from an idea by Derek Lister; executive producer Keith Richardson; produced by Gordon Flemyng.

Main regular cast: Chris Ellison (Ellington), Sean Chapman (Ben Ellington), Maureen O'Farrell (Mary Pitt), Perry Fenwick (Vinnie Done).

	VT Number	Holding / Source
26.10.1994 **Ellington**	D202	DB / V1S

Duration: 75 minutes.

Flanked by his loyal team of brother Ben, minder Vinny and assistant Mary, Ellington steers his clients (a starry-eyed snooker champion and a browbeaten boxer) through shark-infested waters.

Written by Don Webb; directed by Gordon Flemyng.

With Hakeem Kae-Kazim (Tommy Knight), Sarah Jane Hassell (Angie), Joanna Dolan (Belle), Anna Chancellor, Dermot Crowley, Robert Lang, Mairead Carty, Craig Kelly, Jody Saron, Ken Sharrock, Simon Cox, Simon D'Arcy, Julian Firth, Sheila Whitfield, Vicky Murdock, Christopher Owen, Midge Taylor, Chris O'Neill, Mickey Poppins, Eric Mason, Richard Beale.

THE ELUSIVE PIMPERNEL

An ITC production. Not made. Duration: 25 minutes.

Written by Ralph Smart; based on novels by Baroness Orczy.

EMBASSY

A Tiger Aspect production for BBC 2. Transmission details are for BBC 2. Duration: 30 minutes.

Comedy set in the British Embassy of the fictional South American Country- Solandas. The newly appointed ambassador, Peter Nevin, soon finds himself having to juggle with the demands of his government and local politicians.

Written by Cris Cole; executive producer Peter Bennett-Jones; production manager Fiona McGuire; produced by Sophie Clarke-Jervoise; directed by Mark Chapman.

Robert Daws (Peter Nevin), Caroline Langrishe (Belinda Thoimpson), Benjamin Whitrow (Taylor Scot), Edward De Souza (Snr Diace), Candida Gubbins (Sarah Nevin), Robert Portal (Rupert Lightfoot), Arancha De Juan (Maria Escobar), Emil Wolk (Snr Hernandez), Lino Omoboni (Barman), Pedro Hernando (Waiter).

	Holding / Source
26.03.1997	DB-D3 / D3S

EMMWOOD

A BBC production. Untransmitted.

	VT Number	Holding / Source
##.##.#### **Just Jensen**	35/T/5415	J /
Recorded 29th January 1959.		

EMU'S BROADCASTING CORPORATION (EBC 1)

A BBC Manchester production for BBC 1. Transmission details are for BBC 1. Duration varies - see below for details.

Main regular credit(s):	Devised by Rod Hull.
Main regular cast:	Rod Hull and Emu.

SERIES 1

Main regular credit(s):	Written by Rod Hull; designed by Paul Montague; produced and directed by Peter Ridsdale Scott.
Main regular cast:	With Barbara New, Billy Dainty.

	Holding / Source
##.##.#### **[untransmitted pilot]**	DB-D3 / 2"
Duration: 30 minutes.	
Recorded 29.05.1975. No end credits.	

THE ENCHANTED TREE

An Elwyn Ambrose production. made in association with Purnell Books. Untransmitted. Duration: 26 minutes.

Puppetry by Elwyn Ambrose and Desmond Macnamara; directed by Darrel Catling.

J. G. Devlin, Sylvia Tysick.

	Holding / Source
##.##.#### **[untransmitted pilot]**	J / C3
This pilot combined both live actors and puppets (The Stage 02.03.1961).	

END OF PART ONE

An LWT production. Transmission details are for the ATV midlands region. Duration: 25 minutes.

Main regular credit(s):	Written by Andrew Marshall and David Renwick; directed by Geoffrey Sax.
Main regular cast:	Denise Coffey, Tony Aitken, Fred Harris, Sue Holderness, Dudley Stevens.

SERIES 1

Main regular credit(s):	Produced by Simon Brett.

	Production No	Holding / Source
27.05.1979 "BBC East Anglia"	9L/99389	D2 / 2"

ENTERTAINMENT GENERAL

An LWT production. Untransmitted. Duration: 50 minutes.

	Holding / Source
##.##.#### **Romantic Destination**	DB / DBSW
Written by Ian Cross; produced by Ian Cross; directed by Chris Ryder.	
With Sarah Matravers, Ottis Deley, Deborah McKinlay, Jan Vintov, Louise Lauritsen.	

EROS UNLEASHED

A HTV production for ITV 1 Wales. Transmission details are for the ITV 1 Wales region. Duration: 25 minutes.

Written by Tina Glynn; produced by Peter Edwards; directed by Natasha Betteridge.

Rhian Morgan (Mags), Francine Morgan, Margaret John, Rachel Bell, Nia Trussler, Maria Pride, Amy Starling, Shelley Rees.

	Holding / Source
01.12.2006	DB / DBSW

EUROPEAN WOMAN

A RPM Communications production. made in association with Central Television Facilities. Untransmitted.

	Holding / Source
##.##.#### **Taster Tape**	DV / 1"
Duration: 4 minutes.	

##.##.#### [untransmitted pilot]   1" / 1"

1992

EVENING SURGERY

A BBC production. Untransmitted.

	VT Number	Holding / Source
##.##.#### **[pilot 1]**	16/P/15930	J /
Recorded 11th September 1962.		
##.##.#### **[pilot 2]**	16/P/16352/A&B	J /
Recorded 4th October 1962.		

EVERY SECOND COUNTS

A BBC production for BBC 1. made in association with Group W Productions / Talbot TV Ltd. Transmission details are for BBC 1. Duration: 30 minutes.

Main regular credit(s):   Theme music by John Mealing.

Main regular performer(s): Paul Daniels (Quizmaster), Philip Talbot (Voice Over).

SERIES 1

	VT Number	Holding / Source
##.##.#### **[untransmitted pilot]**	LNFK506W	DB / 1"

EXIT - IT'S THE WAY OUT SHOW!

Alternative/Working Title(s): EXIT - IT'S WAY OUT

A Rediffusion Television production. Transmission details are for the Rediffusion Television region. Duration: 25 minutes.

Main regular credit(s):   Devised by Barry Langford.

Main regular performer(s): Pat Campbell (The Major (Voice Only)), Jane Bates [as Jane], Lesley Judd [as Leslie].

	Holding / Source
##.##.#### **[untransmitted pilot]**	J / 40

Produced and directed by Michael Currer-Briggs.

With Barry Langford (Compere), Tony Blackburn, Ed Stewart, Rick Dane, Pete Brady [as Peter Brady], Tony Hawes.

Recorded 22.08.1967.

According to the TV Times, it was intended that Barry Langford would compere the whole series but was unable to do so because of illness. To the best of our knowledge, only the pilot and the Christmas programme featured celebrities, on the other editions members, of the public took part.

F.L.A.P.

A L!ve TV production for LWT. Untransmitted. Duration: 25 minutes.

	VT Number	Holding / Source
##.##.#### **Politicians Should Be Seen**	9L/00767	J / 2"
##.##.#### **I Can Get You Into Pictures**	9L/00766	J / 2"

Untx pilots.

FACE OF SUCCESS

An ABC production. Transmission details are for the ABC midlands region. Duration: 25 minutes.

Main regular performer(s): Alastair Burnet (Interviewer).

	Holding / Source
	J / 40

10.09.1966

With Basil Z. De Ferranti.

THE FALL AND RISE OF REGINALD PERRIN

A BBC production for BBC 1. Transmission details are for BBC 1. Duration: 30 minutes.

Main regular credit(s):   Written by David Nobbs; music by Ronnie Hazlehurst.

Main regular cast: Leonard Rossiter (Reginald Perrin), Pauline Yates (Elizabeth Perrin), John Barron (C.J.).

SERIES 1

	Holding / Source
	DB-D3 / 2"

08.09.1976 "Ravioli, ravioli and more ravioli"

Designed by Graham Oakley; produced and directed by John Howard Davies.

With Sue Nicholls (Joan Greengross), John Horsley (Doc Morrissey), Trevor Adams (Tony Webster), Roland Macleod (Morris Coates), Bruce Bould (David Harris-Jones), Jacki Piper (Esther Pigeon), Terence Conoley (Peter Cartwright), Norman Mitchell (Ron Napier), Ray Marioni (Waiter).

See also: THE FUNNY SIDE OF CHRISTMAS* / THE LEGACY OF REGINALD PERRIN* / REGGIE PERRIN*

FAMILIES

A Granada production. Transmission details are for the Central region. Duration varies - see below for details.

Main regular credit(s):   Devised by Kay Mellor; executive producer David Liddiment.

	Production No	Holding / Source
##.##.#### **[untransmitted pilot]**	P1614	J / 1"

Duration: 20 minutes.

Written by Kay Mellor; designed by Tim Farmer; production manager Don Bell; produced by David Liddiment; directed by Oliver Horsbrugh.

Recorded 20-27th April 1989.

A FAMILY AT WAR

A Granada production. Transmission details are for the ATV midlands region. Duration: 50 minutes.

Main regular credit(s):   Created by John Finch.

	Holding / Source
	J / 2"

##.##.#### **[untransmitted pilot]**

Written by Stan Barstow; produced by Richard Doubleday; directed by Michael Cox.

Recorded circa November 1969. John Finch remembers, " I had outlined unmissable events to Denis Forman so we could gauge the likely length of the series.   We had already reached 26 hours and Denis, after reading my early script, was beginning to talk about 52.   It was obvious I couldn't write all of them (I wrote 30 and heavily edited the rest) so we decided to run a pilot and choose an episode by another writer so we could be happy with the plan.   The writer was Stan Barstow, but Stan was a great novelist but not the best of television writers, the casting was patchy, and the pilot didn't work.   So we went into production with half a dozen scripts written (mostly by me).   The entire staff at Granada were gathered in rooms with large monitors and given a pad and a pen to write down their reactions. They were overwhelmingly positive and Denis decided we should go ahead with the plan for 52.   "What happens if you go under a bus, said Denis. "You've got problems," I replied, but while I was quaking somewhat at the size of the enterpise I was also excited by the size of the canvas.

The pilot was never shown, but there were two or three casting errors in the first episode transmitted.   When you spot one in Ep.1 and realise the character will be needed for at least half the series, it makes it very hard work."

FAMILY FORTUNES

An ATV/Central production. made in association with Goodson Todman Productions / Talbot TV Ltd. Transmission details are for the ATV/Central region. Usual duration: 24 minutes.

SERIES 1

An ATV production. Transmission details are for the ATV midlands region.

Main regular credit(s):   Music by Jack Parnell and Dave Lindup; programme consultant Spike Mullins; designed by Richard Plumb; produced by William G. Stewart; directed by Graham C. Williams.

Main regular performer(s): With Bob Monkhouse (Host).

	Production No	VT Number	Holding / Source
##.##.#### **[untransmitted pilot]**	5606/79	174713	J / 2"

Recorded July 1979.

FAMILY GATHERING

A BBC production. Untransmitted.

Gilbert Harding.

	VT Number	Holding / Source
##.##.#### **[pilot Film]**	35/P/7432	J /

Recorded 26th January 1960.

FAMOUS LAST WORDS

A Thames Television production. made in association with Talbot TV Ltd. Untransmitted. Duration: 25 minutes.

Main regular credit(s): Produced and directed by David Clark.

Main regular performer(s): Barbara Windsor, Faith Brown, Henry McGee, Jenny Hanley, John Junkin, Joyce Blair, Kenneth Williams, Lionel Blair, Paula Wilcox, Roy Castle, Sarah Kennedy, Sylvia Syms, Maurice Thorogood.

	Holding / Source
##.##.#### **[first pilot]**	DB / 2"
##.##.#### **[second pilot]**	J / 2"

FANFARE

A Thames Television production. Transmission details are for the ATV midlands region. Duration: 25 minutes.

Main regular cast: Flintlock (Resident Band).

	VT Number	Holding / Source
##.##.#### **[untransmitted pilot]**	14846	D3 / 2"

Produced and directed by Roger Price.

FAWLTY TOWERS

A BBC production for BBC 2. Transmission details are for BBC 2.

Main regular credit(s): Written by John Cleese and Connie Booth; theme music by Dennis Wilson.

Main regular cast: John Cleese (Basil Fawlty), Prunella Scales (Sybil Fawlty), Andrew Sachs (Manuel), Connie Booth (Polly).

SERIES 1

Duration: 35 minutes.

Main regular credit(s): Designed by Peter Kindred; produced and directed by John Howard Davies.

Main regular cast: With Ballard Berkeley (Major Gowen).

	Holding / Source
19.09.1975 **A Touch Of Class**	DB-D3 / 2"

With David Simeon (Mr Mackenzie), Lionel Wheeler (Mr Watson), Robin Ellis (Danny), Terence Conoley (Mr Wareing), Michael Gwynn (Lord Melbury), Martin Wyldeck (Sir Richard Morris).

See also: FAWLTY TOWERS - RE-OPENED*

FEBRUARY TELEVISION SHOW NO.1

Commissioned by ITV. Untransmitted.

	Holding / Source
##.##.#### **What's New?**	DB-R1|n /

With Nanette Newman, Paula Marshall.

	Holding / Source
##.##.#### **'Woman's Own' Advertisement**	DB-R1|n /

With Dennis Price (Noel Coward).

	Holding / Source
##.##.#### **Strange Experiences: Safe And Sound**	DB-R1|n /
##.##.#### **Strange Experiences: Knife Throwing**	DB-R1|n /

The NFTVA acquired this from a film lab.

A pilot production designed to give some idea of how an evening's viewing might appear on the forthcoming I.T.A. channel in London. The programme

includes an introduction to a women's magazine show called "WHAT'S NEW?" by

Josephine Douglas and advertisements for Fry's Caramets, Kleenex Tissues

(featuring Nanette Newman), Frigidaire Refrigerators (featuring Paula

Marshall), Quaker Oats and Alexandre of Oxford Street. In addition, an

advertisement for "Woman's Own" magazine highlights a new autobiographical

series of articles by Noel Coward (played by Dennis Price in the commercial).

Two episodes of the television series "STRANGE EXPERIENCES" are included in

their entirety: "SAFE AND SOUND" and "KNIFE THROWING" (5 minutes each). These

are introduced by Joy Adamson. Both episodes feature Peter Williams, the first

of the two also features Peter Sallis (1348ft).

FELIX AND MURDO

Commissioned by Channel 4. Transmission details are for Channel 4. Duration: 25 minutes.

Written by Simon Nye; produced by Ben Farrell and Saskia Schuster; directed by Christine Gernon.

Ben Miller (Felix), Alexander Armstrong (Murdo), Georgia King (Winnie), Katy Wix (Fanny), Marek Larwood (Archie), Jonathan Coy (Father Of The Family), Pippa Haywood (Mother Of The Family), Lizzie Roper (Mrs Snivel).

	Holding / Source
28.12.2011	HD/DB / HDC

FIBS IS FATTENING

A Witzend production for ATV. Untransmitted. Duration: 25 minutes.

Comedy about a family where one person is dieting.

Written by Laurence Marks and Maurice Gran.

	Holding / Source
##.##.####	J / FNK

May not have got past the script stage. 1980.

FIDDLER'S GREEN

Alternative/Working Title(s): T MAK

A Thames Television production. Untransmitted. Duration: 25 minutes.

Written by John Chapman and Ian Davidson; designed by Philip Blowers; produced and directed by Anthony Parker.

Donald Sinden (Commander Robert Hackforth), Eleanor Summerfield (Nanny), Elspet Gray (Nesta Robbins), Lynette Davies (Jane Powys), Michael Stroud (Truscott), Stephen Hancock (Taxi Driver), Marc Sinden (Restaurant Owner), Kate O'Connell (Rose), Susie McKenna (Waitress).

	VT Number	Holding / Source
##.##.#### The Ladies - God Bless 'Em [untransmitted 1989 pilot]	39544	DB / 1"

FILM ON FOUR

Produced for Channel 4 by a variety of companies (see details below). Transmission details are for Channel 4. Duration varies - see below for details.

SERIES 7

	Holding / Source
12.02.1987 **The Chain**	C1 / C1

A Quinter/Rank production. Duration: 95 minutes.

Written by Jack Rosenthal; produced by Victor Glynn; directed by Jack Gold.

With Maurice Denham (Grandpa), Nigel Hawthorne (Mr Thorn), Bernard Hill (Nick), Denis Lawson (Keith), Phyllis Logan (Alison), Anna Massey (Betty), Leo McKern (Thomas), Warren Mitchell (Bamber), Judy Parfitt (Deidre), Billie Whitelaw (Mrs Andreos), Herbert Norville (Des), Rita Wolf (Carrie), Tony Westrope (Paul), Gary Waldhorn (Tornado), David Troughton (Dudley), John Rowe (Alex), Mark Dignam (Ambrose), Carmen Munroe (Des' Mum), Matthew Blakstad (Mark), Charlotte Long (Rosemary).

See also: MOVING STORY.

Only predominantly British films have been included.

"A Splice of Life - 15 Years of Film On Four" was shown on Channel 4, tx:25.12.97. 40mins.

See also: MOVIE CONNECTIONS*

FILTHY LUCRE

A John Kaye Cooper Productions production for BBC. made in association with Mike Hughes. Untransmitted. Duration: 35 minutes.

Highly amusing sitcom pilot about a tax inspector who is ruthless, but hopeless at his job.

Written by Jennifer Franks and Peter Vincent; costume Linda Martin; make-up Jenny Hughes; music by Alan Parker; designed by Bernard Lloyd-Jones; production manager Garrie Mallen; produced and directed by John Kaye Cooper.

Russ Abbot (Medlock), Les Dennis (Clarence Plum), Terence Rigby (Inspector Pepper), Alison Rose (Loretta), Lia Williams (Fern), Arthur White (Lucan), Stella Moray (Mrs Ashbury), Leila Hoffman (Tea Lady), Alan Hay (Mr Simms), Peter John (Humphrey Bogart).

	Production No	Holding / Source
##.##.#### [untransmitted 1987 pilot]	LLVL012L/71	DB / 1"

The studio recording also exists.

FIRE STATION

A Talkback Thames production for BBC. Untransmitted. Duration: 28 minutes.

Written by Simon Nye; script supervisor Katie Collins; music by Simon Lacey; director of photography James Cairney; titles by Liquid TV [credited as Liquid]; art director Anna Pearce; designed by Steve Groves; assistant producer Matthew Mulot; executive producer Lucy Lumsden; head of production Dean Jones; line producer Kathy Nettleship; produced by Margot Gavan Duffy; directed by Ben Kellett.

John Henshaw (Malcolm), Johnny Vegas (Buzz), Paterson Joseph (Carl), Cristian Solimeno (Dan), Angel Coulby (Alison), Tameka Empson (Sheila), Simon Paris (Terry), John Normington (Caretaker), William Jeffs (Giles), William Nye (Child 1), Bradley Muggeridge (Child 2).

	Production No	VT Number	Holding / Source
##.##.#### [untransmitted pilot]	60/ICE E867F/71	358888	DB / DBSWF

Recorded 2006.

FIREBALL XL5

Alternative/Working Title(s): CENTURY 21 / NOVA X100

An AP Films production for ITC. made in association with ATV. Transmission details are for the ATV midlands region. Duration: 25 minutes.

Main regular credit(s):	Created by Gerry Anderson and Sylvia Anderson; theme music by Barry Gray, Charles Blackwell and Don Spencer; music by Barry Gray; associate producer Reg Hill; produced by Gerry Anderson.
Main regular cast:	Paul Maxwell (Voice of Colonel Steve Zodiac), Sylvia Anderson (Voice of Doctor Venus), David Graham (Voice of Professor Matthew Matic, Lt 90 and Zoony), John Bluthal (Voice of Commander Wilbur Zero), Gerry Anderson (Voice of Robert The Robot).

Holding / Source

25.03.1963 **Planet 46**   DB / B3

Written by Gerry Anderson and Sylvia Anderson; directed by Gerry Anderson.

The opening titles and some sequences from "Planet 46" have been colourised and exist on Betacam.

THE FIRECHASERS

An ITC production. Transmission details are for the ATV midlands region. Duration: 85 minutes.

Toby Collins is a beautiful, persistent reporter who, with press photographer Jim Maxwell, is always the first on the scene of a series of fires ravaging London. One after another, the infernos rage out of control before the fire service arrives. Toby believes an arsonist is to blame, but without any proof she has no story to write. Suave American Quentin Barnaby is one man who may be able to help her.

Quentin, a chief investigation officer for a major insurance company, soon discovers that he has more in common with Toby than the desire to find criminals, and the two begin a passionate affair. But as the flames hit too close to home, the clues begin to point in one direction, and Quentin has to face his greatest fear: is his new lover the deadly arsonist?
- See more at: http://networkonair.com/shop/1216-firechasers-the.html#sthash.otzbJofh.dpuf

Written by Philip Levene; produced by Julian Wintle; directed by Sidney Hayers.

Chad Everett (Quentin Barnaby), Anjanette Comer (Toby Collins), Keith Barron (Jim Maxwell), Joanne Dainton (Valerie Chrane), Rupert Davies (John Prentice), Roy Kinnear (Roscoe), Robert Flemyng (Carlton), John Loder (Routledge), James Hayter (Inspector Herman), Allan Cuthbertson (Jarvis), Joseph Brady (Nightwatchman), Marianne Stone (Neurotic Woman).

Holding / Source

06.03.1977   C3 / C3

See also: FIRE-TEC

FIRE-TEC

An ITC production for ATV. Not made.

Created by Philip Levene; written by Philip Levene.

Holding / Source

##.##.#### **Cause For Alarm [unmade pilot]**   NR / NM

Unmade 1968 pilot about a fire investigator, Quentin Barnaby, who is Chief Investigating Officer, in the Fire Division of the International Federation of Insurance Groups.

Eventually, the project was made into a feature film entitled "The Firechasers". Produced by Julian Wintle, directed by Sidney Hayers and written by Philip Levene. With Chad Everett, Anjanette Comer, Keith Barron, Joanne Dainton, Rupert Davies, Roy Kinnear and Allan Cuthbertson. 101 mins, distributed by ITC Entertainment.
See also: THE FIRECHASERS

FIRST OF THE SUMMER WINE

A BBC production for BBC 1. Transmission details are for BBC 1.

Main regular credit(s):	Written by Roy Clarke.
Main regular cast:	Peter Sallis (Mr Clegg), David Fenwick (Norman Clegg), Maggie Ollerenshaw (Mrs Clegg).

Holding / Source

03.01.1988   DB / 1"

Duration: 45 minutes.

Designed by David Hitchcock; produced and directed by Gareth Gwenlan.

With Paul McLain (Seymour), Paul Wyett (Compo), Richard Lumsden (Foggy), Helen Patrick (Nora), Gary Whitaker (Wally), Paul Oldham (Sherbet), Sarah Dangerfield (Ivy), Joanne Heywood (Dilys), Derek Benfield (Mr Scrimshaw), Adrian Lochhead, Julie Ann Taylor, Patricia England, Barbara Durkin, Annie Raitt, Gillian Goodman, Joanne Rudling, Geoffrey Hodson, Joe Belcher, Alan Starkey.

See also: LAST OF THE SUMMER WINE*

FIST OF FUN

A BBC production for BBC 2. Transmission details are for BBC 2.

Main regular credit(s):	Written by Richard Herring and Stewart Lee; produced by Sarah Smith.
Main regular cast:	Richard Herring (Host), Stewart Lee (Host), Peter Baynham, Kevin Eldon.
Credits:	Additional material by Peter Baynham.

Holding / Source

##.##.#### **[untransmitted pilot]**   DB / D3S

Duration: 37 minutes.

Directed by Dominic Brigstocke.

With Ronni Ancona, Ian Ashpitel, Wendy Danvers, Lucy Edis, Alan Francis, Rebecca Front, Alistair McGowan, Ben Moor, Sue Perkins, John Thomson, Jo Unwin, Lawrence Werber, Philip Whitchurch, David Wolstencroft, Al Murray*.

The pilot is not held by the BBC. It was taped in May 1994 but not transmitted. Also, Al Murray makes an uncredited appearance in the prison comic strip. No dialogue, but we have included him.

See also: FIST OF FUN (RADIO)*

FITZ

An LWT production. Untransmitted. Duration: 25 minutes.

	VT Number	Holding / Source
##.##.#### [untransmitted pilot]	9L/90404	J / 2"

FIVE ALIVE

A TVS production. Transmission details are for the Central region.

Main regular credit(s):   Executive producer John Kaye Cooper; produced by Alan Nixon.

Main regular cast: Brian Conley, Peter Piper.

	Holding / Source
23.08.1986	1" / 1"

Duration: 40 minutes.

Written by Charlie Adams, Geoff Atkinson, Paul Minett and Brian Leveson; designed by John Newton Clarke; directed by Bob Collins.

With Five Star, Andrew Secombe, Sharon Maiden, Eve Ferret, Rent Party, Kevin Devane.

FLEET STREET

An ATV production. Not made.

Research Julian Bond.

Julian Bond was asked to develope this concept into a pilot. It does not appear to have been made.

FOLLOW THE YELLOW BRICK ROAD

A Cinema Verity production for LWT. Untransmitted. Duration: 25 minutes.

Written by Jan Butlin.

Cilla Black.

	Holding / Source
##.##.#### [untransmitted pilot]	J / 1"

Recorded 26.09.1989.

FOR 4 TONIGHT

An LWT production for Channel 4. Transmission details are for Channel 4.

Main regular credit(s):   Written by Ruby Wax; produced and directed by Michael Dolenz.

	Production No	Holding / Source
##.##.#### [untransmitted pilot]	9L/79030	DB|n / 2"

Duration: 28 minutes.

With Paola Dionisotti (Avril Petrie), George Irving (Tony Royale), Nat Jackley (Happy Kyne), David Claridge (Colin Popple), Elizabeth Anson (Tiny McDougall), Olga Lowe (Mrs McDougal), Janine Duvitski (Gaye Farrell), Bill Martin (Voice Over).

Recorded 18/05/1983.

FOREIGN BODIES

A BBC production for BBC 2. Transmission details are for BBC 2. Duration: 30 minutes.

Main regular credit(s):   Written by Bernard Farrell and Graham Reid.

	Production No	Holding / Source
##.##.#### [untransmitted 1986 pilot]	LLCH580X/71	DB / 1"

Costume Anna Stubley; make-up Benita Barrell; designed by Rosemary Hester; production manager Jo Austin; produced and directed by Gareth Gwenlan.

With Kenneth Branagh (Tom), Colum Convey (Alex), Hilary Reynolds (Roisin), Lise-Ann McLaughlin (Septa), John Hewitt (Harry), Trudy Kelly (Madge), Catherine Brennan (Elaine), Tracey Lynch (Carol), Joe McPartland (Soup), Maureen Dow (Lilly), Michael Gormley (Jim), Margaret D'Arcy (Mrs Brown), Toby (Tiger).

FORTUNE'S TIDE

An Anglia production. Transmission details are for the Anglia region. Duration: 25 minutes.

A waterman on the Norfolk Broads helps visitors.

Written by Rose Tremain; executive producer Philip Garner; produced and directed by Michael Edwards.

Frank Middlemass, David Black, Sheila Ruskin, Paul Spurrier.

	Holding / Source
09.08.1982	MII / 2"

Held at EAFA.

Made in April/May 1981.

FOUR FEATHER FALLS

An A.P. Films production for Granada. Transmission details are for the ATV midlands region. Duration: 13 minutes.

Main regular credit(s):   Based on an idea by Gerry Anderson and Barry Gray; music by Barry Gray.

Main regular cast: Kenneth Connor (Rocky), Nicholas Parsons (Tex Tucker), David Graham (Dusty), Denise Bryer (Various Roles).

	Holding / Source
25.02.1960 **How It Began**	DB / B3

Written by Mary Cathcart Borer; directed by Gerry Anderson.

Made in secret during the making of Torchy the Battery Boy to prevent Roberta Leigh finding out.

THE FOX

A Bischoff-Diamond production for ITP. Transmission details are for the ATV midlands region. Duration: 25 minutes.

Written by Crane Wilbur; produced by Samuel Bischoff and David Diamond; directed by Peter Maxwell.

Anthony Dexter (The Fox), Susan Beaumont (Marie Antoinette), Jane Griffiths (Madeline De Charny), Alec Mango (De Charney), Julian Somers (Governor Stanville).

	Holding / Source
03.11.1957	C3 / C3

The pilot script was revised on 14th January 1957. The Fox was described as "in his late twenties or early thirties, swordsman, hypnotist, ventriloquist, magician." The 1957 screening was unbilled, following a reshuffle of programmes that evening which saw THE JACK JACKSON SHOW and ARMCHAIR THEATRE swap start times and BOX OFFICE get dropped completely.

FRANK AND FAIR

An ABC production. Untransmitted.

	Holding / Source
##.##.#### **[untransmitted pilot]**	DV / 40

FRANK SIDEBOTTOM'S FANTASTIC SHED SHOW

A Chameleon TV production for Yorkshire Television. Transmission details are for the Yorkshire Television region. Duration: 25 minutes.

Main regular credit(s):   Executive producers Sarah Doole and Allen Jewhurst; produced and directed by Dave Behrens.

Main regular cast: Chris Sievey (Frank Sidebottom), Caroline Aherne (Mrs Merton), Martin Sievey (Alfonse Allegro), Mark Radcliffe (Emmo Lake), London Beat.

	Holding / Source
11.01.1992	1" / 1"

With No guest cast.

FRANK SKINNER'S OPINIONATED

An Avalon Productions production for BBC 2. Transmission details are for BBC 2. Duration: 30 minutes.

Main regular cast: Frank Skinner (Host).

	Holding / Source
##.##.#### **[untransmitted pilot]**	HD/DB / HDC

FRANKIE HOWERD: UP THE BEEB

A BBC production for BBC 1. Untransmitted. Duration: 28 minutes.

Written by Barry Cryer and Neil Shand; designed by Chris Seagers; production team Terry Pettigrew and Helen Post; produced and directed by Geoff Miles. Frankie Howerd.

	VT Number	Holding / Source
##.##.####	LLV J380H/72	DB / 1"

Frankie Howerd introduces clips from his three 'Up the...' films and recounts amusing stories pretending the clips are showing us how his ancestors behaved. Recorded 19.2.1987. This was the third version made and the only version that was kept.

FREDDI

An Arbie Production production for BBC 4. made in association with Talkback Thames. Untransmitted. Duration: 29 minutes.

Created by Sacha Alexander and Mark Staheli; written by Sacha Alexander and Mark Staheli; script supervisor Hayley Boyd; script assistant Rob Brydon; art directors Mark Everett and Peter Stammers; designed by Rosy Thomas; associate producer Guy Davidson; executive producers Simon Lupton, Rob Brydon, Duncan Hayes and Miles Ross; head of production Beatrice Gay; line producer Kathy Nettleship; produced and directed by Alex Kavallierou.

Sacha Alexander (Freddi), Charity Wakefield (Yasmin), Susannah Wise (Kristiana), Daniel Copeland (Martin), Rory McCann (Mr Thompson), Rob Brydon (Salenko), David Skinner (Cousin Illy), David Sterne [as David Stern] (Uncle Stephen), Richard Li (Bell Boy), Paul Moody (Car Salesman), Tom Knight (Peter Jones's Friend), Simon McCoy (Newsreader), Peter Jones (Himself).

	Production No	VT Number	Holding / Source
##.##.#### **[untransmitted pilot]**	L1192	370716	DB / DBSWF

Recorded 2008.

FREEDOM OF EXPRESSION

A BBC production. Untransmitted.

Pilot about film censorship.

Produced by Tony Whitby.

Holding / Source

##.##.#### [untransmitted pilot]

J /

Shot on 17th March 1967. It may have been funded by the Arts department or Current Affairs. Only stills survive and they are reproduced in this book.

FREEZING

A BBC production. made in association with 39 Steps Ltd. Transmission details are for Various BBC Channels. Duration: 30 minutes.

Main regular credit(s):   Written by James Wood; production executive Sarah Hitchcock; produced by Kenton Allen and Simon Curtis; directed by Simon Curtis.

Main regular cast: Hugh Bonneville (Matt), Lucinda Raikes (Gloria), Ben Miles (Stephen Marshall), Tom Riley (Dave Beethoven), Elizabeth McGovern (Elizabeth), Martin Savage (O'Rourke), Tom Hollander (Leon), Richard E. Grant (Richard), Joely Richardson (Rachel), Andrew Garfield (Kit).

Commissioned by BBC 4. Transmission details are for BBC 4.

Holding / Source

28.02.2007

DB / DBSWF

An actress and her publisher husband wonder where their next jobs will come from.

Script supervisor Judy Gayton.

With Martha Howe-Douglas (P.A.), Alan Yentob (Alan).

FRESH FIELDS

Alternative/Working Title(s): FRESH START

A Thames Television production. Transmission details are for the Central region. Duration: 25 minutes.

Main regular credit(s):   Written by John Chapman; produced and directed by Peter Frazer-Jones.

Main regular cast: Julia McKenzie (Hester Fields), Anton Rodgers (William Fields).

SERIES 1

Main regular cast: With Ann Beach (Sonia Barratt), Fanny Rowe (Nancy Penrose).

Holding / Source

07.03.1984   **Dish Of The Day**

1" / 1"

Designed by Philip Blowers.

With Debby Cumming (Emma), Jackie Lye.

See also: FRENCH FIELDS*

FRIDAY NIGHT PROJECT

A Princess Productions production for Channel 4. Transmission details are for Channel 4. Duration: 50 minutes.

Performer(s):   With Jimmy Carr (Host), Rob Rouse (Host), Sharon Horgan (Host), Lucy Montgomery (Roving Reporter).

Holding / Source

##.##.#### [untransmitted pilot]

DB / DBSW

With Gordon Ramsay (Guest Host), Razorlight.

See also: SUNDAY NIGHT PROJECT*

FRIDAY NIGHT'S ALL WRIGHT

An LWT production. Transmission details are for the London Weekend Television region. Duration varies - see below for details.

Main regular credit(s):   Produced by Ric Blaxill.

Main regular performer(s): Ian Wright (Host).

Holding / Source

23.01.1998

DB / DBSW

Duration: 51 minutes.

Directed by John L. Spencer.

With Pete Tong, Jo Guest, Ray Tizzard, All Saints, Nicole Appleton, Natalie Appleton, Melanie Blatt, Shaznay Lewis, Lennox Lewis, 'Prince' Naseem Hamed, Lionel Richie, Mark Bright, Dion Dublin, Tina Hobley, Dominic Johnson.

FROM GLEN TO GLEN

An Ulster Television production. Transmission details are for the Ulster Televison region. Duration: 25 minutes.

Main regular credit(s):   Music adviser Brian O'Donnell; produced and directed by Andrew Crockart.

Holding / Source

02.11.1964

J / 40

FROST ON SATURDAY

An LWT production. Transmission details are for the ATV midlands region.

Main regular performer(s): David Frost (Host).

SERIES 1

Transmission details are for the London Weekend Television region.

	Holding / Source
##.##.#### **[untransmitted pilot]**	J / 62

FROST ON SUNDAY

Alternative/Working Title(s): FROST VARIETY

An LWT production. Transmission details are for the ATV midlands region.

Main regular performer(s): David Frost (Host).

SERIES 1

Transmission details are for the London Weekend Television region.

Main regular credit(s):   Directed by Michael Peacock.

	Holding / Source
##.##.#### **[untransmitted pilot]**	J / 40

THE FROST PROGRAMME

A Rediffusion Television production. Transmission details are for the Rediffusion Television region.

Main regular credit(s):   Presented by David Frost; theme music by George Martin.

	Holding / Source
##.##.#### **[untransmitted pilot]**	J /

Directed by Ian Fordyce.

Recorded 07.09.1966.

THE FROST REPORT

A BBC production for BBC 1. Transmission details are for BBC 1. Duration varies - see below for details.

Main regular cast: David Frost (Host).

	Holding / Source
##.##.#### **Authority [untransmitted pilot]**	R1 /

Duration: 40 minutes.

Written by David Frost, John Cleese, Antony Jay, Peter Lewis, Peter Dobereiner, Keith Waterhouse and Willis Hall; additional material by Anthony Booth, Anthony Buffery, Graham Chapman, Barry Cryer, Terry Jones, John Law and Denis Norden.

With Ronnie Barker, Ronnie Corbett, John Cleese, Dilys Watling, Nicky Henson, Nicholas Smith, Tim Lehrer, Julie Felix.

See also: FROST'S WEEKLY*

FULL HOUSE

A Thames Television production. Transmission details are for the Central region. Duration: 25 minutes.

Two couples share the same house.

Main regular credit(s):   Created by Johnnie Mortimer and Brian Cooke; music by Harry Stoneham.

Main regular cast: Christopher Strauli (Paul Hatfield), Sabina Franklyn (Marsha Hatfield), Natalie Forbes (Diana), Brian Capron (Murray McCoy).

SERIES 1

	VT Number	Holding / Source
07.01.1985 **First Time Buyers**	30614	1" / 1"

Written by Johnnie Mortimer and Brian Cooke; designed by Colin Andrews; produced and directed by Mark Stuart.

With Diana King (Paul's Mother), Milton Johns, Mike Kemp, Elvis Payne.

FUNNY CUTS

Produced for E4 by a variety of companies (see details below). Transmission details are for E4. Duration: 10 minutes.

	Holding / Source
18.05.2006 **Tank Commander**	DB / DBSWF

A the Comedy Unit production.

Created by Greg McHugh and William Andrews; written by Greg McHugh and William Andrews; costume Carole K. Millar; make-up Gillian Turnbull; edited by Walter J. Grant; director of photography Edward Edwards; art director Joni Clark; production executive April Chamberlain; executive producer Colin Gilbert; production manager Elaine Campbell; produced by Rab Christie; directed by William Andrews.

With Greg McHugh (Gary), Leah Macrae (Jackso's Sister).

FUNNY FOR MONEY: Bob Monkhouse Meets Ben Elton

A BBC production for BBC 2. Transmission details are for BBC 2. Duration: 39 minutes.

Devised by Bob Monkhouse; music by Philip Pope; designed by Louise Jackson; assistant producer Karen Rosie; produced by Tom Webber; directed by John L. Spencer.

Bob Monkhouse (Presenter), Ben Elton.

	Production No	Holding / Source
08.11.1995	LLVT780W	DB-D3 / D3S

FUNNY HA HA

A Thames Television production. Transmission details are for the ATV midlands region. Duration: 25 minutes.

Produced by Ruth Boswell.

	VT Number	Holding / Source
24.05.1974 **Commander Badman**	9081	D3 / 2"

Written by Eric Idle; designed by David Ferris; directed by Darrol Blake.

With Aubrey Woods (Commander Badman), Henry Woolf (Vince), David Battley (Boy Wonder), Bridget Armstrong (Anthea), Roland Macleod (Sergeant Henderson), Martin Clarke (Footballer), John Moore (Man In Library), Terry Wale (A.M. Man).

31.05.1974 **Football Crazy**	9082	D3 / 2"

Written by John Esmonde and Bob Larbey; designed by Tony Borer; directed by Vic Hughes.

With Bob Todd (Arnold), Madge Hindle (Daphne), Liz Gebhardt (Carol), Mike Lucas (Terry), Joe Dunlop (Spadger), John Vyvyan (Edmeades), Sam Kydd (Dickie), William Lawford (Referee).

07.06.1974 **Don't Blame Us!**	9083	D3 / 2"

Designed by David Ferris; directed by Darrol Blake.

With Anne Cunningham, Roddy Maude-Roxby, David Wood, Barry Stanton, Elaine Stritch, Nigel Pegram.

14.06.1974 **Who's Afraid Of The Big Bad Bear?**	9084	D3 / 2"

Written by Adele Rose; designed by John Plant; directed by Leon Thau.

With Barbara Mitchell (Kate Carter), Harry Towb (Geoff Carter), Lynne Miller (Tess Carter), Jane West (Carrie Carter), Richard McVey (Steve Carter), Peter Daly (Joe).

21.06.1974 **The Molly Wopsy**	9085	D3 / 2"

It's wartime. Alan and Linda Musgrove have been evacuated to the small Oxfordshire village of Lewkner. Alan is staying with Mr. and Mrs. Bonnie, little Linda with Mrs. James. Searching for his sister, Alan meets Dinky Dunkley, the village terror, who convinces him that Mrs. James is a witch and will turn Linda into a white rabbit. Together, the two boys try to rescue the girl from this awful fate.

Mr. Smith, the author, is a 50-yearold worker at a Midlands car plant. This is his first play.

Written by Mr Smith; designed by John Plant; directed by Stan Woodward.

With Aubrey Morris (Police Constable Berry), Walter Gotell (Sergeant Needler), Tony Maiden (Dinky Dunkley), Julia Nelson (Mrs Bonnie), Ken Watson (Mr Bonnie), Josie Bradley (Mrs James), Claire Davenport (Mrs Thompson), Mario Renzullo (Alan Musgrove), Jane Powell (Linda Musgrove).

28.06.1974 **Me 'n' Meep**	9086	D3 / 2"

Written by John Kane; designed by John Plant; directed by Leon Thau.

With Jack Haig (Grandad), Roy Barraclough (Mr Tomlin), Alec Bregonzi (Mr Trench), Lesley Goddard (Cilla), Anthony McCaffrey (Barney), John Kane (Meep), Rodney Cardiff (Removal Man), Mark Sheridan (Removal Man).

See also: THE MOLLY WOPSIES*

THE FUZZ

A Thames Television production. Transmission details are for the ATV midlands region. Duration: 25 minutes.

Main regular credit(s):	Written by Willis Hall; designed by Robin Parker; produced and directed by Stuart Allen.
Main regular cast:	Michael Robbins (Detective Sergeant Marble), Nigel Lambert (Police Constable Cordwainer), Mike Savage (Police Constable Dickinson), Lynda Bellingham (Woman Police Constable Purvis), Colin Jeavons (Superintendent Allardyce).

	Holding / Source
08.09.1977 **[untitled]**	D3 / 2"

With Ena Cabayo (Doris), Harry Littlewood, Derek Deadman.

See also: THE CREZZ: A Flash Of Inspiration

THE FUZZ

GAFFER (RADIO)

A BBC production for BBC Radio 4. Transmission details are for BBC Radio 4. Duration: 30 minutes.

Written by Graham White; play production by Betty Davies.

Bryan Pringle (Fred Moffat, The Gaffer), Joyce Latham (Betty), Anthony Jackson (Harry), Brian Hewlett (Charlie), William Eedle (Brother Wagstaff), Henry Knowles (Baxter).

	Holding / Source
17.09.1977	J /

See also: THE GAFFER*

GAGGING FOR IT

An LWT production. Transmission details are for the London Weekend Television region. Duration: 25 minutes.

Created by Garry Bushell; executive producer Liam Hamilton; produced by Bob Massie; directed by Jonathan Glazier.

Garry Bushell (Host), Johnnie Casson, Pauline Daniels, Gary Marshall, Diane James, Andy Ford, Micky Pugh, Rikki Jay, Andy Leach, Al Benson, Mark Peters.

	Holding / Source
24.04.1998	DB / DBS

See also: GAGGING FOR IT*

GALAXY

A Mike Mansfield Television production for ITV. Untransmitted. Duration: 25 minutes.

The following pop videos are also used in the 25 minute edit:
> ABBA (Winner Takes it All video)
> David Bowie (Ashes to Ashes video).

Written by Barry Cryer and Ray Cameron; produced and directed by Mike Mansfield.

Kenny Everett (Presenter), Grace Jones, Mary Stavin, The Average White Band, E.L.O. (Electric Light Orchestra), Hot Chocolate, Catherine Howe, Peter Straker*, The Sweet*.

	Holding / Source
##.##.#### [untransmitted pilot]	UM / 2"

Rx 19/08/1980. Master held by Kaleidoscope, ex-John Henshall collection.

THE GALTON AND SIMPSON COMEDY

An LWT production. Transmission details are for the ATV midlands region. Duration: 25 minutes.

Written by Ray Galton and Alan Simpson; produced and directed by David Askey.

	Production No	Holding / Source
18.04.1969 **The Suit**	9L/00193	DB-R1 / 62

Alternative transmissions: LWT: 19.04.1969.

Designed by John Clarke.

With Leslie Phillips (Howard Butler), Jennie Linden (Penny), Frank Jarvis (Burglar), Bill Oddie (Jimmy), Jan Holden (Wife).

25.04.1969 **Friends In High Places**	9L/00194	DB / 62

Alternative transmissions: LWT: 26.04.1969.

Designed by Barbara Bates.

With Bob Monkhouse (George), Patricia Hayes (Joyce), Sally Geeson (Sandra), Christopher Timothy (Tony), Frank Williams (First Angel), Arthur English (Second Angel), Richard O'Sullivan (Third Angel), Fred McNaughton (George's Friend).

George Gosling is 58, fat, balding and miserable. He wishes he was young again, and his wish is granted.

02.05.1969 **Never Talk To Strangers**	9L/00196	DB / 62

Alternative transmissions: LWT: 03.05.1969.

With Harry H. Corbett (Basil), Rosemary Leach (Olive), Dorothy Frere (Landlady).

09.05.1969 **Don't Dilly Dally On The Way**	9L/00197	DB / 62

Alternative transmissions: LWT: 10.05.1969.

Designed by Barbara Bates.

With Jimmy Edwards (Arthur Croucher), Pat Coombs (Joyce Croucher), Jackie Piper (Avril), David Jason (Gordon), Charles Morgan (Father), Daphne Anderson (Mother).

16.05.1969 **Pity Poor Edie... Married To Him**	9L/00195	DB / 62

Alternative transmissions: LWT: 17.05.1969.

With Milo O'Shea (Alec Hentill), Gwendolyn Watts (Edie Hentill).

23.05.1969 **An Extra Bunch Of Daffodils**	9L/00282	DB / 62

Alternative transmissions: LWT: 24.05.1969.

Designed by John Clarke.

With Stratford Johns (Lawrence Warner), Patsy Rowlands (Mildred Evans), Ronald Govey (Barman), Howard Goorney (Pawnbroker).

THE GALTON AND SIMPSON PLAYHOUSE

A Yorkshire Television production. Transmission details are for the ATV midlands region. Duration: 25 minutes.

Written by Ray Galton and Alan Simpson; music by Ken Jones; associate producers Ray Galton and Alan Simpson; executive producer Duncan Wood.

	VT Number	Holding / Source

17.02.1977 Car Along The Pass — 1" / 2"

Designed by Colin Pigott; produced and directed by Vernon Lawrence.

With Anton Diffring (Heinz Streiber), Arthur Lowe (Henry Livingstone), Maggie Wright (Hilda), Mona Washbourne (Wife), Aubrey Morris, Freddie Earlle, André Maranne, Arnold Diamond, Harry Tardios, John Cazabon.

24.02.1977 Swap You One Of These For One Of These — VT Number 2872 — 1" / 2"

Designed by Andrew Drummond; produced and directed by Ronnie Baxter.

With Henry McGee (Mr Gresham), Richard Briers (Henry), Jan Waters (Sarah), Linda Hayden, Susie Baker, John Sharp, Peggyann Clifford, Michael O'Hagan, Penny Meredith, Geoffrey Davion, Lois Hantz, David Goodland, Nicola Rowley.

03.03.1977 Cheers — 1" / 2"

Designed by Colin Pigott; produced and directed by Vernon Lawrence.

With Charles Gray (Peter), Freddie Jones (Charles), Nicholas Courtney, Edwin Apps, Maria Charles, John Harvey, Pauline Peart.

10.03.1977 Naught For Thy Comfort — 1" / 2"

Designed by Colin Pigott; produced and directed by Ronnie Baxter.

With Roy Kinnear (Richard Burton), Alan Freeman (Voice Only), Fanny Carby (Linda), Robin Hunter, Robert Gillespie, David Rowlands, Claire Faulconbridge, Edward Kemp, Frank Gatliff, John Clive.

17.03.1977 Variations On A Theme — 1" / 2"

Designed by Andrew Drummond; produced and directed by Ronnie Baxter.

With John Bird, Frances de la Tour.

31.03.1977 I Tell You It's Burt Reynolds — VT Number 2874 — 1" / 2"

Designed by Howard Dawson; produced and directed by Ronnie Baxter.

With Leonard Rossiter (Jim), Patricia Hayes (Mrs Davis), Roy Barraclough (Harry), Ed Devereaux (Percy), Gillian Raine (Mrs Davis Junior), Kim Smith, Sally Watkins.

07.04.1977 Big Deal At York City — 1" / 2"

Designed by Colin Pigott; produced by Vernon Lawrence; directed by Len Lurcuck.

With Warren Mitchell (Albert), Gerald Flood, Lockwood West, Robert Dorning, Robin Parkinson, Alister Williamson, Edwin Brown.

GALTON AND SPEIGHT'S TEA LADIES

A BBC production for BBC 1. Transmission details are for BBC 1. Duration: 30 minutes.

Written by Ray Galton and Johnny Speight; lighting by John Farr; sound Larry Goodson; designed by Paul Allen; produced and directed by Dennis Main Wilson.

Mollie Sugden (Lil), Dandy Nichols (Vi), Patricia Hayes (Min), John Quayle (M P).

	Holding / Source
04.01.1979	DB-D3 / 2"

A series was commissioned but was cancelled some time after the 1979 general election as the change of goverment rendered the scripts out of date (the series was set in the House of Commons). A spokesman for the BBC claimed that only "one and a half scripts" had been delivered.

GAMBITS

A BBC production. Untransmitted.

	VT Number	Holding / Source
##.##.#### [untransmitted pilot]	16/P/18992	J /

Recorded 30th June 1964.

GAME FOR A LAUGH

An LWT production. made in association with Action Time / Little Joey Inc / Ralph Edwards Productions. Transmission details are for the Central region.

Main regular performer(s): Jeremy Beadle (Presenter).

SERIES 1

Transmission details are for the ATV/Central region. Duration: 40 minutes.

Main regular credit(s):   Designed by Pip Gardner; associate producer Brian Wesley; produced by Alan Boyd; film sequences directed by John Longley.

Main regular performer(s): With Matthew Kelly (Presenter), Sarah Kennedy (Presenter), Henry Kelly (Presenter).

	Holding / Source
##.##.#### [untransmitted pilot]	J / 2"

GASTANK

A Goldcrest production for Channel 4. Transmission details are for Channel 4. Usual duration: 52 minutes.

Main regular credit(s):   Designed by Bryce Walmsley; associate producer Ralph Tobert; produced by Paul Knight.

Main regular performer(s): Rick Wakeman (Host), Tony Ashton (Host).

	Holding / Source
##.##.#### [untransmitted pilot]	J / 1"

Directed by Philip Casson.

GAYLE'S WORLD

A tv21 production for Carlton UK. Transmission details are for the Central region. Duration: 25 minutes.

Main regular credit(s):   Created by Brenda Gilhooly.

Main regular performer(s): Brenda Gilhooly (Gayle Tuesday).

	Production No	Holding / Source
11.06.1996	CAR0896	D2 / D2S

Page three 'stunna' and rising media star GAYLE TUESDAY takes another step up the show-business ladder when she hosts her first television chat how. Gayle gives viewers a taste of the exciting worlds in which she is now moving and her new famous friends, watched over, as ever, by boyfriend Grant. Viewers will be given an exclusive behind the scenes report from the set of Gayle' first venture into film - a version of the life of Emily Bronte - with co-star SHEILA HANCOCK. RUSSELL GRANT is in the studio to help tackle viewer's emotional problems, while the studio audience is encouraged to join in the singing of Gayle's latest charity record 'Save the Donkey'.

Executive producer Dave Morley; produced by Pete Ward and Dave Morley; directed by Tom Poole.

With Russell Grant, Sheila Hancock, Anna Karen.

THE GENDER GAP

A BBC production for BBC 2. Transmission details are for BBC 2. Duration: 30 minutes.

Howard Hamilton may be an eminent barrister but he is an appalling husband. His first wife divorced him, his second walked out. Blithely unaware that he is the biggest male chauvinist of all time, he considers the fair sex is anything but fair.

Emma Maitland feels much the same way about men, but she needs a barrister - and a job.

Written by Richard Waring and Geraldine Murphy; designed by Stephan Paczai; produced and directed by Harold Snoad.

Francis Matthews (Howard Hamilton), Judy Parfitt (Emma Maitland), Helen Cherry (Louise), Lisa Maxwell (Alison Maitland), Gabrielle Daye (Mrs Bascombe), Heather Tobias (Olive), Victor Maddern (First Taxi Driver), Stuart Sherwin (Second Taxi Driver), Norman Bird (Charles), Ray Gatenby (Sydney), Cyd Hayman (Sarah Hollingsworth).

	Holding / Source
12.12.1985	DB / 1"

Recorded Autumn 1983.

GENERATION FAME

A BBC production for BBC 1. Transmission details are for BBC 1. Duration: 60 minutes.

A celebrity version of The Generation Game.

Programme associates Jon Magnusson and Rob Colley; script supervisor Tony Grech; music by Dan McGrath; associate producer Rob Billington; production executive Claire Bridgland; executive producer Martin Scott; series producer Victoria Ashbourne; produced by Kevin Mundye; directed by Nikki Parsons.

Graham Norton (Host), Davina McCall, Andrew McCall, Rupert Grint, Chris Grint, Kelly Holmes, Pamela Thomson, James Fleet, Stanley Parkinson, Johnny Vegas, Engelbert Humperdinck, Harry Hill, Double-D-Force, Jean-Christophe Novelli, John Hicks, Bruno Tonioli, Vanessa Leigh Hicks.

	Holding / Source
31.12.2005	DB / DBSW

(LARRY GRAYSON'S) GENERATION GAME

A BBC production for BBC 1. Transmission details are for BBC 1. Duration varies - see below for details.

Main regular performer(s): Larry Grayson (Host), Isla St. Clair (Hostess).

	Holding / Source
##.##.#### **[untransmitted pilot]**	DB-D3 / 2"

Initially Isla St Clair was only hired for make the pilot. Other hostesses were being considered if she failed the screen test.

(BRUCE FORSYTH AND) THE GENERATION GAME

A BBC production for BBC 1. Transmission details are for BBC 1. Usual duration: 50 minutes.

"A lawn mower, a set of chef's knives, a basket of fruit, a set of towels, a cuddly toy!" The list seemed endless, but it wasn't. And pity the poor assistant floor manager picking each item up, and putting it on the conveyor belt.

It was, of course, the end of another show of The Generation Game. You may think the format of The Generation Game was evident in its title – different generations of a family competing to win prizes. But no, every quiz show uses that generic concept. If you want to make a new series of The Generation now, you would approach the show's format owners and pay them money for only one consideration – the right to use a conveyor belt to display the prizes. Indeed, the world of copyright is a funny world!

It was a gameshow that launched the Saturday evening careers of three high-profile entertainers – Bruce Forsyth (twice), Larry Grayson and Jim Davidson. All three were well-known entertainers in their own right, but The Gen Game rocketed them to superstar status.

In Brucie terms it was a quiet lull in his career (his Yorkshire TV 1969 series had quietly died) and Bruce was doing guest appearances on different LE shows. Then he was offered The Gen Game, and never looked back. For Larry Grayson it was a blatant poaching of an ITV star to come to the BBC, and Jim Davidson we will discuss in part 3 of this article.

The Gen Game saw members of different families compete through a series of challenges. They were marked and given points. The challenges were diverse – cake making, flower arranging, spelling, and in later rounds appearing in pantomime sketches or dancing with morris dancers. The range of guests from season to season were very diverse - Arthur Negus, Ralph Reader, Larry Ogles, Michael Connick and Josephine Knight were on a typical show. Non-celebrity guests would be represented by Ivor Spencer or Lieutenant Andrew Linsley and divers from HMS Daedalus; or The King's Squad, Royal Marines and Headington Quarry Handbell Ringers. Diverse indeed!

Launching in Autumn 1971, Bruce Forsyth was assisted by Anthea Redfern, later to become his wife. The series did many specials – May 1972 saw The Gen Game mingling with Miss United Kingdom, Christmas Day specials abounded with guests such as Joe Brown, Roy Castle, Leslie Crowther, Jimmy Edwards, Kenny Lynch, Cardew Robinson, Eric Sykes, Amanda Barrie, Melvyn Hayes, Madeline Smith and The Rupert Christmas Show all aided and arranged by Ronnie Hazlehurst and his Orchestra. Ronnie wrote the catchy theme tune as well.

The show weathered a few ups and downs along the way. In October 1974 Anthea was away from the screen and Jenny-Lee Wright was the stand-in hostess. In November 1976 there was a repeat of a 1973 edition due to Bruce's illness, introduced by Anthea Redfern and Arthur Weston. In October 1977 Jenny Lee-Wright returned, because Anthea was away having a baby! And in November 1977 an edition starring The Brother Lees was blacked out after 39 minutes due to industrial action.

When Bruce left to pursue other projects with ITV, the BBC quickly moved Larry Grayson and his new hostess, Isla St. Clair, into the job.

Main regular credit(s):   Theme music by Ronnie Hazlehurst.

Main regular performer(s): Bruce Forsyth (Presenter), Anthea Redfern.

SERIES 1

Duration: 45 minutes.

Main regular performer(s): With Anthea Redfern (Hostess), Ronnie Hazlehurst and his Orchestra.

	Holding / Source
02.10.1971 [re-edited pilot]	R1 / 2"

Programme associates Denis Gifford and Tony Hawes; designed by Andy Dimond.

A pilot was shot and deemed a reasonable success. The first episode proper, however, was felt to be overlong and slow. The pilot was re-edited and transmitted in its place and now survives.

See also: (BRUCE FORSYTH'S) GENERATION GAME* / GENERATION GAME: NOW AND THEN*

GENIUS

A BBC Productions production for BBC 2. Transmission details are for BBC 2. Usual duration: 29 minutes.

Main regular credit(s):   Created by Ali Crockatt and David Scott.

Main regular performer(s): Dave Gorman (Host).

	Holding / Source
##.##.#### [untransmitted pilot]	DB / DBSW

With Stephen Mangan (Guest Genius).

GENTLEMEN IN RETIREMENT

A V-C Productions production for BBC. Untransmitted. Duration: 30 minutes.

Produced by Dennis Vance and Howard Connell.

	Holding / Source
##.##.####	J / B3

GENTLEMEN NEVER TELL

An Ulster Television production. Transmission details are for the Ulster Televison region.

Leila Webster.

	Holding / Source
03.04.1992	1" / 1"

Comedy pilot.

GEORGE AND BERNARD SHAW

Commissioned by BBC 1. Transmission details are for BBC 1. Duration: 30 minutes.

Written by John Finnemore.

Robert Lindsay (George), Richard Griffiths (Bernard).

	Holding / Source
##.##.#### [untransmitted 2011 pilot]	HD/DB / HD/DB

GEORGE MIKES' EVENING CLASSES

An Associated-Rediffusion production. Untransmitted.

Written by George Mikes; directed by Rollo Gamble.

George Mikes (Himself), Deryck Guyler (Various Roles), Robert Nicholls (Various Roles).

	Holding / Source
##.##.#### **Manners**	

Recorded 14.07.1960.

GEORGIE FAME

A BBC Manchester production for BBC 2. Transmission details are for BBC 2. Duration: 45 minutes.

In concert at the Royal Exchange Theatre, Manchester.

Sound Tony Worthington; designed by Paul Laugier; produced by Peter Ridsdale Scott; directed by Mike Stephens.

Georgie Fame, Annie Ross.

	Holding / Source
15.12.1981	DB-D3 / 2"

GET ON A BIKE

A BBC production. Untransmitted. Duration: 29 minutes.

Written by Bill MacIlwraith; costume John Peacock and Lisa Benjamin; make-up Shaunna Harrison; music by Jack Point; designed by Ray London and John O'Hara; production manager Janet Bone; produced and directed by Roger Race.

Jill Kerman (Sally), Gaye Brown (Heather), Robert McBain (Jeff), Michael Osborne (Charles), Michael Stainton (Security Guard), Daniel Hill (Harold).

	Holding / Source
##.##.####	DB / 2"

1980s pilot echoing Norman Tebbit's famous words.

GET RICH QUICK

A BBC Variety production for BBC 1. Never intended for transmission.Duration: 30 minutes.

Designed by Richard Dupré; production manager Charles Garland; produced by Tony Wolfe; directed by David Taylor.

Chris Tarrant (Host), Peter Dixon (Voice Over).

	Production No	Holding / Source
##.##.#### [untransmitted pilot]	1/LEGA450K	DB-D3 / D3S

Recorded 08.08.1995.

GET THE DRIFT

A BBC Manchester production for BBC 2. Transmission details are for BBC 2. Duration: 30 minutes.

	Holding / Source
15.01.1971	J / 2"

Produced by Alfred Bradley; directed by Nick Hunter.

With Henry Livings, Alex Glasgow, Fivepenny Piece, Bernard Cribbins.

See also: CRIBBINS--LIVINGS & CO.* / THE NORTHERN DRIFT*

GET THIS!

A Southern Television production. Transmission details are for the ATV midlands region. Duration: 25 minutes.

SERIES 1

Main regular credit(s):	Music by Jonathan Xavier Coudrille; designed by Greg Lawson; produced and directed by Dave Heather.
Main regular cast:	With Kenny Lynch (Presenter), Harry Fowler (Presenter), Bob Danvers-Walker (Presenter).

	Holding / Source
##.##.#### [untransmitted pilot]	J / 2"

Made in early 1971. It is unclear if Bob Danvers-Walker was in the pilot.

GFI

A Gosh!/inimitable Production production for Link Licensing Ltd. Untransmitted. Duration: 24 minutes.

Script editor Tony Barwick; music by Dave Stewart; executive producers Gerry Anderson and Adam J. Shaw; produced by Bob McKie.

Paul Carrington (Voice of James Gee), Dave Wade (Voice of Wungee), Denise Bryer (Voice of Tugee), Ben Stevens (Voice of Argent), Gary Martin (Voices of D'Or And George Washington).

	Holding / Source
##.##.#### **Warming Warning**	DV / 1"

Written by Tony Barwick; directed by Phil Littler.

Made circa 1991/1992. Animated in Russia but cancelled when it ran into financial problems.

GHOST SQUAD

Produced for ATV by a variety of companies (see details below). Transmission details are for the ABC midlands region. Duration: 50 minutes.

Main regular credit(s):   Inspired by the book by John Gosling.

Made in association with Rank.

	Holding / Source
##.##.#### **[untransmitted pilot]**	J / B3

A foreign president needs protecting.

Written by Lindsay Galloway; based on a script by Lawrence Galaway; story editor Lewis Greifer; associate producer Frank Green; executive producer Connery Chappell; directed by Robert Lynn.

With Donald Wolfit (Sir Andrew Wilson), William Sylvester (Brett), Hazel Court (Jackie).

Scheduled to be made in July 1960. Went into production at Pinewood on 15th August 1960.

See also: G.S.5*

THE GIDDY GAME SHOW

A Yorkshire Television production. Transmission details are for the Central region.

SERIES 1

Main regular credit(s):   Produced and directed by Joy Whitby.

Main regular cast: With Bernard Bresslaw (Gorilla), Bill Fraser.

	VT Number	Holding / Source
##.##.#### **[untransmitted pilot]**	C014	1" / 1"

Duration: 11 minutes.

GIMME 5

A Tyne Tees Television production. Transmission details are for the Central region.

SERIES 1

Main regular cast: With Nobby The Sheep (Host), Jenny Powell (Host), Lewis Macleod (Host).

	Production No	Holding / Source
##.##.#### **[untransmitted pilot]**	T/0036/0001	J / D3S

Duration: 104 minutes.

With Simon Buckley, Matthew Davies, Neil Armstrong, Karina Brian, Ryan Barkatiki, Richard Evans, Paul Moore, Catlow Family, Nick Brownlee, Martin Duffy, Mike Hayley, Della.

A GIRL CALLED FRIDAY

A Tyne Tees Television production. Transmission details are for the Tyne Tees region. Duration: 25 minutes.

Main regular credit(s):   Produced and directed by George Adams.

Main regular performer(s): Friday Brown.

	Holding / Source
12.01.1968	

GIRLS ABOUT TOWN

An ITV Various production. Transmission details are for the ATV midlands region. Duration: 25 minutes.

Main regular credit(s):   Written by Adele Rose; produced by Shaun O'Riordan.

Main regular cast: Denise Coffey (Brenda Liversedge), Julie Stevens (Rosemary Pilgrim), Robin Parkinson (George Pilgrim), Peter Baldwin (Harold Liversedge).

A Thames Television production.

	Holding / Source
02.10.1969	J / 2"

A Thames Television production.

Ladies! Are you feeling run down, neglected and unwanted? If you fall into any of these categories you'll enjoy watching how two housewives, Rosemary and Sylvia, try to solve the seven-year-itch problem when they get involved with an Elegant Escorts Agency.

Designed by Tony Borer; produced and directed by Ronnie Baxter.

With Anna Quayle (Rosemary), Barbara Mullaney (Sylvia), John Clive, Aubrey Morris, Steve Plytas, Frederick Schiller, Joe Ritchie, Maria O'Brien.

GIRLS ON TOP

Alternative/Working Title(s): 4 F'S TO SHARE

A Witzend production for Central. Transmission details are for the Central region. Duration: 25 minutes.

Main regular credit(s):   Written by Ruby Wax, Dawn French and Jennifer Saunders; executive producer Allan McKeown; produced by Paul Jackson.

Main regular cast: Dawn French (Amanda), Jennifer Saunders (Jennifer), Ruby Wax (Shelley).

		Holding / Sourco
##.##.#### [untransmitted pilot]		J / 2"

Four girls sharing a flat in London.

Produced by Tony Charles; directed by Baz Taylor.

With Tracey Ullman.

THE GIST

A BBC production for BBC 4. Transmission details are for BBC 4. Duration: 30 minutes.

Written by John Morton; executive producer Myfanwy Moore; produced by Paul Schlesinger; directed by John Morton.

Emma Fielding (Harriet Gould), Robert Webb (Paul Ashdown), Amelia Bullmore, Edward De Souza, Billy Carter, Julian Bloach, Roy Strong, Mike Leigh, Janet Street-Porter, Jonathan Meades, Paul Morley.

	Holding / Source
02.03.2002	DB / DBSWF

Alternative transmissions: BBC 2: 02.03.2002.

GIVE US A CLUE

A Thames Television production. Transmission details are for the Central region. Duration: 25 minutes.

Main regular credit(s):   Devised by Juliet Grimm and Vince Powell.

Main regular performer(s): Lionel Blair (Team Captain).

	VT Number	Holding / Source
##.##.#### [untransmitted pilot]	18757	DB / 2"
##.##.#### [untransmitted second pilot]	18758	DB / 2"

GIVE YOUR MATE A BREAK

A Granada production. Transmission details are for the Central region. Duration: 51 minutes.

Produced by Richard Woolfe; directed by Tony Prescott.

John Leslie (Presenter).

	Production No	Holding / Source
29.08.1998	P2854/1	DB / DBS

THE GLAMOUR GIRLS

A Granada production. Transmission details are for the ATV/Central region. Duration: 25 minutes.

Main regular credit(s):   Written by David Nobbs; produced by John G. Temple.

	Production No	Holding / Source
##.##.#### [untransmitted pilot]	P989/DR	J / 2"

Designed by Taff Batley; directed by Gordon Flemyng.

With Una McLean (Magda Garstang), Martyn Hesford (Brian), Holly De Jong (Debbie Wilkinson), Victoria Burgoyne (Veronica Haslett), James Warrior (Mr Meredith), Archie Tew (Howard), Anthony Schaeffer (Tom).

Recorded 09.05.1979.

THE GLEN DHU FACTOR

A Scottish Television production. Transmission details are for the Scottish Television region.

Series set on the shores of Loch Lomond, concerning the revitalisation of a country estate when a new manager arrives.

Main regular credit(s):   Written by Don Houghton; produced and directed by Bryan Izzard.

Main regular cast: Edith Macarthur, John Cairney, Vivien Heilbron, Bill Henderson.

	Holding / Source
##.##.#### [first pilot]	J / 2"
##.##.#### [second pilot]	J / 2"

Recorded May 1979. This series was later renamed High Road, Low Road and eventually was re-made and transmitted as Take the High Road.

See also: TAKE THE HIGH ROAD*

GO GIRL

An Action Plus production for HTV. Untransmitted. Duration: 27 minutes.

Music directed by Wayne Bickerton; music composed by Wayne Bickerton and Tony Waddington; director of photography David Holmes; co-produced by Kenneth F. Rowles; directed by Steven Collins and Kenneth F. Rowles.

Luan Peters (Carol), Susan Shifrin (Jackie), Françoise Pascal (Martine), Simon Brent (Adam), George Margo (Rick), Walter Randall (Juan), Leena Skoog.

	Holding / Source
##.##.#### Give Me A Ring Sometime	C1 / C1

Overseas location work was completed for six episodes before problems with the production caused HTV to pull the funding. Only one episode was completed.

THE GOGGLIES

A Bristol Films production. Untransmitted.

Written by Martin Shuttleworth; from an idea by Diana Morrsom; music by Ernst Naser; designed by Corinna Gray; produced by Boyce De Roemer; directed by Martin Shuttleworth.

Martina Mayne (Narrator), Charlotte Black (Child On Farm), Tamsin De Roemer (Child On Farm), Emma Shuttleworth (Child On Farm), Benedict Shuttleworth (Gogglie), Alison Lloyd (Gogglie), Claire Hull (Gogglie), Geoffry Fry (Gogglie), Anthony Edwards (Gogglie).

	Holding / Source
##.##.#### **[untransmitted pilot]**	B1|n / B1

A pilot episode intended to be shown to buyers of material for children's television. A spoken introduction explains that aspects of the script and designs for the programme are based upon the ideas of children, and that it is envisaged as a thirty-nine part series. The Gogglies, a metallic robot race, attempt to fly to Venus in their space ship for a picnic, get lost and end up in the sky above England. A convoluted series of accidents in the craft results in two baby Gogglies abandoning ship and parachuting down in the Cotswolds, to the surprise of three children below.

GOING FOR GOLD

A Reg Grundy Productions production for BBC 1. Transmission details are for BBC 1. Duration: 25 minutes.

General knowledge quiz.

Main regular performer(s): Henry Kelly (Presenter).

SERIES 2

Main regular credit(s):   Executive producer Michael Whyte; directed by Steve Chilver.

	Holding / Source
##.##.#### **[untransmitted pilot]**	DB / 1"

GOLD TOP

A Central production. Untransmitted.

Directed by Derrick Goodwin.

	Holding / Source
##.##.#### **[untransmitted pilot]**	J / 1"

Recorded December 1985.

THE GOLDEN PATHWAY

Alternative/Working Title(s): MAYFAIR THEATRE

A BBC production. Untransmitted. Duration: 60 minutes.

Written by John Harding and John Burrows; make-up Maureen Winslade; designed by Rodney Ford; play production by Gareth Gwenlan.

John Harding, John Burrows, Maggie McCarthy, Mark Wing-Davey.

	Production No	Holding / Source
##.##.#### **[untransmitted pilot]**	1154/2643	DB / 2"

Recorded 29.8.1974.

From the Mayfair Theatre, London. Stage play about post-war Britain adapted for television.

GOLDMASTER

A Thames Television production for UK Gold. Transmission details are for UK Gold. Duration: 25 minutes.

Main regular credit(s):   Consultants Christopher Perry, Richard Down and Simon Coward; designed by Richard McManan-Smith; executive producer John Fisher; produced by David N. Mason; directed by Mike Catherwood.

Main regular performer(s): Mike Read (Presenter).

	Holding / Source
##.##.#### **[untransmitted pilot]**	DV / DBS

With Christopher Perry, Richard McManan-Smith.

Held by Chris Perry.

THE GONG SHOW

A Southern Television production. Untransmitted. Duration: 53 minutes.

Each of the ten acts — some are funny because they are not that good — gets a minimum of forty-five seconds. If the panel likes them, they are allowed to go on and finish their act. The ones who complete the act are marked. The act with the highest mark is the winner. Gary Martin won the pilot.

Created by Chuck Barris and Chris Beard; programme associate Hilary Tipping; additional material by Barry Cryer; music directed by Laurie Holloway; designed by John Dilly; associate producer David Arden; executive producer Terry Henebery; produced and directed by Mike Mansfield.

Frankie Howerd (Host), Russell Harty (Judge), Diana Dors (Judge), Madeline Smith (Judge), Bella Emberg, Caroline Munro, Gary Martin, Gertrude Shilling, Barry Dawson, Vice Versa, Roy Howley, Valerie Braithwaite, Pat Roe, Linda Millington, Charlie Lea.

	VT Number	Holding / Source
##.##.#### **[untransmitted pilot]**	1222	UM / 2"

Television Today - 18/08/1977 :

MIKE MANSFIELD has just finished producing and directing The Gong Show for Southern, a one-off which it is hoped will become a series. The show is described as a sort of talent show with a difference and is based on a format seen in America.

Southern has no transmission date yet either for local showing or networking.

Interestingly, a couple of adverts were placed in December that year asking for acts to apply for an audition for the show - with the address to write to being that of Mike Mansfield Enterprises Ltd, but there don't appear to be any further references to it after that in the paper.

GOOD AFTERNOON

A Thames Television production. Transmission details are for the Thames Television region. Duration: 25 minutes.

Untransmitted.

	VT Number	Holding / Source
##.##.#### [untransmitted consumer pilot]	8016	DB / 2"

Designed by Nevil Dickin; executive producer Ian Martin; produced by Diana Potter; directed by Joe Boyer.

With Allan Hargreaves (Presenter), Carol Binsted (Presenter).

Recorded 13.07.1973.

See also: AFTER NOON PLUS*

THE GOOD DOCTOR

Alternative/Working Title(s): LE FLAIR DU PETIT DOCTEUR

A HTV West production for Hamster. Transmission details are for Unknown. Duration: 52 minutes.

Adapted by Bob Baker; based on a story by Georges Simenon; produced and directed by Sebastian Robinson.

Alain Sachs (Dollant), Pauline Lafont (Anna), Norman Bowler (Jack Ridley), Dave King (Goddard), Sherrie Eugene (Juliet), Stephen Boxer, Valentina Vargas.

	Holding / Source
##.##.####	1" / 1"

The Doctor comes over to England with his assistant to visit an English cousin. During his stay a murder is committed and the doctor, whose hobby is detective work, investigates.

Made as a one-off in the UK, this was one of six editions in a French television series made by Hamster. It seems as though the intention was that this would be shown in the UK as a pilot. In post-production August 1985.

GOOD MORNING CAMPUS

An LWT production. Untransmitted. Duration: 25 minutes.

	VT Number	Holding / Source
##.##.#### [untransmitted pilot]	9L/99470	J / 2"

THE GOOD OLD DAYS

A BBC production for BBC 1. made in association with Stanley and Michael Joseph. Transmission details are for BBC 1. Duration varies - see below for details.

Main regular credit(s):　　　Devised by Barney Colehan; by arrangement with Stanley & Michael Joseph; produced by Barney Colehan.

A BBC production. Transmission details are for BBC/BBC1.

	Holding / Source
20.07.1953	J / Live

Duration: 50 minutes.

Music directed by Alyn Ainsworth; directed by Derek Burrell-Davis.

With Don Gemmell (Chairman), Eric Williams and Mary Harkness, Bill Wareham, Joe King, Pop, White and Stagger, Margery Manners, Geoffrey Hibbert, Joan Sterndale Bennett, Pamile Can-Can Dancers.

See also: GOODBYE TO THE GOOD OLD DAYS*

THE GOON SHOW

A Thames Television production. Transmission details are for the ATV midlands region. Duration: 25 minutes.

Written by Spike Milligan; designed by Harry Clark; produced by Peter Eton; directed by Joe McGrath.

Spike Milligan, Harry Secombe, Peter Sellers, John Cleese, Christine Pryor [as Christine Prior], John Hamilton, Alan Clare.

	VT Number	Holding / Source
08.08.1968 **Tales Of Men's Shirts**	94970	DB-1-C1 / 2"

See also: IT'S A SQUARE WORLD / THE TELEGOONS*

GOTCHA!

Alternative/Working Title(s): GOTCHER

A BBC production. made in association with Lyle McCabe Productions. Untransmitted. Duration: 50 minutes.

Additional material by Jeremy Beadle; music directed by Ronnie Hazlehurst; designed by Roger Cann; production team Mark Lyons, Marie O'Shaunessy, Steve Morris and Yvonne Robinson; production manager Geoff Posner; produced and directed by Michael Hurll.

Paul Daniels (Presenter), David Copperfield, Jeremy Beadle, Jack Scott, Pamela Stephenson, Fiona Richmond, John Conteh, Andrew Sachs.

	Production No	Holding / Source
##.##.#### [untransmitted 1980 pilot]	LLV_C475T/72	DB / 1"

THE GRAHAM NORTON SHOW

A So Television production for Various BBC Channels. Transmission details are for Various BBC Channels. Duration varies - see below for details.

Main regular credit(s):   Theme music by Trellis; series producer Jon Magnusson; directed by Steve Smith.

Main regular performer(s): Graham Norton (Host).

SERIES 1

Transmission details are for BBC 2. Duration: 30 minutes.

	Holding / Source
##.##.#### **[untransmitted pilot]**	DB / DBSW

With Sarah Beeny, Sandi Toksvig.

See also: GRAHAM NORTON UNCUT*

GRANDAD

A BBC production for BBC 1. Transmission details are for BBC 1. Duration: 25 minutes.

Main regular credit(s):   Devised by Clive Dunn; written by Bob Block; produced and directed by Jeremy Swan.

Main regular cast: Clive Dunn (Charlie Quick, billed as Grandad).

SERIES 1

	Holding / Source
##.##.#### **[untransmitted episode - may be pilot]**	DB-D3 / 2"

Music by Roy Civil; designed by Chris Edwards; executive producer Anna Home.

With Maurice Thorogood (Digby Rigby), Colin Rix (Sergeant Stone), Geoffrey Russell (Henry Watkins), Jane Waddell (Mildred), John Cunningham (Donald Charlesworth), Daniel Chasin (Mark).

See also: THE ADVENTURES OF CHARLIE QUICK*

GRANNY'S KITCHEN

A Yorkshire Television production. Transmission details are for the ATV midlands region. Duration: 8 minutes.

Cookery series for children.

Main regular cast: Dorothy Sleightholme (Presenter).

	Holding / Source
##.##.#### **[untransmitted pilot]**	1" / 2"

Produced and directed by Joy Whitby.

Recorded November 1976.

GREASE MONKEY

A BBC production. Untransmitted.

	Holding / Source
##.##.#### **[untransmitted pilot]**	DB / DBSW

GREAT NEWS

A BBC production for BBC 1. Transmission details are for BBC 1. Duration: 31 minutes.

Created by John Morton; written by John Morton; script supervisor Teresa Powick; music by Crunch; art director Nick Harding; designed by Les Stephenson; assistant producer Lucy Armitage; production executive Jez Nightingale; executive producer Jon Plowman; production managers Jane White and Justine Randle; produced by Paul Schlesinger; directed by John Morton.

Kevin R. McNally (Alastair), Laura Solon (Fi), Tim Preece (Brian), Daisy Haggard (Emma), Daniel Mays (Steve), Lucy Briers (Marion), Steve Oram (Police Constable Andy Fleming), Neil McCaul (Simon Hawkins), Sarah Hadland (Jackie), Jordan Long (Man In Office), Lizzie Roper (Woman In Office).

	Production No	Holding / Source
##.##.#### **[untransmitted pilot]**	ENC A008P/01	DB / DBSW

Recorded 2006.

GREEN

A Granada production for BBC 3. Transmission details are for BBC 3. Duration: 30 minutes.

Comedy pilot about three single friends living in Manchester.

Written by Eamonn O'Neill, James O'Neill and Martin Shea; script supervisor Kendall Anderson-Müt; script editor Alison Gordon; production executive Gary Connelly; executive producer Saurabh Kakkar; head of production Marigo Kehoe; produced by Simon Lupton; directed by Alex Hardcastle.

Lyndsey Marshall, Aidan McArdle, Craig Parkinson, Loo Brealey, James D'Arcy.

	Holding / Source
19.02.2007	DB / DBSWF

GRIFFINS

A TVS production. Untransmitted. Duration: 25 minutes.

New soap opera set in a health farm. Griffins is a fashionable health hotel owned by the Chetwyn family.

Main regular credit(s):   Designed by Zandra Rhodes and Murray Arbeid; produced by David Pick.

Main regular cast: Claire Oberman, Debbie Arnold, Simon Oates, Lucy Aston, Timothy Bentinck, Kirsten Hughes, Celia Montague.

	Holding / Source
##.##.#### **[pilot Episode 1]**	1" / 1"

THE GRIMLEYS

A Granada production for ITV 1. Transmission details are for the Central region. Duration varies - see below for details.

Main regular credit(s):   Executive producer Andy Harries.

	Production No	Holding / Source
05.07.1997	1/2387/0001	DB / DBS

Duration: 50 minutes.

"Jericho Council Estate, Dudley, 1975: there were only two sounds that mattered - the Bay City Rollers and the roar of Shane Titley's Vauxhall Viva."

The story revolves round young Gordon Grimley's dreams of getting off with his new English teacher and going to university. However, most enjoyable of all - apart from Planer's Wayne Slobstyle performance as Gordon's gross dad and Dee's macho posturing as his sadistic PE teacher - are seventies references. Who could fail to raise a nostalgic smile at the memory of butterscotch- flavoured
Angel Delight or Lynsey de Paul singing Sugar Me?

Written by Jed Mercurio; produced by Spencer Campbell; directed by Declan Lowney.

With Nigel Planer, Barbara Keogh, James Bradshaw, Ryan Cartwright, Jan Ravens, Corrieann Fletcher, Paul Angelis, Samantha Janus, Noddy Holder, Woody Clements, Jack Dee, James Richard.

GROOVE

An LWT production. Untransmitted. Duration: 25 minutes.

	VT Number	Holding / Source
##.##.#### [untransmitted pilot]	9L/00324	J / 2"

GRUNDY

A Thames Television production. Transmission details are for the ATV midlands region. Duration: 25 minutes.

Main regular credit(s):   Created by Ken Hoare.

Main regular cast: Harry H. Corbett (Leonard Grundy).

Holding / Source
J / 2"

##.##.#### Injured Party [untransmitted pilot]

Written by Ken Hoare.

GUESS WHO'S COMING TO DINNER?

A BBC production for BBC 1. Transmission details are for BBC 1. Duration: 30 minutes.

Main regular credit(s):   Devised by Hugh Rycroft.

Main regular performer(s): Anne Robinson (Host).

Holding / Source
DB / DBS

##.##.#### [untransmitted pilot]

Produced by Phil Bowker; directed by Geraldine Dowd.

With Ricky Gervais.

Recorded 2002.

H. G. WELLS' INVISIBLE MAN

An Official Films production for ITP. made in association with ITC. Transmission details are for the ABC midlands region. Duration: 25 minutes.

Main regular credit(s):   Devised by Larry White; music by Sydney John Kay; production supervised by Aida Young; produced by Ralph Smart.

Main regular cast: Tim Turner (Peter Brady aka The Invisible Man).

Holding / Source

##.##.#### **The Invisible Man [untransmitted pilot]**   DV / B3

Alt. Title(s): *Secret Experiment*

Duration: 26 minutes.

Written by Doreen Montgomery and Ralph Smart; produced and directed by Ralph Smart.

With Robert Beatty (Peter Brady aka The Invisible Man), Lisa Daniely (Diane Brady), Deborah Watling (Sally), Willoughby Goddard, Brian Rawlinson.

Television Today in February 1959 reports that Ralph Smart also made pilots for Robin Hood, The Buccaneers, Sir Lancelot and William Tell. Kaleidoscope has information about The Buccaneers pilot, but has no details about the other three.

Holding / Source

13.06.1959 **Secret Experiment**   DB / B3

Written by Michael Connor and Michael Cramoy; directed by Pennington Richards.

With Lisa Daniely (Diane Brady), Deborah Watling (Sally), Ernest Clark (Sir Charles Anderson), Lloyd Lamble, Bruce Seton, Michael Goodliffe.

According to ITP paperwork, episodes 1-4 must be transmitted first.

H.M.S. PARADISE

A Rediffusion Television production. Transmission details are for the ATV midlands region. Duration: 25 minutes.

Main regular credit(s):   Music by Malcolm Lockyer.

Holding / Source

##.##.#### **[untransmitted pilot]**   J / 40

With Richard Caldicot (Turvey), Frank Thornton (Fairweather), Robin Hunter (Pouter), Ronald Radd (Banyard), Angus Lennie (Murdoch), Jill Curzon (Amanda), Cameron Hall (Admiral), Robert Perceval (Trickett), Lionel Wheeler (Guard).

Recorded 03.01.64.

HAFFERTEE HAMSTER

An Ulster Television production. Untransmitted.

Holding / Source

##.##.#### **(investor Showreel)**   UM /

Proposed children's puppet series possibly for Channel 4 based on a then popular series of books. Investor reel produced seeking co-production partners. Note: Pilot features a a demonstration of the main Haffertee Hamster puppet and an outline of likely adventures.

HAPPILY EVER AFTER

Alternative/Working Title(s): THE DORA BRYAN SHOW

An ABC production. made in association with NBC. Transmission details are for the ABC midlands region. Duration: 25 minutes.

Main regular credit(s):   Written by James Kelly and Peter Miller; designed by Mark James; produced and directed by Philip Jones.

Main regular cast: Dora Bryan (Dora Morgan), Pete Murray (Doctor Peter Morgan), Bryan Coleman (Harry Watkins), Audrey Noble (Grace Watkins).

SERIES 1

Holding / Source

##.##.#### **[untransmitted pilot]**   J / 40

With Myrtle Reed.

According to Television Today (02.02.1961) this first series would run for 13 episodes.

HAPPY TOGETHER

A Chatsworth Television production for Carlton. Transmission details are for the Central region. Duration: 50 minutes.

Bellingham and Johnston play two old school friends who meet up again after a gap of 30 years. Bellingham is Teresa, a smart, sexy singleton (looking totally unlike the Oxo mum) while Johnston is mousy Val, who has never moved out of their home town of Crewe and has "turned into her mum". Then there's Val's husband Doug, who also knewTeresa at school. His life is so humdrum that he thinks an unexpected weekend in a B&B in Rhyl is the height of rash behaviour while a sofa that will last "until we die" is
something to treasure. It's fairly obvious from the outset that Val envies Teresa her sophisticated, carefree lifestyle. And it will come as no surprise that Teresa eventually admits
she rather envies Val her comfortable routine and family life.

Written by Sue Teddern; executive producers Malcolm Heyworth and Nick Symons; produced by Jen Samson; directed by David Wheatley.

Sue Johnston (Val), Lynda Bellingham (Teresa), Bill Paterson (Doug), Gavin Abbott (Roy), Charlotte Roach (Clare), Tom Cameron, Bridget Turner, Sally Bretton.

Holding / Source

01.01.2002   DB / V1SW

HARBEN'S HAPPENING

An ABC production. Transmission details are for the ABC midlands region. Duration: 25 minutes.

Designed by Roger King; produced and directed by Margery Baker.

Philip Harben.

		Holding / Source
24.09.1966		J / 40

THE HARBOUR

A Mersey TV production for TVS. Untransmitted.

A pilot drama set in a fishing harbour. It started with titles over shots of a fisherman leaving the harbour but then went to interiors with dialogue.

Executive producer Phil Redmond.

	Holding / Source
##.##.#### [untransmitted pilot]	J / 1"

Made circa 1989/1990.

HARDEE'S HALF HOUR

A Noel Gay Television production for Channel 4. Untransmitted. Duration: 24 minutes.

Malcolm Hardee.

	Holding / Source
##.##.#### [untransmitted pilot]	J / 1"

HARDWARE

A Thames Television production for ITV 1. Transmission details are for the Central region. Duration: 25 minutes.

Main regular credit(s):   Written by Simon Nye; produced by Margot Gavan Duffy.

Main regular cast: Martin Freeman (Mike), Peter Serafinowicz (Kenny).

	Holding / Source
##.##.#### Finger [untransmitted pilot]	DB / DBS

A Thames Television production.

Script supervisor Julie Church-Benns; designed by Dennis De Groot; line producer Sue Howells; directed by Martin Dennis.

With Emily Woof (Anne), Ken Morley (Rex), Ryan Cartwright (Steve), Steven Alvey (Timid Customer), Peter Heppelthwaite (Builder), Emma Ferguson (Nurse), Gary Sefton (Odd Patient).

Made in 2002.

SERIES 1

Main regular cast: With Susan Earl (Anne), Ken Morley (Rex), Ryan Cartwright (Steve), Ella Kenion (Julie).

	Holding / Source
13.04.2003 Finger	DB / DBSW

Script supervisors Julie Church-Benns and Diane Taylor; music by Richard Attree; art director Sally Gray; designed by Dennis De Groot; line producers Sue Howells and Kathy Nettleship; directed by Martin Dennis and Ben Kellett.

With Steven Alvey, Peter Heppelthwaite, Emma Ferguson, Gary Sefton.

This episode is scenes from the pilot with new footage featuring Susan Earl replacing Emily Woof, hence the two sets of end credits.

HARDWICKE HOUSE

A Central production. Transmission details are for the Central region.

Main regular credit(s):   Written by Richard Hall and Simon Wright; costume Val Thomas; make-up Dianne Joyce; music by Peter Brewis; lighting director John Watt; sound supervisor John Bain; camera operated by Don Perrin; designed by Bryan Holgate; produced by Paula Burdon; directed by John Stroud.

Main regular cast: Roy Kinnear (Mr Wickham), Pam Ferris (Ms Crabbe), Tony Haygarth (Mr Savage), Duncan Preston (Moose Magnusson), Gavin Richards (Dick Flashman), Granville Saxton (Mr Fowl), Roger Sloman (Mr Mackintosh), Nick Wilton (Peter Philpott), Kevin Allen (Slasher Bates), Chris Pitt (Junior), Stephen Arnold, Dylan Champion, Sean George, Ladene Hall, Michael Hutchinson, Sally Johnson, Pui Fan Lee, Phillip Moore, Christiana Norris, Mark O'Connell, Leon Snelgrove.

	Production No	VT Number	Holding / Source
24.02.1987 The Visit	6685	6685/86	DB / 1"

Duration: 50 minutes.

With Deborah Norton (Mrs Van Der Git), Nigel Pegram (Mr Van Der Git), Liz Fraser (Agnes), Paul Spurrier (Spotty), Mickey O'Donoughue (Ernie), Christopher Driscoll (Stan), Pat Doyle (Terry), Cindy Day (Donna), Mark Monero (Leroy), Paul Darlow (John), Courtney Roper-Knight (Smutts Van Der Git), Clive Curtis (Teacher), Annabelle Barker, Faye Maguire, Leslie Mantock, Joachim Shotter, Justine Thornton, Jean Turner, Stuart Wattam.

THE HARRINGHAM HARKER

A BBC production for BBC 2. Transmission details are for BBC 2. Duration: 30 minutes.

Written by Alex Lowe, Tracy-Ann Oberman, Chris Pavlo and Kim Wall; executive producer Jon Plowman; produced by Jon Rolph; directed by David Kerr.

Alex Lowe (Peter Hallam), Tracy-Ann Oberman (Deirdre Portland), Chris Pavlo (Nick Parris), Kim Wall (Gordon Knowles), Craig Giovanelli (Roberto).

	Holding / Source
13.01.2003	DB /

HARRY HILL'S TV BURP

An Avalon Productions production for ITV 1. Transmission details are for the Central region. Duration: 25 minutes.

Main regular credit(s):   Written by Harry Hill.

Main regular cast: Harry Hill (Host).

	Holding / Source
	DB / DBSW

22.12.2001

Additional material by Andrew Collins, Paul Hawksbee and Iain Pattinson; research Jo Envori and Margaret Gordon; script supervisor Nikki Dowbiggin; costume Leah Archer; make-up Jane Walker; music by Steve Brown; edited by Mark Sangster; lighting director Rob Kitzmann [credited as Rob Kitzman]; titles by Be Animation; programme consultant Mark Tinkler; designed by Harry Banks; executive producers Richard Allen-Turner and Jon Thoday; head of production Lee Tucker; line producer Michele Lonergan; produced by Patricia McGowan; directed by Peter Orton.

With Bruce Jones, Simon Day, Alan Halsall, Barry Howard, Jennifer Jamoo, Sally Lindoay, Dave Thompson, Catherine Gee.

See also: COMIC RELIEF - THE BIG ONE*

HAVE I GOT NEWS FOR YOU

A Hat Trick production for BBC. Transmission details are for Various BBC Channels. Duration varies - see below for details.

Main regular credit(s):   Theme music by Big George; titles by Triffic Films.

Main regular performer(s): Ian Hislop (Team Captain).

	Production No	Holding / Source
##.##.#### **John Lloyd's Newsround [untransmitted pilot]**	LDFF257A	DB / 1"

Duration: 27 minutes.

Presented by John Lloyd; programme associate Harry Thompson; designed by Graeme Story; executive producer Denise O'Donoghue; production manager Carrie Fletcher; produced by Jimmy Mulville; directed by Chris Bould.

With Simon Hoggart, Paul Merton, Ian Hislop, Jaci Stephen.

HAVE I GOT YOU... WHERE YOU WANT ME?

A Granada production. Transmission details are for the ATV midlands region. Duration: 25 minutes.

Main regular credit(s):   Written by Philip Harland and Paul Harris; music by Anthony Isaac; designed by Roy Graham; produced by Brian Armstrong; directed by Malcolm Taylor.

Main regular cast: Ian Lavender (Tom), Kim Braden (Valerie), John Alkin (Monty), Jeremy Sinden (Jason).

	Production No	Holding / Source
03.06.1981 **The Anniversary**	P1027/1	DB / 2"

With Joanne Zorian (Vera), Anthony Havering, Josephine Potter.

HEADLINE CHALLENGE

A BBC Birmingham production for BBC 1. Transmission details are for BBC 1 Midlands. Duration: 26 minutes.

Main regular credit(s):   Devised by Julia Mark; research Gillian Statham; produced by John McGonagle; directed by Jim Dumighan.

Main regular performer(s): David Coleman (Presenter).

	Holding / Source
##.##.#### **1976 Untransmitted pilot**	DB-D3 / 2"

With Denis Tuohy (Presenter), Angela Rippon, Anthony Grey, Brian Walden.

HEARTBURN HOTEL

A BBC production for BBC 1. Transmission details are for BBC 1. Duration: 30 minutes.

Main regular credit(s):   Written by John Sullivan and Steve Glover; executive producer John Sullivan; produced by Gareth Gwenlan.

Main regular cast: Tim Healy (Harry Springer), Clive Russell (Duggie Strachan), Peter Gunn (Simon Thorpe), Kim Wall (Baker).

	Holding / Source
##.##.#### **[untransmitted pilot]**	DB /

Recorded October 1995.

THE HEAVY MOB

A Thames Television production. Transmission details are for the ATV midlands region. Duration: 25 minutes.

Bungling George Fletcher goes into the crime-busting business...

Written by Terence Feely; designed by Norman Garwood; produced and directed by Les Chatfield.

Windsor Davies (Inspector George Fletcher), Robert Keegan (Sergeant Ryan), Bernard Stone (Joe Higgins), Michael Robbins (Bert Ramsden), Norman Mitchell (Benny Bates), Ronnie Brody (Lofty Harris), John Flanagan (Alan Parker), Toni Palmer (Sadie Higgins), Lynne Carol (Little Old Lady), Ray Marioni (Traffic Warden).

	VT Number	Holding / Source
24.03.1977	12824	D3 / 2"

HEIL HONEY, I'M HOME

A Noel Gay Television production for BSB Galaxy. Transmission details are for BSB Galaxy. Duration: 25 minutes.

Life with Adolf Hitler at home.

	Holding / Source
30.09.1990	DV / 1"

Written by Geoff Atkinson; research Mark Tinkler; costume Frances Haggett; make-up Sharon Walsh; theme music by Geoff Atkinson and Kate Robbins; theme music composed by Kate Robbins; edited by Graham Hutchings; lighting director Brian Pearce; titles by Kay Eglise; associate director Ivan Douglass; production designer James Dillon; executive producer Paul Jackson; production manager Jeremy Connor; produced by Harry Waterson; directed by Juliet May.

With Neil McCaul (Adolf), Gareth Marks (Arny), Caroline Gruber (Rosa), Denica Fairman (Eva), Patrick Cargill (Neville), Laura Brattan (Ruth).

HELLO... I'M JACK BERRY

A BBC production for BBC 2. Transmission details are for BBC 2. Duration: 30 minutes.

Written by Johnny Daukes; additional material by Patricia Keating; produced by Sandie Kirk; directed by Johnny Daukes and Robert Payton.

Johnny Daukes, Elizabeth Chadwick, Max Digby, Sara Drinkwater, Owen Evans, Anthony MacMurray, Penelope Solomon.

	Holding / Source
07.01.2002	DB /

HER MAJESTY'S PLEASURE

A Granada production. Transmission details are for the ATV midlands region. Duration: 25 minutes.

Main regular credit(s): Devised by Leslie Duxbury; music by Derek Hilton; produced by Peter Eckersley.

Main regular cast: John Sharp (Arnold Clissitt), Ken Jones (Leslie Mills), John Nettleton (Pongo Little), John Normington (Mushy Williams), Tommy Mann (Grizzy Bear Ryan).

SERIES 1

	Production No	Holding / Source
##.##.#### **[untransmitted pilot]**	P573/2	J /

Recorded 7th December 1967.

HERE COMES KANDY

A Pentagon Films production. Untransmitted.

Written by Peter Hayes; story by David White; music by Bruce Campbell and Robin Richmond; designed by Jack Whitehead; produced by Peter Hayes; directed by E. Smith-Morris.

Denise Bryer (Voices), Tessa Clarke (Voices), Tony Sympson (Voices).

	Holding / Source
##.##.#### **[untransmitted pilot]**	DB|n / C3

HEROIC FAILURES

A Witzend production for ATV. Untransmitted. Duration: 25 minutes.

Devised by Ian La Frenais and Dick Clement; written by Lance Percival; based on a book by Stephen Pile; executive producer Allan McKeown; produced by Tony Charles; directed by David Hillier.

Lance Percival (Presenter), Liza Goddard (Presenter), Sheila Steafel, David Quilter, Nigel Planer, Robert Putt, Janette Foggo.

	Holding / Source
##.##.#### **[untransmitted pilot]**	J / 2"

Recorded 23rd November 1980.

HEX

A Shine production for British Sky Broadcasting. made in association with Sony Pictures Television International. Transmission details are for Sky One. Duration varies - see below for details.

Main regular credit(s): Created by Julian Jones; theme music by Garbage; music by James Brett; executive producers Dean Hargrove, Sara Johnson and Elisabeth Murdoch.

DVD version:

Main regular credit(s): Written by Julian Murphy; executive producers Dean Hargrove, Sara Johnson and Elisabeth Murdoch; produced by Julian Murphy and Johnny Capps; directed by Brian Gant.

Main regular cast: With Christina Cole (Cassie), Joseph Morgan (Troy), Jemima Rooper (Thelma), Anna Wilson-Jones (Jo Watkins), Michael Fassbender (Azazeal).

	Holding / Source
##.##.#### **[pilot episode - classed as parts 1 & 2]**	DB / V1SW

Duration: 80 minutes.

With Christina Cole (Cassie), Jemima Rooper (Thelma), Jessica Oyelowo (Rachel McBain), Stephen Yardley (Thomas McBain), Davyd Harries (Sir Stephen), Ram John Holder (Voodoo Priest), Samuel Anderson (Julius), Amber Sainsbury (Roxanne), Zoë Tapper (Gemma), Jamie Davis (Leon), Theo Fraser Steele (Ben Halliday), Colin Salmon (David Tyrel), Kim McGarrity (Jenny), Holly Lumsden (Esther McBain), Julian Jones (Police Inspector), Lorraine Burroughs (Sinead), Alison Newman (Reverand George).

In 5.1 sound.

HEY BRIAN!

A Yorkshire Television production. Transmission details are for the ATV midlands region. Duration: 25 minutes.

Main regular cast: Brian Marshall.

	Holding / Source
	DB / 2"

29.08.1972

Written by Peter Dulay; directed by Keith Beckett.

With Gemma Craven, Design, Keith Harris, Josephine Antoszi, Freda Jeffries, Paul Luty.

HIBBERT AND LONG

An ITV Productions production for ITV 1. Untransmitted. Duration: 25 minutes.

Written by Sam Bain and Jesse Armstrong; executive producer Andy Harries.

	Holding / Source
##.##.####	J /

HI-DE-HI!

A BBC production for BBC 1. Transmission details are for BBC 1. Duration varies - see below for details.

You have been watching…. Simon Cadell, Paul Shane, Ruth Madoc, Jeffrey Holland, Su Pollard, Felix Bowness and Leslie Dwyer. Perhaps the names may be unfamiliar but the faces and characters of this repertory theatre of comedy are instantly recognisable.

The writers Jimmy Perry and David Croft based all their sitcoms on personal experience, and created such hits as Dad's Army and It Ain't Half Hot Mum. So it is perhaps surprising that the famous comedy writers were not automatically guaranteed a series for every new idea they had. In 1977 after the disastrous science-fiction sitcom Come Back Mrs Noah, the BBC were reluctant to commission a new Perry/Croft sitcom. Had the magic run out? Were Perry and Croft good writers of war-based sitcoms or could they broaden their talents?

On New Year's Day 1980 the BBC1 audience saw the pilot to a new sitcom set at Maplin's Holiday Camp. Some of the faces would go on to become instant TV superstars – Simon Cadell as Jeffrey Fairbrother, the University academic; Ted Bovis the loveable rogue; Spike Dixon the new camp comic and potty chalet maid Peggy who wanted to become a yellowcoat. But who remembers Wilf Green aka Marty Storm, the Bill Haley impersonator? Like all TV pilots it set up a potential series but worked as a good stand-alone comedy full of gentle touches like Ted telling Spike he was auditioning for a part in Florizel Street, a new Granada TV soap opera. Florizel Street was the working title for Coronation Street.

A series was commissioned and each episode unravelled another adventure of the yellowcoats, led by Gladys Pugh who lusted after Jeffrey, and tried to stop Ted and all his fiddles. Each episode ended with the familiar You Have Been Watching caption - a tradition that began with Dad's Army and continued on every Perry/Croft sitcom afterwards. Perry admitted later that Croft had the ability to write witty gags but he preferred plotting the episodes and writing character dialogue.

After four seasons Simon Cadell left and was replaced by David Griffin as Squadron Leader Clive Dempster, DFC. Clive was a charming ladies man and initially pursued Gladys until he was forced to announce his engagement to her. Eventually he realised that he did love her and the series ended with their marriage.

Cadell was the first to leave, but others followed. Leslie Dwyer, the drunken punch and judy man Mr Partridge, died and the character 'left to visit a relative'. Barry Howard resigned and Yvonne Stuart-Hargreaves was forced to find a new partner - Julian Dalrymple-Sykes played by Ben Aris. The writing was on the wall when Perry/Croft decided to write You Rang M'Lord and even the addition of Kenneth Connor playing Sammy was not enough to save the series from cancellation. In true Perry/Croft style the series had a proper ending as Maplins was closed by Joe Maplin and it became self-catering chalets.

Such was the popularity of Paul Shane, Jeffrey Holland and Su Pollard that they returned as regulars in You Rang M'Lord? and Oh Doctor Beeching to continue the great Perry/Croft tradition of period-set sitcoms.

Main regular credit(s):   Written by Jimmy Perry and David Croft; theme music by Jimmy Perry.

Main regular cast: Paul Shane (Ted Bovis), Ruth Madoc (Gladys Pugh), Jeffrey Holland (Spike Dixon), Felix Bowness (Fred Quilley), Su Pollard (Peggy Ollerenshaw), Nikki Kelly (Sylvia), Stan Ley (The Webb Twins), Bruce Ley (The Webb Twins), Chris Andrews (Gary).

	Holding / Source
	DB-D3 / 2"

01.01.1980 **Hey Diddle, Diddle**

Duration: 40 minutes.

The year: 1959. The place: Maplin's Holiday Camp. When the entertainment staff assemble for the new season they discover that a university professor is in charge.

Lighting by Peter Winn; sound Michael McCarthy; designed by Garry Freeman; produced and directed by David Croft.

With Simon Cadell (Jeffrey Fairbrother), Leslie Dwyer (Mr Partridge), Richard Cotton (Wilf Green Aka Marty Storm), Penny Irving (Mary), Rikki Howard (Betty), Chris Andrews (Gary), Joyce Grant (Mrs Fairbrother), Harry Markham (Camper), Josephine Antoszi (Camper), Marianne Tollast (Hilda).

See also: STARS REUNITED*

HIGH AND DRY

An LWT production. Untransmitted. Duration: 25 minutes.

	VT Number	Holding / Source
##.##.#### [untransmitted pilot]	9L/90717	J / 2"
##.##.#### [untransmitted pilot]	9L/90591	J / 2"

HIGH STREET BLUES

An LWT production. Transmission details are for the Central region. Duration: 25 minutes.

Main regular credit(s):   Written by Jimmy Perry and Robin Carr; executive producer Marcus Plantin; produced and directed by Robin Carr.

	Holding / Source
##.##.#### [untransmitted pilot]	1" / 1"

THE HIGHLAND QUEEN

A BBC production. Untransmitted. Duration: 29 minutes.

Written by Peter McDougall; music by Ronnie Hazlehurst; designed by Paul Allen; produced and directed by Bernard Thompson.

Billy Connolly (Joe), Kenneth Nelson (Jason), Russell Hunter (Naebrain), John White (Dunnichy Van Gogh), Bill Patterson (Scattercash), Michael Malone (The Boy), Chris Brown (Norseman), Freddie Earlle (Sammy), Peter Thornton (Silvester), George Tovey (Asa), Peter Davidson (Boatman), Nosher Powell (Big Willie), William Hootkins (American Voice), Raymond Boyd (On The Messdeck), Roy Pattison (On The Messdeck), Chris Sanders (On The Messdeck), Terry Duggan (On The Messdeck).

	Production No	VT Number	Holding / Source
##.##.#### 1978 Untransmitted pilot	1146/3261	VTC/6HT/B16329	DB / 2"

HIGHLIGHT: THE SINGING CINEMA

An Associated British Pathe production for Associated-Rediffusion. Transmission details are for Associated-Rediffusion.

Musical numbers from thirty five years of British films.

Dialogue directed by Denis Gifford; written by Denis Gifford; associate producer Lionel Hoare; executive producer Terry Ashwood; produced by Denis Gifford.

Pete Murray (Presenter).

	Holding / Source
##.##.#### [untransmitted pilot]	R1|n /

THE HIGHWAYMAN

Alternative/Working Title(s): STAND AND DELIVER!

A Sapphire Films production for ITC. Transmission details are for the ATV midlands region. Duration: 25 minutes.

Written by Waldo Salt; directed by Robert Day.

Louis Hayward (James Macdonald), Adrienne Corri (Lady Sylvia Marlow), Richard O'Sullivan (Luke), Sam Kydd (Jerry Badger), Peter Coke (Lord Harrington), Anne Blake (Mrs Badger), Thomas Heathcote (Willetts), Carl Bernard (Crouch), Jack May (Cowley), John Dearth (Somers), Michael Peake (Pendleton), Peter Retey (Fletcher), Stanley van Beers (Chief Judge).

	Holding / Source
14.06.1958 **The Chimney Sweep**	B3SEQ / B3
##.##.#### **The Indiscreet Time-Piece**	NR / NM
Written by Waldo Salt.	
##.##.#### **The Devil's Apprentice**	NR / NM
Written by Waldo Salt.	
##.##.#### **Stand And Deliver!**	NR / NM
##.##.#### **The Duel**	NR / NM

Only the opening titles exist. The second and subsequent episodes listed did not go beyond the script/outline stage, as far as we know.

Details acquired from an article in the TVT - issue 03.05.1957, Pages 28/29.

HILARY

A BBC production for BBC 2. Transmission details are for BBC 2. Duration: 30 minutes.

Main regular credit(s):   Written by Peter Robinson and Peter Vincent.

Main regular cast: Marti Caine (Hilary).

	Production No	Holding / Source
##.##.#### [untransmitted pilot]	LLCQ601R/71	DB / 2"

Costume Christine Rawlins; make-up Eileen Mair; music by Donald Fraser; designed by Pamela Lambooy; production manager Jo Austin; produced and directed by Alan J. W. Bell.

With Jack Smethurst, Carolyn Moody, Christopher Good, Philip Fox, Ray Jewers, Sandra Carrier, Jerry Harte, Percy Edwards.

	Holding / Source
10.12.1984	DB / 1"

There is no reason why Hilary's life should be particularly complicated. A divorcee with a 19-year-old son, she works as a researcher on a TV chat show. But somehow things just seem to happen to her.

Lighting by Nigel Wright; sound Alan Stokes; designed by Paul Allen; produced and directed by Harold Snoad.

With Jack Smethurst (Kim), Philip Madoc (George), Carolyn Moody (Lyn), Clinton Greyn (Angel Wonderlight), Sandra Carrier (Angela), Jerry Harte (Sam), Percy Edwards (Arthur), Philip Fox (Wesley).

HIT DANCIN'

A Thames Television production. Transmission details are for the Thames Television region. Duration: 25 minutes.

Street-alert dancers in trendy clothes.

Produced and directed by Keith Beckett.

	Holding / Source
20.08.1987	DB|n / 1"

HIT THE NOTE!

A BBC production for BBC 2. Transmission details are for BBC 2.

Main regular cast: Jonathan Cohen (Host).

Holding / Source
J / 2"

19.03.1977

Designed by Ken Ledsham; executive producer Cynthia Felgate; produced by Ann Reay; directed by Avril Price.

With Kim Goody, Maggie Henderson, Ian Caddy, The Co-Operation Choir.

HIT THE PITCH

A Thames Television production. Transmission details are for the Thames Television region. Duration: 25 minutes.

Written by Alan Whiting; designed by Anne Diamond; produced and directed by John Stroud.

Sam Smart (V-Neck), Vincenzo Nicoli (Michael), Peter Benson (Hector), Angela Catherall (Becky), Ailsa Fairley (Maria), Susannah Hitching (Karina), Stephen Tompkinson (Andy), Lavinia Bertram (Inspector), Sean Gilder (Samaritan).

Holding / Source
1" / 1"

11.12.1989

This pilot was only shown in the London area.

THE HITCH HIKERS GUIDE TO THE GALAXY

A BBC production for BBC 2. Transmission details are for BBC 2. Duration varies - see below for details.

Arthur Dent awakes one day to find the world is about to be demolished. Ford Prefect kidnaps him and takes him off the planet before it is destroyed.

Main regular credit(s):   Written by Douglas Adams; theme music by Bernie Leadon and Tim Souster; music by Paddy Kingsland; designed by Andrew Howe Davies; associate producer John Lloyd; produced and directed by Alan J. W. Bell.

Main regular cast: Peter Jones (Voice of the Book), Simon Jones (Arthur Dent), David Dixon (Ford Prefect).

Holding / Source
J / 2"

##.##.#### **[untransmitted pilot]**

Produced by John Lloyd.

Holding / Source
DB-D3 / 2"

05.01.1981 **Episode One**

Duration: 33 minutes.

With Martin Benson (Vogon Captain), Joe Melia, Steve Conway, Cleo Rocos, Andrew Mussell.

This episode was made several months before the series suggesting it was a second pilot.

HITLISTS

A Pearson Television production. Never intended for transmission. Duration varies - see below for details.

Holding / Source
DV /

##.##.#### **Promo**

Duration: 13 minutes.

DV /

##.##.#### **[untransmitted 1998 pilot]**

Duration: 49 minutes.

HOB Y DERI DANDO

A BBC Wales production. Transmission details are for BBC 1.

Duration: 25 minutes.

Holding / Source
DB-4W / 40

##.##.#### **[untransmitted pilot]**

Young people and their folk music. The 1968 editions had previously been shown on BBC 1 Wales and there are, almost certainly, further editions of this programme which were aired on BBC 1 Wales only.

See also: DERRY DANDO*

HOBSON'S CHOICE

An ATV production. Transmission details are for the ATV midlands region.

Main regular cast: Derek Hobson (Host).

Holding / Source

##.##.#### **[untransmitted pilot]**

Produced by Terry Johnston.

With Jackie Collins, Arthur Askey, Lord Lichfield, Bill Price MP.

Television Today [15.03.1979] reported that a pilot chat show had been recorded under the aegis of ATV's FORMAT V (q.v.) strand and would be broadcast on 12.04.1979.

However the broadcast does not seem to have occurred. Whether this is was one of the results of a number of schedule changes caused by the unexpected General Election which was called on 07.04.1979 we are unsure.

Equally confusing is the fact that the ATV tape logs of the time do not appear to list the pilot either under HOBSON'S CHOICE or under FORMAT V.

HOLD ON IT'S THE DAVE CLARK FIVE

A Big Five Films production. Transmission details are for the ATV midlands region. Duration: 32 minutes.

Written by Dave Clark; music composed by Dave Clark and Mike Smith; choreography by Ralph Talbot; produced and directed by Dave Clark.

The Dave Clark Five, Richard Chamberlain, Lulu, Rita Webb, Toni Palmer, Judith Furse, Terry Day, Joe Cornelius, Rube Martin, Dana Gillespie, Joyce Crossley, The Hold On Dancers.

	Holding / Source
31.08.1968	C3 / C3

Reported as being first of a series of six aimed at the international market. Filming apparently started on 29.01.68 at Pinewood Studios.

HOLDING THE FORT

An LWT production. Transmission details are for the ATV/Central region. Duration: 25 minutes.

The lives of Russell and Penny Milburn, a young couple with a baby, finds them in a quandary. If Russell moves from London with his employers, he'll be promoted — if he stays, he's redundant. But there's no way Penny will leave —so can Russell brew up a solution?

Main regular credit(s):   Created by Laurence Marks and Maurice Gran; music by Denis King.

Main regular cast: Peter Davison (Russell Milburn), Patricia Hodge (Penny Milburn), Matthew Kelly (Fitz).

	Holding / Source
##.##.#### [untransmitted Pilot - dummy run]	J / 2"

Written by Laurence Marks and Maurice Gran; produced and directed by Derrick Goodwin.

The pilot for Holding the Fort was due to be recorded on the day that the 1979 ITV strike started. Only a partial dummy run had been close circuit recorded and this was sent up to Michael Grade who authorised the series.

See also: RELATIVE STRANGERS*

'HOLIDAY CAMP PILOT'

An ABC production. Untransmitted. Duration: 40 minutes.

Directed by Ben Churchill.

Donald Churchill.

	Holding / Source
##.##.#### [untransmitted pilot]	J / 40

Television Today 07.03.1963 reported that a comedy pilot set in a holiday camp had been recorded.

HOME JAMES!

A Thames Television production. Transmission details are for the Central region. Duration: 25 minutes.

Main regular credit(s):   Created by Geoff McQueen.

Main regular cast: Jim Davidson (Jim London), George Sewell (Robert Palmer), Harry Towb (Henry Compton).

SERIES 1

Main regular credit(s):   Written by Geoff McQueen; produced by Anthony Parker.

	Holding / Source
##.##.#### [untransmitted pilot]	1" / 1"
01.07.1987 **Thinkin' On Your Feet**	1" / 1"

Designed by Peter Joyce; directed by Anthony Parker and Mark Stuart.

With Colin Farrell, David Hatton, Suzanne Church, Zoe Rutland, Diana Payan, Barry Killerby.

HOME TONIGHT

Alternative/Working Title(s): THE SUTTONS OF SOUTHPOOL

An Associated-Rediffusion production. Transmission details are for Associated-Rediffusion. Duration: 25 minutes.

Main regular credit(s):   Theme music by Laurie Johnson; produced by Ray Dicks.

Main regular cast: Andrew Laurence (George Sutton), Simon Prebble (Peter Sutton), Patricia Regan (Emma Sutton), David Hemmings (Paul Sutton), Patricia Brake (Dot Sutton).

Untransmitted Dummy Run

Main regular credit(s):   Based on an original story by Jimmy Hanley; script editor Jimmy Hanley; directed by Sheila Gregg.

Main regular cast: With Eric Phillips (Henry Sutton), John Downing (William Sutton).

	VT Number	Holding / Source
##.##.####	W718/137	J / 40

With Peggy Paige (Hilda Andrews), Richard Burnett (Leslie Nicholls), Caroline Mortimer (Tina Botelli), Malcolm Russell, Nicholas Grimshaw, Johnny Fry, Jackie Sawyer, Charles Gilbert.

##.##.####	W719/133	J / 40

With Hilda Campbell-Russell (Mrs Spindle), Peggy Paige (Hilda Andrews), Peter Stockbridge (Chalky White).

##.##.####	W720/92	J / 40

With Richard Burnett (Leslie Nicholls), Peter Stockbridge (Chalky White), Tom Macauley, Joanna Drew, Joan Clevedon.

##.##.####	W721/13	J / 40

With Hilda Campbell-Russell (Mrs Spindle), Peter Stockbridge (Chalky White), Caroline Mortimer (Tina Botelli).

##.##.####	W722/107	J / 40

With Caroline Mortimer (Tina Botelli), Jane Sothern, Pauline Shepherd, Richard Coe.

HOME VIDEO (YOU'VE BEEN FRAMED)

A Granada production. Untransmitted. Duration: 25 minutes.

This pilot was re-made with Jeremy Beadle and became "You've Been Framed".

Richard Madeley (Presenter).

	Production No	Holding / Source
##.##.#### [untransmitted pilot]	P1658	DV / 1"

Held by Kaleidoscope.

THE HONEYMOON'S OVER

A BBC production. Untransmitted. Duration: 30 minutes.

Written by Charlie Higson and Paul Whitehouse; music directed by Peter Brewis; theme music by Hackney Five-O; produced by Paul Whitehouse and Charlie Higson; directed by John Birkin.

Alex Lowe (Phil), Angela Clarke (Helen), Georgina Hale (Norma), Paul Whitehouse (Billy Whizz), Des McAleer (Skippy), Mark Williams (Martin), Jim Moir (Chris Bell), Jacqueline Defferary, Gabrielle Blunt, Sam Stockman, Leon Black.

	Holding / Source
##.##.#### [untransmitted pilot]	DB-D3 / D3S

Made c. 1994.

See also: THE SMELL OF REEVES AND MORTIMER*

HONG KONG HARBOUR

Commissioned by ITC. Not made.

Written by Joyce Bellack.

Reported as an ITC project in Television Today (28.04.1960).

HONGKONG

Alternative/Working Title(s): PASSPORT TO CANTON / PASSPORT TO CHINA

A Hammer Films production. Transmission details are for the Tyne Tees region. Duration: 60 minutes.

Written by Gordon Wellesley; music by Edwin Astley; associate producer Anthony Nelson Keys; produced and directed by Michael Carreras.

Richard Basehart (Don Benton), Lisa Gastoni (Lola Sanchez), Athene Seyler (Mao Tai Tai), Eric Pohlmann (Ivono Kong), Alan Gifford (Charles Orme), Bernard Cribbins (Pereira), Burt Kwouk (Jimmy), Hedger Wallace (Inspector Taylor), Marne Maitland (Han Po), Sorata Ra Fat (Hostess), Ronald Ing (Sentry), Zoreen Ismail (Swee Kim), Robert Lee (Chinese Officer), Paula Li Shiu (Girl Croupier), Milton Reid (Bodyguard), Yvonne Shima (Liong Ti), Gerry Lee Yen (Room Boy).

	Holding / Source
28.11.1967 **Visa To Canton**	C3 / C3

An additional ten minutes of content was shot so the TV pilot could be released as a film, if no one would buy the pilot. Filming began in June 1960, at Pinewood Studios using the set of 'Ferry to Hong Kong' and night shooting on Monkey Island on the Thames and at Bray Studios.

Released theatrically as 'Passport to China'. It only seems to have been shown on British television as a film, rather than a TV production.

HOPE AND KEEN'S CRAZY HOUSE

A BBC production for BBC 1. Transmission details are for BBC 1. Duration: 25 minutes.

Main regular credit(s):   Produced and directed by Paul Ciani.

Main regular cast: Hope and Keen.

	Holding / Source
20.08.1970 **Crazy House**	DB / 2"

Alternative transmissions: ATV: .

Written by Mike Craig and Lawrie Kinsley; additional material by Hope and Keen; music by Martin Goldstein and Ronnie McCrea.

With Colin Edwynn, John Poore, Caroline Deans, Butterscotch.

HORACE

A BBC production for BBC 2. Transmission details are for BBC 2. Duration: 90 minutes.

Written by Roy Minton; music by Almeida; designed by Colin Pigott; produced by Mark Shivas; directed by Alan Clarke.

Barry Jackson (Horace), Stephen Tantum (Gordon), Christine Hargreaves (Ivy), Talfryn Thomas (Dick), Hazel Coppen (Mrs Radford), James Mellor (Sidney), Patricia Lawrence (Miss Bowler), Robert Hartley (Mr Scrimshaw), Howard Goorney (Mr Frankel), Ken Parry (Whitsun), Caleigh Simmons (Brenda), Daphne Heard (Mrs Beal), Eric Francis (Customer), Pamela Miles (Waitress), Jeffrey Gardiner (Jeffries).

	Holding / Source
21.03.1972	C1 / C1

See also: HORACE*

HORNE A'PLENTY

An ABC/Thames production for Various ITV Companies. Transmission details are for Various ITV Companies. Duration: 25 minutes.

Main regular cast: Kenneth Horne, Ken Parry.

	Holding / Source
##.##.#### [first Untransmitted pilot]	J / 40

With Hugh Paddick, Gwendolyn Watts, Norman Chappell, Roddy Maude-Roxby, James Beck, Billy McComb.

Recorded October 1967.

HOT SEAT

An LWT production. Transmission details are for the London Weekend Television region.

	VT Number	Holding / Source
##.##.#### [untransmitted pilot]	9C/03477	J / 2"

THE HOTHOUSE

Produced for Tyne Tees Television by a variety of companies (see details below). made in association with Northern Films & Media / One NorthEast. Transmission details are for the Tyne Tees region. Duration varies - see below for details.

Holding / Source

12.08.2003 **The Dark Lantern - The Devil's Nightglass**   DB / DBSW

A Duchy Parade Films production. Duration: 23 minutes.

Hollywood superstar David Soul stars as the storyteller in a major animation project for television. He's been cast in the role of 'The Projectionist' in The Dark Lantern - which had its live action sequences filmed at Tyne Tees Television studios in Newcastle-upon-Tyne. The actor/singer who found fame with Starsky and Hutch agreed to the project after seeing the work of County Durham animators Robert and Jan Jefferson. The programme is produced by Peter M. Kershaw for Duchy Parade Films and the executive producers are Graeme Thompson and Tom Harvey. The half hour live-action/animation special is being screened by Tyne Tees at 10.30 p.m. on Tuesday 12 August as part of The Hothouse - a series of pilot projects co-financed by Tyne Tees Television and the screen agency Northern Film and Media with support from One NorthEast. The world of the mysterious projectionist was created in TTTV's Studio 5. David Soul is the only live character in the show which tells the story of a magical lantern which brings disturbing morality tales to life. Animators Robert & Jan Jefferson first worked with Peter Kershaw on the cinematic short Wilfred - which also mixed live action with animation to chronicle the death of the war poet Wilfred Owen. Tyne Tees Television's Controller of Programmes Graeme Thompson commented: 'This is a very dark and visceral tale of demons and loss of innocence which has its roots in the folklore of Northumbria. 'The casting of David Soul gives the project a real focus. He brings humour, authority and of course real box office star quality. 'Once the programme has been screened on ITV1 in the North East we will be looking to develop the project further for national and international markets.' Tom Harvey of Northern Film and Media said: 'The North East region has a wealth of animation talent and we hope this broadcast pilot will result in a long running animation series for the region.'

Executive producers Graeme Thompson and Tom Harvey; produced by Peter M. Kershaw; directed by Robert Jefferson.

With David Soul (The Projectionist).

This live-action/animation special had its live sequences filmed in Studio 5 at Tyne Tees.

HOW

Alternative/Working Title(s): KNOW HOW

A Southern Television production. Transmission details are for the Southern Television region. Duration: 25 minutes.

Holding / Source

22.03.1966   J / 40

With Jack Hargreaves (Presenter).

See also: PLAYBACK

HOW NOT TO LIVE YOUR LIFE

A Brown Eyed Boy Production production for BBC 3. Transmission details are for BBC 3. Duration: 30 minutes.

Main regular credit(s):	Written by Dan Clark.
Main regular cast:	Dan Clark (Dom).

Holding / Source

27.09.2007 **Home Sweet Home**   HD/DB / HD/DB

Alternative transmissions: BBC 2: 13.07.2009.

Script supervisor Rebecca Rycroft; script editor Drew Pearce; executive producer Simon Wilson; produced by Gary Reich and Dan Clark; directed by Gary Reich and Dan Clark.

With Arnab Chanda, Tim Key, Clare Keelan, Sally Bretton, Bruce MacKinnon, Buddy, Eliot Carroll, Isabel Fay, Rich Fulcher, Ben Goodman, Leila Hoffman, Alyssa Kyria, Dave Parton, Tom Price, John Rose.

HOW ODD! ODD ADVENTURES

A Moondream Films production. Untransmitted.

Written by George Evans; music by Joe & Co; assistant director Peter Darrell; produced by Mark Jones and David Barnes; directed by Martin Bower.

Holding / Source

##.##.#### [untransmitted pilot]   C1|n / C1

Pre-print production material only.

Pilot episode for a children's television series. A young alien creature takes off in his spaceship, leaving his family behind. He travels through an asteroid belt and lands on Earth, where he is discovered by two young boys. After a brief visit he returns to his spaceship and takes off once again into space.

HR: AN APPRAISAL

A BBC production for BBC 4. Transmission details are for BBC 4. Duration: 30 minutes.

A boss and his HR assistant find their jobs under threat after a disastrous performance review.

Written by Nigel Williams; executive producer Jon Plowman; produced by Christopher Morahan; directed by Justin Davies.

Jonathan Pryce (Peter), Nicholas Le Prevost (Sam).

Holding / Source

07.03.2007   DB / DBSWF

THE HUMAN JUNGLE

An Independent Artists production for ABC. made in association with Independent Artists. Transmission details are for the ABC midlands region. Duration: 50 minutes.

Main regular credit(s):   Theme music by Bernard Ebbinghouse and John Barry; produced by Julian Wintle and Leslie Parkyn.

Main regular cast: Herbert Lom (Doctor Roger Corder M.D., D.P.M.), Sally Smith (Jennifer Corder), Michael Johnson (Doctor Jimmy Davis), Mary Yeomans (Nancy Hamilton), Mary Steele (Jane Harris).

SERIES 1

Holding / Source

15.06.1963 **The Two Edged Sword**   B3 / B3

Postponed from 25.03.1963.

Written by Bill MacIlwraith; directed by Vernon Sewell.

With Susan Burnet, Pauline Yates, Beatrice Varley, Frederick Piper, Freda Bamford, Glynn Edwards, Roger Delgado, William Kendall.

THE HYPNOTIC WORLD OF PAUL MCKENNA

A Celador production for Carlton. Transmission details are for the Central region. Duration varies - see below for details.

Main regular performer(s): Paul McKenna (Host).

Holding / Source

12.04.1993   D2 / D2S

Duration: 50 minutes.

Top comedy hypnotist Paul McKenna.

Introduced by Eamonn Holmes; produced by Nic Phillips; directed by Paul Smith.

With Gloria Estefan, Bobby Womack, Lulu, Bob Holness, Linda Lusardi.

I FEEL FINE

A Granada production. Transmission details are for the Central region. Duration: 50 minutes.

All the acts were Liverpool-centred.

Main regular credit(s):   Designed by Nick King; executive producer John Hamp.

Main regular performer(s): Stan Boardman (Presenter), Mick Miller.

	Production No	Holding / Source
12.07.1986	P1334/1	1" / 1"

Directed by Tim Sullivan and Noel D. Greene.

With Faith Brown, Kate Robbins, Vicki Brown, David Harwood Smith, John Lord, Ringo Starr, Liverpool Ladies Barbershop Chorus, Eddie Flanagan, Terry Sylvester, The Kat Band, Pauline Daniels, Harry Black, Greg Rogers, Peter Goodwright, George Melly, John Chilton's Feetwarmers.

The inserts directed by Tim Sullivan recorded 4-5th March 1986.

I LOVE KEITH ALLEN

A Noel Gay Television production for BSB Galaxy. Transmission details are for BSB Galaxy. Duration: 45 minutes.

	Holding / Source
29.03.1990	DVSEQ / 1"

Presented by Keith Allen; written by Keith Allen; costume Frances Haggett and Pam Downe; make-up Wendy Freeman; theme music by The Backroom Boys; choreography by Jeff Thacker; edited by Graham Hutchings; lighting director Brian Pearce; designed by James Dillon; production team Ross Ciappessoni, Genevieve Robinson and Jeremy Skeet; associate producer Rory Sheehan; production manager Julian Scott; produced by Keith Stewart; directed by Tom Poole.

With Gary Beadle, Paul-Mark Elliott, Linda Henry, Kirkland Laing, Josie Lawrence, Steven O'Donnell.

25mins revised repeat survives as VHS off-air with Laurence Piper. Episode features a studio audience which suggests this was a pilot.

Laurence Piper is a private TV collector.

Shortened repeats followed, but they're so hard to ID from TV Month listings alone. A stretch of half hour episodes from 07/07/90 - 25/08/90 would be eight selected episodes (no idea on order), with four more broadcasts (possibly of the first eight?) on 08/09/90, 15/09/90, 21/09/90 and 28/09/90.

I SAW YOU

A Granada production for ITV 1. Transmission details are for the Central region. Duration: 50 minutes.

Written by David Nicholls; executive producers Christine Langan and Andy Harries; produced by Christine Langan; directed by Tom Vaughan.

Paul Rhys (Ben Walters), Fay Ripley (Grace Bingley).

	Holding / Source
22.05.2000	DB / V1SW

Ben is an inept loser who whinges so much when his girlfriend chucks him that even his long-suffering driving instructor just wants to give him the elbow. Fortunately for Ben, an optician whose idea of a romantic date is to give his girlfriend an eye-test, Grace, played by Fay Ripley from Cold Feet, could prove to be his saviour.

With Jeff Rawle (Frank), Lidija Zovkic (Angel), Alex Graham (Oscar Bingley), Caroline Carver (Zoe), Rachel Isaac (Francesca), Francesca Hunt (Janet), Adam James (Kevin), Jonathan Bond (Paul), Kate Byers (Mary), David Holdaway (Keith), Roger Sloman (Mr Frost), Michael Simkins (Doctor).

I THOUGHT YOU'D GONE

A Central production. Transmission details are for the Central region. Duration: 25 minutes.

A newly-retired insurance broker finds life problematic.

Main regular credit(s):   Written by Peter Jones and Kevin Laffan; designed by Michael Eve; produced by Shaun O'Riordan; directed by Paul Harrison.

Main regular cast: Peter Jones (Gerald), Pat Heywood (Alice), Ian Gelder (Tony), Rosalind Knight (Ruby Pugh).

	Production No	Holding / Source
##.##.#### [untransmitted pilot]	9353	J / 2"

Designed by Stanley Mills; produced and directed by Shaun O'Riordan.

Recorded 13th September 1982.

I WISH I'D SAID THAT

A Polo Productions production. Untransmitted. Duration: 24 minutes.

Written by Barry Cryer; music by John Patrick; designed by Anna Ridley; produced and directed by Paul Stewart Laing.

Dickie Henderson (Host), Kenneth Williams, Peter Goodwright, Johnny More, Karen Kay [as Karen Kaye], Lionel Murton.

	Holding / Source
##.##.#### Untransmitted pilot	DV / 1"

I.A.G.O.

A Rediffusion Television production. Untransmitted.

	Production No	Holding / Source
##.##.#### [untransmitted pilot]	ENT/47/19	J /

Originally scheduled for 15.12.1965.

With Georgie Fame and The Blue Flames, The Walker Brothers, Wilson Pickett, The Small Faces, Kiki Dee, Boz, The Breakaways.

Recorded 18.11 & 19.11.1965.

Material re-edited to become HERE COME THE POPS (q.v.).

IF I RULED THE WORLD

A Hat Trick production for BBC 2. Transmission details are for BBC 2. Duration: 30 minutes.

Main regular credit(s):   Devised by Richard Osman; music by Dave Hewson; titles by Richard Norley and Kate McNamara; production designer Jonathan Paul Green; executive producers Mary Bell and Jimmy Mulville; production manager Sarah McHarry; series producer Anne Marie Thorogood; produced by Richard Osman; directed by John F. D. Northover.

Main regular performer(s): Clive Anderson (Host), Graeme Garden (Team Captain), Jeremy Hardy (Team Captain).

SERIES 1

Main regular credit(s):   Associate producers Juliette Otterburn-Hall and Ruth Phillips.

	Holding / Source
##.##.#### **[untransmitted pilot]**	D3 / D3S

With Graeme Garden.

THE ILLUSTRATED WEDNESDAY REVUE

A Central production. Transmission details are for the Central region. Duration: 25 minutes.

A comedy revue which shows that just when you thought it was safe to turn on the television...

Written by Glen Cardno; designed by Giovanni Guarino; produced by Glen Cardno; directed by Shaun O'Riordan.

Glen Cardno.

	Production No	Holding / Source
15.02.1984	1861/82	1" / 1"

Recorded 7.4.1982 and re-mounted 7.11.1982.

I'M WITH STUPID

A BBC Manchester production for BBC 3. Transmission details are for BBC 3. Duration: 30 minutes.

Main regular credit(s):   Written by Daniel Peak; from an idea by Peter Keeley; script supervisor Sue Wild; story consultant Peter Keeley; script editor Paula Hines; theme music by The Wannadies; music by Dru Masters; production executive Claire Asbury; executive producer Kenton Allen; produced by Jon Mountague; directed by Christine Gernon.

Main regular cast: Mark Benton (Sheldon), Paul Henshall (Paul), Ruth Jones (Jean), Steve Edge (Sergeant Switchenback), Cherylee Houston (Dorothy), Belinda Everett (Police Constable Sarah Madden), Kevin Davids (Syd), Alan Martin (Graham).

	Holding / Source
21.03.2005 **[BBC New Talent Week]**	DB / DBSWF

A Granada production.

See also: BBC NEW TALENT WEEK

IMPRO

A BBC production. Untransmitted. Duration: 35 minutes.

Costume Tessa Philips; make-up Nicola Bellamy; designed by Eric Walmsley; produced by Bill Wilson; directed by Tony Newman.

Josie Lawrence, Steve Steen, Jim Sweeney, Pete Wear, John Dowie, Mac McDonald, Tony Robinson, Steve Brown, Scum of The Earth.

	Production No	Holding / Source
##.##.#### **[untransmitted 1989 pilot]**	LLVL904X	DB / 1"

IN LOVING MEMORY

A Yorkshire Television production. Transmission details are for the ATV/Central region. Duration: 25 minutes.

Oldshaw, 1929 - when you could have a night out at the Theatre Royal, a pint of ale in the interval, a hot pie on the way home - and still have change out of a shilling. You could also have an argument with a brewer's dray and end up as a client of Jeremiah Unsworth and Co., Undertakers and Monumental Masons... and be the subject of the most disastrous funeral in the long and noble history of undertaking.

Main regular credit(s):   Created by Dick Sharples; written by Dick Sharples; produced and directed by Ronnie Baxter.

Main regular cast: Thora Hird (Ivy Unsworth), Christopher Beeny (Billy Henshaw).

A Thames Television production. Transmission details are for the ATV midlands region.

	VT Number	Holding / Source
04.11.1969	1800	J / 2"

The scene: Oldshaw, Lancs., 1929- a time when the horse and cart still outnumbered the two-ton truck, when the tramcar clanged its way down cobbled streets and the gas mantle
reigned supreme. When Jeremiah Unsworth (Undertaker and Monumental Mason—Established 1881) was asked to handle
Oldhaw's biggest, most important funeral since Alderman Jackson fell into the canal. It was the begining of the greatest chapter of accidents in the history of
Undertaking.

Designed by Sylva Nadolny.

With Marjorie Rhodes (Ivy Unsworth), Harold Goodwin (Harold Henshaw), Edward Chapman (Jeremiah Unsworth), Rose Power (Miss Jenkinson).

SERIES 1

Transmission details are for the ATV midlands region.

Main regular credit(s):   Designed by Colin Pigott.

	VT Number	Holding / Source
21.05.1979	2946	1" / 2"

With Avis Bunnage (Amy Jenkinson), Freddie Jones, Paul Luty.

IN SUSPICIOUS CIRCUMSTANCES

A Granada production. Transmission details are for the Central region. Duration: 50 minutes.

Introduced by Edward Woodward; music by Matthew Scott.

Pilot

Duration: 51 minutes.

Main regular credit(s):   Produced by Sue Durkan; directed by Ian White.

	Production No	Holding / Source
03.06.1991 **Mrs Bravo Regrets**	1/1780/0001	D2 / V1

Written by Julian Roach.

With Rory Edwards (Charles Bravo), Kate Gartside (Florence Bravo), Anthony Schaeffer (Mr Harrison), Ted Richards (Doctor Gully), James Tomlinson (Sir William Gull), Gillian Cally (Mrs Cox), Richard Cole (Royes Bell).

	Production No	Holding / Source
03.06.1991 **No Smoke Without Fire**	1/1780/0001	D2 / V1

Written by Barry Woodward.

With Anthony Cairns (Peter Luckhurst), Olive Pendleton (Gwendoline Marshall), Tony Turner (Policeman), Keith Ladd (Policeman), Martin Reeve (Policeman).

	Production No	Holding / Source
03.06.1991 **The Jewel And The Magpie**	1/1780/0001	D2 / V1

Written by Glenn Chandler.

With Mark Spalding (Tony Maffia), David Ross (Stephen Jewell), Peter Armitage (Detective), Jeremy Pearce (Superintendent Drury), David Bond (Scarneck), Derrick Gilbert (Joe the Printer), Marcus Romer (Lan).

The total running time for each episode was fifty minutes. The length of each segment varied.

IN THE DARK

A BBC production. Untransmitted.

	Holding / Source
##.##.#### **[untransmitted pilot]**	DB / D3S

IN THE LION'S DEN

A Rapide Productions production for Channel 4. Transmission details are for Channel 4. Duration: 25 minutes.

Produced by Amanda Feldon; directed by Roger Thomas.

Pattie Coldwell (Presenter), George Gale.

	Holding / Source
23.09.1989	DB|n / 1"

Columnist George Gale is brought face to face with the targets of his forthright views about homosexuality and AIDS. Pattie Coldwell hosts a debate from the Edinburgh AIDS centre, where Gale is questioned by angry AIDS victims, their relatives, doctors and gay campaigners.

THE INBETWEENERS

A Bwark Production production for E4. made in association with Young Films. Transmission details are for E4. Duration: 25 minutes.

Main regular credit(s):   Written by Damon Beesley and Iain Morris; script editor Robert Popper; designed by Richard Drew; head of production Leo Martin; produced by Christopher Young.

Main regular cast: Simon Bird (Will), James Buckley (Jay), Blake Harrison (Neil), Joe Thomas (Simon).

SERIES 1

Main regular credit(s):   Script supervisor Angelica Pressello; executive producers Damon Beesley and Iain Morris; directed by Gordon Anderson.

Main regular cast: With Henry Lloyd-Hughes (Mark Donovan).

	Holding / Source
##.##.#### **Baggy Trousers [untransmitted pilot]**	DB / DBSWF

The cast were very different.

INMATES

A BBC production for BBC 2. Transmission details are for BBC 2. Duration: 30 minutes.

Written by Stuart Morris and Allan Sutherland; produced by Sue Bysh; directed by Sue Longstaff.

Robert Gillespie (The Director), Janet Henfrey (Mrs Prendergast), Roger Bryan (Barney), Nabil Shaban (Sparky), Jag Plah (Gobbo), Colum Convey (Nurse), Mik Scarlet (Wayne), Joan Hooley (Irma), Paddy Ward (Mr Allan).

	Holding / Source
20.07.1992 **Animal Crackers**	DB / 1"

INSIDE STORY

An ABC production. Transmission details are for the ABC midlands region. Duration: 50 minutes.

Main regular credit(s):   Based on an idea by G. R. Mitchell; story editor Ted Willis.

Main regular cast: Robert Brown (Jack Brooks), Mary Peach (Kathie Webb), Brian Phelan (Mike Steele).

	Holding / Source
28.02.1960 **A Touch Of Brimstone**	J / Live

Written by Ted Willis; designed by Voytek; directed by Dennis Vance.

With Edward Woodward (Stanislaw Krasinski), Jane Eccles (Miss Chalmers), Ronald Leigh-Hunt (George Paine), Sonia Fraser (Paula Krasinski), William Kendall (Mr Hartley), June Monkhouse (Mrs Paine), Annette Kerr (Mrs Hartley), Billy Milton (Nobby Clark), Margaret Courtenay (Doctor Edgard).

THE INSPECTOR PITT MYSTERIES

An Ardent Productions Ltd production for Yorkshire Television. made in association with Arts & Entertainment Network. Transmission details are for the Central region. Duration: 100 minutes.

Adapted by T. R. Bowen; based on the book by Anne Perry; executive producers Keith Richardson, Eben Foggitt and Delia Fine; produced by June Wyndham-Davies; directed by Sarah Hellings.

Eoin McCarthy (Inspector Pitt), Keeley Hawes (Charlotte Ellison), Peter Egan (Edward Ellison), John Castle (Reverend Prebble), Richard Lintern (Dominic Corde), Sheila Ruskin (Caroline Ellsion), Patsy Rowlands (Mrs Dunphy), Robert Reynolds (Doctor Hope), Judy Campbell (Grandmama), Sarah Woodward (Sarah Ellison), Katie Ryder Richardson (Emily), David Roper (Maddock), Hannah Spearritt (Lily), Anna Winslett (Dora), Janet Maw (Martha Prebble), Jack Tarlton (Detective Sergeant Webster), Amanda Elwes (Mrs Abernathy), Robert Swann (Superintendent Drummond), Oliver Montgomery (Lord Ashworth), Johnathon Newman (Jack Brody), Stuart Richman (Ferriby), Jessica Turner (Alice Barker), Rachel Heaton (Polly Roberts), Laura Cox (Big Jen), David Fleeshman (Renshaw), Alan Partington (Doctor), Alan Rothwell (Duty Sergeant), Mark Pepper (Constable Benn), Sally Adams (Tate), Benjamin James (Constable Benchley), Alan French (Constable Wetherby), Jessica Grace Bell (Child Singer), Helen Groom (Child Accompanist), Stuart Hall (Tenor).

	VT Number	Holding / Source
23.09.1998 **The Cater Street Hangman**	D982	DB / V1S

Prince Edward appeared on "Des O'Connor Tonight", tx: 18.09.98, to discuss the TV-film, which was made by his production company. Produced by Colin Fay, directed by Paul Kirrage. Thames, colour VT.

INTO INFINITY

A Gerry Anderson production for BBC 1. Transmission details are for BBC 1. Duration: 47 minutes.

Prototype spaceship Altlares accelerates from Earth's polluted
atmosphere to attain maximum speed 186,000 miles a second, as fast as light-on its unique family mission many millions of miles to another solar system. But fate is to take it much further into a new universe.

Written by Johnny Byrne; produced by Gerry Anderson; directed by Charles Crichton.

Brian Blessed (Doctor Tom Bowen), Joanna Dunham (Doctor Anna Bowen), Nick Tate (Captain Harry Masters), Katherine Levy (Jane Masters), Martin Lev (David Bowen), Don Fellows (Jim Forbes), Ed Bishop (Narrator / TV Announcer).

	Holding / Source
11.12.1976	DB / C1

Originally, 'Into Infinity' was the individual episode title for a proposed series, entitled 'The Day After Tomorrow'. When the BBC transmitted the pilot, they chose to cut the series title from the print.

See also: THE DAY AFTER TOMORROW

THE INVESTIGATOR

A Starkits Production production for NBC. Untransmitted. Duration: 23 minutes.

Devised by Gerry Anderson; theme music by Vic Elmes; music by John Cameron; produced and directed by Gerry Anderson.

Peter Dyneley (Voice of the Investigator), Shane Rimmer (Voice of John), Sylvia Anderson (Voice of Julie), Charles Thake (Stavros Karanti), Peter Borg (Christoph).

	Holding / Source
##.##.#### **[untransmitted pilot]**	C1 / C1

IS HARRY ON THE BOAT?

Commissioned by Sky Pictures. made in association with Rapido TV. Transmission details are for Sky One.

Main regular credit(s):   Based on a book by Colin Butts.

A Ruby production for Sky Pictures.

	Holding / Source
08.07.2001	DB / C3SW

Duration: 96 minutes.

Adapted by Eitan Arussi and Colin Butts; executive producers Jamie Roberts, Paul Trijbits and Peter Stuart; produced by Alison Owen, Neris Thomas and Tim Cole; directed by Menhaj Huda.

With Danny Dyer (Brad), Rik Young (Mario), Des Coleman (Mikey), Davinia Taylor (Alison), Will Mellor (Greg), Kate Magowan (Carmen), Daniela Denby-Ashe (Lorraine), Donna Grant (Heather), Sage Pearson (Patricia), Ralf Little (Nick), Keith Allen (Trevor), Carrie Iddon (Jenny), Julian Gonzalez (Spanish Policeman), Caroline Flack (Blonde), Wendy New (Sarah), Unity Brennan (Tracey), Stewart Sinclair Blythe (Jim), Wes Shearer (Robbie), Seth Allan (Jason), Anouska Bolton Lee (Linda), Jodie Clarke (Emma), Bepe (Frank), Phillipa Lett (Maria), David Girvan (Russell), Kate Sanderson (Belinda), Helen Dunning (Jane), Emma Wilson (Sammy), Lyndsey Elcombe (Julie), Michelle Lemoniata (Twin 1), Nicole Lemoniata (Twin 2), Cressy Chandler (Mel), Jakki Degg (Claire), Lianne Wilson (Trudy), Samantha Dodds (Desk Clerk), Laura Hayes (Jackie), Steve Chaplin (Pitbull), Shaun Stone (Kempy), Susan McArdle (Pacemaker Peggy), Jonathan Natynczyk (Trannie 1), Nat Udon (Trannie 2), Danielle Ogilvie (Tanya), Rebecca Hazlewood (Girl With Brad), Lucy Knight (Girl With Mikey).

ISLA... IN WALES

A BBC production. Untransmitted. Duration: 36 minutes.

Written by Peter Robinson; research Gill Stribling-Wright and Fran Landsman; make-up Cissian Rees; music by Ronnie Hazlehurst; choreography by Irving Davies; designed by Alan Taylor; produced by Paul Ciani; studio sequences directed by Paul Ciani; film sequences directed by Peter Campbell.

Isla St. Clair (Presenter), Lady Amabel Williams-Ellis, Victor Spinetti, Eddie Kidd, Ruth and Paul Ruck, Meinir Heulyn, Jackie Pallo [as Jackie Mr TV Pallo].

	Production No	Holding / Source
##.##.#### **[untransmitted 1980 pilot]**	LLVC290/71	DB-D3 / 2"

IT HAPPENED NEXT YEAR

A BBC production for BBC 2. Transmission details are for BBC 2. Duration: 25 minutes.

Written by Mark Burton, John O'Farrell and Pete Sinclair; produced by Phil Clarke; directed by Dominic Brigstocke and Simon Delaney.

Roger Blake, Melanie Hudson, Pauline McLynn, Sally Phillips, Kim Wall, Brian Perkins.

	Holding / Source
04.10.1996	DB-D3 / D3S

IT MUST BE... LOVE

A Yorkshire Television production. Untransmitted. Duration: 27 minutes.

Written by Paul Minett and Brian Leveson; script supervisor Sarah Cockcroft; theme music by Madness; music by Ray Russell; executive producer David Reynolds; produced by Andrew Benson; directed by Roy Gould.

Paula Wilcox (Irene), Kellie Bright (Allie), Benedict Sandiford (Pete), Elizabeth Estensen (Valerie), Lucy Briers (Marnie), Jason Done (Dougie), Nick Stringer (Clifford), Alan David (Uncle Rex).

	Production No	Holding / Source
##.##.####	L634	B / BS

Made in 1996.

IT STICKS OUT HALF A MILE (RADIO)

A BBC production for BBC Radio 4. Transmission details are for BBC Radio 4. Duration varies - see below for details.

The original pilot episode, set in 1948, involved former bank manager and Home Guard Captain George Mainwaring (Arthur Lowe) deciding to renovate a decrepit seaside pier in the fictional town of Frambourne-on-Sea, only to find when applying for a bank loan that the manager of the local branch is his former chief cashier and Home Guard Sergeant Arthur Wilson (John Le Mesurier).

The pilot, recorded in 1981, was not used and Lowe died in April 1982, ending production.

The new revised series involved William Hodges (Bill Pertwee), former ARP warden and nemesis of Mainwaring's Home Guard unit, approaching "stupid boy" and former Home Guard Private Frank Pike (Ian Lavender) with a proposal to renovate the pier at Frambourne. In order to finance this plan Pike has to approach bank manager Wilson (Le Mesurier), who just happens to be his "uncle" (publicly a friend of his mother's, but strongly hinted to the audience to be Pike's father), for a loan. Wilson suspects the only reason Hodges approached Pike was to get to the bank's money through him. Nevertheless, Pike and Wilson put aside their wartime quarrel with Hodges - more or less - and the renovation begins.

Some different actors were used for some of the minor parts, for example Mrs Fox, who was played here by Mollie Sugden.

Due to the death of Arthur Lowe, the original pilot was not broadcast. The master recording was apparently wiped, but co-writer Snoad kept a copy which he later returned to the BBC. The pilot episode was recovered during the BBC's Treasure Hunt campaign. BBC Radio 7 included it as part of a three hour marathon SOME OF OUR ARCHIVES WERE MISSING - first transmitted the morning of 29th May 2004.

Main regular credit(s):   Based on characters created by Jimmy Perry and David Croft.

Transmission details are for BBC 7.

Credits: Written by Harold Snoad and Michael Knowles; produced and directed by Jonathan James Moore.

Cast: With Arthur Lowe (Captain Mainwairing), John Le Mesurier (Arthur Wilson), Josephine Tewson (Miss Baines), Timothy Bateson (Guthrie), Anthony Sharp, Duggie Brown, Sydney Bromley, Haydn Wood.

	Holding / Source
29.05.2004	DA /

Duration: 27 minutes.

With Arthur Lowe (George Mainwaring).

The pilot episode for a sequel to Dad's Army featuring the last performance of Arthur Lowe as Captain Mainwaring.

The pompous old muddler's swansong comes in a pilot episode for a sequel to Dad's Army. Called It Sticks Out Half a Mile, it was a little-remembered radio spin-off about Mainwaring's attempt to restore a neglected pier. The show was recorded in 1982 but never broadcast, out of respect for Lowe, who died of a stroke just weeks later.

The planned series was eventually recast, with Bill Pertwee reprising his Dad's Army role as Warden Hodges in place of Mainwaring's bumptious bank manager, and ran for 13 episodes.

The original pilot disappeared from the BBC archives, and has only now resurfaced after its creator, the veteran sitcom writer and producer Harold Snoad, discovered a copy at home.

The half-hour episode featuring Lowe is significant for several reasons. Not only does it boast the actor's last recorded performance, but periodically he can clearly be heard slurring his words - a symptom of the narcoleptic disorder that he was suffering from at the time.

The pilot is more amusing and poignant than the Pertwee version. In it, a retired Mainwaring is forced to beg for a loan to finance his unlikely pier venture from his sceptical bank manager - none other than John Le Mesurier's Sergeant Wilson, his former deputy.

Mr Snoad, who sent the episode back to the BBC following one of its periodic appeals for the return of lost archive material, explained: "I came up with this idea about Captain Mainwaring wanting to buy a pier. After the war, he had moved to Switzerland where he had been working in a cuckoo clock factory, but had decided to return to England because the climate didn't agree with his wife's chest.

"I rang up Arthur Lowe and he finally said yes, he'd like to do it. Initially, the idea was to do it for TV, but the BBC suggested it would work better on radio."

Though Lowe delivered a typically well-timed turn as the pompous Mainwaring, newly humbled by his subservience to Wilson, his failing health meant that the recording of the pilot was not without its difficulties.

"Arthur was suffering from narcolepsy, and he would start to doze off part-way through the recordings," said Mr Snoad. "We got it in the can in the end, but before we could transmit it, Arthur sadly died."

That a version of It Sticks Out Half a Mile did finally make it on to the radio was largely down to the enthusiasm of Lowe's widow, Joan. The programme eventually came off the air a year later, after Le Mesurier's death. A year or so later, Mr Snoad persuaded the BBC to commission a TV comedy play based on the same premise. Walking the Planks starred the late Michael Elphick with Richard Wilson in the bank manager role, though the names of their characters were changed to avoid upsetting the Dad's Army faithful.

It failed to make a full series on BBC1, but in 1987 it re-surfaced finally as High and Dry, a six-part sitcom on ITV, again starring Wilson, this time alongside Bernard Cribbins. This really was an end-of-the-pier show: when viewers complained about stagey-looking seaside sets the series was swiftly axed.

See also: DAD'S ARMY* / DAD'S ARMY (RADIO)* / HIGH AND DRY* / LAST NIGHT AT THE PARIS (RADIO)* / WALKING THE PLANKS

IT TAKES A WORRIED MAN...

A Thames Television production for ITV/Channel 4. Transmission details are for Channel 4. Duration: 25 minutes.

At the age of 35, Roath is premature menopausal.

Main regular credit(s):　　　Created by Peter Tilbury; music by Ron Grainer.

Main regular cast:　　　Peter Tilbury (Philip Roath).

Commissioned by Thames Television.

	Holding / Source
##.##.####　Roath [untransmitted pilot]	J / 2"

Written by Peter Tilbury; produced and directed by Anthony Parker.

With Christopher Benjamin, Nicholas Le Prevost, Diana Payan, Andrew Tourell.

The real name of Roath's analyst is revealed, in stages, to be Simon Collins though the character is always just listed as 'Analyst'. The Old Man's true name is never divulged.

IT'S A HOOT

An LWT production. Untransmitted.

Pilot for Blind Date.

Duncan Norvelle (Presenter).

	Holding / Source
##.##.####	J / 1"

IT'S A SQUARE WORLD

A BBC production for BBC 1. Transmission details are for BBC. Duration: 30 minutes.

Main regular credit(s):　　　Devised by Michael Bentine and John Law.

Main regular cast:　　　Michael Bentine (Various roles).

Transmission details are for BBC.

	Holding / Source
16.09.1960	J /

Music by The Square Seven; produced and directed by G. B. Lupino.

With Dick Emery, Clive Dunn, Benny Lee, Frank Thornton, Bruce Lacey.

See also: THE GOON SHOW

IT'S ALL IN LIFE

Alternative/Working Title(s): THE AL READ SHOW

An ATV production. Transmission details are for the ATV midlands region. Duration: 25 minutes.

Main regular credit(s):　　　　Written by Ronnie Taylor; produced and directed by Les Chatfield.

Main regular cast:　　　　　　Al Read (Host), Design.

Holding / Source

08.08.1972　　　　　　　　　　　　　　　　　　　　　　　　　　　　　　J / 2"

The brighter side of life? You'll be lucky . . I say, rou'll be lucky! Al Read makes a rare television appearance to bring you a comedy close-up of matters of the moment, turning life around to show you its funny side.

Music directed by Dennis Wilson; designed by Michael Bailey.

With No guest cast.

IT'S CRICKET

A Thames Television production. Untransmitted.

Jimmy Cricket.

Holding / Source

##.##.#### **[untransmitted pilot]**　　　　　　　　　　　　　　　DB / 1"

IT'S GOING TO BE ALRIGHT

Alternative/Working Title(s): WE'RE GOING TO BE ALRIGHT

A Yorkshire Television production for Channel 4. Transmission details are for Channel 4. Duration: 25 minutes.

Written by Peter Liney; produced and directed by Graeme Muir.

June Whitfield (Margie Hansen), Anna Dawson (Renata Dwyer), Ronnie Stevens (Cyril), Vanessa Knox-Mawer (Sarah Hansen).

Holding / Source

10.12.1984　　　　　　　　　　　　　　　　　　　　　　　　　　　　　DB / 1"

IT'S GOING TO PENALTIES

An Objective Productions production for Sky One. made in association with North One Television. Untransmitted. Duration: 25 minutes.

James Nesbitt (Referee), David Ginola (Team Captain), Jodie Kidd (Team Captain), Shane Warne (Team Captain), Kevin Bridges.

Holding / Source

##.##.#### **[untransmitted 2009 pilot]**　　　　　　　　　　　　DB / DBSW

IT'S NEVER TOO LATE

A Yorkshire Television production for Channel 4. Transmission details are for Channel 4. Duration: 24 minutes.

Written by Ian Masters; music directed by Ken Jones; designed by Tony Jones; produced and directed by Graeme Muir.

Peggy Mount (Winifred Walker), Pat Coombs (May Priggs), Hugh Lloyd (Geoffrey Wicks), Harold Goodwin (Jimmy Jackson), Tony Hughes (First Labourer), Charles Pemberton (Second Labourer), Susie Johns (Waitress).

Holding / Source

03.12.1984　　　　　　　　　　　　　　　　　　　　　　　　　　　　　1" / 1"

IT'S ONLY TV.

A Talkback production for LWT. Untransmitted. Duration: 38 minutes.

Written by Angus Deayton and Harry Thompson; research Margaret Frank and Franny Moyle; designed by Andrew Howe Davies; executive producer Peter Fincham; production manager Julian Scott; produced by Harry Thompson; directed by Pati Marr.

Angus Deayton (Host), Nick Hancock, Alison Craig, Tony Hawks, Chris Morris, Clive Anderson.

A Talkback production.

Holding / Source

##.##.#### **[untransmitted 1992 pilot]**　　　　　　　　　　　　DB / DBSW

Although it has a similar title and is based around television as a subject, it appears to have no connection with IT'S ONLY TV BUT I LIKE IT.

IT'S ULRIKA!

A Channel X production for BBC 2. Transmission details are for BBC 2. Duration: 30 minutes.

Written by Vic Reeves and Bob Mortimer; additional material by Steve Burge and Rhys Thomas; executive producer Alan Marke; directed by John Birkin.

Ulrika Jonsson, Laura Brattan, Steve Burge, Charlie Higson, Matt Lucas, Jim Moir, Bob Mortimer, Steve Brody, Rhys Thomas, David Walliams.

Holding / Source

25.08.1997　　　　　　　　　　　　　　　　　　　　　　　　　　　　　D3 / D3S

ITV PLAYHOUSE

Produced for ITV by a variety of companies (see details below). Transmission details are for the ATV midlands region. Duration varies - see below for details.

SERIES 1

14.06.1977 **The Bass Player And The Blonde** DB / 2"

An ATV production. Duration: 75 minutes.

Written by Roy Clarke; produced and directed by Dennis Vance.

With Edward Woodward (Mangham), Jane Wymark (Terry), Ronald Fraser (Charlie), Betty McDowall (Beth), Mary Kerridge (Mrs Merino), Jeremy Sinden (Nigel), Eddie Reindeer (Larry), Sam Kydd (Max), Stanley Lebor (Lenny), Barry Linehan (Platt), Brian Haines (Father Denham), Billy Milton (Pianist), William Dysart (Drummer), Robert Hartley (Art Dealer), Richard Aylen (First Goon), Jeff Hall (Second Goon), Marcia Warren (Barmaid), Chris Sullivan (First Taxi Driver), Peter Thornton (Second Taxi Driver), Mischa de la Motte (Butler).

See also: THE BASS PLAYER AND THE BLONDE.

See also: THE NEARLY MAN

IVANHOE

A Screen Gems production for ITV. made in association with Columbia Tristar / Sydney Box Television. Transmission details are for the ABC midlands region. Duration: 25 minutes.

Main regular credit(s): Based on a novel by Sir Walter Scott; executive producer Peter Rogers.

Main regular cast: Roger Moore (Ivanhoe), Robert Brown (Gurth).

05.01.1958 **Freeing The Serfs** C3 / C3

Written by Benedict Berenberg; assistant director Douglas Hermes; art director Robert Jones; associate producer Benedict Berenberg; produced by Seymour Friedman; directed by David MacDonald.

With John Pike (Bart), Anthony Dawson (Sir Maurice), Norah Gorsen (Lady Rowena), Henry Vidon (Sir Cedric), Jack Lambert (Geoffrey), Andrew Keir (Prince John), Robert Cawdron (Bailiff).

The pilot episode was filmed in colour at the cost of $130,000 at Associated British Elstree Studios.

Made at Beaconsfield Studios, Buckinghamshire.

The majority of the information detailing the real writers behind the on-screen pseudonyms was collated by Steve Neale and has previously been published in "Pseudonyms, Sapphire and Salt" (Historical Journal of Film, Radio and Television, Vol. 23, No. 3, 2003), "Swashbucklers and Sitcoms, Cowboys and Crime, Nurses, Just Men and Defenders: Blacklisted Writers and TV in the 1950s and 1960s" (Film Studies, Issue 7, Winter 2005) and "Un-American Hollywood: Politics and Film in the Blacklist Era" (Rutgers University Press, 2008).

JACK AND JEREMY'S POLICE 4

An Open Mike production for Channel 4. Transmission details are for Channel 4. Duration: 25 minutes.

Dee and Hardy play special constables at Hedlow Police HQ where viewers are invited to join in a mass swearing-in and an uncomfortably topical Spare or Chair vote to decide the fate of a young offender. There's also an interview with actor Jimmy Hard - Hardy looking uncommonly like Jimmy Nail - plugging his sci-fi drama Spacecop 2010.

Written by Jack Dee and Jeremy Hardy; additional material by Richard Morton; produced by Dave Morley; directed by Ed Bye.

Jeremy Hardy (Special Constable Hardy), Jack Dee (Special Constable Dee), Meera Syal (Woman Police Constable April), Richard Morton (Smeggers), Stephen Frost, Norman Lovett, Maria McErlane, Pat Roach.

	Holding / Source
28.04.1995	D3 / D3S

See also: JACK AND JEREMY'S REAL LIVES*

JACK DEE'S SUNDAY SERVICE

An Open Mike production for Granada. Transmission details are for the Central region. Duration: 25 minutes.

Mostly JACK DEE stand-up comedy, with the occasional sketch.

Main regular credit(s):   Written by Jack Dee, Richard Morton and Rob Colley; executive producers Addison Cresswell and Andy Harries; series producer Spencer Campbell; produced by Andy Davies; directed by Steve Smith.

Main regular cast: Jack Dee (Host), Rich Hall.

	Production No	Holding / Source
##.##.#### [untransmitted pilot]	1/8288/0010	DB / DBS

This recording has no end credits.

JACKANORY PLAYHOUSE

A BBC production for BBC 1. Transmission details are for BBC 1. Usual duration: 25 minutes.

SERIES 1

Main regular credit(s):   Executive producer Anna Home.

	Holding / Source
	J / 2"

15.12.1972 **Lizzie Dripping And The Orphans**

Try as she might Lizzie simply could not help thinking about what it would really be like to be an orphan: ' All by yourself with no one to love you ...

Written by Helen Cresswell; designed by Paul Munting; directed by Angela Beeching.

With Hannah Gordon (Narrator), Tina Heath (Lizzie), Barbara Mitchell (Patty Arbuckle), Geoffrey Matthews (Albert Arbuckle), Jane Lowe (Aunt Blodwen).

JAMESON

A Euston Films production. Not made.

Executive producer Johnny Goodman.

Proposed 1978 pilot for a series about a newspaper journalist in London.

JAMESON SHOW

A Granada production. Transmission details are for the Granada region. Duration: 25 minutes.

Derek Jameson presents the pilot edition of a programme which takes a humorous look at current affairs. Jameson interviews The Daily Star's royal correspondent James Whittaker about his role in the recent reporting of the engagement of Prince Charles to Lady Diana Spencer. Later in the programme, to mark the 500th issue of Private Eye magazine, Jameson talks to Richard Ingrams. Throughout the interview Ingrams refers to Jameson as Sid (a reference to the Private Eye character Sid Yobbo - a Cockney newspaper editor and thinly disguised caricature of Jameson himself). The programme also features sketches, and stand up comedy from Rik Mayall (in the guise of Kevin Turvey investigative reporter) and Alexei Sayle.

Script associates Bryan McCallister and Neil Shand; research Jon Plowman, Katie Woods and Eugenie Verney; series editor Steve Hawes; music directed by Bill Connor; designed by Nick King; produced by Geoff Moore; directed by Graham C. Williams.

Derek Jameson (Host), Alexei Sayle, Rik Mayall, Earl Okin, Sally Grace, Royce Mills, Philip Trewinnard, Richard Ingrams, James Whitaker.

	Holding / Source
##.##.#### [untransmitted pilot]	DB / 2"

Rx: 19.2.1981.

THE JEWEL IN THE CROWN, SOUTHALL, MIDDX

Alternative/Working Title(s): SYKES + MILLIGAN

A BBC production. Untransmitted. Duration: 34 minutes.

Written by Johnny Speight; costume Michael Burdle; make-up Sheelagh Wells; designed by John Stout; production manager Tony Dow [credited as Anthony Dow]; produced and directed by Martin Shardlow.

Eric Sykes (Eric), Spike Milligan (Spike), Josephine Tewson (Mrs Gabbitt), Keith Smith (VAT Man), Denise Distel (Girl), Peter Russell (Customer).

	Production No	Holding / Source
##.##.#### [untransmitted pilot]	LLCH291D/71	DB / 1"

Made in 1985.

THE JIM DAVIDSON SHOW

A Thames Television production. Transmission details are for the ATV/Central region. Duration: 25 minutes.

Main regular cast: Jim Davidson (Compere).

	Holding / Source
##.##.#### [untransmitted pilot]	2"|n / 2"

See also: STAND UP JIM DAVIDSON*

THE JIMMY YOUNG TELEVISION PROGRAMME

A Yorkshire Television production. Transmission details are for ITV Various. Duration: 33 minutes.

Main regular performer(s): Jimmy Young (Presenter).

Holding / Source
J / 2"

##.##.#### **[untransmitted pilot]**

Outside broadcast pilot for a chat show, made at Bradford University Theatre in the Mill.

Produced by John Wilford.

Recorded August 1983.

JO BRAND THROUGH THE CAKEHOLE

A Channel X production for Channel 4. Transmission details are for Channel 4.

Main regular credit(s):   Executive producer Katie Lander.

Main regular cast: Jo Brand (Host).

Holding / Source
D3 / D3S

30.12.1993

Duration: 30 minutes.

Produced and directed by Marcus Mortimer.

THE JOCKEYS OF NORFOLK

A Tyne Tees Television production. Untransmitted. Duration: 37 minutes.

Written by Andy Taylor, Chris Lang and Hugh Grant; designed by Eric Briers and Ashley Wilkinson; associate producer Paul Black; produced and directed by Royston Mayoh.

Andy Taylor, Chris Lang, Hugh Grant, The Flying Pickets.

Holding / Source
B / 1"

##.##.#### **[untransmitted pilot]**

Recorded 19.12.86.

JOE

Produced for BBC 1 by a variety of companies (see details below). Transmission details are for BBC 1. Duration: 15 minutes.

Main regular credit(s):   Written by Alison Prince; drawings by Joan Hickson; music by Laurie Steele; produced and directed by Diana Potter.

Holding / Source
R1 /

##.##.#### **[untransmitted pilot]**

Pilot.

JOE

An LWT production. Transmission details are for the London Weekend Television region. Duration: 25 minutes.

Main regular credit(s):   Written by Brian Cooke and Johnnie Mortimer; designed by Bryce Walmsley; produced by Mark Stuart; directed by Bruce Gowers.

Main regular performer(s): Joe Brown (Host), The New Temperance Seven, The Shandy Garr, The Breakaways.

Holding / Source
J / 2"

##.##.#### **[untransmitted pilot]**

Recorded May 1969.

JOE LONGTHORNE ENTERTAINS

A Thames Television production. Transmission details are for the Central region. Duration: 25 minutes.

Written by Roy Tuvey; additional material by Colin Edmonds; music directed by Alan Braden; produced and directed by Keith Beckett.

Joe Longthorne (Host), Kate Robbins, Wayne Dobson.

Holding / Source
1" / 1"

26.08.1987

JOE PASQUALE'S FUNNY FARM

An ITV Productions production for ITV 1. Untransmitted.

Holding / Source
DB / DBSW

##.##.#### **[untransmitted pilot]**

JOHN BULL

A BBC Children's Department production for BBC 1. Untransmitted. Duration: 30 minutes.

A SISTER MAGAZINE TO APPEAL TO OLDER CHILDREN. TITLED JOHN BULL, IT WAS PRODUCED BY BIDDY BAXTER, EDWARD BARNES AND ROSEMARY GILL AND FEATURED JOHN NOAKES AS A REPORTER. NO SERIES FOLLOWED. IT WAS PRESENTED BY TERENCE EDMOND AND BRITT ALLCROFT (THEN ONE OF THE BLUE PETER PRODUCTION TEAM - LATER THE WOMAN BEHIND THE RETURN OF THOMAS THE TANK ENGINE) - THE CONTENT OF THE PILOT RAN: VICTORIAN BATHS DEMO'D/GOLD MOON BATH WITH GOLD SHOWER CHANDELIER/THE LONDON SEASON - STORY OF THE DEBS + TK/INTERVIEW WITH JENNIFER OF 'QUEEN' MAGAZINE TK (Britt)/CELEBRITY DOG TRAINING COMPETITION (with June Whitfield, Peter Byrne, Dave Dee, Linda Ludgrove and Derek Freeman)/PORTOBELLO MARKET TK (John Noakes)/HAT WHICH CAN BE WORN 50 DIFFERENT WAYS/PRESENTERS LEAVE STUDIO ON ELEPHANT.

Production team Robin Kerr, Tim Byford and Alan Russell; produced by Biddy Baxter, Edward Barnes and Rosemary Gill; directed by Biddy Baxter, Edward Barnes and Rosemary Gill.

Terence Edmond (Presenter), Britt Allcroft (Presenter), John Noakes (Reporter), June Whitfield, Peter Byrne, Dave Dee, Linda Ludgrove, Derek Freeman.

	Production No	VT Number	Holding / Source
##.##.#### [untransmitted 1967 pilot]	3317/9520	VTM/4P/4051	DB-4W / 40

JOHN SHUTTLEWORTH'S WORLD OF MUSIC

A BBC production. Untransmitted.

John Shuttleworth.

	Holding / Source
##.##.#### [untransmitted pilot]	DB-D3 / 2"

THE JOHNNY SPEIGHT SHOW

Alternative/Working Title(s): A JAUNDICED VIEW OF LIFE / DOES THIS TRAIN STOP AT WATFORD JUNCTION? / WATFORD

An LWT production. Untransmitted. Duration: 25 minutes.

Recorded 09.08.77. Sub-titled "A jaundiced view of life created and written by Johnny Speight". After the end credits there is one further sketch lasting almost 12 minutes. This sketch features the only appearance of some of the credited cast members and so would appear to be part of the programme but the gap between the end of the credits and the (slightly shaky) start of the sketch would suggest otherwise.

Created by Johnny Speight; written by Johnny Speight; designed by Bill McPherson; production manager Brian Penny; produced and directed by William G. Stewart.

Patricia Hayes, Derek Newark, Toni Palmer, Jonathan Cecil, Dermot Kelly, Eric Sykes, Frank Coda, Bill Treacher, John Lyons, Ronnie Brodie, Geoffrey Lumsden, Leo Dolan, Joy Harrington, Harold Goodwin, Anthony Barnett, Rose Power.

	Production No	Holding / Source
##.##.#### [untransmitted pilot]	99074	DB / 2"

Cartoons by Franklin.

THE JOHNNY VEGAS GAME SHOW

A BBC production for BBC Choice. made in association with Big Eye Film & Television. Transmission details are for BBC Choice. Duration: 43 minutes.

Devised by BBC and Big Eye Film & Television; written by Johnny Vegas; additional material by Mobashir Dar and Hugh Rycroft; titles by Moov; art director Sara Hawden; designed by Jonathan Paul Green [credited as Jonathan Green]; associate producer Johnny Vegas; production executive Andrew Wiltshire; executive producers Steve Lock, Lisa Clark and Myfanwy Moore; production manager Stan Matthews; produced by Mobashir Dar; directed by David G. Croft.

Johnny Vegas (Host).

	Holding / Source
22.12.2002	DB / DBSW

JOKER IN THE PACK

An Action Time production for BBC 1. Transmission details are for BBC 1. Duration: 30 minutes.

Jokes and jokers from around the country feature in this new series of programmes with Marti Caine. Marti has scoured the land to discover ordinary people with a natural joke-telling talent. In the studio, two teams compete in a comedy contest, and members of the audience join in with their own favourite jokes.

On her travels, Marti found that "Comic coppers, witty city slickers and humorous hairdressers prove that Britain is a cut above the rest when it comes to cracking jokes. We uncover comedians in every corner - proving that talent will out wherever it lies."

Main regular cast: Marti Caine (Host).

	Production No	Holding / Source
##.##.#### [untransmitted pilot]	LLVQ268H	DB-D3 / D3S

Additional material by Terry Morrison; script associate Charlie Adams; designed by Anthony Ainsworth; assistant producer Tom Webber; executive producer Stephen Leahy; production manager Guy Freeman; produced and directed by Michael Leggo.

Recorded 29.09.91.

No guest cast - just members of joe public.

JOKERS WILD

A Yorkshire Television production. Transmission details are for the ATV midlands region. Duration varies - see below for details.

Joke-telling competition.

Main regular credit(s):   Devised by Ray Cameron and Mike King.

Main regular performer(s): Barry Cryer (Chairman).

Untransmitted.

	VT Number	Holding / Source
##.##.#### **[untransmitted pilot]**	2069	B / 62

Duration: 29 minutes.

Designed by Richard Jarvis; directed by David Mallett.

With Ted Ray, Charlie Chester, Les Dawson, Ray Martine, Bobby Pattinson, Jimmy Marshall, Ann Coates, Louisa Ravaiotti.

Recorded 15.04.1969.

JOKING APART

A Pola Jones Film production for BBC 2. Transmission details are for BBC 2. Duration: 29 minutes.

Main regular credit(s):   Written by Steven Moffat; produced by André Ptaszynski.

Main regular cast: Robert Bathurst (Mark Taylor), Fiona Gillies (Becky Johnson/Taylor), Tracie Bennett (Tracy Glazebrook), Paul Raffield (Robert Glazebrook).

SERIES 1

Main regular credit(s):   Theme music by Chris Rea; theme sung by Kenny Craddock; incidental music by Kenny Craddock and Colin Gibson; designed by John Anderson; directed by Bob Spiers.

	Holding / Source
07.01.1993 "The story so far" [refilmed version of pilot]	D3 / D3S

Co-directed by John Kilby.

With James Greene, Frank Lee, Rhoda Lewis.

This episode reuses some footage from the pilot, hence John Kilby's credit as co-director.

THE JULIE GOODYEAR TALK SHOW

A Granada production. Transmission details are for the Granada region.

Julie Goodyear (Host), Max Clifford, Nina Myskow.

	Holding / Source
19.08.1994	DB / D3S

JUMP

An LWT production. Untransmitted. Duration: 25 minutes.

	VT Number	Holding / Source
##.##.#### **[untransmitted pilot]**	9L/79202	J / 2"

JUNIOR KICKSTART

A BBC production for BBC 1. Transmission details are for BBC 1.

Main regular cast: Peter Purves (Presenter).

	Holding / Source
29.12.1980	DB-D3 / 2"

JUNIOR THAT'S LIFE

A BBC production for BBC 1. Transmission details are for BBC 1.

	Holding / Source
##.##.#### **[untransmitted pilot]**	DB-D3 / 2"

Directed by Peter Campbell.

With Esther Rantzen (Presenter), Chris Serle (Presenter), Paul Henley (Presenter).

Recorded July 1979.

JUST A MINUTE

A BBC production. Untransmitted.

	Holding / Source
##.##.#### **[untransmitted 1969 pilot]**	DB /

JUST HIS LUCK

A BBC production. Untransmitted. Duration: 30 minutes.

Written by Harold Snoad and Ivor Burgoyne; costume Dennis Brack; make-up Deanne Turner; music by Nick Ingman; designed by David Buckingham; production manager Stacey Adair; produced and directed by Harold Snoad.

Enn Reitel (Kent Eden), Liza Goddard (Liz Holness), Michael Cochrane (Charles), Peter Childs (Alan Winters), Anthony Dawes (Bookshop Assistant), Angus Barnett (Terry Rogers), Debra Beaumont (Hazel), Carolyn Allen (Pamela), Anna Tzelniker (Madame Poweroski), James Bryce (Window Cleaner), Les Clack (Bill Matthews), John Dair (Man In Pub).

	Production No	Holding / Source
##.##.#### [untransmitted 1989 pilot]	LLCK400S/71	DB / 1"

JUST LIKE MUM

An LWT production. Transmission details are for the London Weekend Television region. Duration: 25 minutes.

Main regular credit(s):	Written by John Stevenson; designed by Michael Oxley; produced and directed by Stuart Allen.
Main regular cast:	Peggy Mount (Edith Jordan).

	Production No	Holding / Source
27.08.1976 [Comedy Showcase]		DB|n / 2"

With Leonard Preston (Edward Unsworth), Mike Grady (Alwyn Williams), Roderick Smith (Billy Norris), Frances Bennett (Mrs Fairfax).

rx 23/12/75

##.##.#### [untransmitted pilot]	9767	D2 / 2"

With Mike Grady (Alwyn Williams), David Neville (Edward Unsworth), David Moran (Billy Norris), Linda Cunningham (Girl in Betting Shop), Keith Marsh (Selwyn Halliwell), Joy Stewart (Mrs Hazeldine).

rx 19/11/1976

JUSTICE

A Yorkshire Television production. Transmission details are for the ATV midlands region. Usual duration: 50 minutes.

Main regular cast:	Margaret Lockwood (Harriet Peterson).

	VT Number	Holding / Source
04.09.1969 **Justice Is A Woman [Playhouse]**	1018	1" / 62

Postponed from 14.07.1969.

Adapted by Stanley Miller; based on a play by Jack Roffey and Ronald Kinnoch; executive producer Peter Willes; directed by Joan Kemp-Welch.

With Iain Cuthbertson, John Laurie, Allan Cuthbertson, David Langton, Roddy McMillan, Cavan Kendall, Elizabeth Knight, David Garth, Russell Waters, Daphne Anderson, Prentis Hancock, John Dunbar, Elizabeth Burger, Raymond Farrell, John Young, Arthur Jeffrey, Jack Thomson.

In this play, Lockwood's character is called Julia Stanford.

124

K.9 AND COMPANY

Alternative/Working Title(s): SARAH AND K9

A BBC production for BBC 1. Transmission details are for BBC 1. Duration: 50 minutes.

Christmas at Moreton Harwood. All is peaceful. Or is it?

Written by Terence Dudley; script editors Eric Saward and Antony Root; theme music by Ian Levine and Fiachra Trench; music by Peter Howell; designed by Nigel Jones; production associate Angela Smith; production manager Robert Gabriel; produced by John Nathan-Turner; directed by John Black.

Elisabeth Sladen (Sarah Jane Smith), John Leeson (Voice of K-9), Bill Fraser (Commander Bill Pollock), Ian Sears (Brendan Richards), Colin Jeavons (George Tracey), Mary Wimbush (Aunt Lavinia), Linda Polan (Juno Baker), Sean Chapman (Peter Tracey), Gillian Martell (Lilly Gregson), Neville Barber (Howard Baker), John Quarmby (Henry Tobias), Nigel Gregory (Sergeant Wilson), Stephen Oxley (Police Constable Carter).

	Holding / Source
28.12.1981 **A Girl's Best Friend**	DB-D3 / 2"

Alt.Title(s): *One Girl and her Dog*

See also: DOCTOR WHO / THE SARAH JANE ADVENTURES

KANGAROO VALLEY

A BBC production. Untransmitted. Duration: 30 minutes.

Written by Ronnie Wolfe and Ronald Chesney [credited as Ronnie Chesney]; costume Mary Husband; make-up Gillian Thomas; designed by Derek Evans; production manager Adrian Pegg; produced and directed by Ray Butt.

Peter O'Brien (Greg), Sara Griffiths (Chrissie), Alastair Cumming (Rod), Nick Stringer (Bas), Annie Treadwell (Shirl), Kaleem Janjua (Mr Gupta), Michael Fenton Stevens (Doctor James), Michael Jenner ('Aus' In Camper).

	Production No	Holding / Source
##.##.#### **[untransmitted 1990 pilot]**	LLCA298F	DB / 1"

THE KATHY KIRBY SHOW

A BBC production for BBC 1. Transmission details are for BBC 1. Duration: 45 minutes.

Main regular performer(s): Kathy Kirby (Host).

SERIES 1

Main regular credit(s): Produced and directed by Ernest Maxin.

Main regular performer(s): With Peter Gordeno, The George Mitchell Singers.

	Holding / Source
03.05.1964	J /

Orchestra conducted by Harry Rabinowitz; designed by Keith Norman.

With Stratford Johns, Carlo Dini, Wilf Todd and his Combo, Carl Gonzales, The Six Dancing Showmen.

KATIE AND PETER: UNLEASHED

An ITV Productions production for ITV 2. made in association with Can Associates Television. Transmission details are for ITV 2. Duration: 48 minutes.

Main regular credit(s): Script associate Richard Easter; script supervisors Lindsay O'Mahony and Annie Griffiths; music by Mcasso; designed by Chris Webster; associate producers Frank Smalley, James Howard and Caroline Roseman; executive producers Mike Parkinson, Brent Baker and Neville Hendricks; head of production Leah Milton; senior producer Gareth Davies; series producer Amanda Sangorski; produced by Rick Murray; directed by Rick Murray and Matthew Amos.

Main regular performer(s): Katie Price, Peter André.

	VT Number	Holding / Source
##.##.#### **[untransmitted pilot]**	9L/51178/A	DB / DBSW

KEEP IT IN THE FAMILY

A Thames Television production. Transmission details are for the ATV/Central region. Duration: 25 minutes.

Main regular credit(s): Created by Brian Cooke.

Main regular cast: Robert Gillespie (Dudley Rush), Stacy Dorning (Susan Rush).

	Holding / Source
##.##.#### **[untransmitted pilot]**	J / 2"

Written by Brian Cooke; produced and directed by Mark Stuart.

With Pauline Yates (Muriel Rush), Jenny Quayle (Jacqui Rush).

Recorded early 1979.

THE KEITH BARRET SHOW

Produced for BBC 2 by a variety of companies (see details below). Transmission details are for BBC 2. Duration: 29 minutes.

Main regular cast: Rob Brydon (Keith Barret).

	Holding / Source
##.##.#### **[untransmitted pilot]**	DB / DBSW

A Baby Cow / Jones the Film production.

This is an untransmitted pilot version of ep.1, but Kaleidoscope thinks it is just a longer edit.

See also: MARION & GEOFF*

THE KEITH HARRIS SHOW

A BBC production for BBC 1. Transmission details are for BBC 1. Duration varies - see below for details.

Main regular performer(s): Keith Harris (Host), Bucks Fizz.

	Holding / Source
	DB / 2"

31.12.1982

Duration: 30 minutes.

Written by George Martin; music directed by Ronnie Hazlehurst; choreography by Norman Maen; produced and directed by Paul Ciani.

With Bucks Fizz, Ray Dondy, Jacqui Scott, The Norman Maen Dancers.

See also: KEITH AND ORVILLE'S CHRISTMAS CIRCUS*

KEITH LEMON'S LEMONAID

A Talkback Thames production for ITV 1. Transmission details are for the Central region.

Main regular performer(s): Leigh Francis (Keith Lemon).

	VT Number	Holding / Source
	384841	HD/DB / HDC

##.##.#### [untransmitted pilot]

Duration: 27 minutes.

With Emma Bunton, Flawless.

No end credits.

KEN DODD AND THE DIDDYMEN

A BBC North/Manchester production for BBC 1. Transmission details are for BBC 1. Duration: 10 minutes.

Main regular cast: Ken Dodd and The Diddy Men.

	Holding / Source
	J /

##.##.#### [untransmitted pilot]

Puppetry by Roger Stevenson.

THE KENNETH WILLIAMS SPECTACULAR

A BBC production for BBC 1. Untransmitted. Duration varies - see below for details.

Main regular credit(s):   Written by John Law and Kenneth Williams; designed by Colin Green; produced and directed by David O'Clee.

Main regular cast: Kenneth Williams.

	Production No	VT Number	Holding / Source
##.##.####			DB-R1 / 2"

Duration: 17 minutes.

With No guest cast.

	Production No	VT Number	Holding / Source
##.##.####	1219/1058	16H/6P/49895	DB-R1 / 2"

Duration: 48 minutes.

With No guest cast.

THE KENNY EVERETT VIDEO SHOW

A Thames Television production. Transmission details are for the ATV midlands region. Usual duration: 25 minutes.

Main regular performer(s): Kenny Everett, Hot Gossip.

	Holding / Source
	J / 2"
	J / 2"

##.##.#### [untransmitted pilot]

##.##.#### [untransmitted pilot]

KENYA

An United production for HTV. made in association with Robert Halmi Incorporated. Untransmitted. Duration: 50 minutes.

Written by Hal Sitowitz; executive producers Robert Halmi Jnr, Patrick Dromgoole and Johnny Goodman; produced by Robert Halmi; directed by Simon Langton.

Lisa Eichhorn (Jennifer), David Huddleston (Will), Robert Swales (Duncan), Mary Alice Griffin (Chelsea), Kimber Shoop (Terry), Caroline Langrishe (Roe), Janice Oats (Paula), Leslie Ann MacInnes (Adrienne), Martin Akelo (Matthew), Gideon Nzoka (Elijah), Conga Mbandu (Simon), Kuldup Barkoo (Duka), Lydia Kigada (Ayah / Housekeeper), Abdullah Sunado (Elder), Alois Aloo (Worker 1), Jan McCoy (Air Stewardess).

	Holding / Source
	DB / 1"

##.##.####

Pilot for an unmade series.

KETCH! & HIRO-PON GET IT ON

Alternative/Working Title(s): GAMARJOBAT - GET IT ON

A Baby Cow Manchester production for BBC 3. made in association with Komedia. Transmission details are for BBC 3. Duration: 30 minutes.

Written by Gamarjobat and Ben Gregor; additional material by Alex Spiro and Dave Savage; music by Sniffydog; designed by Dick Lunn; assistant producer Ruth McCarthy; associate producers Ketch! & Hiro-Pon and Lindsay Hughes; executive producers Richard Daws and Henry Normal; produced by David Lambert; directed by Ben Gregor.

Gamarjobat (Themselves), Graham Duff (Cafe Manager), Eleanor Lawrence (Chav Girl), Natasha Granger (Chav Girl), Elle Dillon-Reams (Chav Girl), Jo Neary (Tramp), Laura Patch (Hot Woman), Joe Rice (Hot Woman's Boyfriend).

	Holding / Source
06.02.2009	DB / DBSWF

KILLING TIME

A Brown Eyed Boy Production production for BBC 3. Transmission details are for BBC 3. Duration: 28 minutes.

Pilot of new comedy set in a woman's prison. Features unrequited love, lesbianism; covert and uncovered, drug running and racial disharmony, as Victorian values vie with the rough in the outside world.

Written by Amymay Bowes, Shelley Cooper, Tanya Crawford, Tracey Groves, Morgan Lloyd Malcolm, Lucy Montgomery, Barunka O'Shaugnessy, Terrian Oudjar, Leila Serrao, Chloe Wilson and John F. D. Northover; script editor Jenny Landreth; music by Paul Bradbury; designed by Philip Barber; executive producer Gary Reich; produced and directed by John F. D. Northover.

Amymay Bowes, Shelley Cooper, Tanya Crawford, Tracey Groves, Morgan Lloyd Malcolm, Lucy Montgomery, Barunka O'Shaugnessy, Terrian Oudja, Leila Serrao, Chloe Wilson, Melanie Kilburn.

	Holding / Source
24.03.2004	DB /

KISS AND TELL

An LWT production. Transmission details are for the Central region. Duration: 105 minutes.

Graham is a man suspected of doing away with his wife and several other women: the key to the mystery lies in a lonely hearts column. Enter policewoman Jude, former lover of a disturbed detective, who answers Graham's ad and becomes hopelessly involved with the suspect and his loveable son.

Written by Heidi Thomas; executive producer Sally Head; produced by Sarah Wilson; directed by David Richards.

Rosie Rowell (Jude Sawyer), Peter Howitt (Graham Ives), Daniel Craig (Matt Kearney), Ralph Ineson (Sergeant Beddowes), Nicola Stephenson (WPC Alex Reynolds), David Bradley (Superintendent Hines), Gillian Bevan (Barbara Ives), Danny Worters (James Ives), Hilda Braid (Gloria Sumner), Peter Pacey (Roland Burke), Clare Cathcart (Steph), Helena Little (Doctor Garnett), Rosie Cavaliero (Maggie Wallace), Caroline John (Avril Owens), Mark Tandy (Barrister), Stephen Ilett (Solicitor), Liam McKenna (Constable), Patsy Peters (Singer), Felicity Chilver (Child), Annelies Lovell (Child's Mother).

	Holding / Source
09.11.1996	D2 / V1S

THE KIT CURRAN RADIO SHOW

A Thames Television production. Transmission details are for the Central region. Duration: 25 minutes.

Main regular credit(s):	Written by Andy Hamilton; theme music by David Mackay and Ian La Frenais; theme sung by Denis Lawson; produced and directed by Derrick Goodwin.
Main regular cast:	Denis Lawson (Kit Curran), Brian Wilde (Roland Simpson), Paul Brooke (Les Toms), Clive Merrison (Damien Appleby).

	Holding / Source
##.##.#### **[untransmitted pilot]**	J / 1"

Produced and directed by James Gilbert.

See also: KIT CURRAN*

KITCH'S CLUB

A Scottish Television production. Transmission details are for the Scottish Television region.

Written by Dick Vosburgh; produced and directed by Clarke Tait.

Chic Murray (Host), Vivian Stanshall (Host), The Tremeloes, Arrival, Clodagh Rodgers, Sandy Brown, The Rhada Krishna Temple.

	Holding / Source
##.##.####	J / 2"

The Stage, 04.06.70, reported that a pilot, under this provisional title, was to be recorded that same day.

THE KLANG SHOW

A BBC Productions production for BBC 3. Transmission details are for BBC 3. Duration: 30 minutes.

Written by Greg Davies, Marek Larwood and Steve Hall; script supervisor Louise Johnson; script consultant Logan Murray; theme music by Daniel Pemberton TV Orchestra; art director Thorin Thompson; designed by Simon Rogers; production executive Sarah Hitchcock; executive producer Jo Sargent; production manager Judith Bantock; produced by Lucy Robinson; directed by Tim Kirkby.

We Are Klang.

	Holding / Source
16.08.2010	HD/DB / HD/DB

KNOWING ME, KNOWING YOU... WITH ALAN PARTRIDGE

A Talkback production for BBC 2. Transmission details are for BBC 2. Duration: 30 minutes.

Main regular credit(s):   Written by Steve Coogan, Armando Iannucci and Patrick Marber; music directed by Steve Brown; produced by Armando Iannucci; directed by Dominic Brigstocke.

Main regular performer(s): Steve Coogan (Alan Partridge), Steve Brown (Glenn Ponder).

Credits: Executive producer Peter Fincham; produced by Armando Iannucci; directed by Dominic Brigstocke.

Holding / Source

##.##.#### **[untransmitted pilot]**   1" / 1"

A Granada production.

With Rebecca Front (Patty Blake).

Recorded 14.04.1994.

See also: I'M ALAN PARTRIDGE*

THE KRYPTON FACTOR

A Granada production. Transmission details are for the ATV/Central region. Duration: 25 minutes.

Main regular performer(s): Gordon Burns (Presenter).

SERIES 1

Transmission details are for the ATV midlands region.

Holding / Source

##.##.#### **[untransmitted pilot]**   J / 2"

The competition in the pilot, was won by a woman.

LADIES AND GENTLEMEN

Alternative/Working Title(s): MODERN MEN

A Talkback Thames production for Channel 4. Untransmitted. Duration: 25 minutes.

Created by James Bobin, Jesse Armstrong and Sam Bain; written by Jesse Armstrong and Sam Bain; script supervisor Rowena Ladbury; script editor Arthur Mathews; music by Ben Bartlett; director of photography Rob Kitzmann; titles by Sharon Lock; art director Jane Shepherd; designed by Dennis De Groot; executive producers Phil Bowker, Jesse Armstrong and Sam Bain; head of production Beatrice Gay; production manager Isibeal Ballance; produced by Derrin Schlesinger; directed by Becky Martin.

Darren Boyd (The Honourable Horatio Densborough), Adam Buxton (Doctor Jack Carlton), Rosie Cavaliero (Miss Louisa Stokes), Cara Horgan (Emily), Lucy Punch (Mrs Alice Fairfax), Reece Shearsmith (Mr Freddy Kilburn), Christina Cole (Elizabeth), Dominic Coleman (Police Constable Jackson), Neil Edmond (Servant), Karl Johnson (Uncle Philip), Jessica Regan (Susanna), Jonathan Slinger (Mr Lupton), Geoffrey Whitehead (Lawyer).

	Production No	VT Number	Holding / Source
##.##.#### [untransmitted pilot]	44277/001	357597	DB / DBSWF

Recorded 2007.

LANGLEY BOTTOM

A Yorkshire Television production. Transmission details are for the Central region. Duration: 25 minutes.

Main regular credit(s):	Written by Barry Cryer and John Junkin; produced and directed by Alan Tarrant.
Main regular cast:	Bernard Cribbins (Seth Raven), Tim Barrett (Reverend Denis Claybourne), Elvi Hale (Mrs Wentworth), Barbara Hicks (Madge Howarth), Rhoda Lewis (Hilda Howarth), Kaleem Janjua (Mr Patel), Jamila Massey (Mrs Patel), Don Crann (Vernon Nobbs), Lisa David (Brenda).

Holding / Source

1" / 1"

14.07.1986 **PC Blues**

PC Wren - Langley Bottom's custodian of law and order, with one arrest in 30 years - is being transferred.

With Christopher Clarke (Herbert), John Junkin, Peter Martin, Arthur Griffiths, Ian Bleasdale, Paul Jaynes, Pat Grainger, Noel Crowder, Baroness Gavioli, Baron Woolfgang, Jennifer Andrews.

THE LARKINS

Alternative/Working Title(s): LOOK IN WITH THE LARKINS

An ATV production. Usual duration: 25 minutes.

Main regular credit(s):	Created by Fred Robinson.
Main regular cast:	Peggy Mount (Ada Larkins), David Kossoff (Alf Larkins).

SERIES 1

An ATV Midlands production. Transmission details are for the ATV midlands region.

Main regular credit(s):	Written by Fred Robinson; music by Jackie Brown; designed by Pembroke Duttson; produced and directed by Bill Ward.
Main regular cast:	With Ronan O'Casey (Jeff Rogers), Ruth Trouncer (Joyce Rogers), Shaun O'Riordan (Eddie Larkins).

	Production No	Holding / Source
##.##.#### **Dry Run**	7787	J / R1

Recorded 15.09.1958.

LARRY GRAYSON'S HOLIDAY GAME

A Sunset and Vine plc production for Thames Television. Not made.

Quiz show.

Produced and directed by Keith Beckett.

Larry Grayson (Presenter).

Intended pilot for May 1984.

THE LAST DETECTIVE

A Meridian production for ITV 1. Transmission details are for the Central region. Duration varies - see below for details.

Main regular credit(s):   Based on novels by Leslie Thomas; executive producers Michele Buck and Tim Vaughan.

Main regular cast: Peter Davison (Detective Constable 'Dangerous' Davies).

SERIES 1

Main regular credit(s):   Produced by Nick Hurran.

Main regular cast: With Sean Hughes (Mod), Rob Spendlove (Detective Inspector Aspinall), Emma Amos (Julie Davies), Charles De'Ath (Detective Sergeant Pimlott), Billy Geraghty (Detective Constable Barrett).

	Holding / Source
07.02.2003 **The Last Detective**	DB / V1SW

Duration: 95 minutes.

Detective Constable Davies is an old-fashioned kind of copper. Grateful little old ladies give him boxes of biscuits because he's good-hearted and thoughtful. He's thorough and assiduous, but is seen as a bit of a plodder by his colleagues, who have given him the tongue-in-cheek nickname of "Dangerous" Davies.

Davies is separated from his wife (though they obviously still love each other), he lives in grotty digs and he has occasional custody of a lolloping great dog.

But "Dangerous" Davies is not a man who should be dismissed lightly. His methods may seem cumbersome and slow, particularly to his nasty boss, a bully who gives Dangerous all the rotten jobs, but Dangerous gets his man. (Though no one thanks him for it ...)

Dangerous accidentally finds himself on the trail of a woman who vanished without trace 20 years earlier, aged 17. Davies meets the woman's haunted mother and the sister she never knew. Dangerous's relentless digging back into the past, with the help of a cheery Irish friend, reveals that the solution to the case is very close to home.

Dramatised by Richard Harris; directed by Nick Hurran.

With David Troughton, Joanne Froggatt, Rachel Davies, Leslie Schofield, Ingrid Lacey, Rupert Farley, Ian Targett, Andy Greenhalgh, Desmond McNamara, Kenneth McDonald, Peter Czajkowski, Mohammad George, Natalie Dakin, Jalaal Hartley, Jason Heppenstall, Mike Smith, Leon Black.

THE LAST LAUGH

A BBC Scotland production for BBC 3. Transmission details are for BBC 3. Duration varies - see below for details.

Main regular credit(s):   Presented by Dara Ó Briain.

	Holding / Source
19.03.2005	DB / DBSWF

Duration: 60 minutes.

Alternative transmissions: BBC 1: 13.04.2005.

Assistant producer Lucy Bacon; executive producer Gary Chippington; series producer Alison Black; produced by Abi Judge; directed by Mike Prince.

With Susan Nickson (Writer and Creator), Natalie Casey (Actress), Adam Chase (Writer and Creator), Ash Atalla (Producer), Drew Carter-Cain, Anne Downie, Steve Furst, Samantha Janus, Jane Stabler.

Main regular credit(s):   Script editor Dan Evans; executive producer Gary Chippington; series producer Alison Black.

	Holding / Source
21.01.2006 **Last Quango In Harris**	DB / DBSWF

Duration: 50 minutes.

Written by Maurice Gran and Laurence Marks; directed by Lucy Bacon.

28.01.2006 **Love For Sale**	DB / DBSWF

Duration: 50 minutes.

Written by Jonathan Harvey; directed by Ewan Torrance.

04.02.2006 **Annie's People**	DB / DBSWF

Duration: 50 minutes.

Written by Ian Pattison; directed by David Aitken.

11.02.2006 **Mike Davis PI**	DB / DBSWF

Duration: 50 minutes.

Written by Ian Brown and James Hendrie; directed by Andrea Miller.

18.02.2006 **Some Day I'll Find Me?**	DB / DBSWF

Duration: 50 minutes.

Written by Carla Lane; directed by Maria Stewart.

26.02.2006 **Being Dad?**	DB / DBSWF

Duration: 45 minutes.

Written by Trix Worrell; directed by Dearbhla McNulty.

04.03.2006 **The Old Guys**	DB / DBSWF

Duration: 55 minutes.

Written by Jesse Armstrong and Sam Bain; directed by Marcus Harben.

11.03.2006 **Good Morning Miss Milton**	DB / DBSWF

Duration: 60 minutes.

Written by Paul Mayhew-Archer; directed by Iain Ross.

A competition in which eight sitcom authors wrote the first twenty minutes of a pilot script and members of the public were invited to write the ending with the prize of a full sitcom pilot for the winner.

See also: THE OLD GUYS

LAST OF THE BEST MEN

A Thames Television production. Transmission details are for the ATV midlands region. Duration: 25 minutes.

Once they were the magnificent seven. Seven footloose and fancy-free bachelors. Now they are only two—Henry and Geoff. And when Geoff announces his defection, Henry has problems.

Written by Richard Waring; designed by Rod Stratfold; produced and directed by Michael Mills.

Derek Fowlds (Henry), Prunella Gee (Annette), Geoffrey Whitehead (Geoff), Jacqueline Clarke (Pamela), Jeannie Collings (Margaret), John Scott Martin (Vicar), Catherine Riding (Linda), Eunice Black (Mother).

	Holding / Source
19.05.1975	D3 / 2"

THE LAST VARIETY SHOW

An LWT production. Untransmitted. Duration: 25 minutes.

Produced and directed by David Bell.

Kenny Smiles.

	VT Number	Holding / Source
##.##.#### [untransmitted pilot]	9L/99133	2"|n / 2"

Recorded 29th November 1977.

LATE EXPECTATIONS

A BBC production for BBC 1. Transmission details are for BBC 1. Duration: 30 minutes.

Main regular credit(s):   Written by John Gleeson; produced by John B. Hobbs.

	Production No	Holding / Source
##.##.#### [untransmitted 1986 pilot]	LLCI650E/71	DB / 1"

Costume Lisa Benjamin; make-up Christine Greenwood; theme music by Ronnie Hazlehurst; designed by Suzy Lawrance; production manager Bill Ersser; directed by John B. Hobbs.

With Christopher Timothy (Ted Jackson), Anna Carteret (Liz Jackson), Caroline Mander (Suzie), Siobhan Boa (Polly), Paul McCarthy (George), Peter Hughes (Doctor Anderson), Mary Maude (Pauline), Norman Eshley (Harry), Neil West (Bruce), Sally Hughes (Joyce).

LATE NIGHT LYNAM

A BBC production. Untransmitted.

Desmond Lynam (Host).

	Holding / Source
##.##.#### [untransmitted pilot]	DB / DBS

Recorded in 1997.

LAURA, BEN AND HIM

An Avalon Productions production for ITV 2. Transmission details are for ITV 2. Duration: 22 minutes.

Main regular credit(s):   Written by Marek Larwood, Laura Solon and Ben Willbond; script supervisor Suzanne Baron; music by Robert Wix; designed by Dennis De Groot; associate producer Alison Carpenter; executive producers Richard Allen-Turner and Jon Thoday; head of production Bluey Richards; produced by Sioned Wiliam; directed by Ben Kellett.

Main regular cast: Marek Larwood (Performer), Laura Solon (Performer), Ben Willbond (Performer).

	Holding / Source
##.##.#### [untransmitted pilot]	DB / DBSWF

See also: THE 3RD XI

THE LAW

A Thames Television production for ITV 1. Transmission details are for the Central region. Duration: 75 minutes.

A pairof detectives investigate the murder of a respected doctor, who has been stabbed nine times and hurled from the balcony ofa seedy block of flats. They soon have a suspect on their hands —a heroin-addicted teenage prostitute who seems to have been rather more than just one of the doctor's patients. It also appears that the good
doctor led something of a double life. But just how much does his poisened headmistress wife know about that?

Written by Matthew Hall; executive producer Chris Parr; produced by Mary Gibson; directed by Juliet May.

Douglas Hodge (Detective Inspector Jack Raleigh), Joseph McFadden (Detective Constable Connor), Amita Dhiri (Helen Galloway), Sharon Duce (Linda Farrer QC), Barbara Flynn (Eleanor Kimbrough), Sam Loggin (Anna Damon), William Gaminara (Alan Vine), Nicola Redmond (Detective Chief Inspector Denby), Sarah Malin (Dawn Trent).

	Holding / Source
12.06.2002 **Trial And Error**	DB / V1SW

LE PRIX DE LEEDS

A Yorkshire Television production. Transmission details are for the ATV midlands region. Duration: 25 minutes.

Television sends itself up in this comedy. It is set in Leeds' first International Festival of Television which has the theme of "Peace and Goodwill between Nations."

However, there is a mass walkout by delegates over unsatisfactory accommodation, so that only a handful of small nations is left.

Written by John Bird and John Wells; designed by Peter Caldwell; produced by John Duncan; directed by David Mallet and Len Lurcuck.

John Wells (Guy Peverett), John Bird (Nick Nax), John Wells (Ilona Harpy), John Bird (Herr Klopstick), Harry, The Intelligent Rook.

	Holding / Source
23.07.1974	1" / 2"

See also: DEADLINE LEEDS* / LEEDS ATHLETIC* / THE PLAY'S THE THING - A DRAMA IN THE MAKING* / RETURN TO LEEDS - THE MAKING OF A DOCUMENTARY*

LEAD BALLOON

An Open Mike production for Various BBC Channels. Transmission details are for Various BBC Channels. Duration: 30 minutes.

Main regular credit(s):   Created by Jack Dee; produced and directed by Alex Hardcastle.

Main regular cast: Jack Dee (Rick Spleen), Sean Power (Marty), Raquel Cassidy (Mel), Antonia Campbell Hughes (Sam), Anna Crilly (Magda), Tony Gardner (Michael), Rasmus Hardiker (Ben).

	Holding / Source
##.##.#### [untransmitted pilot]	DB / DBSWF

THE LEAD ZEPPELIN SHOW

A BBC production. Untransmitted. Duration: 30 minutes.

Mick Sadler, Clement Freud, Chris Serle, Joanna Van Gyseghem.

	Holding / Source
##.##.####	J /

Recorded March 1968.

A LEAGUE OF THEIR OWN

A CPL (Celador) production for Sky One. Transmission details are for Sky One. Usual duration: 25 minutes.

Comedy sports panel show.

Main regular credit(s):   Executive producers Danielle Lux, Duncan Gray and Murray Boland.

Main regular performer(s):   James Corden (Referee).

	Holding / Source
##.##.#### [untransmitted pilot]	DB / DBSW

With Stuart Broad (Team Captain), Jamie Redknapp (Team Captain).

LEAPY LEE

An LWT production. Untransmitted. Duration: 25 minutes.

	VT Number	Holding / Source
##.##.#### [untransmitted pilot]	9L/00190	2"|n / 2"

LEGIT

A the Comedy Unit production for BBC 1 Scotland. Transmission details are for BBC 1 Scotland. Duration: 29 minutes.

Main regular credit(s):   Written by Robert Florence and Iain Connell; produced and directed by Iain Davidson.

Main regular cast: Steve McNicoll (Fox), Jordan Young (Danny), Clare Grogan (May).

	Holding / Source
16.09.2006	DB /

LET'S PRETEND

A Central production. Transmission details are for the Central region. Duration: 18 minutes.

Main regular credit(s):   Devised by Michael Jeans.

SERIES 1

	Production No	VT Number	Holding / Source
##.##.#### [untransmitted pilot]	9157/81	9537x6	J / 2"

Recorded 5.8.1981.

LEWIS

Produced for ITV 1 by a variety of companies (see details below). made in association with WGBH Boston. Transmission details are for the Central region. Duration: 100 minutes.

Main regular credit(s):   Based on characters created by Colin Dexter; produced by Chris Burt.

Main regular cast: Kevin Whately (Detective Inspector Robert Lewis), Laurence Fox (Detective Sergeant (llater Inspector) James Hathaway), Clare Holman (Doctor Laura Hobson), Rebecca Front (Chief Superintendent Jean Innocent).

A Granada production.

	Holding / Source
29.01.2006	DB / V1SW

The ghost of John Thaw looms large over this handsome Inspector Morse sequel. But between them, Kevin Whately as Lewis, now promoted to inspector, and a shrewd new sidekick in the shape of Laurence Fox, pick up
his torch and run with it.

Here, a student is shot dead at a sleep laboratory and the story behind her killing has elaborate parallels with a certain Shakespeare play - parallels that are there to flatter our intelligence but are nonetheless carefully spelt out, in case our intelligence isn't quite up to it. Whateiy's weary everyman act works as well as ever and Fox looks like he could single-handedly make up the charisma deficit left by Thaw.

Written by Stephen Churchett; based on a story by Russell Lewis; script supervisor Pauline Harlow; music by Barrington Pheloung; production executive Gail Kennett; executive producers Rebecca Eaton, Michele Buck, Ted Childs and Damien Timmer; co-produced by Kate McKerrell; directed by Bill Anderson.

With Charlie Cox (Danny Griffon), Sophie Winkleman (Regan Peverill), Colin Starkey (Bernard Beech), Jack Ellis (Rex Griffon), Jemma Redgrave (Trudi Griffon), Dennis Matsuki (Mr Tanigaki), Flora Spencer-Longhurst (Jessica Pollock), Danny Webb (Tom Pollock), Rosalyn Wright (Air Stewardess), Alex Knight (Detective Inspector Knox), Lizzy McInnerny (Kate Jekyll), Marc Elliott (Hal Bose), Michael Maloney (Ivor Denniston), Michael Hobbs (Club Secretary), Adam Smethurst (Locksmith), Mark Small (Uniformed Police Constable), Janet Maw (Secretary).

See also: INSPECTOR MORSE*

THE LIFE OF RILEY

A Granada production. Transmission details are for the ATV midlands region. Usual duration: 24 minutes.

Main regular credit(s):   Designed by Denis Parkin; produced and directed by Eric Prytherch.

Main regular cast: Bill Maynard (Frank Riley).

	Production No	Holding / Source
##.##.#### Untransmitted pilot: Happy Days	P795/1	J / 2"

Written by H. V. Kershaw.

With Bill Maynard (Frank Smith), Eileen Kennally (Ethel Goodchild), Carrie Kirstein (Janice Butcher), Peter Pratt (George Pollitt), Wensley Pithey (Clifford Pringle), Frank Lincoln (Brian Smith).

Recorded 23.04.1974.

LIFE SPAM

A Jones The Film production for BBC 3. Untransmitted. Duration: 30 minutes.

Written by Rob Brydon; executive producer Simon Wilson.

Alice Lowe (Host), Rob Brydon.

	Holding / Source
##.##.####	DB /

LIFE'S A PITCH

A Michael Hurll Television production for BBC 1. Transmission details are for BBC 1. Duration: 30 minutes.

Pilot programme for a sporting comedy show. The programme combines a sitcom about the making of a sports review with a stand-up featuring Jimmy Tarbuck performing in front of a studio audience.

Devised by Michael Hurll and Colin Bostock-Smith; programme associate Mark Tinkler; script associates Colin Bostock-Smith and Nigel Crowle; script supervisor Lulu Haggerty; music by David Arch; assistant producer Nigel Jones; executive producer Jon Plowman; production manager Gillian Goodlet; produced by Michael Hurll; directed by Peter Orton.

Jimmy Tarbuck (Host), Peter Brackley, Kevin Day, Gary Richardson, Jon Culshaw, Ted Robbins, Lucy Porter, Josephine Caulfield, Simon Evans.

	Holding / Source
19.03.2000	DB / DBSW

LIFESPAM: MY CHILD IS FRENCH

An Arbie production for BBC 3. made in association with Talkback Thames. Transmission details are for BBC 3. Duration: 30 minutes.

Written by Alice Lowe; music by Jane Watkins; designed by Rosy Thomas; associate producer Guy Davidson; executive producers Rob Brydon, Miles Ross and Duncan Hayes; production managers Karen Turner and Clare Casey; produced by Daisy Robertson; directed by Jacqueline Wright.

Sharon Horgan (Narrator), Steve Brody, Margaret Cabourn Smith, Justin Edwards, Simon Farnaby, Richard Glover, Alice Lowe, Tom Meeten, Steve Oram, Clare Thomson, Rosalyn Wright, Joel Coussins, Leo Henry, Susannah Slevin.

	Holding / Source
23.01.2009	DB / DBSWF

Spoof documentary pilot.

LIKE IT OR NOT

A Southern Television production. Transmission details are for the Southern Television region. Duration: 25 minutes.

	Holding / Source
11.05.1979 **Open Dors**	J / 2"

See: OPEN DORS.

18.05.1979 Dance Crazy   DB-DV / 2"

Produced by Britt Allcroft; directed by John Kaye Cooper.

The surviving DB-DV is of an earlier 45 minute edit of the programme. David King recalls, "Jeremy Wallington, Southern's Director of Programmes said at the time [Dance Crazy] was expensive to make and something may come of it when they had more sophisticated editing facilities. However, nothing happened before the loss of the franchise. The first three shows were all half hour but "Dance Crazy" was made to 45 mins with 2 x centre breaks. Strangely, they cut it down to 30 mins for transmission. The VT Editor, Ken McLeod-Baikie, was very proud of his work on this one and tried to thwart all attempts to wipe the show after transmission. However, they did succeed in wiping the master but a VHS copy of the full length version was kept which has been transferred to DVD and to Digibeta. The latter is now in the Wessex archive."

25.05.1979 Anna, Helene and Sue   J / 2"

With Anna Raeburn, Helene Hayman, Sue Slipman.

See: POLLY, HELENE AND SUE.

01.06.1979 My Favourite Things   J / 2"

With Trevor Baker, Candlewick Green.

See also: POLLY, HELENE AND SUE*

LILY SAVAGE'S BLANKETY BLANK

A Fremantle production for BBC 1. made in association with Wildflower Productions. Transmission details are for BBC 1. Duration: 30 minutes.

Main regular credit(s):   Theme music by Ronnie Hazlehurst.

Main regular performer(s): Lily Savage (Host).

	Holding / Source
26.12.1997	DB / DBS

Written by Charlie Adams and Dennis Berson; script supervisor Anthea Dudley; designed by Andy Walmsley; executive producers Brendan Murphy and Keith Stewart; production manager Paul Kelly; produced by Dean Jones; directed by Geoff Miles.

With Adrian Finighan (Voice Over), Ronan Keating, Christopher Cazenove, Gwen Taylor, Elizabeth Dawn, Gareth Hale, Carol Vorderman.

SERIES 2

	Holding / Source
28.12.1999 **Christmas Special**	DB / DBS

With Donald Sinden, Roy Barraclough, Honor Blackman, Barbara Windsor, Anthea Turner, Tim Vincent.

LIMMY'S SHOW

A the Comedy Unit production for BBC 2 Scotland. Transmission details are for BBC 2 Scotland. Duration: 30 minutes.

Main regular cast: Brian Limond, Debbie Welsh, Tom Brogan, Raymond Mearns.

	Holding / Source
18.02.2009	HD/DB / HDC

Written by Brian Limond; designed by Ewen Duncan; executive producers Jacqueline Sinclair, Iain Davidson and Ewan Angus; produced by Rab Christie; directed by Brian Limond.

With Debbie Welsh, Tom Brogan, Raymond Mearns.

THE LITTLE AND LARGE "TELLYSHOW"

A Thames Television production. Transmission details are for the ATV midlands region. Duration: 25 minutes.

Main regular cast: Little and Large (Hosts).

	Holding / Source
20.12.1976	D3 / 2"

Written by Tony Hawes, Syd Little and Eddie Large; programme associate Tony Hawes; music by Sam Harding; designed by Anthony Cartledge; produced and directed by Royston Mayoh.

With Tom Shelley.

A LITTLE BIG BUSINESS

Alternative/Working Title(s): HEART OF GOLD

A Granada production. Transmission details are for the ATV midlands region. Duration: 25 minutes.

Main regular credit(s):   Written by Jack Pulman.

Main regular cast: David Kossoff (Marcus Lieberman).

Credits: Designed by Bernard Carey; produced by Peter Eton; directed by Graeme McDonald.

Cast: With James Maxwell (Simon Lieberman).

	Production No	Holding / Source
08.08.1963	P395/6	DB / 40

Alternative transmissions: Granada: 11.07.1963.

With David Langton (Basil Crane), John Cater (Laslo), Charles Lamb (Charlie), Joyce Marlow (Miss Stevens), Sydney Gatcum [as Sydney Gatcumb], John Adams, Donald Fraser [as Donald Fraszer].

See also: COMEDY FOUR

LITTLE BIG TIME

A Southern Television production. Transmission details are for the ATV midlands region. Duration: 25 minutes.

Main regular cast: Freddie and The Dreamers.

Holding / Source

##.##.#### **[untransmitted pilot]**   J / 2"

Format by Jack Hargreaves and Angus Wright; produced and directed by Angus Wright.

Recorded at the Nuffield Theatre, Southampton, in March 1968.

LITTLE BRITAIN

A BBC production for BBC 3. made in association with Pozzitive Television. Transmission details are for BBC. Duration: 30 minutes.

Character-based sketches satirising modern life written and performed by Matt Lucas and David Walliams.

Main regular credit(s):   Created by Matt Lucas and David Walliams; written by Matt Lucas and David Walliams; music by David Arnold.

Main regular cast: Matt Lucas, David Walliams, Tom Baker (Narrator, Voice Only).

SERIES 1

Transmission details are for BBC 3.

Main regular credit(s):   Produced by Myfanwy Moore.

Holding / Source

09.02.2003   DB / DBSWF

Alternative transmissions: BBC 2: 09.02.2003.

Directed by Graham Linehan.

With Anthony Head, Stirling Gallacher, Clare Boland, Paul Putner, David Foxxe.

The BBC1 'repeats' were re-edited for a mainstream audience.

See also: COMIC RELIEF - THE BIG ONE* / LITTLE BRITAIN (RADIO) / LITTLE BRITAIN ABROAD*

LITTLE BRITAIN (RADIO)

A BBC production for BBC Radio 4. Transmission details are for BBC Radio 4. Duration: 30 minutes.

Main regular credit(s):   Written by Matt Lucas and David Walliams; music by David Arnold.

Main regular cast: Matt Lucas, David Walliams.

Holding / Source

03.08.2000   DA /

Matt Lucas and David Williams preview their forthcoming sketch show which takes a look at life in Britain in the new millennium by following the lives of some less than ordinary folk.

Produced and directed by Ashley Blaker.

With Jean Ainslie, Tom Baker, Samantha Power, Paul Putner.

See also: LITTLE BRITAIN / LITTLE BRITAIN ABROAD*

LIVING LIFE LATELY

A BBC production. Untransmitted. Duration: 30 minutes.

Written by Martyn Hesford; costume Kathryn Ayerst; make-up Yvonne Brockbank; designed by Jim Hatchard; production manager Jim Capper; produced and directed by John Gorrie.

Barbara Keogh (Alice), Liz Smith (Winnie), Joan Sims (Mrs Mullins), Constance Chapman (Monica), Elizabeth Bradley (Jessie), Helen Blakeman (Camille), Tina Earl (Camille's Mother), Jeni Ward (Miss Cartwright), Mary Duddy (Mrs Cartwright), Joe Holroyd (Old Man), Sam Webster (Bus Driver), Georgina Lane (Girl On Bus), Colin Meredith (Bus Passenger), Joy Blakeman (Supermarket Cashier), Mark Jordon (Window Cleaner), Mark Chatterton (Window Cleaner's Mate), Malcolm Hebden (Radio Doctor), Joan Campion (Radio Caller).

	Production No	Holding / Source
##.##.#### **[untransmitted 1990 pilot]**	LLCA380N/71	DB / 1"

LIVING WITH TWO PEOPLE YOU LIKE INDIVIDUALLY BUT NOT AS A COUPLE

A Channel K production for BBC 3. Transmission details are for BBC 3. Duration: 28 minutes.

Martin is an out-of-work actor. He moves in with his brother and brother's girlfriend in their swanky flat in Manchester. They are both lovely people but, as Martin discovers, they make a nightmare couple to share with!

Written by Mark Watson; music by Augustin Bousfield; designed by Jim Holloway; executive producers Cheryl Taylor, Alan Marke and Matt Tiller; produced by Sally Martin; directed by David Sant.

Tom Basden (Martin), Abigail Burdess (Millie), Sara Crowe (Lyn), Marek Larwood (Hugo), Tom Price (Craig), Sarah Soleman (Antonia), James Bachman (Literary agent), Leah Chillery (Beyoncé), Phoebe Soteriades (Hitler).

Holding / Source

12.02.2007   DB /

LIZZIE AND SARAH

A Baby Cow Productions production for BBC 2. Transmission details are for BBC 2. Duration: 30 minutes.

Written by Julia Davis and Jessica Hynes; script supervisor Angelica Pressello; music by Julia Davis, Martin Coogan and Michael Hall; director of photography George Richmond; assistant director Ben Glickman; art director Nick Murray; designed by Dave Ferris; associate producers Julia Davis and Jessica Hynes; executive producers Henry Normal and Lindsay Hughes; head of production Kerry Waddell; production manager Lyndsay Robinson; produced by Alison MacPhail; directed by Elliot Hegarty.

Jessica Hynes (Sarah / Ellie), Julia Davis (Lizzie / Faith), David Cann (John), Kevin Eldon (Rick), Claire Rushbrook (Fiona), Lilly Ainsworth (Podge), Jessica Gunning (Branita), Mark Heap (Michael), Pravin Sunwar (Quarm), Stephen Evans (Barry), Amanda Rawnsley (Shop Assistant).

	Holding / Source
20.03.2010	HD/DB / HD/DB

THE LOCKED BOOK

A Winwell Productions Ltd production. Untransmitted. Duration: 25 minutes.

Based on the papers and case histories left by the late Harry Price. In production January 1959.

Written by Paul Tabori; executive producer Derek Winn; co-produced by Bill Luckwell and Paul Tabori.

Ann Todd (Narrator), Dennis Price (Harry Price), Ellen Pollock, Jean Dawnay.

	Holding / Source
##.##.#### The Case Of The Devil Girl	J / B3

Further scripts were written by Paul Tabori and ITV seemed interested, but the pilot failed to impress. Winwell approached the BBC and made 'Maigret' instead.

LONDON BRIDGE

An LWT production. Transmission details are for the London Weekend Television region. Duration: 26 minutes.

Main regular cast: Michael Wale (Presenter).

	Holding / Source
28.08.1974	2"|n / 2"

Dialogue directed by Alan Wallis; research Alan Lubin; designed by Bryce Walmsley; produced by Mike Smith.

With Leo Dolan (Presenter), Brian Connolly, Dougie Squires, Lindsay Kemp.

Presenter Leo Dolan leads studio discussions on topics such as school uniforms and modern dance. He takes a group of students to a dance class in Covent Garden led by Lindsay Kemp and gives information on local events for the youth of London.

LONDON SHOUTING

A BBC production for BBC 2. Transmission details are for BBC 2. Duration: 35 minutes.

Written by Simon Munnery and Graham Linehan; produced by Jon Rowlands; directed by Nick Wood.

Simon Munnery (Alan Parker - Urban Warrior), Jason Freeman, Kevin Eldon, Mel Giedroyc, Bill Cashmore, Peter Serafinowicz, Julian Barratt, Tim Hope, Waen Shepherd.

	Holding / Source
02.08.1996	DB / DB

LONDON TALKING

An LWT production. Transmission details are for the London Weekend Television region.

Similar to the BBC's Talkback show.

	Holding / Source
07.10.1981	

Edited by Malcolm Southan.

LONDON'S BURNING

An LWT production. Transmission details are for the Central region. Duration varies - see below for details.

Main regular credit(s):   Devised by Jack Rosenthal.

	VT Number	Holding / Source
07.12.1986	10619	D2 / C1

Duration: 100 minutes.

Written by Jack Rosenthal; music by November One; executive producer Linda Agran; produced by Paul Knight; directed by Les Blair.

With Mark Arden (Vaseline), Gary McDonald (Ethnic), Jerome Flynn (Rambo), James Hazeldine (Bayleaf), James Marcus (Tate), Sean Blowers (Hallam), Rupert Baker (Malcolm), Richard Walsh (Sicknote), Gerard Horan (Charisma), Katharine Rogers (Josie), Eric Deacon (Gerry), Hetty Baynes, Corinne Skinner-Carter, Joy Richardson, Jason Rose, Mary Jo Randle, James Saxon, Peter McNamara, Brenda Cowling, Gary Webster, Eve Bland, George Sweeney, Helen Blizard, Nigel Louis-Marie, Astley Harvey, Patrick Henry, Tricia Thorns, Cynthia Powell, Kenneth Breinburg, Leonard Hay, Stephen Brigden, Norman Warwick, Robert East, Betty Romaine, Jean Leppard, Bill Spencer, Winston Crooke, Steve Emerson, Richard Cordery, John Joyce, Clive Shilson, Marsha Millar, Gavin Brown, Reginald Stewart, Sammy Blair, Joe Blair, Leon Davis, P. J. Nicholas, Jelena Budimir, Leon Silver, Kit Jackson, A. J. Clark, Joanne Zorian, Rory O'Connor.

THE LONELYHEARTS KID

A Thames Television production. Transmission details are for the Central region. Duration: 25 minutes.

Main regular credit(s):   Written by Alex Shearer; designed by Jan Chaney; produced by Anthony Parker; directed by Douglas Argent.

Main regular cast: Robert Glenister (Ken), George Winter (Ray), Julia Goodman (Ros).

	Holding / Source
17.07.1984 Old Acquaintance	1" / 1"

With Paul Chapman, Deborah Farrington.

LOOK AROUND YOU

Produced for BBC 2 by a variety of companies (see details below). Transmission details are for BBC 2. Duration varies - see below for details.

Main regular credit(s):   Written by Robert Popper and Peter Serafinowicz; music by Gelg; produced by Robert Popper and Peter Serafinowicz; directed by Tim Kirkby.

A Mivvin production.

		Holding / Source
##.##.#### **Calcium**		DB / DBSW

Duration: 22 minutes.

Narrated by Nigel Lambert; edited by Chris Dickens; director of photography John E. Walker; art director Rosy Thomas; production manager Daisy Robertson.

With Peter Serafinowicz, Jonny Popper, James Serafinowicz*.

All the live action material in this programme was shot on genuine film, albeit "dirtied-up" in post, so it's not filmised in the conventional sense - i.e. deinterlaced.

LOOKING BACK AT...

An ABC production. Transmission details are for the ABC midlands region. Duration: 25 minutes.

Narrated by Garry Marsh; written by James Thomas; produced and directed by Margery Baker.

Tommy Trinder, Emile Littler, Basil Dean, Eddie Latta.

	Holding / Source
20.08.1966 **George Formby**	J / 40

LOOKS FAMILIAR

A Thames Television production. Transmission details are for the ATV midlands region. Duration: 25 minutes.

Main regular credit(s):   Devised by Denis Gifford.

Main regular performer(s): Denis Norden (Presenter).

Credits: Designed by Sylva Nadolny; produced and directed by Alan Tarrant.

	VT Number	Holding / Source
25.08.1970	2203	DB / 62

Research Denis Gifford; designed by Sylva Nadolny [credited as Sylva Madolny]; produced and directed by Alan Tarrant.

With Humphrey Lyttelton, Jessie Matthews, Cardew Robinson, Alfred Marks, Jimmy Wheeler.

LOVE STORY

A Central production. Untransmitted.

Directed by Nic Phillips.

	Holding / Source
##.##.#### **[untransmitted pilot]**	J / 1"

Recorded November 1985.

LOVE THY NEIGHBOUR

A Thames Television production. Transmission details are for the ATV midlands region. Duration: 25 minutes.

Main regular credit(s):   Created by Vince Powell and Harry Driver.

Main regular cast: Jack Smethurst (Eddie Booth), Rudolph Walker (Bill Reynolds), Nina Baden-Semper (Barbie Reynolds), Kate Williams (Joan Booth).

	VT Number	Holding / Source
##.##.#### **[untransmitted pilot]**	4787	DB / 2"

Written by Vince Powell and Harry Driver; music by Stuart Gillies; produced and directed by Stuart Allen.

With Gwendolyn Watts (Joan Booth), George Roderick (Removal Man), Harry Littlewood (Foreman), Geoffrey Denton (Estate Agent).

Kate Williams role was played by another actress. The general tone of the pilot was more middle-class.

LUCIAN

A BBC production. Untransmitted. Duration: 30 minutes.

Written by Carla Lane; costume Lynda Woodfield; make-up Frances Needham; designed by Nigel Curzon; produced and directed by Bernard Thompson.

Michael Angelis (Lucian Boswell), Christopher Guard (Conrad), Colin Higgins (Glynn), Heather Wright (Kate), Ray Dunbobbin (Mr Boswell), Paula Tilbrook (Liverpudlian Lady), Louis Mahoney (Coloured Speaker), Brian Vaughan (Policeman), Michael Strinton (Police Driver), Oscar Peck (Youth In Crowd), Mark Holmes (Man In Crowd), Gertan Klauber (Foreigner), Graham Hamilton (Man In Pub), Zena Dare (Woman In Pub).

	Production No	VT Number	Holding / Source
##.##.#### **You, Me And Him**	LLCB401J/71	VC189284	DB-D3 / 2"

Recorded in October 1979.

See also: THE LIVER BIRDS*

LUCKY 7'S WITH THE NATIONAL LOTTERY

A BBC production for BBC 1. Transmission details are for BBC 1. Duration: 24 minutes.

Format by Mike Beale and Andy Culpin; additional material by Colin Edmonds; music by Horizon Music Media; designed by Chris Webster; production team Katie Jeffs, Honor Newton, Kate Rea and Amanda Wood; assistant producer Louise Ellard; production executive Erika Leonard; executive producer David Young; production manager Peter Hall; series producer Claire Horton; produced by Suzy Lamb; directed by David Coyle.

Bob Monkhouse (Presenter), Alan Dedicoat (Voice of the Balls).

	Production No	Holding / Source
##.##.#### **[untransmitted pilot]**	50/LEG V163Y	DB / DBSW

Alan Dedicoat announces the pilot is live from the BBC Television Centre, but the time clock reveals it was pre-recorded at the London Studios of LWT. :-)

LUCKY FELLER

An LWT production. Transmission details are for the ATV midlands region.

The tangled romantic lives of two brothers living at home with their mum in south-east London. - See more at: http://networkonair.com/shop/2012-lucky-feller-the-complete-series-5027626427245.html#sthash.mY5cD7vP.dpuf

Main regular credit(s):   Written by Terence Frisby; produced by Humphrey Barclay.

Main regular cast: David Jason (Shorty Mepstead), Cheryl Hall (Kathleen Peake).

	Production No	Holding / Source
##.##.#### **Lucky Fella [untransmitted pilot]**	9L/09560	DB-UM|n / 2"

Duration: 28 minutes.

Designed by John Clements; directed by Bryan Izzard.

With Elizabeth Spriggs (Mrs Mepstead), Nicky Henson, Burt Kwouk, Sylveste McCoy.

Recorded 03.06.75.

M•A•W•

An Absolutely production for Channel 4. Transmission details are for Channel 4.

	Holding / Source
##.##.#### **[untransmitted 2001 pilot]**	DB /

Recorded 2001.

M A W stands for Model, Actress, Whatever.

MAD MOVIES

A Mitchell Monkhouse Eyeline production for Comex Films Ltd. made in association with De Lane Lea / Mitchell Monkhouse Associates. Transmission details are for the ABC midlands region. Duration: 24 minutes.

Main regular credit(s):   Created by Bob Monkhouse; written by Bob Monkhouse; research Philip Jenkinson; music by Malcolm Mitchell; associate producer Raymond Rohauer; executive producer Henry Howard; directed by Jeff Inman.

Main regular cast: Bob Monkhouse (Presenter).

	Holding / Source
##.##.#### **Sports [untransmitted pilot]**	B3 / B3

A MMA Production production.

Titles by Biographic; associate producer Tony Hawes; produced by Henry Howard; directed by Jeff Inman.

Made at Halliford Studios, Shepperton.

The synopses included here are Bob's own. We have tried to work out the correct transmission dates for the episodes in these three series but at times it has come down to educated guesswork as the synopses in the ITV listings magazines are often vague. Where there are no tx dates it isn't that we think the edition remains unshown just that we really don't have a clue.

MADE IN SPAIN

A Central production. Transmission details are for the Central region. Duration: 50 minutes.

Intended to be a female version of 'Auf Wiedersehen Pet'.

Written by Tony Grounds; produced by Nicholas Palmer; directed by Herbert Wise.

Lill Roughley (Jacqui), Camille Coduri (Rosy), Jill Benedict (Estelle), Ella Wilder (Tolla), Vincenzo Nicoli (Johnie), Roger Lloyd Pack (Den), Breffni McKenna (Ray), Gurdial Sira (Hanif), Teris Hebrew (Taxi Driver), Adam French (Hooligan), David Keys (Hooligan), Jonathan Lacey (Hooligan), Joe Searby (Hooligan), Andy Serkis (Hooligan), Jay Simpson (Hooligan).

	Holding / Source
20.06.1989	1" / 1"

MAGGIE AND HER

An LWT production. Transmission details are for the ATV midlands region. Duration: 25 minutes.

Main regular credit(s):   Written by Leonard Webb; theme music by Laurie Holloway and Julia McKenzie.

Main regular cast: Julia McKenzie (Maggie).

Transmission details are for the London Weekend Television region.

	Production No	Holding / Source
13.08.1976 **Poppy And Her**	9L/09628	DB|n / 2"

Produced by Humphrey Barclay.

THE MAGIC BOX

An ABC production. Transmission details are for the ABC midlands region. Duration: 25 minutes.

Each week well-known personalities are asked what people, places or things they would choose to keep forever in a magic box. The box is big enough to contain The Taj Mahal but might just hold a snapshot, a voice, an atmosphere or a fragrance.

	Holding / Source
03.09.1966	J / 40

Produced and directed by Pamela Lonsdale.

With Robin Ray (Presenter), Wilfred Pickles.

THE MAGIC COMEDY STRIP

A Thames Television production. Transmission details are for the Central region.

Main regular credit(s):   Produced by John Fisher; directed by Paul Kirrage.

Main regular performer(s): Rudy Cody (Presenter), Jeff Hobson (Presenter).

	Holding / Source
11.09.1991 **Magic Comedy Hour**	1" / 1"S

Duration: 50 minutes.

With David Williamson, Vladimir Danilin.

MAGIC MOMENTS

A SAM Productions production. Untransmitted. Duration: 25 minutes.

Consultant Ali Bongo; produced by Stan Blackman.

Frankie Howerd, Terry Herbert, Terry Burgess, Robert Knight, Simon Lovell, Stevie Starr.

	Holding / Source
##.##.#### **[untransmitted pilot]**	J / 1"

Recorded 1987 at Foxhunters mobile caravan park, Minster, Thanet.

MAGNUS HAWKE

A BBC production. Not made.

Devised by Richard Harris.

Holding / Source

##.##.####   NR /

Untitled pilot by Richard Harris.

17 one-line story ideas by Philip Chambers.

The First Tycoon by Donald Cotton.

See also: ADAM ADAMANT / ADAM ADAMANT LIVES!*

MAIGRET

Alternative/Working Title(s): INSPECTOR MAIGRET / TALES OF INSPECTOR MAIGRET

A BBC production. made in association with Winwell Productions. Transmission details are for BBC. Duration: 55 minutes.

Main regular credit(s):   Based on novels by Georges Simenon; theme music by Ron Grainer.

Main regular cast: Rupert Davies (Chief Inspector Maigret), Ewen Solon (Lucas), Neville Jason (Lapointe), Victor Lucas (Torrance).

SERIES 1

Main regular credit(s):   Script editor Giles Cooper; associate producer Bill Luckwell; executive producer Andrew Osborn.

Main regular cast: With Helen Shingler (Madame Maigret).

Holding / Source

31.10.1960 **Murder In Montmarte**   R3 /

Adapted by Giles Cooper; directed by Andrew Osborn.

With April Olrich, Thomas Gallagher, Freda Jackson, Maria Andipa, Leonard Graham, Helen Shingler, Michael Hitchman, Ernst Ulman, Peter Grisewood, Aubrey Woods, Joan Young, Linda Castle, Stan Simmons.

An uncut R1 also exists.

Rupert Davies appeared as Maigret on stage in "Maigret And The Lady" in 1965.

See also: MAIGRET (RADIO)* / PLAY OF THE MONTH* / SUNDAY NIGHT THEATRE*

MAKE A DATE

A Yorkshire Television production. Transmission details are for the Central region. Duration: 25 minutes.

A light-hearted celebration of New Year's Days, past and present.

Designed by Robert Scott; produced by John Bartlett; directed by Terry Henebery.

Anne Diamond (Presenter), Nick Owen (Presenter), John Wells (Denis Thatcher), Sarah Brightman, Barbara Dickson, Andrew O'Connor, Jimmy Savile, The Stranglers.

Holding / Source

01.01.1988   1" / 1"

MAKE 'EM LAUGH

An ATV production. Transmission details are for the ATV midlands region. Duration: 40 minutes.

Holding / Source

07.06.1977   J / 2"

Readings by Garry Chambers; written by Philip Parsons and Tony Hawes; music associate Derek Scott; designed by Malcolm Stone; produced and directed by Peter Harris.

With Eve Adam, Michael Barrymore, Trevor Chance, Jim Davidson, Al Dean, Roger de Courcey, Mike Felix, Jodi Grey, Johnny Hammond, Lee Harding, Monopoly, Pat Mills, Simone, 20th Century Steel Sound, Jack Parnell and his Orchestra.

MAKE ME LAUGH

A Tyne Tees Television production. made in association with Action Time. Transmission details are for the Central region. Duration: 25 minutes.

Main regular credit(s):   Created by Mort Green and George Foster; script associate Garry Chambers; consultant Jeremy Fox.

Main regular performer(s): Bernie Winters (Host).

Holding / Source

##.##.#### **[new format - untransmitted pilot]**   1" / 1"

Produced by Heather Ging; directed by Royston Mayoh.

With Clive Webb, Bobby Davro, Lambert & Ross, Lennie Bennett, John Conteh.

An article in The Stage in August 1983 mentions thirteen editions made so far and it also mentions a pilot being made as a result of a change in the show's format with a view to making a further 13 shows in January and February 1984. Recorded 13.08.83.

MAKING GOOD

A BBC production for BBC 1. Untransmitted. Duration: 34 minutes.

Written by Stanley Price and Roger Lloyd Pack; designed by Jan Spoczynski; production manager Richard Boden; produced and directed by David Askey.

Liza Goddard (Kate), Francis Matthews (Max), Roger Lloyd Pack (Eddie), Patrick Newell (James), Helen Blatch (Mrs Cox), Anna Wing (Landlady), Gloria Connell (Inge), David Killick (Barman).

Holding / Source

##.##.####   DB-D3 / 2"

MAKING GOOD

Recorded 29.06.1982.

Untx comedy pilot.

MAMA'S BACK

Alternative/Working Title(s): NEXT

A BBC production for BBC 1. Transmission details are for BBC 1. Duration: 30 minutes.

The story of a temperamental Hollywood TV superstar who finally goes too far. Fired from the set, she finds herself shipped back to London - where she has to face the family she left behind.

Written by Ruby Wax; produced by Justin Judd; directed by Ed Bye.

Joan Collins (Tamara Hamilton), Michael Gambon (Ian Hamilton), Clive James (Himself), Samantha Janus (Sharon Emanuel), Rupert Everett (Stephen), Dana Ivy (Maureen).

	Holding / Source
06.12.1993	DB-D3 / D3S

MAN ABOUT THE HOUSE

A Thames Television production. Transmission details are for the ATV midlands region. Usual duration: 25 minutes.

Main regular credit(s):   Written by Johnnie Mortimer and Brian Cooke; produced and directed by Peter Frazer-Jones.

Main regular cast: Richard O'Sullivan (Robin Tripp), Paula Wilcox (Chrissy Plummer), Sally Thomsett (Jo), Brian Murphy (George Roper), Yootha Joyce (Mildred Roper).

SERIES 1

	VT Number	Holding / Source
15.08.1973 **Three's A Crowd**	7187	D3 / 2"

Designed by Gordon Toms.

With Helen Fraser.

See also: GEORGE & MILDRED* / ROBIN'S NEST*

A MAN IN HIS TIME

A Scottish Television production. Transmission details are for the Scottish Television region.

Play about Dundee poet William McGonagall.

	Holding / Source
##.##.#### **[untransmitted pilot]**	J / 40

Not networked, circa 1965. More plays were planned.

THE MAN IN THE VAN

A Yorkshire Television production. Untransmitted.

He's the new consumer champion, running an undercover team that will tell you how to avoid getting ripped off and secure the best deal. And he'll expose those offering bad deals or bad service. Living in a white van equipped with hi-tech devices, Jonathan, in the name of decency, travels up and down the country searching for rip-off merchants. His targets? Anyone who takes our money for goods and services, particularly for purchases like cars, holidays and houses.

Produced by Jessica Fowle.

Jonathan Maitland (Presenter), Pat Hoy (Presenter), Vince Rogers (Presenter).

	Holding / Source
##.##.#### **Secret Service [untransmitted pilot]**	DB / DBS

A MAN OF OUR TIMES

A Rediffusion Television production. Transmission details are for the ATV midlands region. Duration: 53 minutes.

Main regular credit(s):   Created by Julian Bond; story editor Julian Bond; executive producer Stella Richman; produced by Richard Bates.

Main regular cast: George Cole (Max Osborne).

	Holding / Source
01.01.1968 **The Name Of The Man**	R1|n / 40

Alt.Title(s): *You Leave It To Me*

Alternative transmissions: Granada: 02.01.1968; LWT: 25.04.1969; Rediffusion Television: 04.01.1968; Yorkshire Television: 11.07.1969.

Today is a day full of promise for Max Osborne. The company he works for is being taken over by a larger organisation, a move which promises opportunities for all. As Max brought the two companies together he is looking forward to some kind of reward. A share of the profits? A seat on the board? A company car? But Max still hasn't learnt that you shouldn't count your chickens before they're hatched .. .

Written by Julian Bond; designed by Frank Nerini; directed by Michael Lindsay-Hogg.

With Douglas Livingstone (Ron Banks), Charles Tingwell (David Somes), Clive Morton (Henry Somes), Peter Barkworth (Roberts), Jennifer Wilson (Muriel), Diana Beevers (Gwen), Zuleika Robson (Lucy), Gabrielle Blunt (Shirley), Mary Hignett (Mrs Carr), Sheridan Grant (Miss Carew), Michael Lomax (Bank Clerk).

TV Today claimed Gwen Cherrell was also in the cast. Recorded 04.07.1967.

MAN OF THE WORLD

Alternative/Working Title(s): MAN ABOUT THE WORLD

A Pimlico Films production for ATV. Transmission details are for the ABC midlands region. Duration: 48 minutes.

Main regular credit(s):	Story editor Ian Stuart Black; produced by Harry Fine.
Main regular cast:	Craig Stevens (Michael Strait).

SERIES 1

Main regular cast:	With Tracy Reed (Maggie).

Holding / Source

06.10.1962 **Masquerade In Spain**   C3 / C3

Written by Lindsay Hardy; directed by David Greene.

With Graham Stark, Clifford Evans, Marie France, Christina Gregg, George Coulouris, George Pastell, Guy Kingsley Poynter, Noel Coleman, Andreas Malandrinos, Malou Pantera.

This series featured a merchandising deal with the London Fashion House Group, giving the audience the chance to buy copies of outfits seen on the show. And who said BBC Worldwide invented tacky merchandising opportunities...

A report in The Stage (21.12.61) claimed that the first episode was being shot in colour and quoted an unnamed ITC spokesman who said, "It is useful to have a few TV films ready for colour transmission tests when they begin in earnest." Production of this series was held up by the 1961/62 Equity actors' strike, but unlike a couple of its contemporaries THE AMAZING DR. THORNDYKE and COLLECTOR'S ITEM, this delay was not fatal.

See also: THE SENTIMENTAL AGENT*

A MAN OF THE WORLD

An Ubangi Film Productions Ltd production. Untransmitted.

Executive producers Dan Jackson and Russell Enoch.

William Russell, Balbina Enoch.

Holding / Source

##.##.#### [untransmitted pilot]   J / B3

Production company formed by the actors, Russell Enoch and Dan Jackson, to sell a pilot to the BBC. The pilot was shot in Naples in January 1959.

MAN TO MAN WITH DEAN LEARNER

An Avalon Productions production for Channel 4. Transmission details are for Channel 4. Duration: 24 minutes.

Main regular cast:	Richard Ayoade (Dean Learner).

Holding / Source

##.##.#### **Deano's [untransmitted pilot]**   DB / DBSW

Songs by Matthew Holness; script supervisor Emma John; costume Claire Finlay; make-up Eva Marieges Moore; music by Steve Holness [credited as Steven Holness]; edited by Adam Windmill; director of photography Martin Hawkins; sound supervisor Kevin Paice; camera supervisor Tony Keene; assistant director Leon Coole; art directors Jane Shepherd and Andrea Simpson; designed by Dennis De Groot; executive producers Jon Thoday and Richard Allen-Turner; line producer Stephen Abrahams; produced by Nick Symons; directed by Richard Ayoade and Ben Kellett.

With Matthew Holness (Merriman Weir), Sally Hawkins, Kim Noble, Stuart Silver, Matt Berry.

THE MAN WHO WALKS BY NIGHT

A Vizio Ltd production. Transmission details are for BBC. Duration: 26 minutes.

Written by Duncan Ross; from an idea by Dennis Holman; produced by Roy Plomley; directed by Eric Fawcett.

Patricia Jessel, Roy Plomley, Robert Ayres, Campbell Cotts, James Cairncross.

Holding / Source

28.09.1950 **A Dinner Date With Death**   J / B3

Always listed as DINNER DATE WITH DEATH (no 'A' at the start) and is billed as though a short thriller or crime film. There's no hint in the Radio Times that it was made for television. Repeated on 01/02/1951 and 19/03/1952.

Shooting started at Marylebone Studios on 11th July 1949. US networks and the BBC showed the pilot. A freeze on US funding prevented a series. 26 episodes were written but not made.

MANSIONS

A RPM Communications production. made in association with Central Television Facilities. Untransmitted.

Main regular credit(s):	Written by John Stoker.
Main regular cast:	Diane Keen (Lorna), Alexandra Bastedo (Contessa Maria Valdez), Simon Williams (Hal), Edward Jewesbury (Sir George Trevelyan), Freddie Stuart, Caroline Williams, Phillip Sidney.

Holding / Source

##.##.#### **The Homecoming**   1" / 1"

Duration: 8 minutes.

Taster episode made as a pilot.

A MANY SPLINTERED THING

A Lucky Dog production for BBC 1. Transmission details are for BBC 1. Duration: 30 minutes.

Main regular credit(s):   Written by Geoff Deane.

Main regular cast: Alan Davies (Russel Boyd).

	Holding / Source
25.12.1998	DB / DBSW

The last thing you need as a married man is to wake up naked and hungover next to another woman. But when Russel meets Elly, somehow good intentions go out the window.

Music by Keith Miller; executive producer Danielle Lux; produced by Geoff Deane and Kenton Allen; directed by Paul Harrison.

With Kate Ashfield (Elly Rawsthorn), Victor McGuire (Luis Banks), Paul Trussell (Alistair Cranwell), Kate Isitt (Susanna Boyd), Steve Robling, Vanessa Feltz.

In 2001 Lucky Dog made a US pilot for the Paramount Channel.

MARGIE AND ME

A Yorkshire Television production. Transmission details are for the ATV midlands region. Duration: 25 minutes.

Written by John Graham; music by Peter Husband; designed by Mary Rea; produced and directed by Stuart Allen.

Arthur Mullard (Arthur), Betty Marsden (Margie), Vanessa Ford (Lilian), Nigel Lambert (Dennis), Norman Bird (Cheeseman), Richard Hope (Police Constable), Roger Avon (Landlord), Jimmy Young (Himself).

	Production No	Holding / Source
06.07.1978	Y/1051/0001	2" / 2"

Postponed from 22.05.1978.

Originally, Georgina Melville was billed to play Lilian.

MARK MY WORDS

An LWT production. Untransmitted. Duration: 25 minutes.

	VT Number	Holding / Source
##.##.#### [untransmitted pilot]	9L/00223	2"|n / 2"

MARK'S BRILLIANT BLOG

A Hat Trick North production for BBC 3. Transmission details are for BBC 3. Duration: 28 minutes.

Written by Darren Dutton and Zoë Galloway; additional material by Andy Mettam; edited by Joe Varley and Will Hodgson; director of photography Chris Burton; assistant director Paul Tigue; art director Sami Khan; assistant producer Kriston Jackson McKeown; production executive Jason Crosby; executive producers Jonathan Davenport and Helen Williams; production manager Julie Rose; produced and directed by Kirsty Smith.

Chris Hannon (Mark Padley), Lee Fenwick (Phillip Hughes), Jayne Tunnicliffe (Louise Moorcroft), Susan Vale (Maureen), Toby Hadoke (Terry Cartwright), Seymour Mace (Ratman / Simon), Lou Conran (Kate), Holliday Grainger (Mary Padley).

	Holding / Source
24.03.2009	DB / DBSW

THE MARSHA HUNT SHOW

A Granada production. Untransmitted.

Music directed by Derek Hilton; designed by Denis Parkin; produced by Simon Albury; directed by Nicholas Ferguson.

Marsha Hunt (Host), Julie Walters, Ian La Frenais, James Fox, Darts.

	Production No	Holding / Source
##.##.#### [untranmitted pilot] Rx: 02.07.83	P1204/0	DB / 1"

Proposed chat show.

See also: LIVE AT THE MILLIONAIRE*

THE MARSHAL

Alternative/Working Title(s): THE MARSHAL AND THE MAD WOMAN

A Portobello Films production for HTV. Transmission details are for the Central region. Duration: 100 minutes.

Adapted by John Goldsmith; based on a book by Magdalen Nabb; executive producers Alan Clayton and Eric Abraham; produced by Manny Wessels; directed by Alan Clayton.

Alfred Molina (Marshal Salvatore Guarnaccia), Gemma Craven (Teresa), Anna Cropper (Clementina), Vincenzo Ricotta (Di Nuccio), Jude Law (Bruno), Paul Humpoletz (Franco), Brenda Kempner (Pina), Kerry Peers (Linda), Robin Soans (Angelo), Gillian Hanna (Maria Pia), Neil Boorman (Pippo), Gerard Logan (Rossi), Jonathan Coy (Mannucci), Helen Baxendale (Anita), Al Ashton (Bruti), Frank Baker (Spicuzza).

	Holding / Source
24.04.1993	1" / V1S

Pilot for unmade series.

MARTI

An ATV production. Transmission details are for the ATV midlands region.

Main regular performer(s): Marti Caine (Host).

	Holding / Source
04.05.1977	DB / 2"

Duration: 50 minutes.

Written by Wally Malston, Barry Cryer, Sid Green and Dick Hills; music by Derek Scott; designed by Malcolm Stone; produced and directed by Peter Harris.

With The Three Degrees, Keith Harris & Cuddles, Gilbert O'Sullivan, The Norman Maen Dancers, The Tony Mansell Singers, Jack Parnell and his Orchestra, Christopher Good, Sandra Michaels, Royce Mills, Derek Fowlds, Colette Gleeson.

MARTIN KANE PRIVATE INVESTIGATOR

A Towers of London Productions production for ABC. made in association with Towers of London Productions / Ziv Television. Transmission details are for the ABC midlands region. Duration: 25 minutes.

Main regular credit(s):   Associate producer Frank Sherwin Green; produced by Harry Alan Towers.

Main regular cast: William Gargan (Martin Kane), Brian Reece (Superintendent Page).

	Holding / Source
##.##.#### **Missing Daughter**	J / B3

Alt.Title(s): *Diamond Ring*

Written by Art Wallace; story by Paul Dudley; directed by David MacDonald.

With Macdonald Parke, John Warwick, Martin Benson, Kay Callard, Basil Dignam, Guido Lorraine.

Brian Reece does not appear in this episode.

The episodes are listed in the correct transmission order.

THE MARY WHITEHOUSE EXPERIENCE

A BBC production for BBC 2. Transmission details are for BBC 2. Duration: 30 minutes.

Main regular credit(s):   Written by David Baddiel, Steve Punt, Rob Newman and Hugh Dennis; produced and directed by Marcus Mortimer.

Main regular performer(s): David Baddiel, Steve Punt, Rob Newman, Hugh Dennis.

	Holding / Source
03.10.1990	DB / 1"

A Spitting Image Productions production.

With No guest cast.

MASTER OF INNOCENTS

A BBC Birmingham production for BBC. Untransmitted. Duration: 30 minutes.

Written by Ian Davidson and Peter Vincent; costume Mecheal Taylor; make-up Tracy Drury; designed by Lynda Kettle; production manager Gavin Clark; produced and directed by David Askey.

Ronnie Corbett (Lamb), Jane Downs (Millie Lamb), Peter Cellier ('W'), Terrence Hardiman (The Brigadier), Pippa Page (Major Craxton), Tim Meats (The Master), Alan Penn (Doctor Harbinger), Vanessa Ray (Professor Shillibeare), John Burgess (Minister Of Defence), Michael Cochrane (Captain Seton), Peter Moran (Corporal), Hugh Armstrong (Sergeant), Richard Bates (Padre), Denis Agnew (Bennett), Frank Vincent (The Steward).

	Holding / Source
##.##.#### **[untransmitted 1988 pilot]**	DB / 1"

THE MASTERSPY

An ATV production. Transmission details are for the ATV midlands region. Duration: 40 minutes.

Main regular credit(s):   Devised by Ronnie Taylor.

	Production No	Holding / Source
##.##.#### **[untransmitted pilot]**	2321	J / 2"

Produced and directed by Alan Tarrant.

In Television Today 02.02.1978 Francis Essex recalled, "We made a pilot of The Masterspy to transmit. decided it wasn't exactly what we wanted, threw it away and made another series with Bill Franklyn."

All the surviving VHS recordings (ex-Phillips tapes) were made by William Franklyn.

MATCH THE BABY

An LWT production. Never intended for transmission. Duration: 6 minutes.

Creepy pilot.

Jeremy Beadle (Presenter).

	Holding / Source
##.##.#### **[untransmitted 1990s pilot]**	DV / 1"

A MATTER OF EXPRESSION

A Scottish Television production. Transmission details are for the ATV midlands region. Duration: 25 minutes.

Scottish mime show with jazz and dance.

Main regular credit(s):   Devised by Alex McAvoy; music by Andy Park; developed by Bryan Izzard; produced and directed by Bryan Izzard.

	Holding / Source
##.##.####	J / 40

Alternative transmissions: Scottish Television: 08.07.1967.

MAVIS - WANTING TO KNOW

Alternative/Working Title(s): MAVIS ON MORALS

A Thames Television production. Transmission details are for the Thames Television region. Duration: 25 minutes.

Main regular credit(s):   Interviewer Mavis Nicholson.

SERIES 1

Main regular credit(s):   Executive producer Diana Potter; produced by Catherine Freeman; directed by Margery Baker.

	Holding / Source
##.##.#### **Mavis [untransmitted pilot]**	2"|n / 2"

rx 25/1/77

MAX BOYCE AND FRIENDS

A BBC production for BBC 1. Transmission details are for BBC 1. Duration: 40 minutes.

Main regular credit(s):   Written by Max Boyce; produced and directed by Jack Williams.

Main regular performer(s): Max Boyce, Ruth Madoc, Aiden J. Harvey.

	Holding / Source
##.##.#### **[untransmitted pilot]**	DB / 2"

Recorded June 1982.

MAX HEADROOM

A Chrysalis TV production for Channel 4. Transmission details are for Channel 4. Duration: 60 minutes.

How Edison Carter took on the might of Network 23 bosses, discovered the truth about Blipverts and had his brain patterns reproduced to give Max Headroom the computer-character a mind.

Written by Steve Roberts; from an idea by George Stone, Rocky Morton and Annabel Jankel; music by Midge Ure and Chris Cross; executive producer Terry Ellis; produced by Peter Wagg; directed by Annabel Jankel and Rocky Morton.

Matt Frewer (Edison Carter / Max Headroom), Nickolas Grace (Grossman), Hilary Tindall (Dominique), Morgan Shepherd (Blank Reg), Amanda Pays (Theora Jones), Roger Sloman (Murray), Paul Spurrier (Bryce Lynch), Hilton McRae (Breugal), George Rossi (Mahler), Anthony Dutton (Gorrister), Constantine Gregory (Ben Cheviot), Lloyd McGuire (Edwards), Elizabeth Richardson (Ms Formby), Gary Hope (Ashwell), Joane Hall (Body Bank Receptionist), Howard Samuels (ENG Reporter), Roger Tebb (Helipad Reporter), Val McLane (Eye Witness), Michael Cule (Exploding Man).

	Holding / Source
04.04.1985 **20 Minutes Into The Future**	C1 / C1

There was also an American dramatic series, featuring a re-made version of this episode for its pilot. Matt Frewer and Amanda Pays reprised their roles.

Channel 4 used the character Max Headroom in its pop video promo show, "The Max Headroom Show".

MAY CONTAIN NUTS

A Tiger Aspect production for BBC 3. Transmission details are for BBC 3. Duration: 30 minutes.

Inventor Chris is passionately continuing the work of her apparently dead parents. Her nocturnal lodger George, oblivious to the world around her, is surprised to find that due to an infestation of cockroaches, they have embarked on an impromptu road trip. With George's loyal lapdog and stalker extraordinaire Matt in tow, the three end up mysteriously trapped in a disused roadside cafe, and are forced to find their own ways of getting through the night.

Devised by Mirren Delaney, Kirsten O'Brien and Karen Taylor; written by Mirren Delaney and Karen Taylor; script supervisor Emma John; costume Claire Finlay; make-up Eva Marieges Moore; edited by Richard Halladay; director of photography Andy Hollis; art director Dick Lunn; designed by Dennis De Groot; executive producers Jon Thoday and Richard Allen-Turner; line producer Stephen Abrahams; produced by Nick Symons; directed by Dominic Brigstocke.

Karen Taylor (Performer), Mirren Delaney (Performer), Lawry Lewin (Performer), Matt Green (Performer), Emory Ruegg (Performer), Elinora Shearer (Performer).

	Holding / Source
21.02.2006	DB /

MCCALLUM

A Scottish Television production. Transmission details are for the Central region. Duration varies - see below for details.

	Holding / Source
28.12.1995 **The Key To My Heart [first pilot]**	DB / V1S

Duration: 80 minutes.

McCallum is called in to investigate the death of a Vietnamese banker, whose body is washed ashore on the Isle of Dogs. It could be suicide - except for a bullet hole in the skull.

Written by Stuart Hepburn; script supervisor Elaine Matthews; script editor Nicole Cauverien; music by Daemion Barry; executive producer Robert Love; produced by Murray Ferguson; directed by Patrick Lau.

With John Hannah (Doctor Iain McCallum), Suzanna Hamilton (Joanna Sparks), Gerard Murphy (Detective Inspector Bracken), Zara Turner (Doctor Angela Moloney), James Saxon (Fuzzy Brightons), Richard O'Callaghan (Bobby Sykes), Alex Walkinshaw (Detective Constable Small), Richard Durden (Sir Paddy Penfold), Simon Slater, Cathryn Harrison, Gary Lammin, Patricia Garwood, Anita Parry, Miriam Leake, Bruce Barnden.

Holding / Source

07.12.1998 **Beyond Good And Evil [second pilot]**   DB / V1SSW

Duration: 100 minutes.

Written by Russell Gascoigne; produced by Robert Banks Stewart; directed by Richard Holthouse.

With Nathaniel Parker (Doctor Dan Gallagher), Eva Pope (Doctor Charley Fielding), Arkie Whiteley (Catrin), Richard Moore (Professor Paddy Penfold), Sian Martin, Daniel Betts, Peter Lee Wilson, Lee Whitlock, Eric Barlow, Sara Stephens, Trevor Thomas, Anna Jaskolka, William Key, Julia Worsley, Gyuri Sarossy, Hannah Green, Jack Healey, Paul Birchard, Robin Cameron, Yasmin Marley.

MCCREADY AND DAUGHTER

An Ecosse Films production for BBC Northern Ireland. Transmission details are for BBC 1. Duration: 50 minutes.

Main regular credit(s):   Created by Ming Ho and Robert Jones; executive producers Robert Bernstein, Robert Cooper, Douglas Rae and Kate Triggs.

Main regular cast: Lorcan Cranitch (Michael McCready), Patsy Palmer (Clare Cooper), Brendan Coyle (Donal), Kim Thomson (Laura).

Holding / Source

15.06.2000   DB / V1SW

A one-off drama about London-based private detective, Michael McCready, who attempts to reconcile his differences with his estranged daughter.

Written by Robert Jones; script editor Ming Ho; music by Michael Storey; associate producer Terry Reeve; production executive Kevin Jackson; produced by Louise Berridge; directed by A. J. Quinn.

With Michelle Fairley, Daragh O'Malley, Paolo Dionisotti, Gary Lilburn, Roy Holder, Karl Glenn Stimpson, Brian Bovell, Romolo Bruni, Alice Redmond, Peter Hanly, Mia Soteriou, David Westhead, Mark Letheren, David McDade, Paddy Glynn.

Lorcan Cranitch replaced Tony Doyle who died during pre-production of the pilot.

MCPHEE, THE MOTHER AND ME!

A Scottish Television production. Transmission details are for the Scottish Television region. Duration: 25 minutes.

Written by Jon Watkins; produced and directed by Bryan Izzard.

Iain Cuthbertson (Charles Proudfoot), John Grieve (McPhee), Bill Denniston (Police Constable Brodie), Daphne Heard (Lady Proudfoot), Jon Croft (Gilchrist), Magda Miller (Janet Mackay), Willy Joss (Murdoch).

		Production No	VT Number	Holding / Source
02.01.1979	**Mother Superior**	PN3460A	VC6231	DB / 2"

Recorded 7th February 1978.

THE MDCLXXVII SHOW

A BBC production for BBC 2. Transmission details are for BBC 2. Duration: 30 minutes.

Written by Ian Davidson and Dick Vosburgh; choreography by Nigel Lythgoe; designed by Kenneth Sharp; produced and directed by Stewart Morris.

Rolf Harris, Guys & Dolls [as Guys 'N' Dolls], Bonnie Tyler, Les Cascadeurs De Paris.

Holding / Source

06.08.1977 **The 1677 Show**   DB-D3 / 2"

MEADOWLARK

An LWT production for Channel 4. Untransmitted. Duration: 36 minutes.

Sitcom based in Brixton, about a black husband and wife sharing their flat with a white Irish woman.

Written by Michael Hastings; designed by Michael Minas; production manager Myra Hersh; produced by John Reardon; directed by Horace Ové.

Oscar James (Meadowlark), Joan-Ann Maynard (Edna), Nichola McAuliffe (Irene), Stefan Kalipha (Reverend Henry Paul), Nina Baden-Semper (Joan), Mark Monero (Cyril), Albert Moses (Mustafa Khan), Tim Meats (Mr Morse), T-Bone Wilson (Horace), Philip Manikum (Bailiff), Christopher Driscoll (Policeman).

		Production No	VT Number	Holding / Source
##.##.####	**Brixton Tree Of Life**	79001	9L/79001	D2 / 2"

Recorded 03.09.82.

This sitcom developed from the LWT comedy play 'Gloo Joo'.

See also: GLOO JOO*

MEET RICKY GERVAIS

A Talkback production for Channel 4. Transmission details are for Channel 4. Duration: 25 minutes.

Main regular credit(s):   Produced by Iain Morris.

Main regular cast: Ricky Gervais (Host).

	Production No	VT Number	Holding / Source
09.06.2000	30802	356428	DB / DBS

VT director Damon Beesley; written by Ricky Gervais; additional material by Robin Ince and Jimmy Carr; script supervisor Pam Wylde; art director Michael Wright; designed by Richard Drew; assistant producer Spencer Millman; executive producer Peter Fincham; head of production Joanna Beresford; directed by Andy De Emmony.

With Stephen Merchant [as Steve Merchant], Tony Green, Bonnie Langford, Jonathan Morris, Terry Nutkins.

MEET THE DOYLES

Untransmitted.

Will Mellor, Niky Wardley, Warren Clarke.

	Holding / Source
##.##.#### **[untransmitted pilot]**	HD/DB /

MEET THE RENT BOY

A Wonderdog Productions production for Channel 4. Transmission details are for Channel 4. Duration: 25 minutes.

Written by Julian Clary and Paul Merton; lighting by John Henshall.

Julian Clary (Terry), Paul Merton (Julian).

	Holding / Source
##.##.#### **[untransmitted pilot]**	DV / 1"

Held by Kaleidoscope in the John Henshall archive.

No end credits. This pilot was re-shot and launched the series Terry and Julian.

See also: TERRY AND JULIAN*

MEET YOURSELF

A BBC production. Untransmitted.

	VT Number	Holding / Source
##.##.#### **[pilot Film]**	16/P/8424	J /

Recorded 22nd May 1960.

MEN BEHAVING BADLY

A Hartswood Films production for BBC/ITV. Duration varies - see below for details.

Main regular credit(s): Written by Simon Nye; theme music by Alan Lisk; produced by Beryl Vertue; directed by Martin Dennis.

Main regular cast: Martin Clunes (Gary Strang), Leslie Ash (Deborah), Caroline Quentin (Dorothy).

SERIES 1

Commissioned by Thames Television. Transmission details are for the Central region. Duration: 24 minutes.

Main regular cast: With Harry Enfield (Dermot).

	Holding / Source
##.##.#### **[untransmitted pilot]**	DB-D3 / 1"

With Ian Lindsay (George), Valerie Minifie (Anthea).

This pilot has no titles. The cast is the same as is the plot, but some of the lines are different. Sets, costumes, camera angles and hairstyles are very different.

SERIES 7

Commissioned by BBC 1. made in association with Pearson Television International. Transmission details are for BBC 1. Duration: 45 minutes.

Main regular credit(s): Script editor Elaine Cameron; director of photography John Rosenberg; art director Susie Ayton; designed by David Buckingham; line producers Chris Griffin and Debbie Vertue.

	Holding / Source
25.12.1998 **Performance**	DB / DBSW

With Ian Lindsay (George), Valerie Minifie (Anthea), John Thomson (Ken), Marcia Ashton, Ian Kelsey, Rory Tapsell.

26.12.1998 **Gary In Love**	DB / DBSW

With Amanda Drew, Lucy Speed, Peter Shea.

28.12.1998 **Delivery**	DB / DBSW

With Ian Lindsay (George), John Thomson (Ken), Valerie Minifie (Anthea), Dido Miles, Eileen Dunwoodie.

See also: COMIC RELIEF*

THE MICHAEL BARRYMORE SHOW

A Thames Television production. Untransmitted.

Written by Sid Green; produced and directed by Robert Reed.

Michael Barrymore.

	Holding / Source
##.##.#### **[untransmitted pilot]**	J / 2"

Recorded November 1982.

MICKEY DUNNE

A BBC production for BBC 1. Transmission details are for BBC 1. Duration: 50 minutes.

Main regular credit(s): Produced by John Frankau.

Main regular cast: Dinsdale Landen (Mickey Dunne).

	VT Number	Holding / Source
##.##.#### **The Black And White Shoes**	35/6P/34180	J / R3

Produced and directed by David Proudfoot.

Recorded 11th July 1966, and never shown.

MIDSOMER MURDERS

A Bentley Films production for ITV/ITV 1. made in association with Arts & Entertainment Network. Transmission details are for the Central region. Duration varies - see below for details.

Main regular credit(s):   Based on the character created by Caroline Graham; theme music by Jim Parker; music by Jim Parker.

Commissioned by Yorkshire Television.

	VT Number	Holding / Source
	D975	B / V1S

23.03.1997   The Killings At Badger's Drift

Duration: 102 minutes.

The peace of idyllic Badger's Drift is shattered by an inexplicable murder. It falls to DCI Brnaby and doughty Sgt Troy to hunt down the killer. Their investigation uncovers a web of sinister events, some long buried in the past.

Adapted by Anthony Horowitz; based on a book by Caroline Graham; script supervisor Ann Gallivan; associate producer Patricia Greenland; produced by Betty Willingale and Brian True-May; directed by Jeremy Silberston.

With Daniel Casey (Sergeant Troy), Laura Howard (Cully Barnaby), Marlene Sidaway (Mrs Bundy), Neil Conrich (Police Constable Angel), Barry Jackson (Doctor Bullard), John Nettles (Detective Chief Inspector Barnaby), Jane Wymark (Joyce Barnaby), Renée Asherson, Jonathan Firth, Rosalie Crutchley, Julian Glover, Selina Cadell, Richard Cant, Avril Elgar, Diana Hardcastle, Emily Mortimer, Elizabeth Spriggs, Bill Wallis, Christopher Villiers, Jessica Stevenson, Barbara Young, Cory Pulman, Peter Jordan, Jonathan Oliver, Simon Godwin, Paul Putner, Nigel Asbridge.

THE MIGHTY BOOSH

A Baby Cow Productions production for BBC 3. Transmission details are for BBC 3. Duration: 28 minutes.

Main regular credit(s):   Written by Julian Barratt and Noel Fielding; music by Julian Barratt.

Main regular cast: Julian Barratt, Noel Fielding.

	Holding / Source
	DB / DBSWF

20.05.2003   The Boosh - Tundra

Script supervisor Chrissie Bibby; director of photography Robert Kitzmann; associate producers Julian Barratt, Noel Fielding and Edgar Wright; executive producers Henry Normal and Steve Coogan; production manager Sally Cooper; line producer Kerry Waddell; produced by Alison MacPhail and Ted Dowd; directed by Steve Bendelack.

With Rich Fulcher [as Richard Fulcher], Richard Ayoade, Dave Brown, Michael Fielding.

In the pilot Julian Barratt was credited as Howard Moon and Noel Fielding was Vince Noir.

A MIND TO KILL

Produced for S4C by a variety of companies (see details below). made in association with ACI. Transmission details are for S4C.

Main regular credit(s):   Created by Lyn Ebenezer and Sion Eirian.

Main regular cast: Philip Madoc (Detective Chief Inspector Noel Bain).

A Lluniau Lliw Cyf production. made in association with Yorkshire International Films. Transmission details are for the Yorkshire Television region. Duration: 100 minutes.

	Holding / Source
	1" / V1S

14.12.1994   Night Of The Hunter

Alt.Title(s):   *Noson Yr Heliwr*

A young girl is found brutally murdered in a small seaside town. The police are baffled; the town's inhabitants are panic-stricken. A serial killer is on the loose, and as yet more horrific murders take place, the search for clues becomes a desperate race against time. - See more at: http://networkonair.com/shop/1250-mind-to-kill-a.html#sthash.5RpOGxaP.dpuf

Written by Lyn Ebenezer and Sion Eirian; executive producers Dafydd Huw Williams and Brian Harries; produced and directed by Peter Edwards.

With Sue Jones-Davies (Professor Gareth Lewis), Hywel Bennett, Nicola Beddoe, Margaret John, Robin Davies.

See also: HELIWR* / YR HELLWR*

MIRACLES TAKE LONGER

A Thames Television production. Transmission details are for the Central region. Duration: 25 minutes.

Main regular credit(s):   Produced by Brenda Ennis.

Main regular cast: Polly Hemingway (Paula Sheardon), Patsy Byrne (Betty Hackforth).

SERIES 1

Main regular credit(s):   Written by John Kershaw; directed by John Michael Phillips.

Main regular cast: With Jeffrey Robert (Frank Sheardon), Rosemary Williams (Sue), Gillian Martell (Georgina Brew), Elaine Lordan (Mandy Anderson), Terence Harvey (David Lewis), Morris Perry (Barry Goodson), Roland Oliver (Michael), Nigel Anthony (Kirk).

	Holding / Source
	D3 / 2"

25.07.1983   Episode 1 [pilot 1]

With Tim Meats, Nan Munro, Henry Moxon.

26.07.1983   Episode 2 [pilot 2]

D3 / 2"

Thames made 3 two-part pilots in 1983. Smiffs became Gems, Miracles Take Longer was commissioned under the same name, and The GPs was only shown as a pilot.

MIRANDA

A BBC Productions production for BBC 2. Transmission details are for BBC 2.

| Main regular credit(s): | Created by Miranda Hart. |
| Main regular cast: | Miranda Hart (Miranda). |

	Production No	Holding / Source
##.##.#### **Miranda Hart's Joke Shop [untransmitted pilot]**	ENT B613T/01	DB / DBSW

Duration: 29 minutes.

Written by Miranda Hart and Tony Roche; additional material by Leisa Rea and Paul Kerensa; script supervisor Katie Wilkinson; script editor Richard Hurst; director of photography Pete Rowe; art directors Margaret Spohrer and Joanna King; designed by Harry Banks; production executive Eirwen Davies; executive producer Pete Thornton; production manager Francis Gilson; produced by Nerys Evans; directed by Gareth Carrivick.

With Tom Ellis (Gary), Sarah Hadland (Stevie), Elizabeth Bennett (Penny), Katy Wix, Belinda Stewart-Wilson, Susy Kane, Jason Watkins, Stephen Evans, Ben Forster, Daniel Edwards, Josie D'Arby, Simon Baines-Norton, Thomas Farries.

Recorded 26.03.2008.

See also: MIRANDA HART'S JOKE SHOP (RADIO)

MIRANDA HART'S JOKE SHOP (RADIO)

A BBC production for BBC Radio 2. Transmission details are for BBC Radio 2. Duration: 30 minutes.

| Main regular cast: | Miranda Hart (Miranda). |

	Holding / Source
26.05.2007	DA /

Written by Miranda Hart; additional material by Richard Hurst, Leisa Rea and Tony Roche; produced and directed by Lucy Armitage.

With Morwenna Banks (Stevie), Alison Steadman (Penny), Katy Brand, Jim Howick, Charlotte McDougall, Ellis Hart, Vincenzo Pellegrino.

See also: MIRANDA

MIRRORBALL

A BBC production for BBC 1. Transmission details are for BBC 1. Duration: 29 minutes.

Vivienne Keill is a West End singer and Jackie Riviera a seventies disco diva, both of whom have fallen on hard times. But then along comes an audition for Angela's Ashes - the Musical.

Written by Jennifer Saunders; script editor Ruby Wax; theme music by Hugh Cornwell; designed by Dennis De Groot; produced by Jon Plowman; directed by Adrian Edmondson.

Jennifer Saunders (Vivienne Keill), Joanna Lumley (Jackie Riviera), Julia Sawalha (Freda Keill), Jane Horrocks (Yitta Hilberstam), Harriet Thorpe (Cat Rogers), Tim Wylton (Brice Michaels), June Whitfield (Dora Vermouth), Matthew Francis (Theatre Producer), Sean Chapman (Mark), Alan Corser (Johnny), Andy Clarkson (Postman), Rupert Bates (Gordon), Nigel Ellacott (Jackie's Fan 1), Peter Robbins (Jackie's Fan 2), George Hall (Pianist), Bonnie Langford (Herself).

	Holding / Source
22.12.2000	DB / DBSW

MISS JONES AND SON

A Thames Television production. Transmission details are for the ATV midlands region. Duration: 25 minutes.

| Main regular credit(s): | Created by Richard Waring; theme music by Roger Webb; produced by Peter Frazer-Jones. |
| Main regular cast: | Paula Wilcox (Miss Elizabeth Jones). |

	Holding / Source
##.##.#### **[untransmitted pilot]**	J / 2"

MISSING SCENE

A Fletcher Wilson production for a variety of companies (see details below). Untransmitted.

Written by David Bussell, Matthew Stott and Ben Ricketts; script editor Alice Lowe; produced and directed by Rollo Hollins.

Alice Lowe, Isabel Fay, Steve Furst, Kevin Eldon, David Bussell, Matthew Stott, Sam Cullingworth.

	Holding / Source
##.##.####	DB / DBSW

MOG

A Central production. made in association with Witzend. Transmission details are for the Central region. Duration: 25 minutes.

| Main regular credit(s): | Based on a book by Peter Tinniswood; executive producer Allan McKeown; produced by Glen Cardno and Tony Charles; directed by Nic Phillips. |
| Main regular cast: | Enn Reitel (Mog). |

	Holding / Source
##.##.#### **[untransmitted pilot]**	J / 2"

Mog is a petty thief and on the run from the police. He finds refuge with his Mum in the most unlikely of places.

Adapted by Dick Clement and Ian La Frenais; designed by Norman Smith.

With Billy Connolly (Mog).

Recorded on 29th October 1984 at Central's Lenton Lane studios.

Made as one series block.

THE MONDAY SHOW

A Toff Media production for BBC 1. Untransmitted. Duration: 30 minutes.

Alexander Armstrong (Presenter), Jon Richardson, Graham Fellows [as John Shuttleworth].

	Holding / Source
##.##.#### [untransmitted pilot]	HD/DB / HDC

Satire show looking at events in the news in the week ahead. Commissioned 30.9.09.

MONGRELS

Alternative/Working Title(s): THE UN-NATURAL WORLD / WE ARE MONGRELS

A BBC Productions production for BBC 3. Transmission details are for BBC 3. Duration: 30 minutes.

Main regular credit(s):   Created by Adam Miller.

	Holding / Source
##.##.#### [untransmitted pilot]	HD/DB / HD/DB

Adult puppet comedy. Puppets created by Talk To The Hand.

THE MORTICIAN'S TEA PARTY

A Yorkshire Television production. Untransmitted. Duration: 52 minutes.

Written by Hugh Ellis.

Peter Ellis (Jed Miller), Ben Roberts (Will Miller).

	Holding / Source
##.##.####	1" / 1"

Surviving material is held by Hugh Ellis.

A black comedy set in the North of England during the early 1950s. Two brothers, Jed and Will Miller, working owners of the family undertaking business, go on holiday with their wheelchair bound mother, to inspect crematoria. Ma dies in suspicious circumstances which lead to recriminations between the brothers, whilst embalming the corpse. Some dark family secrets come out and developments include a probable murder, a Shakespearean haunting and premature death.

(JULIAN FELLOWES INVESTIGATES) A MOST MYSTERIOUS MURDER

A Touchpaper Television production for BBC 1. made in association with RDF Media. Transmission details are for BBC 1. Duration: 60 minutes.

Julian Fellowes (Host).

	Holding / Source
16.10.2004 **The Case Of Charles Bravo**	DB / V1SW

Julian Fellowes pops up like the genial headmaster of a minor public school, to cast light on a case of poisoning that rocked Victorian society. Of course, it didn't take much to rock Victorian society, as it was probably the most rockablc society of them all, but still, the mysterious death of one Charles Bravo had everyone agog.

Written by Tina Tepler and Julian Fellowes; script supervisor Caroline O'Reilly; music by Philip Appleby; executive producers Liz Hartford, Rob Pursey and Adam Kemp; produced by Clare Alan; directed by Michael Samuels.

With Nadia Cameron-Blakey (Florence), Michael Bassbender (Charles Bravo), Elizabeth McKechnie (Mrs Cox), Michael Cochrane (Doctor Gully), Alex Palmer (George Griffiths), Laura Strachan (Mary Ann Keeber), Nicholas Hutchison (Royes Bell), Nigel Hastings (Coroner), Peter Penry Jones (Sir William Gull), Andrew Bridgmont (Rowe), Laurence Hobbs (George Younger), Rachel Bavidge (Fanny).

MOTORING MAGAZINE

A BBC production. Untransmitted.

	VT Number	Holding / Source
##.##.#### [untransmitted pilot]	16/INT/19656	J /

Recorded 25th September 1963.

MOUTH TO MOUTH

An Avalon Productions production for BBC 3. Transmission details are for BBC 3. Duration: 30 minutes.

The lives of the three members of a fictional girl group. Wannabe pop star Meeshell Reeves wants nothing more than to be famous, so when her girl group, Cats Eyes, is accepted on TV talent show Fame Search, she feels her destiny is about to be fulfilled. Alongside lifelong friend Devine and new member Chloe, the girls prepare for their big moment, but with a tragedy marring her past and her mother pushing her onward the pressure on Meeshell begins to grow.

Main regular credit(s):   Written by Karl Minns.

	Holding / Source
07.11.2008	HD/DB / HD/DB

Executive producers Jon Thoday and Richard Allen-Turner; produced by Mark Iddon.

With Alex Price (Tyler), Anna Nightingale (Meeshell), Shane Zaza (Rakim), Simon Coombs (Luke), Ayesha Antoine (Devine), Pippa Duffy (Chloe).

This was BBC3's first multiplatform comedy-drama, which aired on the web and mobile phones before moving to TV.

THE MOVIE QUIZ

A BBC Manchester production for BBC 1. Transmission details are for BBC 1. Duration: 30 minutes.

	Holding / Source
##.##.#### **Untransmitted pilot**	DB-D3-2" / 2"

Introduced by Michael Parkinson.

Rx October 1971.

MR MELLY AND COMPANY

Alternative/Working Title(s): MR MELLY & CO.

A Granada production. Transmission details are for the Granada region. Duration: 25 minutes.

Main regular performer(s): George Melly (Host), Reginald Bosanquet, Tommy Burton, Sheila Collier and The Smoky City 7.

	Production No	Holding / Source
##.##.#### [dry run]	P778/8901	DB / 2"

Produced by Arthur Taylor [credited as Arther Taylor]; directed by Alan Grint.

Although the dry-run/pilot does not appear to have ever been intended for broadcast, four episodes of were scheduled for late evening transmission but were then hit by the government restriction on electricity usage which required television output to finish by 10:30pm. The series was remounted with a slightly different format and a different title: GEORGE.

See also: GEORGE*

MR. AITCH

Alternative/Working Title(s): MISTER AITCH / THE HARRY CORBETT SERIES

A Harry H. Corbett Productions Ltd production for Rediffusion Television. Transmission details are for the Rediffusion Television region. Duration: 25 minutes.

Main regular credit(s):   Theme music by Glen Mason and Keith Miller; produced by Peter Eton.

Main regular cast: Harry H. Corbett (Harry Aitch), Norman Chappell (Albie), Gordon Gostelow (Lefty).

	VT Number	Holding / Source
##.##.#### We Shall Not Be Moved [untransmitted pilot]	T4574/1	J / 40

Written by Dick Clement and Ian La Frenais; directed by Dick Clement.

Recorded 14.10.66. We have no record of the cast for this version of "We Shall Not Be Moved", it may be that even the regular characters – apart from the title one – were played by different actors. The VT number would seem to indicate that it was recorded at Television House rather than Wembley where most, possibly all, of the remaining episodes were.

MR. BEAN

A Tiger Television/Tiger Aspect production for a variety of companies (see details below). Transmission details are for the Central region. Usual duration: 25 minutes.

Main regular credit(s):   Theme music by Howard Goodall.

Main regular cast: Rowan Atkinson (Mr Bean).

	Holding / Source
01.01.1990 Mr. Bean	D3 / 1"

A Tiger Television production for Thames Television.

Written by Richard Curtis, Rowan Atkinson and Ben Elton; music by Howard Goodall; designed by Gillian Miles; production executive Peter Bennett-Jones; produced and directed by John Howard Davies.

With Richard Briers, Paul Bown, Rudolph Walker, Roger Sloman, Howard Goodall.

See also: COMIC RELIEF - THE BIG ONE* / COMIC RELIEF 1991 - THE STONKER*

MR. FIXIT

A Grampian Television production. Transmission details are for the ATV midlands region. Duration: 25 minutes.

Written by Watt Nicoll; produced and directed by John Sichel.

Russell Hunter (Fixit), Colette O'Neil (Jenny), Molly Weir (Ginty), Callum Mill (Barman), Derek Anders (Official).

	Holding / Source
01.10.1974	J / 2"

MR. PETTY

An Associated-Rediffusion production. Untransmitted. Duration: 25 minutes.

Written by Keith Waterhouse and Willis Hall; produced and directed by James Ormerod.

Roy Kinnear (Mr Petty), Johnny Lockwood (Mr Proudfoot), June Munro (Mrs Proudfoot), Joan Newell (Mrs Milliner), Peggy Thorpe-Bates (Lady Mayor), Thomas Baptiste (Chief Obuto), Richard Caldicot (Mr Bingley).

	VT Number	Holding / Source
##.##.#### The Inspector	W1726/255	J / 40

Recorded 26.04.63.

Untransmitted pilot.

MR. RIVIERA

Alternative/Working Title(s): SIROCCO

An ITC production. Transmission details are for the ATV midlands region. Duration: 25 minutes.

Featuring the adventures of Neil McCrea, a freelance writer and photographer, who travels aboard his yacht 'Sirocco'.

Written by Bill Strutton; produced by Denis O'Dell; directed by Peter Graham Scott.

Charles Drake (Neil McCrea), Anna Gaylor (Annette Brosse), Harry Locke (Marius), Kenneth Griffith (Martin), Warren Mitchell (Valgo), Michael Peake (Sancha).

	Holding / Source
12.06.1964	J / B3

Alternative transmissions: ATV London: 10.02.1962.

The yacht Sirocco sails into the harbour at Monte Carlo and Neil McCrea, free-lance writer and photographer, receives a message:
'Planning feature on plastic surgeon, Jules Grosse killed in crash over Corniche. Appreciate new piece on him'. The request is from one of his editors and it sets McCrea on to one of the most sensational stories of his career.

Repeated ATV London 26.12.1965.

At a time when the project was still known as Sirocco, Television Today (26.05.1960) reported that it "goes on the floor" on June 14. Television Today (22.12.1960) confirmed that the pilot had been made 'this summer', so it seems to have taken almost four years after production before it was shown.

See also: SIROCCO

THE MRS BRADLEY MYSTERIES

A BBC production for BBC 1. made in association with BBC America / WGBH Boston. Transmission details are for BBC 1.

Main regular credit(s):	Based on novels by Gladys Mitchell; music by Matthew Scott; executive producers Mal Young, Rebecca Eaton and Ruth Caleb; produced by Deborah Jones.
Main regular cast:	Diana Rigg (Mrs Adela Bradley), Neil Dudgeon (George Moody).

Holding / Source

31.08.1998 **Speedy Death**   DB-D3 / V1SW

Duration: 90 minutes.

Adapted by Simon Booker; directed by Audrey Cooke.

With John Alderton (Alastair Bing), Simeon Andrews (Family Doctor), Lynda Baron (Mrs MacNamara), Tom Butcher (Bertie Philipson), Tyler Butterworth (Ferdinand Bradley), John Conroy (Henry Baxter), Emma Davies (Hermione Bradley), Sue Devaney (Mabel Jones), Emma Fielding (Eleanor Bing), Tristan Gemmill (Garde Bing), Andrew Hallett (Constable), Andrew Grainger (Vicar), Alec Linstead (Wedding Vicar), Carmela Marner (Pamela Storbin), William Oxborrow (Everard Mountjoy), Russell Tovey (Stable Boy), Eleanor Tremain (Dorothy Manners), Michael Troughton (Inspector Starkey).

MRS IN-BETWEENY

A Tightrope North production for BBC 3. Transmission details are for BBC 3. Duration: 60 minutes.

A look at family life.

Created by Paul Abbott and Caleb Ranson; written by Caleb Ranson; script supervisor Angie Pontefract; music by Johnny Clifford; designed by Andrea Hughes; executive producers Lucy Richer, Keith Halsall and Paul Abbott; produced by Barbara McKissack; directed by Paul Norton Walker.

Amelia Bullmore (Emma), Craig Parkinson (Neil), Sarah Parks (Deborah), Jay Simpson (Kevin), Charlotte Dixon (Holly), George Whitton (Charlie), James Greene (Mr Wilson), Rebekah Staton (Kathleen), Pam Shaw (Marie), Dominic Holmes (Brendan), Oliver Goulden (Young Ben), Joseph Barratt (Young Neil), Jamie Doyle (Ryan), Adjoa Andoh (Ellen), Sean McKenzie (Graham), Katey Siddall (Lynne), Lisa Hammond (Isobel), Angela Murray (Alison), Matt Chapman (Policeman), Trevor Williams (House Owner), Kitty Simpson (Tanya).

Holding / Source

03.03.2008   DB / DBSWF

THE MRS MERTON SHOW

A Granada production for BBC North. Transmission details are for BBC 2. Duration varies - see below for details.

Main regular performer(s): Caroline Aherne (Mrs Merton).

	Production No	Holding / Source
06.12.1993 **That Nice Mrs Merton**	1/2092/1	D2 / D2S

Duration: 25 minutes.

Written by Caroline Aherne, Craig Cash and Henry Normal; designed by Christopher Wilkinson; executive producer Andy Harries; produced by Peter Kessler; directed by Richard Signy.

With Carol Thatcher, Doctor Mark Porter, Terry Christian, Steve Halliwell, CNN.

MRS OSBOURNE PRESENTS

A Talkback Thames production for Thames Television. Untransmitted.

Holding / Source

##.##.#### [untransmitted pilot]   DB /

MRS. BROWN'S BOYS

A BBC Productions production for BBC 1. made in association with BocPix / RTE. Transmission details are for BBC 1. Usual duration: 30 minutes.

Main regular credit(s):	Written by Brendan O'Carroll.
Main regular cast:	Brendan O'Carroll (Agnes Brown), Jennifer Gibney (Cathy Brown), Dermot O'Neill (Grandad Brown), Paddy Houlihan (Dermot Brown), Elish O'Carroll (Winnie McGoogan).

Holding / Source

##.##.#### **Dermot's Dilemma [untransmitted pilot]**   HD/DB / HDC

Recorded 2009.

MUMBAI CALLING

An Allan McKeown Presents Ltd production for ITV 1. Transmission details are for the Central region. Duration: 25 minutes.

Main regular credit(s):	Created by Allan McKeown; based on an idea by Allan McKeown.
Main regular cast:	Sanjeev Bhaskar (Kenny Gupta), Adhir Bhat, Shaun Williams, The Stewart Curtis Band.

Holding / Source

30.05.2007   DB / DBSWF

Written by Laurence Marks, Maurice Gran and Sanjeev Bhaskar; script supervisors Linda Baker and Shubha M. Ramachandra; script consultant Anuvab Pal; music by Sanjeev Bhaskar; executive producer Allan McKeown; head of production Ned Parker; directed by Nick Wood.

With Nitin Ganatra (Dev), Sophie Hunter (Tiffany Glass), Andres Williams (Anthony), Peeya Rai Choudhuri (Sarika), Namit Das (Amar), Henry Goodman (Philip Glass), Suzanne Bertish (Jacqui), Twiggy (Herself), Yvonne D'Alpra (Booba Glass), Imran Mirza (Waiter), Scarlett Lesley (Young Tiffany), Sam Marzell (Simon), Sudha Mehta (Auntie).

MUM'S THE WORD

A Thames Television production. Untransmitted. Duration: 25 minutes.

Written by Vince Powell; designed by David Richens; produced and directed by Anthony Parker.

Irene Handl (Amy Collins), Kate Williams (Joyce Collins), Doris Hare (Nora), Robert Gillespie (Postman), John Graham (Mr Turner), Elizabeth Sinclair (Miss Lloyd).

	VT Number	Holding / Source
##.##.#### **[untransmitted pilot]**	1235	DB / 2"

Recorded 1977.

MURKY WATERS

A Central production. Untransmitted.

Directed by Malcolm Taylor.

	Holding / Source
##.##.#### **[untransmitted pilot]**	

Recorded July and August 1987.

MUSIC MATCH

A BBC production for BBC 1. Transmission details are for BBC 1.

Musical quiz series featuring competing celebrity teams.

Main regular credit(s):   Devised by Wally Mardell; drawings by Rod Jordan; music directed by Laurie Holloway; designed by Paul Allen; produced by Keith Stewart; directed by Andrea Conway.

Main regular performer(s): Barry Cryer (Presenter), Liza Goddard, Willie Rushton.

	Holding / Source
##.##.#### **Untransmitted pilot: Stop The Music**	DB / 1"
##.##.#### **Second Untransmitted pilot**	DB / 1"

MUSICAL CHAIRS

A BBC production for BBC 2. Transmission details are for BBC 2. Duration: 30 minutes.

Executive producer Herbert Chappell; produced by David Buckton, Ian Engelmann and Bob Lockyer; studio sequences directed by Peter Butler.

Floella Benjamin (Presenter), Martin Best (Presenter).

	Holding / Source
07.03.1979	DB-D3 / 2"

With Keef Macmillan, John Williams, Sky, Adrian Hope, Isobel Buchanan.

NAME THAT TUNE

A Thames Television production. Transmission details are for the Central region. Duration: 25 minutes.

	Holding / Source
##.##.#### [untransmitted pilot]	2"|n / 2"
rx 7/4/76	

NANNY KNOWS BEST

A Granada production. Transmission details are for the Thames Television region. Duration: 25 minutes.

Nanny Price takes a new post in Kensington. Mistress of the house Lucinda Botsky finds her a great comfort. Property speculator Billy Benson, who lives with Lucinda, isn't so sure. The children, Perry and Pandora, believe their new nanny is a witch.

Written by Anne Valery; designed by Steve Fineren; executive producer Brian Armstrong; produced by Susi Hush; directed by Bob Hird.

Beryl Reid (Nanny Price), Wanda Ventham (Lucinda Botsky), Matthew Fryer (Perry), Ronald Fraser (Colonel Smythe-Roberts), Patricia Lawrence (Mrs Smythe-Roberts), Emma Jane Kennedy (Pandora), Peter Bowles (Billy Benson), Matthew Butcher (Fido Botsky), Carol Gillies (Mrs Steiner).

	Production No	Holding / Source
14.10.1980	P851/1	DB / 2"

THE NAUGHTY NAUGHTY HYPNO SHOW

A the Comedy Unit production for Channel 5. Transmission details are for Channel 5.

The hypnotist's art takes on a new dimension in this show, which sees hypnotised audiences revealing somewhat more than is customary in front of the television camera.

Main regular credit(s):	Produced by Colin Gilbert; directed by Michael Hines.
Main regular cast:	Peter Powers (Host).

	Holding / Source
16.05.2000	DB /
Duration: 25 minutes.	

NEAREST AND DEAREST

A Granada production. Transmission details are for the ATV midlands region. Duration varies - see below for details.

Main regular credit(s):	Devised by Vince Powell and Harry Driver; music by Derek Hilton.
Main regular cast:	Hylda Baker (Nellie Pledge), Jimmy Jewel (Eli Pledge), Joe Gladwin (Stan), Madge Hindle (Lily), Edward Malin (Walter).

SERIES 1

Main regular credit(s):	Produced by Peter Eckersley; directed by June Howson.
Main regular cast:	With Bert Palmer (Bert).

	Production No	Holding / Source
15.08.1968 **It Comes To Us All**	P573/1	DB-4W / 40

Alt.Title(s):   *Thicker Than Water*

Duration: 27 minutes.

Written by Vince Powell and Harry Driver; designed by Michael Grimes.

With John Barrett, Tim Barrett, Ivor Dean, Julie Goodyear.

This first episode was made as a pilot and has a different opening title sequence and an alternative arrangement of the theme. The episode title does not appear on-screen.

THE NEARLY MAN

A Granada production. Transmission details are for the ATV midlands region. Duration: 50 minutes.

Main regular credit(s):	Written by Arthur Hopcraft.

	Production No	Holding / Source
04.08.1974	P760/21	DB / C1

Some of his party workers think that Labour M.P. Chris Tomlinson has developed rather too much of a "cocktail sausage image". And, with a General Election imminent, he faces a critical weekend. Once he had perfect credentials for a candidate - "a brain box from Transport House with a wife and first-born just right for electioneering pictures . ." But does his face still fit in this working-class constituency ? And whose loyalty can he still depend on ? Can he even rely on his wife ?

Edited by Stan Challis; sound Arthur Payne; camera operated by David Wood; designed by Alan Price; produced by Peter Eckersley; directed by John Irvin.

With Tony Britton (Chris Tomlinson), Ann Firbank (Alice Tomlinson), Wilfred Pickles (Bernard King), Michael Elphick (Ron Hibbert), Barrie Gosney (Peter Barry), Richard Butler (Geoff), Jean Rimmer (Ethel), Chris Canavan (Billy), Beth Morris (Deirdre), Joby Blanshard (Mr Deakin), Joe Holroyd (Club Secretary), Bernard Atha (Photographer), Barbara Moore-Black (Miss Dawson).

See also: ITV PLAYHOUSE

NEVER MIND THE BUZZCOCKS

A Talkback production for BBC 2. Transmission details are for BBC 2. Usual duration: 30 minutes.

SERIES 1

Main regular performer(s): With Mark Lamarr (Host), Sean Hughes (Team Captain), Phill Jupitus (Team Captain).

	Holding / Source
##.##.#### **Now That's What I Call A Pop Quiz** [untransmitted pilot]	J / DBSW

NEVER MIND THE QUALITY, FEEL THE WIDTH

An ABC/Thames production.

Main regular credit(s):   Created by Vince Powell and Harry Driver.

Main regular cast: John Bluthal (Manny Cohen), Joe Lynch (Patrick Kelly).

An ABC production. Transmission details are for the ABC midlands region.

	Holding / Source
18.02.1967 **[Armchair Theatre]**	J / 40

Duration: 55 minutes.

Written by Vince Powell and Harry Driver; story editor Terence Feely; produced by Leonard White; directed by Patrick Dromgoole.

With Frank Finlay (Patrick Kelly), Dudley Foster (George Gladwin), Venetia Maxwell (Rita), Charles Lamb (Wally), Michael McKevitt (Clerk), Christopher Benjamin (Rabbi Levy), Denis Carey (Father Ryan).

NEVER THE TWAIN

Alternative/Working Title(s): BETWIXT AND BETWEEN

A Thames Television production. Transmission details are for the ATV/Central region. Duration: 25 minutes.

Main regular credit(s):   Created by Johnnie Mortimer and Brian Cooke.

Main regular cast: Donald Sinden (Simon Peel), Windsor Davies (Oliver Smallbridge).

	VT Number	Holding / Source
##.##.#### **Families At War [untransmitted pilot]**	22636	DB / 2"

Written by Johnnie Mortimer; produced and directed by Peter Frazer-Jones.

With Robin Kermode (David), Julia Watson (Lyn), Elizabeth Tyrrell (Customer).

NEW FACES

An ATV production. Transmission details are for the ATV midlands region. Duration varies - see below for details.

	VT Number	Holding / Source
31.05.1973	7084/73	J / Live

Written by Bryan Blackburn; music directed by Johnny Patrick; designed by Jay Clements; produced by Les Cocks; directed by Dicky Leeman.

With Leslie Crowther (Compere), Tony Hatch (Judge), Noele Gordon (Judge), Clive James (Judge), John Smith (Judge).

This edition seems to have been broadcast in the ATV region only. The remainder appear to have been shown across most or all of the ITV network, albeit not necessarily in a networked slot.

07.07.1973 **The New Faces**	7237/73	J / Live

Music directed by Johnny Patrick; designed by Jay Clements; produced by Les Cocks; directed by Dicky Leeman.

With Derek Hobson (Compere), Noele Gordon (Judge), Dickie Hurran (Judge), Clive James (Judge), The Country Cousins, Finn and Jones, Doris Gill, Danny and Dereth, Peter de Wint, The Mighty Atom, Trevor Chance.

See also: AFTER ALL I'VE BEEN THROUGH*

'NEW GOON SHOW'

An ABC production. Untransmitted. Duration: 25 minutes.

Spike Milligan, Valentine Dyall, Graham Stark.

	Holding / Source
##.##.#### **[untransmitted pilot]**	J / 40

A pilot was filmed at Teddington Studios in March 1960.

NEW LOOK

An ATV production. Transmission details are for the ATV midlands region. Duration: 50 minutes.

Main regular credit(s):   Devised by Brian Tesler; written by Jimmy Grafton, Alan Fell and Jeremy Lloyd; dance direction by Lionel Blair; produced and directed by Brian Tesler.

Main regular performer(s): Roy Castle, Joe Baker, Jack Douglas, Ronnie Stevens, Gillian Moran, Joyce Blair, Stephanie Voss, The Vernons Girls, Jack Parnell and his Orchestra.

	Production No	VT Number	Holding / Source
##.##.#### **[untransmitted pilot]**	7559	16/CC/218	R1N / R1

Designed by Richard Lake.

With Roy Castle, Bruce Forsyth.

Recorded 06.08.1958 and listed, at that time, as "New Look No. 4", although only one edition appears to have been recorded before it. ATV paperwork appears to log further telerecording code against this edition - 36a.

THE NEW STATESMAN

A BBC production for BBC 2. Transmission details are for BBC 2. Duration: 30 minutes.

Main regular credit(s):   Written by Douglas Watkinson; produced and directed by David Askey.

	Holding / Source
03.12.1984	DB / 1"

George Vance, curator of Aylesbury Museum, has always known that greatness would be thrust upon him some day. That day arrives and George sets out to change the world....

Designed by Cecilia Brereton.

With Colin Blakely (George Vance), Gwen Taylor (Enid Vance), Ivor Roberts (Phillip Thomas), Derek Benfield (Mr Walmsley), Richard Davies (Steffan Caradoc), Paula Tilbrook (Mrs Walmsley), Elian Wyn (Owen Vance).

See also: COMEDY CLASSICS*

NEW TRICKS

A Wall to Wall Television production for BBC 1. Transmission details are for BBC 1. Duration varies - see below for details.

UCOS - the Unsolved Crimes Case Unit of the Metropolitan police force. Retired coppers led by an ambitious Detective Superintendent.

Main regular credit(s):   Created by Roy Mitchell and Nigel McCrery; theme music by Mike Moran and Dennis Waterman.

Main regular cast: Alun Armstrong (Brian Lane), James Bolam (Jack Halford), Amanda Redman (Detective Superintendent Sandra Pullman), Dennis Waterman (Gerry Standing), Susan Jameson (Esther (mis-spelt Ester occasionally) Lane).

	Holding / Source
27.03.2003	DB / V1SW

Duration: 86 minutes.

Serving officers call them 'NUCRAP' and show them no respect. Sandra Pullman had a rising career until she shot a Chinese man's dog. Now she is leading a team of ex-officers trying to prove the guilt of Roddy Wringer. It transpires Roddy did not kill a Polish waitress but they do arrest him for another murder, and his wife is arrest for killing the waitress.

Written by Roy Mitchell; script supervisor Sarah Garner; director of photography Lukas Strebel; titles by Huge Design; art directors Edward Andres and Teresa Weston; designed by Grant Hicks; production executive Julie Scott; executive producers Alex Graham and Mike Dormer; line producer Charles Hubbard; produced by Gina Cronk; directed by Graham Theakston.

With Chiké Okonkwo (Police Constable Clark), Leanne Wilson (Amelia), Natalie Forbes (Jayne), Heather James (Alison), Jodie Kelly (Caitlin), Jon Finch (Roddy Wringer), Jill Baker (Gaynor Wringer), Sarah Berger (Mrs Collard), Tim Woodward (Donald Bevan), Michael Culver (Ian Lovett), Zena Walker (Mrs Dubrovski), Carolyn Kelly (Carole), Philip Bretherton (Doug Standeven), Steve Darts (Raid Officer), George Keeler (Duty Sergeant), Leo Dolan (Tom Braham), David Spinx (File Sergeant), Charlie Beall (Matthew Talbut), Logan Wong (Chinese Gang Leader), Peter Harding (Vicious Ex-detective), Peter Geddis (Racist Ex-Detective), Andrew Burt (Drunk Ex-Detective), Hi Ching (Chinese Diner), Andy Armour (Scots Ex-Detective), Wynfydd Chase (Woman Ex-Detective), Peter Gordon (Heart Attack Ex-Detective), Chris Jenkinson (Garage Detective), Martin Bashir (Himself).

NEWSHOUR

An Ulster Television production. Untransmitted.

Pilots for UTV Live at Six.

	Holding / Source
##.##.#### [first pilot]	1" / 1"
##.##.#### [second pilot]	1" / 1"
##.##.#### [third pilot]	1" / 1"

Note: These are fascinating, consisting of full mock bulletins featuring graphics, music and a set which were never subsequently used. The stories were sourced from UTV's then current news programmes. One reason why the concept may have been shelved is the prominent use of the Oscilloscope logo throughout which senior management was already planning to shelve.

NICE DAY AT THE OFFICE

A BBC production for BBC 1. Transmission details are for BBC 1.

Main regular credit(s):   Written by Paul Shearer and Richard Turner; produced by Stephen McCrum.

Main regular cast: Timothy Spall (Phil Bachelor), John Sessions (Tippit), Anna Massey (Janice Troutbeck), Brian Pettifer (Dave Morrison).

	Production No	Holding / Source
##.##.#### Dressing To The Right [untransmitted pilot]	LLC E911W/71	DB / D3S

Duration: 29 minutes.

Music by Debbie Wiseman; designed by David Buckingham and Richard Hogan; executive producer Richard Boden; production manager Francesca Gilpin; directed by Nick Bye.

With Timothy Spall (Phil Bachelor), John Sessions (Tippit), Anna Massey (Janice Troutbeck), Nicholas Le Prevost (Chris Selwyn), Sylvestra Le Touzel (Lizzie Kershaw), Brian Pettifer (Dave Morrison), Nicholas Pritchard (Jeremy Fforbes-Winterton), Togo Igawa (Mr Yokoshima).

NICE GUY EDDIE

A BBC Northern Ireland production for BBC 1. Transmission details are for BBC 1. Duration: 60 minutes.

Main regular cast: Ricky Tomlinson (Eddie McMullen), Elizabeth Spriggs (Vera McMullen), Rachel Davies (Ronnie McMullen).

Credits: Written by Johanne McAndrew and Elliot Hope; executive producers Robert Cooper and Carol Ann Docherty; produced by Colin McKeown; directed by Douglas Mackinnon.

Cast: With Stephen Walters (Scott), Debra Redcliffe (Carol).

	Holding / Source
14.06.2001	DB / V1SW

Eddie is easy-going and endlessly affable and his life rolls along pleasantly enough until a handsome young man comes knocking at the door of the family home. The young man claims that Eddie could be his dad. And that's about it, really.

NICE TIME

A Granada production. Transmission details are for the Granada region. Duration: 25 minutes.

Zany, frothy magazine programme.

Main regular credit(s):   Produced by John Birt.

Main regular performer(s): Kenny Everett, Germaine Greer, Jonathan Routh.

	Holding / Source
##.##.#### **[untransmitted pilot]**	J / 40

The pilot included a competition to find the man who looked most like George Brown.

Edited by John Birt; produced by Brian Armstrong and Mike Murphy; directed by Stacy Waddy.

With Kenny Everett (Presenter), Jonathan Routh (Presenter), Germaine Greer (Presenter).

Recorded May 1968.

NICK REVELL

A John Kaye Cooper Productions production for BBC 1. Transmission details are for BBC 1. Duration: 50 minutes.

Written by Nick Revell; music by Tim Whitnall; designed by Ray Langhorn; produced and directed by John Kaye Cooper.

Nick Revell, John Stapleton, Black, Draylon Underground.

	Holding / Source
24.06.1989	DB / 1"

NIGHT TIME

A TSW production. Untransmitted. Duration: 56 minutes.

Music by Ed Welch; designed by Duncan Cameron; produced and directed by Paul Stewart Laing.

Andy Price (Presenter), Judi Spiers (Presenter), Ian Calvert (Presenter), Michelle Casey (Presenter), Gray Jolliffe, Lal Hardy, Sydney Green, Robbie Martin.

	VT Number	Holding / Source
##.##.#### **1986 Untransmitted pilot**	NTI/2570/ED	UM / 1"

'Instant Sex' cartoon by Bob Godfrey Films Ltd.

Made for the new late night schedule but never commissioned.

NIGHTINGALES

An Alomo/SelecTV production for Channel 4. Transmission details are for Channel 4. Duration: 25 minutes.

Main regular credit(s):   Closing theme sung by Robert Lindsay; music by Clever Music.

Main regular cast: Robert Lindsay (Carter), David Threlfall (Bell), James Ellis (Sarge).

	Holding / Source
##.##.#### **[untransmitted USA Pilot]**	D3 / D3S

Written by Tony Sheehan; produced by Allan McKeown; directed by James Burrows.

With Trevor Eve.

NIGHTSPOT

A Yorkshire Television production. Transmission details are for the Yorkshire Television region.

Produced and directed by Barry Cawtheray.

Ronnie Hilton, Lester and Smart, Deena Webster, Nick Taylor, Isabel Bond.

	Holding / Source
##.##.####	J /

Report of pilot being recorded in The Stage, 11.07.1968.

NIMMO AND FREUD

An LWT production. Untransmitted. Duration: 41 minutes.

Derek Nimmo, Clement Freud.

	VT Number	Holding / Source
##.##.#### **[untransmitted pilot]**	00283	J / 2"

NIPPERS

An LWT production. Untransmitted. Duration: 25 minutes.

	VT Number	Holding / Source
##.##.#### **[untransmitted pilot]**	9L/00678	J / 2"

NO EXCUSES

A Central production. Transmission details are for the Central region. Duration: 50 minutes.

Main regular credit(s):   VT editor John Hawkins; written by Barry Keefe; lyrics by Andy J. Clark; graphics by George Wallder; costume Stuart Currell; make-up Sheila Mann; keyboards Andy J. Clark; guitars Ross McGeeney and Dave Flett; bass Matt Irving; drums Paul Turner; saxophone Patrick Neuburg; harmonica Mark Hughes; music by Andy J. Clark; lighting camera Clive Tickner; lighting by Tony Hudspith; sound Ted Scott; camera supervisor Mike Whitcutt; film editor Nigel Mercer; designed by Michael Eve and Jeff Tessler; produced by Simon Mallin; directed by Roy Battersby.

Main regular cast: Charlotte Cornwell (Shelley Maze), Alex Norton (Howard), Bob Critchley (Alun), Richard Warwick (Mike), Peter Hugo Daly (Steve).

	Production No	Holding / Source
17.05.1983 **One Easy Lesson**	9895/81	1" / 2"

With David Swift (Bill), Donald Sumpter (Trev), Alfred Burke (Max), Jana Shelden (Caryl), Daniel Flynn (Billy), Cherith Mellor (Sandy), David Hargreaves (Dave), Hilton McRae (Pimm), Clare Kelly (Joyce), Alexandra Stordy (Ricky), John Maloney (Jim).

Recorded 5.12.1981.

NO PROBLEM!

An LWT production for Channel 4. Transmission details are for Channel 4. Duration: 25 minutes.

Main regular credit(s):   Created by The Black Theatre Co-Operative; produced by Charlie Hanson.

SERIES 1

Main regular credit(s):   Written by Farrukh Dhondy and Mustapha Matura.

Main regular cast: With Victor Romero Evans (Bellamy), Janet Kay (Angel), Judith Jacob (Sensimilia), Shope Shodeinde (Terri), Chris Tummings (Tosh).

	Holding / Source
07.01.1983 **Rome Was Not Built**	D2 / 1"

Welcome to Willesden. The Powell kids are celebrating — their parents have returned to Jamaica and they have the run of the house.

Designed by Quentin Chases; directed by Michael Dolenz.

With Roy Macready (The Man), Nigel Gregory (Gent 1), David Rolfe (Gent 2).

NO SKILLZ

A Kayak Productions production. Untransmitted. Duration: 25 minutes.

Written by Alex Newman and Nicola Cotter; directed by Alex Newman.

Alec Christie (Christie), Stephen Merchant (Damien Kingstar), Rufus Wright, Bob Cryer, Karen Taylor, Anthony MacMurray, Nicola Cotter, Dan Warren, Toby Mace, Andrew Turner, Andrew Christie, Sam Chapman, Keiron Crook.

	Holding / Source
##.##.#### **[untransmitted pilot]**	DB / DBSW

NO. 13 GOLDEN SQUARE

An ATV production. made in association with ABC. Not made.

Written by Alex Guinness.

A light comedy series, mentioned in Television Today on 11.02.1960.

THE NO.1 LADIES' DETECTIVE AGENCY

A BBC production for BBC 1. made in association with Mirage / The Weinstein Company. Transmission details are for BBC 1.

Main regular credit(s):   Based on books by Alexander McCall Smith.

Main regular cast: Jill Scott (Precious Mma Ramotswe).

	Holding / Source
23.03.2008	DB / HD/DB

Duration: 105 minutes.

Alexander McCall Smith's bestseller about Precious Ramotswe, a "traditionally built" woman who runs Botswana's only female private investigation agency, have delighted readers with their gentle stories that are more about human nature than crime.

The cases (no murders or car chases, just investigations into philanderers, missing children and fraud) progress slower than a lethargic Achatina fulica (that's a giant African snail to you and me).

Adapted by Richard Curtis and Anthony Minghella; script supervisor Dianne Dreyer; produced by Timothy Bricknell, Anthony Minghella and Amy J. Moore; directed by Anthony Minghella.

With Anika Noni Rose, Lucian Msamati, Nikki Amuka-Bird, Idris Elba, David Oyelowo, Desmond Dube, Bongeka Mpongwana, John Kani, Vusi Kunene, Percy Matemela, Kudrah Alabi, Tumisho Masha, Harriet Manamela, Colin Salmon, Lindani Nkosi, Vasco Shoba, Kabelo Thai, Tau Maseramula, Thabo Malema, Tshepo Maphanyane, Shombi Ellis, Brendan Kupa, Motsheresanyi Sefanyetso, Khuduga Kagiso, Kgomotso D. Tshwenyego, Karabo Mpai, Pascar Proctor, Sandiswe Mdiza, Vusiele Otukile, Rebagamang Sekgekge, Sapphire Seeletso, Mpho Pheko, Keeletaang Pelaelo, Seingwaeng Kgafela, Ikanyeng Dipatane, Pauline Letsatle, Thatayaone Mongwedisle, Losika Seboni, Kgosi Goodwill.

In memory of Anthony Minghella CBE 1954-2008.

THE NOEL EDMONDS SATURDAY ROADSHOW

A BBC production for BBC 1. Transmission details are for BBC 1.

Main regular performer(s): Noel Edmonds (Presenter).

	Production No	Holding / Source
##.##.#### **[untransmitted 1988 pilot]**	LLVL451N/72	DB / 1"

Duration: 44 minutes.

Written by Martin Booth, Steve Brown, Crowbar, Russel Lane, John Machin, Paul Minett and Brian Leveson; additional material by Noel Edmonds; script associate Martin Booth; research Jane Simon; costume Les Lansdown; make-up Denise Baron; theme music by Ernie Dunstall; designed by Martin Methven; production associate Anne Gilchrist; production manager Colin Fay; produced and directed by Michael Leggo.

With Anneka Rice, Gloria Hunniford, Gorden Kaye, Barbara Sutton, Adam Wide.

Gotcha - Gloria Hunniford. The tape also contains remounts.

NORMAN GEORGE

A BBC production. Untransmitted.

Norman George.

	VT Number	Holding / Source
##.##.#### **[untransmitted pilot]**	35/P/10995	J /

Recorded 8th March 1961.

NORTHCLIFFE

A BBC production. Not made.

Written by Robert Holmes.

Unmade BBC pilot for Playhouse, circa 1977.

NOT GOING OUT

An Avalon Productions production for BBC 1. Transmission details are for BBC 1. Duration: 30 minutes.

Main regular credit(s):   Created by Andrew Collins and Lee Mack.

Main regular cast: Lee Mack (Lee).

	Holding / Source
##.##.#### **[untransmitted pilot]**	DB / DBSW

Written by Andrew Collins and Lee Mack.

With Catherine Tate (Kate).

NOT SO MUCH A PROGRAMME MORE A WAY OF LIFE

Alternative/Working Title(s): THE LATE SHOW

A BBC production for BBC 1. Transmission details are for BBC 1. Usual duration: 45 minutes.

Main regular credit(s):   Produced and directed by Ned Sherrin.

	VT Number	Holding / Source
##.##.#### **[first pilot]**	16/4P/24101	R1 /

Duration: 67 minutes.

Written by Caryl Brahms, Ned Sherrin, Eleanor Bron, David Frost, Gerald Kaufman, Kenneth Tynan, Clive Goodwin and Donald Webster; music by Ron Grainer and Dave Lee; edited by Max Wheeler; film sequences directed by Jack Gold.

With David Frost (Presenter), Robert Kee (Presenter), Eleanor Bron, Barbara Evans, Peter Jeffrey, David Kernan, Quentin Crewe, Frank Dickens, Kenneth Griffith [as Kenneth Griffiths], Denis Norden [as Dennis Norden], Albert Stevenson, Steven Vinaver.

	VT Number	Holding / Source
##.##.#### **[second pilot]**	16/4INT/25034	R1 /

Duration: 62 minutes.

With David Frost (Presenter), P. J. Kavanagh (Presenter), Jonathan Routh (Presenter), Josephine Blake, Eleanor Bron, Doug Fisher, Roy Hudd, Victor Spinetti, Vanora Walters, Harvey Orkin, Bernard Levin.

No end credits on the print.

	VT Number	Holding / Source
##.##.#### **[third pilot]**	16/4INT/25038	J /
##.##.#### **[fourth pilot]**	16/INT/25161	R1 /

Written by Christopher Booker, Caryl Brahms, David Frost, Jonathan Routh, David Nathan, Dennis Potter, Stephen Sondheim and Gerald Kaufman; music directed by Conn Bernard; music by Ron Grainer and Stephen Sondheim; designed by Darrol Blake; associate producers Elizabeth Cowley and John Stoneman.

With David Frost (Presenter), P. J. Kavanagh (Presenter), Gerald Kaufman (Presenter), Barbara Evans, Eleanor Bron, Roy Hudd, Doug Fisher, David Walsh, Alun Owen, Patrick Campbell, Norman St. John Stevas.

NOT THE NINE O'CLOCK NEWS

Alternative/Working Title(s): SACRED COWS

A BBC production for BBC 2. Transmission details are for BBC 2.

Main regular cast: Rowan Atkinson (Various Roles).

Duration: 30 minutes.

Holding / Source

##.##.#### **[untransmitted 1979 pilot]**   DB-D3 / 2"

Originally scheduled for 02.04.1979.

Written by Peter Spence, Chris Miller, Andy Hamilton, Barry Pilton, Chris Allen, Laurie Rowley, Rowan Atkinson, Richard Curtis, Mike Burgess and Andy Stevenson; script associate Ian Davidson; music by Nic Rowley; choreography by Arlene Phillips; designed by Janet Budden; produced by John Lloyd and Sean Hardie; studio sequences directed by Bob Spiers [credited as Bob Speirs].

With Willoughby Goddard, John Gorman, Chris Emmett, Christopher Godwin, Andrew Sachs*, Jonathan Hyde, Chris Langham, John Cleese*, Wanda Rokicki, Libby Roberts, Teresa Lucas, Claire Lutter, Chrissy Wickham.

See also: NOT AGAIN: NOT THE NINE O'CLOCK NEWS*

NOT WITH A BANG

An LWT production. Transmission details are for the Central region. Duration: 25 minutes.

Main regular credit(s):   Written by Tony Millan and Mike Walling; designed by Richard Dunn; produced and directed by Robin Carr.

Main regular cast: Ronald Pickup (Brian Appleyard), Stephen Rea (Colin Garrity), Mike Grady (Graham Wilkins), Josie Lawrence (Janet Wilkins).

Holding / Source

##.##.#### **[untransmitted pilot]**   1"|n / 1"

With Stephen Rea.

See also: ROBIN'S NEST*

NOTHING BY CHANCE

A BBC Birmingham production for BBC 2. Transmission details are for BBC 2. Duration: 30 minutes.

A mixture of songs & comedy in front of a live audience at the Palace Theatre, Redditch.

Keith Donnelly, Gilly Darbey.

Holding / Source

27.10.1988   DB / 1"

162

O.T.T.

Alternative/Working Title(s): OVER THE TOP

A Central production. Transmission details are for the Central region. Duration: 50 minutes.

Tiswas for adults.

Main regular credit(s):   Script associate Howard Imber; produced by Chris Tarrant; directed by Peter Harris.

Main regular performer(s): Lenny Henry, Chris Tarrant, Bob Carolgees, Helen Atkinson-Wood, John Gorman.

	VT Number	Holding / Source
##.##.#### **[untransmitted pilot]**	9582/81	DB / 2"

Recorded 28th November 1981.

All the one inch tapes are transfers of two inch recordings.

See also: SATURDAY STAYBACK*

OBIT

A BBC production. Untransmitted. Duration: 30 minutes.

Written by Tony Bagley; designed by Sue Tanner; produced by Justin Sbresni; directed by Andy Smith.

Philip Jackson (Michael Sands), Amanda Root (Gill Ashdown), John Forgeham (Donald Osmond), Tim Barlow (Paul Disney), Nick Palliser (Charles Goodwin), Melanie Kilburn (Anna Sands), Bernard Latham (Bill Sharkey).

	Production No	Holding / Source
##.##.#### **[untransmitted 1992 pilot]**	LLCD690X/71	DB / 1"

ODD MAN OUT

A Thames Television production. Transmission details are for the ATV midlands region. Duration: 25 minutes.

Main regular credit(s):   Written by Vince Powell; directed by Anthony Parker.

Main regular cast: John Inman (Neville Sutcliffe), Josephine Tewson (Dorothy).

	VT Number	Holding / Source
##.##.#### **[untransmitted pilot]**	15347	D3 / 2"

Designed by Harry Clark; produced by Anthony Parker.

With Nat Jackley, Kevan Sheehan, Betty Alberge, Richard Davies, John Welsh, Iris Sadler, Debbie Arnold, Cheryl Branker, Charlie Stewart, Maureen Norman, Sean Armstrong.

ODD ONE OUT

A BBC production. Untransmitted. Duration: 40 minutes.

Costume Valerie Spooner; make-up Jennifer Hughes; music by Ronnie Hazlehurst; designed by Richard McManan-Smith; production team John Birkin, Helen Gartell and Gabrielle Jackson; production manager Mandie Fletcher; produced by James Moir; directed by John Bishop.

Paul Daniels (Presenter).

	Production No	Holding / Source
##.##.#### **[untransmitted 1981 pilot]**	LLVD467W/71	DB / 2"

Quiz show.

ODD SOCKS

An Alomo production for Thames Television. Untransmitted. Duration: 24 minutes.

Sitcom set in a launderette.

Main regular credit(s):   Written by Sam Lawrence.

	Production No	VT Number	Holding / Source
##.##.#### **[untransmitted pilot] Hogwash**	L5863	127717	DB / DBSW

Script supervisor Julie Church-Benns; script editor Amy Humphrey; costume Lucia Santa Maria; make-up Nichola Bellamy; theme music by Richard Trevor and Neil Cowley; lighting by Rob Kitzmann; sound Keith Nixon; camera supervisor Tony Keene; art director Liz Lander; designed by Graeme Story; production executive Jessica Sharkey; executive producer Claire Hinson; supervising producers Laurence Marks and Maurice Gran; production manager Chris Liffe; produced by Tony Charles; directed by Tristram Shapeero.

With Linda Robson (Magdalena), Rosemary Leach (Velma), Sarah Churm (Trisha), Vas Blackwood (Carson Pinkney), Sophie Stanton (Tina Moody), Mark Bazeley (Lance Moody), Garry Cooper (Terry), John Axon (Marion), Patrick Drury (Policeman), Peter Geddis (Priest).

THE ODDITORIUM

A Celador production for ITV 2. Untransmitted.

	Holding / Source
##.##.#### **[untransmitted pilot]**	HD/DB /

Created by Margaret Cabourn-Smith and Zoe Gardner; designed by Rudi Thackray.

With Margaret Cabourn Smith (One of the Sisters Lloyd Haemorrhage), Zoe Gardner (The other one of the Sisters Lloyd Haemorrhage).

Recorded in 2007.

OFF PEAK

A Granada production. Transmission details are for the Granada region. Duration varies - see below for details.

	Production No	Holding / Source
16.07.1983 **Queen Of Clubs**	P1153/16	DB / 2"

Duration: 25 minutes.

Produced by David Jenkins; directed by David Liddiment and Sarah Harding.

With Nell Campbell (Host), Simon Drake, Tamsin Heatley, Paul Davies, The Joeys, Pookiesnackenburger.

18.09.1983 **Just A Little Bit Of**	P1153/13	DB / 2"

Duration: 25 minutes.

Produced by Jon Plowman; directed by Gareth Morgan.

With Dick Vosburgh (Host), Sheila Steafel, Paul Macguire, Paul Jones, The Bouncing Czechs.

Made for the Showcase series in Autumn 1982.

25.09.1983 **One Man Band**	P1153/12	DB / 2"

Duration: 25 minutes.

Music by Bruce Thompson; produced by David Jenkins; directed by Patrick Lau.

With Madge Hindle (Host), Walter Zerlin Jnr, Patrick Barlow, Paul Davies, Tony Slattery.

06.10.1984 **An Evening With Doris Stokes**	P1153/11	DB / 2"

Duration: 25 minutes.

Psychic medium Doris Stokes has a huge following in Britain and abroad. She holds a public sitting before a studio audience and attempts to communicate with their friends and relatives in the world beyond the grave. There are a number of moving moments in the programme when Mrs Stokes uncannily unearths facts that could only be known to the individuals concerned.

Produced by Jon Plowman; directed by Lorne Magory.

With Roger Royle (Host), Doris Stokes.

Made for the Showcase series in Autumn 1982.

Series that mixed music, variety, comedy and drama editions.

OFF THE HOOK

Alternative/Working Title(s): FRESH

A Greenroom Entertainment production for BBC 3. Transmission details are for BBC 3. Duration: 30 minutes.

Main regular credit(s):   Created by Simon Maxwell; written by Dean Craig; titles by Greenroom@Momentum; associate producer Dean Craig; executive producers Geoff Goodwin, Simon Lupton and Jon Hamm; produced by Nick Hamm and Simon Maxwell.

	Holding / Source
##.##.#### **[online pilot]**	HD/DB / HD/DB

OFF THE WALL

A John Kaye Cooper Productions production for BBC 1. Transmission details are for BBC 1. Duration: 30 minutes.

Serious comedy with poetry, sex, gratuitous violence and even death — something for all the family.

Written by Nick Revell, John Langdon, Barry Cryer and James Hendrie; executive producer John Kaye Cooper; produced and directed by Marcus Mortimer.

Nick Revell, Doon Mackichan, Owen Brenman, John Hegley.

	Holding / Source
02.12.1989	DB / 1"

THE OFFICE

A Richmond Films and Television production for Carlton UK. Transmission details are for the Central region. Duration: 25 minutes.

Terrified of getting the sack, Norman goes to outrageous lengths to impress his new boss, the man-eating Hillary. But when an interview goes horribly wrong, desperate measures are needed.

Written by Steven Moffat; executive producer Bill Ward; produced by Sandra C. Hastie; directed by Paul Jackson.

Robert Lindsay (Norman Platt), Isla Blair (Hillary), Rebecca Front (Pru), Toby Longworth (Gordon), Stefan Dennis (Nigel), Sara Powell (Joan), Clive Graham (CEO), Belinda Lang (Voice of Mrs Platt).

	Holding / Source
02.07.1996	D3 / D3S

OFFSIDE

A BBC Scotland production for BBC Choice Scotland. Transmission details are for BBC Choice Scotland.

SERIES 1

	Holding / Source
##.##.#### **Talking Balls [untransmitted pilot]**	DB / DBS

Recorded October 1998.

OH DOCTOR BEECHING!

A BBC production for BBC 1. Transmission details are for BBC 1. Duration: 30 minutes.

Main regular credit(s):   Created by David Croft and Richard Spendlove; produced by David Croft.

Main regular cast: Paul Shane (Jack Skinner), Su Pollard (Ethel Schumann), Jeffrey Holland (Cecil Parkin), Julia Deakin (May Skinner), Barbara New (Vera Plumtree), Stephen Lewis (Harry Lambert), Perry Benson (Ralph), Ivor Roberts (Arnold), Lindsay Grimshaw (Gloria Skinner).

	Holding / Source
14.08.1995	DB / D3S

1963: life seems simple at Hatley railway station. But the newspaper has grave news...

Written by David Croft and Richard Spendlove; directed by Roy Gould.

With Sherrie Hewson (May Skinner), Terry John (Percy), Paul Aspden (Wilfred Schumaann), John D. Collins (Man), Daphne Goddard (Lady).

OH NO IT'S SELWYN FROGGIT

A Yorkshire Television production. Transmission details are for the ATV midlands region. Duration: 25 minutes.

Written by Roy Clarke; designed by Gordon Livesey; produced and directed by Derrick Goodwin.

Bill Maynard (Selwyn Froggit), Daphne Heard (Florrie), David Lodge (Morris Froggit), Liz Edmiston (Sylvia), Ian Thompson (Newton), James Cossins (Chairman), Michael Bilton (Horace), Anthony Boden (Frank), Kenneth MacDonald (Buzz), Dorothy Gordon (Nellie), Peter Ellis (Milkman).

	Holding / Source
30.09.1974	1" / 1"

See also: OH NO IT'S SELWYN FROGGITT*

THE OLD BOY NETWORK

A BBC production for BBC 1. Transmission details are for BBC 1. Duration varies - see below for details.

Main regular credit(s):   Produced and directed by Don Sayer.

	Holding / Source
31.12.1978	DB-D3 / 2"

Duration: 40 minutes.

Written by Jimmy Perry.

With Arthur Askey.

	Holding / Source
10.12.1981 **Eric Sykes: One Of The Great Troupers**	DB-D3 / 1"

Duration: 45 minutes.

Assistant producer Timothy Marshall.

With Eric Sykes, Eddie Lester, John Evans, Tony Hayes.

See also: SPOTLIGHT*

THE OLD GUYS

A BBC Scotland production for BBC 1. Transmission details are for BBC 1.

Main regular credit(s):   Created by Jesse Armstrong and Sam Bain.

Main regular cast: Clive Swift (Roy).

	Production No	Holding / Source
##.##.#### **[untransmitted pilot]**	01/NGW H432L/71	DB / DBSW

Duration: 29 minutes.

Written by Jesse Armstrong and Sam Bain; additional material by James Donohue; script supervisor Bernadette Darnell; script editor John Finnemore; art director Suzanne Field; designed by Iain McDonald; executive producer Alan Tyler; production manager Debbie Holley; produced by Gregor Sharp; directed by Dewi Humphreys.

With Geoffrey McGivern (Tom), Lucinda Raikes (Amber), James Rawlings (Reverend Phil).

Recorded 2006.

See also: THE LAST LAUGH

OM2

An LWT production. Untransmitted. Duration: 49 minutes.

	VT Number	Holding / Source
##.##.#### **[untransmitted pilot]**	9L/79258	1" / 1"

ON SQUARED

An LWT production. Untransmitted.

	Holding / Source
##.##.#### **[untransmitted pilot]**	1"|n / 2"

ON THE BRADEN BEAT

Alternative/Working Title(s): WEEKEND ROUND-UP

An ATV London production for ATV. Transmission details are for the ATV London region.

Main regular performer(s): Bernard Braden (Presenter).

SERIES 1

Duration: 16 minutes.

Main regular credit(s): Written by James Thomas and Kenneth Cavander; additional material by Dick Vosburgh; research Mike Townson.

	Production No	Holding / Source
##.##.#### **[dry run]**	2195	NR /

Designed by Richard R. Greenough; produced by Jock Watson.

Recorded 24.09.1962 in Elstree studio A.

Most episodes were taped on the day of transmission, but we are not sure that the programme was actually live. Aside from the name of the producer, TV Times credits are patchy and inconsistent, and it may well be that other writers and researchers were involved and/or those listed here did not work on every single episode.

At least one set of title sequences survives on B3.

ON THE RUN

An LWT production. Untransmitted. Duration: 25 minutes.

Produced and directed by Derrick Goodwin.

Bob Hoskins (Welsh Convict), James Cossins (Posh Convict).

	VT Number	Holding / Source
##.##.#### **[untransmitted pilot]**	9L/99071	DB|n / 2"

ON THE UP

A BBC production for BBC 1. Transmission details are for BBC 1.

Main regular credit(s): Written by Bob Larbey.

Main regular cast: Sam Kelly (Sam), Joan Sims (Mrs Fiona Wembley), Jenna Russell (Maggie).

Untransmitted.

	Production No	Holding / Source
##.##.#### **[untransmitted pilot]**	9L/92119	B / 1"

An LWT production. Duration: 35 minutes.

A pilot episode of the sitcom that went out on BBC with different lead characters : Self-made millionaire Tony Carpenter struggles his way through life, dealing with a snooty wife, troublesome daughter, opinionated mother and quirky domestic staff.

Designed by Colin Monk; production manager Peter McKay; produced and directed by John Reardon.

With Tony Selby (Tony Carpenter), Jill Benedict (Ruth Carpenter), Jenny Lee (Mrs Purves), Ron Aldridge (Taxi Driver), Nevana Kaley (Stephanie Carpenter), Garrie J. Lammin (Police Constable), Ian Collier (Neighbour).

Recorded August 1989.

ONE FOR THE MOON

A BBC production. Untransmitted.

	VT Number	Holding / Source
##.##.#### **[untransmitted pilot film]**	16/P/8423	J /

Recorded 20th May 1960.

THE ONE SHOW

A BBC production for BBC 1. Transmission details are for BBC 1. Duration: 30 minutes.

SERIES 1

A BBC Birmingham production.

	Holding / Source
##.##.#### **[untransmitted pilot]**	DB / DBSW

ONE-COAT WILKIE

A Scottish Television production. Transmission details are for the Scottish Television region. Duration: 25 minutes.

Antics of a jobbing painter.

Produced and directed by Liam Hood.

Larry Marshall (One-Coat Wilkie).

	Holding / Source
02.01.1973	J / 2"

Recorded November 1972.

ONLY MOLONEY

An ABC production. Transmission details are for the ABC midlands region. Duration: 25 minutes.

Produced and directed by Tom Clegg.

Peter Moloney (Presenter).

	Holding / Source
	J / 40

27.08.1966

See also: MOLONEY ON...*

THE OTHER 'ARF

Alternative/Working Title(s): NOTHING IN COMMON

An ATV production for ATV/Central. made in association with Witzend. Transmission details are for the ATV/Central region. Duration: 25 minutes.

Main regular cast: Lorraine Chase (Lorraine Watts), John Standing (Charles Latimer).

SERIES 1

An ATV production. Transmission details are for the ATV midlands region.

Main regular credit(s): Written by Trevor Howard; script editors Dick Clement and Ian La Frenais; designed by Michael Perry; executive producer Allan McKeown; produced by John Kaye Cooper and Tony Charles; directed by John Kaye Cooper.

Main regular cast: With John Cater (George Watts).

	VT Number	Holding / Source
30.05.1980 **Shooting The Germans**	5657/80	DB / 2"

Alt.Title(s): *Poles Apart*

With Patricia Hodge (Sybilla Apthorpe), Natalie Forbes (Astrid Lindstrom), Christopher Scoular, James Villiers, Jack Klaff.

THE OTHER HALF

A BBC Entertainment production for BBC 1. Transmission details are for BBC 1. Duration: 40 minutes.

Main regular performer(s): Dale Winton (Presenter).

	Holding / Source
##.##.#### **Couples [untransmitted first pilot]**	DB-D3 / D3S

Recorded April 1996.

	Holding / Source
##.##.#### **[untransmitted second pilot]**	DB-D3 / D3S

Recorded December 1996.

OUCH!

A Cabal Productions production. Transmission details are for the London Weekend Television region. Duration: 28 minutes.

Written by Anthony Marriott and Alistair Foot; music by Max Harris; assistant director Roland Brinton; executive producers Roger Hancock and Brian T. Codd; produced by Robert Angell; directed by Gerald Bryant.

Peter Butterworth (Jonah Whale), Dennis Castle (Shopkeeper), Bob Todd (Policeman), Ian Wilson (Outfitters Man), Totti Truman Taylor (Auntie), Erik Chitty (Vicar), Garry Marsh (Father), Johnny Wade (Bridegroom), Dilys Watling (Bride), Bill Shine (Father), Michael Ward (Photographer), Tutte Lemkow (Waiter), Nicola Pagett (Bridesmaid), Caron Gardner (Bridesmaid), Janet Webb (Wedding Guest), Michael Darbyshire (Wedding Guest), Glenn Beck, Janet Burnell, Sonny Farrar, Marie Makino, Louis Mansi.

	Holding / Source
09.03.1986	C3 / C3

Production of the pilot began on 07.02.1966 with filming starting 14.03.1966. A number of cast names have come from IMDB and the BFI's SIFT database, nevertheless the identities of the actors playing the tractor driver, the man leaving the pub and the two men on the country code elude us. It would appear that having failed to lead to a series in 1966, the production was released into UK cinemas in mid 1967 – it was classified (U) on 24.04.1967 and seems to have been considered to be a short film (rather than a television programme) ever since.

OUR KID

A Yorkshire Television production. Transmission details are for the ATV midlands region. Duration: 25 minutes.

Comedy about two brothers.

Main regular credit(s): Theme music by Johnny Pearson; designed by Mary Rea; produced and directed by Ian Davidson.

Main regular cast: Barrie Rutter (Bob), Ken Platt (Ben), Sylvia Brayshay (Lynda).

	Holding / Source
##.##.#### **[untransmitted pilot]**	B / 2"

Written by Keith Waterhouse and Willis Hall.

With Brian Marshall.

OUR MAN AT ST MARK'S

Alternative/Working Title(s): THERE WAS A YOUNG VICAR

An Associated-Rediffusion production. Transmission details are for the ATV midlands region. Duration: 25 minutes.

Main regular credit(s): Written by James Kelly and Peter Miller; music by Gordon Franks; produced by Eric Maschwitz.

Main regular cast: Joan Hickson (Mrs Peace).

An Associated-Rediffusion production.

	VT Number	Holding / Source
##.##.#### **The Facts Of Life [untransmitted pilot]**	W1730/11	J / 40

Directed by Bill Hitchcock.

Recorded 30.04.63 - junked under working title.

See also: OUR MAN FROM ST. MARK'S*

OUR MAN IN MISCILY

The companies who commissioned and produced this production are not known. Untransmitted. Duration: 6 minutes.

First in a planned series of demented cartoon documentaries of the fabled Island of Miscily where "ancient ethicold and ordery go hand in hand with Ban the Bomeroo, grape gathery and tip sippers".

Written by Stanley Unwin; drawings by Roy Dewar; theme music by The Bunch; film camera Li Pearce; produced and directed by Guy Robinson.

Stanley Unwin (Narrator).

	Holding / Source
##.##.#### [untransmitted pilot]	J / C3

OUT OF THE TREES

A BBC production for BBC 2. Transmission details are for BBC 2. Duration: 30 minutes.

'Wallooming ' and 'pauntley' are just two of the words that have been used to describe this staunchly ludicrous show in which a series of wallooming sketches are held together in pauntley fashion by two fugitives from television who are in search of the perfect film commentary.

Written by Graham Chapman, Douglas Adams and Bernard McKenna; lighting by Peter Booth; sound Len Shorey; designed by Ian Rawnsley; produced and directed by Bernard Thompson.

Maria Aitken, Graham Chapman, Roger Brierley, Jennifer Guy, Maggie Henderson, Marjie Lawrence, Simon Jones, Tim Preece, Mark Wing-Davey.

	Holding / Source
10.01.1976	DB-DV|n / 2"

The BBC only have the film sequences not the complete programme.

OUT OF TOWN

A Southern Television production. Transmission details are for the Southern Television region. Usual duration: 25 minutes.

Main regular cast: Jack Hargreaves (Presenter).

SERIES 1

	Holding / Source
##.##.#### [untransmitted pilot]	J / C3

Southern made this colour pilot in August 1965 for reasons that remain unknown. Perhaps they thought it could boost sales?

OUT OF TUNE

A BBC production for BBC 1. Transmission details are for BBC 1. Duration: 25 minutes.

Main regular credit(s):   Executive producer Christopher Pilkington.

Main regular cast: Tim Downie (Street), Jotham Annan (Ice D), Louise Sullivan (Sheri).

	Holding / Source
##.##.#### The Whole Tooth [untransmitted pilot]	DB / D3S

Written by Brian Jordan.

With Jane Danson (Chas).

Recorded 17.11.1995.

OVER THE MOON

A BBC production. Transmission details are for BBC. Duration: 30 minutes.

Written by John Sullivan; costume Dinah Collin; make-up Jean Steward; designed by Rochelle Selwyn; production manager Michael Jackley; produced and directed by Ray Butt.

Brian Wilde (Ron Wilson), George Baker (Major Gormley), Paula Tilbrook (Mrs Allardyce), Teddy Turner (Byron), Matthew Scurfield (Maurice).

	Production No	Holding / Source
##.##.#### [untransmitted 1980 pilot]	LLCC321T/71	DB-D3 / 2"

Pilot about a football manager. A planned series was scrapped and replaced by Seconds Out, another sporting sitcom.

OWNER OCCUPIED

A Thames Television production. Transmission details are for the ATV midlands region. Duration: 25 minutes.

Written by Robert Banks Stewart; designed by David Richens; produced and directed by Robert Reed.

Robert Hardy (Major Friedrich Schmidt), Hannah Gordon (Angela Plaquet), Richard Murdoch (Colonel Washbrook), George Innes (Sergeant Watts), Nigel Plaskitt (Corporal Klein), Rose Power (Landlady).

	Holding / Source
25.07.1977	D3 / 2"

OYSTERS

A Witzend production for Central. Untransmitted. Duration: 25 minutes.

An unemployed man takes a small business course and a lecturer introduces him to capitalism.

Written by Stan Hey; executive producer Allan McKeown; produced and directed by Baz Taylor.

Alfred Molina, Jim Broadbent.

	Holding / Source
##.##.#### [untransmitted pilot]	J / 1"

OYSTERS

Recorded on 25th September 1984 at Central's Lenton Lane Studios.

P.O.S.H

An ATV production for Central. made in association with Witzend. Transmission details are for the Central region. Duration: 25 minutes.

Written by Terence Howard; script editors Dick Clement and Ian La Frenais; theme music by Rod Stewart; designed by Stanley Mills; executive producer Allan McKeown; produced by Tony Charles; directed by Christopher Baker.

John Cater (Jack Scratch), Steve Alder (Steve Martini), Ronald Lacey (Mr Vicarage), Lesley Duff (Miss Humphreys), Michael Cashman (Mr Poppy), Kevin Lloyd (Ronnie Strumper), Patrick Durkin (Rosie O'Grady), Lesley Duff (Tannoy).

	Production No	VT Number	Holding / Source
05.04.1982 **A Room With A View**	9124	9124/81	DB / 2"

PAGE ONE PLAYHOUSE

An Associated-Rediffusion production. Transmission details are for Associated-Rediffusion.

	Holding / Source
##.##.#### **Inside Story - Yob At Sea**	J / 40

Written by Allan Prior; produced by Michael Ingrams; directed by John Frankau.

With Geoffrey Bayldon (Magistrate), Geoffrey Denton (Clerk of Court), Alan Rothwell (Yob), Philip Grout (Reporter), Douglas Malcolm (Mr Trippe), Moray Watson (Sergeant), Petra Davies (Miss Friend), Michael Earll (Constable), Olwen Brookes (Wife), Jack May (Narrator).

Recorded on VT on 25.05.64.

	Holding / Source
##.##.#### **Inside Story**	J / 40

Written by Julian Bond; produced by Anthony Kearney; directed by Ronald Marriott.

With Guy Doleman (Narrator), Ursula Howells (Ann Richard), Sarah Amos (Jane Richards), Richard Thorpe (Phipps), Ronald Ibbs (Phipps' Chief), John Paul (Richards), David Langton (1st Businessman/QC), David Bauer (Embassy Official/Interpreter).

Recorded 29.06.64.

Tony Purdy, Robert Tyrell, Alistair Foot and Tudor Gates all submitted outlines entitled Inside Story.

These pilots were never transmitted.

PAMELA STEPHENSON'S ROCK - PAMORAMA

A BBC production. Untransmitted. Duration: 38 minutes.

Produced by John Lloyd.

Pamela Stephenson, Barry Norman, Michael Parkinson, The Hee Bee Gee Bees, Hot Gossip, David Van Day, Jon Glover, David Coker.

	Holding / Source
##.##.#### **[untransmitted October 1981 pilot, though the tx tape was finalised in January 1982]**	DB-D3 / 2"

PAPARAZZO

A Yorkshire Television production. Transmission details are for the Central region. Duration: 75 minutes.

Nineties London and a sharp suit to star as ace snapper Rick Caulker, the man whose candid portraits of the stars grace the front pages of the nation's tabloids.

Written by Guy Andrews; executive producer Keith Richardson; produced by David Lascelles; directed by Edward Bennett.

Nick Berry (Rick Caulker), Fay Masterton (Sadie Prince), Michael J. Shannon (Denis Prince), Anthony O'Donnell (Terry), Philip Wright (Mung), Jimmi Harkishin (Spike), Brian Regan (Chute), Kevork Malikyan (Mackenzie), Gary Beadle (Tony Kambona), Jeff Nuttall (Lionel), Anna Zapparolli (Lilian), Carmen Du Sautoy (Marjorie), Alex Baillie-Hamilton (Denis' Bodyguard), Brett Fancy (Steve), Race Davies (Gloria), Geno Washington (Geno).

	VT Number	Holding / Source
25.10.1995	D204	DB-1" / V1S

THE PARADISE CLUB

A Zenith Films production for BBC 1. Transmission details are for BBC 1. Duration: 55 minutes.

Two unlikely brothers - a streetwise priest and a reluctant villain - are reunited by the death of their notorious gangster mother. But who will inherit the Paradise Club?

Main regular credit(s):	Theme music by Dave Lawson; produced by Selwyn Roberts.
Main regular cast:	Don Henderson (Frank Kane), Leslie Grantham (Danny Kane).

SERIES 1

Main regular credit(s):	Music by Dave Lawson.
Main regular cast:	With Barbara Wilshere (Carol Kane), Leon Herbert (Polish Joe).

	Holding / Source
19.09.1989 **Unfrocked In Babylon**	DB / C1

Written by Murray Smith; directed by Lawrence Gordon Clark.

With Ian Lindsay (Deputy Chief Superintendent Torrance), Kevin Williams (Ron Blythe), Kitty Aldridge (Detective Inspector Rosy Campbell), Philip Martin Brown (Peter Noonan), David Swift (Max Wartbug), Malcolm Terris, Freddie Earlle, David Ryall, Sheila Keith, Frank Vincent, Malcolm Raeburn, Ben Daniels, Nick Dawnay, Annie Scott-Horne.

See also: THE DETECTIVES*

PARADISE ISLAND

A Thames Television production. Transmission details are for the ATV midlands region. Duration: 25 minutes.

Main regular credit(s):   Designed by William Laslett.

Main regular cast: Bill Maynard (Reverend Alexander Goodwin), William Franklyn (Cuthbert Fullworthy).

	Holding / Source
21.04.1977	D3 / 2"

The Reverend Alexander Goodwin and Entertainments Officer Cuthbert Fullworthy—
sole survivors of a shipping disaster in the Pacific Ocean — are deposited on a desert island. They react in different ways to their plight. Mr. Goodwin is more philosophical than Fullworthy, a lover of the sweet life, who is
all for making a raft to get to Australia.

Written by Michael Haley; produced and directed by Stuart Allen.

There were no guest cast in any episodes.

PARDON THE EXPRESSION

A Granada production. Transmission details are for the ATV midlands region. Usual duration: 26 minutes.

Main regular cast: Arthur Lowe (Leonard Swindley).

	Production No	Holding / Source
##.##.#### [first pilot]	P477/1	J / 40
##.##.#### [second pilot]	P477/2	J / 40

Script - The Presentation by Jack Rosenthal. Note says 'Not to be transmitted'. This may be a script for the pilot?

See also: CORONATION STREET / TURN OUT THE LIGHTS*

PARKINSON

A BBC production for BBC 1. Transmission details are for BBC 1. Duration varies - see below for details.

Main regular performer(s): Michael Parkinson (Host).

SERIES 4

Duration: 60 minutes.

Main regular credit(s):   Music by Harry Stoneham; produced by Roger Ordish.

	Holding / Source
##.##.#### Raindrops And Roses [untransmitted pilot]	DB-D3 / 2"

Directed by Colin Strong.

Recorded January 1975.

PARKY

A Thames Television production for ITV. Transmission details are for the Thames Television region. Duration: 50 minutes.

Main regular credit(s):   Executive producer John Fisher; produced by David Clark.

Main regular performer(s): Michael Parkinson (Host).

Credits: Directed by David Clark.

	VT Number	Holding / Source
##.##.#### [untransmitted pilot]	48666	DB /

Main regular credit(s):   Series editor Neil Shand; designed by Bill Palmer; associate producer Caroline Blackadder; directed by John Birkin.

Main regular performer(s): With William Rushton, Frances Edmonds, Dillie Keane, Melina Day, Sophie Heyman.

	VT Number	Holding / Source
02.10.1989	49279	DB / 2"
09.10.1989		DB / 2"
With Paul Boateng.		
16.10.1989		DB / 2"
23.10.1989		DB / 2"
30.10.1989		DB / 2"
06.11.1989		DB / 2"

PASSION KILLERS

A Granada production. Transmission details are for the Central region. Duration: 50 minutes.

Written by Charles Peattie and Mark Warren; executive producer Christine Langan; produced by Rob Bullock; directed by David Evans.

Ben Miller (Nick), Georgia Mackenzie (Kim), Nicholas Sidi (George), James Weber Brown (Joe), Claire Bullus (Jasmine), Deborah Cornelius (Female Executive), Nrinder Dhudwar (Stunt Arranger), Sasha Maya Djurkovic (Maria), Stephen Giffin (Male Candidate), Helen Grace (Maggie), Sidney Livingstone (Fred), Peter McNamara (Riley), Dido Miles (Michelle), Ilario Bisi Pedro (Moses), Michael Simkins (Bill), Paul Venables (Ralph).

	Holding / Source
03.04.1999 [pilot film]	DB / V1SW

PATHFINDERS

A Toledo Film Organisation production for Warboys Film Productions. Transmission details are for the Thames Television region. Duration: 50 minutes.

Drama about the RAF Pathfinder force in World War II.

Main regular credit(s): Devised by Gerry Brown; script supervisor Chris Penfold; script editor Geoff Jones; music by Malcolm Lockyer; titles by Coppin/Maluta Graphimation; associate producers Chris Davies and Frank Green; produced by Gerry Brown.

Main regular cast: Robert Urquhart (Wing Commander MacPhearson), Jack Watling (Doc Saxon).

	Holding / Source
##.##.#### [untransmitted pilot]	J / C1

Directed by Don Chaffey.

Recorded Summer 1971.

PAUL DANIELS' SECRETS

A BBC production for BBC 1. Transmission details are for BBC 1. Duration: 50 minutes.

Main regular credit(s): Produced by Roger Ordish.

Main regular performer(s): Paul Daniels (Host), Debbie McGee (Hostess).

	Holding / Source
29.12.1994 **Secrets**	DB-D3 / D3S

Directed by Babara Jones.

With Philippe Socrate, Chinese State Circus, Ronn Lucas, Scorch the Dragon.

PAUL GAMBACCINI

A BBC production. Untransmitted.

Paul Gambaccini (Host).

	Holding / Source
##.##.#### [untransmitted pilot]	DB / 1"

PAUL O'GRADY'S GOT TALENT

A Talkback Thames production for ITV 1. made in association with Syco TV. Untransmitted. Duration: 75 minutes.

Paul O'Grady (Host), Piers Morgan (Judge), Fern Britton (Judge), Simon Cowell (Judge).

	Production No	VT Number	Holding / Source
##.##.####	L8515	356263	DB / DBSW

No end credits.

PAUL O'GRADY'S THE GENERATION GAME

A BBC production for BBC 1. Untransmitted.

Paul O'Grady (Host).

	Holding / Source
##.##.#### [untransmitted 2004 pilot]	DB / DBSW

PAUL STARR

A National Interest Pictures production for Wonderama. Untransmitted. Duration: 26 minutes.

Created by Roberta Leigh; written by Roberta Leigh; lyrics by Roberta Leigh; drama consultant Roy D. Baker; theme sung by Jerry Dane; music by Roberta Leigh; produced by Roberta Leigh and Arthur Provis.

Patricia English, Dick Vosburgh [as Dick Vosborough], Peter Reeves, Edward Bishop.

	Holding / Source
##.##.#### [untransmitted pilot]	HD/DB / C3

Copyrighted 1964.

PAULINE'S PEOPLE

A Thames Television production. Transmission details are for the Thames Television region.

Main regular credit(s): Produced and directed by Roger Price.

Main regular cast: Pauline Quirke (Host), Linda Robson, Martyn Day.

	VT Number	Holding / Source
##.##.#### **People And Pauline** [untransmitted pilot]	17130	DB / 2"

Duration: 28 minutes.

With Allan Hargreaves, Linda Robson, Rosetta Stone, David Mason [as Dave Mason].

David Mason was the producer of Goldmaster and Funny You Ask!

After the end credits there is an 'alternative comedy' version with Pauline Quirke as a punk rocker! It only lasts 2 minutes and is quite offensive :-)

PEAK PRACTICE

A Central production. Transmission details are for the Central region. Duration varies - see below for details.

Main regular credit(s):   Created by Lucy Gannon; executive producer Ted Childs.

Main regular cast: Margery Mason (Alice North).

SERIES 1

Main regular credit(s):   Produced by Tony Virgo.

Main regular cast: With Kevin Whately (Doctor Jack Kerruish), Amanda Burton (Doctor Beth Glover), Simon Shepherd (Doctor Will Preston), Esther Coles (Kim Beardsmore), Sharon Hinds (Ellie Ndebala), Sylvia Syms (Isabel de Gines), Jacqueline Leonard (Sarah Preston).

	Holding / Source
10.05.1993 **Sharp Practice**	D2 / V1S

Duration: 75 minutes.

Disillusioned inner-city doctor Jack Kerruish returns from three years in Africa looking for a quiet job in the country. He joins a run-down medical practice in the Peak District, and finds his new colleagues are unimpressed both with him and by his plans for their future.

Written by Lucy Gannon; directed by Gordon Flemyng.

With Tom Beard (Doctor Daniel Acres), Andrew Ray (Doctor John Reginald), Richard Platt (James White), Hazel Ellerby (Chloe White), Melanie Thaw, Shaun Prendergast, Agathe Husle, Walter Mupasutsa, Amelda Brown, Christopher Brown, Rebecca Callard, Ross Holland, Andrew Wilde, David Credell, Beth Goddard, Stuart Mackenzie, John Pennington, Desmond Stokes, Craster Pringle, Gail Kemp, Iain Mitchell, Vass Anderson, Tim Briggs, Nada Sharpe.

No Jacqueline Leonard.

PEBBLE MILL AT ONE

A BBC Birmingham production for BBC 1. Transmission details are for BBC 1. Duration varies - see below for details.

	Production No	VT Number	Holding / Source
##.##.#### **Pebble Mill [second untransmitted 1972 pilot]**	4424 BM	VTC/6HP/BM	DB / 2"

Duration: 36 minutes.

Produced by Roy Ronnie.

With Suzanne Hall* (Presenter), Asha Parekh*, Gopi Krishna*, Judith Dahl*, Rachel Heyhoe-Flint*, Molly Price-Owen*, Trevor Wood*, Susan Ashcroft*, Chief Inspector Ron Baston*.

No end credits.

Editions would occasionally be scheduled in slightly earlier or, more likely, later timeslots. These would generally be billed under the name PEBBLE MILL, but in all other respects these programmes were no different to any others. After a while someone must have become fed up with this and for a few years it was billed as PEBBLE MILL for a number of years. When it returned as PEBBLE MILL

See also: PEBBLE MILL*

PEBBLE MILL SHOWCASE

A BBC Birmingham production for BBC 2. Transmission details are for BBC 2.

	Holding / Source
18.08.1976	J / 2"

Duration: 50 minutes.

Music by Johnny Howard and his Orchestra; produced by Colin Farnell; directed by Terry Henebery.

With Don Maclean (Host), Fiddlygig, Don Crann, Maria, Billy Howard, Paul Daniels, Elaine Cameron, David Sebastian Bach, Gentle Persuasion.

PENN & TELLER: FOOL US

A Setpember Films / 1/17 Productions production for ITV 1. made in association with Buggs & Rudy Discount Corp. Transmission details are for ITV 1.

Main regular performer(s):   Jonathan Ross (Host), Penn and Teller (Judges), Johnny Thompson* (Adjudicator), Dominic Byrne, Ali Cook, Richard Bellars, Michael Vincent, John Archer, James More, Benjamin Earl.

	Holding / Source
07.01.2011	HD/DB / DBSW

Duration: 75 minutes.

Written by Peter Davey and Christine Rose; script supervisor Vikki French; music by Nick Foster and Ken Bolam; titles by Component Graphics; consultants Johnny Thompson and Paul Stone; art director Charlotte Pearson; production designer Andrew Gates; executive producers Peter Adam Golden, David Green, Peter Davey and Andrew Golder; production manager Viki Carter; produced by Katharine Begg; directed by Richard Vant Riet [credited as Richard Van't Riet].

According to this programme's Wikipedia entry, three other acts - Morgan & West, Damien O'Brien and Noel Qualter - were filmed but not included in the broadcast edit.

PETE VERSUS LIFE

An Objective Productions production for Channel 4. Transmission details are for Channel 4. Duration: 25 minutes.

Main regular credit(s):   Written by George Jeffrie and Bert Tyler-Moore; script supervisor Kendall Anderson-Müt; script editor Saskia Schuster; designed by Jeff Sherriff; production executive Jenny Hay; executive producers Ben Farrell and Andrew Newman; head of production Debi Roach; line producer Carla McGilchrist; produced by Phil Clarke.

Main regular cast: Rafe Spall (Pete Griffiths), Chris Geere (Kurt), Simon Greenall (Colin), Ian Kirkby (Terry).

	Holding / Source
06.08.2010 **Eco Warrior**	HD/DB / HD/DB

Director of photography Martin Hawkins; art director Lucy Spink; designed by Jeff Sherriff; directed by Simon Delaney.

With Pippa Duffy (Anna), Susannah Fielding (Chloe), Daniel Ings (Jake), Joseph Kloska (Rob), Reece Ritchie (Ollie), Michael Fenton Stevens, Rufus Jones, Catherine Russell.

Made as a pilot for Comedy Lab, but then held back to become the first episode of a series.

THE PETER PRINCIPLE

A Hat Trick production for BBC 1. Transmission details are for BBC 1. Duration: 30 minutes.

Main regular credit(s):	Executive producer Denise O'Donoghue.
Main regular cast:	Jim Broadbent (Peter Duff (pilot), Peter Duffley (series)).

Holding / Source

04.09.1995   DB-D3 / D3S

The Peter Principle states that "everybody is promoted to their level of incompetence and stays there". Bank manager Peter Duff is sent on a time management course, but he hasn't the time to go on it.

Written by Mark Burton, John O'Farrell and Dan Patterson; produced by Dan Patterson; directed by Terry Kinane.

With Clive Russell (Kevin Mott), Linda Bassett (Iris), Lesley Sharp (Susan Harvey), Zoë Heyes (Brenda), Stuart McQuarrie (David), David Schneider (Bradley), David Gant (Geoffrey), Nicola Sanderson (Receptionist), Michael J. Shannon (Milton Macrae), Dan Strauss (Neil).

PETS

A Fit 2 Fill Productions production for Channel 4. Transmission details are for Channel 4.

Main regular credit(s):	Written by Andrew Barclay and Brian West; music by Stacey Smith; produced by Andrew Barclay and Brian West; directed by Mike Stephens.
Main regular cast:	Ian Angus Wilkie (Hamish), Andrew Barclay (Trevor), Petros Emanual (JP), Sally Elsden (Davina).

Holding / Source

##.##.#### [untransmitted pilot]   DB /

Adult puppet sitcom.

PHILIP HARBEN

A BBC production. Untransmitted.

Main regular performer(s): Philip Harben.

	VT Number	Holding / Source
##.##.#### [pilot A]	16/P/18912	J /
##.##.#### [pilot B]	16/P/18913	J /

Recorded 21st June 1963.

PHONESHOP

A Talkback Thames production for E4. Transmission details are for E4. Duration: 25 minutes.

Transmission details are for Channel 4.

Holding / Source

13.11.2009 **New Man**   HD/DB / HD/DB

Written by Phil Bowker; additional material by The Cast and Jon MacQueen; script supervisor Penelope Chong; script editor Ricky Gervais; director of photography Martin Hawkins; art director Holly Berk; designed by Simon Rogers; head of production Beatrice Gay; line producer Caroline Wyard; produced and directed by Phil Bowker.

With Andrew Brooke (Ashley), Javone Prince (Jerwayne), Tom Bennett (Christopher), Emma Fryer (Janine), Martin Trenaman (Lance), Ellena Stacey, Paul Pariser, Claire Vousden, Kobna Holdbrook-Smith.

PHOO ACTION

A BBC Scotland production for BBC 3. made in association with Deadline. Transmission details are for BBC 3. Duration: 60 minutes.

Written by Mat Wakeham and Peter Martin; based on characters created by Jamie Hewlett; script supervisor Margaret Graham; script editor Lizzie Gray; script consultant Jessica Hynes; theme music by Nomad Al Arban; music by Mike Smith and David Coulter; designed by Will Field; production associate Cara Speller; executive producers Tom Astor and Anne Mensah; produced by Matthew Read; directed by Euros Lyn.

Eddie Shin (Terry Phoo), Jaime Winstone (Whitney Action), Talulah Riley (Lady Eleanor Rigsby), Robert Craigs (Footballer), Geraldine James (Doctor Evelyne Conan-Bell), William Chubb (Sir George Conan-Bell), Danny Webb (Lord Rothwell), Richard Woo (Sifu Chlen), Ed Weeks (William), Theo Cross (Harry), Andrew Brooke (Sergeant Copy), Jason Tompkins (Jimmy Freebie), Steve Haze (Marlon Freebie), Spencer Wilding (Burk Freebie), David Goodall (F-Bouncer), Sanjeev Kohli (Alan Arthanayake), Phil Cornwell (Voice of Jimmy Freebie), Carl Weathers (Chief Benjamin Benson).

Holding / Source

12.02.2008   DB / DBSWF

PICK OF THE PAST

A BBC Bristol production for BBC. Untransmitted. Duration: 25 minutes.

Designed by Chris Robilliard; produced by Brian Hawkins; directed by Cynthia Paul.

Tom Salmon (Chairman), Donald Firth, Gyles Brandreth, Barbara Griggs.

	VT Number	Holding / Source
##.##.#### **1973 Untransmitted pilot**	6HP 85041	DB / 2"

PICK OF THE WEEK

A BBC production. Untransmitted.

Holding / Source

##.##.#### [untransmitted pilot]   C1N|n / C1

PICTURE ME

Alternative/Working Title(s): KE

A BBC production. Untransmitted. Duration: 29 minutes.

Written by Ken Hoare; costume Julia Bridgwater; make-up Diane Roberts; designed by Graham Lough; associate producer Lyn Took; production manager Adrian Pegg; produced and directed by Gareth Gwenlan.

Richard Briers (Stephen), Ross Thomson (Stephen As A Boy), Sandra Payne (Mrs Barrett), Abigail McKern (Mother), Joyce Grant (Mrs Darch), Marlene Sidaway (Miss Frazer), Stephen Ludman (Rudolph Valentino), Karen Clegg (Girl).

	Production No	Holding / Source
##.##.#### **A Double Bill: Picturegoer And Mrs Barrett** [untransmitted 1990 pilot]	LLCA150L/71	DB / 2"

PILOT MAGAZINE PROGRAMME

A BBC production. Untransmitted.

	VT Number	Holding / Source
##.##.#### **[untransmitted pilot]**	16/P/15508	J /

Recorded 19th July 1962.

THE PINK MEDICINE SHOW

An LWT production. Transmission details are for the ATV midlands region. Duration: 25 minutes.

Main regular credit(s):   Devised by Chris Beetles, Rob Buckman and Humphrey Barclay; written by Chris Beetles and Rob Buckman; graphics by Tony Oldfield; music directed by Max Harris; titles by Ted Rockley; designed by Jack Robinson; production manager Myra Hersh; produced and directed by Paul Smith.

Main regular cast: Chris Beetles, Rob Buckman, Lynda Bellingham, Nickolas Grace, Peter John.

	Production No	Holding / Source
##.##.#### **[untransmitted pilot]**	9L/09897	J / 2"

PLAY FOR TODAY

A BBC production for BBC 1. Transmission details are for BBC 1. Duration varies - see below for details.

SERIES 4

	Holding / Source
	DB-D3 / 2"

14.03.1974   Headmaster

Duration: 60 minutes.

Fisher is good at his job but in new circumstances that isn't enough : he has to face all the risks of competition for something bigger.

Written by John Challen; script editor Ann Scott; designed by Paul Allen; produced by Graeme McDonald; directed by Anthony Page.

With Frank Windsor (Fisher), Michael Byrne (Russell), Colin Douglas (Philips), Terence Burtenshaw (David), Anthony Douse (Geoff Edwards), Paul Smithers (Gerry), Mary Macleod (June Wade), Pearl Page (Mrs Evans), Auriol Smith (Mrs Russell), Gerald Sim (Carter), Kevin Hourigan (Peter), Patricia Lawrence (Margaret Fisher), Anthony Roye (Harvey), Hugh Thomas (Dickinson), Perry Benson (Nicky), Alan Cullen (Chairman), Margot Boyd (Miss Williams), Arnold Diamond (Andrews).

See also: HEADMASTER.

SERIES 5

	Holding / Source
	C1 / C1

09.01.1975   Gangsters

A BBC Birmingham production. Duration: 110 minutes.

Blackmail, extortion, drug-peddling and the 'Blackbird Run ' of illegal immigrants to the West Midlands. . . . How involved is Rafiq, the respected Indian community leader? Rawlinson, the night-club owner? In this hard adventure story, released prisoner John Kline comes up against his old enemies - the gangsters.

Written by Philip Martin; script editor William Smethurst; theme music by Dave Greenslade [credited as Greenslade]; film editor Henry Fowler; designed by Ian Ashurst; produced by Barry Hanson; directed by Philip Saville.

With Maurice Colbourne (John Kline), Philip Martin (Rawlinson), Ahmed Khalil (Khan), Saeed Jaffrey (Rafiq), Elizabeth Cassidy (Anne Darracott), Tania Rogers (Dinah Carmichael), Paul Satvendar (Kuldip), Paul Barber (Malleson), Paul Antrim (Dermor Macavoy), Goutam Choudhury (Servant), Graham Weston (Billy Rawlinson), Gordon Bilboe (Tommy Rawlinson), Tariq Yunus (Jashir Singh Mahall), Hans Mater (Van Der Staay), Alan Towers (Interviewer), Romi Arora (Mangit), Bunny Johnson (Rawlinson's Accomplice), Larry Brown (Rawlinson's Accomplice), Rolf Day (Comedian), Mohammed Ashiq (Comedian), Ethel Coley (Shadette), Joanne White (Shadette), Earlene Bentley (Shadette), Marie Dali (Sandra), Leon Terroll, Jonny Wong, Jarnail Singh, Ashok Kumar, Gerry Foley, Hinat Solanki.

See also: GANGSTERS.

SERIES 6

	Holding / Source
	DB-D3 / 2"

16.12.1975   Rumpole Of The Bailey

Alt.Title(s):   *Rumpole And The Confession Of Guilt*

Duration: 61 minutes.

"I could win most of my cases if it weren't for the clients . They will waltz into the witness box and blurt things out!" Horace Rumpole, Old Bailey hack, appears for the defence in an assault case.

Written by John Mortimer; designed by Fanny Taylor; produced by Irene Shubik; directed by John Gorrie.

With Leo McKern (Horace Rumpole), Joyce Heron (Mrs Rumpole), David Yelland (Nick Rumpole), Noel Willman (Mr Justice Bates), Herbert Norville (Ossie Gladstone), Peter Spraggon (Prison Officer), Tommy Wright (Man in Cell), John Byron (George), George Sweeney (Jo), Artro Morris (Mr Sinter), Sarah Thomas (Grace), Edwin Brown (Detective Inspector Arthur), Vernon Dobtcheff (Magnus Piecan), Paul Greenhalgh (Reverend Eldred Pickersgill), Eric Hillyard (Court Usher), Richard Wardale (Young Barrister), John Beardmore (Court Clerk), Douglas Auchterlonie (Jury), Jonathan Keays (Jury), Doris Kitts (Jury), Fran Pomeroy (Jury), Lionel Wheeler (Jury), Peter Hugo Daly (Ginger).

See also: RUMPOLE OF THE BAILEY (ITV).

SERIES 8

	Holding / Source
03.01.1978 **Scully's New Year's Eve**	DB-D3 / 2"

A BBC Birmingham production. Duration: 75 minutes.

Scully's mother is having a New Year's Eve party, unaware that her son has invi- ted most of his friends along. Surprises are in store...

Written by Alan Bleasdale; script editor Michael Wearing; produced by David Rose; directed by Michael Simpson.

With Andrew Schofield (Franny Scully), Jane Freeman (Mrs Scully), Avis Bunnage (Florrie), John Junkin (Jack), Stan Stennett (Ms Scully), Kate Binchy (Marie), Arthur Kelly (Barney), Janine Duvitski (Vera), Paul Kelly (Tony), Angela Curran (Rita), Gil Brailey (Carol), Mick Miller (Joey), Ray Kingsley (Mooey), Roger Phillips (Henry), John Anderson (Harry), Daisy Bell (Mrs Riley), Spencer Gurley (Darryl), Jimmy Coleman (First Gatecrasher), Bill Rourke (Second Gatecrasher).

See also: BRIMSTONE AND TREACLE* / GANGSTERS* / RUMPOLE OF THE BAILEY* / SCULLY* / SCUM*

PLAY SCHOOL

A BBC production for BBC 2. Transmission details are for BBC 2. Duration varies - see below for details.

Main regular credit(s):   Created by Joy Whitby.

	Holding / Source
##.##.#### **[untransmitted pilot]**	DB-R1 / 62

More details in Paul R Jackson's book.

PLAYBACK

A Southern Television production. Transmission details are for the Southern Television region. Duration: 25 minutes.

A nursery for new ideas. Whether all were, realistically, pilots for a longer run is hard to determine.

	Holding / Source
04.01.1966 **The One Year Of Miss World**	J /
11.01.1966 **The Cricketers**	J /
18.01.1966 **Big Ships In Narrow Waters**	J /
25.01.1966 **The Boys With The Noise**	J /
01.02.1966 **Quiz In Question**	J /
08.02.1966 **The Star Who Went Pop**	J /
15.02.1966	J /
01.03.1966 **Nearly Made It – Didn't Quite – Will Do One Day**	J /
08.03.1966 **Music For Her Majesty**	J /
15.03.1966 **Royal Film Performance**	J /
22.03.1966 **How**	J /
29.03.1966 **Big Ships In Narrow Waters**	J /
05.04.1966 **Music In Person**	J /
12.04.1966 **Fashion Photographer**	J /
26.04.1966	J /
10.05.1966 **Mid-Atlantic Men 1**	J /
17.05.1966 **Mid-Atlantic Men 2**	J /
24.05.1966 **The Biggest Man**	J /

	Holding / Source
17.04.1969 **Firsts**	J /

Pioneers in a famous field.

Devised by Jimmy Thompson.

With Jimmy Thompson (Presenter), Fay Compton, Commander Leonard Burt, Peter Twiss.

24.04.1969 **Bright's Boffins: Friends Or Foe?**	J /

Space age situation comedy.

01.05.1969 **Now And Then**	J /

08.05.1969 **Junkin**	J /

With John Junkin (Presenter).

15.05.1969 **Travel Abroad**	J /

With René Cutforth (Presenter).

See also: BRIGHT'S BOFFINS* / HOW / JUNKIN*

PLAYHOUSE

Produced for ITV by a variety of companies (see details below). Transmission details are for the ATV midlands region. Duration varies - see below for details.

SERIES 2

	Production No	Holding / Source
30.09.1968 **There's A Hole In Your Dustbin Delilah**	P560/15	DB-R1 / B1

A Granada production. Duration: 80 minutes.

A refuse-collector nicknamed "Cheese and Egg" (because his initials are CE, and "Church of England" would hardly be appropriate) is the main character in this play. He leads a motley crew of dustbinmen.

Written by Jack Rosenthal; music by Derek Hilton; executive producer H. V. Kershaw; produced by John Finch; directed by Michael Apted.

With Jack MacGowran (Cheese and Egg [C. E. Petty]), Frank Windsor (Bloody Delilah [Mr Sinclair]), Harold Innocent (Heavy Breathing), Graham Haberfield (Winston Platt), Henry Livings (Eric Llewellyn), Marjie Lawrence (Mrs Pride of Jutland), Priscilla Morgan (6 Shakespeare Street), Angela Crow (21 Chaucer Street), John Barrett (Smellie Ibbotson), Pitt Wilkinson (Matthew Pride of Jutland), William Maxwell (Coalman), Maggie Jones (4 Shakespeare Street), Louise Jervis (2 Shakespeare Street), Irlin Hall (19 Chaucer Street), James Beck (Police Sergeant), Peter MacKriel (Milkman), Judy Evans (Helpless Woman), Sheila Irwin (Nurse), Kate Brown (Melanie), JRJ 233D (Thunderbird 3).

In the TV Times, Barbara Young is credited as playing No. 6 Shakespeare Street and Betty Hardy was the Helpless Woman. Made as part of City '68/The System.

See also: THE DUSTBINMEN.

See also: JACK SQUALER'S TIME (RADIO)* / MURDER* / STABLES THEATRE COMPANY*

PLAYING FOR TIME

A BBC production. Untransmitted. Duration: 30 minutes.

Barry Moss is an ex-footballer turned media star. David Smith was a better player, now he is a tramp, looking for somewhere to stay...

Written by Gary Seabrook; costume Jackie Pinks; make-up Christine Vidler; designed by Geoff Nawn; associate producer Christopher Bond; production manager Simon Spencer; produced and directed by Richard Boden.

Peter Blake (David Smith), John Challis (Terry Horn), Ray Winstone (Barry Moss), Celia Imrie (Donna Moss), Della Finch (Layla Fell), Howard Goorney (Old Tramp), David Warwick (1st Cab Driver), Alan Renwick (2nd Cab Driver), John Moorhead (Bike Courier).

	Production No	Holding / Source
##.##.#### [untransmitted 1990 pilot]	LLCA250N	DB / 1"

PLAYLAND

A BBC production. Untransmitted. Duration: 32 minutes.

Dick Fiddy remembers, "Oh dear - my sordid past catches up with me. Yes, it was an interesting experience but not a happy one. Producer Dennis Main Wilson came to blows (literally) with the director Martin Shardlow. It was our first produced sitcom though so not all bad."

Written by Mark Wallington and Richard Fiddy; costume Barbara Kidd; make-up Lisa Westcott; music by Ronnie Hazlehurst; designed by John Stout; production manager Evan King; produced by Dennis Main Wilson; directed by Martin Shardlow.

Charles Rea, Norman Rodway, Michael Deeks, John Tordoff, Peter Woodthorpe.

	Holding / Source
##.##.#### [untransmitted 1981 pilot]	DB / 2"

POETRY PROGRAMME

A BBC production. Untransmitted.

	VT Number	Holding / Source
##.##.#### **Men & Women [pilot film]**	16/P/9000	J /

Recorded 5th August 1960.

POINTLESS CELEBRITIES

A Remarkable Television production for BBC. Transmission details are for BBC. Duration varies - see below for details.

Can you find a pointless answer?

Main regular credit(s):   Presented by Alexander Armstrong.

Main regular performer(s): Richard Osman (Co-Host).

Transmission details are for BBC 2.

	Holding / Source
22.12.2010	HD/DB / HDC

Duration: 40 minutes.

Research Rachel Armitage, Oliver Breckon, Rose Dawson, Carl Earl-Ocran, Rebecca Greenwood, Chris Hale, Julia Hobbs, Alex Kessie, Liam Nugent, Benjamin Polya and Helen Price; script supervisor Maria Trevers; graphics by Saint; music by Marc Sylvan; designed by Dominic Tolfts; assistant producers Nazia Butt, Paul Hepplewhite and Terri Marzoli; production executive Hana Canter; executive producers Pam Cavannagh, Tom Blakeson and David Flynn; production manager Tara Ali; series producer Michelle Woods; produced by Tom Cuckson; directed by Nick Harris.

With Richard Osman, Deborah Meaden, Theo Paphitis, Bill Turnbull, Sian Williams, Ginny Buckley, Rav Wilding, Tim Lovejoy, Simon Rimmer.

This was actually a standard edition of the main POINTLESS series.

POLICE DOG

A Crestview production for ABC. Untransmitted. Duration: 25 minutes.

Shay Gorman.

	Holding / Source
##.##.####	J / B3

Television Today reported on 5.5.1960 that this pilot would be made at ABC, Elstree. It seems to have morphed into The Pursuers.

See also: THE PURSUERS*

POP CIRCUS

A BBC production. Untransmitted.

Don Maclean (Host).

	Holding / Source
##.##.#### **[untransmitted pilot]**	J / 2"

Recorded late 1971/early 1972.

POP DOGS

Commissioned by ITV 1. Untransmitted.

ITV music quiz pilot.

Bill Bailey.

	Holding / Source
##.##.####	J /

POP QUIZ

A BBC production for BBC 1. Transmission details are for BBC 1. Duration: 30 minutes.

Main regular credit(s):　　　Produced by Jill Sinclair.

	Holding / Source
04.01.1994　**Top Of The Pops Night**	DB-D3 / D3S

Directed by Phil Chilvers.

With Mike Read (Presenter), Alan Freeman.

POPADOODLEDANDY

A tv21 production for Channel 4. Transmission details are for Channel 4. Duration: 25 minutes.

Written by Vic Reeves and Bob Mortimer; programme associate Dave Morley; produced by Graham K. Smith; directed by David G. Hillier.

Vic Reeves, Bob Mortimer, Cud, Kym Mazelle, Milan, Denim, Strawberry's Tarts.

	Holding / Source
21.08.2012	DB / 1"

POSSESSION

A BBC production for BBC 2. Untransmitted.

Contestants moved around the set by a hydraulic lift!

Associate producer Glen Middleham.

Mariella Frostrup (Host).

	Holding / Source
##.##.#### **[untransmitted pilot]**	DB-D3 / D3S

POTTER

A BBC production for BBC 1. Transmission details are for BBC 1. Duration: 30 minutes.

Main regular credit(s):　　　Written by Roy Clarke; theme music by Ronnie Hazlehurst.

	Production No	VT Number	Holding / Source
##.##.#### **[untransmitted 1978 pilot]**	1148/3231	VTC/6HT/B22698	DB-D3 / 2"

Costume Janet Tharby; make-up Suzan Broad; designed by Carol Golder; produced and directed by Peter Whitmore.

With Arthur Lowe (Potter), Margery Mason (Aileen), Michael Ripper (Commissionaire), John Warner (Tolliver), Madeleine Orr (Mrs Hemming), Jo-Anne Good (Office Girl), Michael Sharvell-Martin (Postman), Jay Neill (Commuter), Philip Ryan (Lorry Driver), Derek Martin (Boilerman).

THE PREVENTERS

An Absolutely production for Carlton. Transmission details are for the Central region. Duration: 20 minutes.

Comedy spoof about a trio of sixties troubleshooters who battle evil wherever they find it.

Written by Morwenna Banks, Chris England and Robert Harley; graphics by Triffic Films; music adviser Pete Baikie; edited by Steve Tempia; director of photography John Walker; designed by Chrysoula Sofitsi; executive producer Miles Bullough; production manager George Cole; line producer Terry Bamber; produced by Nick Symons; directed by Liddy Oldroyd.

Morwenna Banks (Penelope Gold), Robert Harley (Craig Sturdy), Chris England (Mike Stallion), William Gaunt (The Controller), Simon Williams (Lord Belvoir St Nash), Ed Devereaux (Roger Stavro Mordick), Chris Langham (Doctor Keelover), Richard Simpson (Sir Norman Quimby), Andy Smart (Hippy on Gate), Richard Turner (Doctor Beatnik), Mark Heap (Fritz), Neil Mullarkey (Croupier), The Adventures of Parsley (Popstock Band).

	Holding / Source
16.12.1996　**Hippy Daze**	D2 / V1S

THE PRICE IS RIGHT

A Central production. Transmission details are for the Central region. Duration varies - see below for details.

Performer(s):   With Leslie Crowther (Presenter).

	Holding / Source
08.04.1988 **Ep 18**	1" / 1"
Duration: 51 minutes.	

PRIVATES

A Richmond Films and Television production for ITV. Untransmitted. Duration: 48 minutes.

Written by Steven Moffat.

Brian Conley (?).

	Holding / Source
##.##.#### **[untransmitted November 1999 pilot]**	DB /

THE PRODIGAL MOTHER

A Granada production. Transmission details are for the Central region. Duration: 25 minutes.

Written by Arline Whittaker; designed by David Buxton; executive producer David Liddiment; produced by James Maw; directed by Nic Phillips.

Liz Smith (Mrs Tyler), Rosalind Ayres (Marjorie), Diana Weston (Pauline), Claire Skinner (Susan), Tony Doyle (Roy).

	Production No	Holding / Source
##.##.#### **[untransmitted pilot]**	P1471	1" / 1"

THE PROFESSOR & ME

An LWT production. Untransmitted. Duration: 25 minutes.

Written by Colin Callender and Peter Vincent; produced and directed by Les Chatfield.

Tony Britton, Lesley Duff.

	VT Number	Holding / Source
##.##.#### **[untransmitted pilot]**	9L/99526	DB|n / 2"
Recorded October 1980.		

THE PROSECUTORS

A BBC production. Untransmitted.

Drama series about lawyers.

Devised by Philip Levene; produced by Eric Price.

Patrick Allen, David Langton, Basil Henson, Ann Lynn.

	Holding / Source
##.##.#### **[untransmitted pilot]**	J / 2"
Recorded June 1969.	

PUBLIC EYE

An ABC/Thames production. Duration: 50 minutes.

Main regular credit(s):   Created by Anthony Marriott and Roger Marshall; theme music by Robert Earley.

Main regular cast: Alfred Burke (Frank Marker).

	Holding / Source
##.##.#### **The Public Eye: Dig You Later**	J / 40

Frank Marvin is asked by a police inspector to find his missing daughter who mixes in bad company.

Written by Roger Marshall; produced and directed by Don Leaver.

With Alfred Burke (Frank Marvin).

Recorded at Didsbury in June 1964. This episode was re-made for the first series.

PULASKI

A BBC production for BBC 1. made in association with Arts & Entertainment Network. Transmission details are for BBC 1.

Main regular credit(s):   Created by Roy Clarke; theme music by The Shadows; music by Brian Bennett; production associate Ian Brindle; produced by Paul Knight.

Main regular cast: David Andrews (Larry Summers), Caroline Langrishe (Kate Smith / Briggsy), Kate Harper (Paula), Rolf Saxon (Jerome).

	Holding / Source
02.10.1987 **The Fictional Detective**	DB / C1

Duration: 75 minutes.

Written by Roy Clarke; directed by Christopher King.

With Timothy Carlton (Hilary), Nigel Pegram (Director), Terry Cade (Brad), Peter McNamara, Elspet Gray, Donald Hewlett, Gary Shail, Deborah Grant, Valentine Pelka, Helen Burns, Nigel Humphreys, Forbes Collins, Debbie Greenwood, Vincent Keane, Gillian Martell, Brian Hewlett, Bernadette Milnes, Terence Conoley, Lowri Ann Richards, Gayle Coleman, Ron Tarr, Richard England, Desmond Askew.

PULL THE PLUG

Alternative/Working Title(s): THE FLIP SHOW

A Noel Gay Television production for BSB. Untransmitted. Duration: 25 minutes.

Talent show pilots never aired. It caused controversy when revealed that artists would be plunged into darkness on the stage if their acts did not meet with the celebrity panel's approval.

		Holding / Source
##.##.####	[pilot 1]	J / 1"
##.##.####	[pilot 2]	J / 1"

Made February 1990.

PULSE

A World production for BBC 3. made in association with Screen Yorkshire. Transmission details are for BBC 3. Duration: 55 minutes.

Created by Paul Cornell, Tom McRae and Ben Teasdale; written by Paul Cornell; based on a story by Ben Teasdale; script supervisor Jemima Thomas; production executive Hugo Heppell; executive producers Polly Hill and Simon Heath; line producer Thea Harvey; produced by Helen Gregory; directed by James Hawes.

Stephen Campbell Moore (Nick Gates), Alan Williams (Charlie Maddox), Arsher Ali (Adam Hussein), Emily Beecham (Stella Hamilton), Claire Foy (Hannah Carter), Gregg Chillin (Rafee Hussein), Natti Houghton (Jess Black), Eileen Davies (Mrs Maddox), Caroline Goodall (Juliette Randall), Ben Miles (Joe Sennet), Jo Hartley (Loz Westmoor), Emma Stansfield (Nurse).

	Holding / Source
03.06.2010	HD/DB / HD/DB

THE PUNCH REVIEW

A BBC production for BBC 2. Transmission details are for BBC 2. Duration: 30 minutes.

	Holding / Source
21.12.1975	DB-D3 / 2"

Written by Alan Coren, Miles Kington, Sheridan Morley and E. S. Turner; adapted by Barry Took; music by Wally Fawkes and The Troglodytes; designed by Fiona Comrie; produced and directed by Gareth Gwenlan.

With Bill Grundy, Robin Bailey, John Bird, Chris Emmett, Patricia Hayes, Julian Holloway, Roy Kinnear, Sheridan Morley, Gwen Taylor.

Q.E.D.

Alternative/Working Title(s): MASTERMIND / QUENTIN E. DEVERILL

A Consolidated Productions production for ITV. Transmission details are for the Central region. Duration: 50 minutes.

Main regular credit(s):	Created by John Hawkesworth and Robert Schlitt; music by Ken Howard and Alan Blaikley; art director Fred Carter; executive producer John Hawkesworth; supervising producers Ronald Austin and James David Buchanan; production manager Clifton Brandon; produced by Christopher Neame.
Main regular cast:	Sam Waterston (Quentin E. Deverill), A. C. Weary (Charlie Andrews), George Innes (Phipps).

Holding / Source

17.01.1984 Target London   C3 / C3

Written by Robert Schlitt; music directed by Zack Laurence; director of photography Ted Moore; film editor Ralph Sheldon; assistant director Barry Langley; directed by Don Sharp.

With Sarah Berger (Betsy Stevens), Julian Glover (Doctor Stefan Kilkiss), Richard Morant (Richard Stevens), Ronald Lacey (Medium), Frederick Jaeger (Kaiser), John Abineri (Staff Officer), Robert Harris (Judge), Robert Arden (University President), Billy J. Mitchell (Professor), Robert Henderson (Old Professor), Edward Wiley (Young Professor), David Baron (Guest at Seance), Michael Stroud (Guest at Seance), Jean Burgess (Lady at Seance), Michael N. Harbour (Fisherman), Constantin De Goguel (German Commander), Paul Jerricho (German Sergeant), Kenneth Owens (German Corporal), Wolf Kahler (Technician), Steve Ubels (Technician), Paul Humpoletz (Flunkey).

Sarah Berger is credited in the opening title sequence like the other regulars but only appears in this episode. Her role, though not her actual character, is taken by Caroline Langrishe in the other episodes.

The pilot episode was made at Twickenham Studios and is copyrighted, on-screen, to the European Banking Company Ltd. The other five episodes are copyrighted to W. & G. Industrial Leasing Ltd and were made at Lee International Studios.

QI

A talkbackThames production for BBC. Transmission details are for BBC Various. Duration: 29 minutes.

Main regular credit(s):	Created by John Lloyd; theme music by Howard Goodall; production designer Jonathan Paul Green.
Main regular performer(s):	Stephen Fry (QI Master), Alan Davies.

Holding / Source

##.##.#### [untransmitted pilot]   DB / DBSW

Script supervisor Alice Osborne; associate producer Arabella McGuigan; production executive Jenny Hay; executive producer Peter Fincham; production manager Vicky Winter; produced by John Lloyd.

With Bill Bailey, Kit Hesketh-Harvey, Eddie Izzard.

No on-screen credits appear on the pilot.

Titles in quotation marks are official but appear to have been retro-fitted. Titles without were billed on original transmission. None of them appear on-screen.

QUANDARIES

An LWT production. Untransmitted. Duration: 25 minutes.

	VT Number	Holding / Source
##.##.#### [untransmitted pilot]	9L/79238	J / 2"

TVS later made a quiz series using this format in 1988.

A QUESTION OF SPORT

A BBC Manchester production for BBC 1. Transmission details are for BBC 1. Duration: 30 minutes.

Transmission details are for BBC 1 North.

Holding / Source

02.12.1968   J /

With Fred Trueman, Stuart Hall (Presenter), Mary Rand, Henry Cooper (Team Captain), Cliff Morgan (Team Captain), Bobby Moore, Roger Taylor.

QUICK ON THE DRAW

A Thames Television production. Transmission details are for the ATV midlands region. Duration: 25 minutes.

Main regular credit(s):	Devised by Denis Gifford.
Performer(s):	With Bob Monkhouse (Host), Jan Rennison.

Holding / Source

02.01.1974   DB / 2"

Designed by Lawrence Collett; produced by David Clark; directed by Anthony Parker.

With Michael Bentine, William Rushton, Bill Tidy, Frank Dickens.

All editions featured three cartoonists who take part in all of the rounds. Most shows also featured a surprise guest from the world of cartooning who the celebrities had to identify. This latter guest was not billed in the TV Times and so we are unable to list him/her unless we have access to other sources for this information. Where known, we list the surprise guest last in the programme's cast list.

QUIZ BALL

An ATV production. Untransmitted. Duration: 25 minutes.

Devised by George Woolley.

Shaw Taylor (Host).

Holding / Source

##.##.#### Aston Villa v Celebrities [untransmitted pilot]   R1 /

With Joe Mercer, George Graham, Alan Deakin, Charles Aitken, Phil Woosnam, Tony Parker, David Lloyd, Simon Smith, Norman Horner, Rex Alston, Elizabeth Pearsall, Karen Gardner.

QUIZ BINGO

A BBC North production for BBC 1. Transmission details are for BBC 1. Duration: 20 minutes.

Main regular credit(s):   Devised by Ron Crawford and Cecil Korer; produced by Cecil Korer; directed by Bob Toner.

Main regular performer(s): Jimmy Savile (Host).

Holding / Source

##.##.#### [untransmitted pilot] Stockport v. Cheadle   R1 / 40

Research Olga Kersner; illustrated by Eric Ilett; designed by Tony Snoaden.

With Mary Bartley (Assistant), Jackie Lister (Assistant).

QUIZ JOB

A Border Television production. Untransmitted. Duration: 25 minutes.

Devised by Stephen Leslie; designed by Ian Reed; produced by Derek Batey; directed by Norman Fraser.

Derek Batey (Quizmaster).

Holding / Source

##.##.#### [untransmitted pilot] The Shops V The Post Office   2"|n / 2"

Recorded 30/05/1978. Quiz hosted by Derek Batey between two teams of workers from a particular industry.

QUIZ OF THE WEEK

A BBC production. Untransmitted. Duration varies - see below for details.

Holding / Source

##.##.#### Parliamentarians v Private Eye [first untransmitted pilot]   R1 / 2"

Duration: 34 minutes.

Designed by Colin Green; produced by Anthony Smith; directed by Peter Chafer.

With Ned Sherrin (Chairman), Malcolm Ingram (Actor), Miriam Margolyes (Actor), Lady Antonia Fraser, Lena Jeger M.P., Margaret Thatcher [as Margaret Thatcher M.P.], Paul Foot, Richard Ingrams, William Rushton.

Recorded 27.7.1968

##.##.#### Residents v 24 Hours [second untransmitted pilot]   R1 / 2"

Duration: 31 minutes.

Designed by Colin Green; produced by Anthony Smith; directed by Peter Chafer.

With Ned Sherrin (Chairman), Malcolm Ingram (Actor), Miriam Margolyes (Actor), Mary Kenny, Neil Shand, William Rushton, Linda Blandford, Fyfe Robertson, Denis Tuohy.

Only the untransmitted pilots are listed here.

RAB C. NESBITT

A BBC Scotland production for BBC 2. Transmission details are for BBC 2. Duration varies - see below for details.

Main regular credit(s):   Written by Ian Pattison; produced and directed by Colin Gilbert.

Main regular cast: Gregor Fisher (Rab C. Nesbitt).

	Holding / Source
31.12.1989 **Rab C. Nesbitt's Seasonal Greet**	DB / 1"

Duration: 45 minutes.

Alternative transmissions: BBC 1 Scotland: 21.12.1988.

Music by David McNiven.

With Elaine C. Smith (Mary Nesbitt), Tony Roper (Jamesie Cotter), Andrew Fairlie (Gash), Brian Pettifer (Andra), Eric Cullen, Andy Gray, Alex Norton, Charlie Sim, Mary Riggans, Gerard Kelly, Iain Cuthbertson, Rikki Fulton, Jonathan Watson, David McNiven, Gerry Sadowitz, Robert McGowan, Peter Capaldi, Viv Lumsden, Andy Cameron, Russell Hunter, Susan Gilmore, Elaine Collins.

See also: NAKED VIDEO*

RAFFLES

A Yorkshire Television production. Transmission details are for the ATV midlands region.

Main regular credit(s):   Adapted by Philip Mackie; based on stories by E. W. Hornung.

Main regular cast: Anthony Valentine (A. J. Raffles), Christopher Strauli (Bunny Manders).

	VT Number	Holding / Source
10.09.1975 **The Amateur Cracksman**	1804	DB / 2"

Duration: 75 minutes.

Designed by Roger Andrews; executive producer Peter Willes; directed by Christopher Hodson.

With James Maxwell (Inspector Mackenzie), John Junkin (Crawshay), Michael Barrington (Earl of Milchester), Eric Francis (Newsvendor), Edward Palmer (Albany Porter), Osmund Bullock (Viscount Crowley), Anthony Dawes (Landlord), Margot Lister (Dowager Marchioness of Melrose), Belinda Carroll (Lady Margaret), Julia Sutton (Miss Melhuish), Sandra Berkin (French Maid), Ken Halliwell (Policeman), Philip Voss (Albany Manager), Brian Nolan (Second Policeman).

Based on the short story "Gentlemen and Players" from the collection "The Amateur Cracksman".

THE RAG TRADE

Produced for BBC/LWT by a variety of companies (see details below). Duration varies - see below for details.

By the start of the sixties, Ronnie Wolfe and Ronnie Chesney had been writing for BBC radio for a number of years and had several radio shows behind them. This was at a time when almost everybody working in radio was trying to get into television. The general consensus was that radio was becoming old hat; telly people were trendy and that's where the action was.

From their experiences working in factories the two Ronnies always felt there was a good television show to be made out of working in a factory. Ronald Chesney's family had also worked in the textile business and he also had a business share in a clothing factory, so together Wolfe & Chesney thrashed out an idea about a series with a factory background allied to the clothing and fashion industry. They finally settled on a small dressmaking factory.

The series became an instantaneous winner. Wolfe & Chesney think the show, featuring real working people in real working conditions, must have been something of a breakthrough. It is still fondly remembered, as many years later, an article in "The Listener" about "The Rag Trade" ventured that 'it was the funniest comedy of all time".

Full of confidence, the writers took the idea to one of the commercial TV companies – Associated Rediffusion. They thought it was good. Rediffusion didn't. Their reaction was "millions of people spend all day working in a factory; they want to come home, relax and forget it. They'll never switch on to watch a series about factory life." Then they remembered that Frank Muir and Denis Norden, the brilliant writing team that penned so many great sitcoms, had been appointed comedy advisors to the BBC, so Wolfe & Chesney made a quick trip down to the Television Centre at White City where they were based. Being successful writers, they were immediately able to realise the format's potential.. Happily, they both loved the idea; commissioned some scripts, and then the casting started.

Miriam Karlin played the part of the Shop Steward, Paddy. But why Paddy? Well, the script was first sent to Alfred Marks asking if he'd play the part of the Boss, and, as an added inducement to his saying Yes, the part of the Shop Steward was offered to Alfred's wife, Paddy O'Neill. They both turned it down. The script was then sent to Miriam, but the typist forgot to change the name. Miriam didn't query it; she thought it rather amusing that a nice Jewish actress should be named Paddy.

Peter Jones and Reg Varney were soon cast without too many problems. Peter was a fine actor and a known commodity, and perfect for the part of Mr. Fenner - indecisive, untrustworthy, and just slightly dishonest. Ronald Chesney had worked with Reg in variety theatre and knew his worth as an actor and a comic.

For the other smaller parts, the producer, Dennis Main Wilson, didn't hold auditions. He just booked actors who were successfully appearing in shows at that moment. There was Ann Beach who was appearing in Billy Liar; Esma Cannon from Sailor Beware; and Toni Palmer from Fings Ain't Wot They Used to Be. How did the producer manage to get these talented actresses into the show to play such small parts, with maybe only two or three lines? It was easy. He lied. He promised that each week one of them would have the entire show written around them. They would virtually be the star for that week. But of course, it never happened and in the second or third series, quite disheartened and disgruntled, they left.

For the first few episodes, Barbara was put in a low-cut blouse showing lots of cleavage, a very tight miniskirt, and her hair piled up in what was known as the beehive style. But Barbara wasn't happy; she complained to the writers, "Ron, I'm fed up with this outfit. It's like a uniform. Can't you fix it that I wear something different? Have my hair done another way?" Ronnie Wolfe said "Look, you're playing a comedy character and you don't have many lines. You want to be noticed? Stay with that one outfit throughout the series". Then he added, "Think of Chaplin. He always wore the same clothes - the bowler hat, the baggy trousers, the cane. This sort of uniform seems to work for comedy characters". Barbara thought for a minute, then said "O.K. Ron, you could be right. I'll stay with it. Tits, Bum and Beehive!" Barbara did stay with it, and that get-up became her trademark – helped her into films, and started her carrying on in many a 'Carry On'!

After three successful seasons for the BBC, Wolfe & Chesney moved on to write 'Meet the Wife' and 'On The Buses'. Interested in a remake, the BBC commissioned a new pilot in 1975 with Tony Robinson in the Reg Varney role as Anthony. The BBC decided against going further so LWT picked up the idea and did two popular seasons in 1977-78. Two seasons of the BBC original and all the LWT remake is available to watch again on commercial DVD.

Main regular credit(s):   Written by Ronald Wolfe and Ronald Chesney.

Main regular cast: Peter Jones (Mr Fenner), Miriam Karlin (Paddy).

A BBC production. Untransmitted. Duration: 30 minutes.

	Production No	VT Number	Holding / Source
##.##.#### **Versus**	1145/3261	B01635/ED	DV / 2"

Music by Alex Welsh and his Band; produced and directed by Dennis Main Wilson.

With Tony Robinson (Anthony), Gaye Brown, Jumoke Debayo, Diane Langton, Annabel Leventon, Jamila Massey, Mollie Maureen, Trixie Scales, Ahmed Khalil.

Made in 1975, this pilot was never transmitted.

RAINBOW

A Thames Television production. Transmission details are for the ATV midlands region. Usual duration: 15 minutes.

Main regular credit(s):   Created by Pamela Lonsdale.

SERIES 1

Main regular credit(s):   Produced by Pamela Lonsdale.

Main regular cast: With David Cook (David), John Leeson, Roy Skelton, Telltale.

	Holding / Source
##.##.#### **[untransmitted pilot]**	J / 2"

Recorded January 1972.

Puppets by Violet Philpott.

"Sally & Jake" / "Curly & Straight" by Stop Frame Animations Limited.

RAINBOW CITY

A BBC Birmingham production for BBC 1. Transmission details are for BBC 1. Duration: 25 minutes.

Racial issues examined through the eyes of a Jamaican man and his white wife living in Birimingham.

Main regular credit(s):   Created by John Elliot; music by Ram John Holder and Michael McKenzie; designed by Margaret Peacock.

Main regular cast: Errol John (John Steele).

	Holding / Source
05.07.1967 **What Sort Of Boy?**	R1 / 40

Alternative transmissions: Central: .

Written by Horace James and John Elliot; produced and directed by John Elliot.

With Horace James (Dennis Jackson), Gemma Jones (Mary Steele), Graham Weston, Colin Skipp, Calvin Butler, Ianthe Agelasto, Frank Veasey, Yolande Fermin, Leslie Dunn, Myrtle Robinson, Frances Dunn, Nina Baden-Semper, Dolores Mantez, Ian Cooper, Calvin Lockhart, Ann Curthoys, Lloyd Reckord.

	Holding / Source
12.07.1967 **Why You Marry?**	DB-4W|n / 40

Alternative transmissions: Central: .

Written by John Elliot and Horace James; produced and directed by John Elliot.

With Horace James (Dennis Jackson), Gemma Jones (Mary Steele), George Woolley, Raymond Hill, Annie Perkins, Ian Cooper, Mitzi Townshend, Cecil Gray, Leonie Forbes, Buddy Pouatt, Yvonne Jones, Beverley Anderson, George Madden.

BBC hold 16mm telerecording.

	Holding / Source
19.07.1967 **A Better Fortune**	DB-4W / 40

Alternative transmissions: Central: .

Written by Horace James and John Elliot; produced and directed by John Elliot.

With Horace James (Dennis Jackson), Gemma Jones (Mary Steele), Carmen Munroe, Clifton Jones, David Stevens, George Woolley.

The first three editions were made in one batch as pilot episodes.

RAISED BY WOLVES

A Big Talk Productions production for Channel 4. Transmission details are for Channel 4. Duration: 24 minutes.

Comedy set on a Wolverhampton council estate, following the fortunes of a single mother and her six children.

Written by Caitlin Moran and Caroline Moran; costume Kat Willis; make-up Juliet Jackson; edited by Nigel Williams; director of photography Laurie Rose; titles by Yianni Papanicolaou; assistant director Lee Trevor; art director Andrea Coathupe; production designer David Butterworth; post production supervisor Alistair Hopkins; executive producers Matthew Justice, Kenton Allen and Caroline Leddy; head of production Rhian Griffiths; production supervised by Benjamin Richards; line producer Samantha Milnes; produced by Caroline Norris; directed by Ian Fitzgibbon.

Philip Jackson (Grampy), Rebekah Staton (Della Garry), Helen Monks (Germaine Garry), Alexa Davies (Aretha Garry), Molly Risker (Yoko Garry), Kaine Zajaz (Lee Rind), Lucie Brown (Mariah Garry), Caden-Ellis Wall (Wyatt Garry), Violet Maple (Cher Garry), Daisy Maple (Cher Garry).

	Holding / Source
23.12.2013	HD/DB / HDC

RALF RALF THE SUMMIT

A Quay Brothers production for Channel 4. Untransmitted.

Ralf Little (Host).

	Holding / Source
##.##.####	DV|n / 1"

Performance art piece first performed in 1987. This pilot was made in 1995 but rejected by Channel 4.

RAP

A Yorkshire Television production. Transmission details are for the Thames Television region. Duration: 25 minutes.

Produced by John Meade and Barbara Macdonald; directed by Norman Fenton.

Mike Dornan (Presenter).

	Holding / Source
04.08.1974	2"|n / 2"
rx 21/5/74	

Discussion programme in which teenagers talk about things that affect them.

RAT TRAP

A Granada production. Transmission details are for ITV 1. Duration: 35 minutes.

	Production No	Holding / Source
08.03.2000	1/3223/0001	DB / DBS

Kirsty Young hosts this one-off programme which secretly films thieves as they commit crimes. The programme lays traps to catch the crime "rats" and records them as they take the bait. That footage is shown tonight in the hope viewers can identify the thieves.

Presented by Kirsty Young; executive producer Sarah Caplin; produced by Kate Middleton.

THE RAVE

A Granada production. Transmission details are for the Granada region. Duration: 25 minutes.

from the book
Echoes: The Complete History Of Pink Floyd.

Monday 6 March: TV SHOW, Granada Studios, Manchester, England.

Pink Floyd were filmed on this date performing Arnold Layne live for the pilot episode of a new 30 minute Granada TV music programme called The Rave. A proposed replacement for Rediffusion's Ready Steady Go! and hosted by The Move, the series was not commissioned and this pilot show was never broadcast The Move (Hosts), Pink Floyd.

	Holding / Source
06.03.1967	J /

REALLY REALLY

An Ulster Television production. Transmission details are for the Ulster Televison region.

	Holding / Source
25.10.1998	DV / DBS

REBUS

A Clerkenwell Films production for Scottish Television. Transmission details are for the Central region. Duration: 100 minutes.

Main regular credit(s):   Based on novels by Ian Rankin; produced by Murray Ferguson.

Main regular cast: John Hannah (Detective Inspector John Rebus), Sara Stewart (Detective Chief Inspector Templer), Stuart Hepburn (Detective Superintendent McCaskill), Gayanne Potter (Detective Sergeant Clarke), Ewan Stewart (Detective Inspector Morton).

	Holding / Source
26.04.2000 **Black And Blue**	DB / V1SSW

Set in Edinburgh, and within the first few minutes we have a particularly gruesome scene that ends up with a body impaled on a set of railings. Hannah's voiceover gives it the feel of a Raymond Chandler novel, as does Joanna Roth's portrayal of "gangster's moll" Eve, who has an attitude as harsh as her hair colour. If you like your murder mysteries set against a backdrop of seedy nightclubs, gloomy tenement buildings and constant rainfall, this is for you.

Written by Stuart Hepburn; music by David Ferguson; designed by Campbell Gordon; executive producers John Hannah and Philip Hinchcliffe; directed by Martyn Friend.

With Jim Norton, Joanna Roth, Clare McCarron, David Lyon, Fish, Robert McIntosh, Lewis Howden, Jenny Foulds, Stevie Hannan, David Gallacher, Gilbert Martin, Jenny Ryan, Stephen McCole, Michael Carter, Russell Anderson, Graeme Mearns, Andrew McCulloch, Anthony Donaldson, Malcolm Shields, Tam White, Bill Barclay, Molly Innes, Faroque Khan.

REDCAP

An ABC production. Transmission details are for the ABC midlands region. Duration varies - see below for details.

Main regular credit(s):   Devised by Jack Bell; produced by John Bryce.

Main regular cast: John Thaw (Sergeant John Mann).

SERIES 1

Main regular credit(s):   Story editor Ian Kennedy Martin.

	VT Number	Holding / Source
24.10.1964 **A Town Called Love**	3772	DB-R1 / 40

Duration: 51 minutes.
Alternative transmissions: Anglia: 12.12.1965; Rediffusion Television: 28.07.1965.
Written by Anthony Steven; story by Jack Bell; directed by Ray Menmuir.

With Peter Copley, Gwendolyn Watts, Michael Robbins, Glynn Edwards, Malcolm Douglas, Tony Steedman, Yootha Joyce, Garfield Morgan, Edwin Finn, Robert Arnold, Valentino Musetti, Avril Wheatley, Geraldine Hart.

Recorded at Didsbury in June 1964.

RELEASE

A BBC production for BBC 2. Transmission details are for BBC 2. Duration: 45 minutes.

	Holding / Source
##.##.#### **[untransmitted pilot] New Release**	R1 /

It was a magazine programme.

With Francis Bacon.

NB: Throughout this series directing credits, where given, generally relate to one of the main features within the programme rather than the main programme itself.

Often only inserts survive, not complete shows.

RESPECT

A Yorkshire Television production. Transmission details are for the Central region. Duration: 75 minutes.

A boxer struggling to get back into the ring after an injury is desperate for money, Bobby Carr (Berry) falls in with a bad lot down at the local pool hall and turns to crime, much to the disgust of wife Rosie (Jayne Ashbourne). Can he turn aside from his wicked ways and win back the respect of family and fans?

Written by Richard La Plante; executive producer Keith Richardson; produced by Peter Waller; directed by Terry Marcel.

Nick Berry (Bobby Carr), Jayne Ashbourne (Rosie Carr), Mark Addy (Joe Carr), Dean Williamson (Trevor Nye), Rachel Victoria Roberts (Janine), Nicholas Ball (Ronnie Ellis), Carol Harrison (Veronica), Garey Bridges (Billy Price), Philip Woodford (Stephen Ruther), Adam Searles (Kevin Murphy), Karl Moffatt (John Simpson), Kenneth Cope (Stan Peters), Nicholas Beveney (Ralph Grandistone), Paul Kember (Tipper Donovan), Graham Bryan (Oliver Wright), Lee Macdonald (Danny Phillips), Ayo Taiwo (Ayo), Richard Driscoll (Steve Ellis), Glynis Brooks (Betty Murphy), Oscar Soiza (Baby Ben), Brian Miller (Boxing Doctor), Martyn Read (Ray Green), Owen Scott (Doctor Lane).

	VT Number	Holding / Source
17.12.1996	D212	DB-1" / V1S

REST ASSURED

A Granada production. Untransmitted. Duration: 25 minutes.

Graham Haberfield and Neville Buswell star as insurance salesmen Jerry and Raymond in a series of adventures with their clients.

Written by H. V. Kershaw; produced by H. V. Kershaw; directed by Nick Burrell-Davis.

Graham Haberfield (Jerry Booth), Neville Buswell (Ray Lampton), Gwyneth Powell (Mrs Johnson), Betty Hardy (Mrs Heywood), Margaret Shevlin (Beryl), Fred Feast (Lift Engineer), Ruth Kettlewell (Mrs Minto), Bruce Watt (Boy).

	Production No	Holding / Source
##.##.#### **Lift Off [untransmitted pilot]**	P756/8901	DB / 2"

Recorded 20.11.72.

See also: CORONATION STREET

REVOLTING WOMEN

A BBC Manchester production for BBC 2. Transmission details are for BBC 2.

Feminist revue series.

Main regular credit(s):   Assistant producer Jackie Spreckley; produced by Lyn Webster.

Main regular cast: Jeni Barnett, Philip Bird, Linda Broughton, Alison Skilbeck.

	Holding / Source
22.01.1981	DB-D3 / 2"

Duration: 25 minutes.

Directed by Geoff Posner.

With Marcella Evaristi, Helen Glavin.

REVOLVER

An ATV production. Transmission details are for the ATV midlands region. Duration: 35 minutes.

"The rock just keeps coming round" was the way TVTimes described ATV's short-lived 1978 music show Revolver which was marketed as a home for new wave music – the midlands' answer to Granada's So It Goes, if you like.

It certainly wasn't Top of the Pops, and distinguishing itself from that venerable institution (which then wasn't even fifteen years old) was a key part of Revolver's identity.

Chart music was out – or at least coincidental – because the programmes were recorded well in advance of transmission. For the pilot programme, sixty minutes' worth of material was recorded during a seven-hour session at ATV in Birmingham on Sunday 19th March, and this would be further compacted to just under 40 minutes by the time it was broadcast. This was originally going to be on 15th July, but the programme was brought forward – perhaps fearing it might be too out of date by then – to 20th May. The acts on this first programme included Kate Bush, XTC, The Tom Robinson Band, The Rich Kids, Steel Pulse and local band Ricky Cool and the Icebergs. Even in the pilot, despite the visual trappings being very much new wave there was musical variety in the form of Kate Bush along with some reggae and rock 'n' roll.

The idea for the programme came from Mickie Most – a long-time record producer, though best known to the public as a member of the New Faces judging panel. Wanting the show to be the antithesis of Top of the Pops, which had been described by its producer Robin Nash as a programme all the family could enjoy, Most envisaged Revolver to have the life and immediacy of a club, and that was the basis of the show's appearance – a former ballroom now 'forced' to put on modern bands while retaining its revolving stage. Introducing most of the acts was comedy veteran Peter Cook playing the role of the faded ballroom's manager who didn't like the raucous music played by the bands.

Two other regulars were also involved: popular local radio DJ Les Ross, then with BRMB, served up hamburgers and dispensed news and information. One of the acts each week would be a 'support act' currently without a recording deal. Les would introduce these groups and would regularly report that 'after being seen on Revolver, so-and-so had been offered a recording contract'. The other regular was DJ Chris Hill whose involvement in the finished programme is next to non-existant but presumably played more of a role in the studio.

Each programme had much the same format – it would start with one of the headline acts just finishing a number, thus giving the impression that things were already underway rather than waiting for the viewer to arrive before kicking-off. There would generally be seven acts each week. Two of these would have 'star' status and would perform two songs apiece with one of these playing either side of the centre ad-break and the other closing the show. Whether it was the original intention to broaden the scope of the programme, or 'division one' new wave bands were hard to find isn't clear, but the type of band on the show changed quite dramatically around half-way through as can be seen in the list of headline acts. So, after Rich Kids and TRB in the pilot, it was The Stranglers and Boomtown Rats, then Buzzcocks and Ian Dury, while the fourth edition had Nick Lowe and Elvis Costello – so far so new wave-ish. The next edition saw funk band Heatwave headlining with The Jam; show six had midlands stalwarts The Steve Gibbons Band plus Suzi Quatro; folk-rockers Lindisfarne provided an interesting contrast to Eddie and the Hot Rods in the penultimate show and the final edition saw the return of The Rich Kids along with 50's revivalists Darts. John Lydon's Public Image Ltd were supposed to appear on the last show but instead of travelling to Birmingham they apparently spent the day enjoying themselves on Camber Sands instead. In making the show less than family-friendly, producer Mickie Most had, as a result, forced a more out-of-the-way time-slot on the programme and, the pilot aside, the programme was shown after 11pm for the whole of its summer 1978 run. As a result, it sadly didn't pick up enough viewers to get renewed for a second season. The whole series survives, as do some out-takes and while there's no DVD release it has had the occasional repeat on VH1.

Main regular credit(s):   Designed by Martin Davey; produced by Mickie Most; directed by Chris Tookey.

Main regular performer(s): Peter Cook (Host), Chris Hill, Les Ross.

	VT Number	Holding / Source
20.05.1978	6083	DB / 2"

Brought forward from 15.07.1978.

With XTC, Steel Pulse, Kate Bush, John Dowie, The Rich Kids, Ricky Cool and The Icebergs, The Tom Robinson Band.

RICH HALL'S BADLY FUNDED THINK TANK

An Open Mike production for BBC Choice. Transmission details are for BBC Choice. Duration: 30 minutes.

Written by Rich Hall, Mike Wilmot and Mike Dugan; theme music by Pat Fish; music by Damian Coldwell and Christian Reilly; titles by Tom Messenger; art director Julian Nagel; production team Jeremy Hall, Emily Hudd, Andrew Parkin, Alison Vann and Helen Wurzer; executive producer Addison Cresswell; head of production Andrew Beint; production manager Lucy Eagle; produced by Rob Baker; directed by Paul Wheeler.

Rich Hall, Mike Wilmot.

	Holding / Source
13.11.2001	DB / DBSW

RICHARD LITTLEJOHN LIVE AND UNCUT

Alternative/Working Title(s): LITTLEJOHN TAKES ON THE WORLD

An LWT production. made in association with NPC Productions. Transmission details are for the London Weekend Television region. Usual duration: 55 minutes.

Main regular performer(s): Richard Littlejohn (Presenter).

	VT Number	Holding / Source
##.##.#### [untransmitted pilot]	9C/26020	DB / DBSW

With Paul Ross, Ann Andrews, Jean Richie, Rabbi Yitzhak Schochet, Jane Couch, The Fraud Monty.

RINGS ON THEIR FINGERS

A BBC production for BBC 1. Transmission details are for BBC 1. Duration: 30 minutes.

Main regular credit(s):   Written by Richard Waring.

	Production No	Holding / Source
##.##.#### What Difference Does A Piece Of Paper Make? [untransmitted pilot]	1148/3021	DB-D3 / 2"

Produced and directed by Mark Cullingham.

With David Troughton (Oliver Pryde), Diane Keen (Sandy Bennett), Roger Brierley (Victor Brown), Daphne Oxenford (Mrs Bennett), Keith Marsh (Mr Pryde).

RIPPING YARNS

A BBC production for BBC 2. Transmission details are for BBC 2. Duration: 30 minutes.

Written by Michael Palin and Terry Jones.

	Holding / Source
07.01.1976 **Tomkinson's Schooldays**	DB / 2"

A ripping yarn from the pens of two of Monty Python's creators: a tale set in the Edwardian era - the heyday of school stories. It has all the authentic ingredients of absolutely topping

schoolboy fun: excitement, adventure,

heroes and bullies.

Lighting by Duncan Brown; sound Michael McCarthy; film camera Peter Hall; film editor Ray Millichope; designed by Martin Collins; produced and directed by Terry Hughes.

With Michael Palin (Tomkinson / Headmaster / TV Introducer / Mr Craffitt), Terry Jones (Mr Ellis / Director), Gwen Watford (Mummy), Ian Ogilvy (Grayson, the School Bully), John Wentworth (Chaplain), Sarah Grazebrook (Maid), Chai Lee (Suki), Terence Denville (Man).

RISING DAMP

A Yorkshire Television production. Transmission details are for the ATV midlands region. Duration: 25 minutes.

Comedy set in a seedy house where Rigsby rents rooms.

Main regular credit(s):   Written by Eric Chappell; music by Dennis Wilson.

Main regular cast: Leonard Rossiter (Rupert Rigsby), Don Warrington (Philip Smith), Frances de la Tour (Ruth Jones).

	VT Number	Holding / Source
02.09.1974 **The New Tenant**	2721	DB / 2"

Alt.Title(s):   *Rooksby*

If you've ever been a student, or had one in the family, you'll have probably made the acquaintance of someone like Rigsby.

Rigsby is the landlord of a seedy. down-at-heel boarding house, catering mainly for students. The sort of bloke who's always snooping at the door, or popping in and out to make sure no one

is fiddling the gas meter. There are two lodgers in residence, Hallam, a medical student Rigsby reckons will never qualify, and Miss Jones,

who will-but always gives "no" as an answer. It's little wonder there are always vacancies at Rigsbys'.

Then a new arrival comes to take over the best room, but it's not the good news it might seem at first .

Designed by Colin Pigott; produced and directed by Ian Macnaughton.

With Richard Beckinsale (Hallam).

Dennis Wilson's name was spelt Denis Wilson on the credits.

See also: COMEDY CLASSICS*

THE RIVER

A BBC production for BBC 1. Transmission details are for BBC 1.

Main regular credit(s):   Written by Michael Aitkens.

	Production No	Holding / Source
##.##.#### **Up The River [untransmitted 1987 pilot]**	LLCJ400N/71	DB / 1"

Duration: 28 minutes.

Costume Inez Nordell; make-up Ann Humphreys; designed by John Coleman; production manager Jenny Leah; produced and directed by Ray Butt.

With Paul Nicholas (Davey Jackson), Julia Dow (Sarah MacDonald), Toni Palmer (Betty Willson), Anthony Jackson (Tom Davis), Timothy Kightley (The Vicar), Debbi Blythe [as Debbie Blythe] (Girl On Barge), Michael Aitkens (Fisherman).

RIVERSIDE

A BBC production for BBC 2. Transmission details are for BBC 2.

	Holding / Source
##.##.#### **[untransmitted pilot]**	DB / 1"

ROADRUNNER

A Tiger Aspect production for Central. Untransmitted.

	Holding / Source
##.##.#### **[untransmitted 1989 pilot]**	B / 1"

THE ROB BRYDON SHOW

Produced for BBC 2 by a variety of companies (see details below). made in association with Talkback Thames. Transmission details are for BBC 2. Duration: 30 minutes.

Main regular performer(s): Rob Brydon (Host).

	Holding / Source
##.##.#### **[untransmitted pilot]**	DB /

An Arbie production.

ROBBINS

Alternative/Working Title(s): ROBBINS FAMILY

A Granada production. Transmission details are for the Granada region.

Main regular credit(s):   Produced by Trish Kinane.

Main regular cast: Ted Robbins, Kate Robbins, Jane Robbins, Emma Robbins, Amy Robbins.

	Production No	Holding / Source
27.08.1986	P1285/1 & 2	1" / 1"

Duration: 50 minutes.

Designed by Paul Danson; executive producer John Hamp; production manager Graham Wild; produced by Trish Kinane; film sequences directed by Mike Adams; directed by Tom Poole.

With Emma Robbins, Amy Robbins, Jane Robbins.

Two 25-minute episodes combined together.

See also: CHRISTMAS ROBBINS* / THE KATE ROBBINS SHOW*

ROBIN HOOD

Alternative/Working Title(s): THE NEW ADVENTURES OF ROBIN HOOD

A Trident production. Untransmitted. Duration: 30 minutes.

Produced by Robert Cardona; directed by Peter Duffell.

Barry Andrews (Robin Hood), Briony McRoberts (Maid Marion), Michael Culver (Sheriff Of Nottingham), Barry Stanton (Friar Tuck), Michael Jones (Little John), Peter Duncan (Much).

	Holding / Source
##.##.#### **[untransmitted pilot]**	C3 / C3

In 1976 Trident made this pilot for £100,000 as the first product of the new Trident-Anglia Sales company. It was shown in the USA as The New Adventures of Robon Hood.

ROCK AND CHIPS

Alternative/Working Title(s): SEX, DRUGS & ROCK 'N' CHIPS

A BBC Productions production for BBC 1. made in association with Shazam Productions. Transmission details are for BBC 1. Duration varies - see below for details.

Main regular credit(s):   Written by John Sullivan; director of photography John Sorapure; designed by David Hitchcock; production executive Sarah Hitchcock; executive producers Mark Freeland and John Sullivan; produced by Gareth Gwenlan; directed by Dewi Humphreys.

Main regular cast: Nicholas Lyndhurst (Freddie Robdal), Kellie Bright (Joan Trotter), James Buckley (Del Trotter), Phil Daniels (Ted Trotter), Shaun Dingwall (Reg Trotter), Stephen Lloyd (Boycie), Lewis Osborne (Trigger), Ashley Gerlach (Denzil), Lee Long (Jumbo Mills), Jonathan Readwin (Albie Littlewood), Paul Putner (Gerald 'Jelly' Kelly), Robert Daws (Ernie Rayner), Billy Seymour (Raymond), Bobby Bragg (Don), Alison Pargeter (Val).

	Holding / Source
24.01.2010	HD/DB / HDC

Duration: 90 minutes.

Script supervisor Chrissie Bibby; titles by Louise Hillam; art director Jane Shepherd; line producer Jane Harrison.

With Emma Cooke (Reenie Turpin), Roger Griffiths (Clayton), Jodie Mooney (Pam), Colin Prockter (Mr Johnson), Simon Ludders (Mr Manley), Emily Atack (Marion), Martin Delaney (Chief Biker), Claire Lubert (Receptionist), Stephen Bent (Ron Cran), Gemma Salter (Kathleen), Sandra Bee (Midwife), Calum Macnab (Roy Slater), Katie Griffiths (Glenda).

In High Definition the pilot was shot and looked like videotape but shown on terrestial television it appeared filmised.

See also: ONLY FOOLS AND HORSES....*

THE ROCK 'N' ROLL YEARS

A BBC production for BBC 1. Transmission details are for BBC 1. Duration: 30 minutes.

A year, seen and heard through its newsreels, headlines, broadcasts and popular music.

	Holding / Source
03.05.1984 **1966**	DB / 1"

Alt.Title(s):   *Those Rock 'N' Roll Years*
THE ROCK 'N' ROLL YEARS 1966
Spencer Davis Group - Keep on running
Overlanders - Michelle
Stevie Wonder - Uptight
Walker Brothers - The sun ain't gonna shine anymore
Who - Substitute
Beach Boys - Good vibrations
Beatles - I feel fine
Manfred Mann - Just like a woman
David & Jonathan - Lovers of the world unite
Hollies - I can't let go

Research Sue Gagan and Denise Smith; produced and directed by Ann Freer.

When they got to 1966 in the normal run a couple of years later it's marked as a repeat in RT, but it was re-edited when it was shown in series 2. Both versions exist.

ROCKERS

A Southern Television production. Untransmitted. Duration: 25 minutes.

This pilot was set in 1955, on the night when ITV began transmissions.

	Holding / Source
##.##.#### **The Night Grace Archer Died**	J / 2"

Written by Tony Bilbow; executive producer Terry Henebery; directed by John King.

With Bernard Cribbins, Liz Fraser.

Recorded mid November 1977.

ROGER ROGER

Alternative/Working Title(s): PASSENGERS ON BOARD

A BBC production for BBC 1. Transmission details are for BBC 1.

Comedy-drama about a cab firm.

Main regular credit(s):   Written by John Sullivan; executive producer John Sullivan; produced by Gareth Gwenlan.

Main regular cast: Robert Daws (Sam), Pippa Guard (Reen), David Ross (Baz), Terence Maynard (Andre), Paul Sharma (Rajiv), Jude Akuwudike (Henry), Ricci Harnett (Marlon).

	Holding / Source
26.08.1996	DB-D3 / V1S

Alt.Title(s):   *POB*

Duration: 60 minutes.

Cresta Cars is a disorganised cab firm.

Directed by Tony Dow.

With Neil Morrissey (Phil), Lesley Vickerage (Chrissie), Chris Larkin (Cambridge), Sandra Payne (Pam), Sally Dexter (Maddie Price), Anthony Head (Jimmy Price), Robert Daws (Sam), Pippa Guard (Reen), David Ross (Baz), Ricci Harnett (Marlon), John Thomson (Barry), Paul Sharma (Rajiv), Terence Maynard (Andre), Jude Akuwudike (Henry).

ROMANY JONES

An LWT production. Transmission details are for the ATV midlands region. Duration: 25 minutes.

Main regular credit(s):   Created by Ronald Wolfe and Ronald Chesney.

	Production No	Holding / Source
15.02.1972	9L/04975	J / 2"

A Thames Television production.

The trouble with Bert Jones is that he has too much gipsy in his soul. After all, it is a husband's duty to provide his wife with a decent, comfortable bedroom, not a shakedown in a caravan crawling with ants—especially on the wedding night.

Written by Ronald Wolfe and Ronald Chesney; designed by Frank Gillman; produced and directed by Stuart Allen.

With James Beck (Bert Jones), Jo Rowbottom (Betty Jones), Queenie Watts (Lily Briggs), Arthur English (Wally Briggs), Kevin Brennan (Mr Gibson), Bruce Wells (Farmhand).

See also: YUS, MY DEAR*

ROME, SWEET HOME

An ITC production for ATV. Transmission details are for the ATV London region. Duration: 25 minutes.

Created by Irving Taylor and Jack Harvey; written by Irving Taylor and Jack Harvey; associate producer John Pellatt; produced and directed by Hal Stanley.

Lois Maxwell (Megadorus), Peggy Mount (Lippia), Susan Baker (Faith), Jennifer Baker (Hope), Hughie Green (Braggius), Kip King (Philoxenus), Del Moore (Cashio), Peter Brace (Spartacus), Murray Kash (Lambus), Melvyn Hayes (Pentamus), Aubrey Morris (Tailor), Paul Whitsun-Jones (Flavius), Kevin Scott (First slave), Ivor Salter (Second slave), Vic Wise (Connivus), Keith Marsh (Demosthenes), Vicky Smith (First girl), Monica Lewis (Second girl), Pat Finch (Third girl), Tommy Reeves (Chariot driver), John Scripps (Chariot driver).

	Holding / Source
25.12.1966	C3N / C3

Alternative transmissions: ATV Midlands: 24.06.1970; Southern Television: 09.04.1970; Tyne Tees Television: 26.03.1967.

THE RONNIE BARKER PLAYHOUSE

A Rediffusion Television production. Transmission details are for the ATV midlands region. Duration: 25 minutes.

Main regular credit(s):   Associate producer Paul Knight; executive producer David Frost; produced by Stella Richman; directed by Michael Lindsay-Hogg.

	Production No	VT Number	Holding / Source
23.04.1968 **Tennyson**	SS/13/29	W4780/5391	J / 40

Alternative transmissions: Granada: 02.04.1968; Rediffusion Television: 03.04.1968.

Written by Alun Owen; designed by Frank Nerini.

With Ronnie Barker (Tennyson Elias Williams), Dudley Jones (Cecil), Gwendolyn Watts (Mrs Cecil), Talfryn Thomas (Lecher Lewis), Meredith Edwards (The Policeman), Richard O'Callaghan (Shelley Longfellow Morgan).

Recorded 28.03.1968.

	Production No	VT Number	Holding / Source
07.05.1968 **Ah! There You Are**	SS/12/20	W4766/5304	R3N|n / 40

Alternative transmissions: Granada: 09.04.1968; Rediffusion Television: 10.04.1968.

Written by Alun Owen; designed by John Emery.

With Ronnie Barker (Lord Rustless), George A. Cooper (Badger), Bill Shine (Willy), Sandra Michaels (Jane), Victor Winding (Director), Donald Groves (First Assistant), Mark Moss (Carpenter), Walter Swash (Electrician), William F. Sully (Sound Man), Michael Guest (Props Man), John Wilder (Lighting Cameraman).

Recorded 20.03.1968.

The play spawned numerous Rustless appearances including Hark at Barker and His Lordship Entertains.

14.05.1968 **The Fastest Gun In Finchley**	SS/15/9	W4800/5536	J / 40

Alternative transmissions: Granada: 16.04.1968; Rediffusion Television: 17.04.1968.

Written by Johnnie Mortimer and Brian Cooke; designed by Henry Federer.

With Ronnie Barker (Ronald Winterbourne), Colin Jeavons (Gostling), Charlotte Mitchell (Beatrice), Sheila Keith (Mrs Granville).

Recorded 17.04.1968.

21.05.1968 **The Incredible Mister Tanner**	SS/10/7	W472/5266	R3N|n / 40

Alternative transmissions: Granada: 23.04.1968; Rediffusion Television: 24.04.1968.

Written by Johnnie Mortimer and Brian Cooke; designed by Henry Federer.

With Ronnie Barker (Cyril Tanner), Alec Clunes (Peregrine), Richard O'Sullivan (Arthur), Lionel Wheeler (First Policeman), Doris Hare (Ma), Frank Gatliff (Official), Martin Pilcher (Reporter), Leonard Brockwell (Boy Scout), Bill Cornelius (Sailor).

Recorded 07.03.1968.

Thames made this series many years later in 1982!

04.06.1968 **Talk Of Angels**	SS/16/19	T5568/5592	R3N|n / 40

Alternative transmissions: Granada: 30.04.1968; Rediffusion Television: 01.05.1968.

Written by Hugh Leonard; designed by Frank Nerini.

With Ronnie Barker (The Monk), David Kelly (Matthew), Maureen Toal (Doreen), Donald Hewlett (Nigel), Elizabeth Crowther (Deirdre), Gillian Fairchild (Ramona).

Recorded 19.04.1968.

15.07.1968 **Alexander**	SS/18/1	T5593/5574	R1|n / 40

Alternative transmissions: Granada: 07.05.1968; Rediffusion Television: 08.05.1968.

Written by Alun Owen; designed by John Clarke.

With Ronnie Barker (Alexander Hamish Macgregor), Pauline Yates (Lesley Crown), Molly Urquhart (Marmsie), Pamela Ann Davey (Miss Craig), Tony Trent (Youth), Maggie Lynton (Secretary).

Recorded 01.05.1968.

See also: HARK AT BARKER* / THE INCREDIBLE MR. TANNER*

ROOM 101

A Hat Trick production for BBC 2. Transmission details are for BBC 2. Duration: 30 minutes.

SERIES 1

Main regular credit(s):   Research Zita Foley, Genevieve Robinson and Belinda Harris; costume Sharon Lewis; music by Peter Salem; titles by Mighty; designed by Dennis De Groot; production team John O'Farrell, Mark Burton, Polly Hope, Barrie McCulloch, Adrian O'Brien and Rachel Lyon; associate producer Kate Anthony; executive producer Denise O'Donoghue; production manager Sarah McHarry; series producer Dan Patterson; produced by Lissa Evans; directed by John F. D. Northover.

Main regular cast: With Nick Hancock (Host).

	Holding / Source
08.08.1994	D3 / D3S

Make-up Eve Marieges Moore; lighting director Mike Sutcliffe.

With Tony Slattery.

It's pretty clear that the Tony Slattery show is the pilot. The regular props are different and the show generally lacks polish. However, Bob Monkhouse's vewing tape states that his show was recorded twice as a pilot.

ROOM SERVICE

A Thames Television production. Transmission details are for the ATV midlands region. Duration: 25 minutes.

Main regular credit(s):   Written by Jimmy Perry; designed by John White; produced and directed by Michael Mills.

Main regular cast: Bryan Pringle (Charles Spooner), Freddie Earlle (Aldo De Vito), Jeillo Edwards (Mrs McGregor), Chris Gannon (Horace Murphy), Matthew Kelly (Dick Sedgewick).

	VT Number	Holding / Source
##.##.#### **[untransmitted pilot]**	18784	DB / 2"

With Derek Newark (Mr Charlie Spooner), Penelope Nice (Marlene), Matthew Kelly (Dick Sedgewick), Judi Maynard (Freda), Jeillo Edwards (Mrs McGregor), Harry Webster (Horace Murphy), Basil Lord (Mr Morris), Freddie Earlle (Mr Aldo DeNito), Michael Petrovitch (Fedros), Gertan Klauber (Gustav), Neville Rofaila (Ahmed), Ric Young (Tin Tin).

ROUGH MAGIK

A Bubblehead Productions production for BBC. Untransmitted. Duration: 41 minutes.

Created by Stephen W. Parsons; written by Stephen W. Parsons; theme music by Stephen W. Parsons and F. Haines; executive producer Bob Lawrie; produced by Stephen W. Parsons; directed by Jamie Payne.

Paul Darrow (Mr Moon), Gerrard McArthur [as Gerrad Mc Arthur] (Kenneth Reece Warren), Justine Glenton (Mrs Machen), Oliver Banks (Thomas), Eleanor Gellard (Julie), Wayne Cater (Police Photographer), Katy Secombe (Woman Police Constable), Eamonn Clarke (Enforcer), Stacy Gough (Enforcer), David Flack (Prison Warder), Jennifer Harnett (Fiona), Tim Kirby (Colonel Shaw), Andrew Sweeney (Radio Operative), Robert Smith (Lumley), Ricco Se (Bren Gunner), Adam ? (Sergeant Davis), John O'Brien (Soldier), Regan Hutchings (Soldier), Des Kirby (Soldier), Michael Poole (Mr Wilson), Veronica Duffy (Mrs Wilson).

	Holding / Source
##.##.#### **An Age Of Wonders**	DB / C1SW

This pilot, made in 2000, remains untransmitted in the UK.

Other planned episodes:
Deep Waters
The Soft Dog
She Prays Like A Roman
Blue
The Tide Wood Flower
Doncaster Poison
The Institute
The Sleeping God
Black Grail
Skin
Agents Of Midnight
The Stars Are Right
Dreamer.

ROUND ABOUT TEN

An ATV production. Transmission details are for the ATV London region. Duration: 25 minutes.

Main regular credit(s):   Written by John Law and Bill Craig; additional dialogue by Barry Took; produced and directed by Peter Glover.

Main regular performer(s): Barry Took (Host), Bobby McGee and his Music.

	Holding / Source
##.##.#### **[untransmitted pilot]**	J / Live

With Patti Lewis, Malcolm Goddard, Jim Dale.

THE ROWAN ATKINSON SHOW

A Thames Television production. Untransmitted. Duration: 24 minutes.

Rowan Atkinson (Host), Peter Wilson.

	VT Number	Holding / Source
##.##.####	20571	DB / 2"

Untx pilot with no end credits.

ROY'S RAIDERS

A BBC production for BBC 1. Transmission details are for BBC 1. Duration: 30 minutes.

Main regular credit(s):   Written by Michael Aitkens.

	Production No	Holding / Source
##.##.#### **[untransmitted 1989 pilot]**	LLCA100F/71	DB / 1"

Costume Maggie Partington-Smith; make-up Shauna Harrison; designed by George Kyriakides; production manager Gavin Clark; produced and directed by Susan Belbin.

With Philip McGough (Roy), Julia Watson (Jill), Anthony Head (Jack), Shane Withington (Bazza), Tony Hughes (Wingco), William Vanderpuye (Henry), Emma Myant (Daisy), Simon Pearsall (Chris), Des McAleer (Gavin Bailey), Richard Ireson (Towtruck Driver), Tariq Yunus (Voice of Mr Singh).

RULE OF THREE

An Avalon Productions production. Untransmitted. Duration: 30 minutes.

Based on the radio comedy series BANTER.

Rebecca Front (Host).

	Holding / Source
##.##.#### **[untransmitted pilot]**	DB / DB

RULES OF ENGAGEMENT

A Yorkshire Television production. Transmission details are for the Central region. Duration: 50 minutes.

The National Crime Task Force, an elite force drawn from police and intelligence personnel with almost unlimited powers. Frances Barber is the ministerial controller, and Douglas Hodge a nervous MI5 graduate. Together they tackle
drugs barons, terrorists and bank robbers, cutting up the conventional police authorities as they do so, with Commander Ferguson in charge.

Written by Geoff McQueen; story consultant Patrick Stoddart; script editor Lizzie Taylor; music by Rick Wentworth; associate producer David Noble; executive producer David Reynolds; produced by Peter Norris; directed by Charles McDougall.

Ciaran Hinds (Commander Campbell Ferguson), Frances Barber (Harriet Saunders), Douglas Hodge (Moorhead), Holly Aird (Dawn Bell), Fraser James (Razz), Peter Sullivan (Greaves), Grant Masters (Lancer), Andrew Schofield (Eric), Nigel Terry (Preston), Sean McGinley (O'Donnell), Steve Nicolson (Detective Inspector Packer), George Anton (Burke), Lalor Roddy (Mahoney), Hannah Miles (Claire), William Hoyland (Chief Superintendent), Brian Hayes (TV Interviewer), Hamish McColl (MI5 Man), Glyn Grimstead (Gavin Hammond), Stephen Billington (Gary), Jonathan Barlow (James Forsyth), Christopher Glover (Ranji), Hakeem Kae-Kazim (Reporter), Abigail Bond (Reporter), Razaaq Adoti (Dave), Gary Oliver (Police Officer), Mark Lacey (Police Officer), Paul Whitby (Police Officer), Nick Miles (Police Officer), Dermot Keaney (Police Officer), Mason Phillips (Police Officer).

	Holding / Source
24.04.1995	D3 / C1SW

This pilot, for an unmade series, was dedicated to Geoff McQueen, 1947-1994, who died before its transmission.

RUNNING WILD

An LWT production. Transmission details are for the Central region. Duration: 25 minutes.

Main regular credit(s):   Written by Philip Trewinnard.

Main regular cast: Ray Brooks (Max Wild), Janet Key (Babs Wild).

Holding / Source

##.##.#### **[untransmitted pilot]**   1" / 1"

THE RUSS ABBOT SHOW

A BBC production for BBC 1. Transmission details are for BBC 1. Duration varies - see below for details.

Main regular cast: Russ Abbot (Various roles).

Holding / Source

26.05.1986   DB / 1"

Duration: 33 minutes.

Written by Barry Cryer, Dick Vosburgh, Gary Clapperton, Mike Burton, David Hurst, Paul Minett and Brian Leveson; script associates Barry Cryer and Neil Shand; music directed by Alyn Ainsworth; music by Alyn Ainsworth; choreography by Tudor Davies; designed by Chris Hull and Gary Williamson; production manager Mike Pearce; produced and directed by John Bishop.

With Les Dennis, Gordon Kennedy, Bella Emberg, Maggie Moone, Tom Bright, Suzy Aitchison, Julia Gale, Chrissie Ling, Paul Robinson, Paul Tomkinson, Susie Waring, Aiden Waters.

RUSSELL HOWARD'S GOOD NEWS

An Avalon Productions production for BBC 3. Transmission details are for BBC 3. Duration: 30 minutes.

Main regular cast: Russell Howard.

Holding / Source

##.##.#### **[untransmitted pilot]**   HD/DB / HDC

Commissioned 8th May 2009.

* Acts marked with the asterisk appeared only on the longer extended Saturday evening shows.

SADIE, IT'S COLD OUTSIDE

A Thames Television production. Transmission details are for the ATV midlands region. Duration: 25 minutes.

Main regular credit(s):   Written by Jack Rosenthal.

Main regular cast: Rosemary Leach (Sadie), Bernard Hepton (Norman).

	VT Number	Holding / Source
##.##.#### "Anything Left?" [untransmitted pilot]	9696	D3 / 2"

Designed by John Plant; produced and directed by Anthony Parker.

With Patrick Newell, Kathleen St. John, Julie Peasgood.

THE SAINT

Produced for ITC by a variety of companies (see details below). Transmission details are for the ATV midlands region. Usual duration: 48 minutes.

Main regular credit(s):   Based on characters created by Leslie Charteris; music by Edwin Astley.

Main regular cast: Roger Moore (Simon Templar aka The Saint).

SERIES 5

A Bamore Productions production.

Main regular credit(s):   Produced by Robert S. Baker.

	Holding / Source
	1" / C3

14.10.1966   **The Russian Prisoner**

Alternative transmissions: ATV London: 09.10.1966.

The Saint is instrumental in helping a Russian professor escape his captors in Geneva—in an adventure that has a far from inevitable conclusion.

Adapted by Harry W. Junkin; based on a story by Leslie Charteris; directed by John Moxey.

With Joseph Furst, Penelope Horner, Guy Deghy, Sandor Elès, Raymond Adamson, Robert Crewdson, Yootha Joyce, Godfrey Quigley, Anthony Booth, Alexis Chesnakov, William Buck.

When production finished on the monochrome Saint episodes, Roger Moore considered continuing but without Monty Berman. Robert S. Baker and Berman parted company and after production on The Baron ran into difficulties, Moore was approached to form a new production company with Robert S. Baker and begin colour episodes. This pilot was made at the end of production for The Baron.

If the episode was adapted from a Leslie Charteris story this is noted, as is the original story title, if different from the transmitted one.

Val Kilmer played Simon Templar in a 1997 film re-make. The film featured the remixed Saint theme (by Edwin Astley, performed by Orbital) and Roger Moore's voice made a cameo appearance as a radio newsreader. Starring Elisabeth Shue (Doctor Emma Russell), Alun Armstrong (Chief Inspector Teal), Rade Serbedzija (Ivan Tretiak) and Charlotte Cornwell (Inspector Rabineau). Written by Jonathan Hensleigh and Wesley Strick from a story by Jonathan Hensleigh, produced by William J. MacDonald, Mace Neufeld, David Brown and Robert Evans, the Executive Producers were Robert S. Baker and Paul Hitchcock, and it was directed by Phillip Noyce. 116 minutes widescreen stereo colour. Paramount Pictures / Rysher Entertainment.

See also: RETURN OF THE SAINT* / THE SAINT*

SANCTUARY

A Rediffusion Television production. Transmission details are for the ATV midlands region. Duration: 50 minutes.

Main regular credit(s):   Created by Philip Levene; executive producer Stella Richman; produced by John Harrison.

Duration: 46 minutes.

	VT Number	Holding / Source
##.##.#### **Few Are Chosen [untransmitted pilot]**	T4644/613	J / 40

Written by Elaine Morgan; directed by Joan Kemp-Welch.

With Pamela Gravett, Lila Kaye (Sister Hilary), Margot Thomas (Sister Veronica), Sara Aimson, Patricia Healey (Sister Bernadette), Denise Buckley, Susan Whitnell, Robert Sansom, Jeremy Burnham.

Recorded 25.11.66.

SERIES 1

Main regular credit(s):   Story editor Reuben Ship.

	VT Number	Holding / Source
29.06.1967 **The Mission**	W4189/5013	R1N|n / 40

Alt.Title(s):   *Few Are Chosen*

Written by Philip Levene and Noel Robinson; designed by William McCrow; directed by Joan Kemp-Welch.

With Fay Compton (Sister Juliana), Alison Leggatt (Sister Ursula), Peggy Thorpe-Bates (Sister Paul), Joanna Dunham (Sister Benedict), Mona Bruce (Sister Frances), Michael Williamson (African Boy), Rudolph Walker (African Doctor), Alan Stuart (Taxi Driver), Hilda Fenemore (Sister Agnes), Bonnie Hurren (Sister Joan), Bridget Brice (Sister Vincent), Tracy Rogers (Vicky Mason), Ursula Hirst (Sister Bridget), Coral Fairweather (Sister Luke), Robert Sansom (Father Jeremy), Susan Richards (Mrs Green), Carol Macready (Woman), Barbara Bolton (Housewife), Ruth Porcher (Nurse), Jeremy Burnham (Doctor).

Inserts were used from the untransmitted pilot.

Outside Broadcast material was shot on videotape. God Is A God Of Love written by Maureen Duffy was commissioned, but not made.

SANCTUARY

An ATV production. Untransmitted. Duration: 25 minutes.

Designed by Michael Perry; produced and directed by Bob Spiers.

	VT Number	Holding / Source
##.##.####	5841/80	

Monoculus 01.08.1980; filming 02-03.08.1980; studio recording 10.08.1980.

SARA AND HOPPITY

A P.P. Productions production for Roberta Leigh. Transmission details are for Associated-Rediffusion. Duration: 13 minutes.

Main regular credit(s):   Written by Roberta Leigh; lyrics by Roberta Leigh; music by Roberta Leigh; produced by Roberta Leigh; directed by Arthur Provis.

Holding / Source

##.##.#### **[untransmitted pilot]**   B3 / B3

See also: SMALL TIME*

THE SARAH JANE ADVENTURES

A BBC Wales production for BBC Children's Department. Transmission details are for CBBC.

Main regular credit(s):   Created by Russell T. Davies; theme music by Murray Gold; production executive Julie Scott.

Main regular cast: Elisabeth Sladen (Sarah Jane Smith), Tommy Knight (Luke Smith).

Transmission details are for BBC 1.

Holding / Source

01.01.2007 **Invasion Of The Bane**   DB / DBSWF

Duration: 60 minutes.

Doctor Who's former assistant Sarah Jane Smith is now working as an investigative journalist. She joins forces with her 13-year-old neighbour Maria to fight evil alien forces at work in Britain. Their first case sees the duo come up against the Scheming Ms Wormwood.

Written by Russell T. Davies and Gareth Roberts; script editor Simon Winstone; music by Sam Watts; executive producers Julie Gardner, Russell T. Davies and Phil Collinson; produced by Susie Liggat; directed by Colin Teague.

With John Leeson (Voice of K.9), Yasmin Paige (Maria Jackson), Samantha Bond (Mrs Wormwood), Porsha Lawrence-Mavour, Jamie Davis, Joseph Millson, Juliet Cowan, Rungano Nyoni, Philip North, Alexander Armstrong, Sydney White, Olivia Hill, Konnie Huq, Gethin Jones.

See also: DOCTOR WHO / K.9 AND COMPANY

SATELLITE CITY

A Fiction Factory production for BBC 2 Wales. Transmission details are for BBC 2 Wales. Duration: 30 minutes.

Sitcom set in Wales.

Main regular credit(s):   Written by Boyd Clack and Jane Clack; produced by Michael Parker and Edward Thomas.

Main regular cast: Islwyn Morris (Idris Price), Michael Neill (Randy), Boyd Clack (Gwynne), Ri Richards (Moira), Rhodri Hugh (Dai), Shelley Miranda Barrett (Mandy).

Holding / Source

12.12.1995   DB-D3 / D3S

Directed by Edward Thomas.

Originally a radio series that transferred to TV.

SATSUMA & PUMPKIN

The companies who commissioned and produced this production are not known. Untransmitted.

Written by Jeremy Engler; additional material by Bob Monkhouse; edited by Jeremy Engler; production manager Nicola Scott; produced and directed by Jeremy Engler.

Bob Monkhouse OBE (Ernst Vetterlein), Tony Hawks (Frank Dirch), Neil Gibbs (Donald), Marie Newey (Mrs Cribbens), Sean Halligan (Alistair Cartwright), Cara Sweeney (Ms Shaft), Miranda Raison (Gloria), Richard Batt (Admiral Hugh Alexander), Richard Helm (Air Raid Warden), Keith Hoskins (German Pilot), Stephen Astley-Jones (German Commander), Keith Hoskins (German Spy), Richard Batt (German Spy), Toby Aldon (German Spy), Neil Gibbs (German Spy), Gary O' Brien (German Spy), Toby Stronge (German Spy), Kadie-Marie Plumridge (Precocious Child), Fran Davies (Child's Mother), Brian Elliot (Vicar), Renee Sears (Distraught Mother), Russell Leak (Soldier), Gary O'Brien (Soldier), DH (Soldier), James DeHavailand (Soldier), Toby Aldon (Soldier), Keith Hoskins (Soldier), Ann King, Jackie Straw, Graham Richardson, John Goreham, Barbara Scanton, Bob Macdonald, Irene Macdonald, Phil Davies, Karen Nott, Murlyn Hakon MBE.

Holding / Source

##.##.#### **If The Invader Comes**   DV /

Promo edit, interviews and news reports re this project are included. The source was DVCAM - i.e. that's what it was shot on.

SATURDAY LIVE

An LWT production for Channel 4. Transmission details are for the Central region. Duration varies - see below for details.

	VT Number	Holding / Source
12.01.1985	79159	D2 / 1"

Duration: 82 minutes.

Written by Kim Fuller, Geoff Atkinson, Garry Chambers, Adrian Edmondson, Dawn French, James Hendrie, Chris Langham, Rik Mayall and Jennifer Saunders; theme music by Kenny Clayton; lighting director Teddy Fader; sound Graham Hix; designed by James Dillon; production manager Glen Jennings; produced and directed by Paul Jackson.

With Lenny Henry, Helen Atkinson Wood, Chris Barrie, 20th Century Coyote, Robbie Coltrane, Smiley Culture, Andy de la Tour, French & Saunders, Chris Langham, Carla Mendonca, Raw Sex, Christopher Ryan, Slade, Mel Smith, Abby Stein, The Style Council.

See also: FRIDAY NIGHT LIVE*

THE SATURDAY NIGHT ARMISTICE

A BBC production for BBC 2. Transmission details are for BBC 2. Duration varies - see below for details.

Main regular cast: Armando Iannucci (Presenter), Peter Baynham (Presenter), David Schneider (Presenter).

	Production No	Holding / Source
##.##.#### Saturday Night Armistice [untransmitted 1995 pilot]	LLCF7505/71	DB-D3 / D3S

Duration: 40 minutes.

Written by Armando Iannucci, Peter Baynham, David Schneider, Kevin Cecil, Graham Linehan [credited as Graham Linnehan], Arthur Matthews and Andy Riley; costume Leah Archer; make-up Vanessa White; designed by Dennis De Groot; production manager Terry Pettigrew; produced by Sarah Smith; directed by Steve Bendelack.

With Ben Moore, Bill Cashmore, Kevin Eldon, Mel Giedroyc, Melanie Hudson, Jonathan Guy Lewis, Sue Perkins, Sir Teddy Taylor [as Sir Teddy Taylor M.P.], The Jeremy Hanley Fan Club.

See also: THE FRIDAY NIGHT ARMISTICE*

SATURDAY NIGHT OUT

A BBC production for BBC 1. Transmission details are for BBC 1. Duration: 55 minutes.

Late-night entertainment in the electrifying atmosphere of one of London's top disco nightspots.

Designed by Mel Bibby; produced and directed by Alan Walsh.

Janet Street-Porter (Presenter), Steve Blacknell (Presenter), Peter Stringfellow (Presenter), Kim Wilde, Jim Diamond, The Vicious Boys, Dusty Springfield, Vanderbilt And Bergdorf.

	Holding / Source
27.04.1985	DB / 1"

SATURDAY NIGHT WITH CILLA

A Thames Television production. Untransmitted.

Cilla Black (Host).

	Holding / Source
##.##.#### [untransmitted pilot]	DB /

SATURDAY ZOO

A Channel X production for Channel 4. Transmission details are for Channel 4.

Main regular credit(s): Produced by Kenton Allen; directed by Ian Hamilton.

Main regular performer(s): Jonathan Ross (Host).

	Holding / Source
##.##.#### [untransmitted pilot]	D3 / D3S

Written by Kevin Day, Steve Coogan, Geoff Deane, Patrick Marber, Lise Mayer, David Quantick, Jez Stevenson and Mark Thomas; script editor Steve Punt; executive producer Alan Marke; production manager Alison MacPhail.

With Steve Coogan, Simon Day, Graham Fellows, Rebecca Front, Patrick Marber, John Sparkes, Mark Thomas, John Thomson.

SAUCERFUL OF SECRETS

A Baby Cow Productions production for BBC. Untransmitted.

Directed by Ben Wheatley.

Roy Hudd.

	Holding / Source
##.##.#### Recorded May 2012 [untransmitted pilot]	HD/DB / HDC

There are three copies logged, one is logged as missing, one went out to someone and never came back (possibly Baby Cow?) and the third one is logged as being in the store at TVC where things awaiting transmission live – but if it's been there since May 2012 it should have come to the BBC archive by now.

SCANDAL

An ABC production. Untransmitted. Duration: 50 minutes.

Written by Allan Prior; designed by Stan Woodward; associate producer Michael Chapman; directed by Guy Verney.

Andrew Faulds (Bill Ballard), Christine Finn (Jean Rhys), Nan Marriott Watson (Becky Heron), Allan Cuthbertson (George Gravely), Kenneth Farrington (Con Chandler), Malcolm Russell (Jock), Patrick Bedford (Luke Heron), Isobel Black (Torry Dewar), John Standing (Jimmy Benedict), Irene Sutcliffe (Louise Gravely), Joby Blanshard (Allen), Gerald Young (Mosby), Bill Cornelius (Smith), Lynne Ashcroft (Rene), Barbara Bolton (Maid).

	Holding / Source
##.##.#### Lawful Force	R1N / 40

Controversial pilot for a series that was 'frowned upon' by the ITA, and ABC was forced to cancel it. They replaced it with 'The Protectors'.

SCENE BY SCENE WITH....

A BBC Scotland production for BBC 2. Transmission details are for BBC 2.

Main regular credit(s): Directed by Mark Cousins.

Main regular cast: Mark Cousins (Interviewer).

	Holding / Source
10.05.1997	DB / DBS

Executive producer May Miller.

With Sean Connery.

SCHOFIELD'S QUEST

A Michael Hurll Television production for LWT. Transmission details are for the Central region. Duration: 50 minutes.

Main regular credit(s):   Executive producer Michael Hurll.

Main regular performer(s): Phillip Schofield (Presenter).

	Holding / Source
26.06.1994	D2 / D2S

Produced by Colman Hutchinson.

With Caron Keating (Co-Presenter), Kay Ainsworth, Joe Callan, Rick Calmert, Alison Craig, Reverend Abbotsford Hubble, Moira Kelsey, Philip Mantle.

Investigative programme covering a variety of human interest stories all linked by a missing element. Includes Tony Dorite at the Elvis auction at Las Vegas and Caron Keating visiting Odiham in Hampshire reputed to be the most mysterious place in Britain. Studioguests include Nell Jones a psychic.

SCOOP

A BBC Bristol production for BBC 2. Transmission details are for BBC 2.

Main regular credit(s):   Produced by Colin Godman; studio sequences directed by Mike Derby.

Main regular performer(s): Barry Norman (Presenter), Diane Harron, Derek Jameson, Miles Kington, Alan Whicker.

	Holding / Source
13.06.1981	DB / 2"

SCOTLAND YARD REPORTER

A Vizio Ltd production. Untransmitted. Duration: 26 minutes.

Executive producer James A. Carter; produced by Edgar Blatt; directed by Malcolm Baker-Smith.

	Holding / Source
##.##.####	J / B3

A freeze on US funding prevented a series. Shown in the USA.

SCOTTISH COMEDY PLAYHOUSE

A BBC Scotland production. Transmission details are for BBC 1 Scotland. Duration: 30 minutes.

Main regular credit(s):   Produced by Eddie Fraser.

	Holding / Source
22.09.1970 **Stand-In For A Hearse**	J / 62

Written by Jack Gerson; based on stories by James Wood; directed by Ian Christie.

With Russell Hunter, James Grant, Phil McCall, Douglas Murchie, Angus Lennie, Jean Taylor Smith, Margaret Milne.

29.09.1970 **The Siege Of Castle Drumlie**	J / 62

Written by Kenneth Little; directed by John Crowther.

With Una McLean, Walter Carr, Alex McAvoy, Michael O'Halloran, James Gibson, Clem Ashby, Roy Boutcher.

20.10.1970 **The Dinner Party**	J / 2"

Written by John Lawson; directed by Ian Christie.

With Eileen McCallum, Victor Carin, Madeleine Christie, Leon Sinden, Morag Forsyth, Paul Kermack.

27.10.1970 **To Gracie A Son**	J / 2"

Written by John Temple and Pat Flynn; directed by Ian Christie.

With John Grieve, Gracie Clark, Nancy Mitchell, Clem Ashby.

03.11.1970 **Stobo Takes The Chair**	J / 2"

Written by Tom Wright; directed by Ian Christie.

With Jonathan Kaye, Joe Dunlop, Jameson Clark, Carol Ann Dunigan.

10.11.1970 **Made In Heaven**	J / 2"

Written by John Lawson; based on an idea by Edward Boyd [credited as Eddie Boyd]; directed by Ian Christie.

With Rikki Fulton, Edith Macarthur, John Inman, Pat Keen, Saria Ballintyne, Callum Mill, Mary Riggans, Robin Lefevre.

SCRABBLE

A BBC Bristol production for BBC. Untransmitted. Duration: 30 minutes.

Devised by Ian Messiter; designed by Pamela Lambooy; produced by Mark Patterson; directed by Rosalind Gold.

Mike Neville (Host), Colin Baker, Pete Murray, Patricia Murray, Liza Goddard, Leonard Sachs, Eleanor Summerfield, Brian Rix, Elspet Gray, Pippa Page.

	VT Number	Holding / Source
##.##.#### [untransmitted 1977 pilot]	VTC/6HP/B17183	DB / 2"

SCREEN TEST

A Central production. Transmission details are for the Central region. Duration: 25 minutes.

Written by Colin Edmonds; produced by John Gorman and Peter Harris; directed by John Gorman and Peter Harris.

Bob Monkhouse (Host), Samantha Norman, Baz Bamigboye.

	Production No	Holding / Source
##.##.#### [untransmitted pilot]	011022	DV / D2S

This pilot is filmed on the set of 'Blockbusters'. Rx: 13.3.1992.

SCREENPLAY

A Granada production. Transmission details are for the ATV midlands region. Duration varies - see below for details.

	Production No	Holding / Source
23.12.1979 **Waxwork**	P790/19	D2 / 2"

Duration: 75 minutes.

Postponed from 19.08.1979.

Adapted by Pauline Macaulay; based on a book by Peter Lovesey; music by Derek Hilton; designed by Alan Price; produced and directed by June Wyndham-Davies.

With Alan Dobie (Sergeant Cribb), David Waller (Chief Inspector Jowett), Carol Royle (Miriam Cromer), David Ashford (Simon Allingham), Gerald Sim (Inspector Waterlow), Elizabeth Burger (Bell), Barbara Bolton (Hawkins), Susie Blake (Lottie Piper), Joanne Zorian (Judith Hunnicutt), Elspeth March (Dorothea Davenant), Laurence Payne (Howard Cromer), Geoffrey Larder (Josiah Perceval), James Warrior (James Berry), Ursula Mohan (Mrs Berry), Ernest Hare (Mr Justice Colbeck), Alick Hayes (Clerk of the Court), Stuart Latham (Prison Doctor), Bernard Archard (Governor of Newgate), Peter MacKriel (Wallis), Jacob Witkin (Brodski), Lesley Nightingale (Maid), Paul Williamson (Headmaster), Roy Evans (Shopkeeper), William Abney (Joseph Tussaud), John Quarmby (Inspector Moser), Mark Hudson (Call Boy), Mike Mungaven* (Police Constable).

See also: CRIBB.

See also: CITY SHORTS* / CRIBB

SCRIBBLE

A Thames Television production. Untransmitted. Duration: 25 minutes.

Programme associate Eric Merriman; designed by Graham Probst; produced and directed by Robert Reed.

Brian Marshall (Host), Robert Gillespie, Stacy Dorning, Angie Butler, Sheila White, David Janson, Dick Clark.

	VT Number	Holding / Source
##.##.#### **[untransmitted pilot]**	26109	DB / 2"

1982 pilot, similar to Give Us A Clue where contestants draw and the artistes have to guess what they are trying to say.

THE SCUM ALSO RISES

A Bwark Production production for BBC 4. Transmission details are for BBC 4. Duration: 30 minutes.

Set in the offices of wealthy ad agency HHH&H, following the misadventures of writer's block sufferer Billy, hapless account executive Greg and a neurotic producer.

Written by Jonathan Thake; script supervisor Vicky Cole; designed by Rosy Thomas; production executive Leo Martin; executive producers Damon Beesley and Simon Wilson.

Chris Barrie (Mr Broom), Kevin Bishop (Keaton), Joanna Bobin (Chloe), Adam Buxton (Greg), Daisy Haggard (Emma), Ruth Keeling (Jane), Tom Price (Billy), Catherine Skinner (Claire).

	Holding / Source
28.05.2007 **[BBC 4 pilot]**	DB / DBSWF

Produced by Iain Morris; directed by Tim Kirkby.

	Holding / Source
##.##.#### **[BBC 2 untransmitted pilot]**	DB / DBSWF

Produced by Jon Rolph; directed by Tristram Shapeero.

With Iain Lee.

SEARCH

A BBC Bristol production for BBC 1. Transmission details are for BBC 1. Duration: 25 minutes.

SERIES 1

Main regular credit(s):   Presented by John Craven; produced by David Turnbull.

	Holding / Source
##.##.#### **[untransmitted pilot]**	J / 2"

Film inserts mainly.

See also: COUNTRY SEARCH* / SEARCH REPORT*

SEARCH FOR A STAR

A Rediffusion Television production. Transmission details are for the Rediffusion Television region. Duration: 45 minutes.

Main regular credit(s):   Introduced by Keith Fordyce; choreography by Leo Kharibian; directed by Peter Croft.

	Holding / Source
##.##.#### **[untransmitted pilot]**	J / 40

With Eden Kane (Judge), Rex Garner (Judge), Pam Elliott (Judge), James Swann (Judge), Elkan Allan (Judge).

Recorded 01.09.1964.

Talent show - searching for a "girl who will star in a big song-and-dance television spectacular" in 1965. Entrants had to be British, aged between 16 and 23, be able to act, mime and dance - and "look smashing". Things appear to have moved quite quickly: the earliest advertisement seems not to have appeared until 27.08.1964 where it stated that entrants may not "be a professional actress". By 10.09.1964 a new, re-worded, advertisement appeared removing the bar to professionals but requiring no more than one year's professional experience. A fortnight further on, and the contest was now open to all.

See also: WISH UPON A STAR*

THE SECRET KEEPERS

A Kenneth Hume (International) Productions production. Untransmitted.

Written by David Hebden and Kenneth Hume; music by Tony Osborne; assistant director David Giffard; art director Duncan Sutherland; associate producer Geoffrey Forster; produced and directed by Kenneth Hume.

Harold Lang, Alma Cogan, Peggyann Clifford, Ann Lancaster, Tom Gill, Frankie Howerd, Shirley Bassey, Jess Conrad, Cardew Robinson.

	Holding / Source
##.##.#### **[untransmitted 1962 pilot]**	B3|n / B3

Pilot for TV comedy series about a detective.

THE SECRET LIFE OF A NEBBISH

A Kayak Productions production. Untransmitted. Duration: 27 minutes.

Written by Rob Hitchmough and Alec Christie; directed by Esta Charkham.

Holding / Source

##.##.#### **[untransmitted pilot]**   DB / DBSW

As of November 2014, Kayak's website reports that scripts are "in development".

SEEDS OF LOVE

A Harlech production. Transmission details are for the Harlech region. Duration: 25 minutes.

Main regular performer(s): The Rainbow People.

Holding / Source

05.06.1969

SET 'EM UP, JOE!

An LWT production. Transmission details are for the ATV midlands region.

Main regular credit(s):   Music directed by Harry Rabinowitz; choreography by Denys Palmer; designed by Cephas Howard; produced and directed by Philip Casson.

Main regular performer(s): Joe Brown (Host).

Holding / Source

##.##.#### **[untransmitted pilot]**   J / 2"

Duration: 38 minutes.

SEVEN OF ONE

A BBC production for BBC 2. Transmission details are for BBC 2. Duration: 30 minutes.

Executive producer James Gilbert.

Holding / Source

25.03.1973 **Open All Hours**   DB-D3 / 2"

Written by Roy Clarke; music by Max Harris; designed by Tim Gleeson; produced and directed by Sydney Lotterby.

With Ronnie Barker (Arkwright), David Jason (Granville), Sheila Brennan (Nurse Gladys Emmanuel), Yootha Joyce (Mrs Scully), Keith Chegwin (Keith), Elissa Derwent (Petrol Pump Girl), David Valla (Breadman).

01.04.1973 **Prisoner And Escort**   DB-D3 / 2"

Written by Dick Clement and Ian La Frenais; music by Max Harris; produced and directed by Sydney Lotterby.

With Ronnie Barker ('Fletch'), Fulton Mackay (Mr McKay), Brian Wilde (Mr Barraclough), Hamish Roughead (Police Officer).

08.04.1973 **My Old Man**   DB-D3 / 2"

Written by Gerald Frow; produced and directed by Sydney Lotterby.

With Ronnie Barker (Sam), Graham Armitage (Arthur), Ann Beach (Doris), Robin Parkinson (Cyril), John Sanderson (Andrew), Leslie Dwyer (Willy Price), Peter Clay (Andrew), Roy Denton (Old Man), John Rudling (Old Man).

YTV made this series with Clive Dunn in the lead role.

15.04.1973 **Spanner's Eleven**   DB-D3 / 2"

Written by Roy Clarke; produced and directed by Harold Snoad.

With Ronnie Barker (Albert), Bill Maynard (Councillor Mortimer), Christopher Biggins (Cyril), Priscilla Morgan (Wife), John Cater, Louis Mansi, Geoffrey Todd, John Rutland, Brian Godfrey, Stephen Calcutt, Melanie Jane, Ian Gray.

22.04.1973 **Another Fine Mess**   DB-D3 / 2"

Written by Hugh Leonard; produced and directed by Harold Snoad.

With Ronnie Barker (Harry Norvel), Roy Castle (Sydney Jefferson), Avis Bunnage (Doris Norvel), Margery Mason (Cissie), Pearl Hackney (Neighbour), Sally Brelsford (Dinah Norvel), Pauline Delany (Edwina), Dennis Ramsden (Finlay).

29.04.1973 **One Man's Meat**   DB-D3 / 2"

Written by Ronnie Barker [credited as Jack Goetz]; produced and directed by Harold Snoad.

With Ronnie Barker (Alan Joyce), Joan Sims (Mrs Dawkins), Prunella Scales (Marion Joyce), Glynn Edwards (Police Sergeant), Sam Kelly (Policeman), Barbara New (Woman), Iris Fry (Shop Assistant).

06.05.1973 **I'll Fly You For A Quid**   DB-D3 / 2"

Postponed from 25.03.1973.

Written by Dick Clement and Ian La Frenais; music by Max Harris; produced and directed by Sydney Lotterby.

With Ronnie Barker (Mr Evan Owen), Margaret John (Mrs Owen), Beth Morris (April Owen), Ronnie Barker (Grandpa Owen), Talfryn Thomas (Tommy Pugh), Gwyneth Owen (Auntie), Emrys James (Rev Simmonds), Richard O'Callaghan (Mortlake Owen).

See also: MY OLD MAN* / OPEN ALL HOURS* / PORRIDGE*

SEVEN SECOND DELAY

A Granada production. Untransmitted. Duration: 25 minutes.

'Seven Second Delay is about that window of opportunity which allows us pause to think clearly, weigh up the pros and cons - and then make the wrong decision'.

Katie Lyons, Chris Langham, Sally Phillips, Cavan Clerkin, Stewart Wright, Ben Crompton.

Holding / Source

##.##.#### **[untransmitted pilot]**   J / DBSW

The series was axed when Chris Langham was arrested, convicted and went to jail.

SEVEN TO ONE

A BBC Manchester production for BBC 2. Transmission details are for BBC 2. Duration: 30 minutes.

	Holding / Source
##.##.#### [untransmitted pilot]	DB / 2"

Originally scheduled for 26.07.1978.

SHADES OF DARKNESS

A Granada production. Transmission details are for the Central region. Duration: 50 minutes.

Music by Derek Hilton; produced by June Wyndham-Davies.

SERIES 1

Main regular credit(s):   Executive producer Michael Cox; produced by June Wyndham-Davies.

	Production No	Holding / Source
10.06.1983 **Feet Foremost**	1/1127/1	C1 / C1

Adapted by Alan Plater; based on a story by L. P. Hartley; directed by Gordon Flemyng.

With Jeremy Kemp (Charles Ampleforth), Joanna Van Gyseghem (Mildred Ampleforth), Carol Royle (Maggie Winthrop), Peter Machin (Antony Fairfield), Heather Chasen (Eileen Turnbull), Ken Kitson (Wilkins).

Recorded Winter 1981.

THE SHADOW OF THE TOWER

A BBC production for BBC 2. Transmission details are for BBC 2. Duration: 50 minutes.

	Holding / Source
31.07.1969 **The Tower Of London - The Innocent**	R1 / 2"

A BBC production for BBC 1.

After the bloodshed of civil war, the White Rose and the Red Rose have been united and there has been peace in England for fourteen years. But however strong the King may seem, many still plot to take away his crown. And in the Tower is a prisoner who could well claim to be the rightful King of England.

Written by Derek Ingrey; designed by Stanley Morris; produced by Jordan Lawrence; directed by Jonathan Alwyn.

With James Maxwell (Henry VII), Bernard Archard (Earl of Oxford), Paul Bacon (Court Chamberlain), Wolfe Morris (Doctor Puebla), Simon Turner (Prince Arthur), Peter Copley (Archbishop Morton), Robert Powell (Earl of Warwick), Philippa Urquhart (Lady Catherine), Corin Redgrave (Perkin Warbeck), Edward Kelsey (Clerk of the Court), Peter Welch (Robert Cleymound), John Abineri (Thomas Astwood), Roy Patrick (Gaoler), Laurence Jeffrey (Prince Henry).

SHADOWS

A Thames Television production. Transmission details are for the ATV midlands region. Duration: 25 minutes.

Plays for youngsters, incorporating the supernatural, fantasy and magic.

SERIES 3

Main regular credit(s):   Produced by Pamela Lonsdale.

	VT Number	Holding / Source
11.10.1978 **The Boy Merlin**	18656	D3 / 2"

Set in Saxon times, it deals with the boyhood of Merlin, an apprentice magician soon to become a legend. "Their names shall be spoken together a thousand years hence . . . Merlin and Arthur." So says Merlin's grandmother Myfanwy, who sees a vision.

Adapted by Stewart Farrar; based on a book by Anne Carlton; designed by Bill Palmer; directed by Vic Hughes.

With Donald Houston (Dafydd), Rachel Thomas (Myfanwy), Ian Rowlands (Merlin), Margaret John (Blodwen), Archie Tew (Octa), Cassandra Harris (Ismena).

See also: THE BOY MERLIN* / DRAMARAMA

SHADOWS OF FEAR

A Thames Television production. Transmission details are for the ATV midlands region. Duration: 52 minutes.

	VT Number	Holding / Source
17.06.1970 **Did You Lock Up?**	2747	D3 / 2"

Written by Roger Marshall; produced and directed by Kim Mills.

With Michael Craig (Peter Astle), Gwen Watford (Moira Astle), Mark McManus (Cox), Malcolm Kaye (Pierce), Ray Smith (Newman), Charles Leno (Jeweller).

SHAPING UP

A HTV Wales production. Transmission details are for the HTV West region. Duration: 25 minutes.

Jack Dixon is made redundant. His wife persuades him to invest his redundancy money in a health studio.

Written by Ronald Wolfe and Ronald Chesney; executive producer Peter Elias Jones; produced and directed by Bryan Izzard.

Ruth Madoc (Shirley Dixon), Gareth Hunt (Jack Dixon), Elizabeth Morgan (Gwyneth), Lesley Guinn (Annabel), Peter Greenwell (Freddy), Guinevere John (Mrs Price Jones).

	Holding / Source
22.12.1988	1" / 1"

Lizzie Webb was the Exercise Consultant.

SHARMAN

A World production for Carlton UK. Transmission details are for the Central region. Duration varies - see below for details.

Main regular credit(s):   Based on novels by Mark Timlin; music by Mike Moran; executive producer Tony Garnett; produced by Bill Shapter.

Main regular cast: Clive Owen (Nick Sharman), Roberta Taylor (Aggie).

	Production No	Holding / Source
05.04.1995 **The Turnaround**	CAR/00422/0001	DB / C1SW

Duration: 75 minutes.

Nick Sharman is an ex-policeman currently earning a precarious living as a detective for hire. A lucrative contract is offered by the shady Mr Webb to investigate the murder of his family, but no sooner has Sharman agreed to the job than his first witness is bumped off and his daughter kidnapped.

Written by Tony Hoare; script supervisor Julie Robinson; directed by Suri Krishnamma.

With Bill Paterson (James Webb), John Salthouse (Detective Inspector Jack Robber), Isabella Marsh (Judith), Rowena King (Fiona), Miranda Foster (Laura), Matthew Marsh (Tony Hagan), Sarah Carpenter (Natalie), Ranjit Krishnamma (Ashok Ali), G. Brennan Fox (Detective Sergeant Jackson), Lee Alliston (Lenny), John Alexander, Peter Corey.

SHARON AND ELSIE

A BBC Manchester production for BBC 1. Transmission details are for BBC 1. Duration: 30 minutes.

Main regular credit(s):   Written by Arline Whittaker.

	Production No	Holding / Source
##.##.#### **[untransmitted 1983 pilot]**	LLCF181B/71	DB / 1"

Costume Lisa Benjamin; make-up Caroline Noble; theme music by Ronnie Hazlehurst; designed by Val Warrender; production manager Susan Belbin; produced and directed by Bernard Thompson.

With Susan Tracy (Elsie), Janette Beverley (Sharon), Norman Jones (Stanley), Maggie Jones (Ivy), Peter Martin (Tommy), Paula Tilbrook (Mrs Tibbett), Lee Daley (Elvis), Rita Howard (Lady In Queue), Muriel Lawford (Lady In Queue), Raffles (McQueen, The Dog).

This pilot was made by BBC London.

SHE AND ME

An LWT production. Untransmitted. Duration: 25 minutes.

Written by Terence Brady and Charlotte Bingham; theme music by Labi Siffre; produced by Humphrey Barclay; directed by Simon Langton.

Liza Goddard (Daphne), Colin Baker (Henry), Derek Fowlds (Nigel), Janine Duvitski (Maria), Bridget McConnel (Boo), Joan Heath (Mrs Compton-Wingate), Eric Mason (Firechief), Matthew Brady (Mutty).

	Production No	Holding / Source
##.##.#### **The Man Who Came To Dinner**	9L/99148	UM / 2"

Recorded 29.12.1977.

SHELFSTACKERS

A Conker Media production for BBC Switch. Transmission details are for BBC 2. Duration: 24 minutes.

Main regular credit(s):   Created by Bede Blake.

	Holding / Source
27.03.2010	DB / DBSWF

Written by Bede Blake; script supervisor Billie Hughes; script editor Tim Compton; theme music by Alexis Blue; director of photography Jonathan Smith; art director Pawlo Wintoniuk; associate producer Christopher Wood; production executive Trevor Klein; executive producers Geoffrey Goodwin, Lee Hardman and Tony Wood; production manager Colette Chard; produced by Kristian Smith; directed by Jeremy Wooding.

With Adam Byard (Fitzy), Dan Wright (Roy), Colin Ryan (Dan), John Warburton (Funkhausen), Naomi Everson (Alyssa), Beattie Edmondson (Danni).

SHE'LL HAVE TO GO

An ATV production. Untransmitted. Duration: 25 minutes.

Produced and directed by Alan Tarrant.

	Holding / Source
##.##.#### **[untransmitted 1973 pilot]**	DB|n / 2"

SHE'LL HAVE TO GO

An ATV production. Transmission details are for the ATV midlands region. Duration: 25 minutes.

Written by Ronnie Taylor and Wally Malston; music by Robert Farnon and Jack Parnell and his Orchestra; designed by Ray White; produced and directed by Alan Tarrant.

Moira Lister (Mrs Vicky Labone), Ted Rogers (Peter Merrick), Richard Vernon (Maurice Sheldon), Aubrey Morris (Ernest Goostrey), Belinda Carroll (Audrey Dyson).

	Holding / Source
14.08.1973	J / 2"

SHERLOCK

A Hartswood Films production for BBC Wales. made in association with Masterpiece. Transmission details are for BBC 1.

Main regular credit(s):   Created by Steven Moffat and Mark Gatiss; produced by Sue Vertue.

Main regular cast: Benedict Cumberbatch (Sherlock Holmes), Martin Freeman (Doctor John Watson), Una Stubbs (Mrs Hudson).

Holding / Source

##.##.#### A Study In Pink [untransmitted pilot]   HD/DB / HD/DB

Duration: 60 minutes.

Written by Steven Moffat; music by David Arnold and Michael Price; director of photography Matt Gray; assistant director Paul Judges; production designer Edward Thomas; designed by Arwel Wyn Jones; production executive Julie Scott; executive producers Mark Gatiss, Steven Moffat and Beryl Vertue; line producer Kathy Nettleship; directed by Coky Giedroyc.

With Rupert Graves (Inspector Lestrade), Zawe Ashton (Sergeant Sally Donovan), Loo Brealey (Molly Hooper), Jonathan Aris, Joseph Long, Tanya Moodie, James Harper, Phil Davis.

Untransmitted pilot.

SHILLINGBURY TALES

An ITC production for ATV. Transmission details are for the ATV midlands region.

Main regular credit(s):   Written by Francis Essex; music by Ed Welch; produced by Greg Smith; directed by Val Guest.

Main regular cast: Robin Nedwell (Peter), Diane Keen (Sally), Jack Douglas (Jake).

Holding / Source

06.01.1980 The Shillingbury Blowers   DB / C3

Alt.Title(s):   *And The Band Played On*

An Inner Circle Films Ltd production. Duration: 79 minutes.

Associate producer Frank Bevis.

With Trevor Howard, John Le Mesurier, Miles Anderson, Sam Kydd, Eric Francis, Joe Black, Tony Sympson, Patrick Newell, Diana King.

Francis Essex originally wrote 'The Shillingbury Blowers' in 1974 as a short story while he was on a flight to New York, where he was meeting Tv executive (eg TV-AM and others) Bruce Gyngell.

Gyngell read the story overnight and suggested to Essex the next day that he write it as a screenplay. Essex did just that while he was on holiday, and it then lay in a drawer until September 1978.

Jack Gill of ATV had set up a number of film subsidiaries (eg Inner Circle) and was looking for exclusively English film subjects; he read the Essex screenplay and agreed to put up the money required for the production.

See also: CUFFY

SHINE ON HARVEY MOON

A Witzend production for ATV/Central/Meridian. Transmission details are for the Central region.

Main regular credit(s):   Devised by Laurence Marks and Maurice Gran; executive producer Allan McKeown; produced by Tony Charles.

Main regular cast: Elizabeth Spriggs (Nan), Maggie Steed (Rita Moon), Linda Robson (Maggie Moon), Lee Whitlock (Stanley Moon), Nigel Planer (Lou Lewis).

SERIES 1

A Witzend production for ATV. Duration: 25 minutes.

Main regular credit(s):   Written by Laurence Marks and Maurice Gran; script editors Dick Clement and Ian La Frenais; theme music by Jack Parnell and his Orchestra; music by David Lindup; directed by Baz Taylor.

Main regular cast: With Kenneth Cranham (Harvey Moon).

	Production No	VT Number	Holding / Source
08.01.1982 Hail The Conquering Hero...	5985	5985/81	DB / 2"

With Richard Le Parmentier, Anthony Carrick, George Tovey, Robert Putt, Dawn Perllman.

Recorded 23rd January 1981.

SHOWCASE

Alternative/Working Title(s): SNEAK PREVIEW

A Granada production. Transmission details are for the Granada region. Duration: 25 minutes.

Main regular credit(s):   Produced by John Hamp.

	Production No	Holding / Source
29.03.1983 The Grumbleweeds Radio Show	P1178/4	DB / 1"

Directed by Ian Hamilton.

With The Grumbleweeds.

	Production No	Holding / Source
08.04.1983 Million Dollar Music	P1178/1	DB / 1"

Middle of the road music programme. Following the American trend back towards middle of the road music, Granada's Million Dollar Music programme features 16 of the world's best top selling classic pop songs.

Costume Clive Stuart; choreography by Brian Rogers; designed by Tim Wilding; directed by Ian Hamilton.

With Lisa Stansfield, Sue Glover, Sunny, George Chandler, Jimmy Chambers, Kofi, The Les Reed Orchestra.

18.08.1983 **Born In The 60s - Lisa**	P1178/2	DB / 1"

This programme is about Lisa Stansfield, a young singer. Four of her songs are performed in the studio and there are documentary film inserts looking at her everyday life , and interviewing her family.

Costume Clive Stuart; designed by Tim Wilding; directed by Peter Walker.

25.08.1983 **Born In The 60s - Jade**	P1178/3	DB / 1"

This programme is about Jade, a young singer. Four of her songs are performed in the studio and there are documentary film inserts looking at her career development to date, including interviews with her manager and mother.

Costume Clive Stuart; designed by Tim Wilding; directed by Peter Walker.

All pilots for possible series. Recorded Summer 1982.

See also: BORN IN THE 60'S - LISA* / EGO TRIP / THE GRUMBLEWEEDS RADIO SHOW*

SHUSH

Commissioned by BBC. Untransmitted. Duration: 30 minutes.

Main regular credit(s):   Written by Arthur Mathews and Armando Iannucci; script editor Richard Herring; produced by Armando Iannucci.

Main regular cast: Rebecca Front (Alice), Morwenna Banks (Snoo), Ben Willbond (Library Inspector), Simon Greenall (Seller), Michael Fenton Stevens, Alex Macqueen.

	Holding / Source
##.##.#### **[first pilot]**	HD/DB / HD/DB
##.##.#### **[second pilot]**	HD/DB / HD/DB

SIDNEY YOU'RE A GENIUS

A BBC production. Untransmitted.

	Holding / Source
##.##.####	DB-D3 / 2"

THE SIGHT

An Impact Pictures production for Sky One. Transmission details are for Sky One. Duration: 106 minutes.

Written by Paul W. S. Anderson; script supervisor Sharon Mansfield; music by Jocelyn Pook; executive producers Paul W. S. Anderson, Jeremy Bolt, Mark Freeland and Julia Webb; produced by Chris Symes; directed by Paul W. S. Anderson.

Andrew McCarthy (Michael Lewis), Kevin Tighe (Jake), Amanda Redman (Detective Sergeant Price), David Roper (Detective Sergeant Mills, Formerly David Connor), Alexander Armstrong (Charles Dodgson), Honor Blackman (Margaret Smith), Jessica Oyelowo (Isabelle), Maurice Roëves (Chief Superintendent), Julian Firth (Tourist In New York), Helene Patarot (Mrs Fong), Michaela Dicker (Alice), Tom Knight (Suit 1), Gregg Prentice (Cute Kid), Jason Barnett (Security Guard), Vinta Morgan (Policeman 1), Charlie Watts (Young Man), Kumari Simmons (Friend), Eamon Geoghegan (Priest), Helena Lyons (World War II Ghost), Ian Peck (Construction Worker), Andrew Westfield (Site Manager), Nick Bartlett (Hospital Orderly), Jordon Long (Prison Warder), Oliver Darley (Andrew Norrington), Charles Simon (Mr Douglas), Jeffry Wickham (English Doctor), Jonathan Linsley (Van Policeman 1), Clabe Hartley.

	Holding / Source
10.09.2000	DB / V1SW

SINCE YOU'VE BEEN GONE

An LWT production. Untransmitted. Duration: 24 minutes.

	VT Number	Holding / Source
##.##.#### **[untransmitted pilot]**	9L/94447	DB / 2"

THE SINGING BARN

A BBC Wales production. Transmission details are for BBC Various. Duration: 25 minutes.

Transmission details are for BBC 2.

	Holding / Source
03.06.1967	DB-4W / 40

SINGING IN THE BRAIN

A Granada production. Untransmitted. Duration: 40 minutes.

Main regular credit(s):   Written by John Glashan and Denis Pitts; produced by Peter Eckersley; directed by Peter Jones.

	Production No	Holding / Source
##.##.####	3/227/1	B1|c / B1

With Geoffrey Chater (Boris Cheteton), David Langton (Doctor Mycroft Ferguson), Georgina Cookson (Princess Albert), Ronald Lacey (Ruthven / Doctor Lunga), John Bluthal, Fulton Mackay.

	Production No	Holding / Source
##.##.####	P227/2	NR|c /

With Geoffrey Chater (Brigadier Chesterton), David Langton (Dr Mycroft Ferguson), Georgina Cookson (Princess Albert), Ronald Lacey (Ruthven / Dr Lenyo), John Bluthal (Cranston / Pakistani / Dr Zeiss), Fulton Mackay (Secretary / Labour Exchange Man).

	Production No	Holding / Source
##.##.#### **The Watch-Smashing Party**	P227/3	NR|c /
##.##.#### **A Massive Shot In The Arm**	P227/4	NR|c /

SINGLES NIGHT

A Thames Television production. Transmission details are for the Central region. Duration: 50 minutes.

Written by Eric Chappell and Jean Warr; designed by John Plant; executive producer Lloyd Shirley; directed by Robert Reed.

Robin Nedwell, Jane Carr, Angela Richards, Doug Fisher, Patricia Brake, John Kavanagh, Denis Gilmore, Michael Lees, Jane Bough.

	VT Number	Holding / Source
19.06.1984	30613	1" / 1"

Comedy play set at a hotel "singles night". Made for inclusion in the Storyboard series.

See also: SINGLES*

SIR YELLOW

A Yorkshire Television production. Transmission details are for the ATV midlands region. Duration: 25 minutes.

A mediaeval comedy.

Main regular credit(s):   Written by Johnny Heward; script editor David Nobbs; designed by Howard Dawson; produced by Bill Hitchcock; directed by Ian Davidson.

Main regular cast: Jimmy Edwards (Sir Yellow), Melvyn Hayes (Gregory), Alan Curtis (Sir Griswold), Michael Ripper (Cedric).

	Holding / Source
##.##.#### [untransmitted pilot]	J / 2"

Recorded Autumn 1972.

SIROCCO

An ATV production. Untransmitted. Duration: 25 minutes.

	Holding / Source
##.##.####	B3 / B3

A pilot film was planned to begin production on 14th June 1960. It had a photographer-type hero similar to Bob Cappa, famous life photographer. Casting proved very difficult and production was moved back to August 1960. Filming began shortly after in Monte Carlo.

Eventually re-edited and shown as 'Mr. Riviera'.

See also: MR. RIVIERA

SISTER FRANCES

A Thames Television production for ITV 1. Untransmitted. Duration: 23 minutes.

Written by Jo Brand and Sue Teddern; script supervisor Tessa Kimbell; music by Simon Lacey; art director Clara Morland; designed by Sally Gray; line producer Kathy Nettleship; produced by Margot Gavan Duffy; directed by Ben Kellett.

Jo Brand (Sister Frances), Morwenna Banks (Sister Grace), Honor Blackman (Mother Superior), Kathryn Drysdale (Sister Josephine), Evie Garratt (Sister Faith), Geraldine McNulty (Sister Maria), Tilly Vosburgh (Sioban), Jordan Long (Steve), Alyson Coote (Sister Alice), Arthur Smith (Voice of God), Brian Sewell (Voice of God).

	Production No	VT Number	Holding / Source
##.##.#### [untransmitted pilot]	PC/6167/04	349037	DB / DBSW

Recorded 2004.

A planned series of six episodes never materialised.

SISTERS

A Messenger TV production for BBC North West. Untransmitted. Duration: 30 minutes.

It's a middle class soap, based on the five daughters of a rich architect, living in the Cheshire stockbroker belt of Wilmslow.

Lighting by Peter Nolan; designed by Tim Wilding; produced by June Howson; directed by Gareth Davies.

Judy Loe (Mother), Eamon Boland (Father), Belinda Lang (Aunt), Rebecca Lacey, Sarah Griffiths, Francesca McGregor, Liza Walker, Charley Hayes.

	Holding / Source
##.##.#### [untransmitted pilot]	J / BS

Recorded 31st July 1989. June Howson remembers:
" It was made by Messenger TV - An independent company belonging to Eddy Shah. He had asked me to Head it for him which I was doing at that time - I knew him from my Granada days when he had been my Floor manager and I was one of the few people who listened to him when he said, with total assurance, that he was going to make a lot of money !!
Gareth Davies directed and I produced.

It was devised by Eddy and was about a middle to upper class family living in Cheshire. The mother(Judy Loe) is killed in a car accident in the first episode and the father (Eamon Boland) is left to bring up five girls on his own. The girls were played by Rebecca Lacey, Sarah Griffiths, Francesca McGregor, Liza Walker and Charley Hayes. Belinda Lang played the aunt and was shot entirely on location.

The BBC were looking for a new, long running soap and Messenger were one of several companies commissioned to make a pilot. We made it down to the last three but they chose Eldorado! I still think it had great potential and would have had a strong following but it never happened."

THE SITCOM TRIALS

An ITV Carlton West production for ITV 1 Carlton West. Transmission details are for the ITV 1/Carlton West region. Duration: 24 minutes.

Main regular credit(s):   Created by Kevin F. Sutherland; produced by Mark Ashton; directed by Sally Harvey.

Main regular cast: Kevin F. Sutherland (Presenter).

	Holding / Source
21.02.2003 **Policevets In Casualty / Do You Think They'll Cotton On?**	DB / DBSW

28.02.2003	**The Client / Go Wild In The Country**	DB / DBSW
07.03.2003		DB / DBSW
14.03.2003		DB / DBSW
21.03.2003		DB / DBSW
28.03.2003		DB / DBSW
04.04.2003		DB / DBSW
11.04.2003		DB / DBSW

Interactive show in which two sitcoms were piloted every week, the audience saw the first half of each pilot and then voted for their favourite to watch the ending of the winning entry.

THE SITE

A BBC Productions production for BBC 3. Transmission details are for BBC 3. Duration: 30 minutes.

Martin returns home for the first time in ten years for his father's funeral, and realises nothing has changed in his disfunctional family when his dad sits up in his own coffin.

Written by Henry White; script supervisor Mathilde Bouts; music by Laura Rossi; designed by Harry Banks; production executive Eirwen Davies; production manager Tony Morris; produced by Pete Thornton; directed by Tristram Shapeero.

Chris Hannon (Martin), Paul Kaye (Douglas), Danny Kirrane (Chobb), Annette Badland (Mother), Clive Russell (Ironweed), Andrew Lawrence (Morris), Colin Proctor (Father), William Travis (Salesman), Richard Katz (The Speaking Clock), Charlie Kenyon (Rock Throwing Kid), Harry Herring (Digby Grittleton), Rae Baker (Enid Grittleton), Paul Barber (Tom Cruise), Roger Bingham (Stationmaster), Paul Hawkyward (Head Engineer), John Branwell (Breathless Man), Leader Hawkins (Torn Man), Rod Arthur (Barman).

		Holding / Source
30.01.2009	**No Place Like Home**	DB / DBSWF

Comedy pilot.

SITTING PRETTY

A BBC production for BBC 1. Transmission details are for BBC 1. Duration: 30 minutes.

Main regular credit(s):	Written by John Sullivan.
Main regular cast:	Diane Bull (Annie).

		Production No	VT Number	Holding / Source
##.##.####	**Welcome To Sitting Pretty [untransmitted pilot]**	LLCC3005	T0188998	DB / 1"

Costume Richard Winter; make-up Vanessa Poulton; designed by Grenville Horner and Richard Dupré; production manager Adam Tandy; produced by Gareth Gwenlan; directed by Susan Belbin.

With Brenda Bruce (Kitty), Charlotte Cornwell (Sylvie), Pippa Hinchley (Tiffany), David English (Trevor).

SIX O' ONE - DEAR MR BRADBURY

A Granada production. Untransmitted.

	Production No	Holding / Source
##.##.#### **[untransmitted pilot]**	P/696/8901	J / 2"

SIX OF THE BEST

An ATV production. Transmission details are for the ATV midlands region. Duration: 25 minutes.

Main regular credit(s):   Produced by Alan Tarrant.

		Production No	VT Number	Holding / Source
11.08.1965	**Annie Doesn't Live Here Anymore**	7488	7648	J / 40

Recorded 29.07.1965.

		Production No	VT Number	Holding / Source
18.08.1965	**Me And My Big Mouth**	7497	7707	J / 40

Written by Fred Robinson; designed by Eric Shedden; directed by Shaun O'Riordan.

With Alfie Bass (Alfie Smith), Peter Bowles (Tom Brown), Barry Linehan (Barman), Douglas Ditta (Scot), Hazel Coppen (Mum), Alan Rolfe (Mr Fiske), David Davenport (Doctor), Michael Corcoran (Agitated Man), Joanna Wake (Sheila).

Recorded 17.06.1965.

		Production No	VT Number	Holding / Source
25.08.1965	**Charlie's Place**	8142	7819	J / 40

Written by Alan Plater; designed by Lewis Logan; directed by Dicky Leeman.

With Ray Brooks (Charlie), Francis Matthews (Jack), Yootha Joyce (Doris), John Junkin (Sid), Helen Fraser (Vanessa).

Recorded 20.08.1965.

Like Plater's earlier play "So Long, Charlie" this features a character called Jack played by Francis Matthews and another called Charlie. Are these intended to be the same characters? We don't know.

		Production No	VT Number	Holding / Source
01.09.1965	**Porterhouse - Private Eye**	7827	7777	J / 40

Written by Maurice Wiltshire; designed by Ray White; directed by Albert Locke.

With Peter Butterworth (Edwin Porterhouse), June Whitfield (Daffodil), Dudley Foster (Otto Mulchrone), John Glyn-Jones (Sir Gregory Bowles), Cicely Hullett (Lady Bowles), Bryan Mosley (Hargreaves), Elizabeth Counsell (Irma), Frank Sieman (Inspector).

Recorded 20.07.1965.

		Production No	VT Number	Holding / Source
08.09.1965	**Are There Anymore At Home Like You?**	8331	7857	J / 40

Written by Tony Hawes.

With Graham Stark, Barbara Mitchell.

Recorded 03.09.1965.

15.09.1965 **These Four Walls**	8476	8033	J / 40

Designed by Richard R. Greenough; directed by Alastair Reid.

Recorded 13.09.1965.

##.##.#### **Man With A Mission**	8143	7820	J / 40

Originally scheduled for 08.09.1965.

Written by Richard Harris and Dennis Spooner; directed by Dicky Leeman.

With Ronald Lacey (Wilfred Hicks), Thorley Walters (Forbes-Glanville), Avis Bunnage (Mrs Whittaker), Derek Nimmo (Hope-Weston), Harry Locke (Security Guard), Denise Buckley (Carol).

Recorded 27.08.1965. Television Today reported that this edition was replaced by Are There Anymore At Home Like You?

SLATER'S DAY

A Yorkshire Television production. Transmission details are for the ATV midlands region. Duration: 25 minutes.

Freddy Slater has his ups and downs as a public relations man.

Written by Chris Boucher; designed by Colin Pigott; produced and directed by Paddy Russell.

John Junkin (Freddy Slater), Mary Miller (Jean Slater), Peter Mayock (Jack), Maureen Sweeney (Muriel), James Cairncross (Frogley), Warwick Sims (Jason), Rio Fanning (Van Driver), John Who (Waiter), Roy Alon (Waiter), Robin Parkinson (Agent).

	Holding / Source
	1" / 2"
03.12.1974	

Postponed from 07.10.1974.

A SLIGHT HITCH

A Thames Television production. Transmission details are for the Central region. Duration: 25 minutes.

Written by Adrienne Conway; produced and directed by John Howard Davies.

Nigel Havers (Simon), Joanna Kanska (Anna), Nancy Nevinson (Katerina), Helen Christie (Helen), Sarah-Jane Varley (Susie), David Lloyd (Police Inspector), Marilyn Finlay (Registrar).

	VT Number	Holding / Source
28.03.1991	50717	1" / 1"

SMIFFS

A Thames Television production. Transmission details are for the Central region. Duration: 25 minutes.

A fashion design company in London.

Main regular credit(s):	Written by Tessa Diamond; produced by Brenda Ennis; directed by Neville Green.
Main regular cast:	Christina Jones (Christina Scott), Brian Capron (Stephen Smith), Cornelius Garrett (Alan Smith), Sandy Ratcliff (Cally Brown), Jonty Miller (George), Aaron Harris (Paul), Margo Cunningham (Shirley), Maggie Ollerenshaw (Mrs Scott), Della Finch (Joy Fuller), Mark Tandy (Ben Coleman), Lillian Silverstone (Chloe), Alibe Parsons (Buyer).

	Holding / Source
01.08.1983 **Episode 1 [pilot 1]**	D3 / 2"
02.08.1983 **Episode 2 [pilot 2]**	D3 / 2"

Pilot for the Thames soap opera Gems.

See also: GEMS*

SO HAUNT ME

A Cinema Verity production for BBC 1. Transmission details are for BBC 1. Duration: 30 minutes.

Main regular credit(s):	Written by Paul A. Mendelson.
Main regular cast:	Miriam Karlin (Yetta Feldman), Tessa Peake-Jones (Sally Rokeby), George Costigan (Pete Rokeby), Laura Howard (Tammy Rokeby), Jeremy Green (Daniel Rokeby).

	Production No	Holding / Source
##.##.#### **[untransmitted pilot]**	LLCB100K/71	DB / 1"

The pilot had no end credits, but it included roles for a neighbour and two removal men.

SOB SISTERS

A Central production. Transmission details are for the Central region. Duration: 25 minutes.

Main regular credit(s):	Written by Andrew Marshall; music by Dave Cooke; produced by Christopher Walker.
Main regular cast:	Gwen Taylor (Liz), Polly Adams (Dorothy), Freddie Jones (Leo), Philip Bird (Charlie), Beryl Cooke (Edna).

	VT Number	Holding / Source
26.05.1989 **I Don't Think We're In Kansas Anymore**	2966/88	1" / 1"

Designed by Ann Croot-Hawkins; directed by Ray Butt.

With Sue Holderness, Nigel Lambert, Jeillo Edwards, Jeff Stevenson.

SOFTLY SOFTLY

A BBC production for BBC 1. Transmission details are for BBC 1. Duration: 50 minutes.

Main regular credit(s):   Format by Elwyn Jones.

SERIES 1

Main regular credit(s):   Produced by David E. Rose.

	Production No	VT Number	Holding / Source
02.02.1966 **Talk To Me**	22/1/5/7193	VT/4T/29946	J / 40

Written by Kenneth Ware; directed by Shaun Sutton.

With Stratford Johns (Detective Chief Superintendent Charles Barlow), Frank Windsor (Detective Inspector John Watt), Robert Keegan (Mr Blackitt), John Welsh (Assistant Chief Constable Calderwood), Garfield Morgan (Detective Chief Inspector Lewis), Norman Bowler (Detective Sergeant Hawkins), Gilbert Wynne (Detective Constable Reg Dwyer), Alexis Kanner (Detective Constable Matt Stone), Cavan Kendall (Police Constable Greenly), Barry Letts (Detective Sergeant Reed), Colin Douglas (Detective Chief Inspector Rawlings), Garth Adams (Station Sergeant), Ivor Salter, Milton Johns, Douglas Blackwell, John Woodnutt, Norman Mitchell.

There was a test pre-record of a Softly Softly episode on 16th November 1965, which was transmitted as episode 5 – "Talk to Me" - on 2nd February 1966. They'd already pre-recorded a Z Cars episode so that show could take the studio day.

Unmade episode: 'Safe Conduct' by Brian Wright.

See also: BARLOW* / BARLOW AT LARGE* / JACK THE RIPPER* / SECOND VERDICT* / Z CARS*

THE SOLARNAUTS

A Wonderama production for ABC TV Films. Untransmitted. Duration: 25 minutes.

Created by Roberta Leigh; music by John Hawksworth; production supervised by Johnny Goodman; produced by Roberta Leigh and Arthur Provis.

John Garfield (Power), Derek Fowlds (Tempo), John Ringham (Tri-S), Alex Scott (Logik), Martine Beswick (Kandia), George Roubicek, Virginia Wetherell, Jan Leeming, Les Crawford, Frank Maher, Cliff Diggins, Romo Gorrara, Peter Blair Stewart, John Connell.

	Holding / Source
##.##.#### **[untransmitted pilot]**	DB / C3

SOME YOU WIN

A Granada production. Transmission details are for the Central region. Duration varies - see below for details.

Main regular credit(s):   Produced by Nick Turnbull; directed by David G. Hillier.

Main regular performer(s): With Frank Carson, Stan Boardman, Cheryl Murray, Mike Goddard, Geoff O'Neil, Peter Skellern, The Thompson Twins, Sonny Hayes & Co.

	Production No	Holding / Source
30.07.1983 **[first pilot]**	P1205/1	DB / 1"

Duration: 38 minutes.

Script associate Mike Goddard; produced by Nick Turnbull; directed by David G. Hillier.

With Mike Goddard (Presenter), Frank Carson, Stan Boardman, Cheryl Murray, Geoff O'Neil, Peter Skellern, The Thompson Twins, Sonny Hayes & Co, Graham Jarvis.

	Production No	Holding / Source
06.08.1983 **[second pilot]**	P1205/2	DB / 1"

Duration: 38 minutes.

Script associate Mike Goddard; produced by Nick Turnbull; directed by David G. Hillier.

With Frank Carson, Stan Boardman, Cheryl Murray, Mike Goddard, 10cc, Bob Williamson, Sonny Hayes & Co, Kate Robbins, The Bootleg Beatles.

SOMETHING ELSE

A Community Programmes Unit Production production for BBC 2. Transmission details are for BBC 2. Duration varies - see below for details.

Magazine programme for teenagers.

	Holding / Source
11.03.1978	DB-D3 / 2"

Duration: 45 minutes.
With The Clash, Joan Lestor, M.P., Patricia Mann.

SONGWRITER

A Tyne Tees Television production. Transmission details are for the Tyne Tees region. Duration: 45 minutes.

Produced by Heather Ging; directed by James Goldby.

Ralph McTell (Presenter).

	Holding / Source
02.09.1982	1" / 2"

Recorded 29th July 1982.

SORRY, I'M A STRANGER HERE MYSELF

A Thames Television production. Transmission details are for the ATV/Central region. Duration: 25 minutes.

Main regular credit(s):   Produced and directed by Anthony Parker.

Main regular cast: Robin Bailey (Henry Nunn), David Hargreaves (Tom Pratt), Christopher Fulford (Alex), Diana Rayworth (Doreen Pratt), Nadim Sawalha (Mumtaz).

SERIES 1

Transmission details are for the ATV midlands region.

Main regular credit(s):   Written by David Firth and Peter Tilbury; designed by Jan Chaney.

	VT Number	Holding / Source
29.06.1981 **All Friends**	24046	D3 / 2"

With Neil McCarthy.

SOUND

A BBC Manchester production for BBC 3. Transmission details are for BBC 3. Duration: 30 minutes.

Following two Manchester lads who set up their own record label.

Created by Damian Lanigan; written by Damian Lanigan; script supervisor Eileen Wood; designed by Andrea Hughes; production executive Sarah Hitchcock; executive producer Kenton Allen; produced by Jim Poyser; directed by David Kerr.

Sam Riley (Shay), Tony Mooney (Shay's Dad), Ben McKay (Danny), Olwen May (Danny's Mum), Lorraine Cheshire (Shay's Mum), Honor Blackman (Danny's Gran), Joel Fry (Swing), Christine Bottomley (Lou), Matthew Forrest (Losey), Sam Stockman (Paul), Craig Storrod (Kemps), Denise Kennedy (Mrs Schofield), Ian Puleston-Davies (Strange Pete), John Thomson (Terry Frayne).

	Holding / Source
28.03.2007	DB / DBSWF

See also: MASSIVE*

THE SOUND OF LAUGHTER

An ABC production. Transmission details are for the ABC midlands region. Usual duration: 25 minutes.

	Holding / Source
29.01.1967 **No Strings**	J / 40

Written by Fred Robinson; designed by Harry Clark; produced and directed by Milo Lewis.

With Arthur Askey, Ann Lancaster, Jack Haig, Muriel Zillah, Arthur Hewlett, Norman Mitchell, Bob Todd, Shirley Stelfox.

05.02.1967 **Mister Misfit**	J / 40

Alternative transmissions: Anglia: 16.02.1967.

Written by George Evans and Derek Collyer; theme music by Roger Sharples; designed by Roger Burridge; produced and directed by Peter Frazer-Jones.

With Jim Dale (Jim Didsbury), Hugh Morton, Ken Parry, Damaris Hayman, Amy Dalby, Deborah Watling, Joanna Wake, Warren Clarke, Constance Milligan Dancers.

12.02.1967 **That's Show Business**	J / 40

Written by Vince Powell and Harry Driver; designed by Roger Allen; produced and directed by John Paddy Carstairs.

With Billy Dainty, Kenneth Connor, June Whitfield, Harold Berens, Julian Holloway, Joe Gladwin.

19.02.1967 **Gentleman Jim**	J / 40

Alternative transmissions: Anglia: 30.03.1967.

Written by Jimmy Grafton and David Climie; designed by Bryan Graves; produced by Peter Dulay; directed by Malcolm Morris.

With Jimmy Edwards (Squire Jim), Clive Dunn (Bules), Richard Wattis, Alison Frazer, Eddie Malin, Damaris Hayman, Walter Sparrow, Marion Wilson, Bob Todd, Will Stampe.

26.02.1967 **Stiff Upper Lip**	J / 40

Duration: 35 minutes.

Adapted by Giles Cooper; based on a book by Lawrence Durrell; designed by Philip Harrison; produced by Robert Banks Stewart; directed by Michael Mills.

With Robert Coote, Donald Churchill, James Villiers, David Kernan, Penny Morrell, Judith Furse, David Phethean, Raymond Clarke, Edward Caddick, Hugo de Vernier, Rose Alba, Michael Trubshawe, Tom Macaulay.

05.03.1967 **Around With Allen**	J|a / 40

Duration: 30 minutes.

Alternative transmissions: Anglia: 23.03.1967.

Written by Alistair Foot, Anthony Marriott [credited as Tony Marriott] and Eric Merriman; designed by Darrell Lass; produced and directed by Malcolm Morris.

With Dave Allen, Patrick Cargill, Ronnie Stevens, Victor Maddern, Arthur Mullard, Penny Anne France, Bob Todd, Marian Montgomery, Ted Brennan and his Orchestra.

12.03.1967 **Hooray For Laughter**	J / 40

Duration: 30 minutes.

Alternative transmissions: Anglia: 20.04.1967.

Written by Ted Ray and John Junkin; designed by Terry Gough; produced and directed by Peter Frazer-Jones.

With Ted Ray, Reg Varney, Rosemary Squires, Ray Alan, John Junkin, Mike Felix, Bob Sharples and his Music.

19.03.1967 **Did You See Una?**	J / 40

A Scottish Television production.

Devised by Eric Merriman; written by Eric Merriman; designed by Ron Franchetti; produced and directed by Clarke Tait.

With Una McLean, Margery Dalziel, Paul Kermack, Doris McLatchie, Glen Michael, Malcolm Ingram, Alex McAvoy, Glenys Marshall.

26.03.1967 **Hicks And Stokes**	J / 40

Alternative transmissions: Anglia: 27.04.1967.

Written by Ronnie Taylor; designed by Tony Borer; produced and directed by Ronnie Baxter.

With Rodney Bewes (Billy Hicks), Norman Rossington (Norman Stokes), James Cossins (Mr Bowling), Barry Halliday (Jenkins), Didi Sullivan (Valeria Dobbs).

THE SOUND OF LAUGHTER

An ATV production. Transmission details are for the ATV midlands region. Duration: 25 minutes.

	VT Number	Holding / Source

28.07.1977 A Sharp Intake Of Breath   2333   D3|n / 2"

Written by Ronnie Taylor.

With David Jason (Peter Barnes), Patricia Brake (Sheila Barnes).

04.08.1977 Young At Heart   2332   DV / 2"

Postponed from 28.07.1977.

Written by Ronnie Taylor; designed by Stanley Mills; produced and directed by Les Chatfield.

With Stratford Johns (Albert Sculley), Richard Pearson (Leonard Jarvis), Joan Scott (Gladys), Ellis Dale (Shop Assistant).

11.08.1977 Bricks Without Straw   2334   DV / 2"

Builder Ernie Randle at last finds a job —to make the Potter family's new home habitable. And if it's speed you require, it's Randle you hire. Or is it?

Written by Andrew McCulloch and John Flanagan; designed by Gerry Roberts; produced and directed by Les Chatfield.

With Michael Elphick (Ernie Randle), Amanda Reiss (Phoebe), James Wooley (Peregrine Potter), Peter Childs (Sydney Lennox), Richard Domfe (Reg Cooper), Declan Mulholland (Charles Leek), Tony Sympson ('Pop' Young), Toni Palmer (Doris).

18.08.1977 What A Performance   2335   DV / 2"

A situation comedy about an amateur dramatic society — everyday characters who gather together to create a realm of fantasy and grandeur—for three performances only. Their current production is put in jeopardy when T.G. storms out and it's left to Brian to direct the important new play. But T.G. also wants the play for a rival group . .

Written by Kenneth Cope; designed by Sue Nash; produced and directed by Shaun O'Riordan.

With Robin Bailey (David), Noel Davis (Thomas G. Read), Rosemary Martin (Victoria), Anna Quayle (Vera), Andrew Sachs (Brian Jones), Stan Stennett (Arnold Bingham), Marjie Lawrence (Brenda), Debbie Farrington (Helen), Spencer Banks (Stephen), Gerald James (Mr Tandy), Kathleen Heath (Betty), Trixie Scales (Freda).

Planned to become a series in 1978.

25.08.1977 After The Boom Was Over   2336   DV / 2"

The misadventures of two young people as an hilarious hunt for bargain homes. It all seems so simple to Sally and Jack Tatham . Settle on a distict that's not too expensive , then find an estate agent. But events are to prove otherwise.

Written by Connor Fraser; designed by Stanley Mills; produced and directed by Les Chatfield.

With Tim Wylton (Jack Tatham), Gabrielle Lloyd (Sally Ashcroft), Martin C. Thurley (Mr Airedale), Jonathan Pryce (Mr Ambrose).

Planned to become a series in 1978.

01.09.1977 The Best Of Friends   2337   DV / 2"

When little old Miss Vaughan's nephew and girlfriend arrive for a visit, the double bed poses an embarrassing problem . . . especially when the Lloyd sisters, Miss Vaughan's friends for over 60 years, become too inquisitive ...

Written by Linette Purbi Perry; designed by James Weatherup; produced and directed by Shaun O'Riordan.

With Jessie Evans (Miss Vaughan), Margaret Courtenay (Olwyn Lloyd), Peter Blythe (Nicholas Barry), Catherine Chase (Sally Morton), Gerald James (Doctor Hamer), Megs Jenkins (Emily Lloyd).

Until the late 1990s, all of this series existed at ITC / Polygram on low-band Umatic. At some point after 1997 they were all wiped, and only VHS copies (purchased and held by Kaleidoscope) exist. Due to restrictions placed by the artist on the purchase of David Jason's material, we were not given a copy of his pilot, so that one has been wiped for ever. :-(

See also: A SHARP INTAKE OF BREATH*

SOUNDS LIKE MUSIC

A TSW production. Untransmitted.

Members of the public give their views and sing songs from musicals.

	Holding / Source

##.##.#### [untransmitted pilot]   B / 1"

Recorded in 1987. Held by SWFTA.

SPACE POLICE

An Anderson-Burr Pictures production for TVS. Untransmitted. Duration: 53 minutes.

Created by Gerry Anderson and Christopher Burr; written by Gerry Anderson and Tony Barwick; associate producer Bob Bell; produced by Gerry Anderson and Christopher Burr; directed by Tony Bell.

Shane Rimmer (Lieutenant Chuck Brogan), Catherine Chevalier (Officer Cathy Costello), Christine Glanville (Officer Tom), Lyn Beardsall (Officer Harry), Jan King (Officer Dick), Tina Werts (Officer Bats).

	Holding / Source

##.##.#### Star Laws   1" / C1S

David Healy, Jeff Harding, Kate Harper, Desiree Erasmus and Gary Martin provided voices for the puppets used.

TV Today 13.3.1986 claimed this pilot was commissioned by TVS.

Untransmitted pilot made in 1986. Re-edited into a 24-minute version and a 7-minute trailer in 1993 which led to the production of the series 'Space Precinct'.

SPEARHEAD

A Southern Television production. Transmission details are for the ATV midlands region.

Main regular credit(s):   Format by Nick McCarty; from an idea by Simon Theobalds; executive producer Lewis Rudd; produced by James Ormerod.

Main regular cast: Roy Holder (Sergeant Bilinski), Gordon Case (Private Mayhoe), Stafford Gordon (Company Sergeant Major Gilby), George Sweeney (Private Twiss), Charles Cork (Private Gadd).

SERIES 1

Duration: 52 minutes.

Main regular credit(s):   Theme music by Anthony Isaac.

Main regular cast: With Michael Billington (Colour Sergeant Jackson), Jacqueline Tong (Mary Jackson), Peter Turner (Private Adams), Lawrence Davidson (Major Taylor).

	VT Number	Holding / Source
18.07.1978 **Suspect**	1401	DB / 2"

Written by Nick McCarty; designed by John Dilly and John Shergold; directed by James Ormerod.

With Stephen Leigh, Tim Swinton, Paul Keown, Brian Anthony, Judi Lamb, Mollie Maureen, John Kearney, Peter Holt.

Made in 1976.

See also: SPEARHEAD IN HONG KONG*

SPIN-A-DISC

An ABC production. Transmission details are for the ABC midlands region. Duration: 25 minutes.

ITV version of Juke Box Jury for children.

	Holding / Source
17.06.1961	J /

Designed by Patrick Downing; produced by Philip Jones; directed by Helen Standage.

With Jimmy Young (Presenter), Alan Freeman (Guest Disc Jockey), Gloria Johnson, Keith Knight, Delia Seaborn, Melvin Sims.

SPITTING IMAGE

A Central production. made in association with Spitting Image Productions. Transmission details are for the Central region. Usual duration: 25 minutes.

Main regular credit(s):   Created by Roger Law and Peter Fluck.

SERIES 1

Main regular credit(s):   Designed by Ken Ryan and Giovanni Guarino; associate producer Richard Holloway.

Main regular cast: With Anthony Asbury (Puppeteer), Chris Barrie (Puppeteer), Kevin Bradshaw (Puppeteer), Alistair Fullarton (Puppeteer), Richard Robinson (Puppeteer), Louise Gold (Puppeteer), Steve Nallon (Puppeteer), Terry Lee (Puppeteer).

	Holding / Source
##.##.#### **[untransmitted pilot]**	DVSEQ / 1"

Held in a private collection.

Puppet Workshop Supervisor - Stephen Bendelack.

Puppets created by Luck and Flaw, based on an original lunch with Martin Lambie Nairn.

See also: BEST EVER SPITTING IMAGE* / MUST SEE TV*

SPONTANEOUS COMBUSTION

A HTV production. Transmission details are for the HTV region.

A night of live, uncensored comic improvisation. Viewers themselves will control the action, through an on-the-spot phone-in.

Cardiff Comedy Explosion.

	Holding / Source
27.07.1989	1" / 1"

SPOONER'S PATCH

A Regent Productions production for ATV. Transmission details are for the ATV/Central region. Duration: 25 minutes.

Main regular credit(s):   Written by Ray Galton and Johnny Speight; produced and directed by William G. Stewart.

Main regular cast: Peter Cleall (Police Constable Bulsover), John Lyons (Police Constable Killick).

	VT Number	Holding / Source
##.##.#### **[untransmitted pilot]**	5180/78	DB / 2"

SPRING AND AUTUMN

A Thames Television production. Transmission details are for the ATV midlands region. Duration: 25 minutes.

Main regular cast: Jimmy Jewel (Tommy Butler).

	VT Number	Holding / Source
23.10.1972	6099	D3 / 2"

Not every widower of 70 is lucky enough to have a daughter willing to provide him with a home in his declining years, and not every daughter is unlucky enough to have a father as awkward, cantankerous and mischievous as Tommy Butler.

Tommy resisted moving from the slums until the bricks began to fall about his ears. Now, with his hand luggage of a stuffed parrot and a chamberpot, he arrives at his daughter's modern highrise flat. Having left all his friends behind, he characteristically chooses a new one - 60 years his junior.

Written by Vince Powell and Harry Driver; designed by Allan Cameron; produced and directed by Stuart Allen.

With Larry Martyn (Joe Dickinson), Gaye Brown (Betty Dickinson), Gary Williams (Colin Harris), Meadows White (Wally), George Tovey (Mr Duffy), John Lyons (The Man).

SPROUT

A Thames Television production. Transmission details are for the ATV midlands region. Duration: 25 minutes.

Out of work Darwin Sprout and his flatmate, John Russell, face rent, phone and every other bill imaginable. In his desperate search for work, Sprout has already failed nine interviews on the trot. But surely the tenth one, coming up, will be the answer to all their problems? After all, his only weakness is for the truth... and women! And with John's expert advice on what and what not to say, success is
only a mere interview away . . .

Written by Anthony Matheson and Peter Tilbury; designed by Bill Palmer; produced and directed by Anthony Parker.

John Alderton (Darwin Sprout), Julian Holloway (John Russell), Geoffrey Chater (Mr Barker), Clare Sutcliffe (Emily Braithewaite), Jenny Cox (Carol).

	VT Number	Holding / Source
01.07.1974	9322	D3 / 2"

A series was commissioned, but did not go into production.

SQUARE DEAL

An LWT production. Transmission details are for the Central region. Duration: 25 minutes.

Main regular credit(s):   Written by Richard Ommanney; executive producer Marcus Plantin; produced and directed by Nic Phillips.

Main regular cast: Lise-Ann McLaughlin (Emma Barrington), Timothy Bentinck (Nigel Barrington).

	Holding / Source
##.##.#### **[untransmitted pilot]**	1" / 1"

THE SQUIRRELS

An ATV production. Transmission details are for the ATV midlands region. Duration: 25 minutes.

Main regular credit(s):   Created by Eric Chappell.

	Holding / Source
08.07.1974	J / 2"

It was a bad day for Rex when he trod on the budgerigar. Who would expect the bird to be walking across the lino instead of flying through the air? But worse awaits Rex when he arrives at the office—Fletcher the boss has discovered a £17,000 deficit . .

Written by Eric Chappell; designed by Vic Symonds; produced and directed by Shaun O'Riordan.

With Bernard Hepton (Mr Fletcher), Ken Jones (Rex), Alan David (Harry), Patsy Rowlands (Susan), Ellis Jones (Burke), Susan Tracy (Carol).

Many of the same scripts were later re-used for "Fiddlers Three".

THE STAND UP SHOW

A BBC production for BBC 1. Transmission details are for BBC 1. Usual duration: 30 minutes.

Main regular credit(s):   Executive producer Jon Plowman.

	Holding / Source
18.08.1994	DB-D3 / D3S

Produced by Claudia Lloyd; directed by Peter Howitt.

With Barry Cryer (Host), Phill Jupitus, Phil Kay, John Thomson.

See also: BBC NEW COMEDY AWARDS*

STAR CHAMBER

A Yorkshire Television production. Never intended for transmission.Duration: 25 minutes.

Game show in which a panel made up of a palmist, graphologist and astrologer attempt to identify celebrities.

Produced and directed by John Bartlett.

Kenny Everett (Host), Freddie Trueman (Star Guest), Kate Robbins (Star Guest), Madame Rosina (Palmist), Peter West (Graphologist), Jonathan Cainer (Astrologist), Rebecca Trueman (Star Witness), Martin ??? (Star Witness), Carmen Rogers (Clairvoyant).

	Holding / Source
##.##.#### **[untransmitted pilot]**	DB / 1"

Although only the pilot was made, it seems that production of a series got far enough down the line for at least one of the experts to be contracted, and paid, for a season of 13.

STAR CHOICE

A Yorkshire Television production. Untransmitted. Duration: 25 minutes.

Duggie Brown, Alvin Stardust, Nerys Hughes.

	VT Number	Holding / Source
##.##.#### **[untransmitted pilot]**	Y/1647/0001	1" / 1"

THE STAR SHOW

A Granada production. Untransmitted.

	Holding / Source
##.##.#### **[untransmitted pilot]**	DB / DBSW

STARCRUISER

A Group 3 production for CBS. Not made.

Created by Gerry Anderson and Fred Freiburger.

Planned live-action series that became an Airfix kit and Look-In cartoon strip after its rejection by the CBS network in 1976.

STARLIGHT BALLROOM

A Granada production. Transmission details are for the Granada region. Duration: 25 minutes.

Every week The Starlite Ballroom is the location for the most successful BBC radio show of its time featuring UMBERTO ROSSI with the Starlite Orchestra, The Starlite Singers, The Starlite Radio dancers, The Starlite Fountain and special guests.

Produced by Simon Albury.

Umberto Rossi.

	Production No	VT Number	Holding / Source
08.08.1983	P576/8901	OB567/PILOT	DB / 1"

Re-edited 12.09.1982.

STARS AND GARTERS

An Associated-Rediffusion production. Transmission details are for the ATV midlands region. Usual duration: 25 minutes.

Main regular performer(s): The Alan Braden Band and Quartet.

	Holding / Source
##.##.#### **[first pilot]**	J / 40

Directed by John P. Hamilton.

	Holding / Source
##.##.#### **[second pilot]**	J / 40
##.##.#### **[third pilot]**	J / 40

See also: THE NEW STARS AND GARTERS*

STARS IN A SPIN

An ITV Studios production. Untransmitted. Duration: 50 minutes.

	Holding / Source
##.##.#### **[untransmitted pilot]**	DB /

STARTING NOW

An LWT production. Untransmitted.

	Holding / Source
##.##.#### **[untransmitted pilot]**	J / 2"

STEPTOE AND SON

The companies who commissioned and produced this production are not known. Untransmitted. Duration: 25 minutes.

	Holding / Source
##.##.#### **[untransmitted pilot]**	DB / B3

1967. Held by Ray Galton and Kaleidoscope.

THE STEVE WRIGHT SHOW

A Granada production. Untransmitted. Duration: 49 minutes.

Feature on British Rail fares. Chat with Richard Madeley and Judy Finnigan in the studio. Feature on record stores. Talent Takes a holiday in the studio: this week the Rockin' Gorby singing 'Achey Breaky Heart'. Steve links up with the Fashion Gurus Bob and Jackie. Showbiz gossip - this week Madonna's book 'Sex'. Nick Wilty talks about meeting up with Bobby Brown. Steve wrestles with Mr Sumoin the studio. Feature on cashing cheques, 'Cash a Cow'. Steve chats to Jeremy Beadle in the studio. Tasmin Archer sings live in the studio - Sleeping Satellite.

Produced by Mark Wells; directed by Jonathan Glazier.

Steve Wright (Presenter), The Posse, Judy Finnigan, Richard Madeley, Rockin' Gorby, Jeremy Beadle.

	Production No	Holding / Source
##.##.#### **[untransmitted pilot]**	1/1966	J / 2"

STILL - WILLIAM

A Thames Television production. Untransmitted. Duration: 25 minutes.

Whatever happened to William Brown from the 'Just William' stories? 25 years later William has a family.

Written by Laurence Marks and Maurice Gran; based on characters created by Richmal Crompton.

Dennis Waterman (William Brown), Julian Fellowes (Hubert Lane), Henry Blofeld (Cricket Commentator).

	VT Number	Holding / Source
##.##.#### **William And The Old Barn** [untransmitted pilot]	37108	DB / 1"

Who wants to knock down the old barn? Violet Elizabeth?

There are no end credits. A caption says the opening titles are temporary as well! From circa 1986.

STILL OPEN ALL HOURS

A BBC production for BBC 1. Transmission details are for BBC 1. Duration: 30 minutes.

Written by Roy Clarke.

David Jason (Granville).

	Holding / Source
26.12.2013	HD/DB / HDC

Granville has inherited the emporium from his Uncle Arkwright and runs it with his son Leroy. But some things never change: Nurse Gladys Emmanuel and the Black Widow are still regulars.

Produced by Gareth Edwards; directed by Dewi Humphreys.

With Lynda Baron (Gladys Emmanuel), Stephanie Cole (Mrs Featherstone), Maggie Ollerenshaw (Mavis), Johnny Vegas (Wet Eric), Mark Williams (Planter's Salesman), James Baxter (Leroy), Brigit Forsyth (Madge), Kulvinder Ghir (Cyril), Sally Lindsay (Mrs Agnew), Nina Wadia (Mrs Hussein), Barry Elliot (Mr Marshall), Kathryn Hunt (Vera), Misha Timmins (Cindy), Cathy Breeze (Mrs Hemstock), Sally Womersley (Mrs Travis), Emily Fleeshman (Hayley), Nadine Mulkerrin (Ashley).

See also: OPEN ALL HOURS*

STINGRAY

An AP Films production for ITC. made in association with ATV. Transmission details are for the ATV midlands region. Duration: 25 minutes.

Main regular credit(s):   Theme music by Barry Gray and Gary Miller; music by Barry Gray; associate producer Reg Hill; produced by Gerry Anderson.

Main regular cast: Don Mason (Voice of Captain Troy Tempest and others), Robert Easton (Voice of Lieutenant George Phones Sheridan and others), Ray Barrett (Voice of Commander Sam Shore and others), Lois Maxwell (Voice of Lieutenant Atlanta Shore), David Graham (Various Voices).

	Holding / Source
06.10.1964 "The Pilot"	DB / C3

Troy and Phones are sent to investigate the destruction of a WSP submarine. They are soon captured by an enemy submarine in the form of a gigantic fish, which takes them to the underwater city Titanica. There, they meet Titan for the first time.

Written by Gerry Anderson and Sylvia Anderson; directed by Alan Pattillo.

STOMPING ON THE CAT

An LWT production for Channel 4. Transmission details are for Channel 4. Duration: 25 minutes.

Designed by Alison Humphries; produced and directed by Paul Jackson.

Chris Barrie, The Oblivion Boys, The Dialtones, Simon Fanshawe, John Hegley, Paul Martin, Pauline Melville.

	Holding / Source
04.01.1984	D2 / 1"

STORYBOARD

A Thames Television production. Transmission details are for the Central region. Duration: 50 minutes.

Executive producer Lloyd Shirley.

SERIES 1

	VT Number	Holding / Source
26.07.1983 **Inspector Ghote Moves In**	28624	1" / 1"

Written by H. R. F. Keating; consultant George Markstein; produced by John Bryce; directed by Peter Duguid.

With Alfred Burke (Colonel Bressingham), Sam Dastor (Inspector Ghote), Irene Worth (Mrs Bressingham), Zohra Segal (Ayah), Barbara Hicks (Nurse), Tony Doyle (Harold Hellford), Patrick Durkin (Detective Sergeant Phillips), Maev Alexander (Jo).

	VT Number	Holding / Source
02.08.1983 **Judgement Day**	28623	1" / 1"

Written by James Doran; produced by Michael Chapman; directed by Christopher Hodson.

With Carol Royle (Jane Alexander), Tony Steedman (Augustus Rook), Leslie Schofield (John Lloyd), John Normington (Walter Warley), David Beames (Detective Sergeant Gray), Arthur Cox (Inspector Kirby), Leo Dolan (Hopkins).

	VT Number	Holding / Source
09.08.1983 **Secrets**	28626	1" / 1"

Written by Robert Muller; produced by Michael Chapman; directed by Peter Sasdy.

With John Castle (Miles Longstreet), Barbara Kellerman (Eve Hanning), Anna Palk (Sally Longstreet), Holly De Jong (Tina Collings), Clifford Rose (DAD), Gwen Taylor (Angie Powers), Clive Merrison (Peter Hanning), David Langton (Sir Robert Grayne).

16.08.1983 **Woodentop**   28625   D3 / 1"

Written by Geoff McQueen; produced by Michael Chapman; directed by Peter Cregeen.

With Robert Pugh (Detective Inspector Galloway), Mark Wingett (Police Constable Jimmy Carver), Trudie Goodwin (Woman Police Constable June Ackland), Colin Blumenau (Police Constable Morgan), Peter Dean (Sergeant Wilding), Jon Croft (Inspector Deeping), Paul McKenzie (Winston Summers), Gary Hailes (Reg Taylor), Colin McCormack (George Taylor), Gary Olsen (Police Constable Litten), Chris Jenkinson (Duty Sergeant), Richard Huw (Duty Police Constable), Dawn Perllman (First Neighbour), Maryann Turner (Second Neighbour), Derek Parkes (Caretaker), Larry Dann (Policeman).

23.08.1983 **The Traitor**   28627   1" / 1"

Written by George Markstein; production designer David Ferris; produced by Michael Chapman; directed by Christopher Hodson.

With Alec McCowen (Palfrey), Tim Pigott-Smith (Fawkes), Antony Brown (Kilpeck), Gary Watson (Gorsky), Keith Edwards (American), Georgine Anderson (Mrs Rennie), Ian Barritt (Jordan), Michael Sheard (Dorian), David Gillies (Channing), John Quarmby (Slade), Simon Watkins (Commissionaire).

30.08.1983 **Lytton's Diary**   28628   1" / 1"

Written by Ray Connolly; from an idea by Peter Bowles and Philip Broadley; produced by Michael Chapman; directed by Brian Parker.

With Peter Bowles (Neville Lytton), Frances Tomelty (Laura Grey), Ralph Bates (Jonathan Burridge), Iain Cuthbertson (Editor), Naomi Buch (Suzie), John Michie (David Armstrong), Abigail Cruttenden (Emma), Jonny Lee Miller (Christopher).

SERIES 2

Main regular credit(s):   Produced by Peter Duguid.

	VT Number	Holding / Source

20.08.1985 **King And Castle**   32976   1" / 1"

Written by Ian Kennedy Martin; directed by Richard Bramall.

With Derek Martin (Detective Sergeant King), Nigel Planer (David Castle), Martin Fisk (Detective Sergeant Enright), James Lister (Detective Sergeant Causton), John Challis (Billy Cato), Eric Mason (Mr Grant), Wensley Pithey (Vicar), Peter Cellier (Herbert Parrish QC).

27.08.1985 **Ladies In Charge**   32977   1" / 1"

Adapted by Alfred Shaughnessy; based on a book by Kate Herbert-Hunting; directed by John Davies.

With Carol Royle (Diana Granville), Julia Hills (Babs Palmer), Amanda Root (Polly Swift), Rosemary Williams (Alice Manders), Orlando Wells (Tommy Manders), Terrence Hardiman (Charles Carmichael), Raymond Francis (Jack Carmichael).

17.02.1986 **Thank You, Miss Jones**   32978   1" / 1"

Written by Scott Forbes; directed by Mervyn Cumming.

With Susie Blake (Miss Susan Jones), Linda Marlowe (Yvonne Cavaye), Ian McCurrach (Roger), Patrick Barlow (Mr Manning), Virginia Denham (Detective Sergeant Wicks), Michael Hughes (Detective Chief Inspector Haynes), Maggie Ollerenshaw (Mrs Phelps).

SERIES 3

	Production No	VT Number	Holding / Source

09.05.1989 **Making News**   47614   1" / 1"

Written by Michael Aitkens; produced by Robert Banks Stewart; directed by Geoffrey Sax.

With Tom Cotcher (Eddie), Nichola McAuliffe (Carrie), Bill Nighy (Sam), Jack Klaff (Hendry), Peter Settelen (Roger), Charlotte Attenborough (Lucy), Paul Darrow (George), Celia Imrie (Sylvia), David Baron (Sir Ian Fenton), Ian Bleasdale (Cameraman), Tony Osoba (Soundman), Susan Kyd (Jill), Jeremy Nicholas (Pelham), Deborah Grant (Greta), Joseph Blatchley (Larry), Michael Aitkens (Foreign Office Mole), Andrew Hawkins (Fortescue), Terence Alexander (Himself), Peter Sands (Fillary), George Little (Deaf Man), Pavel Douglas (Lawyer), Angus Banks Stewart (Studio Director), Stephen Churchett (Weatherman), Dieter Bratsch (Neidermeyer), Stephen Tiller (Washington Reporter), Kate O'Connell (Editor), Colin Dudley (Tramp), Susan Graham (Secretary), Robert Lister (Lucy's Cameraman).

16.05.1989 **Snakes And Ladders**   47616   1" / 1"

Written by Jeremy Burnham; produced by Robert Banks Stewart; directed by Baz Taylor.

With Peter Blake (Max), Bruce Payne (Gerald), Dermot Crowley (Rowlands), Alphonsia Emmanuel (Anne), Judi Trott (Amy), Doran Godwin (Stella), Liz Crowther (Paula), Duncan Preston (Thornton), John Bluthal (Van Der Moeuwe), Victoria Wicks (Virginia), Richard Moore (Andrews), Jonathan Linsley (Security Man), Jack Carr (Bill), John Scholes (First Director), Roger Hammond (Second Director), Barrie Cookson (Sir Anthony), Michael Mascoll (Bellboy), Tommy Eytle (Servant), Sally St David (Lois), Peter Symonds (Professor), John Forgeham (McPhee), Alan Hunter (Roger), Carol Leader (Peggy), Bruce McGuire (Phillips), Francesca Hall (Sandra), Michael Baish (Waiter).

23.05.1989 **A Question Of Commitment**   D.4191   47615   1"|c / 1"

Written by Philip Broadley; designed by Robin Parker; produced by Michael Chapman; directed by Gareth Davies.

With Clive Wood (Blair), Donald Burton (Cromer), Amanda Elwes (Caroline Carshalton), Tim Wylton (John Backman), Jeffrey Chiswick (Pavlicek), Charles Kay (Spender), Carolyn Pickles (Clare), Eric Dodson (George), Dorothea Phillips (Mary), Penny Brownjohn (Alice), Christine Ellerbeck (Janet), Helen Horton (American Lady), Willoughby Gray (Sir John), Matthew Radford (Waiter (Jean-Paul)).

30.05.1989 **Hunted Down**   47617   1" / 1"

Adapted by Hugh Leonard; based on a story by Charles Dickens; produced by Michael Chapman; directed by Michael Simpson.

With Alec McCowen (Sampson), Stephen Moore (Skipton), Nicholas Gecks (Alfred Beckwith / Charles Meltham), Polly Walker (Margaret Niner), Clive Swift (Hewes), John Southworth (Adams), Richard Beale (Krane), Jo Abercrombie (Woman), Jim Holmes (Man), Philip Dunbar (Vicar), Maggie McCarthy (Landlady).

See also: THE BILL* / KING AND CASTLE* / LADIES IN CHARGE* / LYTTON'S DIARY* / MAKING NEWS* / MR. PALFREY OF WESTMINSTER*

THE STORY-SHOP

Commissioned by Clapham Park Studios. Untransmitted.

Produced by Honoria Plesch; directed by Peter Zadek.

Bernadette O'Farrell.

	Holding / Source

##.##.#### **[untransmitted 1958 TV pilot]**   J / B3

THE STORYTELLER

A TVS production for Channel 4. Transmission details are for Channel 4. Duration: 24 minutes.

Adapted by Anthony Minghella; based on the stories of Folk Artists; music by Rachel Portman; associate producer Martin G. Baker; executive producer Jim Henson.

John Hurt (The Storyteller), Brian Henson (Voice of Storyteller's Dog).

	VT Number	Holding / Source
12.06.1988 **Hans My Hedgehog**	17135	DB / V1

Produced by Mark Shivas; directed by Steve Barron.

With Eric Richard (Farmer), Maggie Wilkinson (Farmer's Wife), David Swift (King), Helen Lindsay (Queen), Abigail Cruttenden (Princess), Jason Carter (Man), Robin Summers (Jailer), Ailsa Berk (Grovelhog).

See also: THE STORYTELLER - GREEK MYTHS*

STRAMASH

A BBC Scotland production for BBC 1. Transmission details are for Various BBC Channels. Duration: 30 minutes.

Main regular performer(s): The Stramashers, The Lindolla Movers.

	Holding / Source
##.##.#### **[untransmitted pilot]**	J / 40

Produced and directed by David Bell.

Recorded in August 1965.

The Stramashers were five female dancers, the Lindolla Movers were walk-ons!

STRANGE

A Big Bear Films production for BBC 1. Transmission details are for BBC 1. Duration: 60 minutes.

John Strange is a defrocked priest with a deep interest in the occult.

Main regular credit(s):   Written by Andrew Marshall; executive producers Sophie Clarke-Jervoise and Andrew Marshall; produced by Marcus Mortimer.

Main regular cast: Richard Coyle (John Strange), Ian Richardson (Canon Black), Samantha Janus (Nurse Jude Atkins), Timmy Lang (Kevin), William Tomlin (Joey).

	Holding / Source
09.03.2002	DB / V1SW

Odd things start happening in a hospital ward. An elderly clergyman is admitted, barely able to speak. He communicates enigmatically through Scrabble tiles, spelling out the word "Azar — something that resonates with the demon-hunting Strange.

Directed by Joe Ahearne.

With Alastair Mackenzie, Abi Eniola, Bryan Dick, Samuel Barnett, Peter Copley, John Delaney, Charles Simon, Richard Manson, Kerry Elkins.

STRICTLY COME DANCING

A BBC production for BBC 1. Transmission details are for BBC 1. Duration varies - see below for details.

Main regular credit(s):   Created by Fenia Vardanis; theme music by Dan McGrath and Josh Phillips.

	Holding / Source
##.##.#### **[untransmitted pilot]**	DB / DBSW

See also: STRICTLY AFRICAN DANCING* / STRICTLY COME DANCING CHRISTMAS SPECIAL*

STRICTLY FOR LAUGHS

An ABC production. Transmission details are for the ABC midlands region. Duration: 25 minutes.

Members of the public try to tell jokes better than the professionals.

Main regular credit(s):   Programme associate Len Marten; based on an idea by Terry Hall; produced by Pat Johns.

Main regular cast: Kenneth Horne (Chairman), June Murdoch.

	Holding / Source
##.##.#### **[untransmitted pilot]**	J / 40

Recorded in Birmingham on 11th June 1967.

Seems to have been shown in the Midlands and Border only! Dates and cast (apart from 24/09) from The Times.

STRICTLY PERSONAL

An LWT production. Untransmitted. Duration: 25 minutes.

Studio-based show where three presenters follow up on small ads from newspapers, involving the studio audience along the way.

Produced by Nina Donaldson; directed by Simon Staffurth.

Aonghus McAnally, Philippa Forrester, Ainsley Harriott.

	Production No	VT Number	Holding / Source
##.##.#### **[untransmitted pilot]**	LWT0000101805	9L/93346	DB / D2S

Made in 1996.

STRIKE IT RICH

A Lamplight Film Productions production for Channel 4. Untransmitted.

Contestants buy and sell shares and make takeover bids for companies.

Devised by Andrew Wood; theme music by Martin Lee; produced by Andrew Wood.

Dave Ismay (Host).

	Holding / Source
##.##.#### **[untransmitted pilot]**	J / 1"

Recorded on 1st February 1985.

See also: THE STOCKS AND SHARES SHOW*

STRUGGLE

An LWT production for Channel 4. Transmission details are for Channel 4.

Main regular credit(s):   Written by Peter Jenkins; script editor Bernard McKenna; designed by Rae George; produced and directed by Graham Evans.

Main regular cast: Tim Pigott-Smith (Steve), Ray Smith (Sir Bert), Paul Rogers (Reg), Clare Clifford (Caroline).

Cast: With Jack Shepherd (Steve), David Kelly (Reg), Barry Stanton (Sir Bert), David Neville (Robin), Derek Thompson (Alan), Bernard Hill (Stanley).

	Production No	Holding / Source
##.##.#### **One Step Forward Two Steps Back**	79017	D2 / 2"

Duration: 23 minutes.

Recorded 10.09.82. The pilot does not feature any location filming, just captions where the film sequences would be inserted. It has no end credits.

STUDIO SERVICE

A BBC production. Untransmitted.

	VT Number	Holding / Source
##.##.#### **[Dry Run No.4 - pilot]**	16/P/9182	J /

Recorded 28th August 1960.

STUFF THE WEEK

An LWT production. Transmission details are for the Central region. Duration: 25 minutes.

Main regular credit(s):   Written by Dan Gaster, Will Ing, Paul Powell and Ben Silburn; executive producer Humphrey Barclay; produced by Gareth Edwards.

Main regular cast: Dan Gaster, Will Ing, Paul Powell, Ben Silburn.

	Holding / Source
26.09.1997	DB / DBS

Directed by Jonathan Glazier and Richard Bracewell.

STUFF THE WHITE RABBIT

A Granada production. Transmission details are for the Granada region. Duration: 29 minutes.

Magic series.

Main regular credit(s):   Devised by Peter Kessler; consultants Anthony Owen and Dynamic FX; executive producer Andy Harries; produced by Peter Kessler; directed by David G. Croft.

Main regular performer(s): John Lenahan, Jerry Sadowitz.

	Production No	Holding / Source
28.11.1994	1/2168/1	D2 / D2S

JOHN LENAHAN presents a magic show, including some spoof tricks such as making cooling towers disappear (ie they're demolished). JERRY SADOWITZ performs card tricks, DAVID WILLIAMSON plays with people in the audience, RICHARD MCDOUGALL does a mime and a spoof trick to music. They all come back to do more slots.

With David Williamson, Richard McDougall.

SUMMER ARMCHAIR THEATRE REPLACEMENT PILOTS

A Towers of London Productions production for ABC. Untransmitted. Duration: 50 minutes.

Produced by Harry Alan Towers.

	Holding / Source
##.##.#### **The Saint**	J / FNK

Based on books by Leslie Charteris.

In May 1959 ABC commissioned Towers of London to make four pilots to show during August when Summer Armchair Theatre would be rested. The pilots were due to be made in June-July. Three of these pilots were made and shown by Summer Armchair Theatre. Whether The Saint was made is unclear, it may have become 'Invitation to Murder' when Towers was unable to secure the rights.

SUPERCAR

Alternative/Working Title(s): MIKE MERCURY AND THE SUPER CAR

An AP Films production for ITC. made in association with ATV. Transmission details are for the ATV midlands region. Duration: 24 minutes.

Main regular credit(s):	From an idea by Gerry Anderson and Reg Hill; theme music by The Mike Sammes Singers; music by Barry Gray; produced by Gerry Anderson.
Main regular cast:	Graydon Gould (Voice of Mike Mercury), David Graham (Voice of Doctor Horatio Beaker), Sylvia Anderson [as Sylvia Thamm] (Voice of Jimmy Gibson).

	Holding / Source
14.09.1961 **Rescue**	DB / B3

Written by Martin Woodhouse and Hugh Woodhouse; directed by David Elliott.

With George Murcell (Voice of Professor Rudolph Popkiss).

The opening titles and some sequences have been colourised and exist on Betacam.

SUPERSONIC

An LWT production. Transmission details are for ITV. Usual duration: 25 minutes.

Main regular credit(s):   Produced and directed by Mike Mansfield.

Transmission details are for the London Weekend Television region.

	Production No	Holding / Source
01.03.1975	9C/05614	D2 / 2"

With Status Quo, Rod Stewart, Maggie Bell, The Bay City Rollers, Gary Glitter, Alvin Stardust, Sunny, Gilbert O'Sullivan.

Entries marked thus - ° - look to have been recorded - possibly for inclusion in another edition - but not included in the final edit.

SUPPLY AND DEMAND

A Lynda La Plante (LLP) Productions production for Granada. Transmission details are for the Central region. Duration varies - see below for details.

Ethnically-mixed police undercover force operating in the world of drugs.

	Holding / Source
05.02.1997	DB / V1S

Duration: 100 minutes.

Written by Lynda La Plante; produced by Lynda La Plante; directed by Peter MacDonald.

With Eamonn Walker (Jake Brown), Ade Sapara (Carl Harrington), Freddie Starr (Lance Izzard), Juliet Aubrey (Chomsky), Anthony Higgins (Lloyd St. John), Benedict Wong (Frankie Li), Ramon Tikaram (Irwin), Jonathan Phillips (Teller), Colin McCormack (Superintendent Harper), Fintan McKeown (Detective Chief Inspector Smith), Ron Donachie (Superintendent Brent), Gary Francis Hope (Eric), Fiona Ramsay (Julia Summers), Carl Cieka (Ewan Reece), David Kennedy (Michael Carter), Andreas Wisniewski (John Howard), Ariyon Bakare (Willy Boy), Tony Armatrading (Scotty), Femi Elufowoju Jr (Crack Head), Shango Baku (Crack Head), Sasha Alexander (Jazzy), Mike Sarne (Bruce), Sean O'Callaghan (Alex), David Verrey (Ronny), Danny Midwinter (Barry).

SURPRISE SURPRISE

An LWT production. Transmission details are for the Central region. Duration varies - see below for details.

Main regular performer(s): Cilla Black (Presenter).

	VT Number	Holding / Source
##.##.#### [untransmitted pilot]	90792	D2 / 1"
Duration: 51 minutes.		
06.02.1984	90922	D2 / 1"
Duration: 52 minutes.		

CILLA BLACK stars in the first of six programmes in a brand new family entertainment series in which the unexpected is always just around the corner. You'll be surprised at who Cilla meets and what she finds; and her right-hand man CHRISTOPHER BIGGINS, has some strange encounters of the unpredictable kind, too. Unsung heroes? Long-lost pals? Who knows who will get the Surprise Surprise! this week? Plus a chance for viewers at home to join the studio audience in the Phone Game.

With Christopher Biggins.

SWAPPING

A BBC production. Untransmitted. Duration: 30 minutes.

Written by Angela Ince and Shirley Lowe; costume Christian Dyall; make-up Pauline Cox; designed by Bryan Ellis; production manager Gavin Clark; produced and directed by Sue Bysh.

James Faulkner (Antony Forester-Jones), Alison Fiske (Ann Forrester-Jones), Sharon Maughan (Felicia Harman), Bob Sherman (Donald Harman), Debbie Paul, Julie Selwood, Rupert Degas, Colette Gleeson, Robin Lermitte, Carole Mowlam, Richenda Carey, Beryl Cooke, Carol Gillies, Heather Tobias, Katharine Page, Louisa Janes, Caroline Lee Johnson, Frank Coda.

	Production No	VT Number	Holding / Source
##.##.#### [untransmitted 1989 pilot]	CK150T	T0130917	DB / 1"

SWEET AND SOUR

An LWT production. Not made.

Written by Ken Hoare.

Mentioned in an article in The Stage 17.02.1977 about new LWT sitcoms. Other programmes mentioned were CLIP JOINT and the as yet unnamed MIND YOUR LANGUAGE.

SWEET CHARITY

A the Comedy Unit production for ITV 1. Transmission details are for the Central region. Duration: 25 minutes.

A couple of ladies run a charity shop. Will the police catch the persistent handbag snatcher bothering Agnes?

Written by Donald McLeary; script editor Niall Clark; produced by Colin Gilbert; directed by Michael Hines.

Thelma Barlow (Jan), Anne Reid (Agnes), James Ryland (Dan), Jay Manley (Tony).

	Holding / Source
07.05.2002	DB / DBSW

Recorded July 2001.

SWEET LIFE

A Granada production. Transmission details are for the Granada region. Duration: 25 minutes.

Series based around Victor, a gay hairdresser, and his beautiful trainee assistant.

Written by Adele Rose.

	Production No	Holding / Source
##.##.#### [untransmitted pilot]	P801/1	DV / 1"

Kaleidoscope hold a VHS master of this untx comedy pilot. The digibeta is apparently lost and the library are trying to trace it.

SWEET 'N' SOUR

A Baby Cow Productions production for BBC 3. Transmission details are for BBC 3. Duration: 27 minutes.

Comedy sketch show predominantly written by and starring British Chinese performers.

Additional material by Mirren Delaney and Robert Mills; associate producers Tony Dow and Paul Hyu; executive producers Mark Freeland, Henry Normal and Ted Dowd; produced and directed by Neil MacLennan.

Paul Hyu, Lobo Chan, Su Looi, Paul Chan, Ria Lina, Karen Taylor, Michelle Lee, Matthew Wilkinson.

	Holding / Source
23.03.2004	DB / DBSWF

SWEET SIXTEEN

A BBC production for BBC 1. Transmission details are for BBC 1.

Main regular credit(s):   Written by Douglas Watkinson; produced and directed by Gareth Gwenlan.

Main regular cast: Penelope Keith (Helen Walker).

	Production No	Holding / Source
##.##.#### [studio recording of untransmitted1983 pilot]	LLCF101X	DB / 1"

Duration: 67 minutes.

Costume Dorinda Rea; make-up Frances Needham; music by Ronnie Hazlehurst; designed by Gerry Scott and Jo Day; production team Olivia Cripps and Martin Dennis; associate producer John B. Hobbs; production manager Bill Ersser; produced and directed by Gareth Gwenlan.

With Peter Settelen (Peter Morgan), Michael Grady (Doctor Ballantine), David Neville (Tony Hartshorn), Joan Blackham (Jane), Glynn Edwards (Mr Barnicoat).

SWEETHEARTS

An Anglia production. Transmission details are for the Anglia region. Duration: 25 minutes.

Three couples tell Larry the story of how they met. Only one couple is genuine. The genuine couple won a weekend in Paris, the fakes received a candlelit dinner.

Main regular credit(s):   Devised by Terry Mardell and David Moore; theme music by Ed Welch.

Main regular performer(s): Larry Grayson (Host).

	Holding / Source
##.##.#### [untransmitted pilot]	J / 1"

Produced and directed by Peter Townley.

SWINGS AND ROUNDABOUTS

An Ulster Schools production for Channel 4. Transmission details are for the Ulster Televison region. Duration: 25 minutes.

Schools series featuring Jane Cassidy and a somewhat sinister puppet called Barney.

Jane Cassidy (Presenter).

	Holding / Source
##.##.#### [untransmitted 1986 pilot] Barney Goes Fishing	UM /

Note: It's easy to see why the pilot was never transmitted: while Barney was ultimately a reasonably elaborate puppet, he is a mere sock puppet in the pilot. In addition, the pilot borrowed footage liberally from an episode of Let's Look At Ulster called Fishing (1977), meaning that it was a decade out of date in some respects.

SWITCH

A BBC production for BBC 2. Transmission details are for BBC 2.

	Holding / Source
15.12.2001 [See Hear On Saturday]	DB / DBSW

Shown as part of the See Hear strand for hearing-impaired people.

THE SYD LAWRENCE BAND SHOW

A Yorkshire Television production. Transmission details are for the Yorkshire Television region. Duration: 25 minutes.

Music directed by Syd Lawrence; designed by Ian McCrow; produced by John Duncan; directed by David Mallet.

Syd Lawrence and his Orchestra, Kevin Kent, The Skylarks, Les Dawson.

	Holding / Source
31.12.1970	DB / 62

SYKES

A BBC production for BBC 1. Transmission details are for BBC 1. Duration: 30 minutes.

Main regular cast: Eric Sykes (Eric), Hattie Jacques (Hattie).

SERIES 10

Transmission details are for BBC 1.

Main regular credit(s):   Written by Eric Sykes; music by Ken Jones; executive producer Dennis Main Wilson; produced and directed by Roger Race.

Main regular cast: With Richard Wattis (Mr Brown).

	Production No	VT Number	Holding / Source
##.##.#### **Ankle**	1142/3021	VTC/6HT/75675	DB / 2"

Designed by Colin Green.

With No guest cast.

"The South Bank Show: Eric Sykes", LWT, 50 mins. Tx:18.09.2005. Directed and produced by Aurora Gunn. With Ken Dodd, Michael Palin and Jimmy Tarbuck.

TABLE TALK

A BBC production. Transmission details are for BBC.

Monday lunchtime programme.

	VT Number	Holding / Source
##.##.#### **Mainly For Women [untransmitted pilot]**	16/P/12532	J /

Recorded 14th August 1961.

TAKE MY WIFE

A Granada production. Transmission details are for the ATV midlands region. Duration: 25 minutes.

Main regular credit(s):   Written by Anthony Couch; music by Alan Parker; designed by Steve Fineren; produced by John G. Temple; directed by Gordon Flemyng.

Main regular cast: Duggie Brown (Harvey Hall), Victor Spinetti (Maurice Watkins), Elisabeth Sladen (Josie Hall), Joan Benham (Mabel Norrington).

	Production No	Holding / Source
##.##.#### **[untransmitted pilot]**	P935/8901	J / 2"

TAKE ONE PLUS ONE

A Take One Productions production. Untransmitted.

Produced by Steve Turner.

Yes, Stephen Stills.

##.##.#### **[untransmitted pilot]**

According to 22nd May 1971 NME this music pilot was similar in style to 'Colour Me Pop' and had already been bought by Australia!

TAKE THE STAGE

A Granada production. Transmission details are for the Granada region. Usual duration: 25 minutes.

	Production No	Holding / Source
##.##.#### **[untransmitted pilot]**	P1064/8801	1" / 2"

With Michael Hordern (Host), Eleanor Bron, Robert Lindsay, Trevor Peacock.

	Production No	Holding / Source
##.##.#### **Royal Exchange Theatre, Manchester v The Everyman Theatre, Liverpool**	1/1064/8801	DB / 2"

Directed by Peter Walker.

With Michael Hordern (Chairman), Trevor Peacock (Royal Exchange), Robert Lindsay (Royal Exchange), Eleanor Bron (Royal Exchange), Jonathan Barlow (Everyman), Andy Rashleigh (Everyman), Eithne Hannigan (Everyman).

TAKE TWO

A BBC production for BBC 1. Transmission details are for BBC 1.

	Holding / Source
07.08.1981 **[untransmitted pilot]**	DB-D3 / 2"

Described by Frances Whitaker as "the son of Ask Aspel".

TALES OF FRANKENSTEIN

A Hammer Films production. made in association with Columbia Pictures. Untransmitted. Duration: 25 minutes.

Frankenstein creates a monster, but the humanity of the creature leads it to commit suicide.

Written by Catherine Kutter and Henry Kutter; based on a story by Curt Siodmak; associate producer Curt Siodmak; produced by Michael Carreras; directed by Curt Siodmak.

Anton Diffring (Baron Von Frankenstein).

	Holding / Source
##.##.#### **The Face In The Tombstone Mirror [untransmitted pilot]**	B3 / B3

Recorded in 1957.

Held in the USA. The lack of a sponsor for the pilot meant the series was never made.

THE TALES OF SIR WAGALOT

A David Henley and Associates production. Untransmitted. Duration: 15 minutes.

Devised by Dick Sharples and Gerald Kelsey.

	Holding / Source
##.##.#### **[untransmitted pilot]**	J /

Written by Dick Sharples and Gerald Kelsey.

According to The Stage (15.12.1960) this was made in 'Visimotion' – an animation process involving magnets. The eponymous character was a Canine Knight.

TALES OF THE UNEXPECTED

An Anglia production. Transmission details are for the ATV/Central region. Duration: 25 minutes.

SERIES 1

Transmission details are for the ATV midlands region.

Main regular credit(s):   Music by Ron Grainer; executive producer John Woolf; produced by John Rosenberg.

	Holding / Source
	1" / C1

24.03.1979 Man From The South

The flamboyant stranger (JOSE FERRER) goads a young sailor (MICHAEL ONTKEAN) into taking a frightening bet while on holiday in Jamaica. The stakes are high. He could win an expensive car or lose a finger. What will be the outcome of this gruesome gamble, and who is the mysterious woman (KATY JURADO) with a macabre secret?

Adapted by Kevin Goldstein-Jackson; based on a story by Roald Dahl; associate producer Kevin Goldstein-Jackson; directed by Michael Tuchner.

With José Ferrer (Carlos), Katy Jurado (Woman), Michael Ontkean (Tommy), Cyril Luckham (Rawlsden), Pamela Stephenson (Cathy), Angela Malcolm (Maid).

12.05.1979 A Dip In The Pool   1" / C1

A tourist (JACK WESTON) on his way home from Europe on a trans-Atlantic liner. He stakes it all on one last desperate gamble in the auction pool, betting how far the ship will travel by noon the following day. But his plan to scoop the jackpot looks doomed when there is a sudden change in the weather. Somehow he must slow the ship down......

Adapted by Ronald Harwood; associate producer Kevin Goldstein-Jackson; directed by Michael Tuchner.

With Jack Weston (William Botibol), Gladys Spencer (Sylvia), Don Fellows (Renshaw), David Harries (Purser), Jana Shelden (Mrs Renshaw), Michael Troughton (Steward), David Healy (Auctioneer), Paula Tilbrook (Maggie), Bill Reimbold (Bidder), Elaine Ives-Cameron (Woman Bidder), Ken Buckle (Sailor).

The two pilot films were recorded Summer 1977.

TALKABOUT

A BBC Schools production for BBC 1 Schools. Transmission details are for BBC 1.

For 5-7 year olds. Stories to stimulate oral development.

	Holding / Source
	DB-D3 / 2"

11.05.1979 The King's Hiccups

Duration: 24 minutes.

Introduced by Jill Shilling; produced by Moyra Gambleton.

TARBUCK LATE

A Talbot Television production for LWT. Transmission details are for the London Weekend Television region.

Main regular performer(s): Jimmy Tarbuck (Host).

	Production No	Holding / Source
01.07.1994	9L/93029	D2 / D2S

Duration: 51 minutes.

Written by Mark Leigh, Mike Lepine and Patrick Stoddart; produced by John Kaye Cooper; directed by Chris Ryder.

With Kate Hoey, David Mellor, Rory McGrath, Lawrie McMenamie, Sean Meo, Paulette Ivory.

TARBUCK'S LUCK

A BBC production for BBC 1. Transmission details are for BBC 1.

Main regular credit(s):   Written by Mike Craig, Lawrie Kinsley and Ron McDonnell.

Main regular cast: Jimmy Tarbuck (Host).

	Holding / Source
29.05.1970	J / 2"

Duration: 50 minutes.

Additional material by Austin Steele and Bob Hedley; music by Ronnie Hazlehurst; choreography by Lionel Blair; designed by John Burrowes; produced by Freddie Carpenter and Peter Whitmore; directed by Freddie Carpenter and Peter Whitmore.

With Anita Harris, Carol Raye, Clovissa Newcombe, Carolyn Seymour, Lucille Gaye, Katherine Kessey, Jackie Poole, Renée Corbé.

TARRANT BYTES BACK

Alternative/Working Title(s): TARRANT PILOT 93

An LWT production. Untransmitted.

Studio-based show in which Chris Tarrant looks at daft and unusual inventions, helped by members of the studio audience. Inventions include (for example) Unsinkable Soap, and a Relaxation Computer Game.

Produced by Mark Tinkler; directed by Alasdair MacMillan.

Chris Tarrant (Host).

	Production No	VT Number	Holding / Source
##.##.#### [untransmitted pilot]	9L/92760	LWT0000086428	D2 / D2S

Recorded 1993.

Studio-based show in which Chris Tarrant looks at daft and unusual inventions, helped by members of the studio audience. Inventions include (for example) Unsinkable Soap, and a Relaxation Computer Game.

TAYLOR MADE

A HTV production. Transmission details are for the HTV region. Duration: 30 minutes.

Main regular performer(s): Alan Taylor (Host).

		Holding / Source
20.06.1968		J /

TEENAGE KICKS

A Phil McIntyre Television production for ITV 1. Transmission details are for the Central region. Duration: 25 minutes.

The original radio series was broadcast on BBC Radio 2, recorded in The Drill Hall in late 2006. Originally a pilot was to be made for BBC Two. However, ITV took control of the project and commissioned eight episodes. Paul Jackson, ITV's director of entertainment and comedy said, "From the moment I arrived in this job I have made it my mission to bring quality sitcom back to ITV, this project absolutely does that and I'm very excited about having Ade back on our screens."

A pilot version of the first episode was shot in 2007 with the notable difference of Ben Elton in the role Bryan, the same role he had played in the original radio version. Elton was replaced by Mark Arden in the transmitted version and the following season for reasons unknown.

Main regular credit(s):   Written by Adrian Edmondson and Nigel Smith; script supervisor Valerie Letley; theme music by Simon Brint; designed by Harry Banks; executive producers Phil McIntyre and Lucy Ansbro; produced by Joan Schneider; directed by Dewi Humphreys.

Main regular cast: Adrian Edmondson (Vernon), Ed Coleman (Max), Laura Aikman (Milly), Jonathan Chan Pensley (David).

		Holding / Source
##.##.#### [untransmitted pilot] Sex		J / DBSW

With Ben Elton (Bryan).

Main regular cast: With Mark Arden (Bryan).

	VT Number	Holding / Source
28.03.2008 **Sex**	368154	DB / DBSW

With Abigail Cruttenden.

THE TELEVISION PROGRAMME

A Westward Television production. Transmission details are for the Thames Television region. Duration: 25 minutes.

Main regular credit(s):   Presented by Peter Fiddick; written by Peter Fiddick.

SERIES 1

Main regular credit(s):   Produced by Michael Reinhold; directed by David R. Scott.

	Holding / Source
29.02.1980 **Style**	J / 2"

Research Tom Goodison.

With Piers Haggard.

TELEVISION WORKSHOP

A Tyne Tees Television production. Transmission details are for the Tyne Tees region. Duration: 25 minutes.

Pilots included a folk series and a children's show.

	Holding / Source
01.11.1968 **Protest**	J /
08.11.1968	J /
15.11.1968	J /
22.11.1968	J /
29.11.1968 **Moloney's Place**	J /

In a pub setting a light-hearted and irreverent look at British institutions.

With Peter Moloney.

The pilot for Moloney's Place aired at 4pm, but the series went out at 10.30pm.

06.12.1968	J /
13.12.1968	J /
20.12.1968	J /
27.12.1968	J /

See also: MOLONEY'S PLACE*

THE TEN SHOW

An Avalon Productions production for BBC 2. Untransmitted.

Frank Skinner (Host), Adrian Chiles (Host).

	Holding / Source
##.##.#### [untransmitted pilot]	HD/DB / HDC

Late night version of The One Show recorded 7.11.09 after two run-throughs.

THANK GOD YOU'RE HERE

A Talkback Thames production for ITV 1. Transmission details are for the Central region. Duration: 48 minutes.

Main regular credit(s):	Written by John Irwin, Paul Merton and Victoria Payne; script supervisor Helena Taylor; theme music by Media Industry Audio; designed by Dominic Tolfts; assistant producer Oli Head; production executive Ian Liddington; executive producer Dave Morley; head of production Darina Healy; production manager Isobel Oram; series producer Victoria Payne; produced by Leon Wilson; directed by Steve Smith.
Main regular cast:	Paul Merton (Host), Tara Flynn, Cicely Giddings, Nick Haverson, Rufus Jones, Richard Katz, Dan Mersh, Aimee Parkes.

Holding / Source

##.##.#### **[untransmitted pilot]**   DB / DBSW

With Clive Anderson, Phil Nichol, Kirsten O'Brien, John Thomson.

The four (or first four) cast names against each edition are the contestants, any further names are additional cast members in the scenarios.

'THANKS A MILLION'

A Central production. Transmission details are for the Central region. Duration: 25 minutes.

Associate producer Kathy Nelson; produced and directed by Bob Cousins.

Leslie Crowther, Bob Warman, Jim Bowen, Jimmy Cricket, Michael Elphick, John Caine, Andy Craig, Bob Hall, Bill Tidy.

Holding / Source

22.12.1988   1" / 1"

THAT ANTONY COTTON SHOW

An ITV Productions production for ITV 1. Transmission details are for the Central region. Duration: 48 minutes.

Main regular credit(s):	Script associate Richard Easter; theme music by Jackie Cline and Al Collingwood; designed by Chris Webster; assistant producers Alan Thorpe and John Nichols; production executive Helen Bratt; executive producers Rachel Ashdown and Mark Wells; head of production Leah Milton; senior producer Gareth Davies; series producer Amanda Sangorski; produced by Sian Grundy; series director Jonathan Bullen.
Main regular performer(s):	Antony Cotton (Presenter).

Holding / Source

##.##.#### **[untransmitted pilot]**   DB / DBSW

With Pauline Quirke, Marsha Thomason, Neil Ruddock.

THAT WAS THE WEEK THAT WAS

A BBC production. Transmission details are for BBC. Duration: 50 minutes.

Main regular credit(s):	Produced and directed by Ned Sherrin.
Main regular cast:	David Frost (Presenter), Millicent Martin (Presenter), Kenneth Cope (Presenter), David Kernan (Presenter), Bernard Levin (Presenter), Lance Percival (Presenter), William Rushton (Presenter).

Holding / Source

##.##.#### **[first pilot]**   J /

With Brian Redhead.

##.##.#### **[second pilot]**   R1 /

Duration: 88 minutes.

Written by Christopher Booker, Caryl Brahms, David Frost, Willis Hall, Keith Waterhouse, Steven Vinaver and Geoffrey Paxton; music directed by Norman Perceval; music by Ron Grainer, Norman Perceval and Hugh Macdonald; associate producer John Bassett; produced and directed by Ned Sherrin.

With David Frost, Lance Percival, William Rushton, Millicent Martin, Roy Kinnear, David Kernan, Rose Hill, Bernard Levin, Norman St. John Stevas, Colin Renfrew.

That Was The Week That Was - Goodbye TW3 (Production Tape) containing unbroadcast material in audio form is held by Kaleidoscope.

THAT'S FOR ME

A Rediffusion Television production. Transmission details are for the Rediffusion Television region. Duration: 45 minutes.

Main regular credit(s):	Written by Clive Goodwin and Francis Hitching.

	VT Number	Holding / Source
##.##.#### **[untransmitted pilot]**	W3253/54	J / 40

Directed by Peter Croft.

With Daniel Farson (Host), Anne Nightingale (Host), Fenella Fielding, Annie Ross, Evelyn Laye, Val Doonican.

Television's request show.

THAT'S LIFE

A BBC production for BBC 1. Transmission details are for BBC 1.

Main regular performer(s): Esther Rantzen (Presenter).

Holding / Source

##.##.#### **[untransmitted pilot]**   DB-D3 / 2"

See also: BRADEN'S WEEK* / THAT'S LIFE REPORT*

THEATRE BOX

A Thames Television production. Transmission details are for the ATV midlands region. Usual duration: 25 minutes.

Executive producer Pamela Lonsdale; produced by Sue Birtwistle.

	VT Number	Holding / Source
02.11.1981 **Marmalade Atkins In Space**	24693	D3 / 2"

Written by Andrew Davies; music by Andy Roberts; designed by Jan Chaney; directed by Colin Bucksey.

With Charlotte Coleman (Marmalade Atkins), John Bird (Mr Atkins / Potsmasher), Lynda Marchal (Mrs Atkins), Gillian Raine (Mrs Allgood / Reeny of Spacehols), Dudley Sutton (Colonel Perry), Dicken Ashworth (Sister Conception / Captain Conch), Freddie Jones (Voice of Nodding Dog).
SEE: EDUCATING MARMALADE

THE THEATRE QUIZ

A BBC production for BBC 2. Transmission details are for BBC 2. Duration: 30 minutes.

Main regular credit(s):   Devised by Rosemary Wilton; designed by Bernard Lloyd-Jones; produced by Peter Butler.

Main regular performer(s): Alfred Marks (Questionmaster).

	Holding / Source
##.##.#### **[untransmitted pilot]**	DB-D3 / 2"

With Alfred Marks.

Recorded October 1979.

THEATRE ROYAL

An ATV production. Transmission details are for the ATV midlands region.

Music directed by Johnny Patrick.

Bernie Clifton (Host), Russ Abbot, Su Pollard, Dustin Gee, Ray Alan and Lord Charles, Noele Gordon, Dave Ismay, Dave Blakeley, Fred Evans, Petra Siniawski, The Dirty Dozen, Ray C. Davis, Stephanie Voss.

	Holding / Source
26.08.1980	UM / 2"

THEN CHURCHILL SAID TO ME

A BBC production for BBC 2. Transmission details are for UK Gold. Usual duration: 27 minutes.

Main regular credit(s):   Written by Maurice Sellar and Lou Jones; theme music by Ronnie Hazlehurst and Anne Shelton; designed by Vic Meredith and Barrie Dobbins; production manager Jo Austin; produced by Roger Race; directed by Martin Shardlow.

Main regular cast: Frankie Howerd (Private Potts / General Fearless / Freddy Hollocks), Nicholas Courtney (Colonel Robin Witherton), Joanna Dunham (Petty Officer Joan Bottomley), Michael Attwell (Norman).

	VT Number	Holding / Source
##.##.#### **Operation Panic: Untransmitted Original Version**	LLC M431T/72	DB-D3 / 2"

Additional material by Terry Ravenscroft and Jim Eldridge; designed by Barrie Dobbins; production manager Evan King.

With Beryl Nesbitt, Shaun Curry, James Chase, Linda Cunningham, Roger Avon, Brian Haines, Frank Gatliff.

The original version of the tx'd episode "Operation Panic". It is the same script but a different performance, evident because one of the characters has a different costume.

Made in 1982 but postponed due to the Falklands conflict.

Studio recordings exist on DB-2" for every episode.

THESE TWO FELLAS

A Granada production. Untransmitted. Duration: 25 minutes.

Written by John Temple; produced by John Hamp; directed by Les Chatfield.

Duggie Brown (Himself), Frank Carson (Himself), Liz Fraser (Olive).

	Production No	Holding / Source
##.##.#### **[untransmitted pilot]**	P754/DR	DB / 2"

Rx 24.08.1972.

THICK AS A... PLANK

A Talkback production for BBC. Untransmitted. Duration: 30 minutes.

Main regular credit(s):   Programme associates Mike Barfield and Ged Parsons; additional material by Mark Brisenden, Steve Punt and Dan Gaster; designed by Colin Piggot; executive producer Peter Fincham; head of production Sally Debonnaire; production manager Darina Healy; produced by Richard Wilson; directed by Steve Smith.

Main regular performer(s): Jack Docherty (Host), Tony Hawks (Guest), Mariella Frostrup (Guest), Hugh Dennis (Guest), Germaine Greer (Guest), Fred Macaulay (Guest), Peter Serafinowicz (Guest), Andy Lever (Male Model), Kevin Cardine (Male Model).

	VT Number	Holding / Source
##.##.#### **Programme 2**	367665	DB / DBS
##.##.#### **Programme 2 Remount**	367667	DB / DBS

With Brian Bowles (Voice Over Artist).

1996 untx pilot for a celebrity game show.

THICK AS THIEVES

An LWT production. Transmission details are for the ATV midlands region. Usual duration: 24 minutes.

Main regular credit(s):　　　Written by Dick Clement and Ian La Frenais; music by Mike Hugg and Ian La Frenais; produced by Derrick Goodwin.

Main regular cast:　　　John Thaw (Stan), Bob Hoskins (George Dobbs), Pat Ashton (Annie Dobbs).

	Production No	Holding / Source
01.06.1974　**The Home Coming**	9L/09287	DB / 2"

Directed by Derrick Goodwin.

With Reg Lye (Norman), Johnny Briggs (Spiggy), John J. Carney (Rainbow), Winnie Holman.

THIEF TAKERS

A Central production for Carlton UK. Transmission details are for the Central region. Duration: 50 minutes.

The elite Armed Robbery Squad - known to their colleagues as the best "thief takers" in London.

Main regular credit(s):　　　Created by Roy Mitchell; theme music by Hal Lindes.

Credits:　Associate producer Ron Purdie; executive producer Ted Childs; produced by Gina Cronk.

Cast:　　With Robert Reynolds (Detective Inspector Mickey Dawes), Lynda Steadman (Detective Sergeant Helen Ash), Lennie James (Detective Constable Alan Oxford), Sophie Dix (Detective Constable Angela Prudhoe), David Sterne (Detective Chief Superintendent Ian Uttley), Robert Willox (Detective Constable Ted Donachie), Brendan Coyle (Detective Sergeant Bob Tate).

	Production No	Holding / Source
01.02.1995　**Cash And Carry**	915032	DB / V1SS

When the Flying Squad gets tipped off about a supermarket heist, it mounts a stakeout in what should have been a textbook operation - but the villains fail to comply with the instructions.

Written by Roy Mitchell; script supervisor Pauline Harlow; associate producer Ron Purdie; directed by Colin Gregg.

With Beatie Edney (Cathy Worsley), Edward O'Connell, Lee Ross, Niall Refoy, Paul Kynman, Roger Leach, Fred Pearson, Robin Summers, Glyn Grimstead, Florence Guerin, Elaine Loudon, Stephen Ullathorne, Jackson Leach, Abigail Ansell, Tamsin Levett, Grace Martin, Scott Baker.

THINK OF A NUMBER

A BBC Bristol production for BBC 1. Transmission details are for BBC 1. Duration: 28 minutes.

Main regular credit(s):　　　Written by Johnny Ball.

Main regular cast:　　　Johnny Ball (Host).

Transmission details are for BBC 2.

	Holding / Source
02.04.1977	DB-D3 / 2"

Executive producer Cynthia Felgate; produced by Ann Reay; directed by Albert Barber.

THE THINLY SLICED TOAST AND FRUIT JUICE SHOW

A BBC Home Service production. Untransmitted.

Written by Terry Nation and Dennis Potter.

	Holding / Source
##.##.####　**[untransmitted pilot]**	J / 40

Recorded April 1963.

THIRTY MINUTES

An LWT production. Untransmitted. Duration: 50 minutes.

A spoof news magazine show.

Written by Chris Beetles, Rob Buckman, Colin Bostock-Smith, Mike Goddard, Chris Miller, Terry Palmer, Len Richmond, Steve Thorn and Paul Wolfson; music by Max Harris; designed by Roger Hall; associate producer Mike Goddard; production manager Myra Hersh; produced and directed by Paul Smith.

Russ Abbot, Linda Lou Allen, Jim Davidson, Les Dennis, Berni Flint, Pat Mills.

	Production No	Holding / Source
##.##.####　**[untransmitted pilot]**	99136	DB / 2"

Recorded 11.11.77. A discontinuous studio recording of approximately 50 minutes duration seems to be all that exists.

THIS AND THAT

An Ulster Television production. Transmission details are for the Ulster Televison region. Duration: 15 minutes.

Main regular credit(s):　　　Produced by John Scholz-Conway.

Main regular performer(s):　Rog Whittaker.

	Holding / Source
25.09.1963	R1N / 40

THIS IS IRELAND

A BBC production for BBC 2. Transmission details are for BBC 2. Duration: 30 minutes.

A comedy pilot featuring brand new comedy writers and performers from the emerald isle under the stewardship of Arthur Mathews.

Arthur Mathews.

	Holding / Source
19.03.2004	DB / DBSW

THIS IS JINSY

A Welded Tandem Production production for BBC 3. Transmission details are for BBC 3. Duration: 30 minutes.

Comedy pilot written by and starring Justin Chubb and Chris Bran as Maven and Sporrall - the hapless adminstrators of Jinsy Island. They watch over the residents, carrying out the instructions of the unseen but all-powerful 'Great He', dispensing punishment, propaganda and pelch to the 762 inhabitants of Jinsy. Maven is agitated by a dirty spoon and is given the honour of making the inaugural speech at a ceremony linking Jinsy to Old Jinsy - a mythic place populated by barely civilised natives.

Written by Chris Bran and Justin Chubb; script supervisor Caroline Bowker; script editor Emma Kennedy; music by Tim Bran and Nik Albumen; director of photography Ole Bratt Birkeland; designed by Dan Gardner, Ed Perkins and Nic Pallace; executive producer Simon Lupton; line producer Stephanie Burke; produced by Chris Carey and James Dean; directed by Chris Bran and Justin Chubb.

Chris Bran, Justin Chubb, Christopher Fairbank, David Hatton, David Mounfield.

		Holding / Source
01.03.2010 **Bandy Dog Red**		HD/DB / HD/DB

THIS WAY UP

A Granada production. Transmission details are for the Granada region. Duration: 23 minutes.

A comedy in which graduates Nonny, Clive and Ben start a new business called "This Way Up" which is a general consultancy/information centre, and is a series of Zany sketches.

Written by Clive Anderson, Ben Jacobs and Nonny Williams; designed by Paul Danson; produced by John G. Temple; directed by Ric Mellis.

Nonny Williams, Ben Jacobs, Clive Anderson.

	Production No	Holding / Source
21.12.1984 **Nonnie**	P1287	1" / 1"

THREE FLIGHTS UP

A BBC production. Untransmitted. Duration: 30 minutes.

Written by Paul Powell.

Mel Smith, Griff Rhys Jones.

	Holding / Source
##.##.####	

Recorded c. 2000.

THREE IN A BED

A Thames Television production. Transmission details are for the ATV midlands region. Duration: 25 minutes.

Rivalry between pubs is as traditionally British as fish and chips, Yorkshire pudding, and discussions about the weather.
Everyone thinks that his local is the best. And the leaners and lifters at The Ploughman's Boots and The Lady's Garter are no exception.

Perhaps the inter-pubs darts match will resolve the problem. Syd and Eddie of the "Boots", and Bert of the "Garter" hope so, but much depends on the out-of-town visitor who throws a deadly "arrer".

Written by Brian Chasser and Mike Firman; music by Jackie Brown and Carol Scott; designed by David Ferris; associate producer David Clark; produced and directed by Royston Mayoh.

Eddie Large (Eddie), Syd Little (Syd), Les Noyes (Arnold), Roy Barraclough (Percy), Jacqueline Clarke (Olive), Norman Chappell (Mr W. Ernest Johnson), John Barrard (Frederick), Anthony Jackson (Bert), Jackie Brown (Organist).

	VT Number	Holding / Source
22.02.1972	4579	D3 / 2"

THREE ON A COUCH

A BBC production. Untransmitted. Duration: 30 minutes.

Written by Adele Rose; costume Barbara Kronig; make-up Viv Riley; designed by Bryan Ellis; production team Kathryn Foulkes and Sylvie McRoberts; production manager Richard Boden; produced and directed by Gareth Gwenlan.

Judy Carne (Judy), Patrick Mower (Harry), Edward Wilson (Sam), Frederick Jaeger (Waldo), Christina Matthews (Angela), Simone Welch (Little Girl).

	Holding / Source
##.##.#### **Strays [untransmitted pilot]**	DB / 2"

THREE ON FOUR-CH FOUR TALK

An LWT production. Untransmitted.

	VT Number	Holding / Source
##.##.#### **[untransmitted pilot]**	9L/79240	J / 1"
##.##.#### **[untransmitted pilot]**	9L/79241	J / 1"

THROUGH THE KEYHOLE

Commissioned by ITV. Transmission details are for the Central region. Duration: 25 minutes.

Panellists try to guess whose home they are watching on film.

A Yorkshire Television production.
Main regular credit(s):   Produced by Kevin Sym; directed by Ian Bolt.

Main regular performer(s): With David Frost (Host).

	Holding / Source
##.##.#### **[pilot 1]**	J / 1"

##.##.#### [pilot 2]   J / 1"

THUNDERBIRDS

Alternative/Working Title(s): INTERNATIONAL RESCUE

An AP Films production for ITC. made in association with ATV. Transmission details are for the ATV midlands region.

Main regular credit(s):	Created by Gerry Anderson and Sylvia Anderson; theme music by Barry Gray.
Main regular cast:	Ray Barrett (Voice of Alan Tracy / John Tracy / The Hood / guest voices), Peter Dyneley (Voice of Jeff Tracy), David Graham (Voice of Brains / Aloysius Parker / guest voices), Sylvia Anderson (Voice of Lady Penelope), Christine Finn (Voice of Tin-Tin Kyrano), David Holliday (Voice of Virgil Tracy), Shane Rimmer (Voice of Scott Tracy), Matt Zimmerman (Voice of Alan Tracy / guest voices).

SERIES 1

Duration: 48 minutes.

Main regular credit(s):	Script editor Alan Pattillo; associate producer Reg Hill; produced by Gerry Anderson.

Holding / Source

30.09.1965 **Trapped In The Sky**   D5Hrv/DB / C3

Alternative transmissions: ATV London: 02.10.1965; Granada: 19.10.1966.

The Thunderbird machines rocket into their first adventure when a mysterious extortionist, know only as The Hood, plants a bomb aboard the supersonic airliner Fireflash. The rescue operation is complicated when The Hood escapes from the airport police with detailed photographs of Thunderbird 1. Utilising radio-controlled elevator cars, International Rescue attempts to catch the Fireflash on its landing approach without disturbing the bomb. Meanwhile, Lady Penelope is called into action to stop The Hood.

Written by Gerry Anderson and Sylvia Anderson; directed by Alan Pattillo.

TICKET TO RIDE

Produced for LWT by a variety of companies (see details below). Transmission details are for the Central region.

Holding / Source

16.07.1988   1" / 1"

An LWT production. Duration: 60 minutes.

Written by Peachey Markowitz; executive producers Bruce Sallan and Peachey Markowitz; produced by Nick Elliott and Lee Miller; directed by Richard Franklin.

With Margaret Whitton (Louisa), Kevin Moore (Miles), Lucia Faucett (Martha), Kharis Faucett (Jill), George Rossi (Jock), David Griffin (Nate), Massiomo Sarchielli (Alexandros), Oscar James (Terence), Dinah Lenny (Friday), Ernie Sabella (George), Anthony Andrews (Michael), Susan Wooldridge (Anne), Cyril Shaps (Metzinger), Romano Puppo (Alfredo), Mike Edmonds (Carlo), Ron Houck (Red), Geoffrey Copplestone (Krueger), Domenico Fiore (Man), Buck Herron (Clerk), Robert Stephens (Consul), Rossano Brazzi (Castello), Antonio Iorio (Police Chief), Molly Weir (Birdie).

TIGER BASTABLE

A Mike Mansfield TV production for Central. Transmission details are for the Central region. Duration: 25 minutes.

Comedy set in the 1930s. Maverick private-eye Tiger Bastable is called in by Scotland Yard to investigate the mysterious disappearances of young men and women from English public schools.

Written by Tony Slattery and Richard Turner; executive producer Paul Spencer; produced and directed by Mike Mansfield.

Tony Slattery (Tiger Bastable), Graham Stark (Guffer), Jim Sweeney (Herr Von Schtupp).

Holding / Source

28.09.1995 **The Case Of The Nazi Mindbender**   D3 / D3S

TIME AFTER TIME

An LWT production. Transmission details are for the Central region. Duration: 25 minutes.

Main regular credit(s):	Written by Paul Minett and Brian Leveson; theme music by Andy Street, Paul Minett, Brian Leveson and Brian Conley; produced by John Kaye Cooper.
Main regular cast:	Brian Conley (Kenny Conway), Richard Graham (Jake Brewer), Kate Williams (Ma Conway), Georgia Allen (Donna), Neil McCaul (Mr Michael Tredwell), David Shane (Robbie Conway), Deddie Davies (Auntie Dot).

	Production No	VT Number	Holding / Source
##.##.#### **Outside Chance** [untransmitted pilot]			J / D2S
Directed by John Kaye Cooper.			
With Carla Mendonca (Gillian Walcott).			
03.07.1993 **Outside Chance**	P/N 9L/92784	92971	DB / D2S

Script associate Mark Robson; directed by John Kaye Cooper.

With Kim Thomson (Gillian Walcott), Al Ashton (Mr Eaton), William Vanderpuye (Disc Jockey).

TIME FOR ACTION

A Thames Television production. Untransmitted. Duration: 48 minutes.

Devised by Tom Brennand and Roy Bottomley; written by Tom Brennand and Roy Bottomley; programme associate Kay Bird; designed by Robin Parker and John White; produced by Andy Allan; directed by Terry Yarwood.

Eamonn Andrews (Host), Ray Fell, Jim Bowen.

	VT Number	Holding / Source
##.##.#### [untransmitted 1977 pilot]	17224	DB / 2"

The videotape is damaged.

See also: STAR GAMES*

TIME OF MY LIFE

A BBC production for BBC 1. Transmission details are for BBC 1. Duration: 30 minutes.

Main regular credit(s):   Written by Jim Eldridge; music by Ronnie Hazlehurst; produced by Dennis Main Wilson; directed by Martin Shardlow.

Main regular cast: Mark Kingston (Ken Archer), Amanda Barrie (Joan Archer).

	Production No	Holding / Source
##.##.#### [untransmitted 1979 pilot]	LLCA731H/71	DB-D3 / 2"

Costume Romayne Horton; make-up Jill Shardlow; designed by Ken Starkey.

With Mark Kingston (Ken Armitage), Amanda Barrie (Joan Armitage), Dudley Long, George Tovey, Cyril Cross, Tony Millan, Rosemary Williams, Andrew Paul, Mollie Maureen, Eddie Tagoe, Harry Fielder.

THE TIME THE PLACE

A Granada production for Anglia. Transmission details are for the Granada region. Duration: 35 minutes.

	Production No	Holding / Source
##.##.#### "Aircraft noise" [pilot?]	1/1446/0001	1" / 1"

Presented by Mike Scott; produced by David Jenkins; directed by Eric Harrison.

TIMESLIP - THE BLOCK

A The Callender Company production for Yorkshire Television. Transmission details are for the Central region. Duration: 25 minutes.

Adapted by Jim Hawkins; based on a story by Robert Holmes; associate producer Carol Williams; produced by Colin Callender; directed by Willi Paterson.

John Taylor (The Hacker), Jeff Harding (Greg), Virginia Hey (Jenny), Liza Ross (Candy), Manning Redwood (Lee), Blain Fairman (Billy).

	VT Number	Holding / Source
28.12.1985	D040	1" / C1

TIN PAN ALICE

A Granada production. Transmission details are for the ATV midlands region. Duration: 25 minutes.

Written by Peter Coke; song by Steve Race; script editor Barry Took; settings by Stanley Mills; produced by Peter Eton; directed by Eric Fawcett.

Athene Seyler (Alice Lacey), Warren Mitchell (Gerry Goldbind), Carole Carr (Belinda), Nancy Nevinson (Mrs Pasqualina), Neville Becker (Tom), Charles Farrell (Ted), Anne Blake (Mrs Porterhouse), Dallas Cavell (Alf), Patricia Clapton (June), Fred Kitchen (First Song Plugger), Tommy Godfrey (Second Song Plugger), Steve Race (Steve).

	Production No	Holding / Source
15.08.1963	P395/2	DB / 40

Postponed from 13.06.1963.

Recorded 31.05.63.

Made as part of COMEDY FOUR and originally scheduled in place of "Fit For Heroes".

See also: COMEDY FOUR

TISWAS

Produced for ATV/Central by a variety of companies (see details below). Transmission details are for the ATV/Central region. Duration varies - see below for details.

SERIES 1: Today is Saturday or The Tiswas Show

Transmission details are for the ATV midlands region.

	Holding / Source
##.##.#### [untransmitted pilot]	J / 2"

Made in Studio 4 at ATV.

TITTYBANGBANG

A Pett Productions production for BBC 3. Transmission details are for BBC 3. Duration: 30 minutes.

Main regular credit(s):   Created by Jill Parker; head of production Anne Cafferky; produced by Lisa Clark.

	Holding / Source
20.09.2005	DB / DBSWF

Bare-bottomed embroiderers and a necrophilic pathologist are among the characters in the female-comedy pilot.

Written by Jill Parker; additional material by Lucy Montgomery; script supervisor Emma John; directed by Angie De Chastelai Smith.

With Lisa Clark, Lucy Montgomery, Debbie Chazen, Lorraine Cheshire, Shelley Longworth, Veille Tshbalala, Tony Way.

TO THE MANOR BORN (RADIO)

A BBC production for BBC Radio 4. Transmission details are for BBC Radio 4. Duration: 30 minutes.

Grantleigh Manor may have to be sold... Audrey is determined to stop it. An American millionnaire expresses interest in buying the manor.

Written by Peter Spence.

Penelope Keith (Audrey), Bernard Braden.

	Holding / Source
##.##.#### [untransmitted 1978 pilot]	J /

After hearing the pilot, Peter Spence was commissioned to create a version for TV.

TOAST OF LONDON

An Objective Productions production for Channel 4. Transmission details are for Channel 4. Duration: 22 minutes.

Main regular credit(s):   Created by Arthur Mathews and Matt Berry; written by Arthur Mathews and Matt Berry; music composed by Matt Berry; director of photography Peter Edwards; production designer Rosy Thomas; production executive Jenny Hay; head of production Debi Roach; directed by Michael Cumming.

Main regular cast: Matt Berry (Steven Toast).

	Holding / Source
20.08.2012 **The Unspeakable Play**	HD/DB / HD/DB

Assistant director David Stafford; art director Rosanna Westwood; executive producers Ben Farrell and Andrew Newman; line producer Carla McGilchrist; produced by Phil Clarke and Rachel Springett.

With Robert Bathurst (Ed Howzer-Black), Fiona Mollison (Jane Plough), Harry Peacock (Ray Purchase), Tracy-Ann Oberman (Mrs Purchase), Theresa Watson (Goodhouse), Lee Cornes (Flasher), Geoff McGivern (Cliff Promise), Paul Marlon (Scowling Prisoner), Howard Ward (Prison Officer), Adrian Lukis (Blair Toast), Tim Downie (Danny Bear), Shazad Latif (Clem Fandango), Ginny Buckley (Crimewave Presenter), Jiggy Bhore (Protester).

TOGETHER

A Southern Television production. Transmission details are for the ATV midlands region. Duration: 25 minutes.

	Holding / Source
##.##.#### **People Together [untransmitted pilot]**	J / 2"

Written by Adele Rose; executive producer Lewis Rudd; directed by Hugh David.

Recorded Summer 1979.

An end of series spoof show for the cast and crew exists on VHS, ex 2".

TOKSVIG

A TVS production. Transmission details are for the Central region.

Main regular cast: Sandi Toksvig (Presenter).

	VT Number	Holding / Source
##.##.#### **[untransmitted pilot]**	12050	1" / 1"

TOM DEVISES

A BBC production. Not made.

	Holding / Source
##.##.#### **Tom Devises Saves The Home Secretary [unmade pilot]**	NR / NM

Written by Donald Cotton.

See also: ADAM ADAMANT / ADAM ADAMANT LIVES!*

THE TOM O'CONNOR SHOW

A Thames Television production. Transmission details are for the ATV midlands region. Duration: 25 minutes.

Four times winner of Opportunity Knocks!, comedian Tom O'Connor reflects the funny side of life to a packed studio audience.

Written by Spike Mullins and Pat Finan; music directed by George N. Paterson; designed by Robin Parker; produced and directed by Keith Beckett.

Tom O'Connor (Host), The New Faces.

	VT Number	Holding / Source
12.10.1976	13703	DB / 2"

TOM, DICK AND HARRIET

A Thames Television production. Transmission details are for the Central region. Duration: 25 minutes.

Main regular credit(s):   Written by Johnnie Mortimer and Brian Cooke; theme music by Syd Lawrence and his Orchestra and Stephanie Lawrence; produced and directed by Michael Mills.

Main regular cast: Lionel Jeffries (Thomas Maddison), Brigit Forsyth (Harriet Maddison).

	VT Number	Holding / Source
##.##.#### **[untransmitted pilot]**	24600	DB / 2"

Designed by Robin Parker.

With Martin Jarvis (Richard Maddison), John Southworth, Robbie Coltrane, Louise English, Carl Andrews, Anita Graham, Susie Silvey.

Recorded 1981.

TOM, DICK AND HARRY

A Yorkshire Television production. Transmission details are for the ATV midlands region. Duration: 8 minutes.

Main regular credit(s):   Written by Jim Bywater; designed by David McDermott; produced and directed by Lesley Smith.

Main regular cast: Jim Bywater (Tom), Ted Richards (Dick), Pete Ivatts (Harry).

	VT Number	Holding / Source
##.##.#### **[untransmitted pilot]**	E239	B / 2"

THE TOMORROW PEOPLE

Produced for Thames Television by a variety of companies (see details below). Transmission details are for the ATV midlands region. Usual duration: 25 minutes.

Main regular credit(s):   Created by Roger Price.

	Holding / Source
##.##.#### **A Bad Dream Gets Real [untransmitted pilot]**	1" / 1"

A Tetra Films production.

Written by Roger Damon Price; music by Clever Music; director of photography Mike Thomson; art director Charles Collum; designed by Andrew Rothschild and Alan Muraoka; executive producers Michael Yudin, Jay Mulvaney, Roseanne Lopopolo and Alan Horrox; production managers Brenda White and Susan Bradley; produced and directed by Roger Damon Price.

With Kristian Schmid (Adam Newman), Stephen Pollard (Kevin), Kristen Ariza (Lisa), Christian Tessier (Megabyte), Hugh Quarshie (Professor Galt), Ted Decker (Masterman), Linda Goens (Mrs Davis), Callum Dixon (Ray), Tom Kerridge (Hulk), Eryl Maynard (Kevin's Mother), Sally McClaren (Newscaster), Jeff Farmer (Big Man).

Recorded 1990.

See also: TOMORROW PEOPLE (SPIN OFF AUDIOS)*

TONI BASIL

Alternative/Working Title(s): TONI BASIL - DO YOUR THING!

A BBC Manchester production for BBC 2. Transmission details are for BBC 2. Duration: 30 minutes.

Executive producer Ken Stephinson; produced and directed by Alan Walsh.

Toni Basil.

	Holding / Source
	DB / 2"
19.01.1982	

Recorded September 1981.

TONIGHT WITH BRADEN

Alternative/Working Title(s): BRADEN

A Thames Television production. Untransmitted.

Bernard Braden (Host), Anita Harris, Michael Attwell, Harry Fowler, The Kenny Clayton Band.

	VT Number	Holding / Source
##.##.#### **[untransmitted pilot]**	23661	DB / 1"

TOO MANY CROOKS

A Granada production. Not made. Duration: 25 minutes.

Written by Marty Feldman and Maurice Richardson.

A planned twenty-six episode, half-hour comedy series with Marty Feldman and Maurice Richardson as lead writers. Mentioned in The Stage in August 1961, it was presumably a victim of the six month Equity strike which ran started a couple of months later.

TOP OF THE FORM

A BBC production for BBC 1. Transmission details are for BBC 1.

	VT Number	Holding / Source
##.##.#### **Television Top Of The Form [untransmitted pilot]**	35/P/14431	J /

Recorded 16th May 1962.

Surviving items only.

TOP OF THE POPS

A BBC production for BBC 1. Transmission details are for BBC 1. Duration varies - see below for details.

Other Top of the Pops related material:

	VT Number	Holding / Source
##.##.#### **[1980 untransmitted re-versioned pilot]**	LLV/C95A	DB / 2"

Duration: 32 minutes.

Designed by John Holland; production team Hilary Bennett, Annie Ogden and Mark Williams; executive producer Michael Hurll; produced and directed by Phil Bishop.

With Peter Powell (D.J.), B. A. Robertson (D.J.), Paul McCartney, Darts, Olivia Newton-John, Legs & Co..

The acts credited appeared only on pop videos. Other bands were identified as being live on the show, but crew stood in their places pretending to be the real musicians. Legs & Co. appeared performing a proper dance routine in groovy legwarmers!

Acts marked with an asterisk indicate they were not live in the studio.

Kaleidoscope's "Top Pop" book provides full information on every show.

See also: BOB PRATT ENGINEERING TAPES* / CHEGWIN CHECKS IT OUT* / STARS REUNITED* / TOP OF THE POPS: THE STORY OF 1976*

TOP OF THE SHOP

Alternative/Working Title(s): BOB'S BINGO / THE BOB MONKHOUSE GAME SHOW

A BBC production for BBC 1. Untransmitted. Duration: 30 minutes.

Format by Terry Mardell and David Moore; script associates Spike Mullins and Johnny Pearson; music by Johnny Pearson; designed by Bob Cove; production team John Birkin and Georgina Don; production manager Robert Randell; produced by Marcus Plantin; directed by John Bishop.

Bob Monkhouse (Host).

	Production No	Holding / Source
##.##.#### **[untransmitted pilot]**	LLV E140/71	DB / 1"

Recorded 16.03.84.

Unbroadcast pilot for a BBC quiz show that eventually became BOB'S FULL HOUSE.

TOP OF THE WORLD

A Thames Television production. Untransmitted.

A Mastermind with money as contestants compete across the globe.

Produced by Malcolm Morris.

Eamonn Andrews (Presenter).

	Holding / Source
##.##.#### **[untransmitted pilot]**	DB-D3 / 2"

Recorded October 1980.

TOP PUB

A BBC production. Untransmitted.

	Holding / Source
##.##.#### **[untransmitted pilot]**	R1 /

Warwick Cross remembers, " remember doing an OB for two days in a pub in Carshalton, Surrey for a pilot for a programme called 'Top Pub'. Pilot never went out to my memory and no series ensured. This idea was a variation on the established Top Form format of the mid 60s.

Best guess for date was June or July 1967. It was an KA scanner/crew. Best guess is it was OB Events from Ken House.

Never mind the pilot, though – a pub for two days solid is an excellent location! Even the tea served between licensing hours was delivered in pint mugs!"

TOP SECRET

A BBC production for BBC 1. made in association with Goodson Todman Productions / Talbot TV Ltd. Transmission details are for BBC 1. Duration: 30 minutes.

Celebrities are challenged to guess people's secrets.

Main regular performer(s): Barry Took, Jan Leeming, Chris Kelly.

	Holding / Source
25.08.1982	DB / 1"

Produced by Roger Mackay; directed by Antonia Charlton.

With Barry Took (Host), Mollie Sugden, Frank Windsor, Chris Kelly, Jan Leeming.

TOUCH ME, I'M KAREN TAYLOR

An Avalon Productions production for BBC 3. Transmission details are for BBC 3. Duration: 30 minutes.

Main regular credit(s):	Script supervisor Kendall Anderson-Müt; script editor David Quantick; designed by Dennis De Groot; executive producers Richard Allen-Turner and Jon Thoday; head of production Bluey Richards; produced by Richard Grocock; directed by Ben Kellett.

Main regular cast:	Karen Taylor (Host).

	Holding / Source
28.03.2006	DB / DBSWF

A TOUCH OF MARTELL

A BBC Scotland production for BBC 1 Scotland. Transmission details are for BBC 1 Scotland.

Glasgow singer Lena Martell made her comeback to television after serious illness.

Produced and directed by Iain MacFadyen.

Lena Martell, Marmalade, Don Maclean.

	Holding / Source
05.01.1971	J / 2"

See also: PRESENTING LENA MARTELL*

TOWN HALL TV

A Yorkshire Television production. Untransmitted. Duration: 25 minutes.

Hughie Green (Host).

	Holding / Source
##.##.####	J /

Made in Sheffield in late 1968.

TRIVIAL PURSUIT

A BBC production. made in association with David Paradine Productions Ltd / Mike Mansfield Enterprises. Untransmitted. Duration: 31 minutes.

Written by Fred Metcalf and Martin Kelner; make-up Monica Ludkin; consultants Bob Merrilees and Keith Stewart; designed by Tim Gleeson; associate producer Hilary Stewart; produced by Mike Mansfield and Phil Chilvers; directed by Phil Chilvers.

David Frost (Quizmaster), Lord Chalfront, Lord Lichfield [as Earl Of Lichfield], Lord Stockton, Sue Arnold, Alan Coren, Nigel Dempster.

	Production No	Holding / Source
##.##.#### [untransmitted 1988 pilot]	LLVL920D	DB / 1"

TROUBLE IN MIND

A Hightimes Productions production for LWT. Transmission details are for the Central region. Duration: 25 minutes.

Main regular credit(s):	Based on an idea by Greg Brenman; music by Richard O'Sullivan; music arranged by Laurie Holloway; designed by Quentin Chases and Su Chases; executive producer Robin Carr; produced by Al Mitchell; directed by Terry Kinane.

Main regular cast:	Richard O'Sullivan (Adam Charlesworth), Susan Penhaligon (Julia Charlesworth).

	Holding / Source
##.##.#### [untransmitted pilot]	1" / 1"

Written by Colin Bostock-Smith; produced by Robin Carr; directed by Terry Kinane.

With Richard O'Sullivan (Adam Green), Susan Penhaligon (Julia Green), Sally Cookson (Lucy Green), Simon Schatzberger (Joe Green), Sarah K. Crowe (Hilary Molesworth), Virginia Denham (Woman 1), Hollie Garrett (Woman 2), Richard Cordery (Man 1), Andrew Branch (Man 2).

(MICHAEL WINNER'S) TRUE CRIMES

An LWT production. Transmission details are for the Central region. Duration: 25 minutes.

Introduced by Michael Winner; series editor Jeff Pope; executive producer Simon Shaps.

	Holding / Source
04.08.1991 **The Golden Rule**	D2 / D2

The story of ex-detective Rodney Whitchelo, the man behind the baby food scare that made the headlines in 1989. The 'consumer terrorist' used his police experience to keep one step ahead of his former colleagues. But he forgot the golden rule - don't be greedy - and he paid for it. He is currently serving a 17-year sentence for his crime.

Produced by Jeremy Phillips; directed by Kathryn Wolfe.

With Philip Goldacre (Rodney Whitchelo), Michael Redfern (Chief Superintendent Flemming), Alan Leith (Robertson), Edward Phillips (Lecturer), Martin Matthews (Managing Director), Ken Sharrock (Leacey), John Dryden (Garner), Frank Taylor (Superintendent), Gary Lammin (Detective), Adam Ray (Detective), Steve Emerson (Detective), Tony Ryan (Detective), Robert Crake (Detective), David Cann (Donnelly), Kevin O'Brien (Kiarton), Colin Mace (McDowell), Richard Ashley (Journalist), Penny Howatt (Mum), Sydnee Blake (Woman In Mobile Home), John Bromley (Barman).

There were no writers credited on-screen, in listings magazines or on any LWT paperwork.

TRUE LOVE

A Granada production. Transmission details are for the Central region. Duration: 51 minutes.

Written by Simon Nye; executive producer Andy Harries; produced by Brian Park; directed by Simon Massey.

Emma Wray (Donna), Douglas Hodge (James), Philip Glenister (Phil), Scott Handy (Christopher), Nisha K. Nayar (Olive), Elizabeth Earl (Shirley), Hannah McVeigh (Rhiannon), Maggie Jones (Martha), James Bannon (Duane), Garth Napier Jones (Man In Blazer), Richard Dixon (Theatre Director).

	Holding / Source
25.02.1996	DB / V1SW

See also: MY WONDERFUL LIFE (comedy guide)

See also: G.B.H.* / MY WONDERFUL LIFE*

TURNING YEAR TALES

A BBC Bristol production for BBC 2. Transmission details are for BBC 2. Duration: 30 minutes.

Theme music by Dave Greenslade; produced by Alastair Reid.

	Holding / Source
24.06.1979 **Big Jim And The Figaro Club**	C1 / C1

In the early 1950s `College' comes down from Cambridge to work for the summer with his old mates on the buildings only to find a seething passion gripping the Figaro Club. What is the dark secret of Harold Perkins, Clerk of the Works? What mysterious device is Big Jim building in his workshop the other side of town?

Written by Ted Walker; music by Dave Greenslade; film camera Bernard Hedges; film editor David Altband; designed by Chris Robilliard; directed by Colin Rose.

With Bob Hoskins (Narrator), Patrick Murray (College), David Beckett (Chick), Sylvester McCoy (Turps), Norman Rossington (Big Jim), Helen Keating (Glad), Roland Curram (Perkins), Gordon Rollings (Ned).

See also: BIG JIM AND THE FIGARO CLUB*

TV HELL

A BBC production for BBC 2. Transmission details are for BBC 2.

	Holding / Source
31.08.1992 **Mainly For Men**	DB-D3 / 62

Pilot programme for what was meant to be the televisual equivalent of a sixties "girlie" magazine. Recorded in 1969.

With George Best, David Bailey.

TV OFFAL

An Associated-Rediffusion production for Channel 4. Transmission details are for Channel 4.

| Main regular credit(s): | Written by Victor Lewis-Smith and Paul Sparks; produced by Victor Lewis-Smith and John Hayward-Warburton; directed by Victor Lewis-Smith. |

Main regular performer(s): Victor Lewis-Smith (Presenter).

Holding / Source

31.10.1997   DB / DBS

Duration: 35 minutes.

TV SQUASH

A WTTV Production production for Yorkshire Television. Transmission details are for the Central region. Duration: 25 minutes.

Main regular credit(s): Executive producer John Bartlett; produced by Simon Wright and Angelo Abela; directed by Vic Finch.

Main regular cast: Angelo Abela, Gabrielle Cowburn, Andrew Dunn, Treva Etienne, Lucinda Fisher, Caroline Gruber, Geraldine McNulty, Phil Nice.

Holding / Source

##.##.####   **[untransmitted pilot]**   1" / 1"

TWO BIRDS IN THE BUSH

A Granada production. Untransmitted. Duration: 15 minutes.

Written by Dennis Woolf; produced and directed by Richard Everitt.

Pauline Collins (Honey), Amber Kammer (Candy), William Maxwell (Police Constable), Arthur Barclay (Old Man).

	Production No	Holding / Source
##.##.#### **The Birds meet the Old, Bald, Ugly man with a Beard and a Monocle.....**	P490/DRI Team A	DB-4W / 40

The voice-over during the count-down clock describes this as a dry-run.

TWO BIT

A HTV Wales production. Transmission details are for the HTV Wales region. Duration: 25 minutes.

Written by David Anthony.

Holding / Source

30.11.1993   D3 / D3S

Comedy-drama. A rock band has a shot at the big time.

TWO FOR ONE

A Thames Television production. Untransmitted. Duration: 25 minutes.

Written by Charlotte Bingham and Terence Brady; produced and directed by Les Chatfield.

Holding / Source

##.##.####   **[untransmitted pilot]**   J / 2"

THE TWO OF US

An LWT production. Transmission details are for the Central region. Duration: 25 minutes.

Main regular credit(s): Written by Alex Shearer.

Main regular cast: Nicholas Lyndhurst (Ashley), Janet Dibley (Elaine).

Holding / Source

##.##.####   **[untransmitted pilot]**   DB / 1"

Produced and directed by Marcus Plantin.

With Patrick Troughton (Perce).

TWO OLD DEARS

Alternative/Working Title(s): THE TWO DEARS

A Thames Television production. Transmission details are for the ATV midlands region. Duration: 25 minutes.

Old Edie and Dorothy are sisters-in-law. They share Dorothy's house, but after a now about their domestic status, Edie declares she is moving out. Dorothy calls her bluff by advertising the room.

Written by Ken Levison; designed by Jack Robinson; produced and directed by John Robins.

Wynne Clark (Dorothy Trevelyan), Joan Hickson (Edie Trevelyan), David Battley (Ron), Michael Ripper (Mr Miller), Nina West (Assistant).

Holding / Source

15.01.1973 **Edie's Lovely Room**   J / 2"

Billed in the TV Times as "The Two Dears" but in newspapers as "Two Old Dears". A repeat, on 08.08.73 was also billed as "Two Old Dears" so the title has been changed to reflect the 'majority' position.

THE TWO RONNIES

A BBC production for BBC 1. Transmission details are for BBC 1. Duration varies - see below for details.

Main regular performer(s): Ronnie Corbett (Various roles), Ronnie Barker (Various roles).

		Holding / Source
20.03.1971 **The Ronnie Barker Yearbook**		J|a / 2"

Duration: 45 minutes.

Written by Gerald Wiley, Dick Vosburgh, Eric Idle, John Cleese and Graham Chapman; music by Ronnie Hazlehurst; choreography by Pamela Devis; designed by Keith Cheetham; executive producer James Gilbert; produced and directed by Terry Hughes.

With John Cleese, New World, Billy Dainty, Jerold Wells, John Gower, Len Lowe, Jan Rossini, Olive Mercer, Noël Dyson, The Pamela Devis Dancers, The Fred Tomlinson Singers.

27.03.1971 **Ronnie Corbett In Bed**	DB-1" / 2"

Duration: 45 minutes.

Written by John Antrobus, Barry Cryer, Doug Fisher, Eric Idle, David Nobbs, Spike Mullins and Dick Vosburgh; based on an idea by Barry Cryer; music directed by Ronnie Hazlehurst; designed by John Burrowes; executive producer James Gilbert; produced and directed by Terry Hughes.

With Howard Keel, Blossom Dearie and her Trio.

See also: 6 DATES WITH BARKER / BY THE SEA* / THE PICNIC* / THE TWO RONNIES (IN AUSTRALIA)* / THE TWO RONNIES SKETCHBOOK*

TWO WHEELS ON MY WAGGON

A BBC production. Untransmitted. Duration: 30 minutes.

Comedy pilot about a guy who loses his legs in a road accident, but wants to buy a flat and move out of home.

Written by Pam Valentine.

Ian Lindsay, Jaye Griffiths.

	Production No	Holding / Source
##.##.#### **[untransmitted pilot]**	LLCA200H/71	DB / 1"

No end credits, no way to identify many actors.

THE TYNE SLIDES BY

A BBC production for BBC 2. Transmission details are for BBC 2. Duration: 20 minutes.

Written by Alex Glasgow; song by Alex Glasgow; music by Alex Glasgow and Bill Southgate; produced and directed by John Bird.

Alex Glasgow.

	Holding / Source
	DB / 2"
24.07.1972	

It exists, but only in the recut version tx'd 3/2/74 in "The Camera and the Song".

UNDER AND OVER

A BBC production for BBC 1. Transmission details are for BBC 1. Duration: 30 minutes.

Three Irish labourers working on a new London Underground tunnel.

Main regular credit(s):   Written by David Climie and Austin Steele; produced by Austin Steele.

Main regular cast: Dec Clusky [as The Bachelors] (Dec), Con Clusky [as The Bachelors] (Con), John Stokes [as The Bachelors] (John), Tommy Godfrey (Landlord).

	Holding / Source
08.01.1971 **[Comedy Playhouse]**	J / 2"

Designed by Brian Tregidden; directed by David Askey.

With Robert Keegan (Lord Brentwood), Jack Smethurst, Therese McMurray, Patrick Laffan, Gordon Peters, Jim O'Connor, James Appleby, Michael Cooper.

This new pilot was shown unscheduled and replaced the first episode of 'That's Your Funeral'. So many viewers missed the pilot it was shown as episode 1 of the actual series.

UNDER ONE ROOF

A BBC production for BBC 3. Transmission details are for BBC 3. Duration: 30 minutes.

Created by Siobhan Rhodes-Johnson and Sally Hawkins; written by James Bachman, Katy Brand, Mark Evans, Rufus Jones, Oriane Messina and Fay Rusling; additional material by David Mitchell; script supervisor Lucy Crayford; music by Jane Watkins; production executive Sarah Hitchcock; executive producer Micheal Jacob; produced by Siobhan Rhodes-Johnson; directed by Paul King.

James Bachman, Naomi Bentley, Kevin Bishop, Katy Brand, Akemnji Ndifornyen, Rufus Jones, Alice Lowe, Alan Corser, Melissa Elliot.

	Holding / Source
26.02.2007	DB / DBSW

UNDER THE MOON

A BBC production for BBC 1. Transmission details are for BBC 1. Duration: 30 minutes.

Written by Paul A. Mendelson; produced and directed by Paul Harrison.

Samantha Bond (Francesca), Mark Aiken (Mr Thackeray), Geraldine Fitzgerald (Megan), Malcolm Sinclair (Hugo Tripp), Nicholas Boulton (Alex), Kacey Ainsworth (Sarah), Peter Moreton (Gavin), Cliff Parisi (Clifford), Archie Panjabi (Heena), Helen Fraser (Miss Prudhomme), Amanda Symonds (Midwife), Bobby Bragg (First Man), Stephen Crane (Second Man), Suzanne Sinclair (Woman), Arthur Nightingale (Joe), Tristan Hickey (Harvard Man), Christabelle Dilks (Nurse).

	Holding / Source
18.09.1995	DB-D3 / D3S

UP CLOSE AND PERSONAL

A Talkback Thames production for ITV 2. Untransmitted. Duration: 25 minutes.

Written by Andrew Rattenbury; directed by David Schneider.

Raquel Cassidy.

	Holding / Source
##.##.#### **[untransmitted pilot]**	DB /

Recorded September 2007.

Up Close and Personal was a planned sitcom for ITV2, set in the office in a celebrity-based magazine, similar to Heat Magazine.

UP THE POLE

A Kudos Productions production. Untransmitted.

Directed by John Henderson.

Nigel Plaskitt.

	Holding / Source
##.##.####	J / D3S

Recorded in 1994.

UP THE WORKERS

An ATV production. Transmission details are for the ATV midlands region. Duration: 25 minutes.

Main regular credit(s):   Written by Tom Brennand and Roy Bottomley; from an idea by Lance Percival.

	Holding / Source
04.09.1973	J / 2"

This half-hour comedy programme, based on an idea by Lance Percival, is all about industrial relations at Cockers Ltd. And what relations! A token stoppage over a broken boiler in a heat wave is eventually settled by a "conference" which takes place between management and union in the loo!

Music by Jack Parnell; designed by Lewis Logan; produced and directed by John Scholz-Conway.

With Lance Percival (Bernard Peck), Henry McGee (Richard Bligh), Norman Bird (Sid Stubbins), Gordon Rollings (Bert Hamflitt), Ivor Dean (Sir Henry Carmichael), Lynn Smith (Deirdre), Peter Hill (Arthur Henthorne).

UPSTAIRS DOWNSTAIRS

Alternative/Working Title(s): 165 EATON SQUARE / 75 EATON SQUARE / BELOW STAIRS / THE SERVANTS' HALL / TWO LITTLE MAIDS IN TOWN

An LWT production. made in association with Sagitta. Transmission details are for the ATV midlands region. Duration: 50 minutes.

This series joins a fashionable household in Eaton Place in 1903, to follow the trials of those in service and the human dramas being played out above stairs.

Main regular credit(s):   Script editor Alfred Shaughnessy; theme music by Alexander Faris; executive producer Rex Firkin; produced by John Hawkesworth.

Main regular cast: Gordon Jackson (Hudson), Jean Marsh (Rose), Angela Baddeley (Mrs Bridges), David Langton (Richard Bellamy), Simon Williams (James Bellamy), Christopher Beeny (Edward).

Holding / Source

##.##.####   **On Trial [untransmitted pilot]**   J / 62

A strange little Cockney girl calling herself Clemence and claiming a French background, comes to the house to apply for the position of under-parlourmaid.

Written by Fay Weldon; designed by John Clements; directed by Derek Bennett.

With George Innes (Alfred), Evin Crowley (Emily), Brian Osborne (Pearce), Beatrice Greeke.

Although recorded the episode was never transmitted as it was remounted and recorded in colour to enable foreign sales.

See also: MUST SEE TV* / THOMAS AND SARAH*

US GIRLS

A BBC production for BBC 1. Transmission details are for BBC 1. Duration: 30 minutes.

Holding / Source

##.##.####   **[untransmitted pilot]**   DB / 1"

Written by Lisselle Kayla; script editors Heather Peace and Justin Sbresni; costume Paula Bruce; make-up Yvonne Brockbank; designed by Rob Hinds; production manager Johanna Kennedy; produced and directed by David Askey.

With Joanne Campbell (Bev), Carmen Knight (Selina), Nick Pickard (Sean), Marlaine Gordon (Aisha), Kerry Potter (Catherine), Mona Hammond (Grandma), Allister Bain (Grandad), Nirjay Mahindru (Vijay).

See also: COMIC ASIDES

VACANT LOT

An ABC production. Transmission details are for the ABC midlands region. Duration: 25 minutes.

Main regular cast: Alfie Bass (Alf Grimble), Bill Fraser (William Bendlove).

Holding / Source

13.05.1967 Criminal Negligence   J / 40

Written by Ian La Frenais and Dick Clement; designed by Roger King; produced and directed by Dick Clement.

With Arthur Mullard (Chippy), Murray Melvin, Wensley Pithey, Harry Brunning, Mike Newman, Charles Bird, Pat Crowther, Vi Kane, Trudy Nichols, Arnold Yarrow.

Made as the pilot episode, shown last!

THE VANISHING MAN

An ABTV production for Meridian. Transmission details are for the Central region.

Executive producer Nick Barton; produced by Linda Agran.

Neil Morrissey (Nick Cameron), Mark Womack (Joe Cameron), Lucy Akhurst (Alice Grant).

Holding / Source

02.04.1997   DB / V1S

Duration: 100 minutes.

Written by Anthony Horowitz; directed by Maurice Phillips.

With Barbara Flynn (Ms Jeffries), Dominic Jephcott (Doctor Chivers), Nadia Sawalha (Catherine), Peter Eyre, David Hemmings, David Brierley, Shaun Prendergast, William Chubb, Elizabeth Jasicki, Michael McKell, Julian Sims, Melissa Connell, Tara MacGowran, Rikke Steffensen, Gerald Dwight, Steve Edwin, Frank Ellis, James Laurenson, Graham Cull.

VARIETY CLUB

Alternative/Working Title(s): NIGHTSPOT

A Yorkshire Television production. Transmission details are for ITV. Duration: 25 minutes.

Produced by Barry Cawtheray.

Ronnie Hilton, Lester and Smart, Deena Webster, Nick Taylor, Isabel Bond.

Holding / Source

08.08.1968   J / 2"

Recorded at Batley Variety Club on 4th July 1968. This programme became the source of a spat between James Corrigan, the owner of the club, and Yorkshire Television because of the perceived quality of the acts. The intention, apparently, was that the pilot was made very much as a technical test to see how what results could be obtained by shooting the entire programme at the club and it wasn't intended for broadcast. The technicians' strike which affected the ITV network in August 1968 meant that the pilot was one of all too few completed programmes available for screening and so it was used on the date shown. This despite Yorkshire's Head of Light Entertainment, Sid Colin, saying that, "... the pilot show was not suitable for public viewing, not even on a regional basis."

VARIETY MADHOUSE

An LWT production. Transmission details are for the London Weekend Television region. Duration: 25 minutes.

Described by Michael Grade as "visual comedy".

Produced and directed by Jon Scoffield.

	Production No	Holding / Source
22.10.1977	9L/09867	DB / 2"

VIC REEVES BIG NIGHT OUT

A Channel X production for Channel 4. Transmission details are for Channel 4. Duration varies - see below for details.

Main regular credit(s): Written by Vic Reeves and Bob Mortimer.

Main regular cast: Vic Reeves (Various Roles), Bob Mortimer (Various Roles), Fred Aylward (Les).

Holding / Source

##.##.#### [untransmitted pilot]   1" / 1"

Duration: 41 minutes.

Music by Steve McGuire, Vic Reeves, Dave McLeod, Mark Narayn and Patrice Serapiglia; edited by Mykola Pawluk; designed by Andrew Howe Davies; production team Angelo Faria, Hilary Henderson, Tanya Jackson and Harriet Williams; executive producers Alan Marke and Jonathan Ross; production manager Sue Hancock; produced and directed by Geoff Posner.

With Emma Cafferty, Charles Higson, Paul Whitehouse.

Although untransmitted, the pilot's end caption states it is "A Channel X production for Channel 4". Some material was re-used (though also re-shot) in the series proper. It is copyrighted 1989.

Fred Aylward is credited only as "Les" in series one and the New Year's Eve special; only from series two onwards and in the pilot is he listed as Fred Aylward. The musicians, aside from the musical director, are invariably credited en masse as 'The Vic Reeves Orchestra'. Punctuation fans will be disappointed to learn that at no point does an apostrophe appear in the programme's title, a fact particularly galling on the edition broadcast 31.12.1990.

VISION ON

A BBC production for BBC 1. Transmission details are for BBC 1.

Holding / Source

##.##.#### Gallery Exhibition [untransmitted pilot]   C1 / C1

An untransmitted insert exists on T3.
A foreign version of the edition tx'd 04.05.76 exists on D3.

VIVE LA DIFFERENCE

A Thames Television production. Untransmitted. Duration varies - see below for details.

Main regular credit(s):   Devised by Lance Percival.

	VT Number	Holding / Source
##.##.#### **[first pilot]**	1409	DB / 2"

Duration: 37 minutes.

Script by Rupert Cullen; designed by David Richens; produced by Andy Allan; directed by Robert Reed.

With Michael Aspel (Presenter), Maggie Norden (Presenter), Diana Coupland, Jackie Collins, Lesley Smith, William Franklyn, Phil Read, Jeffrey Bailey, Cherida Langford, Alan Harding.

	VT Number	Holding / Source
##.##.#### **[second pilot]**	17580	DB / 2"

Duration: 40 minutes.

Programme associate Dick Vosburgh; research Colin Williams; designed by David Richens; produced by David Clark; directed by Leon Thau.

With Lennie Bennett (Presenter), Jenny Hanley (Presenter), Rachel Heyhoe-Flint, Terry Wogan, Windsor Davies, Liza Goddard, Debbie Ryan, John Healy.

	VT Number	Holding / Source
##.##.#### **[third pilot]**	18222	DB / 2"

Duration: 40 minutes.

With Michael Aspel (Presenter), Lizzie Power (Presenter), Jon Pertwee, Paula Wilcox, Jilly Cooper, Shelley Keen, David Bedford, Paul D'Comamond.

No on-screen credits.

(c) 1977

VOICE OF EUROPE

A Spartan Productions production. Untransmitted.

Gordon Roxburgh says, "ITV tried twice in the 1960s to come up with a rival for the Eurovision Song Contest, with the ITV Song Contest in 1961 and the British Song Festival in 1965, but neither caught the public's imagination.

The Eurovision Song Contest went through something of a crisis around 1969/70, when just 12 countries participated in the 1970 edition, and there were thoughts of ending the contest, however with some changes implemented it survived, and 18 countries participated in the 1971 contest, and since then it has more or less went from strength to strength.

ITV were keen to get their hands on the contest, and when Monaco were unable to host the 1972 contest, ITV put forward an offer to stage the contest (this offer was made in September 1971), however the BBC had got there first, and it was they who organised and broadcast the 1972 contest in Edinburgh."

	Holding / Source
##.##.#### **[untransmitted pilot]**	J /

A pilot made in 1971, seen as an alternative contest to the Eurovision Song Contest. The emphasis would have been on the song, not the singer. Some European countries liked the idea and it was provisionally linked to LWT, HTV and STV. The contest would have taken place over 12 weeks culminating in Cannes at the Festival.

WAKE UP WITH...

An Elephant production for Tyne Tees Television. Transmission details are for the Central region. Duration: 25 minutes.

Latest recruits to television's mid-morning sofa slot are married media darlings Jonathan and Libby Hughes. But behind the sofa there's a different story - their perfect
partnership is on the rocks.

Devised by Nigel Planer; written by Andrew Nickolds; executive producer Christine Williams; produced and directed by Jamie Rix.

Nigel Planer (Jonathan Hughes), Susie Blake (Libby Hughes), Stephen Moore (Jeff), Paul Humpoletz (Dennis), Robert McKewley (Kim), Lucinda Fisher (Grace), Clare Cathcart (Mac), Sukie Smith (Ali), Robert Putt (Tea Van Proprietor), Andrew Dunford (Ned Hawking), Phoebe Scholfield (P.A.).

	Holding / Source
14.07.1994 **Let's Get Divorced!**	D3 / D3S

WAKING THE DEAD

A BBC production for BBC 1. Transmission details are for BBC 1. Duration: 60 minutes.

Main regular credit(s):	Created by Barbara Machin.
Main regular cast:	Trevor Eve (Detective Superintendent Peter Boyd), Sue Johnston (Doctor Grace Foley), Wil Johnson (Detective Sergeant Spencer Jordan).

Waking The Dead
Duration: 50 minutes.

Main regular credit(s):	Written by Barbara Machin; produced by Deborah Jones; directed by Martin Hutchings.
Main regular cast:	With Holly Aird (Doctor Frankie Wharton), Claire Goose (Detective Constable Amelia Silver).

	Holding / Source
04.09.2000 "Schoolgirl killer"	DB / V1SW

With Finbar Lynch (Jimmy Marshall), Amelia Warner (Jodie Whitemore), Sam Loggin (Kelly Caldwell), Adie Allen (Jenny Boyd), Tyler Butterworth (Mr Whitemore), Elaine Claxton (Mrs Whitemore), Steven Elder (Doctor Clive Pearson), Lachlan Ryan (Matt Boyd), John Vine (Superintendent Mavers), Roger Walker (Detective Chief Inspector Connors).

05.09.2000 "Exhuming the first victim"	DB / V1SW

With Finbar Lynch (Jimmy Marshall), Amelia Warner (Jodie Whitemore), Sam Loggin (Kelly Caldwell), Elaine Claxton (Mrs Whitemore), David Sterne (Mr Harvey).

Peter Boyd is a Detective Chief Inspector during this story.

WALK ON THE WILD SIDE

A BBC Productions production for BBC 1. Transmission details are for BBC 1. Duration: 30 minutes.

	Holding / Source
28.03.2009	DB / DBSWF

WALK ON THE WILDSIDE

A Granada production. Transmission details are for the Central region. Duration: 51 minutes.

	Production No	Holding / Source
17.02.1999	P2877/1	DB / DBS

Produced and directed by Daniel Abineri.

With Daniel Abineri (Presenter), Marc Almond, Richard O'Brien, Zandra Rhodes, Malcolm McLaren, Ray Davies, Nina Myskow, Mick Rock, Holly Johnson, David Bowie, Lindsay Kemp, Steve Harvey, Dave Stewart, Herbie Flowers, Sue Blane, Steve Strange, Pete Burns, Freddie Cannon.

WALKING THE PLANKS

A BBC production for BBC 1. Transmission details are for BBC 1. Duration: 30 minutes.

Ron Archer only allowed himself the merest flirtation with the three Rs. However, over the years, he has carefully developed a fourth R - Resourcefulness. This comes to the fore when he decides to buy an old seaside pier. All he needs is the money!

Written by Harold Snoad and Michael Knowles; lighting by Mike Jefferies; sound Dave Thompson; designed by Stephen Mellor; produced and directed by Harold Snoad.

Michael Elphick (Ron Archer), Richard Wilson (Richard Talbot), Vivienne Martin (Miss Baxter), Donald Hewlett (Henry Cummings), Gary Raynsford (Trevor Archer), Jean Cope (Elderly Lady), Ray Gatenby (Townhall Official), John Clive (Derek Rawlings), Robert McBain (Graham Winters), Norman Bird (Frank Short).

	Holding / Source
02.08.1985	DB / 1"

See also: HIGH AND DRY* / IT STICKS OUT HALF A MILE (RADIO)

THE WALL GAME

A Talkback Thames production for Thames Television. Untransmitted.

Designed by Stan Woodward.

Sinitta.

	VT Number	Holding / Source
##.##.#### [untransmitted pilot]	31186	DB /

WALLY

A BBC production. Untransmitted. Duration: 30 minutes.

Written by Bryan Blackburn; costume Christine Rawlins and Mary Husband; make-up Suzan Broad; designed by Austin Ruddy; production manager Alan Mills; produced and directed by Harold Snoad.

Enn Reitel (Wally), Mel Martin (The Duchess of Hampton Wick), David Roper (Frank), Carolyn Moody (Ellen), Michael Denison (The Vicar).

	Production No	Holding / Source
##.##.#### **[untransmitted 1986 pilot]**	LLCI150X/71	DB / 1"

THE WANDERER

A Fingertip production for Sky One. Transmission details are for Sky One. Duration: 75 minutes.

	Holding / Source
##.##.####	DB / V1SW

Pilot for an unmade series.

WATERMAN AND WILSON

A Granada production. Transmission details are for the Granada region.

Discussing this weeks new album and single release.

Take That single - Pray Rupaul Album U2 Album Manic Street Preachers Concert Neil Young Single Shaggy - Album Mica Paris - Album The Lemonheads - Video The Best Dance Album in the World Ever! Moby - Interview

Pete Waterman (Presenter), Tony Wilson (Presenter), Moby.

	Holding / Source
09.07.1993 **Juice [untransmitted pilot]**	D3 / D3S

THE WAY IT IS

A BBC production for BBC 1. Transmission details are for BBC 1. Duration: 35 minutes.

Put a fresh spin on the week's events from a perspective in the newsroom. If some earlier radio incarnations are anything to go by, viewers are in for a stream of topical jokes that can be a little hit-and-miss.

Written by Simon Blackwell, Simon Evans, Jon Holmes, Andy Hurst, Danny Robins and Dan Tetsell; additional material by Terry Franks-Newman, Paul Sassienie and Howard Ricklow; executive producer Jon Plowman; produced by Anil Gupta and Alex Walsh-Taylor; directed by Sue McMahon.

Simon Evans (Richard Richard), Tracy-Ann Oberman (Lolly Swain), Sanjeev Bhaskar, Nina Wadia, Dave Lamb, Chris Pavlo, Laura Shavin.

	Holding / Source
03.08.2000	DB /

WE KNOW WHERE YOU LIVE

A Witzend production for Channel 5. Transmission details are for Channel 5.

Main regular credit(s):	Executive producer Tony Charles; produced by Richard Parker and David Tomlinson; directed by Nick Jones.
Main regular cast:	Simon Pegg, Fiona Allen, Sanjeev Bhaskar, Jeremy Fowlds, Amanda Holden, Ella Kenion.

	Holding / Source
06.04.1997	D3 / D3S

WEAVERS GREEN

An Anglia production. Transmission details are for the ATV midlands region. Duration: 25 minutes.

Weavers Green was the name of a fictitious village of some
800 inhabitants situated in the heart of Anglia's own region. The main character around whom the serial revolved was the local vet, but the intention was that the story lines would take viewers all over the countryside of the east of England.

Main regular credit(s):	Created by Peter Lambda and Betty Lambda; story editor Ian Kennedy Martin; music by Wilfred Josephs; assistant producer Robert Bell; produced by John Jacobs.

	Holding / Source
##.##.#### **[untransmitted Pilot - Episode 1]**	J / 40

Written by Peter Lambda and Betty Paul; directed by John Jacobs.
Made Summer 1965.

##.##.#### **[second untransmitted pilot - episode 2]**	J / 40

Written by Peter Lambda and Betty Paul; directed by John Jacobs.
Made Summer 1965.

WELCOME TO STRATHMUIR

An Absolutely production for BBC 2 Scotland. Transmission details are for BBC 2 Scotland. Duration: 30 minutes.

Written by Moray Hunter and Jack Docherty; produced by Alan Tyler and Jack Docherty; directed by Nick Wood.

John Gordon Sinclair (Andrew), David Kay (Barry), Morwenna Banks (Muriel), Gabriel Quigley (Sheena), Jack Docherty (Reverend Sterne), Moray Hunter (Sheena's Dad), Nitin Ganatra (Deepak).

	Holding / Source
09.02.2007	DB /

John Gordon Sinclair stars in a new comedy pilot set in an information bureau in Strathmuir, a small fictitious Scottish town on the fringes of the Highlands.

WEST END TALES

An ATV production. Transmission details are for the ATV midlands region. Duration: 25 minutes.

Main regular credit(s):   Written by Keith Waterhouse; music by Laurie Holloway; designed by Bryan Holgate; produced by Colin Frewin and Keith Beckett; directed by James Gatward.

Main regular cast: Robin Nedwell (Fiddler), Toni Palmer (Ma), Peter Childs (Sergeant Dobbs).

	Production No	Holding / Source
16.02.1981 **Some You Lose**	5746/80	DB / 2"

With Garfield Morgan (Bishop), Larry Martyn (Checkie), Susan Skipper (Tina), Tom Chatto, Gurdial Sira, Paul Haley, Hedger Wallace, Stuart Myers, John Salpeas, Dave Cooper, John Cannon.

Recorded 10.11.1980.

WHAT A PERFORMANCE!

A Watchmaker Productions production for Carlton UK. Transmission details are for the Central region. Duration: 50 minutes.

Main regular credit(s):   Heads of production Lynn Hodgkinson and Zoe Norman.

Main regular cast: Bob Monkhouse (Presenter).

	Production No	Holding / Source
01.10.1997 **Camp**	CAR/00872/2001	DB / DBS

Written by Bob Monkhouse and Jez Stevenson; designed by Linda Conoboy; assistant producer Mark Turnbull; executive producer Elaine Bedell; production manager Zoe Norman; produced and directed by Karen Steyn.

With Harry Enfield, Julian Clary, Clive James, Matthew Kelly, Lesley Joseph, Kenneth Williams, Chris Tarrant, Paul Vaughan, Barry Took, Jonathan Ross, Claire Rayner, Cleo Rocos, Ned Sherrin, Garry Bushell, John Inman, Wendy Richard.

WHAT MAKES ME LAUGH?

A Talkback Thames production for Thames Television. Untransmitted.

	Holding / Source
##.##.#### **[untransmitted pilot]**	DB /

WHAT SHALL WE DO ON WEDNESDAY?

A BBC Wales production for BBC 1 Wales. Transmission details are for BBC 1 Wales. Duration: 30 minutes.

Written by Michael Davies.

Dermot Kelly, Windsor Davies.

	Holding / Source
11.04.1972	DB / 2"

WHAT THE PUBLIC WANTS

An Associated-Rediffusion production. Transmission details are for Associated-Rediffusion. Duration: 25 minutes.

Main regular credit(s):   Script editors Ken Hoare and Philip Oakes.

	Holding / Source
##.##.#### **[untransmitted pilot]**	J / 40

Originally scheduled for 25.10.1962.

Script editor Ken Hoare; designed by Michael Wield; directed by Don Gale.

With Clemence Bettany, Dorothy Bromiley, Chris Bryant, Allan Scott, Aubrey Woods, The Tubby Hayes Quintet.

Television Today reported 25.10.1962 that A-R executives had vetoed the pilot, because satirical sketches featured Mrs Kennedy, Prince Rainier, Princess Grace and Ernest Marples.

The first two scheduled programmes were billed but then postponed. Apparently, the Television Act which governed ITV (but not the BBC) forced the programme to limit its targets and that, the weekday slot, and the fact that no other ITV regions took it all conspired to give the BBC's THAT WAS THE WEEK THAT WAS the upper hand even though WHAT THE PUBLIC WANTS predated it. According to Humphrey Carpenter's "That Was Satire That Was" Granada Television were considering a similar programme, to be entitled MAN BITES DOG, but on seeing the problems the Act was giving Rediffusion, they gave up on it before transmission.

WHATEVER NEXT...

A BBC production for BBC 1. Untransmitted. Duration: 28 minutes.

Devised by The Unique Group; written by John Machin, Michael Barfield, Martin Booth, Ged Parsons and Mark Brisenden [credited as Mark Brissenden]; research Sarah Jarman; theme music by Ronnie Hazlehurst; designed by Michael Young; production manager James Wynn; produced by Michael Hurll; studio sequences directed by Michael Hurll; film sequences directed by Marcus Mortimer.

Noel Edmonds (Presenter).

	Production No	Holding / Source
##.##.#### **Show 2 [untransmitted 1987 pilot]**	LLVK220N/71	DB / 1"

Quiz show with comedy stunts.

WHEEL OF FORTUNE

A Scottish Television production. Transmission details are for the Central region. Duration: 25 minutes.

Main regular performer(s): Nicky Campbell (Presenter).

	Holding / Source
##.##.#### **[untransmitted Pilot 1]**	J / 1"

Executive producer Sandy Ross; produced by Stephen Leahy.

##.##.#### **[untransmitted Pilot 2]**

J / 1"

Executive producer Sandy Ross; produced by Stephen Leahy.

##.##.#### **[untransmitted Pilot 3]**

J / 1"

Executive producer Sandy Ross; produced by Stephen Leahy.

WHERE THERE'S A WILL

A TSW production. Transmission details are for the London Weekend Television region. Duration: 55 minutes.

Written by Ian Scrivens, Alan Froud and Baz Taylor; designed by Gordon Toms and Sarah Fiddian; associate producer Ian Scrivens; executive producers Michael Reinhold and Larry De Waay; produced and directed by Baz Taylor.

Patrick Macnee (Charles Crow-Ffinch), Michael Howe (Rupert Crow-Ffinch), Louan Gideon (Cavatina Andretti), Amanda Burton (Alice Freemantle), Christopher Benjamin (Terence Hill), Judy Loe (Margaret), Chris Jury (Selwyn), Ellis Dale (Weedon), Arthur Whybrow (Courtenay), Valerie Holliman (Lucy Lake), Philip O'Brien (Tex), Lorna Barton (Traffic Warden), Ian Stirling (Television Reporter), Nicholas Barnes (John), Doel Luscombe (Boatman), Ricky Skyberyou (Demolition Man), Cheryl Hart (Sarah), Colin Burns (Head Waiter), Susan Yorkton (Mrs Freemantle), David Beard (Pub Landlord).

	VT Number	Holding / Source
18.08.1989	FPN/0310/87	1" / C1

Pilot for an unmade series. Where There's A Will was recorded in summer 1987. The Stage, in January 1988, says it will be shown "soon". Courtesy of The Guardian, it looks like LWT showed it at 11.35pm on 18/08/89, but whether this was the first ITV screening (or indeed even the first LWT screening) we have no idea.

WHERE THERE'S BRASS

A Yorkshire Television production. Transmission details are for the ATV midlands region. Duration: 25 minutes.

"It's hard being a Captain of Industry and a Conductor of the Brigthorpe Brass Band."

Some of Britain's top brass band musicians are featured in this comedy about the trials and tribulations of conductor Joe Lockwood and his two errant sons.

Written by Dick Sharples; designed by Colin Pigott; produced and directed by Ronnie Baxter.

Derek Smith (Joe Lockwood), Colin Farrell (Alan Lockwood), Michael Tarn (Neil Lockwood), Peter Denyer (Harry Askwith), Ann Penfold (Hilda Bayliss), Tony Melody (Albert Heyworth), Paul Luty (Billy Armitage), The James Shepherd Versatile Brass.

	Holding / Source
16.03.1980	B / 2"

See also: THICKER THAN WATER*

WHERE THERE'S HOPE THERE'S KEEN

An ABC production. Untransmitted. Duration: 25 minutes.

Described as a type of fantasy comedy show.

Written by George Evans, Derek Collyer, Mike Craig, Lawrie Kinsley and Keith Beckett; designed by Darrell Lass; produced and directed by Darrell Lass.

Hope and Keen, Deryck Guyler, Fiona Fisher Green, Bob Sharples and his ABC Television Showband.

	Holding / Source
##.##.#### **[untransmitted pilot]**	J / 40

Recorded April 1968 at the Didsbury Studios.

WHERE WAS SPRING?

A BBC production for BBC 2. Transmission details are for BBC 2.

Main regular credit(s):	Written by John Fortune and Eleanor Bron; music by North Kensington Festival Wind Ensemble and Stanley Myers; directed by Terry Hughes.
Main regular cast:	Eleanor Bron, John Fortune.

	Holding / Source
09.06.1968 **What Did You Say This Thing Was Called, Love?**	J / 62

Duration: 40 minutes.

Designed by Colin Pigott; produced by Ned Sherrin; directed by Vere Lorrimer.

With No guest cast.

This edition was later re-broadcast as part of WHERE WAS SPRING?

Extract from unknown episode exists in Scene tx:15/02/1973.

WHERE'S THE FIRE

An LWT production. Untransmitted. Duration: 25 minutes.

Michael Robbins.

	VT Number	Holding / Source
##.##.#### **[untransmitted pilot]**	9L/09295	J / 2"

The videotape for this pilot is currently lost.

WHICH WAY TO THE WAR

A Reg Grundy Productions production for ITV. Transmission details are for the Central region. Duration: 24 minutes.

This comedy is set during the Second World War but this time in the Libyan Desert. Two Australian and two British soldiers find themselves accidentally separated from their units. They set up base in a deserted farmhouse. where they are joined by an ambulance-full of Italian nurses - but they turn out to be prostitutes, and the fun begins.

Written by David Croft and Jeremy Lloyd; executive producer Don Reynolds; produced by David Croft; directed by Roy Gould.

William Tapley (Cpl Roy Muller), Simon Baker Denny (Pte Stan Hawke), Terry John (Cpl Tony Genaro), Robert Hands (Pte Jock Stewart), Sarah Payne (Mara), Nadia Sawalha (Lucia), Elisabeth Bolognini (Anna), Amanda Weston (Teresa), Valeria Fabbri (Carla), Jason Hall (Capt Gregory Swift), Martin Sadler (Colonel).

	Holding / Source
19.08.1994	D2 / D2

WHISPERS IN THE AIR

A Granada production. Transmission details are for the Central region. Duration: 51 minutes.

Investigates whether some world war II American bomber pilots suffered from LMF (lack of moral fibre) when they landed their aircraft apparently without justification in neutral countries such as Sweden and stayed there till the end of the war.

Produced and directed by Simon Berthon.

	Production No	Holding / Source
28.11.1989	P1518	DB / 1"

THE WHITE ROOM

An Initial Film & TV production for Channel 4. Transmission details are for Channel 4. Duration: 50 minutes.

A blank canvas against which music can speak for itself.

Main regular performer(s): Mark Radcliffe (Presenter).

	Holding / Source
11.06.1994	D3 / D3S

Reggae concert.

Produced and directed by Chris Cowey.

With Sly Dunbar and Robbie Shakespeare, Jimmy Cliff, Toots, Rico Rodriguez, Chaka Demus, Pliers.

WHITES

A BBC Productions production for BBC 2. Transmission details are for BBC 2. Duration: 30 minutes.

Main regular credit(s):   Written by Matt King and Oliver Lansley.

Main regular cast: Alan Davies (Roland).

	Holding / Source
##.##.#### [untransmitted pilot]	DB /

Recorded 2008 - just rushes and an assembly.

##.##.#### [untransmitted pilot]	HD/DB /

Recorded 2009.

WHO DARES WINS...

Produced for Channel 4 by a variety of companies (see details below). Transmission details are for Channel 4.

	Holding / Source
##.##.#### Qwert [untransmitted pilot 1]	C1 / C1

A Thames Television production.

##.##.#### Qwert [untransmitted pilot 2]	J / 1"

A Thames Television production.

	Holding / Source
04.11.1983 Who Dares Wins A Week In Benidorm [third pilot]	1" / 1"

A Holmes Associates production. Duration: 50 minutes.

Written by Colin Bostock-Smith, Guy Jenkin, Andy Hamilton, Rory McGrath, Jimmy Mulville, Laurie Rowley and Tony Sarchet; produced by Andy Hamilton and Denise O'Donoghue; directed by Graeme Matthews.

With Brenda Blethyn, Bill Hootkins, Rory McGrath, Jimmy Mulville, Philip Pope, Tony Robinson.

See also: COME DANCING WITH JOOLS HOLLAND*

WHO DO YOU DO?

An LWT production. Transmission details are for the ATV midlands region. Duration: 25 minutes.

Main regular credit(s):   Devised by Jon Scoffield.

	Production No	Holding / Source
##.##.#### [untransmitted pilot]	9L/09073	2"|n / 2"

See also: NOW WHO DO YOU DO?*

WHO KNOWS WHO?

An LWT production. Untransmitted. Duration: 28 minutes.

Game show pilot featuring newly-married couples.

Gloria Hunniford (Host).

	Production No	Holding / Source
##.##.#### **[first pilot]**	91399	1" / 1"

WHODUNNIT?

A Thames Television production. Transmission details are for the ATV midlands region. Duration varies - see below for details.

Main regular credit(s):   Devised by Jeremy Lloyd and Lance Percival.

	VT Number	Holding / Source
15.08.1972	5954	D3 / 2"

Duration: 28 minutes.

A brutal murder at a lonely country house, with the victim found in the study.

It's the stuff the best mystery thrillers are made of. Well, who did do it? Armchair detectives get the chance to pit their wits against a panel of studio sleuths, with Edward (Callan) Woodward, Frank (Z-Cars) Windsor and Anne Summer, a real-life private-eye, competing against each other and the studio audience.

All the necessary clues and suspects are pinpointed as Ivor Salter, Ralph Ball, Peter Hughes, Dany Clare, Tirzah Lowen, Ian Dewar, Thee Ranft and Cy Town act out the foul deed, and the subsequent police investigation. One extra clue: it wasn't the butler. There isn't one!

Written by Jeremy Lloyd and Lance Percival; designed by Philip Blowers; produced and directed by Malcolm Morris.

With Shaw Taylor (Host), Ivor Salter (Sergeant Wilkins), Peter Hughes (Jack Harvey), Tirzah Lowen (Madelaine Young), Ralph Ball (George Foreman), Ian Dewar (Bill Williams), Dany Clare (Mrs Foreman), Thea Ranft (Helga Van Eyck), David Hamilton (Radio Announcer), Edward Woodward, Frank Windsor, Anne Summer.

WHOSE LINE IS IT ANYWAY?

A Hat Trick production for Channel 4. Transmission details are for Channel 4. Duration: 25 minutes.

Main regular credit(s):   Devised by Dan Patterson and Mark Leveson; theme music by Philip Pope.

Main regular cast: Clive Anderson (Host).

SERIES 1

Main regular credit(s):   Music by Richard Vranch; designed by Pip Gardner; executive producer Denise O'Donoghue; produced by Dan Patterson; directed by Paul O'Dell.

Main regular cast: With Richard Vranch (Musician), John Sessions.

	Holding / Source
16.12.1988	1" / 1"

With Josie Lawrence, Jimmy Mulville, John Sessions, John Glover.

Pilot, but shown last in series 1!

THE WIND IN THE WILLOWS

A Cosgrove Hall production for Thames Television. Transmission details are for the Central region.

Main regular credit(s):   Produced by Brian Cosgrove and Mark Hall.

	Holding / Source
27.12.1983 **The Wind In The Willows**	C1 / C1

Duration: 75 minutes.

Adapted by Rosemary Anne Sisson; based on a book by Kenneth Grahame; music by Keith Hopwood and Malcolm Rowe; edited by John McManus; executive producer John Hambley; directed by Mark Hall.

With Ian Carmichael (Rat), Richard Pearson (Mole), Michael Hordern (Badger), David Jason (Toad), Jonathan Cecil (Reggie), Beryl Reid (Magistrate), Una Stubbs (Jailer's Daughter), Allan Bardsley, Edward Kelsey, Brian Trueman.

WINDMILL

A BBC production for BBC 2. Transmission details are for BBC 2. Duration: 60 minutes.

Main regular cast: Chris Serle (Presenter).

	Holding / Source
##.##.#### **[untransmitted incomplete January 1985 pilot]**	J / 1"
26.08.1985 **Bank Holiday Special**	DB / 1"

Designed by Martin Methven; assistant producers Mike Seddon and Nel Romano; series producer Albert Barber.

WINGS

A Yorkshire Television production. Untransmitted. Duration: 27 minutes.

Written by David Angell, Peter Casey and David Lee; script supervisor Sarah Cockcroft; music by Ray Russell; executive producer David Reynolds; produced by Andrew Benson; directed by Roy Gould.

Jonathan Cake (Steve), Tony Gardner (Michael), Tim Wylton (Roy), Una Stubbs (Fay), Debra Beaumont (Helen), Bob Mason (Noel), Jason Hall (Passenger), Anthony Schaeffer (Dispatcher).

	Production No	Holding / Source
##.##.#### **The Legacy**	L635	B / BSF

Made in 1996.

WIPEOUT

An Action Time production for BBC 1. Transmission details are for BBC 1. Usual duration: 29 minutes.

Main regular credit(s):   Format by Paramount Pictures Corporation.

1994-1997 series

Main regular performer(s): With Paul Daniels (Host).

	Holding / Source
##.##.#### **[untransmitted pilot]**	D3 / D3S

Recorded 1994.

DLAF shows:

Untransmitted.

	Holding / Source
##.##.#### **[series 5 evening pilot]**	DV / DBS

Commissioned by BBC Manchester. Duration: 29 minutes.

Written by Colin Edmonds; music by Simon Etchell; titles by Triffic Films; designed by Richard Plumb; associate producers Gloria Gee and Barry Hart; executive producer Stephen Leahy; production manager Angela Murgatroyd; series producer John Rooney; line producer Ged Gray.

With Bob Monkhouse (Host), Tom Edwards (Voice Only).

This pilot was pitched to the BBC to move the daytime game show into a primetime slot. Action Time paid for the pilot at its own expense, convinced it would be commissioned. The BBC decided against the move. Recorded 31.07.01.

	Holding / Source
##.##.#### **[australian pilot]**	DV / DBS

Colin Edmonds comments: two non-broadcast speculative pilot shows were also recorded, one for prime time and one for Australia. These shows we called DLAF - "Doing Leahy A Favour". Neither of them is held by the BBC, by ITV or by Action Time.

WISECRACKS

A Yorkshire Television production. Untransmitted. Duration: 25 minutes.

Introduced by Lance Percival; devised by Graham Deykin and Lance Percival; written by Graham Deykin and Lance Percival; designed by Gordon Livesey; produced and directed by Ian Bolt.

Lance Percival (Host), Don Maclean, Roger Kitter, Mike Newman, Jimmy Marshall.

	Holding / Source
##.##.#### **[untransmitted pilot]**	B / 1"

Recorded ??.??.1982

This was a comedy game show in which the contestants would tell jokes about various subjects, would try to complete limericks, put captions to photographs and so on. Two further rounds were recorded but edited from the finished programme, though they still exist at the end of the master tape.

WOGAN

A BBC production for BBC 1. Transmission details are for BBC 1. Duration varies - see below for details.

Main regular performer(s): Terry Wogan (Host).

	Production No	Holding / Source
##.##.#### **Alternative Wogan [untransmitted pilot]**	LLVD390J/71	DB / 1"

Duration: 16 minutes.

With Frazer Hines*, Jane Firbank*, Randy Edelman*, Paula Yates*.

The recording runs out just as Wogan starts to talk to Paula Yates.

SERIES 5

Duration: 40 minutes.

	Holding / Source
##.##.#### **[untransmitted pilot]**	J / 1"

With B. A. Robertson, John Hatt, Lorraine Chase, Cliff Cohen, Doctor Rob Buckman.

See also: TERRY IN PANTOLAND*

WOLFSHEAD

A London Weekend International production for Global Distribution. Never shown on UK TV, given a theatrical release instead. Duration: 53 minutes.

The legendary bow-man who stole from the rich to give to the poor, depicted as a poor struggling man.

Devised by Bill Anderson; written by David Butler; music by Jack Spague, Bernie Sharp and Don Innes; production manager Laurie Greenwood; produced by Bill Anderson; directed by John Hough [credited as Johnny Hough].

David Warbeck (Robert of Locksley), Kathleen Byron (Katherine of Locksley), Dan Meaden (John Little of Cumberland), Ciaran Madden (Lady Marian Fitzwalter), Kenneth Gilbert (Friar Tuck), Joe Cook (Much), Derrick Gilbert (Wat), David Butler (Will Stukely), Patrick O'Dwyer (Tom), Peter Stephens (Abbot of St Mary's), Christopher Robbie (Roger of Doncaster), Roy Boyd (Geoffrey of Doncaster), Pamela Roland (Adele), Inigo Jackson (Legros), Will Knightley (Abbot's Secretary), Roy Evans (Gyrth), Reg Lever (Old Wat), Kim Braden (Alice), Sheraton Blount (Abbie), Nicholas Jones (Squire), Sheelah Wilcocks (Nurse).

	Holding / Source
##.##.#### **[untransmitted pilot]**	C1 / C1

Alternative transmissions: BBC 2: .

Recorded in 1969. Held by Kaleidoscope.

WOOD AND WALTERS

A Granada production. Transmission details are for the ATV/Central region. Duration varies - see below for details.

Main regular credit(s):   Written by Victoria Wood; music by Jim Parker; directed by Stuart Orme.

Main regular cast: Victoria Wood, Julie Walters.

Credits: Produced by Peter Eckersley.

	Production No	Holding / Source
01.01.1981 **"Two creatures great and small"**	P1076/1	2" / 2"

Duration: 26 minutes.

Music directed by Jim Parker; designed by Tim Wilding; produced by Peter Eckersley.

With Robert Longden, Keith Hodiak.

WOODY

Commissioned by BBC. Transmission details are for BBC. Duration: 30 minutes.

Kayvan Novak (Woody), Roger Lloyd Pack, Emma Pierson.

	Holding / Source
##.##.#### **[untransmitted pilot]**	HD/DB / HD/DB

WORD GAMESHOW PILOTS

A TVS production. Untransmitted. Duration varies - see below for details.

Letters come up on screen and two teams compete to complete the word.

Main regular credit(s):   Devised by Armand Jammot.

Main regular performer(s): Fern Britton (Presenter).

	Holding / Source
##.##.#### **[pilot 1]**	J / 1"

Duration: 15 minutes.

##.##.#### **[pilot 2]**	J / 1"

Duration: 25 minutes.

John Kaye Cooper hoped to sell this format to Channel 4. Two pilots were made in February 1985.

THE WORD

A Planet 24 production for Channel 4. Transmission details are for Channel 4. Duration: 52 minutes.

Main regular performer(s): Terry Christian (Host), Dani Behr (Host).

	Holding / Source
##.##.#### **[untransmitted pilot]**	1" / 1"

With Michelle Collins, Whycliffe, Mark Brown.

Pilot, recorded 10.08.1990.

THE WORLD OF BEATRIX POTTER: 1866-1943

An A Four Companies Production production for Border Television. Transmission details are for the Rediffusion Television region. Duration: 25 minutes.

Produced and directed by Douglas Hurn.

Kenneth More (Presenter).

	Holding / Source
15.08.1966	J / C1

The four companies that jointly funded the pilot were Ulster, Border, Westward and Grampian. Three more films were planned after this pilot.

A WORLD OF COMEDY

A Rediffusion Television production. Untransmitted. Duration: 25 minutes.

Introduced by Michael Crawford.

	Production No	VT Number	Holding / Source
##.##.#### **I'll Get It In A Minute**	SS/33/13	W3207/844	J / 40

Written by Keith Waterhouse and Willis Hall; produced and directed by Bill Hitchcock.

With Roy Kinnear (George Webley), Patsy Rowlands (Rosemary Webley).

Recorded 13.08.65. T/R 16/1615.
SEE: INSIDE GEORGE WEBLEY

Only programmes 1 to 7 seem to have been produced although on 03.08.65 Michael Crawford recorded introductions for 'The Celebrity', 'Mutiny At Bella Vista', 'The Telly Room', 'The Only Way To Travel' and 'Fred' - VT W3009/972 and T/R 16/1610.

THE WORLD OF EDDIE WEARY

A Fingertip production for Yorkshire Television. Transmission details are for the Central region. Duration: 100 minutes.

Written by Roy Clarke; music by John Cameron; executive producer Keith Richardson; produced by Terry Mellis and Steve Lanning; directed by Alan Grint.

Ray Brooks (Alex Conway), Celia Imrie (Birdie), Connie Booth (Madge), Anita Dobson (Roxanne), Brian Glover (Strip Club MC), Anthony Daniels (Bruce), Kitty Aldridge (Barbara Daniels), Ella Wilder (Fern), Melanie Kilburn (Mrs Hebdon), Ian Bleasdale (Disco Club Man), Judy Brooke (Rita Hebdon), Martyn Whitby (Mr Hebdon), Sandra Maitland (Mrs McDermott), Judy Flynn (Maureen McDermott), Josephine Antoszi (Gran), Neil Dickson (Raymond Knight), Francesca Ryan (TV Awards Hostess), Anthony Dutton (Police Sergeant), Alex Hall (Disco Club Woman), Greg Powell (Strip Club Bouncer), Marcus Romer (Kevin), Nick Wright (Desmond), Emma Rawson (Emma), Jeffrey Robert (Grave Digger), Yusuf Sultan (Indian Police Officer), Mohammed Ashiq (Fat Accountant).

	Holding / Source
31.08.1990	1" / 2"-C1

WORLDWISE

A TVS production. Transmission details are for ITV.

	Holding / Source
##.##.#### [untransmitted pilot]	1" / 1"

Recorded 18.9.1985.

THE WORST WITCH

A Central production. Transmission details are for the Central region. Duration: 50 minutes.

Adapted by Jill Murphy; based on a book by Mary Pleshette Willis; music by Denis King; executive producers Hilary Heath and Lewis Rudd; produced by Colin Shindler; directed by Robert Young.

Diana Rigg (Miss Hardbroom), Charlotte Rae (Miss Cackle / Agatha), Tim Curry (The Grand Wizard), Fairuza Balk (Mildred), Danielle Batchelor (Maud), Anna Kipling (Ethel), Sabina Franklyn (Miss Spellbinder), Su Elliott (Delilah), Kate Buckley (Donna), Lisa Brice (Zoe Chant-Vestry), Katrina Heath (Sophie Hattrick), Nevena Kaley (Dawn Undercover), Caroline Woolf (Julie Vanishing), Amy Shindler (Spinner Web), Sophie Cook (Natalie Sinister), Sophie Millett (Verity Sinister), Julia Nagle (Bubble Toil), Laura Heath (Misty Meadow), Leila Marr (Pixie Brown), Tara Stevenson (Gloria Hobgoblin), Kathryn Lacey (Goodie Twocharm), Pui Fan Lee (Prefect).

	Holding / Source
01.11.1986	1" / 1"

WYCLIFFE

Produced for HTV by a variety of companies (see details below). Transmission details are for the Central region. Duration varies - see below for details.

Main regular credit(s):   Based on characters created by W. J. Burley.

Main regular cast: Jack Shepherd (Detective Superintendent Charles Wycliffe).

A HTV production.

	Holding / Source
07.08.1993 **Wycliffe And The Cycle Of Death**	1" / C1

Duration: 78 minutes.

Wycliffe investigates a series of deaths in the same family.

Adapted by Julia Jones; based on a book by W. J. Burley; music by Mark Thomas; titles by Mole Burrett; assistant director Chris Dando; production designer Gary Pritchard; executive producer Alan Clayton; produced and directed by Pennant Roberts.

With Gemma Jones (Sara Glynn), Richard Heffer (Maurice Glynn), Carla Mendonca (Detective Sergeant Lane), Kevin Quarmby (Detective Inspector Kersey), Lucy Fleming (Helen Wycliffe), John Turner (Matthew Glynn), John Cater (Alfred Glynn), Siri Neal (Christine Glynn), Steve Jacobs (David Glynn), Joseph Bennett (Gerald Glynn), David Shaw (Detective Inspector Trice), Tim Munro (Sergeant Fox), Peter Settelen (Doctor Franks), Peter Jonfield (Ronnie Swayne), Hubert Rees (Doctor Rees), April Walker (Florence Tremayne), Patrick Jordan (Colonel Armitage), Julie Neubert (Molly Pearce), Frank Docherty (Dippy Martin), Rachel Preece (Paula James), Graham Ryder (Fire Officer), Philip Jacobs (Constable).

Wycliffe holds the rank of Detective Chief Superintendent in the pilot.

WYCLIFFE

YANKS GO HOME

A Granada production. Transmission details are for the ATV midlands region.

SERIES 1

Duration: 25 minutes.

Main regular credit(s):   Produced and directed by Eric Prytherch.

Main regular cast: With Stuart Damon (Corporal Rossi), Alan MacNaughtan (Colonel Kruger), Bruce Boa (Sergeant Pulaski), Meg Johnson (Phoebe Sankey), Harry Markham (Bert Pickup).

	Holding / Source
##.##.#### **[untransmitted pilot]**	J / 2"

Executive producer Brian Armstrong.

Recorded November 1975.

YES MINISTER

A BBC production for BBC 2. Transmission details are for BBC 2. Duration: 30 minutes.

Main regular credit(s):   Written by Anthony Jay and Jonathan Lynn; drawings by Gerald Scarfe; theme music by Ronnie Hazlehurst.

Main regular cast: Paul Eddington (Jim Hacker, M.P.), Nigel Hawthorne (Sir Humphrey Appleby), Derek Fowlds (Bernard Woolley).

SERIES 1

	Holding / Source
25.02.1980 **Open Government**	DB-D3 / 2"

Produced and directed by Stuart Allen.

With Diana Hoddinott (Annie Hacker), Neil Fitzwilliam (Frank Weisel), John Nettleton (Sir Arnold Robinson), Fraser Kerr, Edward Jewesbury, Norman Mitchell, David Moran.

Recorded Summer 1979 and before the General Election prevented its transmission.

See also: COMEDY CONNECTIONS* / THE FUNNY SIDE OF CHRISTMAS* / YES, PRIME MINISTER*

YOU HAVE BEEN WATCHING

A Zeppotron production for Channel 4. Transmission details are for Channel 4. Duration: 37 minutes.

Main regular credit(s):   Theme music by Mat Osman and Alex Lee.

Main regular cast: Charlie Brooker (Host).

	Holding / Source
##.##.#### **[untransmitted pilot]**	DB / DBSW

With Terry Christian, Rufus Hound, David Mitchell, Jamelia.

Recorded 30.01.2009.

YOU MUST BE JOKING!

A BBC production for BBC 1. Untransmitted. Duration: 45 minutes.

Programme associates Jeremy Beadle and Tony Hawes; research Linda Beadle, Helen Fraser, Pat Parrish, Ann Toy and Harvey Woolfe; music by Ronnie Hazlehurst; designed by Bob Cove; production team Greg Childs, Lesley Coulburn and Kathryn Randall; production manager Geoffrey Posner; produced by Marcus Plantin; film sequences directed by Alan J. W. Bell; directed by Keith Stewart.

Terry Wogan (Presenter), Bernard Cribbins, John Burton, Danny Gunnery, Whitelands College, Putney.

	Production No	Holding / Source
##.##.#### **[untransmitted pilot]**	1/LLVC239D	DB / 2"

Recorded Friday 27/3/1981. Quiz show where Terry Wogan tries to fool two teams with improbable objects and facts.

YOU MUST BE JOKING!

A Thames Television production. Transmission details are for the ATV midlands region.

Main regular cast: Ray Burdis, John Blundell, Pauline Quirke, Jim Bowen, Flintlock, Mike Holoway, Elvis Payne.

	VT Number	Holding / Source
##.##.#### **[untransmitted pilot]**	9409	1" / 2"

Duration: 28 minutes.

Written by The Cast; designed by Peter Elliott; produced and directed by Roger Price.

With Kay Humblestone, Chris Leonard, Phil Daniels [as Philip Daniels], Beverley Martin, Linda Robson, Sandra Scott, Fireweed, Brian Jones, Django Wheeler, Bob Edwards, Arthur Latham M.P..

The pilot doesn't feature Flintlock, Mike Holoway, Elvis Payne or Pauline Quirke. Its title caption doesn't feature the exclamation mark.

YOU RANG, M'LORD?

A BBC production for BBC 1. Transmission details are for BBC 1. Duration varies - see below for details.

Main regular credit(s):   Written by Jimmy Perry and David Croft; theme music by Jimmy Perry, Roy Moore, Bob Monkhouse and Paul Shane; produced by David Croft.

Main regular cast: Paul Shane (Alf Stokes), Jeffrey Holland (Jim Twelvetrees), Su Pollard (Ivy Teesdale (aka Stokes)), Donald Hewlett (Lord George Meldrum), Michael Knowles (The Honourable Teddy), Bill Pertwee (Police Constable Wilson), Brenda Cowling (Mrs Blanche Lipton), Perry Benson (Henry Livingstone).

Made in association with Seven Network, Australia.

Holding / Source

29.12.1988   DB / 1"

Duration: 49 minutes.

A hour-long comedy performed in front of an audience, in which Lord Meldrum takes on a new butler who in turn engages his daughter as parlour-maid.

Designed by David Buckingham and Paul Cross; directed by David Croft.

With Mavis Pugh (Lady Lavender), Susie Brann (Poppy), Catherine Rabett (Cissy), Barbara New (Mabel), Angela Scoular (Lady Agatha), Sarah Mortimer, Ken Morley, Alf Pearson, John D. Collins, Karen Westwood, Cameron Stewart, Bob Appleby, Yvonne Marsh.

THE YOUNG ONES

A BBC production for BBC 2. Transmission details are for BBC 2. Duration varies - see below for details.

Main regular credit(s):   Written by Ben Elton, Rik Mayall and Lise Mayer; additional material by Alexei Sayle; music by Peter Brewis; designed by Graeme Story; produced by Paul Jackson.

Main regular performer(s): Adrian Edmondson (Vyvyan), Rik Mayall (Rick), Nigel Planer (Neil), Christopher Ryan (Mike), Alexei Sayle (The Balowski Family).

SERIES 1

Main regular credit(s):   Production team Ed Bye and Jackie Tyler; production manager Marcus Mortimer.

Holding / Source

09.11.1982 **Demolition**   DB-D3 / 2"

Duration: 33 minutes.

Directed by Paul Jackson.

With Nine Below Zero, Paul Bradley, Christine Ellerbeck, Chris Ellis, Ben Elton, Gerard Kelly, Hilary Mason, Pauline Melville, Herbert Norville, Cyril Shaps, Anthony Sharp, Maggie Steed, Andy de la Tour.

Adrian Edmondson was credited as 'Ade Edmondson' throughout series one.

YOUR MOTHER WOULDN'T LIKE IT

A Central production. Transmission details are for the Central region. Duration: 25 minutes.

Revue-style comedy show for children made by the Central's Junior Television Workshop.

Main regular credit(s):   Executive producer Lewis Rudd.

Main regular cast: Ian Kirkby (Loaf), Paul Stark (Lonnie).

SERIES 1

Main regular credit(s):   Written by Bob Hescott and Michael Maynard; programme associate Sue Nott; produced by Peter Murphy.

Main regular cast: With Tom Anderson (Cans), Karen Murden (Mary Rose).

Holding / Source

01.11.1985   1" / 1"

Directed by Tony Cox.

Recorded April 1985.

ZODIAC

A London Weekend International production. Untransmitted.

Anouska Hempel, John Fraser.

Holding / Source

##.##.#### **[untransmitted pilot]**   J /

The Stage, on 20.05.71, reported that this "Avengers style pilot lies uncompleted on the shelf". Anouska Hempel, in an interview published in The Australian Women's Weekly [02.09.1970], mentions that she's soon to be playing an astrologer who assists a policeman, to be played by John Fraser. So clearly this is an antecedent of the Thames Television series of the same name.

See also: ZODIAC*

ZOOM IN

An Ulster Television production. Transmission details are for the Ulster Televison region. Duration: 25 minutes.

Local Top of the Pops meets At Last The 1948 Show.

Main regular credit(s):   Produced by Gordon Burns.

Holding / Source

16.10.1968 **[first pilot]**   J /

23.10.1968 **[second pilot]**   J /

Programme was commissioned for two series in 1969 but was cancelled due to financial crisis caused by Troubles.

Note: These are probably the best known of UTV's pilots. They were co-produced by Gordon Burns who was asked to come up with two programmes to replace UTV's local sports show Sportscast during the 1968 Olympics. He basically came up with the same show twice - a sort of Top of the Pops with comedic elements aimed at twenty-somethings. It was popular although Burns apparently regrets some of the sexism exhibited within it.

HOLDING AND SOURCE FORMAT CODES AND DESCRIPTIONS

1"	625 line PAL colour 1" videotape.
1"-R1	625 line monochrome 1" videotape from 16mm monochrome telerecording.
1"S	625 line PAL colour 1" videotape - transmitted in stereo.
2"	625 line PAL colour 2" videotape.
2"-C1	625 line PAL colour 2" videotape from 16mm colour film.
40	405 line monochrome 2" videotape.
62	625 line monochrome 2" videotape.
B	Betacam SP videotape.
B1	16mm monochrome film.
B3	35mm monochrome film.
B-R1	Betacam SP videotape taken from 16mm monochrome telerecording.
BS	Betacam SP videotape, recorded in stereo.
BSF	Betacam SP 625 line colour videotape which has been filmised - transmitted in stereo.
C1	16mm colour film.
C1S	16mm colour film - transmitted in stereo sound.
C1SW	16mm colour film - transmitted in stereo sound and widescreen.
C3	35mm colour film.
C3SW	35mm colour film - transmitted in stereo widescreen.
D2	D2 digital videotape.
D2S	D2 digital videotape - transmitted in stereo.
D3	D3 digital videotape.
D3S	D3 digital colour videotape - transmitted in stereo sound.
D5Hrv/DB	D5 digital videotape high definition 1080 line reversioned master with 625 line Digital Betacam backup copy for use on standard definition transmissions.
DA	Digital Audio.
DB	Digital Betacam videotape.
DB-1"	Digital Betacam videotape taken from 625 line PAL colour 1" videotape.
DB-1-C1	Digital Betacam videotape taken from 625 line PAL colour 1" videotape transfer of a 16mm colour film.
DB-4W	Digital Betacam videotape copy of converted 405 to 625 line monochrome videotape.
DB-D3	Digital Betacam copy of a D3 digital videotape.
DB-D3-2"	Digital Betacam copy of a D3 dub of a 625 line PAL colour 2" videotape.
DB-D3-R1	Digital Betacam copy of a D3 digital videotape transfer of a 16mm monochrome telerecording.
DB-DV	Digital Betacam copy of a 625 line PAL domestic format videotape including VHS, Betamax and Philips 1500.
DB-R1	Digital Betacam videotape taken from 16mm monochrome film recording.
DBS	Digital Betacam 625 line colour videotape - transmitted in stereo.
DBSW	Digital Betacam 625 line colour videotape - transmitted in stereo widescreen.
DBSWF	Digital Betacam 625 line colour videotape which has been filmised - transmitted in stereo widescreen.
DB-UM	Digital Betacam copy of a 625 line U-Matic videotape.
DV	625 line PAL domestic format videotape including VHS, Betamax and Philips 1500.
FNK	The format on which it is held, or on which it was recorded, is not known.
HD/DB	High Definition master with 625 line Digital Betacam backup copy for use on standard definition transmissions.
HDC	HD-CAM or HD-CAM SR high definition master.
HD-R1	High Definition videotape taken from 16mm monochrome film telerecording (reverse anamorphic)
HF	625 line videotape converted from ½" monochrome open reel domestic system.
J	Does not exist.
Live	Live transmission.
MII	MII videotape.
MXF	Data File held by the broadcaster and/or programme-maker
NM	Not made
NR	Not Recorded.
R1	16mm monochrome film telerecorded from 405/625 line videotape or a live transmission.
R3	35mm monochrome film telerecorded from 405/625 line videotape or a live broadcast.
UM	625 line U-Matic videotape copy.
V1	16mm colour film - edited on videotape.
V1S	16mm colour film - edited on videotape - transmitted in stereo.
V1SS	16mm colour film - edited on videotape - transmitted in stereo surround.
V1SSW	16mm colour film - edited on videotape - transmitted in stereo surround widescreen.
V1SW	16mm colour film - edited on videotape/computer - transmitted in stereo widescreen.

ADDITIONAL FORMAT CODES

|a - Held on Domestic Audio

|c - Held as Script

|n - Held at NFTVA

N - Only survives as film negative

SEQ - Although the complete programme is missing, some sequences survive

SO - Sound only (no picture survives)

Printed in Great Britain
by Amazon